D1252960

THE BOOK OF ACTS IN ITS FIRST CENTURY SETTING

I. The Book of Acts in Its Ancient Literary Setting
II. The Book of Acts in Its Graeco-Roman Setting
III. The Book of Acts and Paul in Roman Custody
IV. The Book of Acts in Its Palestinian Setting
V. The Book of Acts in Its Diaspora Setting
VI. The Book of Acts in Its Theological Setting

Bruce W. Winter

Series Editor

I. Howard Marshall • David W. J. Gill

Consulting Editors

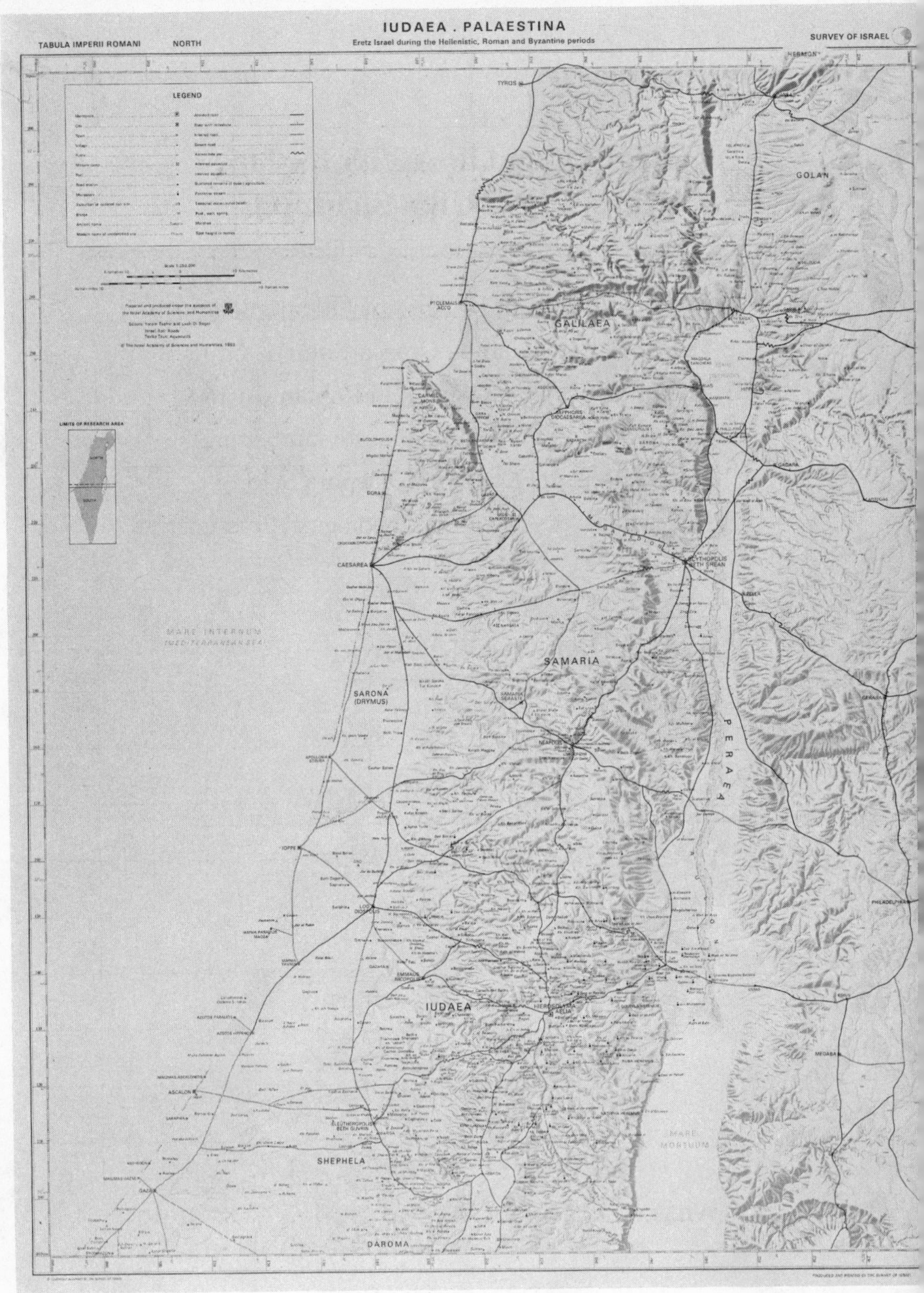

IUDAEA . PALAESTINA

TABULA IMPERII ROMANI NORTH

Eretz Israel during the Hellenistic, Roman and Byzantine periods

SURVEY OF ISRAEL

LEGEND

LIMITS OF RESEARCH AREA

HERMON

TYROS

GOLAN

PTOLEMAIS ACCO

GALILAEA

SEPPHORIS DIOCAESAREA

CAESAREA

MARE INTERNUM (MEDITERRANEAN SEA)

SCYTHOPOLIS BETH SHEAN

SAMARIA

SARONA (DRYMUS)

APOLLONIA

NEAPOLIS

PERAEA

IOPPE

LOD DIOSPOLIS

EMMAUS NICOPOLIS

IUDAEA

HIEROSOLYMA AELIA

PHILADELPHIA

ASCALON

MARE MORTUUM

ELEUTHEROPOLIS BETH GUVRIN

SHEPHELA

GAZA

DAROMA

THE BOOK OF ACTS IN ITS
FIRST CENTURY SETTING

VOLUME 4

The Book of Acts in Its Palestinian Setting

Edited by

Richard Bauckham

William B. Eerdmans Publishing Company
Grand Rapids, Michigan

The Paternoster Press
Carlisle

255 Jefferson Ave. S.E., Grand Rapids, Michigan 49503

First published 1995 jointly
in the United States by
Wm. B. Eerdmans Publishing Company
and in the U.K. by
The Paternoster Press,
P.O. Box 300, Carlisle, Cumbria CA3 0QS

Printed in the United States of America

00 99 98 97 96 95 7 6 5 4 3 2 1

Library of Congress Cataloging-in-Publication Data

The book of Acts in its Palestinian setting / edited by Richard Bauckham.
p. cm. — (The book of Acts in its first century setting ; v. 4)
Includes bibliographical references and indexes.
Contents: The location of cultures in Second Temple Palestine / Tessa Rajak — Acts and Roman policy in Judaea / David W. J. Gill — The geography of Palestine in Acts / Martin Hengel — Palestinian Jewish personal names in Acts / Margaret H. Williams — Chief priests, Sadducees, Pharisees and Sanhedrin in Acts / Steve Mason — Synagogues in Jerusalem / Rainer Riesner — The composition of the Jerusalem church / David A. Fiensy — The population size of Jerusalem and the numerical growth of the Jerusalem church / Wolfgang Reinhardt — Jewish prayer literature and the Jerusalem church in Acts / Daniel K. Falk — The cenacle — topographical setting for Acts 2:44-45 / Jerome Murphy-O'Connor — The Palestinian cultural context of earliest Christian community of goods / Brian Capper — Jewish activity against Christians in Palestine according to Acts / Ernst Bammel — Paul's pre-Christian career according to Acts / Simon Légasse — Peter and Ben Stada in Lydda / Joshua Schwartz — James and the Jerusalem church / Richard Bauckham.
ISBN 0-8028-2436-6 (alk. paper)
1. Bible. N.T. Acts — History of contemporary events. 2. Church history — Primitive and early church, ca. 30-600. 3. Jews — History — 168 B.C.-135 A.D. 4. Palestine — Politics and government. 5. Palestine — Ethnic relations. 6. Palestine in Christianity.
I. Bauckham, Richard. II. Series.
BS2625.2.B66 1995
226.6'067 — dc20 95-12881
CIP

British Library Cataloguing in Publication Data

Book of Acts in Its Palestinian Setting. —
(Book of Acts in Its First Century Setting Series; Vol. 4)
I. Bauckham, Richard II. Series
226.6091
ISBN 0-85364-566-3

TABLE OF CONTENTS

LIST OF CONTRIBUTORS

Ernst Bammel is Professor Emeritus, Westfäl. Wilhelms-Universität, Münster and Reader Emeritus, Cambridge University. Bibliography in: W. Horbury, *Templum Amicitiae* (Sheffield, 1991) 477ff. His latest publication is *Judaica et Paulina* (Tübingen, 1995).

Richard Bauckham holds the chair of New Testament Studies, St Mary's College, University of St Andrew's, Scotland and has recently published *Jude and the Relatives of Jesus in the Early Church* (1990), *The Theology of the Book of Revelation* (1993) and *The Climax of Prophecy: Studies on the Book of Revelation* (1993). He read history as an undergraduate at Cambridge University where he subsequently obtained his doctorate.

Brian J. Capper is Senior Lecturer in Religious Studies, Canterbury Christ Church College, University of Kent at Canterbury. He has previously taught at Edinburgh University, Ripon College Cuddesdon (University of Oxford) and St. Andrews University. He holds his doctorate from Cambridge University, and also researched at the University of Tübingen. His research interest is the social pattern of the New Testament church.

Daniel K. Falk is completing a PhD dissertation at Cambridge University on 'Daily, Sabbath, and Festival Prayers in the Dead Sea Scrolls'. He holds a BA in Bible/Theology from Providence College, Canada, and a Master of Christian Studies (New Testament) from Regent College, Canada.

David A. Fiensy is Senior Minister of the Grape Grove Church of Christ in Jamestown, Ohio. After receiving degrees from the Cincinnati Bible Seminary and Xavier University, he earned the PhD in New Testament from Duke University. His published monographs include: *Prayers Alleged to be Jewish: An Examination of the* Constitutiones Apostolorum (1985); *The Social History of Palestine in the Herodian Period* (1991); and *New Testament Introduction* (1994).

David W.J. Gill obtained his DPhil from the University of Oxford and is presently Lecturer in Ancient History and Honorary Curator of the Wellcome Museum at the University of Wales Swansea. A former Rome Scholar at the British School at Rome, he held a Sir James Knott Fellowship at the University of Newcastle-upon-Tyne. He was previously a member of the Department of Antiquities at the Fitzwilliam Museum, University of Cambridge. He contributed to and co-edited volume 2 in this series, *The Book of Acts in its Graeco-Roman Setting*.

Martin Hengel was until recently Professor of New Testament and Early Judaism at the University of Tübingen, Germany. His many publications on early Judaism and early Christianity include (in their English translations) *Judaism and Hellenism* (1974), *Acts and the History of Earliest Christianity* (1979), *The Cross of the Son of God* (1986), *The Zealots* (1989), *The Johannine Question* (1989), *The 'Hellenization' of Judaea in the First Century after Christ* (1989), *The Pre-Christian Paul* (1991) and *Studies in Early Christology* (1995).

Simon Légasse, Docteur ès Sciences Bibliques (Pontifical Biblical Commission), is Professor of New Testament and Semitic Languages in the Faculty of Theology (Institut Catholique) of Toulouse, France. He has published: *L'Appel du riche* (1966), *Jésus et l'enfant* (1969), *Les Pauvres en esprit* (1974), *'Et qui est mon prochain?' Étude sur l'objet de l'agapè dans le Nouveau Testament* (1989), *Paul apôtre: essai de biographie critique* (1991), *Stephanos: Histoire et discours d'Etienne dans les Actes des apôtres* (1992), *Naissance du baptême* (1993), *Le Procès de Jésus* I: *L'histoire* (1994).

Steve Mason is Associate Professor in the Division of Humanities at York University, Toronto. He earned his PhD at the University of St Michael's College, Toronto, having conducted research at the Hebrew University of Jerusalem and the University of Tübingen. Along with several articles on Josephus, early Judaism, and Christian origins, he has published *Flavius Josephus on the Pharisees* (1991) and *Josephus and the New Testament* (1992). He is the founder of IOUDAIOS, an electronic seminar on Judaism in the Graeco-Roman world.

Jerome Murphy-O'Connor, OP, is a professor of New Testament at the Ecole Biblique et Archéologique, Jerusalem. A graduate of the University of Fribourg, Switzerland, he has published extensively on Paul. His *The Theology of the Second Letter to the Corinthians* (1991) will be joined in 1995 by *Paul the Letter-Writer. His World, His Options, His Skills*. As a sideline he has written *The Holy Land. An Archaeological Guide* (3rd edn., 1992).

Tessa Rajak is Reader in Classics and Head of the Department of Classics in the University of Reading. After her degree in Classics at Somerville College, Oxford, she wrote an Oxford doctorate on the intersection of Greek and Jewish cultures in the works of Josephus. She is the author of *Josephus: the Historian and his Society* (1984), and the co-editor, with Judith Lieu and John North, of *The Jews among Pagans and Christians in the Roman Empire* (1992). She has published widely on Jewish history and historiography, the Jewish Diaspora and Jewish inscriptions.

Wolfgang Reinhardt is a graduate of the universities of Marburg and Göttingen. During his many years pastoring a German Protestant Church, he wrote most of his thesis on 'Das Wachstum des Gottesvolkes' (an abbreviated form is awaiting publication). He obtained his doctorate from the Kirchliche Hochschule Wuppertal and is now a lecturer at the Protestant Seminary for Church Ministry in Bad Salzuflen.

Rainer Riesner is a Lecturer in New Testament at the Protestant Theological Faculty, University of Tübingen. His doctoral thesis was about the earliest oral Gospel tradition (*Jesus als Lehrer. Eine Untersuchung zum Ursprung der Evangelien-Überlieferung*, 3rd edn., Tübingen, 1988). Recently he published *Die Frühzeit des Apostels Paulus. Studien zur Chronologie, Missionsstrategie und Theologie* (Tübingen, 1994), and, together with his former teacher Professor Otto Betz, *Jesus, Qumran and the Vatican: Clarifications* (London, 1994). His research interests also include the sources of Luke, New Testament archaeology and the history of Jewish Christianity in patristic times.

Joshua Schwartz is Associate Professor of the Historical Geography of the Land of Israel at Bar-Ilan University (Ramat-Gan), Chairman of the Department of Land of Israel Studies there and Co-ordinator of the Krauthammer Chair in Archaeology in that university. He received his PhD from the Hebrew University (Jerusalem) and has published *Jewish Settlement in Judaea after the Bar-Kochba War until the Arab Conquest* (1986) (Hebrew) and *Lod (Lydda), Israel: From Its Origins through the Byzantine Period* (1991).

Margaret H. Williams is a Tutor for the Open University in Scotland and was a Lecturer in Ancient History in the Department of Classics at Swansea. She holds her doctorate from Cambridge University, where she read Classics. She has published a number of articles on the Jews in the Graeco-Roman world. Her main interest is the Jewish community of Ancient Rome.

PREFACE

Forty years ago the great American Acts scholar Henry Cadbury, in his still valuable study, *The Book of Acts in History* (London: A. & C. Black, 1955), sketched with broad but expert brush 'how well [the Book of Acts] fits its contemporary setting' (p. v). He classified the contemporary contexts into which Acts fits as Greek, Roman, Jewish and Christian, devoting a chapter to each. These, of course, are not geographical, but cultural distinctions. Cadbury's chapter on the Jewish setting is as much about the western Diaspora as it is about Palestinian Judaism. His chapter on the Roman setting takes some of its major examples from Palestine. Another on the Greek setting perhaps betrays its date in that it does not refer to the hellenization of Palestinian Jewish culture which more recent writers cannot ignore, even if they still debate its extent. All of these cultural settings overlapped in Palestine and therefore impinge on those chapters of Acts which are set in Palestine.

The present series of volumes on the Book of Acts in its contemporary setting divides the material differently from Cadbury's book, and by devoting a volume to the Palestinian setting makes it possible to focus on the particular cross-cultural situation in 1st-century Roman Palestine. More than half of the narrative of Acts is in fact set in Palestine, a fact which makes it surprising that so little sustained attention has been given to this Palestinian context in recent study of Acts. The very considerable advances in our knowledge and understanding of Jewish Palestine in the late Second Temple period which have occurred in recent decades make this a particularly appropriate time to attempt to remedy this neglect, as this present volume does, while the complexity and diversity of the subject make the collaborative approach of this present volume an appropriate method of doing so. As in two of the previous volumes in the series, the collaboration is cross-disciplinary. Ancient historians, New Testament scholars and specialists in the study of early Judaism have all contributed chapters which draw on a very wide range of types of evidence for the Palestinian setting of Acts in order to illuminate many different aspects of the narrative.

Treatment of the speeches of Peter and Stephen has been deferred to volume 6 of the series (*The Book of Acts and its Theology*) where the theological significance of these speeches can be most appropriately discussed.

Thanks are due to Bruce Winter, who, as series editor, has not only taken a constant interest in this volume, but also solved many of the practical problems to which it gave rise. Andrew Warren worked with meticulous care on the final copy-editing and typographical preparation of the volume. Eileen Satterthwaite, Nicole Beale and Margit Siegel helped to produce the indexes.

Richard Bauckham

November, 1994

Translations and Acknowledgements

Chapter 3 was translated from German (published in *ZDPV* 98, 1983) by John Bowden. It first appeared as: 'Luke the Historian and the Geography of Palestine in the Acts of the Apostles', in M. Hengel, *Between Jesus and Paul* (London: SCM Press, 1983), and is reprinted with permission of the publishers.

Chapter 8 was translated from German by Andrew Warren.

Chapter 14 was translated from French by Richard Bauckham.

The map in the front of this volume on Palestine in the Hellenistic, Roman and Byzantine periods is reproduced from Y. Tsafrir, *Judaea Palaestina Survey of Eretz Israel in the Helenistic, Roman and Byzantine Periods-Maps and a Gazetteer* (Israel Exploration Society, 1994) with the kind permission of the Survey of Israel. It forms part of the *Tabula Imperii Romani* project.

The reproduction of the ossuary on the dust jacket is published with the permission of the Israel Antiquity Authority.

CHAPTER 1

THE LOCATION OF CULTURES IN SECOND TEMPLE PALESTINE: THE EVIDENCE OF JOSEPHUS

Tessa Rajak

Summary

For the reader of Acts, it is important to understand the various designations of ethnic and local affiliation present in the work and especially the Jewish-Greek polarity. In 1st-century Palestine, the distinction between Jews and Greeks was of great ideological importance, and it was of political importance at times of crisis. At the same time, the Jews were themselves extensively 'hellenised' and had more in common with the local 'Greeks' than their own construction of their identity might suggest. The picture is further complicated by the presence of other groups in the region, such as Nabataean Arabs and Idumaeans. The approach of Josephus is a valuable guide to the operation of indicators of ethnic and cultural identity in Jewish Palestine. He regularly distinguishes Jews from foreigners and also from Greeks. But he also assigns a prominent place to Syrians. In general, by 'Greeks', he means simply non-Jewish townsmen, usually citizens of Greek cities, and 'Syrians' are the rural population.

The reader of Acts can scarcely fail to notice the abundance of attributions of ethnic, cultural and religious identities present in the text. A linked phenomenon might also strike him or her, the book's marked interest in Greeks and hellenism, as a means of constructing a contrast both with Hebrews and with Christians. When Paul preaches on the Areopagus at Athens, the Athenians' self-identity as deep thinkers is overtly brought into association with a less flattering characterisation in terms of obsession with novelty; the contrast is with the message Paul is proclaiming, of a strikingly non-Greek God, without images, who yet exists in the heart of Greekness (17:16-34). It is noteworthy that, in his Areopagus speech, Paul draws the attention of his hearers to the racial variety of human beings in the world (the Greek word used is *ethnos*), when he tells them that all races were created by God from a common origin (17:26).

Equally, the question of who is a Jew and who a Gentile is of prime importance throughout Acts, theologically and anecdotally. Thus Timothy's delineation as a half-Jew, child of a Jewish-Christian mother and a non-Jewish father (16:1) is made with unparallelled precision for the literature of the period, and constitutes one of our rare pieces of evidence for intermarriage.

Nor is the situation any different in those early parts of the narrative which are set in Palestine. There we find a striking display of attention to ethnicity and provenance, with a variety of labels assigned to individuals. At the Jerusalem Pentecost, the speakers in tongues, referred to as people from Galilee, are allocated a remarkable list of native languages from across the near East (Acts 2:2-12). The congregation in the synagogue of the freedmen, which disputes with Stephen, is said to originate in Cyrene, Alexandria, Cilicia and Asia (6:9). A eunuch going home to Ethiopia from Jerusalem is won over by Philip (8:27-39). The convert Cornelius, a judaising Roman centurion in the Italic cohort, is a man admired by the entire *ethnos* of the Jews (10:1-2, 22).

It is from the scenes set in Jerusalem that comes the unique evidence for a split between the group known as 'hellenists' and the group known as 'Hebraists' in the earliest church (6:1), evidence which has given rise to much theorising over the centuries.[1] This evidence is supplemented by a later statement that Saul in Jerusalem debates exclusively with the hellenists (9:9).

These are concerns which belong, of course, to the author of Acts, writing perhaps in Antioch, and possibly well after AD 70. Yet they purport to describe the situation on the ground in pre-70 Palestine, and, to make sense of them, we need to understand that situation. This study of the cultures of 1st-century Palestine has such understanding as its purpose, and explores the way ethnic and cultural distinctions operated there. The exercise is not to draw a map of cultures: indeed, it would be hard to do so, since on many crucial matters we have no information. And in any case, culture is here understood as a relational matter, essentially a question of description to serve particular purposes, and therefore, perhaps, something too fluid and evasive to map. What is here offered is rather a framework into which evidence can be slotted, and then, in the second part of the study, a more detailed exploration of the ideology of ethnicity in Second Temple Palestine as expressed by an author centrally placed in that world. Any description of 1st-century Palestine which does not allocate a prominent place to Josephus' perceptions misses a golden opportunity.

I. Jew versus Greek

To distinguish between Jews and Greeks was a commonplace in Second Temple Palestine. To Paul this was a primary division in society: he addresses 'the Jew first, but the Greek also', and, writing to the Christian community of Rome, he seems to regard the audience there as composed of Greeks (Rom. 1:14-17). It is precisely because the distinction is so natural to him that Paul can claim that faith abolishes, among other differences between person and person, the difference between Greek and Jew.[2] The implication is that this pair of opposites, whether taken as ethnic, linguistic, religious, social, or all of these, represented familiar identity markers in Paul's world.

The power of Paul's rhetoric should not mislead us. Recent scholarship on the complexity of hellenism and new orientations in Jewish Studies serve as a warning to us against taking a limited and polemical statement at face value, so as to set up Jewish and Greek

---

[1]Recent discussion seems to be agreed that the terms have linguistic reference and distinguish a group of Jews whose mother tongue was Greek and a group whose mother tongue was Aramaic (or Hebrew): see C.F.D. Moule, 'Once More, Who Were the Hellenists?', *ExpT* 70 (1958-59) 100-2; M. Hengel, *Between Jesus and Paul*, tr. J. Bowden (London: SCM Press, 1983) 4-11; R. Pesch, '"Hellenisten" und "Hebräer": Zu Apg. 9.29 und 6.1', *BZ* 23 (1979) 87-92; C.C. Hill, *Hellenists and Hebrews: Reappraising Division within the Earliest Church* (Minneapolis, 1992).

[2]Rom. 10:11-12; Gal. 3:28; *cf.* Col. 3:11, where barbarians and Scythians also figure by way of contrast with Greeks.

cultures as two incompatible, fixed systems, standing centre stage, in opposition to one another. If we do, we end up with caricatures which are all too familiar, in which a central core of Jews is preoccupied with holding back the inroads of an encroaching hellenism, and, on the other side, Christianity emerges in reaction, perhaps out of sparks of Jewish enlightenment, and achieves, after a false start or two, the merging of divergent worlds of thought and practice.

In reality, even if contemporaries were not themselves wholly aware of the strands, Jewish and Greek cultures were deeply intertwined from the early hellenistic period.[3] This is not to say that in the consciousness of participants, the rare occasions of tension may not have loomed larger; and there were, indeed, important historical moments when Jews saw themselves as diametrically opposed to what Greeks stood for, in the broadest sense.[4] At such moments physical conflicts coincided with ideological conflict. The most famous occasion of this kind was the revolt of the Maccabees, in the 160's BC, which was, as is well known, provoked by the promotion of a Greek lifestyle in Jerusalem by the Jewish High Priest Jason and then by his successor, Menelaus, backed by the Seleucid-Greek imperial government. Even after the cleansing of the Temple and the rededication of the altar, the unreconciled members of the Jewish establishment who held out against the Maccabees in Jerusalem's Akra fortress are described in the Maccabaean literature not only as impious and lawless, but specifically as 'hellenisers'. A second striking instance is the quarrel between Jews and Greeks in Caesarea, which Josephus regards as a principal cause of the Jewish Revolt against Rome of AD 66-73/4. This revolved around the question of whether the city was a Greek one with a Greek constitution, or a city for Jews. Cultic divergences caused mutual suspicion too, with Greek mockery of practice in the city's synagogue inflaming the situation.

Those conflicts assume a different meaning, however, when we remember that, by the time of Paul, 'Greekness' had been an intrinsic part of Judaism for some centuries. Around the Roman empire lived Jews who knew no Hebrew, spoke no Aramaic, and lived their lives, heard their Bible and did their reading (if they did it) in Greek—and

---

[3]E.J. Bickerman, *The Jews in the Greek Age* (Cambridge, Mass./London, England, 1988).

[4]See T. Rajak, 'The Hasmoneans and the Uses of Hellenism' in P.R. Davies and R.T. White (eds.), *A Tribute to Geza Vermes: Essays on Jewish and Christian History and Literature* (JSOT Supplement Series 100; Sheffield, 1990) 261-80.

who, we should not forget, contributed significantly to the evolving hellenism of their environments as well as taking from it.

II. The Cultures of Palestine

We might regard Palestine, more than anywhere, as a region divided between Greeks and Jews. To the distinctive groupings among the Jews is attributed a rigidly separate identity, whether as purity-obsessed Pharisees, or as Sadducees insistent on cultic practice, or as monastic Essenes in their strict communities. Yet the historian must question the limits of such schematisation. No one sect represented the whole picture, and all three probably included no more than a small part of Palestinian Jewry. It is worth reflecting what distinctions between types and groups of people might have struck a visitor to 1st-century Palestine, as he or she moved around. We shall find that the distinction between Jews and Greeks is more notional than real, and so unlikely to have been particularly visible. Then we might ask just how far that Jewish-Greek dichotomy will actually have mattered to the diverse local inhabitants in their day-to-day interactions, outside rare historic moments of the kind which we have mentioned, when a sharp polarisation manifested itself—and those moments might not occur even once in a lifetime. There is reason to view them as distinctions activated only intermittently.

In a sense, buildings and institutions spoke more distinctly than people, and here national styles could certainly be observed. Herod's Temple, with its Solomonic proportions and hybrid orientalising style, could scarcely have been mistaken for a Greek shrine. Its sequence of courts and barriers, demarcating separate zones and reflecting the elaborate Jewish purity regulations, are not easy to parallel. And the spectacle of the daily holocaust smoking perpetually on the altar, the constant activity of the numerous priests and Levites, the recitations of Scripture and the benedictions, were undoubtedly unique in the Greek east.[5]

But the situation is not a simple one. We learn from Josephus that the Temple was constructed by exclusively Jewish masons (*Ant.* 15.390), a gesture of respect for the Jewish law designed to placate opponents of the project. Yet it is unlikely that these workmen will

[5]On physical and cultic aspects of the Temple ritual, see E.P. Sanders, *Judaism: Practice and Belief 63 BCE - 66 CE* (London/Philadelphia, 1992) 47-145 (70-1).

have betrayed their religious affiliation in their external appearance—except by their total absence on the Sabbath and at other sacred times and seasons. These workmen probably stemmed from many parts of the Jewish world, and conducted themselves according to the customs of their places of origin. They will not have been recognisable by any head-covering, since covering the head was not the norm for males in this period.

By contrast, if we turn again to buildings, we may think of the temple of the imperial cult at Caesarea, with its huge statue of the emperor and its many inscriptions, or its dark underground Mithraeum: both of these, in their own way, were a far cry from any Jewish cult place.[6] Here were reflected, on the one hand, forms of loyalty made their own by Greeks, and on the other, religious practices specifically associated with the spread of Roman occupation. Yet in Tiberias the Jews had the physical structure of a Greek city built not for Greeks but largely for them (albeit on a polluted site) by Herod Antipas;[7] while the Jewish inhabitants of Caesarea felt a close enough affinity with their city, physical identity included, to make them relentless in disputing control of it with the Greeks with whom they lived.

Among the many identities in Palestine it is hard to say which, if any, made a visible impact. Fergus Millar has now shown us how little justification there is of conceiving the ancient near east in terms of a common, long-standing semitic culture. For the ancients, at any rate, there seems to have been little sense of a common past among the peoples of the region, and it is hard to detect significant elements of a shared culture beyond the linguistic elements.[8]

For various reasons, however, we focus on Greek culture more than on any other, and above all because of the strong reactions evoked by hellenism, a reaction to be accounted for, in turn, by the fact that Greek culture was the most dynamic of those among which the Jews moved, the one that encroached on others. For the Greek culture of our period was the culture of empire. And, indeed, for the Jews, it was the culture of three empires in turn, the Ptolemaic, the Seleucid and the Roman. Roman rule in the east used the Greek language, Greek polit-

---

[6]For an illustrated account of recent discoveries, and further bibliography, see K.G. Holum, R.L. Hohfelder, R.J. Bull and A. Raban, *King Herod's Dream: Caesarea on the Sea* (New York/London, 1988).

[7]H. Hoehner, *Herod Antipas* (Cambridge 1972) 91-9. T. Rajak, 'Justus of Tiberias', *CQ* 23 (1973) 345-68 (345-51).

[8]F. Millar, *The Roman Near East 31 BC - AD 337* (Cambridge, Mass./London, England, 1993).

ical ideas and Greek literature as its instrument; and Roman rule was mediated through Greekness in a particularly noticeable way in Palestine, because of the power of Herod and the Herodian dynasty, who flaunted themselves as benefactors and Philhellenes around cities of the Roman east and even in front of the emperor. It is of great assistance in running an empire to have a culture to sell. And having an empire to run is a stimulus to evolving a superior cultural product. As long as foreign rule was not stabilised in Palestine, the symbols of the culture which was its tool would be at times perceived as a threat and a provocation.

III. Constructed Identities

The Jews of Palestine were both attracted and resistant to the culture of empire. But their resistance was the more spectacular reaction. Their extensive hellenisation is now undeniable: it is the great achievement of Martin Hengel to have demonstrated this, both for the hellenistic and for the Roman period, even if critics have raised objections on many individual issues.[9] And yet those who dispute with Hengel, to stress the distinctiveness of the Jews, are no less justified.[10] In Palestine, Jewry had its own rooted social and cultic organisation, and the Jews' reaction to foreign rule was first to accentuate their uniqueness and eventually to systematise their own religious tradition. If debate about hellenisation of Jews has seemed inconclusive, it is because both sides are right in their own terms and resolution is not needed. In effect, they are talking about different things: Hengel speaks of cultural facts—language, tangible ideas. He reminds us of the literary productivity of Jerusalem: 'between the Maccabaean period and its destruction, the extent of its literary production was greater than that of the Jews in Alexandria'.[11] Some specific attributions of extensive Greek influence may be open to dispute. How, in the end, do we measure the impact of the Greek conception of *paideia* (in itself highly elusive) on the pessimistic wisdom of the Preacher (Ecclesiastes)? Or, again, is there a true parallel between Pythagorean purity regulations

---

[9]M. Hengel, *Judaism and Hellenism* (ET; London, 1974); *idem, The 'Hellenization' of Judaea in the First Century after Christ* (ET; London, 1989). Criticisms in L. Feldman, 'Hengel's *Judaism and Hellenism* in Retrospect', *JBL* 96 (1977) 371-82.

[10]Especially F. Millar in 'The Background to the Maccabean Revolution: Reflections on Martin Hengel's *Judaism and Hellenism*', *JJS* 29 (1978) 1-21.

[11]Hengel, *'Hellenization'*, 29.

(which themselves can only be extrapolated from much later evidence) and those of the Essene community? But the cumulative impact of the data on the pre-Maccabaean period presented in *Judaism and Hellenism* is incontrovertible; and equally so is Hengel's brilliantly focussed analysis, in his short later book, of the Greek culture of Jewish Palestine in the era leading up to 70. For the latter, new archaeological evidence continues to fill out the picture.

The alternative viewpoint prioritises those aspects of Judaism which stand apart, essentially, it might be said, on two grounds: a) the sense of difference was the more significant politically, sparking off both small conflicts and large-scale revolts, b) historical hindsight lends significance to the uniquely Jewish, since Judaism triumphantly survived through its distinctive form, Rabbinism, not through its hellenised manifestations.

For the Jews of the Second Temple period, the Greek-Jewish polarity was, in fact, a central part of the way they constructed their own identity. They needed to see the Greeks as different from themselves in particular respects. Recent work in anthropology helps us understand this: cultures are read as expressions of symbolic identity, relational and shifting with context.[12] In such interpretations, ethnic boundaries are attitudinal, and significant symbols are vital to them. Attitudes to others can be exposed through the human voice, through action or through visual representation.[13] Tension between groups may, but need not necessarily be, entailed by boundary-drawing. Certainly, the importation of Greek culture into Palestine by the Romans was a case where the pressure on the conquered to define new boundaries led not only to tension but to full-scale war.

What we want to know, then, is how the sense of ethnic identity in Second Temple Judaism was expressed through a symbolic opposition with hellenism. And we can find in literature reflections of the symbols of those contrasting entities. In the post-70 era, the emphasis was to change in a revealing fashion. Many of the Rabbis would be overtly relaxed about hellenism, while 'pagan' was to become the main identity-forming label, the obvious antithesis to 'Jewish'. Other aspects of hellenism, such as use of the Greek language and of Greek visual

---

[12]U. Östergard, `What is National and Ethnic Identity?' in P. Bilde, T. Engberg-Pedersen, L. Hannestad and J. Zahle (eds.), *Ethnicity in Hellenistic Egypt* (Aarhus, 1992) 32; B. Anderson, *Imagined Communities: Reflections on the Origins and Spread of Nationalism* (London, 1983) 15.

[13]F. Barth (ed.), *Ethnic Groups and Boundaries: the Social Organization of Cultural Difference* (London, 1969) 9.

iconography, became less of a threat, as, perhaps, did the Roman government itself. Then the idolatry which, after all, was always a very significant part of what Jews did not like in the Greek cultural package, finally stood out from the rest of the distinctive features of the Greek way of life. For the Second Temple period, the challenge for us is to assess what made up that consciousness which the Jews of Palestine held, of standing apart from Greeks and from many things Greek, at the same time as they happily absorbed other aspects of hellenism.

IV. Ethnic Identities in Josephus

Josephus wrote his historical works in Greek, outside Palestine, after AD 70. But he was born, around 37, a member of the Jerusalem priestly aristocracy, and educated in the city as well as with desert sects. In the early part of the Jewish revolt, he operated as a leader in upper and lower Galilee and in the Golan area. Where the population of Palestine figures in his writings, we would expect to find both knowledge and at least the elements of a Palestinian perception, however distorted by hindsight and muffled by the cloak of a Greek writer. A native provincial voice of this kind is a most unusual phenomenon in ancient literature, and we should make the most of it. Moreover, in contrast to the Gospels, where we also find valuable evidence, in Josephus we are dealing with a known author and man of action, of known background and experience in the region (even if we come to learn of this from his own mouth), and known dates (more or less).

In sketching Josephus' definitions of ethnicity, it will be useful to bear in mind a number of separate questions. (1) The question of the real ethnic map of Palestine: Who was where? As has been said, a systematic attempt to fill in this map, to whatever extent possible, is not our concern here, but certain features will emerge. (2) How Josephus himself chose to describe the Jews in relation to other peoples and cultures in the region. (3) A more specific question can be put: how, as Josephus tells it, do those peoples view and react to one other? (4) Who are the Jews in Josephus? (5) How do other relevant identity tags in Josephus operate? Of these, the most significant are: Syrians, Romans, barbarians and Greeks. It is also worth noting, however, that the Jewish historian seems to have been the first to develop a distinct conception of an Arab ethnic identity, developing a line of descent from Hagar, through Ishmael, and Ishmael's eldest son, Nabaiotes, of the circumcised Ishmaelites, whom he identifies exclusively with the

Nabataeans. A certain affinity between the Arab people generally, or perhaps the Nabataeans in particular, and the Jews would seem to be implied in this reconstruction.[14]

V. Jews in Josephus

Josephus says that the Jews acquired the name *ioudaioi* when they returned from Babylon, because Judah was the first tribe to resettle Palestine (*Ant.* 11.173). For him, the Jews are an *ethnos* or *genos* to which affiliation in differing degrees is possible by conversion.[15] The criterion for Jewishness is not primarily linguistic, since for the most part the Jews spoke Aramaic in Palestine, thus sharing the language of the region. Hebrew was adopted in limited circles, for specific, ideological purposes.[16]. The distinction between Jews and Samaritans is notably sharp, probably because of the brutal conquest of Samaria by the Hasmonaean John Hyrcanus. The differentiation from the Idumaeans is also surprisingly clear, considering that this people underwent a peaceful conversion by the Hasmonaeans, and for Josephus they are at best 'half-Jews' (*Ant.* 14.403), though they identify enough with Judaism to fight tenaciously on the rebels' side in the revolt.[17] The boundaries of what may count as Jewish do thus appear relatively non-negotiable.

VI. Jews and Gentiles in Josephus

It is perhaps surprising to find this resonant polarity playing a part in Josephus' thinking, given that, at least in his *Antiquities*, his avowed

---

[14]F. Millar, 'Hagar, Ishmael, Josephus and the Origins of Islam', *JJS* 24 (1993) 233-45. More fully on Arab identity, Millar, *The Roman Near East*, 387-407.

[15]S.D. Cohen, 'Religion, Ethnicity and "Hellenism" in the Emergence of Jewish Identity in Maccabaean Palestine', in P. Bilde, T. Engberg-Pedersen, L. Hannestad and J. Zahle (eds.), *Religion and Religious Practice in the Seleucid Kingdom* (Aarhus, 1990) 204-23.

[16]See S. Schwartz, `Language, Power and Identity in Ancient Palestine', forthcoming in *Past and Present*.

[17]On the conversion of the Idumaeans, A. Kasher, *Jews, Idumaeans and Ancient Arabs* (TSAJ 18; Tübingen, 1988) 44-78. Cohen, 'Religion', 212-21. On Idumaean status in Jewish eyes, and the Idumaean part in the revolt, M. Goodman, *The Ruling Class of Judaea: The Origins of the Jewish Revolt against Rome AD 66-70* (Cambridge, 1987) 222-3.

concern is with 'reconciling the nations'. The representation of the hostile crowd as made up of *allophuloi*, 'other peoples', figures in the description of the Alexandrian troubles under the emperors Caligula and Claudius (*BJ* 2.488). At Scythopolis in AD 66, the same line-up of the Jewish element against the foreign is envisaged (*BJ* 2.466). Castigating the revolutionaries during the siege of Jerusalem, Josephus, in a speech which he puts into his own mouth, paradoxically contrasts foreign respect for the Temple with the Jews' desecration of their own shrine (6.102). Olive oil not produced by Jews is regularly described as *allophulon*, indicating its unsuitability for Jewish use. If Goodman is right, the basis of this practice was not any *halakhah* (legal ruling) of any kind, but, in the first instance, instinctive revulsion.[18] Further examples of this polarity might be cited.

Non-Jews are the 'other', and they may well be hostile. But we find no verbal expression of separatism in Josephus as strong as that of II Maccabees, where the extraordinary term *allophulismos* is devised to describe the process of adopting foreign habits, and associated with the author's more long-lived and famous coinage, *hellenismos*.[19] Indeed, Josephus can even go so far as to reverse the use of the term *allophulos*, suggesting that the concept did not in itself carry strong negative implications for him. In his preface to the *Jewish War* (1.16), Josephus happily describes himself as *allophulos*, a foreigner, addressing Greeks and Romans.

VII. Greeks in Josephus

When Josephus deploys the label 'Greek', this, too, frequently forms part of a 'them' and 'us' dichotomy, at least implicitly. A point which should not be overlooked, however, is that the polarity, far from being consistent, shifts dramatically. Often Greeks are 'them', as we might expect. There is an unusual and intemperate attack on 'native-born' (*gnesioi*) Greek writers in the preface to the *Jewish War* (1.16), in which they are castigated as liars, voluble in the law-courts but silent when expected to bring forth facts: these are the hostile terms in which Roman cultural stereotypes of the Greek character were often expressed.

---

[18]M. Goodman, 'Kosher Olive Oil in Antiquity' in Davies and White (eds.), *A Tribute to Geza Vermes* (see above, n. 3) 227-45.

[19]On *allophulismos*, see Hengel, *'Hellenization'* (see above, n. 8) 22.

The use of the term 'Greeks' as a general description of non-Jews figures regularly in Josephus. The mercenaries of King Alexander Jannaeus—actually, we are told, Pisidians and Cilicians—are also simply called 'Greeks' (*BJ* 1.94). Foreign oil is also Greek oil (*Vita* 94).

Furthermore, in a number of historical episodes, Greeks and Jews are presented as natural antagonists within a city. At Alexandria, Caesarea, Scythopolis and Antioch, Jews are all, in the course of civil disturbances, massacred by Greeks. At Tiberias, Greeks make their only appearance in Josephus' *Life* when all the Greek residents of Tiberias (they are not citizens, since the city is a Jewish one) are said to be massacred by the Jewish pro-revolt party (*Vita* 67).

Yet sometimes in Josephus the Greeks are 'us', contrasted with barbarians. Thus those before Josephus who have translated Jewish writings into Greek can be simply called Greeks, though they were manifestly Jews (*BJ* 1.17). Here there are obvious apologetic considerations: it could be advantageous in writing history designed for Greek readers to identify Jews with Greeks, just as it was the purpose of the 1st-century Greek historian Dionysius of Halicarnassus, who wrote at Rome, to prove that the Romans were Greek by origin. But there is more to it. Josephus is able to deploy a linguistic and cultural rather than an ethnic definition of what is Greek. In terms of such a construction, Greekness, far from being alien to Judaism, can be something in which Jews shared. In any interpretation of Josephus' ability to speak in this way, the important fact of the existence of a large class of Jews whose only language was Greek should not be overlooked. There is certainly no need to ascribe the contradictions in usage to the historian's employment of different sources.

VIII. Greeks and Syrians in Josephus

The most interesting pair of identity labels in Josephus involves assimilation rather than antithesis. It is unexpectedly hard to establish the difference between the element in the population of Palestine described as 'Greek' and that spoken of as 'Syrians'. Syrian identity is a relatively new and arbitrary phenomenon, probably reflecting the Roman provincial division and thus to be regarded as a consequence of Rome's disruption of the area. But for Jews, too, 'Syrian' was a convenient description, and it was used by our author almost interchangeably with 'Greek'. So what significance lay in the difference?

A clear distinction does seem to emerge, and it is an important one. Greeks are urban, Syrians tend to be rural. The cities and towns in and around Palestine are constantly and automatically described as Greek by Josephus, and their inhabitants simplistically as Greeks. There is a real distinction to be made between proper Greek cities and towns which are not, and, when he needs to, Josephus is quite capable of making it. Thus he explains that the Romans took from the ethnarchy of Archelaus the Greek towns of Gaza, Gadara and Hippos and added them to the province of Syria, leaving the ruler with Strato's tower, Sebaste, Joppa and Jerusalem (*BJ* 2.97). The difference between the two groups evidently lies in their foundation and their organisation.

It would seem that technically 'Greeks' are those who live in Greek cities; more loosely, any non-Jewish town-dwellers can be Greek. Syrians, by contrast, are the provincials, and essentially rural. The villagers around Caesarea, attacked by parties of Jews after the troubles in the city, are described as Syrians (*BJ* 2.458). But the neighbouring cities, listed by Josephus, are not included in the Syrian area. The inhabitants of Trachonitis, in the kingdom of Agrippa II, are a mixture of Jews and Syrians (*BJ* 3.57). Troops fighting for the Romans, when not called simply 'Roman', can be admitted as Syrian (*BJ* 38). Deserting Jerusalemites who have swallowed gold coins before escaping the siege are ripped open by the Arabs among the Syrians on the other side (*BJ* 5.549ff.).

In a technical sense, Syrians are those who live in the province of Syria, of which the cities, with their own territories, were, according to Roman arrangements, formally not a part. Perhaps for Josephus the term had few connotations beyond that. But if Greeks are simply the citizens of the cities, then we do not learn much from the term about the ethnicity or culture of those thus described. It is clear that the cities will have had Greek-style constitutions, at least of a rudimentary kind.[20] And Greek was no doubt the public language of these cities. Yet Greek need not even have been the principal spoken language in the earlier stages of Roman rule. It is hard if not impossible to discover how sharp a distinction existed between the two types of city, those that were Greek in the formal sense and those that were not.

In the high empire of the 2nd and 3rd centuries AD, their public architecture clearly marked out the Greek cities of the region. But in the Second Temple period, the process of physical transformation was

[20]A.H.M. Jones, *The Greek City* (1940) 170-91.

far from complete and building activities sporadic. We return to our earlier question, asking what differences a visitor would be likely to perceive, travelling about the area and closely observing the different elements in the population of Palestine. In the real sense, this remains an impenetrable problem. In another sense, we may perhaps have gone some way towards an answer. For, operating like all others with constructed identities, our visitor to some extent sees what he looks for. Thus he will find reasons, if he so chooses, to place Greeks and Jews in worlds diametrically opposed to one another. He will sometimes hear them, if he can understand them, insisting upon their differences. But if he has no need of this constructed polarity, a more integrated scene will lie before him.

CHAPTER 2

ACTS AND ROMAN POLICY IN JUDAEA

David W.J. Gill

Summary

During the course of Acts Judaea was a Roman province under a prefect, a kingdom under Agrippa I, and then a province again under a procurator. The troubles facing Roman governors in the eastern provinces, and specifically in Judaea, are reflected in the state of the province under Felix and Porcius Festus. Roman control was assisted by the ruling members of the Jewish elite, and this is emphasised by Felix's marriage to Drusilla, sister of Agrippa II.

I. The Incorporation of Judaea

The period of the Book of Acts is one when Judaea moved out of and into the sphere of Roman control. Since Pompey's conquests in the east and the formation of Syria as a province in 58 BC, Rome had been a neighbour.[1] It was from this base that Rome intervened in Judaea.[2] Thus when in 4 BC Herod died, it was Sabinus, the *procurator* of Syria, who went to secure the royal treasury at Jerusalem which contained a bequest to Augustus:

> To Caesar he left ten million pieces of coined silver besides vessels of gold and silver and some very valuable garments, while to Caesar's wife Julia and some others he left five million pieces.[3]

At the same time a Jewish uprising meant that Quinctilius Varus, the *legatus* of Syria, had to intervene with all three Syrian legions.[4]

> This outbreak had been foreseen by Varus, who, after the sailing of Archelaus, has gone up to Jerusalem to repress its promoters, and, as it was evident that the people would not remain quiet had left in the city one of the three legions from Syria which he had brought with him; he himself then returned to Antioch.[5]

The intervention of Sabinus further heightened the tension, and large crowds surrounded the Roman troops.[6] Sabinus therefore had to ask Varus for help, and he brought the additional two Syrian legions along with other forces, and proceeded to advance through Galilee and

---

[1]R. Tracey, 'Syria', in D.W.J. Gill and C. Gempf, *The Book of Acts in its First-Century Setting*, vol. 2: *The Book of Acts in its Graeco-Roman Setting* (Grand Rapids: Eerdmans, 1994) 223-78. For a regional history, F. Millar, *The Roman Near East 31 BC - AD 337* (Cambridge, Mass.: Harvard University Press, 1993). See also M. Sartre, *L'Orient Romain: Provinces et sociétés provinciales en Méditerrannée orientale d'Auguste aux Sévères* (Paris: Seuil, 1991). A new study on Roman Syria is in preparation by K. Butcher.

[2]See especially Tracey, 'Syria', 254-57.

[3]Josephus, *Ant*. 17.8.1; see also F. Millar, *The Emperor in the Roman World* (London: Duckworth, 1992) 153; Millar, *Roman Near East*, 41. Sabinus met Archelaus at Caesarea and was temporarily halted by Varus: Josephus, *BJ* 2.16-18.

[4]E. Schürer, *The History of the Jewish People in the Age of Jesus Christ (175 BC - AD 135)* 1, rev. and ed. G. Vermes and F. Millar (Edinburgh: T. & T. Clark, 1973) 331. See also R.D. Sullivan, 'The Dynasty of Judaea in the First Century', *ANRW* 2.8 (1977) 296-354.

[5]Josephus, *BJ* 2.39-41.

[6]Josephus, *BJ* 2.41-44.

Samaria.[7] Eventually the rebels surrendered, prisoners were sent to Rome and Varus returned to Antioch, leaving a legion in Jerusalem.[8]

In AD 6 Archelaus, Herod's heir as king, was deposed and sent into exile at Vienne in Gallia Narbonensis by Augustus.[9] In this way the areas of Idumaea, Judaea and Samaria became a Roman province; the area ruled by the tetrarchs, Herodes Antipas and Philip, remained in their control.[10] From this date the province was administered by *praefecti* of equestrian rank appointed by the emperor and based at Caesarea.[11]

> The territory of Archelaus was now reduced to a province, and Coponius, a Roman of the equestrian order, was sent out as procurator, entrusted by Augustus with full powers, including the infliction of capital punishment.[12]

These officials had wide-ranging powers which included the ability to appoint the High Priests. In the absence of military forces, this allowed the *praefectus* to win the support of the ruling families of the province and thus be assured of their co-operation.[13] With incorporation came the payment of taxes, and by AD 17 both Syria and Judaea were requesting a reduction.[14]

In AD 33/34 Philip died, and his area of control first passed to the province of Syria.[15] The *praefectus* Pontius Pilatus, appointed by Tiberius in 26, had upset the Jews over several issues.[16] He had introduced images of Caesar into Jerusalem by night and refused requests

---

[7]Josephus, *BJ* 2.66-71.

[8]Josephus, *BJ* 2.77-79.

[9]Josephus, *BJ* 2.111; Millar, *Roman Near East*, 44. For Archelaus: Schürer, *History of the Jewish People* I, 353-57.

[10]Josephus, *BJ* 2.167.

[11]Schürer, *History of the Jewish People* I, 357-98. For other provinces with *praefecti*: F. Millar, *The Roman Empire and its Neighbours* (London: Duckworth, 1981) 55.

[12]Josephus, *BJ* 2.117. See also S. Applebaum, 'Judaea as a Roman province; the countryside as a political and economic factor', *ANRW* 2.8 (1977) 355-96; Z. Safrai, *The Economy of Roman Palestine* (London: Routledge, 1993).

[13]M. Goodman, *The Ruling Class of Judaea: the Origins of the Jewish Revolt Against Rome AD 66-70* (Cambridge: Cambridge University Press, 1987), esp. p. 33.

[14]Tacitus, *Ann.* 2.42.7. See also Millar, *Roman Near East*, 47-48; Millar, *Emperor*, 376-77.

[15]Josephus, *Ant.* 18.106; Millar, *Roman Near East*, 51-52. His area included Gaulanitis, Trachonitis, Batanea and the city of Paneas: Millar, *ibid.*, 41.

[16]See J.-P. Lémonon, *Pilate et le gouvernement de la Judée: textes et monuments* (Paris: J. Gabalda, 1981); B. Lifshitz, 'Césarée de Palestine, son histoire et ses institutions', *ANRW* 2.8 (1977) 501, pl. I,1 (for text).

to remove them; they were only removed when it became clear that the crowd of Jews gathered in the stadium were prepared to die rather than transgress their law about images.[17] Pilatus also constructed an aqueduct which was said to have been paid for by the 'Corbanus' treasury; in the ensuing riot many Jews were killed by Roman soldiers planted in the crowd.[18] In 36 Lucius Vitellius, *legatus* of Syria, was forced to intervene in the province over allegations against Pilatus, who was forced to return to Rome.[19] This act also saw the return of the right for the Jews to take their own control of the priestly robes. In 37 the region of Trachonitis was handed over to Agrippa I along with the tetrarchy of Lysanias;[20] Agrippa himself returned to the east from Rome in 38.[21] After suspicions were raised that Herodes Antipas was in league with Artabanus of Parthia, Antipas was exiled, and his territory of Galilee and Peraea was added to those of Agrippa.[22]

Disturbances in 39/40 at Jamnia led to Gaius ordering that a statue of himself should be erected at Jerusalem in the Holy of Holies.

> The insolence with which the emperor Gaius defied fortune surpassed all bounds: he wished to be considered a god and to be hailed as such, he cut off the flower of the nobility of his country, and his impiety extended even to Judaea. In fact, he sent Petronius with an army to Jerusalem to install in the sanctuary statues of himself; in the event of the Jews refusing to admit them, his orders were to put the recalcitrants to death and to reduce the whole nation to slavery.[23]

Petronius, *legatus* of Syria, brought his troops down, and the plan was only reversed by the intervention of Agrippa I who had returned to Rome.[24]

---

[17]Josephus, *BJ* 2.169-74; *Ant.* 18.55.

[18]Josephus, *BJ* 2.175-77; *Ant.* 18.60-62. See also *The Suda* s.v. *Korbanos*: 'Among the Jews (the Korbanos is) the holy treasury. Pilatus spent the holy treasury on an aqueduct and stirred up a riot. It brought in (water) from a distance of 400 stades. Bringing in his soldiers he killed many (Jews)'. The translation is from R.K. Sherk, *The Roman Empire: Augustus to Hadrian* (Cambridge: Cambridge University Press, 1988) 75 no. 39B.

[19]Millar, *Roman Near East*, 54-55; Millar, *Emperor*, 377. Agrippa I had sent a letter to Tiberius about Pontius Pilatus to Gaius over shields dedicated to Tiberius in the palace at Jerusalem: Philo, *Leg.* 38.299-305.

[20]Josephus, *Ant.* 18.237.

[21]Josephus, *BJ* 2.181; Millar, *Roman Near East*, 57.

[22]Josephus, *BJ* 2.183; *Ant.* 18.252; Millar, *Roman Near East*, 58.

[23]Josephus, *BJ* 2.184-85.

II. Judaea Under Agrippa

With Gaius' murder in January 41 and the accession of Claudius, Agrippa's role in these changes was rewarded by the gift of Judaea and Samaria, and thus the loss of the Roman province of Judaea.[25]

> Upon Agrippa [Claudius] forthwith conferred the whole of his grandfather's kingdom, annexing to it from over the border not only the districts of Trachonitis and Auranitis of which Augustus had made a present to Herod, but a further principality known as the kingdom of Lysanias. This donation he announced to the people by an edict, and ordered the magistrates to have it engraved on bronze tablets to be deposited in the Capitol.[26]

This transfer of the province almost certainly explains the fact that the Book of Acts sees Agrippa receiving an embassy from Tyre and Sidon without reference to the *legatus* of Syria.[27] One of his projects was to defend Jerusalem with new walls 'on such a scale as, had it been completed, would have rendered ineffectual all the efforts of the Romans in the subsequent siege'.[28]

III. Judaea Returned to Roman Control

With Agrippa's death in 44 at Caesarea,[29] the whole area reverted to a Roman province with a *procurator* to govern it, rather than being ruled by Agrippa's son, the future Agrippa II, who was only sixteen.[30] Claudius appointed the equestrian Cuspius Fadus.[31] One of his first acts was to demand the right to control the high priestly robes; this led to a

---

[24]Josephus, *BJ* 2.184-87, 192-203; Millar, *Roman Near East*, 58-59; Millar, *Emperor*, 377; Schürer, *History of the Jewish People* I, 395-97. The letter reversing the instruction crossed over another which threatened Petronius with a death-sentence if he delayed in implementing Gaius' command.

[25]Josephus, *BJ* 2.204-17. Millar, *Roman Near East*, 59-60. For Agrippa: Schürer, *History of the Jewish People* I, 442-54; Sullivan, 'Dynasty of Judaea', 322-29.

[26]Josephus, *BJ* 2.215-16.

[27]Acts 12:20-21 (where he is identified as Herod). See Millar, *Roman Near East*, 60.

[28]Josephus, *BJ* 2.218.

[29]Josephus, *BJ* 2.219; *Ant.* 19.351; *cf.* Acts 12:19; see also Schürer, *History of the Jewish People* I, 453.

[30]Josephus, *BJ* 2.220; *Ant.* 19.354; Millar, *Roman Near East*, 61; Sullivan, 'Dynasty of Judaea', 329-45. For the procurators: Schürer, *History of the Jewish People* I, 455-70.

[31]Josephus, *BJ* 2.220.

petition to the *legatus* of Syria, Cassius Longinus, as well as to Claudius himself.[32] The next *procurator*, Tiberius Iulius Alexander, a member of a Jewish family from Alexandria, proved to be a wise appointment as he 'abstained from all interference with the customs of the country and kept the nation at peace'.[33] It was probably during his procuratorship that a food shortage affected Judaea.[34] Herod, the then 'king' of Chalcis and uncle of the younger Agrippa, then obtained the right of control of the Temple as well as the appointment of High Priests.[35] In 50 this Herod died, and Agrippa obtained the kingdom of Chalcis as well as the 'care of the temple'.[36] This kingdom was removed from Agrippa in 53 (when it was presumably added to the province of Syria) and in return Claudius granted Agrippa the region formerly controlled by Philip's tetrarchy as well as the tetrarchy of Lysanias.

This period also saw another intervention by the governor of Syria over a dispute *c.* 51 or 52 surrounding attacks by Samaritans on Jewish travellers moving between Galilee and Jerusalem.[37] Ventidius Cumanus, the *procurator*, had proved to be unsatisfactory in allowing his troops to upset the Jews. Several incidents are recorded:

> The usual crowd had assembled at Jerusalem for the feast of unleavened bread, and the Roman cohort had taken up its position on the roof of the portico of the temple; for a body of men in arms invariably mounts guard at the feasts, to prevent disorders arising from such a concourse of people. Thereupon one of the soldiers, raising his robe, stooped in an indecent attitude, so as to turn his backside to the Jews, and made a noise in keeping with his posture. Enraged at this insult, the whole multitude with loud cries called upon Cumanus to punish the soldier; some of the more hot-headed young men and seditious persons in the crowd started a fight, and, picking up stones, hurled

---

[32]Millar, *Roman Near East*, 62.

[33]Josephus, *BJ* 2.220; *Ant.* 18.8.1, 20.5.2. He was nephew of Philo the philosopher and his father may have been part of the Alexandrian embassy to Gaius. For his life: E.G. Turner, 'Tiberius Iulius Alexander', *JRS* 44 (1954) 54-64, esp. p. 59: 'Rome may have thought him a suitable compromise choice to govern a province that resented direct government after having kings of its own race'; V. Burr, *Tiberius Iulius Alexander* (Bonn, 1955). He went on to be prefect of Egypt: see, for example, his edict from the temple of Hibis at El-Khargeh: Sherk, *The Roman Empire: Augustus to Hadrian*, 118-23, no. 80.

[34]Acts 11:28; *cf.* B.W. Winter, 'Acts and food shortages', in Gill and Gempf, *The Book of Acts in its Graeco-Roman Setting*, 59-78.

[35]Josephus, *Ant.* 20.15-16.

[36]Josephus, *BJ* 2.221, 223; Millar, *Roman Near East*, 63.

[37]Millar, *Roman Near East*, 64-65.

> them at the troops. Cumanus, fearing a general attack upon himself, sent for reinforcements. These troops pouring into the porticoes, the Jews were seized with irresistible panic and turned to fly from the temple and make their escape into the town...upwards of thirty thousand perished....[38]

In another incident, after the robbery by brigands of Stephen, an imperial slave, Cumanus ordered that the local residents be brought to him in chains. During the operation one of the soldiers, 'finding in one village a copy of the sacred law, tore the book in pieces and flung it into the fire'. A delegation was sent to Cumanus at Caesarea and the soldier was sent for execution.[39] In a dispute between the Galileans and the Samaritans, Cumanus did not intervene on the Jews' behalf, and this led to the sacking of various Samaritan villages. Cumanus responded with an attack on the Jews and the arming of the Samaritans. Ummidius Quadratus, the *legatus* of Syria, then intervened and the leaders of both groups as well as Cumanus and Celer the tribune were sent off to Rome for Claudius to hear the case.[40] Agrippa II ensured the exile of Cumanus, the execution of the Samaritan delegation, and the return of Celer to Jerusalem where he was beheaded.[41]

IV. Felix

It was at this point that Felix was appointed by Claudius as *procurator* of the province.[42] He was a freedman and brother of Pallas, perhaps one of the most influential of the freedmen under Claudius.[43] Felix' connections at Rome through his brother Pallas meant that he felt that he could act with impunity in his province. In Tacitus' view, Felix, 'backed by vast influence, believed himself free to commit any crime'.[44] Pallas himself received his freedom from Antonia, the mother

---

38Josephus, *BJ* 2.224-27.
39Josephus, *BJ* 2.228-31.
40Josephus, *BJ* 2.241-44; Millar, *Emperor*, 378.
41Josephus, *BJ* 2.245-46.
42Josephus, *BJ* 2.247. For Felix: Schürer, *History of the Jewish People* I, 459-66. Suetonius, *Claudius* 28, on discussing the freedmen of Claudius, noted, 'For Felix, [Claudius] had an equally high regard, giving him command of infantry battalions and cavalry squadrons, and the governorship of Judaea; this Felix married three queens'.
43S.I. Oost, 'The career of M. Antonius Pallas', *AJP* 79 (1958) 113-39; *cf.* Millar, *Emperor*, 74-75. Oost (p. 132) suggested that Felix obtained his position because of Pallas.

of Claudius, and it has been suggested that the *procurator* was thus Antonius Felix.[45] However, Josephus calls him Claudius Felix.[46] This latter suggestion has been linked to a Greek epitaph found between Dora and Athlit to Titus Mucius Clemens, who was employed by an ἐπίτροπος (the equivalent of the Latin *procurator*) called Tiberius Claudius;[47] Felix is certainly a possibility.

Tension in the eastern provinces was heightened in 54 when Tiridates laid claim to the throne of Armenia.[48] This led to a request for Agrippa to supply forces for an attack on Parthia. Such concerns facing the *legatus* of Syria meant that incidents in Judaea would have to be dealt with sensitivity. The *procurator* could no longer look to Syria for the support of legions and would have to rely on the goodwill of the Jewish elite and his own small number of auxiliary troops. At roughly the same time Nero added part of Galilee to the control of Agrippa.

Felix's procuratorship was marked by a series of incidents. He dealt with the brigand Eleazar and sent him to Rome as punishment; in addition he crucified his associates and punished the common people who were perceived as aiding the brigands.[49] At the same time there grew up a band of assassins, the *sicarii*, whose victims included Jonathan the High Priest.[50] Another group led large numbers into the desert; 'Felix, regarding this as but the preliminary to insurrection, sent a body of cavalry and heavily-armed infantry, and put a large number to the sword'.[51] Around 54 Felix had to deal with a revolt by an Egyptian prophet who planned to storm Jerusalem:

> His attack was anticipated by Felix, who went to meet him with the Roman heavy infantry, the whole population joining him in the defence. The outcome of the ensuing engagement was that the Egyptian escaped with a few of his followers; most of his force were killed

---

[44]Tacitus, *Ann.* 12.54; *cf. Hist.* 5.9: 'Antonius Felix [a freedman] practised every kind of cruelty and lust, wielding the power of a king with all the instincts of a slave'.

[45]As Tacitus, *Hist.* 5.9.

[46]Josephus, *Ant.* 18.6.6.

[47]Schürer, *History of the Jewish People* I, 460 n. 19 for text.

[48]Millar, *Roman Near East*, 66.

[49]Josephus, *BJ* 2.253.

[50]Josephus, *BJ* 2.254-57. Jonathan had been one of the party sent to Rome by Quadratus during the procuratorship of Cumanus: Josephus, *BJ* 2.240. He would thus have been perceived as having been influential in Felix' appointment: Schürer, *History of the Jewish People* I, 463.

[51]Josephus, *BJ* 2.258-60.

> or taken prisoners; the remainder dispersed and stealthily escaped to their several homes.[52]

Indeed, Paul was mistaken by the Roman military tribune for this very Egyptian rebel, 'who recently stirred up a revolt and led the four thousand men of the Assassins out into the wilderness'.[53] In addition there were other internal tensions in part relating to the priesthood.[54]

It is against the background of this tension, both in the Near East and in Judaea, that Paul was arrested in Jerusalem over the allegation that a Gentile had been allowed to enter the Temple.[55] The rapid intervention of the tribune of the cohort shows that the administration did not wish any riot to get out of control.[56] It was to avoid potential trouble in Jerusalem that the tribune, Claudius Lysias, sent Paul with an escort by night to the *procurator* Felix at Caesarea.[57]

Caesarea was established by Herod Antipater on the site of Strato's Tower and was named in honour of Augustus.[58] At Caesarea the provincial administration had taken over the old royal buildings: Paul was sent off to be guarded in Herod's praetorium.[59] The city itself contained important symbols of Rome's authority which included buildings linked to the imperial cult. Josephus described the temple of Roma and Augustus:[60]

> In a circle round the harbour there was a continuous line of buildings constructed of the most polished stone, and in their midst was a mound on which there stood a temple of Caesar, visible a great way off to those sailing into the harbour, which had a statue of Roma and also of Caesar.

---

[52]Josephus, *BJ* 2.261-63. See also Schürer, *History of the Jewish People* I, 464.
[53]Acts 21:38. Josephus (*BJ* 2.261-63; *Ant.* 20.169-72) gives further details of the revolt which was suppressed by the *procurator* Felix, *c.* AD 54.
[54]Schürer, *History of the Jewish People* I, 464-65.
[55]Acts 21:27-36.
[56]Acts 21:31-32. The cohort was garrisoned in the Antonia Fortress. For this unit: Schürer, *History of the Jewish People* I, 366.
[57]On these military units, including the Italic and Augustan cohorts (Acts 10:1; 27:1) see the unpublished paper by F.F. Bruce, 'Roman military units'. I am grateful to Dr Bruce Winter for allowing me to read a copy of this work.
[58]H.K. Beebe, 'Caesarea Maritima: its strategic and political significance to Rome', *JNES* 42.3 (1983) 195-207; Lifshitz, 'Césarée', 490-518. For Josephus' description: *Ant.* 15.331-41; *BJ* 1.405-15.
[59]Acts 23:35. See also Millar, *Roman Near East*, 45. For the place of Caesarea in the province: Schürer, *History of the Jewish People* I, 361.
[60]Josephus, *Ant.* 15.339.

During the term of office of Pontius Pilatus a building dedicated to Tiberius was erected.[61] The city itself was quite substantial, perhaps with a population of some 50,000.[62]

It was probably during Paul's imprisonment at Caesarea that a riot in the city took place. Towards the end of Felix's procuratorship the Jews claimed that Caesarea belonged to them. The Greeks pointed to the statues and temples which Herod had allowed to be erected there as evidence that it was not to be considered a Jewish city.[63] After riots, and the inability of the local magistrates to quell the unrest,

> Felix came forward into the *agora* and ordered them in menacing tones to retire; on their refusing to obey, he sent his troops upon them (*sc.* the Jews), when many were killed, their property being subsequently plundered.[64]

The result was that the leaders of both sides were sent to Nero to argue their case.

Felix's procuratorship illustrates the links between the Roman administration and the Jewish ruling elite. Felix brought his wife, Drusilla, 'a Jewess', to hear Paul.[65] This was in fact the daughter of Agrippa I and sister of Agrippa II. In 44, on the death of her father, she was only six,[66] and so could only have been fourteen when Felix took up his office. She had originally been betrothed to Antiochus (C. Iulius Antiochus Epiphanes) king of Commagene, but Antiochus refused to be circumcised and so she was given to Aziz, king of Emesa.[67] She left him for Felix with the assistance of a magician, Simon, from Cyprus; Aziz must have died shortly afterwards.[68] Felix and Drusilla had a son, Agrippa, who perished in the eruption of Vesuvius in 79.[69] In fact she

---

[61]Schürer, *History of the Jewish People* I, 358 n. 22. Pontius Pilatus is described as *praefectus* of Judaea. The text appears in Sherk, *The Roman Empire: Augustus to Hadrian*, 75 no. 39A.

[62]Schürer, *History of the Jewish People* I, 465, based on the population of 20,000 Jews: Josephus, *BJ* 2.457.

[63]Josephus, *BJ* 2.266-70. A.H.M. Jones, *The Cities of the Eastern Roman Provinces* (Oxford: Clarendon Press, 1937) 273-74; Millar, *Emperor*, 378.

[64]Josephus, *BJ* 2.270.

[65]Acts 24:24.

[66]Josephus, *Ant.* 19.354.

[67]Josephus, *Ant.* 20.139. For Azizus see R.D. Sullivan, 'The dynasty of Emesa', *ANRW* 8 (1977) 198-219, esp. 215-16; Schürer, *History of the Jewish People* I, 462 n. 26. Further on Drusilla: Sullivan, 'Dynasty of Judaea', 329-31.

[68]Josephus, *Ant.* 20.141-4. Aziz died in the first year of Nero, *i.e.* in 53 or 54: Josephus, *Ant.* 20.158.

was his third wife; one of the others was a granddaughter of M. Antonius and Cleopatra.[70]

V. Porcius Festus

Porcius Festus seems to have taken over from Felix *c.* 60 after the riots at Caesarea.[71] Given the troubles under his predecessor, he was eager not to offend the Jews and thus Paul was left in prison;[72] this led Paul to take the decision to appeal to Caesar and thus be sent to Rome. One of Festus' first acts was to move from Caesarea to Jerusalem where he met the chief priests and the leading members of the Jewish community.[73] However, it is at Caesarea, the seat of the Roman administration, that Festus received Agrippa and his sister Berenice.[74] During his governorship there was further trouble by bandits, 'the principal plague of the country'.[75] He died in office,[76] and was followed by Albinus.

VI. Conclusion

The events of the Book of Acts are set against the changing political situation in Judaea. The unstable situation and the reliance on military intervention from Syria meant that the governors of the province sought either to win the support of the Jewish élite or to control the province by force. The growing tension on Rome's eastern frontier may explain the unwillingness of Felix and Porcius Festus to commit themselves to freeing Paul in the face of Jewish opposition.

---

[69]Josephus, *Ant.* 20.7.2.
[70]Tacitus, *Hist.* 5.9 (where she is misleadingly named as Drusilla). Through her Felix was thus related to the emperor Claudius, who was a grandson of Antonius.
[71]For further details: *PW* 22.1, cols. 220-27; *PIR* III, 88, no. 637.
[72]Acts 24:27.
[73]Acts 25:1-2; 'after three days' indicates the priority given to attending to good relations.
[74]Acts 25:13. On Berenice see R. Jordan, *Berenice* (London: Constable, 1974).
[75]Josephus, *BJ* 2.271; Schürer, *History of the Jewish People* I, 467-68.
[76]Josephus, *Ant.* 20.200.

Appendix I: Prefects of Judaea (AD 6 - 41)[77]

1.	*c.* AD 6-9	Coponius
2.	*c.* AD 9-12	Marcus Ambibulus
3.	*c.* AD 12-15	Annius Rufus
4.	AD 15-26	Valerius Gratus
5.	AD 26-36	Pontius Pilatus
6.	AD 36 or 37	Marcellus
7.	AD 37-41	Marullus[78]

Appendix II: Procurators of Judaea (AD 44 - 66)[79]

1.	AD 44-?46	Cuspius Fadus
2.	AD ?46-48	Tiberius Iulius Alexander
3.	AD 48-*c.* 52	Ventidius Cumanus
4.	AD *c.* 52-60?	(Antonius or Claudius) Felix
5.	? AD 60-62	Porcius Festus
6.	AD 62-64	Lucceius Albinus
7.	AD 64-66	Gessius Florus

CHAPTER 3

THE GEOGRAPHY OF PALESTINE IN ACTS

Martin Hengel

Summary

Luke is not interested in precise details of Palestinian geography for their own sake. His inexact knowledge of the geography of Galilee, Samaria and most of Judaea is only what we should expect in a writer who had not visited these areas. But, by contrast, his exact information about the cities of the coastal Plain, the road from Jerusalem to Caesarea, and the relation between the Temple and the Antonia fortress in Jerusalem is striking, and is consistent with the view that he had visited Palestine as a companion of Paul.

I. The Problem

One of the firm convictions of present-day 'critical' exegesis is that the author of the two-volume work dedicated to Theophilus was not at all well versed in the geography of Palestine. Thus D. Gewalt attributes to him 'complete ignorance of geographical conditions in the area of Syria and Palestine'.[1] In H. Conzelmann's well-known monograph *The Theology of St Luke*, the mysterious verse Luke 17:11 is among the evidence which the author uses to support this judgement, and he draws far-reaching consequences from it.[2] In so doing he could refer to the eminent expert on Palestine, C.C. McCown, who some time before had characterised Luke as an 'armchair geographer with no practical experience'.[3]

Of course we make it too easy for ourselves if we compare our modern knowledge (also usually acquired at our desks) with that of ancient writers who had very much less help and far fewer sources of information than we take for granted today. Conzelmann[4] therefore tries to arrive indirectly at a fairer assessment of the 'hellenistic histo-

[1]*Petrus* (Typescript dissertation, Heidelberg, 1966) 48, referring to H. Conzelmann, *The Theology of St Luke* (ET; London, 1960) '18ff. *passim*'. Similarly, most recently, G. Lüdemann, *Paul Apostle to the Gentiles: Studies in Chronology*, tr. F.S. Jones (London, 1984) 35 n. 40: 'Strong doubts about the reliability of Luke as a historian also arise in light of his ignorance of the geography of Palestine, the main setting for his history of the church'. In his often unqualified attacks on Luke the author only shows his inability to pass a reliable historical judgment on ancient texts.

[2]*Op. cit.*, 18-94: 'Part One: Geographical Elements in the Composition of Luke's Gospel'; 13: 'His acquaintance with Palestine is...in many respects imperfect'. More sharply 18 n.: 'At all events the variations in information about the Jordan in Luke arise from the fact that Luke has no personal knowledge of the country'. On Luke 17:11, 'The expression indicates that Luke imagines that Judaea and Galilee are immediately adjacent and that Samaria lies alongside them' (69). I find improbable the hypothesis that there is a fixed christological scheme behind Luke's inaccurate geography. This can only be read into the text with a degree of imagination. The picture sketched out by W. Marxsen, *Introduction to the New Testament* (Philadelphia, 1970) 160, 'According to Luke's geographical conceptions Judaea (alongside the Mediterranean) and Galilee (to the East) are immediate neighbours ...Samaria is thought of as being north of the two territories', turns into a caricature. For criticism of Conzelmann see H.-M. Schenke and K.M. Fischer, *Einleitung in die Schriften des NT* II (Gütersloh, 1979) 132, and I.H. Marshall, *The Gospel of Luke* (Exeter, 1978) 198f., on Luke 4:44; 650 on Luke 17:11. See also below, nn. 5, 28, 123: wrong combinations of names of places and provinces occur relatively frequently in ancient historians.

[3]'Gospel Geography, Fiction, Fact and Central Section', *JBL* 57 (1938) 51-66.

[4]*Theology of St. Luke*, 19 n. 1.

rian' Luke by referring to the work of ancient 'armchair geographers', for example to Strabo's account of Palestine,[5] which has a great many errors in it, and to the confused remarks of Pliny the Elder,[6] who completely muddled up his sources. Tacitus, too, had only very inaccurate ideas of the geographical relationship of Samaria and Galilee within the province of Judaea.[7] Even Ptolemy, who sought to give exact locations of places in Palestine with indications of longitude and latitude, makes serious mistakes: his mention of Idumaea, 'which lies well to the west of the Jordan'(!), is an anachronism in the second century AD and his location of Sebaste and Gaza in Judaea, in contrast to Joppa, Ashkelon and Γαζαίων λιμήν, is also misleading.[8] That even educated Jews had little information about the geography of Palestine is clear from the imaginary description of Judaea and Jerusalem in the Letter of Aristeas[9] or that of the Holy City by Pseudo-Hecataeus;[10] we can presuppose that even Philo had only a vague knowledge of Jerusalem, the Temple and the Holy Land, though he did visit it once in his life.[11] To some extent the valuable geographical details given by an expert in political and military matters like Josephus contrast with this.

---

[5]Strabo, *Geography* 16.2.16-46, pp. 754-65. M. Stern, *Greek and Latin Authors on Jews and Judaism* I (Jerusalem, 1974) 288-311, nos. 112-15 gives a selection relating to Jewish territory. Strabo 16.2.16=754 makes the Antilebanon begin at Sidon and has the inhabitants of Arados travelling on the Lycus and the Jordan in ships, presumably confusing the Jordan with the Orontes (Stern, *Authors*, 289). According to Strabo, Phoenicia is a narrow coastal strip extending from Orthosia to Pelusium (!), 'the interior lying behind this as far as the Arabians, between Gaza and the Antilebanon, is called Judaea' (16.2.21=756). At Joppa the coastline coming from Egypt, which has previously run in an easterly direction, takes a turn to the north; the city is said to be situated at such a height that one can see Jerusalem from it. Gadara in Transjordan is confused with Gadaris (= Gezer) captured by the Jews (16.2.28f.; *cf.* 41f., 45 = 758f., 764), as is the Dead Sea with the Sirbonian Sea east of Pelusium. Jerusalem is said to lie close to the sea. The main places (or territories), 'Galilee, Jericho, Philadelphia and Samaria' (note the sequence), are inhabited by a mixed population of Egyptians, Arabians and Phoenicians (16.2.34=760, 763).

[6]*Hist.Nat.* 5.66-73; Stern, *Authors* I, 468ff. no. 204.

[7]*Annals* 12.54.2; Stern, *Authors* II (Jerusalem, 1980) 76ff., no. 288. *Cf. Hist.* 5.6.1; Stern, *Authors* II, 19 no. 280: Judaea is bounded on the south by Egypt, on the east by the Arabians, and on the west by the Phoenicians and the sea. The miraculous river Belius (5.7.2), which is said to flow into the Jewish (Dead?) Sea, is in fact outside Judaea near Acco-Ptolemais, *cf.* Pliny, *Hist.Nat.* 5.75; 36.190f., and Josephus, *BJ* 2. 189ff.; see Stern, *Authors* II, 45f.

[8]*Geographia* 5.15.1-7 (Müller) = 5.16.1-10 (Nobbe); see Stern, *Authors* II, 166ff., no. 137a, also 163 and M. Linke, 'Syrien und Palästina in der Karte des Ptolemäus', WZ Halle-Wittenberg 14 (1964) 473-77.

[9]Judaea: *Ep. Arist.* 115-18; the Temple and Jerusalem: 83-91, 100-7.

The educated son of a Jerusalem priest, he was a military commander in Galilee in AD 66/67, and could provide very detailed geographical information which is of abiding and inestimable value for the historical geography of Palestine. However, even Josephus is not always reliable and free from error, and draws some of his precise information from Roman sources.[12] The same is true of the unknown author of 1 Maccabees or the five-volume work underlying 2 Maccabees, which was written by Jason of Cyrene, who must have known Palestine quite well.[13] Polybius, too, bases his account of the first conquest of Palestine by Antiochus III in 219/218 BC on a well-informed—military—source.[14] The relatively exact but unfortunately very scanty details of distances in Palestine in the *Itinerarium Antonini Augusti* and the *Itinerarium Burdigalense*, which were important for Christian pilgrims to

---

[10]In Josephus, *C. Ap.* 1.196f.: the Temple is said to be in the middle of the city; similarly Tacitus, *Hist.* 5.8.1. *Cf.* also the imaginary description of the water supplies of Jerusalem in the earlier Philo, according to Eusebius, *Praep. Evang.* 9.37.1-3 (GCS 43/1, pp. 546f.) = A.-M. Denis, '*Fragmenta pseudepigraphorum quae supersunt Graeca*', in M. Black (ed.), *Apocalypsis Henochi Graece*, A.-M. Denis, *Fragmenta pseudepigraphorum quae supersunt Graeca* (Leiden, 1970) 204.

[11]*De prov.* 2.107 = Eusebius, *Praeparatio evangelica* 8.14.64 (GCS 43/1, p. 477): 'There is a city of Syria by the sea called Ashkelon; when I came into this city on the occasion of a journey to my ancestral sanctuary, to pray and to sacrifice there...' For knowledge of this temple see I. Heinemann, 'Philo von Alexandrien', *PW*, XX/1 (1941) col. 3: '...that his description is only correct in so far as it refers to the peribolos of marble and the cedar table and the inner enclosures. Everything else is wrong, false, derived from the description of the tent of meeting in the Old Testament or by transference from the building and arrangement of Greek temples to Jewish ones'. *Cf. idem*, *Philons griechische und jüdische Bildung* (repr. Hildesheim, 1973) 17: 'Doctrinaire people—and Philo is one of these—are taught by life what they already know from books or talk.' I would not condemn Luke as severely as this, but certainly he is a 'tendentious historian' who deals selectively with reality.

[12]There is urgent need for an assessment of Josephus as a geographer of Palestine. For individual details see now C. Möller and G. Schmitt, *Siedlungen Palästinas nach Flavius Josephus*, TAVOB 14 (Wiesbaden, 1976). Among other points see the description of Galilee, Peraea, Samaria and Judaea: 3.35-58; Lake Gennesaret: 3.506-521; the Dead Sea: 4.477f.; Jerusalem and the temple: 5.136-257. *Cf.* also *Ant.* 5.80-87: the division of the land among the twelve tribes. In all probability, for the *Bellum Judaicum* Josephus could refer to Roman military commentaries; *cf.* A. Schlatter, *Zur Topographie und Geschichte Palästinas* (Stuttgart, 1893) 348ff. (I am indebted to G. Schmitt for this reference). See above all his concluding verdict, 360: 'It is strange that he is accurate where he was not present and inaccurate where he was'.

[13]*Cf.* F.-M. Abel, 'Topographie des campagnes Maccabéennes', *RB* 32 (1923) 495-521; 33 (1924) 201-17, 371-87; 34 (1925) 194-216; 35 (1926) 196-222, 510-33. *Cf.* also B. Bar-Kochva, *Judas Maccabaeus: The Jewish Struggle against the Seleucids* (Cambridge, 1989) 138ff., 276, 350; 508ff. (in Hebrew).

Palestine, probably also go back to earlier official Roman military lists.[15] Exact geographical details and information presuppose either eye-witnesses or at least reliable sources which in turn are based on personal experience. In 2.5.10, Strabo refers to extended journeys of his own, *e.g.* from the Black Sea to Ethiopia, but like his predecessors and rivals he obtained most of his information at second hand (ἀκοῇ παραλαβόντες). His serious mistakes are evidence of this.

Even in the early period of the Principate, exact and detailed geographical knowledge on the basis of maps and accurate descriptions of places was limited to a very tiny élite of soldiers, politicians and scholars, and even with them, personal knowledge of a place was irreplaceable.[16] In addition, there were accounts of voyages and journeys, but by themselves they were hardly enough to provide a faithful geographical picture of a distant land. And as, for example, the Peutinger Table[17] and some other fragments of ancient maps indicate, by the standards of our modern cartographic material, ancient maps were not particularly instructive. Furthermore, it is more than doubtful whether evangelists like Mark or Luke ever caught sight of a map of Palestine. The famous Madaba map from the end of the sixth

---

[14]5.61.3-62.6; 66.1-72.12; the quotation of Josephus (*Ant.* 12.135f.) from the lost account of the Fifth Syrian War and the victory over Scopas is not very accurate, see n. 125 below.

[15]O. Cuntz (ed.), *Itineraria Romana* (Leipzig, 1929) 149,5-150,4; 169,2-5; 199,1-4, 11-200,3 (pp. 21, 23, 27) = Stern, *Authors* (n. 5), nos. 470a-71b, 488ff. For the *Itinerarium Burdigalense* see Stern, *Authors*, no. 488, on 150,2.

[16]See now R.K. Sherk, 'Roman Geographical Exploration', *ANRW* 11/1 (Berlin & New York, 1974) 534-61. Military maps: 558-61: 'Although maps and itineraries may not have been readily available to the general public even by the age of Augustus, at least they become more common by the Late Empire' (560). Note 83: 'Knowing that maps exist is not the same thing as being able to acquire them'. *Cf. Anth. Pal.* 9.55f. On the subject see also F. Lasserre, 'Geographie', in *KP* 2 (Munich, 1975) cols. 751ff.; 'Karten', *KP* 3, cols. 131ff., and Kubitschek, 'Karten', in *PW* X/2 (1919) col. 2100, though he overestimates the significance of maps for schools in antiquity. Such maps are found only in a later time and are primarily maps of the world (col. 2133). It is no coincidence that so few maps on papyrus have come down to us. Apart from the fact that the large-scale maps were very inaccurate in detail (see the illustration of Cyprus on the Peutinger Table, col. 2116), they were above all of military importance.

[17]Konrad Miller, *Die Peutinger'sche Tafel* (Stuttgart, 1887, repr. 1962); *idem*, *Itineraria Romana* (Stuttgart, ^{2}1929, repr. 1963); on Palestine, 810ff.; F. Gizinger, 'Peutingeriana', *PW* XIX/2 (1938) cols. 1405ff. They go back to the famous but inaccurate map of the world by Vipsanius Agrippa, the friend and son-in-law of Augustus: see what is probably the ironical verdict by Strabo (2.5.17) and his remarks on the making of maps (2.5.10).

century AD is a special exception. Ultimately it seems to go back to Eusebius' map for his *Onomasticon*. Maps and accounts of travels in Palestine only became more frequent when pilgrims began to flock to Palestine in the fourth century.[18] Although it may be said to be one of the best preserved maps from antiquity, even the Madaba map does not make it very easy for anyone who does not already know Palestine to get an accurate idea of the country. So in the last resort the only sure way of getting to know a place better was to go there and see for oneself.

As we cannot assume that the Greek Luke ever visited Galilee, Samaria or the Jordan valley, we cannot expect that he would have exact knowledge about the course of the frontiers of Samaria and Galilee or about the relationship of Galilee to the area of the Jordan or to Judaea. The same is true of the much-criticised, deficient knowledge of Galilee and the adjacent regions in Mark. Given that the author of the second Gospel had presumably never been there, it is not as bad as all that.[19]

Luke poses a further special problem in that he does not always use the term Judaea in the same sense.[20] In one instance it can denote the Roman province along with Judaea and Samaria, which in contrast to Galilee was subject to the *imperium* of the Roman procurator,[21] but sometimes it can also denote the whole of Palestine.[22] However, it is most frequently used to refer to the part of Palestine inhabited by Jews, apart from Samaria and Galilee, and even excluding Caesarea.[23] Finally, Luke also sometimes makes a distinction between Judaea and Jerusalem.[24] The reason for this vagueness may be, first, that because of the numerous changes in political circumstances and in boundaries, official terminology was itself inconsistent, and secondly, that the old LXX phrase 'the land of Judah'[25] still influenced him.

Luke is much more concerned for a clear pattern than for geographical exactitude. He is strictly selective in writing his two-volume work as a 'monograph' with a purpose, and therefore in the Gospel he simplifies the geographical details in Mark, his model: there they are much richer. Anything that disturbs or distracts is eliminated. Luke is concerned not about the journeys and the places but about

---

[18]*Cf.* M. Avi Yonah, *The Madaba Mosaic Map* (Jerusalem, 1954) and H. Fischer, 'Geschichte der Kartographie von Palästina', *ZDPV* 62 (1938) 169-89. For the historical map as the starting point for the *Onomasticon* see Eusebius, *Onomasticon*, GCS, ed. Klostermann (Leipzig, 1904) pp. 2, 7f.: ἔπειτα τῆς πάλαι Ἰουδαίας ἀπὸ πάσης βίβλου καταγραφὴν πεποιημένος, καὶ τὰς ἐν αὐτῇ τῶν δώδεκα πυλῶν διαιρῶν κληρου(χία)ς.

Jesus' teaching and activity. Furthermore, Jesus' proclamation is concentrated on Israel, so for Luke it makes no sense that the messianic prophet Jesus should spend any time in Gentile territory. Consequently the excursions into Gentile territory have to disappear, apart from an unsuccessful foray into the territory of the 'Gerasenes, which lies over against Galilee' (8:26-39). For the same reason, Luke avoids mentioning the Decapolis and the area 'beyond the Jordan'. Thus Jesus' activity is concentrated in two areas: Galilee, from which the whole movement begins, and Judaea—or more exactly Jerusalem, the place of the last struggle, which takes place primarily in the Temple—and which thus represents a final focal point.[26] It is from Jerusalem that

[19]The verdict by P. Vielhauer, *Geschichte der urchristlichen Literatur* (Berlin/New York, 1975) 346f.; 'But the incorrect geographical views which can often be noted exclude a Palestinian, and therefore John Mark', expresses a widespread view which for its part displays a certain naivety over geographical knowledge in antiquity. From Jerusalem to Capernaum is about 66 miles as the crow flies; only in exceptional circumstances will someone living in Jerusalem have travelled to the distant province of Galilee, as the *Life* of Josephus shows. With the best will in the world one could not expect exact knowledge here about the borders between the city territories of Tyre and Sidon and Galilee or the Decapolis (*cf.* Mk. 7:31). R. Pesch, *Das Markusevangelium* Part 1, HTK (1976) 10, begins from quite incorrect historical presuppositions: 'Mark has...no personal knowledge of Galilean geography around the Sea of Galilee, as might have been expected from a (travelled) inhabitant of Jerusalem.' A journey to Rome—from metropolis to metropolis—would be more likely for a better-class Jerusalem dweller than one to provincial Galilee, which was the back of beyond. The command to go on pilgrimage to the temple naturally made journeys from Galilee to Jerusalem a matter of course, but travelling the other way round was an exception. The people of Judaea despised the uneducated Galileans and were not particularly interested in this remote province; *cf.* H.L. Strack and P. Billerbeck, *Kommentar zum Neuen Testament aus Talmud und Midrasch* I (Munich, [2]1956) 156-9. The geographical question is kept well back in the sadly neglected study by F.G. Lang, '"Über Sidon mitten ins Gebiet der Dekapolis". Geographie und Theologie in Markus 7,31', *ZDPV* 94 (1978) 145-60, which shows that Mark was not as naïve as all that. Still less, of course, should one follow W. Marxsen, *Introduction* (n. 2), 143, in putting the origins of the Second Gospel in Galilee or the Decapolis; S. Freyne, *Galilee from Alexander the Great to Hadrian 323 B.C.E. to 135 C.E.* (Wilmington, 1980) 357ff., is correct here.

[20]See the unfortunately rather one-sided account by M. Bachmann, *Jerusalem und der Tempel*, BWANT 9 (Stuttgart/Berlin/Köln/Mainz, 1980) 67-131.

[21]*Cf.* Luke 3:1 and 23:6.

[22]Luke 1:5; 7:17; 23:5; Acts 10:37.

[23]Luke 4:44; 5:17; Acts 1:8; 9:31; 11:29; 12:19; 15:1; 20:10; 26:20; 28:21. In Luke 1:65; 2:4; 21:21, the old hill country of Judah is meant. For Caesarea see n. 99 below.

[24]Luke 6:17; Acts 1:8; 8:1.

[25]*Cf.* Luke 1:39.

[26]See now M. Bachmann, *Jerusalem* (n. 20), 274ff., *etc.*

the apostolic proclamation goes out after the resurrection. Samaria is only touched on in the Gospel,[27] a reference to the coming mission.

There has been much discussion as to how Luke imagined the geographical relationship of the three areas of Galilee, Samaria and Judaea, which were essential for him because he already found them in the Old Testament. It is no longer possible to give a simple answer. In Luke 17:11, the geographical information over which scholars have argued so much and which tends to be over-interpreted remains utterly obscure. We do not know what the author had in mind here. For 'Luke's only concern is to explain the presence of a Samaritan among the Jews' (17:16).[28] So there is no need to see the reference to the journey to Jerusalem διὰ μέσον Σαμαρείας καὶ Γαλιλαίας as any more than a narrative slip of the kind that can also be found elsewhere in Luke.

None of this is new; indeed it should be stressed more than ever that, given conditions in antiquity, Luke *could* not have had any better knowledge of the places which Jesus frequented, as he had never seen Galilee, Samaria and the area of the Jordan with his own eyes. In his basically kerygmatic 'Jesus biography' he is barely interested in geographical details. That also has its good side. He does not have to improve the tradition by inventing geographical details to deck it out. Consequently he only makes a few stylistic improvements to Mark, his model, by making the 'sea' (θάλασσα) of Galilee—rightly, in fact—an 'inland lake' (λίμνη), while he accurately puts Tyre and Sidon on the sea coast (παράλιος). With the exception of some key passages like 2:1f.; 3:1, he only gives geographical details where he finds them in his sources (*cf.* 4:16, 31; 7:1, 11; 9:10; 10:13); more often he leaves them out.

It is striking that in the Acts of the Apostles the situation is quite different, at least in part. Obviously one could not write the history of a 'mission' from Jerusalem to Rome with so few geographical details as are to be found in the Gospel. This, of course, raises the question where Luke puts the stress in his geographical comments. It is also striking that despite the flood of modern literature on Acts, the geographical detail in the Acts of the Apostles has attracted far less attention from scholars than the sparse notes in the Gospel. So far, this detail has been subjected only to partial investigation—much to the

[27]Luke 9:52; 17:11, 16.

[28]E. Schweizer, *Das Evangelium nach Lukas* (NTD 3; Göttingen, 1982) 177. For the conclusions of Conzelmann and his followers, which go much too far, see n. 2 above. I.H. Marshall, *The Gospel of Luke* (n. 2) 650, considers various other possibilities. For the problem of the sequence see below, n. 125.

detriment of scholarship on Luke.[29] In what follows I shall make a few comments and raise some questions; it should be noted that it is impossible to separate the Gospel and Acts completely. It will emerge how geographical details, historical information and theological tendency can all hang together.

II. The Temple in Jerusalem[30]

The first seven chapters of Acts are exclusively limited to Jerusalem. This is in accordance with the strict pattern of salvation history which governs the whole of the two-volume work: Jesus' career leads from Galilee, where as the 'primal missionary'[31] he himself proclaimed the good news, via Judaea to the Holy City, whereas the preaching of the primitive church begins in Jerusalem, goes on to Judaea and Samaria, and finally even reaches the Gentiles in the wider world. So Luke does not need to go into Galilee again.[32] Acts 1:8, which has been much discussed, describes this development, so we can see it as the programme for the second volume. Of course the last phrase, ἕως ἐσχάτου τῆς γῆς, points beyond what Luke reports, and is essentially a description of the missionary programme of the church in the last decades of the first century, as it is also defined in the Gospels and in non-canonical texts.[33] What we have here is more than a mere table of contents for Acts.[34] For in contrast to his rather bombastic opening statement, Luke shapes the content of his work by a strict, indeed rigorous selection and limitation of the material. The content of his work is not the worldwide mission of the apostles. Once the frontiers of Judaea and Samaria have been crossed, Luke limits himself essentially to one man's, an outsider's, mission to the Gentiles, and his progress from Jerusalem to Rome as the 'thirteenth witness'.[35] Despite Ps. Sol. 8:15, the distinctively Isaianic formula 'to the ends of the

---

[29]Still the best is the brief but full survey in A. von Harnack, *Beiträge zur Einleitung in das N.T.* III, *Die Apostelgeschichte* (Leipzig, 1908) 69-80. The large but somewhat laborious work by M. Bachmann, *Jerusalem* (n. 20), is unfortunately limited to the temple, Jerusalem and the term 'Judaea'.

[30]M. Bachmann (n. 20), 132ff., 171ff.

[31]See pp. 61f.

[32]It is only mentioned in 9:31, to some degree *en passant* (see the note below). It is striking that Paul, too, speaks only of Jerusalem (Rom. 15:19, 20f., 30; 1 Cor. 16:3; Gal. 1:17f.; 2:1) or Judaea (Rom. 15:31; 2 Cor. 1:16; Gal. 1:22; 1 Thes. 2:14). The communities in Galilee no longer seem to have been significant, so we know nothing more about them.

earth'[36] hardly envisages Rome[37] as the conclusion of Paul's activity and the centre of the then known world; the decisive factor is the way in which the Greek reader could understand this statement: 'For the people of antiquity the frontiers lay at the Atlantic, among the Germani, Scythians, Indians and Ethiopians.'[38] In other words, the fulfilment of Acts 1:8 is not described completely in the 'second volume', which contains, rather, what Luke thought to be the most significant events leading to this goal. Acts contains selected scenes, the decisive stages in the course of the message of salvation from the resurrection of Jesus to Paul's Gentile mission and his imprisonment in Rome. Thus we could say that the theme of Acts, indeed of the whole

---

[33]*Cf.* Mk. 13:10; 14:9; 16:15; Mt. 28:19; Lk. 24:47; *cf.* also 1 Clem. 42:3f.; Hermas 69:2 (*Sim.* 8.3.2); Aristides, *Apology* 15:2 (Goodspeed, 19); Justin, *Apol.* 31:7; 39:1ff. following the quotation of Is. 2:3f.; 45:5; 50:12; *Dial.* 53:5; 109:1. There are further partly apocryphal traditions in E. Hennecke, W. Schneemelcher and R. McL. Wilson, *New Testament Apocrypha* II (London, 1965) 25ff. This 'world-wide' universal programme of mission primarily based on Isaianic texts may in the last resort go back to Paul. The other early Christian missionaries—in my view including Peter—took it over from him; *cf.* M. Hengel, *Acts and the History of Earliest Christianity* (London/Philadelphia, 1979) 93f., 97f. By contrast, the deutero-Pauline tradition, like Luke, can stress the universal influence of Pauline preaching: Col. 1:23; 1 Tim. 4:17; *cf.* also 1 Clem. 5:7. *Cf.* O. Bauernfeind, *Kommentar und Studien zur Apostelgeschichte*, ed. V. Metelmann (Tübingen, 1980) 337ff.

[34]Against E. Haenchen, *The Acts of the Apostles*, 144, and H. Conzelmann, *Die Apostelgeschichte*, HNT 7 (Tübingen, ^{2}1972) 27.

[35]See C. Burchard, *Der dreizehnte Zeuge. Traditions- und kompositionsgeschichtliche Untersuchung zu Lukas' Darstellung der Frühzeit des Paulus*, FRLANT 103 (Göttingen, 1970) 174: 'Paul is the only witness who travels around and the only one who appears in person before all the audience mentioned in Acts 1:8.' Luke may very well have been familiar with 'the theme of the spread of the apostles throughout the world, which has become determinative of the historical view of the early church'. If he 'interprets the farewell tradition...as a promise of their being witnesses to the ends of the earth' (Acts 1:8), but not as a sending out, and if he has the apostles remaining in Jerusalem and subsequently makes them fade out of the picture, this must be a deliberate restriction of their role' (175).

[36]Is. 8:9; 48:20; 49:6; 62:11; 1 Mac. 3:9; *cf.* Acts 13:47, where Paul refers Is. 49:6 to himself and Barnabas.

[37]Against H. Conzelmann, *Apostelgeschichte* (n. 34), *loc. cit.*; see J. Roloff, *Die Apostelgeschichte*, NTD 5 (Göttingen, 1981) 23. Similarly already W.M.L. De Wette and F. Overbeck, *Kurze Erklärung der Apostelgeschichte* (Leipzig, ^{4}1870) 6.

[38]W.C. van Unnik, *Sparsa Collecta* I (Leiden, 1973) 400. He points out that Pompey 'had fought against Sertorius in Spain for many years before he came to the East in 66 BC and captured Jerusalem in 63 BC'. Ps. Sol. 8:15 could be a specific reference to this. *Cf.* now also G. Schneider, *Die Apostelgeschichte* I, HTK 5 (Freiburg-Basle-Vienna, 1980) 203 n. 41.

two-volume work, is 'From Jesus to Paul';[39] the secondary title ΠΡΑΞΕΙΣ ΑΠΟΣΤΟΛΩΝ is misleading.

To mention Jerusalem as the starting point is still not exact enough. In reality the proclamation of the crucified and risen Messiah begins at the holy place where according to the salvation history of the Old Testament God was present. Luke already has the Gospel beginning (1:5ff.) with an epiphany scene in the Temple. And just as Jesus, after coming down from the Mount of Olives (Lk. 19:37), immediately appears in the Temple (19:35: without going through the city), to drive out the merchants and to teach there day by day,[40] so in Jerusalem the apostles preach primarily in the Temple. Originally the Temple might possibly have been supposed to be the scene even of the Pentecost story, though it is not mentioned there in so many words.[41]

The Temple, or more precisely the στοὰ τοῦ Σολομῶντος, 'the hall of Solomon' (3:11; 5:12, *cf.* Jn. 10:23), is at the same time the place where the community meet every day (2:46; *cf.* 5:42). We can perhaps identify it from Josephus' description of the Temple. According to this the hall of pillars, with a single nave four hundred cubits long, was situated on the east side of the sanctuary of Solomon dropping steeply to the Kidron valley; that is, this part of the outer forecourt probably dated from before the time of Herod.[42] However, it remains doubtful whether Luke imagined its location in this way.

The second topographical detail about the Temple, the so-called 'Beautiful Gate' (πρὸς τὴν θύραν τοῦ ἱεροῦ τὴν λεγομένην Ὡραίαν 3:2; τῇ

---

[39]See M. Hengel, 'Between Jesus and Paul', in *Between Jesus and Paul*, tr. J. Bowden (London, 1983) 1-29. Also A. Lindemann, *Paulus im ältesten Christentum*, BHT 58 (Tübingen, 1979) 68 n. 117.

[40]*Cf.* Luke 19:47; 20:1; 21:5, 37f. Conzelmann, *Theology* (n. 1), 78, sees the Cleansing of the Temple as a 'means of taking possession', which in contrast to the original in Mark of itself no longer has any eschatological significance.

[41]*Cf.* Luke 24:52; Acts 2:46; 3:1ff.; 5:20ff.; 5:42, and M. Bachmann, *Jerusalem* (n. 20), 160ff. (167 n. 99), 279f. Following B. Reicke and T. Zahn, among others, he sees the οἶκος in Acts 2:2 as a place in the sanctuary. *Cf.* Is. 6:1 [LXX] καὶ πλήρης ὁ οἶκος τῆς δόξας αὐτοῦ and 6:4 καὶ ὁ οἶκος ἐπλήσθη καπνοῦ with Acts 2:2...καὶ ἐπλήρωσεν ὅλον τὸν οἶκον. However, the addition οὗ ἦσαν καθήμενοι tells against the Temple. Possibly the original had this in mind, whereas Luke related the whole event to the 'upper room' (1:13). The subsequent assembly of festival pilgrims from all over the world for the Feast of Weeks can only be imagined as in the outer court of the Temple, which of course in Luke's view was not part of the ἱερόν; see above. As elsewhere in Luke, the account does not give us a really clear idea.

[42]*Ant.* 20. 221; *cf. BJ* 5.185; *cf.* T.A. Busink, *Der Tempel von Jerusalem* II (Leiden, 1980) 1198f. A. Schlatter, *Zur Topographie* (n. 12) 197ff., wanted to put it on the east side of the inner sanctuary, in order to avoid the difficulty with the 'beautiful gate'.

Ὡραίᾳ πύλῃ τοῦ ἱεροῦ, 3:10), is far more difficult to determine because this designation occurs only in Luke, who in 3:1-11 evidently supposes that the apostles go through the 'beautiful gate' in the Temple to the 'hall of Solomon'. Presumably this more specific reference had already been in the pre-Lukan legend of Peter, originally coming from Jerusalem. As the Temple had numerous gates,[43] the gate at which the miracle took place had to be described more precisely. Neither the tractate *Middot* nor Josephus speaks of a 'beautiful gate'. It is usually identified with the Nicanor Gate, for which there is evidence in Talmudic literature; it was made of gleaming 'Corinthian bronze' and took its name from Nicanor of Alexandria, who had endowed it.[44] According to a note in *t. Yoma* 2:4, 'it was as beautiful as gold' (היה יפה כזהב).[45] By contrast Josephus speaks only of the 'bronze'[46] or 'Corinthian' gate.[47] This last piece of information suggests an identification with the Nicanor Gate, but there is a difference in the location. According to *Middot*, the Nicanor Gate lay between the court of the men and the court of the women, whereas the eye-witness details in Josephus (some of which present serious textual problems) are more in favour of the eastern gate between the court of the women and the court of the Gentiles. Since E. Schürer's impressive investigation,[48] the majority of scholars follow the information given in Josephus, as (more recently) does A. Schalit;[49] on the other hand, O. Holtzmann and E. Stauffer, followed by J. Jeremias and H. Conzelmann, have emphatically argued that the account in the Mishnah is original.[50] It is hardly possible to

---

[43]*Cf.* the plural αἱ θύραι, Acts 21:30; Josephus, *BJ* 5.201ff.; *Ant.* 15.410f;*m. Mid.* 1:3f.

[44]*M. Mid.* 2:3, *cf. Ant.* 15.410f.; *m. Mid.* 1:3f. Also *m. Mid.* 1:4; 2:6; *m. Yoma* 3:10; *m. Sheqal.* 6:3.; *m. Sota* 1:5; *m. Neg.* 14:8. See also P. Billerbeck, *Kommentar* (n. 19) II, 623, and the literature in G. Schneider, *Apostelgeschichte* (n. 38) 300 nn. 30, 31. Also the surveys by A. Schalit, *König Herodes* (Berlin, 1969) 387ff.; T.A. Busink, *Tempel* II (n. 42), 1079ff. For Nicanor see also *OGIS* 599 and J.B. Frey, *CIJ* II, 1256.

[45]Zuckermandel (ed.), (repr. Jerusalem, 1962/63) 183. *Cf.* the heightening of detail in *y. Yoma* 2.8.41a l. 40: היה מסחיב ויותר יפה משל זהב, 'it shone and was finer than gold'. In both cases, of course, gold is used only as a comparison.

[46]*BJ* 2.411; 6.293: it was made of bronze and was particularly heavy, needing twenty men to open it.

[47]*BJ* 5.204; *cf.* 201: more valuable than the other silvered and gilded gates of the Temple. R.J. Forbes, *Studies in Ancient Technology* VIII (Leiden, [2]1971) 275, conjectured that the door was made of more valuable brass. See also M. Hengel, *Achilleus in Jerusalem*, SAH (1982) I n. 106.

[48]'Die ΘΥΡΑ oder ΠΥΛΗ ΩΡΑΙΑ Act. 3,2 u. 10', *ZNW* 7 (1906) 51-68; P. Billberbeck, *Kommentar* II (n. 19) 620-5, and G. Dalman, *Orte und Wege Jesu* (Gütersloh, [3]1924) 315, agree.

[49]*Herodes* (n. 44), 393ff.; *cf.* also T. Busink, *Tempel* II (n. 42) 1080ff.

arrive at a really satisfying conclusion. Even if we assume the identity of the Nicanor Gate and the bronze gate—because of the manufacture from precious Corinthian metal—and that the location given by Josephus is more reliable, identification with Luke's 'beautiful gate' remains doubtful. In the first place, we do not know when Nicanor endowed the gate—the only possible period is the time after Herod, between AD 6 and AD 60[51]—and secondly, the reference could be to other gates of the Temple—say, the outer forecourt—because the Mishnah names only some of them. In addition, it is also doubtful whether it would have been possible for a crippled beggar to beg at the main eastern gate of the Temple proper, within the holy precinct, as Levites and priests kept a guard on the gates.[52] Consequently, T.A.

---

[50]O. Holtzmann, 'Tore und Terrassen des herodianischen Tempels', *ZNW* 9 (1908) 71-4; *idem*, *'Middot'*, in *Die Mischna*, V/10 (Berlin/New York, 1913) 15, 26ff., 29f.; E. Stauffer, 'Das Tor des Nikanor', *ZNW* 44 (1952) 44-66; J. Jeremias, πύλη, *TDNT* VI, 921 n. 3; *idem*, *Jerusalem in the Time of Jesus*, ET (London, 1969) 23f., 128f. C. Kopp, *The Holy Places of the Gospels*, tr. R. Walls (Freiburg/Edinburgh/London, 1963) 290, suggested that the 'beautiful gate' was at the east of the Court of the Women and distinguished it from the Nicanor Gate, between the Courtyard of the Women and that of the Men; similarly now B. Mazar, *Der Berg des Herrn* (Bergisch Gladbach, 1979) 110ff. For discussion see also M. Bachmann, *Jerusalem* (n. 20), 292ff. n. 345.

[51]For the dating see E. Stauffer, *ZNW* 44 (1952) 58. The Nicanor ossuary is dated by Sukenik towards the end of the forties on the basis of a coin of Agrippa I and points of style. U. Rappaport, *EJ* 12 (1971) 1133f. suggests a post-Herodian origin 'about the middle of the first century, a generation before the destruction'. We therefore do not know whether the gate was already in existence between AD 30 and 40.

[52]For the problem see J. Jeremias, *Jerusalem* (n. 50), 128f., and T.A. Busink, *Tempel* (n. 42), 186, who also refers to 1QSa 2:55-7 and 2 Sam. 5:8 [LXX]; *cf.* also 1QM 7:4f. and 11QTemple 45:12, where not only the unclean but even the blind are prohibited from staying in Jerusalem. We know nothing of any prohibition against the lame and the crippled stopping in the inner sanctuary; see G. Dalman, *Orte* (n. 48), 406. Lv. 21:21ff. refers to the Temple service of the priests, but if there were always crippled beggars by the main gate of the inner sanctuary this must have caused considerable disruption to the ordering of the Temple. Certainly we should not suppose that Luke had such concerns; they will have been part of the original Jerusalem legend about Peter. M. Bachmann, *Jerusalem* (n. 20) 295f. n. 345, points to the possibility of outer gates. He connects the adjective ὡραῖος as applied to the temple gate with the first-fruits, because he supposes the word to have a chronological and not an aesthetic significance, referring to the same usage in Philo, *Spec. Leg.* 2.220, and Josephus, *Ant.* 4.241. Stephanus-Dindorf, *Thesaurus Graecae Linguae* VIII (Paris, 1829) 2057ff., says on the use of ὡραῖος in connection with sacrificial terminology: '*idemque* ὡραῖα *accipi etiam* ἐπὶ τὸν καθ' ὥραν τελουμένων ἱερόν, *et* ὡραῖον *vocari* τό θῦμα τὸ καθ' ὥραν...'. He also refers to the later instances of ὡραῖαι πύλαι as a designation for the church doors between the narthex and the nave proper (col. 2060). They might be dependent on Acts 3:2, 11. I cannot discover any pre-Christian instances of the use of ὡραῖος for buildings.

Busink, following F. de Saulcy and others, conjectures that the 'beautiful gate' is meant to be the eastern gate of the outer courtyard by the Kidron valley, mentioned only in *Middot* 1:3, which was in the immediate vicinity of the hall of Solomon and above which 'the citadel of Susa' was depicted.[53] In about 570, the pilgrim of Piacenza found the *porta speciosa* in the immediate vicinity of the eastern gate of the city, *i.e.* by what is now Stephen's Gate. A little later, as a result of a misreading of the Greek ὡραῖα, Latin *(h)orea* as *aurea*, the east gate of the old Temple precinct was given the name 'Golden Gate', which is still current today.[54] Josephus knows of four gates without names on the west side of the outer forecourt, of which the two southern ones lead to the city—one of them over a bridge to the royal palace—and the two northern ones lead to the suburbs. By contrast, the tractate *Middot* mentions only one gate in the west, the Qiponos (Coponius?) gate. On the basis of archaeological evidence, B. Mazar even assumes that there were five gates on the west side.[55] One of these western gates could also have been called 'beautiful', perhaps the southernmost gate, which according to Josephus was approached by an attractive flight of stairs, the foundations of which have been excavated very recently. This connected the Temple precinct with the real centre of the city on the southwest corner of Mount Zion, where the great routes from the northwest, north, east and south came together.[56] However, here we are in the realm of conjecture. The whole question is made more difficult by the fact that Luke—like the other New Testament writers—never makes a distinction between the inner sanctuary and the court of the Gentiles. They are all speaking only about the one ἱερόν, the real Temple. This is in some way in accordance with rabbinic terminology, which makes a sharp distinction between the sanctuary proper (מקדש, הבית *etc.*) and the outer courtyard, the 'Temple mount' (הר הבית), which is not called sanctuary. It is also possible that Luke did not regard the outer courtyard—which would be the only place he would have been

[53]*Tempel* II (n. 42), 1185ff., *cf.* 984f., 1178ff. For a description of the gate see also O. Holtzmann, '*Middot*' (n. 50), 50f. T.A. Busink further complicates the matter by wanting to extend the enclosed area of the ἱερόν proper as far as the east gate of the outer wall.

[54]Ch. 17; see H. Donner, *Pilgerfahrt ins Heilige Land* (Stuttgart, 1979) 276 n. 83; C. Kopp, *Holy Places* (n. 50), 288; T.A. Busink, *Tempel* II (n. 49), 984-9.

[55]*Ant.* 15.410; *m. Mid.* 1:3. *Cf.* T.A. Busink, *Tempel* II (n. 49), 968ff., 1178ff.; B. Mazar, *Berg* (n. 50), 119ff.

[56]B. Mazar, *Berg* (n. 50), 121, 126; *Jerusalem Revealed: Archaeology in the Holy City 1968-1974* (Jerusalem, 1975) 26ff. According to *m. Sanh.* 11:2 even legal sessions took place in one of the gigantic gates opening on to the Temple mount.

allowed to enter as a Gentile—as the ἱερόν, although of course he knew that godfearing non-Jews came to Jerusalem 'to worship' (8:27).[57]

The information given by Luke about the 'beautiful gate' in Acts 3:1-11 would correspond better with an identification with the Corinthian or Nicanor Gate and its location at the eastern exit from the Courtyard of the Women if with Zahn, Clark and Lake we could follow the Western text (Cod. D, h and the Middle Egyptian translation).[58] Here according to 3:11, the lame man, who had accompanied the two apostles as they went into the Temple (3:8), went out again with them (ἐκπορευομένου δὲ τοῦ Πέτρου καὶ Ἰωάνου συνεξεπορεύετο κρατῶν αὐτούς οἱ δὲ θαμβηθέντες ἔστησαν ἐπὶ τῇ στοᾷ τῇ καλουμένῃ Σολομῶντος ἔκθαμβοι). However, this was a way in which a later redactor sought to remove a difficulty in Luke's text, in a barbaric style and a way which could again be misunderstood.

Thus it is impossible to conclude from Luke's two topographical details about the Temple either that he was generally ignorant or that he had exact knowledge. Conzelmann's conclusion that 'Luke has no knowledge of locations'[59] can be challenged simply on the grounds that our own knowledge of the Temple of Herod is still too fragmentary for us to demonstrate that Luke has clearly made a mistake. He has taken over the 'beautiful gate' and the 'hall of Solomon' from the tradition and incorporated them in a text which he has fashioned himself, without bothering further about details.[60] In contrast to

---

[57]See below, pp. 42-3. *Cf.* G. Schrenk, τὸ ἱερόν, *TDNT* III, 234ff. The New Testament texts do not know of the distinction between outer and inner sanctuary which Josephus takes for granted. Which part of the sanctuary is meant can only be discovered from the context. On the other hand, there is usually a distinction between ναός and τὸ ἱερόν.

[58]T. Zahn, *Die Apostelgeschichte des Lukas* I, KNT 5 (Leipzig-Erlangen, [3]1922) 147ff., 150; *idem*, *Forschungen zur Geschichte des ntl. Kanons* IX (Leipzig, 1916) 251; A.C. Clark, *The Acts of the Apostles* (Oxford, 1933) 17, on Acts 3:8-11; K. Lake and H.J. Cadbury, *The Acts of the Apostles* V (*Beginnings* I/5; London, 1933), 479-850, 484; J. Duplacy, *REAug* 2 (1956) 231-42. But see B.M. Metzger, *A Textual Commentary on the Greek NT* (London & New York, 1971) 308f., and G. Schneider, *Apostelgeschichte* (n. 38), 303f.: there is a discussion of the various reasons for change.

[59]*Apostelgeschichte* (n. 34), 38; similarly E. Haenchen, *The Acts of the Apostles* (n. 34), 189 n. 12, 204.

[60]*Cf.* G. Schneider, *Apostelgeschichte* (n. 38) 300, 303, conjectures that in the pre-Lukan narrative the 'beautiful gate' was identical with the Nicanor Gate and that Luke understood it as a gate which led into the whole Temple area. He was also the first to connect the Hall of Solomon with the miracle story. *Cf.* already O. Bauernfeind, *Kommentar* (n. 33) 62 on 3:11: 'the whole verse is typical of the carefree way in which Luke often works'.

Josephus he does not attach any importance to a description of the Temple. He simply wants to provide *a* location for the first healing miracle to be performed by the two leading apostles and to give an indication of where the community met. We cannot yet trace in him anything of the 'topographical curiosity' about holy places which is characteristic of the later accounts by pilgrims. At most his interest is in making an effective preparation, by means of the miracle, and the local colouring which goes with it, for Peter's speech in the Temple which he himself has devised. Thus it may be a historical tradition that the earliest community met in the hall of Solomon in the outer fore-court and that Peter preached in public there.

The specific reference to the time of prayer at the ninth hour points to a precise knowledge of Jewish customs in the Temple. This was the time of the *tamid* sacrifice, in the afternoon, which was concluded with an incense offering and the priestly blessing.[61] Luke 1:8-11, 21f. says that the people assembled for prayer in the Courtyard of the Men in front of the Temple building proper (ναός as opposed to ἱερόν).[62] In contrast to Luke 1:8, where in connection with Zechariah's temple service Luke even knows about the assignation of priestly duties by lot, which is attested only in the Mishnah,[63] in Acts he speaks only of the fixed hour of prayer[64] (*cf.* also 10:3, 30: the ninth; 10:9: the sixth). Might this be connected with the fact that Luke knew that for the primitive community in Jerusalem the Temple had changed from being a place of sacrifice to a place of prayer?[65]

So far the details have been isolated and fortuitous, and therefore do not allow of further conclusions. However, in my view Luke's account of Paul's arrest in the Temple (Acts 21:27-40) shows a more extensive knowledge of the location and the legal regulations associated with it: the author knows not only that for non-Jews to enter the sanctuary proper, which was marked off in a special way, was a crime punishable by death because this would be to desecrate the holy places

---

[61]For the offering of the evening *tamid* sacrifice see *m. Pes.* 5:1: between half-past the eighth and half-past the ninth hour. See also Josephus, *Ant.* 14.65: περὶ ἐνάτην ὥραν ἱερουργούντων ἐπὶ τοῦ βωμοῦ. For the evening sacrifice as a time of prayer see already Dn. 9:21 and Jdt. 9:1. *Cf.* M. Bachmann, *Jerusalem* (n. 20) 346ff., 357ff., on the primitive community's prayer in the Temple, and see further the chapter by D. Falk in this volume.

[62]*Cf.* Sir. 50:11ff. and P. Billerbeck, *Kommentar* II (n. 19) 57ff.

[63]*M. Yoma* 2:1-4; *m. Tamid* 1:2; 2:5; 3:1; *t. Yoma* 1.10, 12-13 (Zuckermandel [n. 45], 181); P. Billerbeck, *Kommentar* II (n. 19) 57f.

[64]P. Billerbeck, *Kommentar* II (n. 19) 696ff.

[65]M. Hengel, *The Atonement* (London, 1981) 55, 57.

(*cf.* 24:6, 13), but also that anyone who desecrated the Temple was immediately removed from the sanctuary to be executed—in some circumstances by lynch-law.[66] To have killed the criminal in the Temple itself would have defiled the holy place.[67] Luke also knows that the Roman commandant of the city, *i.e.* the commander of the city cohort in the Antonia, could survey the Temple and its surroundings and could intervene at any time (21:31f.), as the barracks (παρεμβολή: 21:34, 37; 23:10), on a higher level, were connected by stairs (ἀναβαθμοί) with the Temple site (21:35, *cf.* 32: κατέδραμεν; 22:30; 23:10, 20: κατάγειν; καταβαίνειν). The whole description of the event can be illustrated well from the account in Josephus:

> Whereas the tower standing on the south-east corner (of the Antonia) was seventy cubits high (the other towers were only fifty cubits high), so that the whole Temple area could be viewed from there. But at the place where the Antonia joined the two cloisters of the Temple it had stairs down both sides (*i.e.* to the south and to the east), by which the guard went down. For there was always a Roman division in the fortress, the soldiers from which were posted, fully armed, on feast days on the roof of the cloisters of the outer court in order to watch the people, so that no rebellions broke out. If the Temple was set over the city like a fortress, the Antonia formed a guard for the Temple, and the troops posted there watched over all three.[68]

According to 20:16, Paul had wanted to visit Jerusalem for the Feast of Weeks, which in contrast to the Feast of Unleavened Bread lasted for only one day. The accusation against him was made by Jewish pilgrims to the Feast from Asia Minor; however, it was then taken up by the supreme Jewish authorities and pursued further after he had been taken into custody by Roman troops. On several occasions Josephus reports unrest in Jerusalem or in the Temple court at the great festivals, which forced the Roman troops to intervene: after the death of Herod and also at a Feast of Weeks (*Ant.* 17.254ff.). There is a report of a further occurrence some years before Paul's arrest, when Cumanus was procurator: a soldier posted on the roof of one of the

---

[66]P. Billerbeck, *Kommentar* II (n. 19), 761f.; M. Hengel, *The Zealots*, tr. D. Smith (Edinburgh, 1989) 206ff.; E. Schürer, G. Vermes, F. Millar and M. Black, *The History of the Jewish People in the Age of Jesus Christ* II (Edinburgh, 1979) 222; E. Bickerman, *Studies in Jewish and Christian History* II, AGAJU 9 (Leiden, 1980) 210-24.

[67]*Cf.* Mt. 23:35 and P. Billerbeck, *Kommentar* I (n. 19), 942; also Josephus, *Ant.* 18.30; M. Hengel, *Zeloten* (n. 66), 189f.

[68]*BJ* 5.242-5. *Cf.* T.A. Busink, *Tempel* II (n. 49) 1195ff., 1233ff.

cloisters had caused uproar among the crowd at Passover by an obscene gesture (*BJ* 2.223ff. = 20.105f., 108ff.); thereupon Cumanus sent his troops against the crowd.

Luke's account here presupposes some accurate information about conditions, but as elsewhere, he does not reveal an 'archaeological', scholarly interest extending as far as points of detail, which seeks to reproduce events as exactly as possible. Rather, he is concerned to give a vivid, dramatic and psychological account of the conflict. This corresponds to his ideal of a 'solemn' historiography which he shares with numerous historians of the hellenistic period, not least the author of 2 Maccabees.[69] As a result, scenes are depicted in a vivid way for the sake of the effect this makes on the reader and to give a dramatic impression of events; there are divergences from what actually happened, as was allowed and indeed sometimes required by contemporary rhetoric and historiography.[70] Thus, as usual, in 21:30ff. Luke does not make a distinction between the city of Jerusalem and the outer courtyard. In so doing he demonstrates that all Jerusalem and not just the crowd in the Temple had risen up against Paul (ἐκινήθη τε ἡ πόλις ὅλη 21:30; *cf.* 31: ὅτι ὅλη συγχύννεται Ἰερουσαλήμ), to some degree following the motto: the more enemies the greater the glory. This lack of clarity, which can also be noted in all the other Gospels, may seem justified by the fact that the outer court of the Temple essentially replaced the Agora of the city and was the scene of a good deal of very secular activity (see above, pp. 35ff.).

The external circumstances of the speech which Luke has Paul making from the steps leading to the barracks (21:40; 22:24) before a crowd in uproar are required by the course of the narrative as a whole and therefore certainly do not accord with historical reality in the form in which they are recorded.[71] However, the event as a whole and the setting for the scene correspond amazingly to what we know from Josephus and must have a basis in history. In my view, at this point

---

[69]For Luke and hellenistic historiography see E. Plümacher, *Lukas als hellenistischer Schriftsteller*, SUNT 9 (Göttingen, 1972) 80ff.; *idem*, 'Lukas', *PWSuppl* 14 (1974) 255ff. In my view Plümacher's works are the most important contributions to the study of Acts in the German language since Dibelius, because they take research out of the cul-de-sac into which it has been led by the development of Haenchen's theory that Luke was only an edifying writer of devotional theology, more bad than right, with a one-sided redaction-historical perspective. For 2 Maccabees as the 'Old Testament' parallel to the two-volume work see E. Meyer, *Ursprung und Anfänge des Christentums*, I (Stuttgart & Berlin, 1921) 1 n. 1; *cf.* also H. Cancik, *Mythische und historische Wahrheit*, SBS 48 (Stuttgart, 1970) 108ff.: on hellenistic historiography in the Old Testament.

Luke was not just working over an outside source, but may be drawing on his own memories (see below, pp. 76ff.).

III. Jerusalem and the Hill Country of Judah

Although Luke gives us few details about the sanctuary, he does inform us about the topography of Jerusalem and its environs. He is not concerned to praise the splendid Temple and the city in the way we encounter in some Jewish hellenistic writers—that city which his contemporary Pliny the Elder called *longe clarissima urbium Orientis non Judaeae modo*.[72] However, he is able to use what he has taken over from tradition in a straightforward way, and probably also has some

---

[70]For historiography and rhetoric see E. Norden, *Die antike Kunstprosa* I (Darmstadt, [3]1979) 79ff.; H. Strassburger, *Die Wesensbestimmung der Geschichte durch die antike Geschichtsschreibung*, Sitzungsberichte der wissenschaftliche Gesellschaft und der J.W. Goethe Universität Frankfurt/Main 5, no. 3 ([3]1975) 78ff.: 'that history can have its complete content of reality and be fruitful only as *experience*' (78). On the definition of *mimesis*: 'the potential living truth of images which allows the reader to be grasped by events as in the theatre. The idea of mimesis is...an appropriate means of historical realisation in some circumstances even when faithfulness to the facts is replaced by fictitious or potential reality, given that the writer is working only with an authentic experience of life'. See E. Plümacher, 'Die Apostelgeschichte als historische Monographie', in J. Kremer (ed.), *Les Actes des Apôtres*, BETL 48 (Gembloux-Lyons, 1979) 457-66, and his reference to Cicero's letter to Lucceius, *Epp. ad fam.* 5.12, with its invitation to write a special historical study on Cicero's activity as a politician *quasi fabulam rerum eventorumque nostrorum* (6). 'My career will also give you abundant variety, not completely without charm, and could entrance people who read it in your account. Nothing is better suited to captivate the reader than the changing tides of events and fortunes': *multam etiam casus nostri varietatem tibi in scribendo suppeditabunt plenam cuiusdam voluptatis, quae vehementer animos hominum legendo te scriptore tenere possit. Nihil est enim aptius ad delectationem lectoris quam temporum varietatis fortunaeque vicissitudines* (*Epp. ad fam.* 5.12.4). Luke writes about Paul in a comparable way.

[71]Critical scholarship has long and rightly demonstrated that it is historically unlikely that Paul, mistreated (Acts 21:31f.) and in fetters (Acts 21:33), guarded by soldiers, could have quietened the raging crowd (Acts 21:34; 22:22) with one of those gestures of the hand so beloved of Luke and by his speech 'in Hebrew' (Acts 21:40; 22:2). For Luke's story, Paul's account of himself before the people at this dramatic climax is absolutely necessary as testimony by the one called by Christ to the people of Jerusalem and the pilgrims to the festival (Acts 22:15, 21).

[72]*Hist. Nat.* 5.70; see M. Stern, *Authors* I (n. 5), 469f., nos. 477f. *Cf. idem*, in *Jerusalem in the Second Temple Period*, A. Schalit Memorial Volume (Jerusalem, 1980) 257-70 (in Hebrew); H. Heubner and W. Fauth, *Kommentar zu P. Cornelius Tacitus: Die Historien*, V (Heidelberg, 1982) 109.

idea what he is talking about. He knows from Mark that one goes up to Jerusalem from neighbouring Jericho (Lk. 19:1, 11, 28), that Bethphage and Bethany are near to the Mount of Olives and that on coming down from the mountain one can see the city and the Temple in all their grandeur and magnificence. That is reason enough for Jesus to weep over its coming fate, a point which Luke stresses more than any other New Testament author.[73] He also seems to presuppose that one could enter the Temple directly from the side of the Mount of Olives. For pilgrims who came from the East that was the most direct way into the sanctuary.[74]

The mention of two places in connection with the ascension poses a difficulty (which is heightened further by the difference in the time assigned to the event). The best explanation for the difference is that Luke wrote the second book some time after the πρῶτος λόγος had already been produced. The alternative, that 1:3-14, which gives rise to the discrepancy, is a later interpolation, breaking up what was originally one work, is highly improbable. There is no real support for it in the text.[75] According to Luke 24:50, Jesus takes the disciples to Bethany, while according to Acts 1:12, the Ascension takes place on the Mount of Olives, only a 'sabbath day's journey' from Jerusalem. The 2,000 cubits (about 880 metres) which make up a sabbath day's journey are as vague as the two pieces of information provided by Josephus: five stadia (about 1,000 metres, *Ant.* 20.160) or six stadia (about 1200 metres, *BJ* 5.70). The differences can easily be explained from the size of the mountain and a variety of possible points of reference. The term 'a sabbath day's journey', which appears only here in the New Testament, presupposes an amazingly intimate knowledge—for a Greek—of Jewish customs. Evidently Luke wants to make a direct connection between the Ascension—and the Parousia (Acts 1:11)—and the Holy City. G. Lohfink rightly remarks in this connection that this observation, which goes beyond the bounds of what might be expected, is not therefore to be understood 'as the task of a historian interested in detail'. The Ascension took place in the neighbourhood of Jerusalem,

---

[73]Lk. 19:37, 41ff.; 21:24. *Cf.* also David's lament in Josephus, *Ant.* 7.203 and 2 Ki. 15:30.

[74]Lk. 19:45. According to the Mishnah, *Ber.* 9:5, the Temple mount, *i.e.* the forecourt, was not to be trodden by people dressed for travelling with staff, sandals and purse, and the dust of travel on their feet. However, Luke, the Greek author, need not have troubled himself over this at all.

[75]*Cf.* G. Schneider, *Apostelgeschichte* (n. 38), 71f.

'for a sabbath day's journey according to Jewish legal fiction is in fact a negation of any real distance'.[76]

Apart from notes of this kind which have theological importance, Luke continues to be very restrained over details. One could also refer to the village (κώμη) of Emmaus, 60 stadia (about twelve kilometres) from Jerusalem (Lk. 24:13), which the narrator seeks to use to demonstrate the time spent walking with the risen Jesus and the fatigue of the return by night to Jerusalem. This is a place which it has so far proved difficult to identify, since here Luke has possibly made a mistake about the distance. Some manuscripts therefore have 160 stadia (about thirty-two kilometres), which corresponds more closely to the distance of a place called Emmaus of which there is evidence in the books of Maccabees and often in Josephus. It lies twenty-four kilometres west-northwest of Jerusalem as the crow flies, but as the chief place in a toparchy was certainly not a village (24:13, 28). Furthermore, the distance from Jerusalem may be too great for the situation presupposed in the story. Possibly a mistake was made by Luke or the tradition which he took over: perhaps, though, he also means Ἀμμαους, thirty stadia from Jerusalem, where, according to *BJ* 7.217, Vespasian founded a military colony.[77]

The Aramaic designation Ἀκελδαμάχ for 'field of blood' has been correctly handed down in Acts 1:19; this is a place name which is also known by Matthew 27:8 (Aramaic חקל דמא; see H.P. Rüger, *TRE* 3,603). Its exact phonetic transmission probably presupposes a written source. The same is true of the note about the 'synagogue of Libertines, Alexandrians and Cyrenians' (6:9). In the latter case it is not clear

---

[76]G. Lohfink, *Die Himmelfahrt Jesus. Untersuchungen zu den Himmelfahrts- und Erhöhungstexten bei Lukas*, SANT 26 (Munich, 1971) 207. G. Schneider, *Apostelgeschichte* (n. 38) 205, agrees.

[77]*Amwâs* and *Mōṣâ/Qalûnîyâ*. For the two places see C. Möller and G. Schmitt, *Siedlungen* (n. 12), 15ff. (and the bibliography). The reasons given there for identifying it with the second place are illuminating: 'should be added that the distances of thirty (Josephus) and sixty (Luke 24:13) stadia are both round numbers which are used frequently and stand for one and two hours' travelling: *Qalûnîyâ* is only four miles from Jerusalem (the Jaffa gate). For the distance between Jerusalem and Αμμαους 1 one would have to take 150 stadia (as a round—and also more accurate—number) rather than 160 stadia (Origen's text), and it would be remarkable if the traditional round number had arisen by the accidental omission of 100'. E. Schürer, G. Vermes, *etc.*, I (n. 66), 512f. n. 142 arrive at a similar solution: 'Thus, our Emmaus is most probably identical with that mentioned in the NT (Lk. 24:13), even though the distances in both cases...are only roughly correct.' On the other hand we cannot completely rule out an error on the part of Luke or his original. Details of distances are often questionable in the ancient geographers.

whether there was one synagogue or more. Probably there were various synagogues. Possibly the Theodotus inscription found on the Ophel is a reference to this synagogue of Roman freedmen in Jerusalem, mentioned by Luke.[78] The author does not give any further details of place than he does in the case of the mysterious ὑπερῷον (1:13), the 'house' (2:2), unless it is meant to be the Temple—and the homes of some Jerusalem Christians, for example the splendid house of Mary the mother of John Mark (Acts 12:12), distinguished by its forecourt (πυλών), and the abode of James the brother of the Lord (Acts 21:18) who receives Paul only on the day after his arrival like a prince of the church with a court of elders, or the home of the 'old disciple' Mnason from Cyprus, who gives a warm welcome to the new arrival (21:16). We cannot even detect the beginnings in Luke of an interest in 'holy places' in Jerusalem and its surroundings. The 'tomb of David', already mentioned in Nehemiah 3:16 and Josephus, *Ant*. 7.392ff. (*cf*. 13.249; *BJ* 1.161), which is to be located 'on the southern slope of the Ophel above the spring of Siloah near to the eastern wall of the city'[79] is mentioned only in passing in the kerygmatic context of Peter's sermon (2:29) as part of the argument. He merely reproduces tradition even in the case of the place of the Skull (Lk. 23:33) and the tomb[80] (23:53). This refutes modern hypotheses which presuppose fixed 'journeys' to the tomb as early as the first century and a special interest in 'local legends'. The eschatological mood of the communities already tells against this. The note that the place 'Arimathea' is 'a city of the Jews' is an explanation for the Greek reader and does not presuppose any further special knowledge on Luke's part (Lk. 23:51).[81]

There is no further account of the mission in Judaea, either. Leaving aside Jerusalem, with two exceptions, Lydda and Joppa, the communities in Judaea, which, according to the earliest Christian document, 1 Thessalonians 2:14, were undergoing persecution, do not come into the picture. Nor is there mention of any sending out of the

---

[78]J.B. Frey, *CIJ* 2, no. 1404; see also the chapter by R. Riesner in this volume.

[79]See J. Jeremias, *Heiligengräber in Jesu Umwelt* (Göttingen, 1958) 56-60. For Acts 2:29 see also 129. See also ARN vs. A. 35, ed. Schechter, p. 104: there was no tomb in Jerusalem 'apart from the tombs of the House of David and the prophetess Huldah' (= Vs. B 39 p. 107 adds the tomb of Isaiah).

[80]The description of the tomb in Luke 23:53b also appears in John 19:4b. By contrast the Fourth Gospel in 19:20, 41, presupposes further knowledge of the place of the crucifixion and the tomb which could rest on earlier tradition.

[81]Presumably identical with Ramathaim. For the somewhat uncertain identification with *Rentîs* about fourteen kilometres northeast of Lydda see C. Möller and G. Schmitt, *Siedlungen* (n. 12), 158f.

apostles on a mission; compare Galatians 2:8; 1 Corinthians 9:5. Only the hellenists who were driven out of Jerusalem make a missionary journey through Judaea and Samaria (8:1, 4ff.), and then speedily leave Jewish territory behind (11:19ff.). Peter's journey into the coastal regions (9:32ff.) is not really a missionary journey but a tour of inspection, and the important note (12:17) which quite abruptly (indeed, in a way open to misunderstanding, *cf.* 12:2) introduces James (the brother of the Lord) as the later leader of the community, ends with the cryptic comment that the previous head of the group of the Twelve went 'to another place'. In all this, at least on occasion, we may have a certain negligence in writing, though by and large Luke considers very carefully what he says—and what he does not say. At the latest, at this point we are led to wonder whether Luke's restraint is not just caused by deficient geographical or topographical tradition, but is in fact based on a fundamental indifference to geographical details of this kind *in Judaea*. On the one hand, especially if one follows the view popular today that he simply invented facts—he could easily have added such material as illustration and thus could have given colour and concrete detail to the mission in the Holy Land, and on the other hand this restraint is in strange contrast to the fluent information about Paul's mission from chapter 13 onwards, an abundance which when he reaches the 'we' sections increases to become a mass of geographical data which almost confuses the scholar.

All things considered, then, we might conclude from this that in Acts—in the Gospel the situation is different because of the concentration on the person of Jesus—Luke shows by the 'biographical' and the 'geographical' details where his real interest lies. Despite the ideal picture, this is not primarily in the primitive community in Jerusalem or in Judaea, over which he passes rapidly, nor in Peter, who has to leave the stage in an abrupt, enigmatic way in 12:17 and then again in 15:11 with praise for Paul's preaching of grace and faith, but with the 'thirteenth witness', through whom alone the promise of the Lord in 1:8 (put in geographical terms) really comes nearer to fulfilment. Everything else must serve the purpose of describing Paul's mission as far as Rome and preparing for it. The primitive community in Jerusalem is only the connecting link—necessary and indispensable—between Jesus and Paul, between the 'messiah' and 'saviour' (Lk. 2:11) and the mission to the Gentiles apart from the Law.

On this one point, the rigorous narrative organisation of the whole work round the 'chosen instrument' (9:15), progressively suppressing and even misrepresenting everyone else, one could represent Luke as a 'radical Paulinist of a particular kind', even if today we believe that he did not understand much of Paul's theology and take offence that because of his eye-witness theory of salvation history he does not give Paul the title of apostle (except in 14:4, 14). The 'thirteenth witness' 'worked more', indeed for Luke he is more important 'than all of them' (*cf.* 1 Cor. 15:10). Evidently people could be fascinated by Paul even without being able to follow him in all his theology. Perhaps this is connected with the fact that Luke knew Paul from a perspective that we can all too easily neglect for Paul the theologian: as the missionary, the charismatic and the founder of communities.

Luke ignores the communities in Judaea in an almost offensive way, not to mention those in Galilee, which are mentioned in 9:31 only in passing. For him Galilee is interesting only as the place where it all began (10:37; *cf.* 13:31). The mission there had already been carried out through Jesus, while according to Luke missionary work in Judaea took place predominantly in Jerusalem itself: 'the population from the cities round about Jerusalem' bring their sick, who are all healed (5:16).[82] In a way similar to the healing of the lame man (3:1ff.), Philip's mission in Samaria (8:5ff.) and the healing of Aeneas in Lydda by Peter (9:32-35), these miracles are to be understood as the signal for the successful missionary preaching which Luke stresses by a steady increase in numbers. Despite these successes, the future of the church lies neither in Galilee nor in Jerusalem and in Judaea. Therefore the

---

[82]E. Haenchen, *Acts* (n. 34) 243, remarks on the Lukan phrase τῶν πέριξ πόλεων, 'there are of course no real πόλεις in the vicinity' and in n. 4 goes on to conclude: 'Luke had no exact ideas of the geography of Palestine'. The problem is how we understand the term πέριξ, which appears only here in the New Testament. In *BJ* 4.241, Josephus speaks similarly of the 'filth and offscouring of the whole land' which, after it has vented its madness first of all ἐν ταῖς πέριξ κώμαις τε καὶ πόλεσι, 'in the end secretly streamed into the holy city'. As A. Loisy, *Les Actes des Apôtres* (Paris, 1920; repr. Frankfurt, 1973) 27, already observes, the author is thinking 'sans doute...aux villes de Judée'. *Cf.* also *Vita* 81: Josephus conquered the Syrians, who inhabited τὰς πέριξ πόλεις (around Galilee) and took plunder from them. For the stereotyped expression see *BJ* 2.505, 514, 528; 3.134, 430; 4.438, 443, 488 *etc.*: αἱ πέριξ κῶμαι is a phrase from later *koine* (see Liddell and Scott, *s.v.*) which means that the villages are under political control. Luke uses πόλεις instead of the more frequent κῶμαι in Acts 5:16 because this is more appropriate to the status of Jerusalem as the capital of Judaea; moreover, in Hebrew 'city' and 'village' (*ʿîr* and *qiryâ*) are largely interchangeable. *Cf.* A. Schlatter, *Der Evangelist Matthäus* (Stuttgart, 1948) 48, on Josephus, rabbinic texts and the NT. For the formula see also Dio Chrysostom 34.27, of cities with equal rights and indeed hostile cities. On the subject see also Tacitus, *Hist.* 5.8.1: *magna pars Judaeae vicis dispergitur; habent et oppida*; also H. Heubner and W. Fauth (n. 72), 106.

author can leave these areas behind him without laying much stress on them.

IV. The Cities of the Coastal Plain

The first movement in what is a static picture of the primitive community—at least in geographical terms—comes with the expulsion of the hellenists. Those who are driven out of Jerusalem go through 'the districts of Judaea and Samaria' (8:1)—as 8:4 shows, as missionaries. Here Luke does not of course mean that all the churches other than the earliest community in Jerusalem were first founded by the hellenist mission. There were already Christians in Galilee, as there were 'throughout Judaea' (9:31). Peter's 'tour of inspection' in Lydda and Joppa, which follows immediately afterwards, illustrates this situation. The author passes over the way in which the communities came into being and leaves it to the reader to recall that Jesus already had followers at the time of his ministry in places like Emmaus (Lk. 24:13), Jericho (19:9) and perhaps also Arimathea (23:51). He does not dwell on past matters or on incidentals, but hurries his narrative on towards its preconceived goal. Therefore he does not spend further time on the missionizing of Judaea, but immediately has Peter appearing in Samaria (8:5ff.): the winning over of these 'heretics' or 'semi-Jews' is the first step towards the mission to the Gentiles.[83] This becomes completely clear through the second 'Philip legend', the conversion of the eunuch who is the Ethiopian finance minister. Here Luke deliberately leaves it open whether he was a real proselyte or only a godfearer. The detailed description of his high office and his origins, and the commandment in Deuteronomy 23:2 which prohibits eunuchs from being members of the saving community, suggests that the author himself regarded him as a godfearer, even if he does not say as much. Perhaps he sometimes assumes that readers can read between the lines.

In this connection we are particularly interested in the geographical details. O. Bauernfeind already stressed that Philip's activity 'in the city of Samaria' (κατελθὼν εἰς τὴν πόλιν τῆς Σαμαρείας) and the fact that he is sent 'on the way which leads from Jerusalem down to Gaza' (ἐπὶ τὴν ὁδὸν τὴν καταβαίνουσαν ἀπὸ Ἰερουσαλὴμ εἰς Γάζαν) is a direct

---

[83]See Hengel, 'Christology and New Testament Chronology', in *Between Jesus and Paul* (see above, n. 39) 42 ; *idem*, *Acts* (see above, n. 33) 78-79.

contradiction of Jesus' instructions in Matthew 10:5: 'Do not take the road to the Gentiles and do not enter into a city of the Samaritans' (εἰς ὁδὸν ἐθνῶν μὴ ἀπέλθητε καὶ εἰς πόλιν Σαμαριτῶν μὴ εἰσέλθετε).[84] The way which the Ethiopian took from Jerusalem to Gaza on the coast, which brought him via Egypt to his distant homeland at the end of the habitable earth,[85] was a way to the Gentiles. The earliest 'commentator' on this narrative, Irenaeus, stresses twice that the new convert became a missionary there.[86] This may also have been Luke's view, but he says nothing of it and leaves the reader to his own reflections. The κατὰ μεσημβρίαν (8:26) indicates the unusual time of day and is not an indication of direction;[87] the mysterious αὕτη ἐστὶν ἔρημος is not a learned (and at the same time misleading) note copied from Strabo[88] about Gaza, which had once been destroyed by Alexander Jannaeus—the city had been rebuilt long since. Rather, it stresses the unusual nature of the command: there are no people on the road in the heat of the day. Later pilgrims were concerned with questions like which road to Gaza was meant, through the Shephelah in a southwesterly direction or over the hill-country of Judaea southwards in the direction of Hebron, or

---

[84]O. Bauernfeind, *Kommentar* (n. 33), 122.

[85]These facts were known to any Greek with some degree of education. The Greek reader must therefore already have seen here an indirect reference to the fulfilment of Acts 1:8:
Homer, *Odyssey*, 1.22ff.:

> ἀλλ' ὁ μὲν Αἰθίοπας μετεκίαθε τηλόθ' ἐόντας,
> Αἰθίοπας, τοὶ διχθὰ δεδαίαται, ἔσχατοι ἀνδρῶν,
> οἱ μὲν δυσομένου Ὑπερίονος οἱ δ' ἀνιόντος.

'Now he went away to the distant Ethiopians—they are the people at the edge (of the earth); their people is divided: among some Hyperion rises and among others he sets'. See Herodotus 3.25.114; Ephoros, *FGrHist* 70F 30 a/b = Strabo 1.2.28 and Cosmas Indicopleustes, *Top. Christ.* II, p. 117. At the same time the Ethiopians were idealised; see Nicolaus of Damascus, *FGrHist* 90 F 103m = J. Stob., *Anth.* 4.2.142 (ed. Hense IV, 157): ἀσκοῦσι δὲ εὐσέβειαν καὶ δικαιοσύνην.

[86]*Adv.haer.* 3.12.8; 4.22.2.

[87]See W.C. van Unnik, 'Der Befehl an Philippus', in *Sparsa Collecta* I, NTSuppl 29 (Leiden, 1973) 328-39.

[88]Strabo 16.2.30, ἐνδοχός ποτε γενομένή (sc. ἡ πόλις = Gaza) κατεσπασμένη δ'ὑπὸ 'Αλεξάνδρου καὶ μένουσα ἐρημῶς. Here the Greek reader thought of Alexander the Great. In reality the city which he destroyed in 332 BC was quickly rebuilt. So the note refers to the destruction of the place by Alexander Jannaeus in 96 BC after a one-year siege. After the capture of Jerusalem in 63 BC, Gaza was liberated and restored under Gabinius; see M. Stern, *Authors* I (n. 5), 291, 293f., and E. Schürer, G. Vermes *et al.*, II (n. 66), 98ff. (101). The reason for the note by Strabo, who wrote his *Geography* between 7 BC and his death (after AD 23), is that when it was rebuilt under Gabinius the city was constructed rather further south. However, Strabo knows nothing of this new city.

even in what water the Ethiopian was baptised, but they are unimportant to Luke.[89]

Still, this narrative confirms that Luke had a certain basic knowledge of Palestine. The way from Jerusalem to Egypt or Ethiopia runs through Gaza, the first Gentile city, which Luke mentions in Acts in connection with the progress of the mission even before the calling of Paul at Damascus. The mention of Azotus/Ashdod in this context, as the place to which Philip is carried off (8:40), also indicates geographical knowledge. It was just over thirty miles west of Jerusalem and about twenty miles northeast of Gaza and was once a Philistine city. Presumably Luke chose from a larger number of stories about Philip the two which contradicted Matthew 10:5. The brief notes in 8:39a, 40a suggest that here he has summed up a further story in two phrases. The story of Philip's transportation, which is unique for Luke and indeed unique in the New Testament, points to the stormy return of the prophetic Spirit and the way in which there were ecstatic experiences of it in the primitive community and among the hellenists, for whom the miraculous 'divine guidance' of the mission was also connected with the eschatological gift of the Spirit (*cf.* 13:2f.; Gal. 2:1; Acts 16:6; 10:19, *etc.*).[90] We might ask whether the original pre-Lukan story of the transportation of Philip to Azotus might not be meant to express a divine legitimation of the preaching of the missionaries from the 'hellenist' circle in a semi-Gentile city (see below). Luke has allowed the theme of the transportation to stand as an archaic relic—which no longer accorded with his time—but left out the story which went with it.

It is worth our looking more closely at the two places Azotus and Caesarea by the sea, which are mentioned in connection with Philip's further activity. These were no longer Jewish cities in the strict sense of the word, but had a strong Gentile element in their population. There were certainly more 'Greek' citizens than Jews in Caesarea, a polis with a hellenistic constitution and a considerable territory.[91] Conditions in Azotus are not so clear; it is possible that here there were equal

---

[89]For the later legendary 'Philip spring' see H. Donner, *Pilgerfahrt* (n. 54) 63 n. 111; 158f. n. 68; 205; 295 n. 146.

[90]The theme of transportation associates Philip with the Old Testament prophets; *cf.* 1 Ki. 18:12; 2 Ki. 2:16; Ezk. 3:14; 8:3; Bel 36. It continues to have an influence in early Christian prophecy: Hermas 1:3 (*Vis.* 1.1.3); Eusebius, *HE* 5.16.14; the Montanist Theodotus; Mani: the Codex Manichaeus Coloniensis, *ZPapEp* 19 (1975) 51,6ff.; 52,2f.; 55,16ff. *etc. Cf.* also *Gos.Heb.fragm.* 3 (Origen, *Comm. in Joh.* 2, 12, 87) in Hennecke and Schneemelcher and Wilson, *NT Apocrypha* I (n. 33), 158f.

numbers of Jews and Gentiles. Still, the Life of Jonah in the *Vita Prophetarum* says that Jonah came from Kariathmaou, πλησίον πόλεως Ἑλλήνων Ἀζώτον; in other words, the 'Greek' character of the city is deliberately stressed, despite the substantial Jewish element in the population. It is also striking that in contrast to neighbouring Jamnia, it plays no further role in the Talmudic tradition.[92] A look at both cities demonstrates the changed milieu of the missionary activity of Philip as against Jerusalem and Judaea, and at the same time makes it clear that here Luke has worked over traditions which he has also put in the right setting. In supposing that 'v. 40 seems to have been edited by Luke on the basis of accounts of Philip's stay in Caesarea (21:8)',[93] Conzelmann leaves unexplained the decisive introductory Φίλιππος δὲ εὑρέθη εἰς Ἄζωτον. It is also striking that Luke makes Philip, who for him is still the missionary to the Jews (*cf.* 11:19), preach in 'all the cities' as an individual travelling missionary, but mentions only the hellenistic places Azotus and Caesarea as the beginning and end of his journey, whereas predominantly Jewish cities like Joppa and Lydda appear for the first time only on Peter's tour of inspection.

Azotus had been destroyed by Jonathan the Maccabee (1 Mac. 10:84; 11:4) and restored as a polis by Pompey (or Gabinius). It came under the rule of Herod and thus lost its political independence. Presumably it was now just the main city of a taxation district. As Georgius Cyprius gives the city the epithet ἡ Ἵππινος in his *descriptio orbis Romani*, like Gaza it could have been a colony of Herodian cavalry.[94] In his will the king left the place, along with Jewish Jamnia,

---

[91]Josephus, *BJ* 2.266ff.: The Jews 'made the claim that the city belonged to them as its founder was a Jew'; the Greeks pointed out that the statues and temples showed that the city was not Jewish. In the argument the Jews proved to be 'superior in riches and physical strength, the Greeks in the support of the soldiers' (268). L.I. Levine, *Caesarea under Roman Rule* (Leiden, 1975) 22, conjectures a numerical superiority of Jews, but this is not justified by the information given by Josephus. According to Josephus, *BJ* 2.457, at the outbreak of the war, 'in a single hour more than 20,000 were killed, so that the whole of Caesarea was without a Jewish population'. *Cf.* also *Ant.* 20.355ff., 361: the behaviour of the citizens of Caesarea and Sebaste on the death of Agrippa I.

[92]*Liv. Pro.* 10:1; see T. Schermann, *Propheten- und Apostellegende*, TU 31/3 (Leipzig, 1907) 55 ll. 4f. (I am grateful to my colleague Götz Schmitt for this reference). M. Avi-Yonah, *The Holy Land* (Grand Rapids, 1966) referring to Josephus, *BJ* 4.130, conjectures that at that time Azotus was a Jewish city. However, see n. 97 below. The sources in no way indicate that it was a centre for one of the 24 lay divisions responsible for serving in the temple. Herr Gottfried Reeg of the Tübingen Atlas project has pointed out to me its absence from Talmudic literature.

[93]H. Conzelmann, *Apostelgeschichte* (n. 34) 64 *ad loc.*

about nine miles further to the northeast and equally mixed, but more strongly Jewish, to his sister Salome. Probably like Jamnia, after her death it came into the possession of the empress Livia and subsequently directly into that of Tiberius as *patrimonium Caesaris*. With bitter polemic, Philo says that in Jamnia 'there lived a mixed population, the majority of them Jews but the rest a number of foreigners who had nested there as vermin from neighbouring territories'.[95] In AD 39/40 they provoked the Jews by erecting an altar to the emperor Caligula. The Jews tore it down, an act of violence which led the megalomaniac emperor to command that his image should be set up in the temple in Jerusalem. The episode indicates the hatred between Jews and Gentiles in the mixed cities of the coastal plain, which equalled that between Jews and Samaritans.[96] In 67 Vespasian conquered both cities, introduced a garrison as protection and deported the Jewish part of the population, which at the beginning of the revolt had evidently begun to gain the upper hand in Azotus, too.[97]

That hellenists like Philip carried on their missionary work particularly in this mixed area, marked out by hatred between Gentiles and Jews, could be connected with the 'pacifying' character of the gospel. We are better able also to understand traditional statements like Galatians 3:28 (*cf.* Col. 3:11; Eph. 2:11f.) against this background.

The situation in Caesarea was very similar. The Phoenician foundation of Strato's Tower had been conquered by Alexander Jannaeus and regained its freedom from Pompey. Herod refounded it, provided

[94]M. Avi-Yonah, *Land* (n. 91) 149; see Georgius Cyprius, *Descriptio orbis Romani*, ed. H. Gelzer, BT (Leipzig, 1890) 52 l. 1021; A.H.M. Jones, *The Cities of the Eastern Roman Provinces* (Oxford, [2]1971) 273, 275.

[95]*Leg. Gai.* 200. *Cf.* 197-206. On this see E.M. Smallwood, *Philonis Alexandrini Legatio ad Caium*, 262ff.; *idem*, *The Jews under Roman Rule* (Leiden, 1976) 175. According to Josephus, *BJ* 1.166, 'the inhabitants readily returned to each (rebuilt) city'; *cf. Ant.* 14.88. As Azotus was nearer to Gentile Ashkelon, the influence of the non-Jews will have been stronger there than in Jamnia.

[96]*Cf.* Philo, *Leg. Gai.* 205: the hate of the neighbouring Ashkelonites towards the Jews.

[97]Josephus, *BJ* 4.130. Azotus and Jamnia should not be regarded as Jewish places in the same way. It is no coincidence that Josephus mentions Jamnia, with its stronger Jewish stamp, much more frequently above all in the contemporary *BJ* and in the last books of the *Antiquitates*; see C. Möller and G. Schmitt, *Siedlungen* (n. 12) 7f., 97. According to *BJ* 4.444 Vespasian settled 'pacified' Jews in the Jewish towns of Jamnia and Lydda but evidently not in the more markedly Gentile Azotus. For the history of the two places see E. Schürer, G. Vermes *et al.*, *History* (n. 66) 108ff. For the city territory see M. Avi-Yonah, *Land* (n. 91) 149. It was divided into two at a later period.

it with a splendid harbour, and to honour Augustus gave it the name Καισάρεια (Σεβαστή or ἡ πρὸς Σεβαστῷ λιμένι). In AD 6 it became the official capital of Judaea and the official seat of the prefect (from Claudius this official was a procurator). The tensions between Jews and 'Greeks', not least over equal political rights for the former, were intensified in the time of Nero to the point of street fighting and subsequent harsh pogroms, which in the spring of 66 led to the Jewish revolt. At the same time these disputes were of a religious character. Their ultimate cause lay above all in the ancient hatred of the hellenistic Philistines/Phoenicians for the Jews because of Jewish expansion in the Maccabaean and Hasmonaean period.[98] So the situation is not without modern parallels.

For Luke, Caesarea, which he mentions fifteen times, is the second most important city in Palestine, as the residence and seat of the procurator and of a garrison (10:1; 12:19ff.; 23:23-27:1), and also as a harbour and gateway to the *ecumene, i.e.* to the 'world mission' (9:30; 18:22; 21:8ff.; *cf.* 27:1). It is striking that he no longer assigns it to Judaea in the strict sense, since in 12:19 he describes the journey of Herod Agrippa I from Jerusalem to Caesarea as κατελθὼν ἀπὸ τῆς Ἰουδαίας εἰς Καισάρειαν (*cf.* also Agabus, 21:10; 11:1; 10:37). This is an indication that as a 'city state' the predominantly pagan Caesarea had a degree of independence over against the other 'regions', Judaea and Jerusalem, Samaria and Galilee. Agrippa I wanted to negotiate there with the delegations from the city states of Tyre and Sidon; these sought peace with him because they were economically dependent on the hinterland of Galilee and Samaria which was under his control (διὰ τὸ τρέφεσθαι αὐτῶν τὴν χώραν). The Gentile δῆμος of the city hailed him as God (12:22). In other words, for Luke too this was a predominantly pagan city; here he is describing the situation of Caesarea not simply from the perspective of an overseas visitor—who would probably have located the residence in Judaea—but rather from the Jewish

[98]E. Schürer, G. Vermes *et al.*, *History* II (n. 66), 145ff.; L.I. Levine, *Caesarea* (n. 91), 6-32. *Cf.* also I. Heinemann, 'Antisemitismus', in *PWSuppl* 5 (1931) 16ff.; U. Rappaport, 'The Jewish Relations and the Revolt against Rome in 66-70 CE', in *The Jerusalem Cathedra* I (1981) 81-95. For Caesarea as a 'hellenistic' *polis* see also B. Lifshitz, 'Césaré de Palestine, son histoire et ses institutions', *ANRW* II, 8, 490-518.

standpoint,[99] showing his familiarity with the special characteristics of the πόλις.

The hellenistic πόλις of Caesarea, open to the 'great wide world', becomes the permanent abode of the charismatic missionary Philip, who had been the second of the 'Seven' (6:5: τοῦ εὐαγγελιστοῦ, ὄντος ἐκ τῶν ἑπτά, 21:8). Through these precise details, with the title evangelist and the reference to the nucleus of the Seven, Luke puts the representative of the Christian community in Caesarea at a certain distance from that of Peter and the twelve apostles and then from Jerusalem represented by James and the elders, and from the communities in Judaea dominated by Jerusalem (*cf.* 11:1). His four prophetic daughters also give a very distinctive stamp to this 'travelling charismatic', who ultimately becomes firmly established. Presumably—despite Luke's silence on the matter—he carried on the mission to the Gentiles as well in mixed Jewish and Gentile cities like Azotus or Caesarea, *i.e. inter alia* he at least addressed the Gentile godfearers too; that is suggested by the episode with the distinguished Ethiopian. Luke leaves it to the reader to draw the further conclusions which the legends he used may have suggested even more clearly. Finally we should note that in the end Luke, the Greek city-dweller, transfers the activity of the first missionary to be depicted in detail to 'hellenistic' cities. This accords with the course of the expansion of Christianity generally; originally, as Luke knows very well, it had been a Galilean country movement of uneducated people.[100]

Caesarea, which according to Pliny lay on what perhaps was originally Samaritan territory and in the east bordered on the Samaritan villages in the coastal plain, itself had a Samaritan minority.[101] Perhaps Philip had come up against the Samaritan problem there, so that his 'Samaritan mission' developed from the port. In that case it might be even more justified to assume that there was a degree of rivalry between it and the community in Jerusalem and in Judaea. At all events, Luke was concerned to deal with this and to integrate it into

[99]A. von Harnack, *Beiträge zur Einleitung in das NT*, III, *Die Apostelgeschichte* (Leipzig, 1908) 71: 'It is worth noting that Luke is aware that Caesarea is not part of Judaea in the strict sense'. Tacitus, *Hist.* 2.78.4, gives the Roman perspective, as seen from Italy. Mucanius goes to Antioch, Vespasian to Caesarea: *illa Suria, hoc Judaeae caput est. Cf.* also Josephus, *Ant.* 19.351, quoted below, n. 115.

[100]Acts 1:11; 2:7: Γαλιλαῖοι; 4:13: Peter and John: ἄνθρωποι ἀγράμματοι. For the contrast between city and country see M. Hengel, *The Zealots* (n. 66) 326-9; *idem, Judaism and Hellenism* I, 53f.; G. Theissen, *Studien zur Soziologie des Urchristentums* (Tübingen, 1979) 142-59.

his harmonious overall picture of the earliest Christian mission by the sending of Peter and John (8:14ff.). Finally, the friendly reception of Paul and his companions when they arrive in Caesarea on the last journey, described in the 'we report' (21:8ff.), which is clearly contrasted with the more reserved account of the reception by James and the elders in James' 'residence', where the advice, or rather command, of James leads to the subsequent conflict in the Temple (21:18ff.), shows that Philip was also a missionary to the Gentiles. Luke wants to use this background account to demonstrate that in contrast to the threatening situation in Jerusalem, his hero was *persona grata* to Philip and the Christians in Caesarea who accompanied him on his difficult journey to Jerusalem (21:16). It is understandable that, as we can infer from later reports in Papias, Polycrates of Ephesus and so on, Philip and his daughters later left Palestine and settled in Hierapolis in Phrygia. Probably the situation had become impossible for them as a result of the intensification of the conflict between Jews and Gentiles in Caesarea before AD 66.[102]

In the light of all this, Luke's knowledge of the coastal plain seems to be substantially better than that of Galilee, Samaria, the hill-country of Judaea and the territory around Jerusalem. We need only compare with these sensible geographical details the confused geographical accounts in the apocryphal Acts of Philip.[103] This argument can be substantiated by further indications.

---

[101]Pliny, *Hist.Nat.* 5.68: *regio per oram Samaria*; see M. Stern, *Authors*, I (n. 5), no. 204, p. 473: 'Samaria seems to have included the coast from somewhere north of Jaffa up to and including Caesarea; see *Ant.* 19.351.' This was possibly part of the new Roman ordering of the country after Pompey and Gabinius and before Herod. For the Samaritans in Caesarea see L.I. Levine, *Caesarea* (n. 90), 107ff. Although we have no accounts of Samaritans in Caesarea from the first century, we must assume that there was a Samaritan element in the population from the start. According to the later Pseudo-Clementines the clash between Peter and Simon Magus took place in Caesarea, 'the largest city in Palestine'; *Recogn.* 1.12.1ff.; 1.72: Peter is called from Jericho to Caesarea to meet Simon; *cf. Hom.* 1.15.1. See below, nn. 140-2. Samaritan elements in the population were to be found scattered throughout the coastal plain; see M. Avi-Yonah, in M. Safrai and M. Stern (eds.), *The Jewish People in the First Century* I (Assen, 1974) 107; *cf.* also H.G. Kippenberg, *Garizim und Synagoge*, RVV XXX (Berlin & New York, 1971) 80, 142, 155f., 160.

[102]Papias in Eusebius, *HE* 3.39.9, *cf.* the fragment of Philippus Sidetes in F. X. von Funk and K. Bihlmeyer, *Die apostolischen Väter* (Tübingen & Leipzig, 1924) 138f. Polycrates of Ephesus, Eusebius, *HE* 3.31.2-5; 5.24.2; *cf.* the defence against the Montanist reference to Philip's daughters, *HE* 5.17.3. See T. Zahn, *Forschungen zur Geschichte des neutestamentlichen Kanons* VI (Leipzig, 1900) 158-75: 'Philip in Hierapolis'.

V. Peter's Journey (9:32–11:18): Lydda, Joppa and Caesarea

In connection with two miracle stories, Luke in Acts 9:32-43 depicts Peter's tour of inspection round the communities in Lydda and Joppa. Of the numerous 'cities' in Judaea, only these two are of interest to him, as they are the most important almost purely Jewish places on the coastal plain.[104] The geographical details connected with the story are completely correct. If one goes down from Jerusalem into the predominantly Jewish sector of the coastal plain one comes to Lydda, the first large Jewish place in the plain, about twenty-five miles northwest of Jerusalem as the crow flies (*cf.* Josephus, *BJ* 2.244). Joppa, the only Jewish port of any significance, which lost much of its influence as a result of the founding of Caesarea, lies another eleven miles or so further on in the same direction; thus the two places are 'close together' (9:38: ἐγγὺς δὲ οὔσης Λύδδας τῇ Ἰόππῃ). According to Eusebius of Caesarea, the plain of 'Sharon' (9:35), in which, according to Luke's hyperbolic account, the healing of the paralysed Aeneas is said to have had a tremendous effect on the mission, stretched from Caesarea to Joppa; according to Jerome it also comprised the territory of Lydda, Joppa and Jamnia.[105]

Lydda, at the foot of the Shephelah, which cannot always be clearly distinguished from the plain of Sharon (*cf.* Josephus, *Ant.* 15.33,41), had long been settled by Jews.[106] When Cestius Gallus advanced against Jerusalem with his army in 66, he found the 'city' of Lydda 'abandoned by all its inhabitants' (κενὴν ἀνδρῶν πόλιν καταλαμβάνει, *BJ* 2.515). Vespasian settled 'pacified' Jews there (and in Jamnia) two years later (see n. 97 above). In *Ant.* 20.130, Josephus calls it a village, though one 'which in size does not fall short of being a city' (κώμην . . . Λύδδαν πόλεως τὸ μέγεθος οὐκ ἀποδέουσαν). He says this

---

[103]R.A. Lipsius and M. Bonnet, *Acta Apostolorum Apocrypha* II (Leipzig, 1898) 1-90; R.A. Lipsius, *Die apokryphen Apostelgeschichten und Legenden* (Brunswick, 1884) II, 2, 5f., 36ff., 40f.; also O. Bardenhewer, *Geschichte der altkirchlichen Literatur* I (Freiburg, 21913) 584; A. Kurfess, 'Zu den Philippusakten', *ZNW* 44 (1952-53) 145-51. For the apocryphal Philip tradition see especially also T. Zahn, *Forschungen* (see above, n. 102) 18-27.

[104]See already the vivid description by A. Schlatter, *Topographie* (n. 12) 1-43.

[105]See F.-M. Abel, *Géographie de la Palestine* I (Paris, 31967) 414f. (415 n. 1).

[106]A. Schlatter, *Topographie* (n. 12), 29: 'In the Persian period Lydda had vigorously asserted its Jewish character'. For the history see G. Hölscher, 'Lydda', in *PW* XIII/2, cols. 2120ff. and M. Avi-Yonah, *Land* (n. 91), 226f., index *s.v.* Lod, Lydda and Diospolis. For the mention in Josephus see C. Möller and G. Schmitt, *Siedlungen* (n. 12), 131f. (and literature there).

because Lydda, like all other places in Judah, in contrast to the *poleis* of Caesarea, Gaza, Ashkelon and so on, did not have any civic rights. It was significant because, like Joppa, it was the chief centre of one of the ten (or eleven) toparchies of Judaea.[107]

By contrast, Joppa, Hebrew Japho, had originally been a hellenized Canaanite-Phoenician city which—as the only good port on the coast of Palestine before the foundation of Caesarea—had been developed into a strong fortress by the Ptolemies and Seleucids. Even before the time of Alexander the Great, Greek saga had connected it with the myth of Andromeda. It was then conquered by Simon the Maccabee, who drove out all the Gentile population (1 Mac. 12:33; 13:11). In this way the Jews gained a port on the Mediterranean, from which according to Strabo (16.2,28) they also engaged in piracy in the time of the Hasmonaeans. This may be one of the reasons why Pompey detached the city from Judaea (*BJ* 1.156; *Ant*. 14.76). However, in contrast to Azotus it was not re-hellenized, but remained predominantly Jewish, so that Caesar restored it to the Jews. At the beginning of the war in AD 66, unlike Azotus and Jamnia it became a centre of the revolt against Rome and was therefore destroyed by Cestius Gallus (*BJ* 2.508); after his defeat at Beth-horon it was fortified once more and then captured again by Vespasian (*BJ* 3.414ff.).[108]

Thus Peter's activity as 'inspector' of the Jewish-Christian communities in the coastal plain[109] is primarily limited, in contrast to Philip, to expressly Jewish cities. This is hardly a coincidence. Thus to some degree there is confirmation here of the Petrine ἀποστολὴ τῆς περιτομῆς (Gal. 2:7) according to Luke's view. We cannot pursue further here a question which is ultimately insoluble, namely whether and how far in the stories about Peter Luke was working over tradition or shaping it editorially. Presumably, as elsewhere, he did both. If he himself were the one who connected the two miracle stories by the note in 9:38, which is geographically accurate, we would have to say

[107]For the toparchies see A. Schalit, *Herodes* (n. 44), 205-19; Pliny the Elder, *Nat.Hist*. 5.14.70 also mentions a toparchy of Jopica whose existence A. Schalit questions, as under Herod Joppa was not legally incorporated in Judaea (209f.). But see Josephus, *BJ* 2.567: John the Essene as governor of the toparchies of Thamna, Joppa and Emmaus. It is significant that as mixed areas Azotus and Jamnia are not mentioned here (see n. 96 above). For the whole question see also M. Stern, *Authors* I (n. 2), 476f.

[108]For the history of Joppa, see G. Beer, 'Joppe', in *PW* IX/2, cols. 1901f. E. Schürer, G. Vermes *et al.*, *History* II (n. 66), 110ff.; M. Avi-Yonah, *Land* (n. 91), 227, index *s.v.* Joppe. For Josephus see C. Möller and G. Schmitt, *Siedlungen* (n. 12), 105; A. Schalit, *Herodes* (n. 44), 198ff., 206ff.; *EJ* 9, 1250f.

that his knowledge of the coastal area was amazingly good for a Greek who was foreign to the country. Perhaps, however, he already had a whole 'cycle' of stories about Peter which will then of course have included the basic nucleus of the Cornelius story in 10:1–11:18 and which represents the narrative aim of the author in respect of the Philip and the Peter stories, both of which frame the account of the conversion of Saul before Damascus. After the call of the future great missionary to the Gentiles it is time for the conversion of the first Gentiles, by the leading member of the primitive community. Peter's journey to the coast and so to the boundary of the territory of Judah, *i.e.* Judaea according to Acts 1:8, is thus simply geographical preparation for the conversion of the first Gentile, the centurion Cornelius, in Caesarea. The two miracle stories in Lydda and Joppa see to it that this amazing story, to which Luke attaches particular importance, is not too isolated; he could have passed over the two miracles of the apostle in themselves, as over so much else that he had available in the tradition. Thus in connection with the note in 9:31 Luke has reached a clear boundary, both geographically and in the history of the mission. 'Jewish' Palestine—Galilee, Jerusalem, Judaea and Samaria—is missionized; the missionary of the future is called; the gospel is on the threshold of going out 'to the ends of the earth'. The eunuch who travels to Ethiopia; Philip, who works in Caesarea as an 'advance party'; the missionary success of Peter in the plain of Sharon, which extends as far as Caesarea,[110] and in the end the apostle by the sea at

---

[109]The predominant interpretation of this as a tour of inspection has been challenged by W. Dietrich, *Das Petrusbild der lukanischen Schriften*, BWANT (Stuttgart, 1972) 262ff. However, as the spokesman for the community in Jerusalem Peter also had responsibility for the communities in Judaea most closely connected with Jerusalem. For Luke, however, according to 9:31 these together form the one 'church throughout Judaea' (9:31; *cf.* 11:1, 29; 21:10; 26:20; *cf.* Luke's Paul in Acts 28:21; *cf.* 2 Cor. 1:16; Gal. 1:22; 1 Thes. 2:14). Further, Peter has to travel alone because the subsequent Cornelius episode, to which the account as a whole is leading up, is connected only with him. Possibly Luke shaped the whole passage on analogy with the activity of the individual 'travelling charismatic' Philip. It is quite unjustified to see as the reason for the journey 'certain happenings in the Jerusalem community' (W. Dietrich, *Petrusbild*, 264). We can hardly say anything about the historical situation of the community in Jerusalem and Judaea before the persecution by Agrippa I. It simply follows from Gal. 1:18f. that James the brother of the Lord already played an important role—as second-in-command (*cf.* Acts 12:17)—but that Peter's authority was unshaken. For Luke it is only the baptism of the first godfearing Gentile which leads to conflict (Acts 11:1f.).

[110]For the 'plain of Sharon', from the Hebrew *shārôn*, flat land, see K. Elliger, *BHHW* III, cols. 1673f.; *cf.* already Jos. 12:18, but see also n. 105 above.

Joppa, mark out this threshold. From a geographical point of view as well, 'salvation history' is ready for the next stage.

Even the Cornelius story, which, in contrast to the usage of the *auctor ad Theophilum* elsewhere, is elaborated with a great many repetitions and indeed is almost too overloaded with detail, contains some remarkable geographical notes. The report of the angel that the house of Simon the host is 'by the sea' (10:5; *cf.* 9:43; 10:17) may be a novelistic feature prompted by the fact that there was little introduction to the occupation of the tanner; at all events, however, it indicates that from a geographical point of view Peter really had reached the ultimate border of Judaea. His name and the mention of the 'Italian cohort'[111] characterise the hero of the story as a foreigner, as a Roman. Nor is it a coincidence that he and even more the Ethiopian are members of the upper class. Luke stresses both figures in view of the prominent position of the person to whom his two-volume work is addressed, Theophilus, also a member of the upper class. The inclusion of the times of prayer characterises the centurion as a godfearer,[112] who takes things seriously. Cornelius is praying at the ninth hour, about three o'clock in the afternoon; on the command of the angel, without delay he dispatches two slaves and a godfearing soldier to Joppa. They arrive the next day at the time of prayer, the sixth hour, that is, round about noon (10:3, 7-9). The distance between Joppa and Caesarea is about thirty miles; in view of the importance of the mission this is quite a possible journey for a Roman soldier who is used to marching, and able-bodied slaves.[113] For the return journey the day after next Peter and the brothers who accompany him from Joppa are allowed a full day, and perhaps even more, as there is no indication of time; it is part of the colouring of the story that the centurion is already waiting impatiently for him. Even if Luke had made all this up—which I do not believe for a moment—it would have been a good idea: in this case geographically plausible.[114]

Luke gives an accurate description of yet another journey to Caesarea: in the 'we account' in 21:7ff. there is a journey by ship from Tyre to Ptolemais-Akko and from there, after the voyage, a further journey on foot to Caesarea, which again is a march of about thirty miles. Here, however, there are no details of time.

Finally, in 11:1f., we are told: 'Now the apostles and the brethren who were in Judaea (οἱ ὄντες κατὰ Ἰουδαίαν) heard that the Gentiles also had received the word of God. So when Peter went up to Jerusalem, the circumcision party criticised him'. Here there is confirmation that Luke no longer reckoned Caesarea in the strict sense as part of Judaea but as Gentile territory[115] and that with his excursion there Peter had crossed a frontier which had hitherto been forbidden. Furthermore, that the community in Jerusalem and in Judaea form a unity in Luke as they do for Paul. Although Luke sometimes differentiates the two, the Holy City cannot be detached from Judaea (see n. 109 above).

---

[111]The old dispute over the 'historicity' of this information is pointless. It may be an anachronism but need not necessarily be so. Auxiliary cohorts could be posted anywhere in the Roman empire according to need, *cf.* Josephus, *Ant.* 19.364-6: the problem of posting the Sebaste cohorts. For the 'Italian cohort' and on the occupation of Judaea see T.R.S. Broughton in *Beginnings* V (n. 58), 427-45 (441f.); E. Schürer, G. Vermes *et al., History* I (n. 66), 361ff. (365). The epitaph (*loc.cit.*, n. 54 = *CIL* 13483a) of an *optio* (centurion's auxiliary) Proculus Rabili filius, who came from Philadelphia in Palestine, had served in a *cohors secunda civium Romanorum...exercitus Syriaci* and presumably had died on the march of the Syrian army to Italy towards the end of AD 69, indicates the presence of such a cohort in Syria *before* 69. The Philadelphian Proculus son of 'Rabel' (at any rate a Semitic, and presumably a Nabataean name), will probably have begun his service in his homeland, like the people of Sebaste. Finally, a centurion could also be appointed for administrative or other political or police duties, and not just for army service (*cf.* Acts 27:1). This certainly does not prove the historicity of the information. 'Proofs' in the strict sense are impossible, since our knowledge of Roman troops in Syria and Palestine is simply too small. But those who challenge the detail should not make it too easy for themselves. In mentioning the 'Italian' cohort Luke presumably wanted to portray Cornelius as a Roman and not a Jew. He will be right in the fact that the 'historical' centurion Cornelius, whose existence should not be disputed, had virtually nothing to do with the severely anti-Jewish people of Sebastene, who stood out among the Gentile population of the country (particularly in Sebaste). For the social position of the centurion see A.N. Sherwin-White, *Roman Society and Roman Law in the New Testament* (Oxford, 1963) 154ff., and now B. Dobson, 'The Significance of the Centurion and Primipilaris in the Roman Army and Administration', *ANRW* II/1 (1974) 392-434. The rank of a centurion was relatively high. To reach it a capable soldier had to have served in the legions and auxiliaries for between twelve and twenty years (see D.J. Breeze, *ANRW* III/1 [1974] 438-51), for the auxiliary troops in general see D.B. Saddington, 'The Development of the Roman Auxiliary Forces from Augustus to Trajan', *ANWR* II/3 (1975) 175-201 (and the literature there); *idem*, 'The Roman Auxilia in Tacitus, Josephus and Other Early Imperial Writers', *Acta Classica* 13 (1970) 89-124 and 121f. on Acts 10:1; 27:1. A.N. Sherwin-White, *op. cit.*, 156, 160f., sees Cornelius as 'a provincial, living with his kinsmen' (156). At a later stage the *cohors Italicae* also recruited from *peregrini*, as did the other auxiliary cohorts. All in all we know far too little about military conditions in Palestine to be able to draw any clear conclusions.

[112]See the basic study by F. Siegert, 'Gottesfürchtige und Sympathisanten', *JSJ* 4 (1973) 109-64. Neither the eunuch nor the centurion could become full Jews, above all because of their political and social status.

VI. Antipatris and the Road from Jerusalem to Caesarea

One last paradigm can finally round off Luke's knowledge of the coastal region. We had already noted that the account of Paul's arrest in Acts 21 presupposes some knowledge of the connection between the Temple and the barracks in the fortress Antonia. It accords with this that from the beginning of the 'we report' from chapter 20 onwards the historical and geographical details increase in liveliness and content. This is also true of the account of the events which lead the Roman tribune Claudius Lysias to hand Paul over to the procurator Felix in Caesarea. He learns through the nephew of the missionary that religious zealots have made a conspiracy to murder Paul at the next hearing before the Sanhedrin. Thereupon without delay he has the threatened prisoner moved to Caesarea under the protection of two centuries of auxiliary troops, two centuries of lightly armed troops and seventy cavalrymen. In a march which also extends through the night the troops reach Antipatris,[116] about forty-five miles from Jerusalem, a smaller city founded by Herod, who named it after his father. At the same time it served as a military post, being just twelve miles north of

---

[113]For the forced march of Roman troops with full baggage see J. Krohmayer and G. Veith, *Heerwesen und Kriegführung der Griechen und Römer*, HAW (1928) 423: '45 miles in twenty-eight hours with three hours' rest at night' (Caesar, *De bello gallico*, 7, 40f.). According to Plutarch, *Mark Antony*, 47.2, on the return from Media, in adverse conditions, the Roman army covered 240 stadia, *i.e.* about 27 miles, in a night. Josephus bears witness to similar figures for Palestine. According to *Ant.* 15. 293, Sebaste, which was about 42 miles from Jerusalem, could be reached from there in a day. From Sogane (Sichnin) in the northern part of Lower Galilee a large group of travellers could reach Jerusalem itself in just three days. The distance was about 90 miles. *Cf. Vita* 266-70 and C. Möller and G. Schmitt, *Siedlungen* (n. 12) 180f. By contrast we need to be sceptical about the indications of distance in Herodotus, according to which Sinope on the Black Sea, about 360 miles away as the crow flies, could be reached from the hill-country of Cilicia by 'an able-bodied man in five day's journeys'. In 4.101 he assumes more realistically that a day's march would cover a distance of 200 stadia = about 24 miles (I am grateful to Dr Lichtenberger for these references to Herodotus).

[114]The conjecture by E. Haenchen, *Acts* (n. 34), 346ff. (following F.C. Baur and J. Wellhausen, *Kritische Analyse der Apostelgeschichte*, AAG 15, 2 [Berlin, 1914] 10: 'unhistorical fudging') that this is a free, didactic composition by Luke misunderstands his way of working; see F. Bovon, *De vocatione Gentium* (Tübingen, 1967) 304ff.; *idem*, 'Tradition et redaction en Actes 10,1-11,18', *TZ* 26 (1970) 22-45; K. Haacker, 'Dibelius und Cornelius', *BZ* 24 (1980) 234-51; J. Roloff, *Apostelgeschichte* (n. 37) 165f., though he underestimates the distances of marches in antiquity (169).

[115]See above, n. 99. *Cf.* Josephus, *Ant.* 19.351 on Agrippa I: ἐβασίλευσεν καὶ τὴν Ἰουδαίαν προσέλαβεν Σαμαρείαν τε καὶ Καισάρειαν.

Lydda on the border between the territory of Judaea and that of Samaria; its territory in the west ran parallel to that of the hellenistic polis Apollonia, which lay on the coast, and to that of Joppa; in the north it bordered on the territory of Caesarea, in the east on that of Samaria and in the south on the westernmost toparchy of Judaea, Lydda. It was a place which Herod had deliberately sought out for strategic reasons. The next day Paul was brought by the cavalry to Caesarea, which was about twenty-five miles further on, while the infantry returned to their barracks in Jerusalem (23:23-32). We may take the number of troops mentioned by Luke and the capacity of the soldiers for marching to be rather exaggerated—the strong guard and the speed of the undertaking at the same time emphasise the importance of the person under arrest; by and large, however, this account fits admirably into the strange—one might almost say macabre—milieu in Judaea in the time of the last procurators: Felix, under whose long administration the political situation worsened to an acute degree, Festus, Albinus and after them Gessius Florus. As events under Felix's predecessor Cumanus already showed, the charge of defiling the temple was political dynamite, as it could incense the people to the point of open rebellion.[117] Regular events of the time included conspiracies, assassinations by sicarii (21:38) and other manifestations of religious fanaticism, further tumults, street battles, abductions and ambushes.[118] Even before Felix, at the time of Ventidius

---

[116]For its situation and history see E. Schürer,G. Vermes *et al.*, *History* II (n. 66), 107f.; M. Avi-Yonah, *Land* (n. 91), 100, 106, 111, 144-7, where there is also a description of the city territory. The cities founded by Herod, Caesarea, Sebaste, Gaba Heshbon, all also had a strategic character. There are instances from the Mishnah in B.Z. Segal, *hag-gĕôgrafya bam-mishnâ* (Jerusalem, 5739 = 1979) 13f. (in Hebrew): עיר גבול. The strategic significance of the place emerges from *BJ* 2.513, 554, 443: Vespasian begins the expedition against Judaea in early 68 with a march from Caesarea to Antipatris, where he lets the troops rest for two days. *Cf.* also C. Möller and G. Schmitt, *Siedlungen* (n. 12) 20 (lit.).

[117]M. Hengel, *The Zealots* (n. 66) 206-28. E. Haenchen, *Acts*, 650, as usual mocks the inaccurate ideas Luke has of the geography of Palestine. He fails to understand that Luke wants to use the forced march by this substantial unit to stress Paul's importance. For the marching capacity of Roman armies see n. 113 above.

[118]M. Hengel, *The Zealots* (n. 66), 343-58. For the procuratorship of Felix see also E. Schürer, G. Vermes *et al.*, *History* I (n. 66), 460-6. *Cf.* the reference to the Egyptian (Acts 22:38) and his 4,000 sicarii. Apart from Luke, the term σικάριος appears in Greek literature only in Josephus, in his description of conditions in Judaea from Felix to the Jewish War (Masada). This Latin loanword is unknown to all other Greek texts. See M. Hengel, *The Zealots* (n. 67), index of Greek, Hebrew and Latin words *s.v.* His usage was evidently connected with the particular situation in Palestine. Therefore we also find it as a rabbinic loanword.

Cumanus, an imperial slave, perhaps belonging to the financial administration, accompanying a consignment of money, was attacked and robbed on the main route from Jerusalem to Caesarea—*i.e.* the same road along which Paul was probably also taken—on the way up to Beth-horon (*BJ* 2,228: κατὰ . . . τὴν Βαιθωρὼ δημοσίαν ἄνοδον, so PA, Lat, Thackeray, *cf. Ant.* 20.113). In the later years of Felix, at the time of Paul's arrest in, say, the year 57 or 58, the situation in Judaea had become even more unsafe. Eight or nine years later, in October 66, at the same place, the ascent to Beth-horon, *i.e.* the road through the pass which leads down to Lydda, the Governor of Syria, Cestius Gallus, with his army of about 33,000 men was attacked by the badly-equipped Jewish insurgents and only escaped annihilation by withdrawing secretly overnight to the coastal plain, leaving behind his heavier military equipment. The following morning he was pursued by the Jews as far as Antipatris (*BJ* 2.540-555).[119] Against the background of this situation we can understand the action of the Roman commandant in the Antonia in removing as quickly as possible from the danger zone the Jew under special arrest and the Roman citizen who had stirred up resentment among the population of Jerusalem by supposedly desecrating the Temple and leading the people astray. Here the route of march was especially endangered in the hill-country of Judah and the descent to the coastal plain, indeed as far as the boundaries of Judaea, *i.e.* as far as Antipatris. Hence the guard of a detachment of foot soldiers who on the completion of their task returned from Antipatris to Jerusalem. Josephus could hardly have depicted the event more appropriately. In other words, in my view the account must ultimately derive from an eye-witness. It demonstrates the political uncertainty in Judaea towards the end of Felix's period of office. We may forgive Luke for exaggerating some things in the interests of his hero.

This last instance shows in an even more evocative way what we were already able to note in connection with Paul's arrest, namely that at particular points even in the context of Palestine itself the geographical details and the event narrated can very readily be brought together into a unity which needs to be taken seriously in historical terms. In my view this is above all the case where the author, Luke the physician, was close to events. According to Acts 21:15 he himself had gone up

[119]M. Hengel, *The Zealots* (n. 66) 284-5, 368-9. For the defeat of Cestius see E. Schürer, G. Vermes *et al., History* (n. 66) 487f.; M. Smallwood, *Jews* (n. 94), 297f. For upper and lower Beth-horon see C. Möller and G. Schmitt, *Siedlungen* (n. 12), 32f.

the road from Caesarea to Jerusalem. His knowledge of conditions in Judaea during roughly the last fifteen years before the outbreak of the Judaean war and his special concern with the destruction of Jerusalem show how he was affected by these events and stood relatively close to them; this makes it impossible to date his work in the second century. His basic theological problem, namely the rise of the Gentile mission apart from the Law and the separation of the church from the synagogue, was no longer acute in this period.

It was also striking that—in complete contrast to the later romance-like acts of apostles—Luke usually uses exact geographical information only when it is there in the tradition and is significant for the narrative or for his theology. He does not need to invent it to provide novelistic elaboration, since he does not want to display specialist learned knowledge nor does he have the delight of later pilgrims in satisfying curiosity by depicting 'holy places'. The travel account in the first person plural gives his own views; in it the author is demonstrating that he was present at the time. A comparison with Mark, his model for the Gospel, shows that he simply leaves out details which he finds superfluous or open to misunderstanding, or which will not fit into his approach. This is still more the case with Acts, where he had to cope with a longer period and more material. We can also note where he is reporting at second or third hand without having more detailed knowledge, and where he has adopted certain geographical notions on the basis of his own information.

To conclude with, I would like to make a kind of contrary demonstration by considering a complex which we have not looked at so far and over which there is particular dispute among scholars.

VII. Samaria in the Acts of the Apostles

Samaria is strikingly significant within the programme put forward in Acts 1:8. There the mission stands to some degree as a connecting link between the mission (to the Jews) in Jerusalem and Judaea on the one hand and the worldwide mission (to the Gentiles) on the other. This connecting link would not have been at all necessary in itself. The communities in Samaria had no visible influence on the further course of church history, and the only connection which Luke makes between them and Paul (and Barnabas) in 15:3 seems somewhat artificial. At best there remain the Samaritan heresiarchs Simon and Menander. In their case the question is whether their significance does not largely rest on the polemic (and scholarship) of later heresy hunters from Justin[120] and Irenaeus onwards and the imagination of some apostolic romances like the Acts of Peter and the Pseudo-Clementines. In the case of Luke such an influence of the Samaritan church and the heretics on 'church history' cannot be seen at all. For him the 'Samaria' chapter already comes to an end with 9:31.

Basically, so far as Luke's terminology goes, we can say that he always uses the word Σαμαρεία to refer to the territory of the Samaritans, that ethnic religious group whose members are not proper Jews but even less can be counted among the Gentiles. In this sense, in 8:9 he can speak—quite properly in legal terms—of the ἔθνος τῆς Σαμαρείας;[121] this differs completely from his use of δῆμος, which means the civic assembly of a polis (12:22; 17:5; 19:30, 33). The three texts about the Samaritans in the Gospel also show that he is aware of the deep division, indeed of the mutual contempt and hatred, existing between the two kindred religious groups, Samaritans and Jews (*cf.* 9:52ff.; 10:33; 17:16). We may probably understand the reason he gives for the rejection of Jesus and his disciples 'because he was on the way up to Jerusalem' (Lk. 9:53) as an indication that he was also aware of the tensions or clashes between Galilean pilgrims going up for festivals and the Samaritans. Presumably he was also aware of the Samaritan rejection of the Jerusalem cult.[122] In contrast to John 4, however, at no point does he go into the religious peculiarities of the Samaritans. Well as he knew the political significance of the Sadducees and certain doctrinal differences between the Pharisees and Sadducees with whom indeed the Samaritans are compared,[123] he will also have

[120]Justin mentions Simon Magus six times (*Apol.* 26.2 [twice]; 26.4; 56.1, 2; *Dial.* 120.6) and his disciple Menander twice (*Dial.* 100.4; 106.3). K. Beyschlag, *Simon Magus und die christliche Gnosis*, WUNT 16 (Tübingen, 1974) has clearly demonstrated that one may not simply read later Simonian Gnosticism into Luke's Simon Magus. See also the balanced judgment of R. McL. Wilson, 'Simon and Gnostic Origins', in J. Kremer (ed.), *Les Actes des Apôtres*, BETL 48 (Gembloux-Lyons, 1979) 485-91.

[121]For the Jews and Samaritans as ἔθνος see M. Hengel, *Judaism and Hellenism* I, 20, 24f. (II, 18 n. 156), 28. This designation, introduced in the early hellenistic period, lasted on into the Roman period.

[122]For the sharp disputes between Jews and Samaritans under the prefects or procurators see Josephus, *Ant.* 18.30; 20.118-30 = *BJ* 2.232-45. *Cf.* also H.G. Kippenberg, *Garizim* (n. 100) 85-93.

[123]*Cf.* Acts 4:1; 5:17; 23:6ff. For the comparison between Sadducees and Samaritans see Ps.-Clem. *Rec.* 1.54 (ed. Rehm, GCS 51, p. 39); Hippolytus, *Refutatio* 9.29.4 (ed. Wendland, GCS 26, p. 262) *etc.*; see H.G. Kippenberg, *Garizim* (n. 102), 130f., 135.

known of some of the peculiarities of the Samaritans, given that he is the non-Jew with by far the best knowledge of Judaism and the LXX down to the first century AD. However, he does not mention these peculiarities in any way, although by so doing he restricts the revolutionary act represented by the shift of the hellenist mission towards the Samaritans. He is interested only in the 'geographically' visible progress of the mission as a development in 'salvation history', which pursues its divinely directed course despite and indeed because of the persecution of the community in Jerusalem. At the same time the contrast between the hardened inhabitants of Jerusalem and the Samaritans who gladly believe (8:8, 12f.) is brought out in the bas-relief fashion of which Luke is so fond. This contrast in terms of geography and salvation history between Jerusalem and Samaria is probably the most important thing for Luke in his report in chapter 8. Since his narrative reaches a new stage with the conversion of the Ethiopian eunuch and the calling of Saul the persecutor, and since he already has in view the gaining of the first 'real' Gentile, in 9:31 he can close the chapter on Samaria along with Judaea. For him it is only an episode which, if need be, he could have omitted (despite 1:8). The fact that he mentions it at all is connected with the special intermediary role which he has to accord the hellenists, to do justice to historical truth and to provide a bridge to Paul.[124]

The fact that in 15:3 Luke makes Paul and Barnabas travel from Antioch to Jerusalem via the communities of Phoenicia and Samaria—and not through Galilee—is probably an indication that he sees a connection here: they are open to the story of 'the conversion of the Gentiles' and are delighted about it. Furthermore, this note demonstrates over against a widespread interpretation of Luke 17:11 that Luke knows that Samaria lies north of Jerusalem and can be reached directly from there; moreover, that one can travel directly from Samaria to Phoenicia, *i.e.* in the direction of Ptolemais and Tyre (21:7) and back again. The sequence 'all Judaea, Galilee and Samaria' (9:31) in no way means that in Luke's view Galilee lies nearer to Judaea; in accordance with his outline of missionary history he mentions first the Jewish areas and in pride of place among them 'all Judaea' (including Jerusalem), which is so decisive for him.[125]

---

[124]In Acts 26:20, where he makes the Pauline mission follow a scheme similar to Acts 1:8, Samaria can be left out, but not the plerophorous πᾶσάν τε τὴν χώραν τῆς Ἰουδαίας. According to Paul's biography he puts Damascus at the beginning.

The geographical details of the pericope, skilfully divided by Luke, yet disparate, in which he probably combined different and conflicting narratives, begin from a difficult and therefore disputed statement (8:5a): Φίλιππος δὲ κατελθὼν εἰς (τὴν) πόλιν τῆς Σαμαρείας. Against the omission of the article in some late majuscules and the *textus receptus*, reminiscent of Luke 1:39 εἰς πόλιν Ἰούδα or 9:52 εἰς κώμην Σαμαριτῶν, the article should be retained on the basis of the most important Egyptian evidence.[126] However, the sentence is not to be translated, 'He went down into the city (with the name) Samaria', as happens so often in the commentaries, but, 'He went down into the (capital) city of Samaria'. This is not, as in 2 Peter 2:6 (καὶ πόλεις Σοδόμων και Γομόρρας τεφρώσας), an appositional genitive. A number of historical reasons tell against this interpretation. However, the other, better possibility of translation, 'into the (capital) city of Samaria', has its difficulties. In connection with them, here are some basic considerations:

1. Luke never uses Σαμάρεια elsewhere as the name of a city but always only as the designation of the area in which the people of the Σαμαριτεῖς (Lk. 9:52; 10:33; 17:16; Acts 8:25) live. Thus Luke 17:11; Acts 1:8; 9:31; 15:3 and in the context 8:1, 9, 14, together with the reference to the many κῶμαι τῶν Σαμαριτῶν between the anonymous πόλις and Jerusalem (8:25).

---

[125]Lists of territories in an apparently misleading order are not infrequent, *cf.* Josephus, *BJ* 1.302: Idumaea, Galilee, Samaria; 2.247: Judaea, Samaria, Galilee, Peraea and Trachonitis, Batanaea, Gaulanitis; Polybius 16.39.1, 3f. = Josephus, *Ant.* 12.136: Batanaea, Samaria, Abila, Gadara, the Jews in Jerusalem. Eupolemos in Eusebius, *Praep. Ev.* 9.39.5 (4F) on Nebuchadnezzar's campaign: and Scythopolis and 'the Jews settled in Galaditis…'; similarly 9.30.5 (2F) the sequence of David's campaigns: the Syrians on the Euphrates, the Commagenes, the Assyrians and the Phoenicians (?) in the Galadene (Gilead), Idumaeans, Ammonites and Moabites, Ituraeans and Nabataeans. Like Josephus, Eupolemus was a member of the Jerusalem priestly aristocracy; see N. Walter, *Fragmente jüdisch-hellenistischer Historiker*, JSHRZ 1/2 (Gütersloh, 1976) 95f. These results of random reading could easily be increased; see also above, n. 5.

[126]*Cf.* already correctly J. Boehmer, 'Studien zur Geographie Palästinas…Samaria Stadt oder Landschaft', *ZNW* 9 (1908) 216-8. *Cf.* also B.M. Metzger (ed.), *Commentary* (n. 58) 355 and G. Schneider, *Apostelgeschichte* (n. 38) 482 n. 6.

2. The old Macedonian fortress of Samaria,[127] a military settlement founded by Alexander or Perdiccas, no longer existed in Luke's time. After a one-year siege in 108/7 BC, it was completely destroyed by the Jews under John Hyrcanus. In 63 BC Pompey again separated the city territory from Judaea, but the new foundation took place only under Gabinius. Possibly at that time the citizens of the new polis already designated themselves as Γαβινεῖς, after the new κτιστής; *i.e.* the city had been given the name Γαβίνια (or the like) rather than Σαμαρεία. It began to be really significant again only with the second new foundation by Herod in about 25 BC. He made it substantially larger, settled six thousand colonists there, some of them Gentile soldiers and some people from the neighbourhood (including Samaritans), and gave it the name Sebaste. Like Caesarea, it too was a predominantly Gentile city with an enormous temple to Augustus and a sanctuary to Persephone. It was not the religious and ethnic centre for the Samaritans. Scholars argue as to how far the central area of Samaritan settlement was part of the city territory of Sebaste. In all probability the territory of Sebaste was substantially smaller than the territory of the Samaritan *ethnos*. The strongly fortified city became a pillar of Herodian and later Roman rule and along with Caesarea provided an essential part of the auxiliary troops in the country, the so-called Σεβαστηνοί, who were Gentiles and not Samaritan 'semi-Jews'. Whereas in the Jewish War Sebaste was obviously on the Roman side (*BJ* 2.406, *cf. Ant.* 17.289), the Samaritans tried to rebel against the Romans but were overthrown by Vespasian (*BJ* 3.307-315). A consequence of this was the founding of the Roman veterans' colony Flavia Neapolis[128] right next to the ruins of old Shechem. Only now did the territory of the *ethnos* of the Samaritans become the city territory of the newly founded Roman colony, which rapidly surpassed Sebaste because of its considerable extent.[129]

---

[127]For Sebaste see E. Schürer, G. Vermes *et al.*, *History* (n. 66) 160-4; G. Beer, 'Samaria', in *PW*, 2nd edn., 1/2, cols. 2102ff.; A. Schalit, *Herodes* (n. 44) 358-65; A.H.M. Jones, *Cities*, 271ff., 274f., 279ff.; M. Avi-Yonah, *Land* (n. 91), 36, 48, 90, 102, 106, 151-3; *cf.* 153: the map of the city territory in the late Roman period. It will hardly have changed since its foundation. Only the northwest part of the Samaritan area (hardly more than 20%) was part of it.

[128]*BJ* 4.449; Pliny the Elder, *Hist.Nat.* 5.14.69 = M. Stern, *Authors* I (n. 5), 469, 474, no. 204: *intus autem Samariae oppida Neapolis, quod antea Mamortha* (Josephus, *BJ* 4.449 Μαβαρθά from מעברתא, crossing, ford, pass = the col between Gerizim and Ebal) *dicebatur Sebaste in monte, in altiore Gamala.* The last mentioned is a clear mistake: Gamala is to be located in the Gaulanitis, *BJ* 4.4ff. For Neapolis see E. Schürer, G. Vermes *et al.*, *History* I (n. 66), 520f.; G. Hölscher, 'Neapolis 19', *PW* XVI/2, cols. 2128ff.

Thus we must make a distinction between the 'Sebastenes' and the 'Samaritans'.

3. Another factor which tells against the identification of the Σαμάρεια in 8:5 with Sebaste is that the name Sebaste very rapidly suppressed the old city name. Josephus[130] uses Σαμάρεια for the time after Herod only in the sense of Σαμαρεῖτις, *i.e.*, like Luke, for the district and no longer for the city. Strabo (64 BC–AD 23) already mentions the new name alongside the old.

4. The predilection of some scholars for Gentile Sebaste is not least connected with the mysterious figure of Simon Magus. That was thought to be the necessary 'syncretistic milieu' for his alleged identification with the supreme God, or Zeus, and scholars thought that they could demonstrate fantastic relationships between the Kore-Persephone worshipped in Sebaste and his πρώτη ἔννοια Helen.[131] But Luke only gives an account of a magician and wonder-worker, and one should not want to be over-hasty in reading speculations from later Simonian gnosis into his simple report.[132] In addition, supposed Samaritan 'syncretism' is an invention of early Jewish polemic, which already found expression in 2 Kings 17:24-41, but which has a weak historical basis. According to Samaritan sources, this group was no more 'syncretistic' than contemporary Palestinian Judaism. The Samaritans kept as unshakeably as their kindred in Judaea to faith in the 'one God' and his Law despite all persecutions. Finally, and in conclusion, from a traditio-historical and narrative point of view the Simon Magus story is only loosely connected with Philip's mission among the Samaritans. It can be detached without difficulty. As Gitta, Simon's birthplace, is perhaps on the coastal plain and is part of the

---

[129]M. Avi-Yonah, *Land* (n. 91), 112, 115, 152-4: 'This city obtained the whole area to the Samaritans, as well as the toparchy of Acraba, detached from Judaea by Vespasian. Its northern boundary corresponded to the southern one of Sebaste'.

[130]C. Möller and G. Schmitt, *Siedlungen* (n. 12), 164f., count Σαμάρεια as the name of a town even where the territory of Samaria is clearly meant. Josephus has no firm terminology and can use Σαμαρεῖτις (*cf.* Σαμαρίς) and Σαμάρεια interchangeably. Above all in the late mentions after the founding of Sebaste only the province is meant: thus *BJ* 1.213, 302, 303, 314; 2.234, 247; *Vita* 269; *Ant.* 15.246: ἐν Σαμαρείᾳ τῇ κληθείσῃ Σεβαστῇ; 292: τρίτον παντὶ τῷ λαῷ τὴν Σαμάρειαν ἐπενόησεν ἐπὶ τείχισμα, καλέσας μὲν αὐτὴν Σεβαστήν; *cf.* 296; 19.274, 351 (see n. 100 above); 20.118, 129: here Σαμάρεια is confused with Καισαρεία, *cf. BJ* 2. 241. The exception which proves the rule could be *BJ* 2.69 = *Ant.* 17.289 on the invasion of Varus in 4 BC: in my view this means the territory of Samaria *and* the city. Evidently Josephus' source, Nicolaus of Damascus, still follows the old terminology here.

city territory of Caesarea (see n. 141), we might ask whether Simon's activity is not to be located there.[133]

5. Anyone who wanted to address the Samaritans as a religious group had to seek them out at their religious centre on Mount Gerizim. Therefore since Wellhausen,[134] Shechem has regularly been mentioned in the commentaries as a second possibility for 'the city of Samaria'. However, that is even more improbable. For this centre, which the Samaritans had erected on the ruins of the old biblical Shechem after Alexander or Perdiccas had deprived them of Samaria, was also destroyed along with the temple on Gerizim in 128 BC, under John Hyrcanus, too, and as a city vanishes from history.[135] Flavia Neapolis, about a mile further to the northwest and founded by Vespasian as late

---

[131]Any connection between the cult of Persephone-Kore in Sebaste and the Helen of the Simonians (Justin, *Apol.* 26.3) is conjured up completely out of thin air. The tradition connects the latter only with Tyre (Irenaeus, *Adv.Haer.* 1.23.2). The hypotheses which seek to associate with Helen the statue of Kore found in Samaria, with its torch and the inscription, Εἷς θεὸς ὁ πάντων δεσπότης μεγάλη κόρη ἡ ἀνείκητος (J.W. Crowfoot *et al.*, *Samaria-Sebaste* II [London, 1957] 37 no. 12), rest on sheer speculation: thus L.H. Vincent, 'Le culte d'Hélène à Samarie', *RB* 45 (1936) 221-32; D. Flusser, *IEJ* 25 (1975) 13-20; G. Lüdemann, *Untersuchungen zur Simonianischen Gnosis* (Göttingen, 1975) 20, is more restrained. The syncretistic cult of Zeus on Mount Gerizim between the time of Antiochus IV, 167 BC, and the erection of a temple to Zeus-Jupiter there under Hadrian, postulated by G. Lüdemann (52ff.), following H.G. Kippenberg, *Garizim* (n. 101), 80ff., 98ff., 345ff., is another figment of the imagination. At that time Neapolis already existed as a Gentile city, and the building of the temple is to be seen as running parallel to Hadrian's religious policy towards the Jews and the founding of Aelia Capitolina; see the judgment of K. Rudolph, *TR* 42 (1977) 350: 'The return to seeing a syncretistic cult as the earliest foundation of Simonianism does not take us any further, but entangles us even more in the jungle of assumptions and hypotheses which already surrounds the prehistory of this sect'.

[132]In addition to the investigation by K. Beyschlag, *Simon Magus* (n. 116), see R. Bergmeier, 'Qullen vorchristlicher Gnosis', in *Tradition und Glaube,* FS K.G. Kuhn (Göttingen, 1971) 200-20, esp. 205ff.

[133]8:5-8, 12, 13-18 give an excellent context. I regard the remark by the former Gentile Justin from Neapolis, *Apol.* 26.3, that 'almost all Samaritans confess Simon as that God' as excessive exaggeration; possibly Justin confused Simon with the Samaritan eschatological prophet Dositheus, who was also active in the first century, probably before Simon, and for a long time won considerably more support in Samaria. See what is now the basic study by S.J. Isser, *The Dositheans: A Samaritan Sect in Late Antiquity* (Leiden, 1976). For Caesarea as the location of the dispute with Simon see already E. Preuschen, *Die Apostelgeschichte* (Tübingen, 1912), with reference to the Pseudo-Clementines, '...that the source meant the city of Caesarea Pal., with which both Simon and Philip had contacts'.

as AD 72, came to have some significance in the second century. But this cannot be meant, for chronological reasons.

6. For anyone in search of a particular Samaritan 'capital' the most likely place would be the Sychar of John 4.5, present-day 'Askar at the southeastern foot of Ebal, about half a mile northeast of Tell Balata, the ruins of old Shechem. Its significance is attested by Jewish and Samaritan sources,[136] and more recently by the discovery of an interesting tomb from the end of the second and beginning of the third century.[137] At the same time, however, it must be remembered that in the first century the real religious centre for the Samaritans was not a city but the holy mount Gerizim itself.[138] Even Sychar retained its significance after the destruction of Shechem only because it was the nearest substantial place to Gerizim.

---

[134]J. Wellhausen, *Apostelgeschichte* (n. 114) 14; *cf.* J. Boehmer, *Studien* (n. 126) 218; E. Meyer, *Ursprung* III (n. 69) 277; T. Zahn, *Forschungen* (n. 58) 273; A. Wikenhauser, *Die Apostelgeschichte*, RNT 5 (Regensburg, [4]1961); with some hesitation G. Stählin, *Die Apostelgeschichte*, NTD 5 (Göttingen, [10]1962) 252. Against this H.H. Wendt, *Die Apostelgeschichte*, KEK III (Göttingen, [5]1913) 154: 'This can only be the capital of the country, old Samaria, which Herod called Sebaste'; similarly H. Conzelmann, *Apostelgeschichte* (n. 34) 60, on v. 5: 'Luke thinks that the district of Samaria has only one polis (of the same name)'. However, in connection with v. 8 he adds: 'Luke of course thinks of Samaritans in the ethnic and religious sense. . .; he also makes Simon one, hardly rightly. There is no trace of the hellenistic character of the capital Samaria/Sebaste'. One can fully agree with the latter, but that also makes this interpretation of v. 5 questionable. In the two most recent commentaries, J. Roloff, *Apostelgeschichte* (n. 37) 133, leans towards Shechem; G. Schneider, *Apostelgeschichte* I (n. 38), 487, leaves the problem open: 'It is impossible to decide with any certainty whether Luke here is thinking of Shechem or (rather) of the hellenistic city Samaria/Sebaste'. See now also R.J. Coggins, 'The Samaritans in Acts', *NTS* 28 (1982) 423-33, esp. 429f. The historical dubiety of these false alternatives has so far not been recognised.

[135]Josephus mentions Shechem (Σικιμα) only up to the Hasmonaean period; see C. Möller and G. Schmitt, *Siedlungen* (n. 12), 173; *cf. BJ* 1.63, 92; *Ant.* 13.255f., 377. *Cf.* G.E. Wright, *Shechem: The Biography of a City* (London, 1965) 172, 183f.; H.G. Kippenberg, *Garizim* (n. 101), 85ff. Possibly the place was only finally destroyed after the subjection of the Samaritans in connection with the conquest of the Macedonian colony of Samaria in 109 BC. The mention of the place as an assembly point for rebel Jews and Demetrius Eukairos who was allied with them in the fight against Alexander Jannaeus in *BJ* 1.63; *Ant.* 13.377 does not tell against the fact of the destruction. The ruins could be meant here. The col was a highly significant strategic position. At the latest towards the end of the second century BC Shechem disappears from history as an inhabited place. Eusebius, *Onomastikon* (ed. E. Klostermann, GCS 11/1, p. 150, 1), describes it as: Συχὲμ ἡ καὶ Σίκιμα...πόλις Ἰακωβ νῦν ἔρημος.

7. The conjecture, which also appears in commentaries, that this was Gitta, the home village of Simon Magus, is completely wrong.[139] This Samaritan locality,[140] mentioned only in connection with the heresiarch in some old church sources after Justin, was at any rate completely insignificant. Its situation is disputed. A. Alt conjectures

---

[136]Apart from John 4:5, the pilgrim of Bordeaux, H. Donner, *Pilger* (n. 54), 52f.; Sechar = P. Geyer, *Itinera Hierosolymitana Saec. 4-8*, CSEL 39 (Vienna, 1898) 20; Eusebius, *Onomastikon* (n. 135), 164, 1: πρὸ τῆς Νέας πόλεως πλησίον τοῦ χωρίου οὗ ἔδωκεν Ἰακὼβ τῷ υἱῷ αὐτοῦ. For the rabbinic mentions see P. Billerbeck, *Kommentar* II (n. 19), 431; B.Z. Segal, *hag-gĕôgrafyâ* (n. 116), 138f. I am grateful to my colleague G. Schmitt for further references: *m. Menaḥ.* 10:2: מבקעת עין סוכר, the omer sheaf 'from the plain of En Sōker', and *y. Sheqal.* 5.148d.25; *b. Menaḥ.* 64b; *b. Sota* 49b. In the context of the *haggadah* on Jacob's struggles with the Shechemites the place appears in *Yal. Shim Bereshit* para. 135, l. 4, ed. J. Schiloni, II (Jerusalem, 1973) 693: *maḥane seḥir*; *cf.* also para. 134, ll. 76f. (p. 692): *seḥir melek maḥane* and in addition already Jub. 34:4: the king of Maanisakir. On this see K. Berger, *Das Buch der Jubiläen*, JSHRZ II, 3 (Gütersloh, 1981) 492 n. 12. Thus the tradition of the place goes back to pre-Christian times. For the Samaritan accounts see H.G. Kippenberg, *Garizim* (n. 101) 164 from the *Tolida*: (the district of) Sychar up to Tiberias. According to the Chronicles of Abul Fath (ed. E. Vilmar [Gotha, 1865] 151ff.), translated in S.J. Isser, *Dositheans* (n. 133) 77, Dusis (Dositheos) came to a wise teacher in Askar (Sychar). *Cf.* also G. Dalman, *Orte* (n. 48) 226f.; C. Kopp, *Holy Places* (n. 50), 155-66; H.M. Schenke, 'Jakobsbrunnen–Josefsgrab–Sychar. Topographische Untersuchungen und Erwägungen in der Perspektive von Jn. 4:5, 6', *ZDPV* 84 (1968) 159-84: 'Sychar/Askar must have been quite a large and significant place in Roman times, ...before the foundation of Neapolis in AD 72: unfortified and therefore laid out on broad lines, in size presumably greater than Shechem, which had been a fortified town' (182).

[137]Report by E. Damati, *IEJ* 22 (1972) 174, plates 35B/36, a mausoleum with a Greek inscription in Askar: 'It appears that this mausoleum belonged to a wealthy Samaritan family residing in Neapolis at the end of the 2nd or the beginning of the 3rd century AD'. The question is whether the owners of the tomb really lived in Neapolis, about two miles away, and are not rather to be located in Sychar/Askar itself. Neapolis, which was at first Gentile, only appears later as a religious centre of the Samaritans; see the Samaritan synagogue in Thessalonica: B. Lifshitz and J. Schiby, 'Une synagogue samaritaine à Thessalonique', *RB* 75 (1968) 368-78, with the wish: Αὔξι Νεάπολις μετὰ τῶν φιλούντων [αὐτούς or αὐτήν...].

[138]See the Samaritan eschatological prophet in AD 36, *Ant.* 18.85-89, who invites the Samaritans to go with him to Gerizim.

[139]K. Lake and H.J. Cadbury, *The Beginnings of Christianity* IV (London, 1933) 89, *ad loc.*: '...it is tempting to guess that it was Gitta'; I.H. Marshall, *The Acts of the Apostles* (Leicester, 1980) 154 n. 1, lists the three possibilities: 'Sebaste...Shechem or possibly Gitta'.

[140]Justin, *Apol.* 26.2: ἀπὸ κώμης λεγομένης Γίτθων; Ps.-Clem. *Hom.* 2.22.2 (GCS 42, ed. Rehm, p. 44) Σαμαρεὺς τὸ ἔθνος ἀπὸ Γετθῶν κώμης, τῆς πόλεως (Caesarea) ἀεχούσης σχοίνους ἕξ (= about 36 miles, though the detail about distance is useless); *cf.* Ps.-Clem. *Rec.* (GCS, ed. Rehm, p. 55): *ex vico Getthonum*.

that it was at Gett on the coastal plain about eleven miles south-west of Caesarea.[141] That would seem to be the most likely.

8. Linguistically, then, the εἰς τὴν πόλιν Σαμαρείας at any rate remains unusual. We must probably think of a Samaritan 'capital' the name of which Luke either no longer knew or left out as being unimportant.[142] Presumably he found it quite natural that Samaria should have a 'capital', as Judaea did in Jerusalem. However, whereas in Judaea Jerusalem was 'surrounded by cities' (5:16), apart from its anonymous 'capital' Samaria—and this information is by no means incorrect—had only 'villages' (8:25) to show. Gentile Sebaste can be left completely out of account.

The formulation 'the city of Samaria' is already striking because, by contrast, the LXX, which Luke so often follows, often speaks only in the plural of the 'cities of Samaria' and never of 'a' or 'the city of Samaria'.[143] The hypothesis of an Aramaic source in which—as in Luke 1:39—a מדינת שמריין was wrongly rendered by πόλις instead of χώρα (*cf.* 8:1: κατὰ τὰς χώρας τῆς Ἰουδαίας καὶ Σαμαρείας) is not much help, since an Aramaic source is improbable and does not explain the disruptive article.[144]

Here we find that Luke is basically as free over geographical details as we find him in connection with Palestine—leaving aside the 'we narratives' and the coastal plain. There is confirmation of the conjecture that Luke had not visited Samaria any more than Galilee, the Jordan valley or the hinterland of Judaea. That means that those places where he gives exact and well differentiated information deserve special attention, *i.e.* in relation to some of the cities of the coastal region, the road from Jerusalem to Caesarea and the connection between the citadel and the Temple. H. Conzelmann characterised the

---

[141]*Kleine Schriften* II (Munich, [2]1959) 200 n. 2 = *BHHW* IV, 207: *Gett* (map D 6); T. Zahn, *Apostelgeschichte* I (n. 58) 273, on the other hand, conjectures the *Qaryet Ġît* six miles west of Nablus = *BHHW* IV, 207 Gitta? (map D 7). According to A. Alt, Kappareitaia, according to Justin, *Apol.* 26:2, the home of Simon's disciple Menander, should be located in the coastal plain = *Hirbet Kafr Ḥatta*, about two miles northeast of Antipatris, *BHHW* IV, 231 (map C7).

[142]O. Bauernfeind, *Kommentar* (n. 33), 122, assumes that the pre-Lukan tradition already abandoned geographical accuracy because of the 'resonance of the words' in Mt. 10:5, and that Luke 'did not obliterate what was probably a well established peculiarity' (125).

[143]2 Ki. 17:24, 26; 23:19. But *cf.* Is. 36:19. I cannot find any corresponding formulation even in Josephus.

[144]J. Jeremias, Σαμάρεια, *TDNT* VII, 92 n. 29.

geographical picture of Palestine as follows: 'The whole country seems to be viewed from abroad. Luke is familiar with the coastal region of Phoenicia, in Acts with the connection between Judaea and the coast. He appears to imagine Galilee as inland, but adjoining Judaea, and Samaria as being to the north of Judaea; this is suggested by the account of the mission in Samaria in Acts 8 and by the statement in Acts 15:3.'[145] Apart from the observation about Galilee, where the author over-interprets a carelessly formulated remark by Luke, one could happily agree with Conzelmann. But unfortunately he has not sufficiently gone into the more interesting information in Acts, and thus the striking difference in Luke's knowledge of the different parts of the country remains unexplained. I would therefore change Conzelmann's verdict somewhat and in so doing rely on what in this respect is the clear information in Acts. 'The whole country seems to be viewed' with the eyes of a man who comes 'from abroad', more precisely from the 'coastal region of Phoenicia' (Acts 21:3-7: Tyre, Ptolemais), who travelled up to Jerusalem from Caesarea with a party, could stay there for only a few days because of unfavourable conditions and then returned to Caesarea (21:15ff.; 24:11). Chapters 21-24, a vividly written continuous passage, indicates Luke's own view: together with the continuation in chapters 25-28 this is the climax of the whole work which Luke wants to attain in his two volumes and which he hints at a long time before, in the ἐν ἡμῖν of the prologue. Whether as a travelling companion of Paul he stayed in Caesarea for the whole of the two years that the apostle was imprisoned there is in my view improbable.[146] At all events he had no occasion to pay another visit to Judaea, which continued to be unfriendly, disturbed and, for a Gentile-Christian follower of Paul, positively dangerous. The accusation against Paul because of Trophimus (21:29) might well pose a threat to other Gentile-Christian travelling companions of Paul. After the death of Festus in AD 62, the Jewish priestly nobility led by the high priest Annas son of Annas even had James the Lord's brother, a strict observer of the Law, and other leading Jewish Christians, put to death on the charge of transgressing the Law.[147] In prison in

[145]H. Conzelmann, *Theology of St Luke* (n. 2) 70.

[146]*Cf.* A. von Harnack, *Beiträge* (n. 98), 70: 'We may therefore assume that while Luke trod the soil of Palestine and Jerusalem with the apostle, he left it very soon afterwards. Accordingly we expect that he will certainly show himself familiar with the country and the city to the degree that a traveller might be after a short stay. This is confirmed by his account'. *Cf.* above n. 11 and Philo's one visit to Jerusalem.

Caesarea Paul's gaze will have been directed more towards the communities in the West than to those governed by James and his elders in Judaea. Luke then again accompanied the apostle on the journey to Rome (27:1ff.).[148] He may have written his two-volume work some twenty to twenty-five years later, perhaps referring back in the so-called 'source' to earlier notes which he had written himself. The gap in time can explain some obscurities and mistakes, and also his carelessness in narrative must be noted. He could not have been aware how almost two thousand years later his carelessness would have set the pens of critical scholars writing. He did not present his readers with free romance-like invention in the style of the later apostolic acts, and we should not attribute that to him.

In this way we can provide a plausible explanation for the two-level knowledge of Palestine in Luke. We should not require geographical knowledge at an academic level either of him or of the other evangelists; probably none of them had ever so much as seen a map of Palestine, nor did they possess any special geographical interests. Perhaps we New Testament scholars would be more careful if we tried to give an accurate description of the geography of the outer suburbs of our home towns or even to put on a blank map of Palestine those places the location of which Luke knew. Some years ago a graduate secretary in the faculty at Erlangen asked me, 'Tübingen—is that in Hessen?'; since then I have ceased to be surprised about geographical knowledge.[149]

---

[147]Josephus, *Ant.* 20.199-203. For the community in Jerusalem this must have been the most serious catastrophe in their history so far. Jewish Christianity never recovered from the blow.

[148]A comparison with other ancient accounts of sea voyages and the geographical and nautical details shows that despite all the miraculous features this is no romantic fiction. The dedication to Theophilus and the use of the first person singular and plural in Luke 1:1-4; Acts 1:1; 16:10ff. and from Acts 20:6 onwards give the two-volume work its literary consistency, *i.e.* its framework. Theophilus was certainly a historical personality and not a fictitious figure, though his name could be a pseudonym. He must have known the author, who sometimes writes in the first person. If he published the work, he might in the last resort be responsible for the κατὰ Λουκᾶν of the Gospel. Thus the work was in all probability written by an 'eyewitness' of the second, 'post-apostolic' generation and a companion of Paul's on his later journeys. All attempts to explain the traditional name of the author, Luke, as a secondary addition, remain incredible speculation.

[149]The original German version of this chapter was published in *ZDPV* 98 (1983). The English translation by John Bowden was first published in M. Hengel, *Between Jesus and Paul* (London: SCM Press, 1983) 97-128, 190-210.

CHAPTER 4

PALESTINIAN JEWISH PERSONAL NAMES IN ACTS

Margaret H. Williams

Summary

In undertaking this study, I have two objectives: (1) to present, for reference purposes, a profile of the names borne by those men and women in Acts who can be securely identified as having been Palestinian Jews; (2) to reach some understanding of the general character of the 1st-century Palestinian Jewish onomastikon. On the basis of the evidence gathered for (1), it will be argued that the 1st-century Palestinian Jewish onomastikon, with its heavy concentration of Hebrew Hasmonaean names and scattering of Herodian-favoured Greek and Roman ones, was the product of a unique set of historical circumstances and thus unparalleled.

That names regularly operate as social, cultural and, on occasion, political indicators, is an assumption that underlies much modern onomastic research.[1] If that is justified, it follows that the names borne by 1st-century Palestinian Jews ought to (a) reflect their values and aspirations during that troubled time of transition from indirect to direct Roman rule, (b) differ from the names used by contemporary Diasporan Jews (whose non-participation in the great revolt from Rome in AD 66 shows that they were far from identifying with their Palestinian brethren),[2] and (c) vary somewhat from those favoured by Palestinian Jews in other, less turbulent, epochs, such, for instance, as the 3rd century AD, the acme of the Patriarchate.[3] But did they? Before we can answer those questions, we need to examine the evidence. But how are we to approach such a vast mass of material, literary, epigraphic and papyrological? Focussing on the names borne by those people in Acts whose status as Palestinian Jews is absolutely secure is as good a way as any. For not only is there a substantial number of them (around three dozen) but they are generally recognised as constituting a fairly typical sample of the 1st-century Palestinian Jewish onomastikon.[4] (The only serious discrepancies, which we shall return to below, are the absence from the group of the extremely popular nationalistic names Salomezion [Peace over Zion][5] and Eleazar[6] and the presence of a disproportionately high number of Jameses [*i.e.*, Jacobs].) The study, then, begins with a list of those men and women whom I consider to have been Palestinian Jews (nine doubtful cases are discussed separately in the appendix at the end). There follows a profile of each of the names they bore. In the final section, the general character of the 1st-century Palestinian Jewish onomastikon is appraised briefly, using much, but by no means all, of the material presented in the individual name-profiles. (More evidence had to be gathered to meet my first objective than was necessary for my second.)

---

[1]*CPJ* I, 27; N. Cohen, 'Jewish Names as Cultural Indicators in Antiquity', *JSJ* 7 (1976) 97-128; J. Naveh, 'Nameless People', *IEJ* 40 (1990) 108-23.

[2]E.M. Smallwood, *The Jews under Roman Rule from Pompey to Diocletian* (Leiden, 1976) 356-7.

[3]M. Avi-Yonah, *The Jews of Palestine: A Political History from the Bar Kokhba War to the Arab Conquest* (Oxford, 1976) ch. III.

[4]Bagatti-Milik, 108 (with comparative table).

[5]On this, see most recently T. Ilan, 'Notes on the Distribution of Jewish Women's Names in Palestine in the Second Temple and Mishnaic periods', *JJS* 40 (1989) 191-2.

[6]Bagatti-Milik, 92.

I. Palestinian Jews in Acts in English Alphabetical Order

(Names to be profiled below are italicised)

1. *Agabus*—Christian prophet from Jerusalem (Acts 11:28).
2. *Agrippa*—Agrippa II, Roman client ruler (Acts 25:13).
3. *Alexander*—member of the High Priestly party (Acts 4:6).
4. *Alphaeus*—the father of James, one of the Twelve (Acts 1:13).
5. *Ananias*—wealthy member of the early Christian community at Jerusalem (Acts 5:1).
6. *Ananias*—appointed High Priest—*c.* AD 48 (Acts 23:2).
7. *Andrew*—one of the Twelve (Acts 1:13).
8. *Annas*—High Priest—AD 6-15 (Acts 4:6).
9. *Bartholomew*—one of the Twelve (Acts 1:13).
10. *Berenice*—sister of Agrippa II (Acts 25:13).
11. *Caiaphas*—the surname of the High Priest Joseph[7]—AD 18-36 (Acts 4:6).
12. *Drusilla*—daughter of Agrippa I and sister of Agrippa II (Acts 24:24).
13. *Gamaliel*—member of the Sanhedrin, teacher of Saul/Paul (Acts 5:34).
14. *Herod*—Agrippa I, Roman client ruler of Judaea—AD 41-44 (Acts 12:1).
15. *James*—one of the Twelve, the brother of John (Acts 12:2).
16. *James*—one of the Twelve, the son of Alphaeus (Acts 1:13).
17. *James*—the brother of Jesus (Acts 12:17).
18. *James*—the father of Judas (no. 27)— (Acts 1:13).
19. *Jesus*—son of Joseph, called the Messiah (Acts 2:36).
20. *John*—the Baptist (Acts 1:22).
21. *John*—one of the Twelve, brother of James (Acts 12:2).
22. *John* called *Mark*—member of Christian community at Jerusalem (Acts 12:12).

23a. *John*—member of the High Priestly party (Acts 4:6).

23b. *Jonathan*—variant for John (no. 23a) in some MSS (Acts 4:6).

24. *Joseph*—also called both *Barsabbas* and *Justus*—candidate for Judas Iscariot's place (Acts 1:23).
25. *Joseph*—also called *Barnabas*—early Christian from Cyprus[8] (Acts 4:36).
26. *Judas*—former rebel leader from Galilee (Acts 5:37).

---

[7]His first name is given only by Josephus at *Ant.* 18.35 and 95.

27. *Judas*—one of the Twelve, the son of James (no. 18)— (Acts 1:13).
28. *Judas*—surnamed Iscariot[9]—formerly one of the Twelve (Acts 1:16).
29. *Judas*—called *Barsabbas*—member of Christian community at Jerusalem (Acts 15:22).
30. *Mary*—the mother of Jesus (Acts 1:14).
31. *Mary*—the mother of John Mark (Acts 12:12).
32. *Matthew*—one of the Twelve (Acts 1:13).
33. *Matthias*—Judas Iscariot's replacement (Acts 1:23).
34. *Menahem*—brought up with Herod the Tetrarch (Acts 13:1).
35. *Philip*—one of the Twelve (Acts 1:13).
36. *Sapphira*—wife of Ananias, early Christian at Jerusalem (Acts 5:1).
37. *Silas*—early Christian at Jerusalem (Acts 15:22) also known as Silvanus (2 Cor.1:19).[10]
38. *Simon/Simeon*—also known as *Peter*—one of the Twelve (Acts 10:5).
39. *Simon*—the Zealot—one of the Twelve (Acts 1:13).
40. *Simon*—the magician of Samaria (Acts 8:9).
41. *Simon*—the tanner at Joppa (Acts 10:6).
42. *Tabitha*—Christian disciple in Joppa. Her translation name is *Dorcas* (Acts 9:36).
43. *Theudas*—rebel leader (Acts 5:37).
44. *Thomas*—one of the Twelve (Acts 1:13).

Now that we have established the names that are to form the core of this study, we must proceed to the evidence for each one. For ease of reference, I have created two broad categories: first and second names. Each of these is sub-divided into language groups—*viz.* Hebrew (first names only), Aramaic, Greek and Latin. Within each linguistic group, the names are set out in English alphabetical order. For each entry, broadly the same format is used, unless the evidence dictates otherwise. After the name in English, its Greek form(s) in Acts, the Hebrew/ Aramaic original and the basic meaning, references to it are considered

[8]Joseph Barnabas is listed here, even though he was a Cypriot, as his second name, given him by Galilean Jews in Jerusalem, is part of the Palestinian Jewish onomastikon.

[9]As the surname itself does not occur in Acts, it will not be profiled below. Suffice to say that it probably means 'man from Kerioth' (Heb. איש קריות) and is thus one of the many topographical nicknames found in the Palestinian Jewish onomastikon. For other examples and the phenomenon in general, see R. Hachlili, 'Names and Nicknames of Jews in Second Temple Times', *Eretz Israel* 17 (1984) 199 (in Heb.).

[10]Since Silas' Diasporan name Silvanus does not occur in Acts, it will not be given a separate entry. It is considered briefly below, however, along with Saul's alternative name Paul, in the context of John Mark's second name. See n. 277 below.

in first the Palestinian, and then the Diasporan sources. For 1st-century Palestine, these have been culled mainly[11] from (a) Acts, (b) Josephus' *Jewish War* in its entirety and the last six books of his *Antiquities*[12] and (c) the several hundreds of ossuary inscriptions that have been recovered mainly from the Jerusalem area.[13] The last of these constitutes our most important source of information. For brief though these epitaphs are (in most there is little more than the personal name of the deceased and his/her patronymic),[14] they provide the best evidence we have for the names favoured and the name-forms actually used by Palestine's wealthier inhabitants in the century before the destruction of the Temple (AD 70).[15] For the later period, the most fruitful sources are (a) the scores of documents, mostly from the Bar Kokhba period (*i.e.*, the 130's AD), discovered at Murabba'at in the Judaean desert[16] and (b) the

[11]Other sources used are the Gospels and the Masada ostraka and jar inscriptions. For the latter, see Y. Yadin and J. Naveh, 'The Aramaic and Hebrew Ostraka and Jar Inscriptions', and H.M. Cotton and J. Geiger, 'The Greek and Latin Documents', in J. Aviram, G. Foerster and E. Netzer (eds.), *Masada: The Yigael Yadin Excavations 1963-1965*, 2 vols. (Jerusalem, 1989).

[12]Even on a conservative estimate, more than three hundred Palestinian Jews are referred to in these two works. Since space precludes detailed citation of all the relevant evidence, I have decided that the best way of directing the reader's attention to it is to use Feldman's excellent index in vol. IX of the Loeb edition of Josephus. References to Josephus, therefore, generally will take the following form: Loeb index, *s. v.* X, nos. X-Y. Only in special cases will individual passages from either *BJ* or *Ant.* be cited.

[13]The two hundred and fifty texts (approx.) used in this study may be found in the following publications: E.L. Sukenik, 'A Jewish Tomb in the Kidron Valley' , *PEQ* April (1937) 126-30; *idem*, 'The Earliest Records of Christianity', *AJA* 51 (1947) 351-365; *CIJ* II, nos. 1210-1387; Bagatti-Milik, nos. 1-43; N. Avigad, 'A Depository of Inscribed Ossuaries in the Kidron Valley', *IEJ* 12 (1962) 1-12; J. Naveh, 'Ossuary Inscriptions from Giv'at ha-Mivtar', *IEJ* 20 (1970) 33-37; N. Avigad, 'The Burial-Vault of a Nazirite Family on Mount Scopus', *IEJ* 21 (1971) 185-200; R. Hachlili, 'The Goliath Family in Jericho: Funerary Inscriptions from a First Century AD Jewish Monumental Tomb', *BASOR* 235 (1979) 31-66; J. Naveh, 'An Aramaic Consolatory Burial Inscription', *Atiqot* (English series) 14 (1980) 55-59; E. Puech, 'Inscriptions funéraires Palestiniennes: Tombeau de Jason et ossuaires', *RB* 90 (1983) 499-533. These are by no means all the ossuary inscriptions known to exist. However, the non-publication of many reported texts, plus the on-going discovery of others, makes exhaustive coverage impossible.

[14]An exception is the Bethphage ossuary inscription, which is thought to be a name-list of 1st-century ossuary workers. For this, see J.T. Milik, 'Le couvercle de Bethphagé', in A. Caquot and M. Philonenko (eds.), *Hommages à André Dupont-Sommer* (Paris, 1971) 75-94 and Naveh, 'Nameless People', 111-3.

[15]On the ossuaries themselves, see P. Figueras, *Decorated Jewish Ossuaries* (Leiden, 1983).

[16]For these, see *DJD, passim.*

hundreds of (mainly 3rd-century) inscriptions found in the catacombs at Beth She'arim in Galilee.[17] Some useful information is also to be derived from the altogether more limited epigraphic findings at places such as Caesarea Maritima, Jaffa, Gaza and Capernaum.[18] On the Diasporan side, the evidence is not as abundant (for the 2nd century, there is very little at all) but enough exists for comparative purposes. For the 1st century, the tax records from Edfu (Apollinopolis Magna) in Upper Egypt provide the best onomastic data.[19] Almost as valuable is the corpus of Jewish inscriptions from Cyrenaica.[20] For the 3rd, our richest resource is the large body of epigraphic material from the (Jewish) catacombs of Rome.[21] But the inscriptions from Greece and Asia Minor, though comparatively few in number, make a valuable contribution too—especially the recently published Jews and Godfearers text from Aphrodisias with its scores of Jewish names.[22] These are the main sources used in the construction of the name-profiles. Non-Jewish and Talmudic material has been cited only where the discussion demanded (I lack the expertise to handle the latter). References to later Jewish inscriptions (*e.g.* from Venosa)[23] are equally sparse here. In general, they are not relevant to this study.

II. First Names

1. *Hebrew*

Agabus (Ἄγαβος)—חגב ('grasshopper'). A rare name, as its solitary NT appearance in Acts (no. 1 above) implies. In the other sources listed above, it does not occur.[24]

---

[17]*BS* II and III, *passim*.
[18]The older material is to be found in *CIJ* II, nos. 886-90 (Caesarea); 892-960 (Jaffa); 966-70 (Gaza); 982-3 (Capernaum).
[19]*CPJ* II, 116-8 for general discussion; 119-77 for texts. The inscriptions from Leontopolis (Horbury-Noy, nos. 29-105) have barely been used, since their dating is too uncertain.
[20]See Lüderitz, *passim*.
[21]Mainly to be found in *CIJ* I[2] but see also *SEG* 26 (1976-1977) nos. 1157-1202.
[22]See RT, *passim*.
[23]For the Venosa material, see now Noy, nos. 42-116.
[24]For an OT example, see Ezr. 2:46. For the Babylonian family, the בני חגב (sons of grasshopper), see Hachlili, 'Names and Nicknames', 203.

Ananias ('Ανανίας)—חנניה ('Yah has shown favour'). Hanan (חנן), its abbreviated form, appears in Acts 4:6 as Ἄννας and Josephus as Ἄνανος. As popular with 1st-century Palestinian Jews as Acts, with its three cases (nos. 5; 6 and 8 above) implies, and easily the most frequently attested of the many 'God has favoured' names—John excepted. While only rare cases are known of Onias, Elhanan, Hana and Hanin,[25] at least eleven men called Ananias/Ananus are mentioned by Josephus[26] and almost as many appear on the ossuaries.[27] In our later Palestinian sources, the name occurs less often, probably because other *ḥanan*-type names, most notably Hanina, had grown enormously in popularity.[28] At Murabba'at only one Ananias is certainly attested[29] and Beth She'arim has produced just four.[30] In the Diaspora, Ananias and its analogues were never very popular[31] and from the 1st century onwards scarcely occur at all. Acts (9:10-17 and 22:12-16) mentions an Ananias of Damascus and on a 3rd-century graffito from Dura a חננו (Hananu) appears.[32] But in the west, Ananias occurs only once[33] and the related names not at all. In the scattering of Jewish Anniani at Rome[34] there is no need to see anything other than the Latin name Annianus.[35]

---

[25]For Onias (חניה), see Sukenik, 'Jewish Tomb', 127 and *CIJ* II, no. 1394; for Elhanan, Hana and Hanin, see *CIJ* II, nos. 1215 ([א]לחנן), 1218 (חנא), 1373a-c (חנין/'Ανίν/אנין).
[26]Loeb index, *s.vv.* Ananias, nos. 5-12 (possibly some duplication here) and Ananus, nos. 1 and 3-6.
[27]Bagatti-Milik, 93, and Avigad, 'Burial Vault', 194-7.
[28]Discussion at *DJD* 1.20 (comm. on no. 22).
[29]*DJD*, no. 30, l. 10 (חנניה)—AD 134. Possibly also to be read in the undated fragment *DJD*, no. 115 (*verso*)—'Αναν[...].
[30]*BS* II, nos. 69 and 166; *BS* III, nos. 10 (אניאנא/'Ανιανοῦ) and 17 (אניאנה). For discussion of the rendition in *BS* III, no. 10 of the hellenised form of the name Hananiah in Hebrew characters, see W. Horbury, 'A Personal Name in a Jar-Inscription in Hebrew Characters from Alexandria?', *VT* 44.1 (1994) 105.
[31]A few early examples are found in Ptolemaic Egypt. See, for instance,*CP J* I, nos. 24 and 35. For a 2nd-century example from Athens, see *CIJ* I², no. 715c.
[32]*CIJ* II, no. 843.
[33]In a 3rd-century inscription from Cyprus—*DF*, no. 85.
[34]*CIJ* I², nos. 88 and 310.
[35]So, correctly, H. Solin, 'Juden und Syrer im westichen Teil der römischen Welt. Eine ethnisch-demographische Studie mit besonderer Berücksichtigung der sprachlichen Zustände' in W. Haase (ed.), *ANRW*, II.29.2 (Berlin and New York, 1983) 639-40.

Gamaliel (Γαμαλιήλ)[36]—גמליאל ('my reward is God'). A rare and ancient name,[37] which came back into fashion in the 1st century AD. Saul/Paul's teacher (no. 13 above), Hillel's grandson, is among its earliest known bearers.[38] Subsequently it became quite popular in Rabbinical circles in Palestine. Several Jews called Gamaliel are buried at Beth She'arim, some of them quite possibly from the House of Hillel.[39] No Diasporan examples are known.

James (Ἰάκωβος)—יעקוב (a patriarchal name whose meaning is variously explained).[40] Less popular in 1st-century Palestine than its high frequency in Acts (nos. 15-18) suggests. Josephus has only four cases[41] (one of them is the brother of Jesus)[42] and the only ossuary example belongs to a Cyrenaican Jew.[43] Although the name is found occasionally in the Judaean desert documents,[44] it is not until the 3rd century that attestations become frequent. At Beth She'arim, for instance, the name occurs many times and in a wide variety of forms. The commonest is Ἰακώ, but Ἰακώβ, Ἰακώς, Ἰάκ(κ)ωβος and Ἴκουβος also appear.[45] With the Jews of Egypt, the name seems to have been a regular favourite.[46] Attestations range from the 3rd century BC[47] to the

---

[36]One of the rare undeclined Septuagintal name-forms used in Acts. For others, see nn. 78 and 132 below.
[37]Previously borne only by Gamaliel, son of Pedahzur, leader of the tribe of Manasseh, for whom, see Nu. 2:20 and 7:54.
[38]For another Gamaliel (Γαμαλίηλος) of the same period, see *Ant.* 20.213 and 223. Also referred to by Josephus (*BJ* 4.160 and *Vita* 193) as Γαμάλας, this man may be the גמלא mentioned in ossuary inscription *CIJ* II, no. 1353a and b. So Sukenik, cited by Frey *ad loc.*
[39]*BS* III, nos. 9, 15 and 26 for texts and pp. 62-65 for discussion as to their identity. For the name in the House of Hillel, *Encyclopedia Judaica s.v.* Gamaliel.
[40]Compare, for instance, Gn. 25:26 and 27:36.
[41]Loeb index, *s.v.* James.
[42]*Ant.* 20.200 (no. 17 in our list).
[43]See Avigad, 'Kidron Valley', 11. The name does occasionally appear at Masada. See, for instance, Yadin and Naveh, nos. 402, 500 and 501.
[44]See *DJJD*, nos. 40, 42 and 103.
[45]See *BS* II, nos. 83, 126 and 130 for Ἰακώ; no. 75 for Ἰακώβ; no. 203 for Ἰακώς; no. 6 for Ἰάκκωβε (voc.); no. 125 for Ἰακώβου and nos. 94 and 96 for Ἴκουβος. In the towns of the Palestinian littoral, the name, usually in the form Ἰακώ, was also very popular from the 3rd century onwards. See *CIJ* II, nos. 966-7 (Gaza); nos. 910, 927, 929, 946, 950 and 956 (Jaffa). For Caesarea Maritima, see *CIJ* II, no. 890; *SEG* 16 (1959) no. 844 and *IEJ* 3 (1953) 127-9. In the last example, dated to the 5th–6th centuries, the unique form Ἰακῶνος (gen.) appears.
[46]*CPJ* III, 179.
[47]Horbury-Noy, no. 56—comm. *ad loc.*

3rd century AD, most commonly in the form Ἰάκουβος (Ἰάκοβος and Ἰακοῦβις are variant spellings). Only in the late 3rd century AD does the undeclined form Ἰακώβ make an appearance there.[48] In the rest of the Diaspora we find a scattering of cases, mainly of 3rd century date or later. Ἰακώ and Ἰακώβ are the commonest forms[49] but the declinable Ἰάκουβος still crops up now and again.[50]

Jesus (Ἰησοῦς)—ישוע ('Yah is generous or possibly Yah saves'). A far more popular name in 1st-century Palestine than the solitary example in Acts (no. 19 above) implies. In Josephus, many individuals of this name are to be found[51] and on the ossuaries too, where it is written either as ישוע or Ἰησοῦς,[52] it is fairly common.[53] Among 1st-century Diasporan Jews the name was equally popular: many cases have been found both in Egypt and Cyrenaica.[54] Subsequently it underwent a general decline, probably because of its Christian associations. Although a fair number of cases has been discovered at Murabba'at,[55] Beth She'arim has produced only two.[56] And in our Diasporan sources, examples are yet to be found. In other guises, however, the name still appears. Jason, which in hellenistic times had regularly been used in the place of Jesus,[57] is attested at Beth She'arim, Rome and Aphrodisias.[58] And Joshua (יהושע), a form of Jesus which had been neglected for centuries,[59] now enjoys a general renaissance.[60]

John (Ἰωάννης)—יהוחנן/יוחנן ('Yah has shown favour'). An extremely popular name in 1st-century Palestine, as its frequent attes-

---

[48]*CPJ* III, nos. 473 and 475.

[49]*CIJ* I², no. 340 (Rome); RT, 101 (Aphrodisias); *DF*, nos. 14 and 37 (Smyrna and Side); *CIJ* II, no. 787 (Corycus).

[50]*CIJ* II, nos. 801 (Pontus), 820 (Palmyra), 861 (Transjordania) and 879 (Tyre).

[51]Loeb index, *s.v.* Jesus.

[52]For ישוע, see *CIJ* II, nos. 1318, 1345 and 1365a and b; for Ἰησοῦς, see Sukenik, 'Earliest Records', 358, nos. 3 and 4. *Cf. CIJ* II, no. 1327 (Ἰεσοῦς).

[53]For discussion and further examples, see Bagatti-Milik, 94-95.

[54]*CPJ* III, 180 (Egypt); Lüderitz, 222 (Cyrenaica).

[55]*DJD* index, *s.vv.* ישוע and Ἰησοῦς.

[56]*BS* II, nos. 51 and 138-40 (all referring to the same person).

[57]See N. Cohen, 'The Names of the Translators in the Letter of Aristeas: A Study in the Dynamics of Cultural Transition', *JSJ* 15 (1984) 46-48.

[58]*BS* II, no. 154; *CIJ* I², nos. 32, 289 and perhaps 341 (Rome); RT, 101 (Aphrodisias).

[59]Cohen, *ibid.*

[60]For the name in Rabbinical circles in Palestine, see Cohen, *ibid.*; for a Diasporan example, see RT, 5 and 102—Ἰωσούας. *Cf. DF*, no. 73a—Ἴσουος (Gaza—5th century).

tation in all our sources shows.[61] On the ossuaries it occurs in a wide variety of forms. Besides יהוחנן (this is by far the commonest[62]), יוחנן, יחוני and Ἰωάνης also appear.[63] The popularity of the name continues down to the Bar Kokhba period (it is found frequently at Murabba'at),[64] after which it seems to have declined somewhat. In the extensive body of Greek inscriptions from Beth She'arim, for instance, it does not occur.[65] In the Diaspora, it seems never to have been used much. Apart from a handful of examples from Egypt and Cyrene,[66] there is only a single, apparently late, case from Beroea in Macedonia.[67]

Jonathan (Ἰωνάθας)—יהונתן ('Yah has given'). In 1st-century Palestine, the least popular of the early Hasmonaean names (the others were Matthew, Simon, Judas, John and Eleazar).[68] It only occurs once in the New Testament (Acts 4:6) and then not in all MSS. In Josephus there are just six examples[69] and on the ossuaries merely five (always written as יהונתן).[70] Although it is found at Murabba'at fairly often,[71] at Beth She'arim it does not occur at all.[72] In the Diaspora, it was never much used. No Jews of the name are known in 1st-century Egypt[73] and Cyrenaica has produced only two[74] (in both areas, Theodotus was widely used as a substitute).[75] Later Diasporan examples are also rare—an archon called Ἰωνάθας has been found in 3rd-century Greece[76] and at Rome a Ζώναθα and a Pompeius Ionata are attested.[77]

---

[61]For Acts, see nos. 20-23 above; for Josephus, Loeb index, *s.v.* John; for the ossuary evidence, Bagatti-Milik, 88.

[62]See, for instance, *CIJ* II, nos. 1192, 1244, 1245, 1248, 1257 (now Puech, no. 6), 1301, 1335, 1342, 1348.

[63]*CIJ* II, no. 1394 (יוחנן); *CIJ* II, no. 1177 and Bagatti-Milik, no. 12 (יחוני); *CIJ* II, no. 1367b and Bagatti-Milik, no. 18 (Ἰωάνης).

[64]Usually in the form יהוחנן but occasionally as Ἰωάνης. See entries in *DJD* indices.

[65]Note the name, however, in *BS* III, no. 2—an Aramaic inscription.

[66]See *CPJ* III, 182 and Lüderitz, 222.

[67]*CIJ* I², 694a. For the date, see L. Robert in *Hellenica* 3 (1946) 104-5.

[68]For Eleazar, see n. 6 above.

[69]Loeb index, *s.v.* Jonathan, nos. 7-12.

[70]Bagatti-Milik, 87.

[71]See *DJD* indices under יהונתן and Ἰωνάθης.

[72]Two late Palestinian examples, however, are found at Jaffa (*CIJ* II, no. 900) and Scythopolis (*DF*, no. 77b).

[73]For the four Ptolemaic examples, see *CPJ* III, 182.

[74]See Lüderitz, no. 72 and Appendix 1.

[75]*CPJ* III, 177 and Lüderitz, 221.

[76]*CIJ* I², no. 721b = *DF*, no. 9a.

[77]*CIJ* I², nos. 277 and 259.

Joseph (Ἰωσήφ)[78]—יהוסף ('May [God] add [other children to the one just born]'). A perennial favourite with Jews everywhere. In 1st-century Palestine it is found at all social levels (it is one of the few Hebrew names to appear in the Herodian dynasty)[79] and in a variety of forms. Commonest is יהוסף,[80] but both Ἰώσηπος[81] and hypocoristic Ἰωσῆ(ς)[82] also occur occasionally. Though the name was just as popular in later Palestine, there is a shift from the 3rd century onwards in the forms we meet: Ἰώσηπος virtually drops out of use;[83] Ἰωσῆ(ς)/יוסה and Ἰωσήφ[84] now become equally popular. In the Diaspora similar developments are to be observed. Ἰώσηπος, the preferred form in our 1st-century evidence,[85] hardly occurs in our later (predominantly 3rd-century) sources. Instead, the hypocoristic form now prevalent in Palestine dominates.[86] Also to be noted is the appearance in Egypt, Asia Minor and Macedonia of undeclined Ἰωσήφ, a form hitherto not found outside Palestine.[87]

Judas (Ἰούδας)—יהודה (perhaps '[God] be praised'). Enormously popular in 1st-century Palestine, as Acts with its four examples implies (see nos. 26-29 above). Numerous examples of the name can be found both in Josephus[88] and on the ossuaries,[89] where a variety of forms is encountered. Commonest by far is יהודה[90] but a few cases of Ἰούδας

---

[78]Another of the rare, undeclined LXX name-forms retained in Acts. For another, see n. 36 above.
[79]Loeb index, *s.v.* Joseph, nos. 6, 8 and 9.
[80]See, for instance, *CIJ* II, nos. 1190, 1242, 1290, 1291, 1292a and b, 1299, 1343a, 1344, 1348, 1379.
[81]*CIJ* II, nos. 1211, 1355, 1368. *Cf. CIJ* II, no. 1350a and b—יהוסף and Ἰώσηπος (the bilingual ossuary of Joseph Qallon).
[82]*CIJ* II, no. 1283b; *BE* 73 (1960) no. 415; Puech, nos. 4 and 40.
[83]It is not found either at Beth She'arim or Jaffa. Two undated (but latish?) examples from elsewhere in Palestine, however, are cited by Lifshitz at *RB* 76 (1969) 92-94.
[84]Compare *BS* II, nos. 23, 26, 27, 32-33, 44 and 178 (Ἰωσήφ) with nos. 19, 22, 28, 41, 43, 93 and 124 (Ἰωσῆ(ς)). *Cf.* no. 161—Βαριωσῆ.
[85]See *CPJ* III, 182-3 and Lüderitz, 222.
[86]*Inter al.*, note *CIJ* I[2], nos. 126, 209, 347 and 538 (Rome); no. 719 (Argos); no. 721c (Messenia); *BE* 78 (1965) no. 426 (Selinus); *DF*, nos. 16 (Teos) and 82 (Cyprus) andRT, 102 (Aphrodisias).
[87]*CPJ* III, no. 479 (Ἰωσήπ); RT, 102 (Ἰωσήφ); *JSS* 35 (1990) 72, for a Ἰωσήφ at Philippopolis.
[88]Loeb index, *s.v.* Judas, nos. 8-15.
[89]Bagatti-Milik, 85.
[90]See, for instance, *CIJ* II, nos. 1171, 1255a and b, 1262b, 1295, 1301, 1305-1308a and b, 1313b, 1314.

have also been found[91] and occasionally the indeclinable Ἰούδαν.[92] Although attestations of this form increase in later times,[93] in popularity it never overtook either יהודה or Ἰούδας. In the Diaspora, the name fared rather differently. Among the highly hellenised Jews of Egypt and Cyrenaica it was not much favoured. Although a handful of examples has been found in the latter area,[94] only one 1st-century Judas can be securely identified in Egypt (*CPJ* II, no. 235) and not many more at other periods.[95] In other parts of the Diaspora, it was sometimes very popular. Among the rather traditionally-minded Jews of 3rd-century Rome and Aphrodisias, for instance, it is the name most frequently attested.[96] With forms, there is, predictably, a huge preference for those that were declinable—Ἰούδας is the most common, even at Rome.[97] The indeclinables, however, do crop up occasionally—in two latish inscriptions from Egypt, both יודן and Ἰούδα have been found but only once each.[98]

Mary (Μαρία[μ])—מרים (meaning not altogether certain).[99] Salomezion apart,[100] easily the most popular woman's name in 1st-century Palestine,[101] with a social distribution far wider than that implied by Acts and the Gospels. Josephus shows that it was a firm favourite with the Herodian dynasty,[102] whither it was imported by Herod's Hasmonaean bride Mariamme (*BJ* 1.241). And it was heavily used by the ossuary-owning class.[103] Forms vary. Commonest is

---

[91]*E.g. CIJ* II, nos. 1280 and 1282a. The genitive of the declined form varies. Note *CIJ* II, no. 1283a and b and Puech, no. 41 for Ἰούδου; Puech, no. 34 for Ἰούδα and *CIJ* II, no. 1385 for Ἰούδατος.

[92]See, for instance, *CIJ* II, no. 1232 (written ΝΑΔΥΟΙ) and Puech, no. 27.

[93]Examples have been found at Murabba'at (*DJD*, no. 18, l. 12); Beth She'arim (*BS* III, nos. 5, 6 and 22); Jaffa (*CIJ* II, nos. 892 and 900); Corazin (*CIJ* II, no. 981) and Sepphoris (*CIJ* II, nos. 989-90).

[94]Lüderitz, 222. Note the unique forms Ἰουδίον and Ἰουδίων in his nos. 32c and 55b.

[95]*CPJ* III, 180 lists only six other cases.

[96]See, for instance, *CIJ* I^2, nos. 12, 121-2, 206, 345-51 for Rome; RT, 102 for Aphrodisias.

[97]See examples cited in previous note. For Iuda/Iudae at 3rd-century Ostia, see *CIJ* I^2, 534a (now Noy, no. 15).

[98]Horbury-Noy, nos. 118 and 131 (2nd century or later).

[99]See F. Vattioni, 'I Semiti nell'epigrafia cirenaica', *Studi Classici e Orientali* 37 (1987) 538.

[100]See n. 5 above.

[101]Ilan, 191-2.

[102]Loeb index, *s.v.* Mariamme, nos. 2-7.

[103]Ilan, 196-7, nos. 93-125. Note, however, that no. 96 (*CIJ* II, no. 1284) is a Jewess from Capua and no. 101 (*CIJ* II, no. 1390) a proselyte.

מרים,[104] occasionally written as Μαρίαμ.[105] Next in frequency are the two Greek forms Μαριάμ(μ)η and Μαρία;[106] the latter quite often appears as מריה.[107] Μαριάς (gen. -άδος) is attested once.[108] Subsequently the name declines in popularity—by far the commonest woman's name at Beth She'arim, for instance, is Sarah.[109] In the 1st-century Diaspora, the name does not seem to have been particularly popular,[110] unless Μάριον and Μάριν, both of which are found in Egypt and Cyrene, be considered diminutive forms of Μαρία.[111] And there is no general growth in its popularity in later times.[112] 3rd-century Rome provides the sole exception. In that most traditional of communities, Mary was the commonest Jewish woman's name.[113] With regard to forms, Μαρία is easily the most popular with Diasporan Jews, even those at Rome.[114] Μαριάμη and Μαρίαμ are attested only once each—at Alexandria and Dura respectively.[115]

Matthew (Ματθαῖος/Ματθίας)—מתתיה (Mattathiah); מתיה (Matthiah)—('gift of Yah'). A common name among 1st-century Palestinian Jews, with a wider social distribution than Acts (nos. 32-33 above) implies. Josephus has several High Priestly examples[116] and among the ossuary-using class it is well attested.[117] Forms vary. Commonest is מתיה,[118] but מתתיה also occurs,[119] and so does the hypocoristic form מתי (Mattai).[120] At Murabba'at the name crops up several times (the forms used are מתתיה, מתיה and Μαθθαῖος),[121] but at

[104]See, for instance, Ilan, nos. 93, 95, 99, 102 and 103.

[105]Ilan, nos. 106 and 123.

[106]See, for instance, Ilan, nos. 98, 100, 105 for Μαριάμη and nos. 94, 107, 113 for Μαρία. For a [Μαρια]μμη at Masada, see Cotton and Geiger, no. 895 (*SEG* 40 [1990], no. 1500).

[107]As in Ilan, nos. 104, 112, 116. For the fairly rare phenomenon of rendering in Hebrew letters the hellenised forms of Hebrew names, see Horbury (cit. n. 30) 105.

[108]Ilan, no. 97 = *CIJ* II, no. 1328.

[109]See *BS* II, 227-8.

[110]Only two unambiguous examples apiece in Lüderitz (nos. 65 and 66a) and *CPJ* (nos. 223 and 227); for another, see Horbury-Noy, no. 11.

[111]Tcherikover, as cited at *DJD*, 177, and Vattioni, 538-9, consider it to have been a separate semitic name, borne by Jews and Gentiles alike.

[112]There is the odd attestation of the name in Pannonia, Macedonia and Thessaly. See *CIJ* I², nos. 678, 694b and 701.

[113]*CIJ* I², nos. 1, 12, 96, 137, 252, 374, 375, 457, 459 and 511.

[114]See the examples just cited. Note in *CIJ* I², no. 12 the unusual genitive, [Μ]αρίες.

[115]Horbury-Noy, no. 11; R. du Mesnil du Buisson, 'Inscriptions sur jarres de Dura Europos', *MUSJ* 36 (1959) no. 50.

[116]Loeb index, *s.v.* Matthias, nos. 4, 6-8, 10-11.

[117]Bagatti-Milik, 76.

Beth She'arim it appears only once as Μαθᾶς.[122] Diasporan occurrences are exceedingly rare. In Egypt and Cyrene the name does not appear. (Dositheus was used as a substitute.)[123] And there are few certain attestations elsewhere. Alexander, also called Matthew (Rome—probably 3rd century), was definitely a Jew[124] but total certainty is not possible either with Marcus Mathius of 3rd-century Phrygia[125] or the two Syrian immigrants attested at Athens with the name Μαθθαία.[126]

Menahem (Μαναήν)—מנחם ('[God is my] consoler'). A fairly uncommon name in 1st-century Palestine, as the solitary NT reference at Acts 13:1 implies. Only two Menahems appear in Josephus[127] and there are not many more on the ossuaries.[128] The later Palestinian evidence does not evince any upsurge in the popularity of the name either.[129] In material relating to the Diaspora it hardly appears.[130] *BS* II, no. 110 mentions a Μαναή (*sic*!) from Himyar in Arabia but the restoration of the name in *BS* II, no. 37—the epitaph of a Jew of Palmyrene origin—is exceedingly doubtful (only the letters ME are certain). The name-form in Acts is unique. Generally in Greek texts one finds either Μανάημος/Μανάαμος or Septuagintal Μαναήμ.[131]

---

[118]See *CIJ* II, nos. 1240, 1246, 1362a and b; Bagatti-Milik, nos. 3 and 27 (now Puech, no. 19). *Cf. CIJ* II, no. 1275a and b and Figueras 13 n. 88 for the parallel Greek form Μαθίας.

[119]*CIJ* II, no. 1361; Puech, no. 25. *Cf. CIJ* II, no. 1276—Ματταθίου.

[120]*CIJ* II, no. 1365. *Cf.* Bagatti-Milik, no. 23—מתתא.

[121]*DJD*, nos. 10 and 73, 38, 103. *Cf.* no. 74 possibly for the hypocoristic form.

[122]*BS* II, no. 48.

[123]*CPJ* I, 29 for general discussion; for examples, *CPJ* III, 173-4 and Lüderitz, 220.

[124]*CIJ* I², no. 140.

[125]Jewish identification was first suggested by L. Robert in *Hellenica* 11-12 (1960) 411. He is followed by P. Trebilco, *Jewish Communities in Asia Minor* (Cambridge, 1991) 78-79.

[126]*CIJ* I², nos. 715d and 715f—from Antioch and Sidon respectively.

[127]*Ant.* 15.373 (actually of early Herodian date); *BJ* 2.433 (Jewish War leader).

[128]Bagatti-Milik, 90.

[129]Only three attestations at Murabba'at—*DJD*, nos. 10, 21 and 75. From the 3rd century onwards, the synonymous Paregorius does have a certain currency. See, for instance, *BS* II, nos. 31, 61, 83 and 208 (Beth She'arim) and *CIJ* II, nos. 926, 939, 944, 945 (Jaffa).

[130]At 5th-century Elephantine, by contrast, it had been exceedingly popular. Bagatti-Milik, 90.

[131]For the former, see the Josephan references in n. 127 above; *CIJ* II, no. 883 (near Jaffa) and *BE* 81 (1968) no. 561 (Gaza). For the latter, *CIJ* II, no. 1344. *Cf.* 2 Ki. 15:14-22.

Simon (Σίμων/Συμέων)[132]—שמעון ('[Yah] has heard'). A perennial favourite with Jews, especially those in Greek-speaking areas, where it was easily assimilated to Greek Σίμων (snub-nosed)[133] and the commonest male name by far in 1st-century Palestine.[134] On the ossuaries, where it appears dozens of times,[135] it is usually written שמעון,[136] but Σίμων[137] and even hypocoristic Simai[138] occasionally crop up. In the 2nd century, its popularity continued unabated—at Murabba'at it is easily the most frequently attested name.[139] Although from the 3rd century it faced growing rivalry from Isaac, Jacob and Samuel,[140] it still remained a common name—numerous examples have been found both at Beth She'arim and the Greek-speaking cities of the Palestinian littoral—Caesarea, Jaffa and Gaza. Generally it appears as Σύμων (gen. -ωνος/-ονος),[141] but there are occasional variations—*e.g.* Σεμιών[142] and Ψιμίων.[143] With Diasporan Jews, the name was a firm favourite at all times. In Egypt and Cyrene it is one of the most frequently attested names of all[144] and there is a fair scattering of examples from Asia Minor, Greece and Rome.[145] The commonest form is Σίμων (-ονος) but from the 3rd century on a number of variations are

---

132In Acts, Σίμων is the preferred form. Note, however, that at 15:14, in James' direct speech to the early Christians at Jerusalem, Συμέων is used, presumably for 'local colour'. See I.H. Marshall, *The Acts of the Apostles: An Introduction and Commentary* (Leicester, 1980)—comm. *ad loc.* The name Saul is handled likewise: *cf.* Acts 8:1 Σαῦλος (narrative) and 9:4 Σαούλ (the voice from Heaven speaking).

133On this, see now Cohen, 'Names as Cultural Indicators' (cit. n. 1) 112.

134On this our sources are unanimous. Besides the four Palestinian Simons in Acts (nos. 38-41 above), several others are to be found in the Gospels as, for instance, at Mt. 13:55; Mk. 14:3 and Jn. 6:71. Josephus lists over twenty cases: Loeb index, *s. v.* Simon, nos. 6-27. On the ossuaries, it is the most frequently attested name. See Avigad, 'Kidron Valley', 9.

135Bagatti-Milik, 77 for list.

136*Inter al.*, note *CIJ* II, nos. 1254, 1292a, 1298, 1299.

137*CIJ* II, no. 1355a and c; Bagatti-Milik, no. 37d. For Greek Σίμων rendered phonetically in Hebrew, see J. Naveh, 'Giv'at ha-Mivtar' (cit. n. 13) 33-34 (סמון) and Yadin and Naveh (cit. n. 11) nos. 415 (סמון); 561 and 564 (סימו).

138*E.g.* Puech, no. 15 (new reading of Bagatti-Milik, no. 16).

139For details, see J.A. Fitzmyer, 'The Name Simon', *HTR* 56 (1963) 4 n. 11.

140See *BS* II, 227-8.

141See, for instance, *BS* II, no. 220; *CIJ* II, nos. 905, 935, 955 and 956 (Jaffa) and no. 890 (Caesarea).

142*BS* II, no. 46.

143*CIJ* II, no. 923 (Jaffa).

144*CPJ* I, 29-30 for discussion. For examples, see *CPJ* III, 191-2 and Lüderitz, 226.

145*E.g.* *CIJ* II, no. 785 (Corycus); *CIJ* I^2, nos. 165b, 176 and 403 (Rome); and 715c (Athens).

to be noticed. Septuagintal Συμεών, for instance, is found at Aphrodisias[146] and in Egypt, Σεμαιῶν.[147]

2. *Aramaic*

Alphaeus (Ἀλφάιος)—חלפי ('God has replaced [*sc.* a dead child]'). Not a common name among 1st-century Palestinian Jews. The only example apart from the father of James at Acts 1:13 is Alphaeus, the father of Levi/Matthew at Mark 2:14. Among the ossuary-workers of Bethphage, however, there is a בן חלפתא[148]—a man whose patronymic is clearly derived from the same root—חלף. In later Palestinian sources, a number of *ḥalaf*-type names crop up. At Murabba'at, for instance, חליפא appears a couple of times,[149] both Jaffa and Caesarea have each produced an Ἀλάφθα[150] and חלפי has been read by some on a 3rd-century synagogue inscription from Capernaum.[151] In the Diaspora none of these names is attested. Where they do occur is among the Gentile inhabitants of Syria and its neighbours. Emesa has produced several examples,[152] and individual cases are known from Antioch ([Ἄ]λφαι),[153] Arad (Ἀλαφαθα(ς))[154] and Palmyra (Alaphatha).[155]

Bartholomew (Βαρθολομαῖος)—'son (בר) of Tolmai/Talmai (תלמי)'. One of the several "false patronymics" found in the Jewish onomastikon[156] and like them only seldom attested. Apart from the Apostle himself (no. 9 above), there are no other certain Jewish examples. Possibly, though, the [βαρθο]λομεος Ἀλέξα[νδρο]ς mentioned in a recently published inscription from a Christian church on Mount Gerizim was a Jew.[157] Equally rare among Jews is the name Tolmai. Josephus mentions a brigand leader executed by the Romans in the

---

[146]RT, 104.
[147]*CPJ* III, no. 501.
[148]*CIJ* II, no. 1285, l. 13.
[149]*DJD*, nos. 22 and 24.
[150]*CIJ* II, no. 904 (Jaffa); *BE* 84 (1971) no. 694 (Caesarea).
[151]*CIJ* II, no. 982. See Frey's comments *ad loc.* For the rare occurrence of one of these names (חליפא) in Rabbinical circles, see *DJD*, 121—comm. on doc. no. 22, l. 12.
[152]*IGLS* V, nos. 2305, 2310, 2417 and 2570.
[153]*IGLS* III (i), no. 895.
[154]*IGLS* VII, no. 4054.
[155]*CIL* XVI, no. 68—*Hammasaeus Alaphatha f. (domo) Palmyra*. The inscription was actually found at Rome.
[156]See Lifshitz, commentary on *BS* II, no. 161.

40's AD called Tholomaios and a חלמי has recently turned up on an ostrakon at Masada,[158] but no other cases are known. Among the semitic inhabitants of Syria and Arabia, however, the name crops up now and again. Inscriptions of the Roman imperial period mention a Γάϊος Ἰούλιος θολομαῖος at Apamea[159] and a Tholomaeus at Beirut.[160] And from the Lebanon a T(ίτος) X[ορί]κιος Θολομαῖος and a Θολομ are known.[161] Also to be noted is Θολομαῖος Θαιμάλλου ὁ καὶ Μάξιμος of Petra, mentioned on an inscription from Puteoli.[162]

Sapphira (Σάπφειρα)—שפירא ('beautiful'). A name found almost exclusively among the Jerusalem rich of the 1st century. Besides the wealthy Sapphira of Acts 5:1ff., no less than nine other women of this name are known from tombs in the Jerusalem area.[163] The only other case known (also a rich lady) comes from 2nd-century Murabba'at.[164] Spellings vary. Commonest is שפירא—the popular orthography.[165] But שפירה (the historic form) appears twice,[166] and in the Greek we find ΣΑΠΙΡΑ, ΣΑΦΙΡΑ and ΣΑΦΕΙΡΑ.[167] Also attested on the Jerusalem ossuaries is the masculine form of the name שפיר (Saphir)—but far less frequently than the feminine.[168]

Silas (Σίλας)—etymology somewhat uncertain; possibly the Greek form of the Aramaic equivalent of Saul—שאילא ('asked for [from God]').[169] Not quite as popular a name among 1st-century Palestinian

---

157*SEG* 40 (1990) no. 1502. Although the inscription comes from a late 5th-century Christian church, its editors think that it may date from the pre-Christian period of the site and thus possibly be Jewish or Samaritan in origin.

158*Ant.* 20.5; Yadin and Naveh, no. 578.

159*IGLS* IV, no. 1365.

160*AE* (1903) no. 259.

161See R. Mouterde in *MUSJ* 26 (1944-1946) 58-59.

162*IG* XIV, 842a.

163*CIJ* II, nos. 1272a, 1282c, 1378a and b, 1384, 1393b; Bagatti-Milik, no. 13b; J. Naveh, *Atiqot* 14 (1980) 55-59; Puech, nos. 30 and 39.

164*DJD*, no. 29—a property transaction.

165*CIJ* II, nos. 1282c, 1378a, 1384; Bagatti-Milik, no. 13b and possibly *CIJ* II, no. 1393—שפר(א).

166Naveh, *ibid.* and *DJD*, no. 29. For discussion of the forms, see Bagatti-Milik, 85.

167*CIJ* II, no. 1272a; Puech, nos. 30 and 39; *CIJ*, no. 1378b.

168See, for instance, Bagatti-Milik, no. 38. For discussion, see Hachlili, 'Names and Nicknames', 199.

169See H. Conzelmann, *Acts of the Apostles*, tr. J. Limburg, A.T. Kraabel and D.H. Juel (Philadelphia, 1987) 120. For further discussion and examples, see H.J. Cadbury, 'Some Semitic Personal Names in Luke-Acts', in H.G. Wood (ed.), *Amicitiae Corolla* (London, 1933) 50-51.

Jews as Saul itself. While the latter occurs several times on the ossuaries,[170] the only certain cases of Silas, apart from the early Christian of that name (no. 37 above), are two Jewish commanders mentioned by Josephus.[171] In the Diaspora, few Silases are attested. A 1st-century Babylonian example is to be found in Josephus,[172] and inscriptions dated to the 2nd and 3rd centuries (from Antibes and Dura respectively) yield two more.[173] Among semites of the Syrian area the name had a certain currency. Silas was the signum or additional name of the 1st-century Roman client king of Emesa, Gaius Iulius Samsigeramus.[174] The same region has also produced a Σείλας Σαμσαίου.[175]

Tabitha (Ταβιθά)—טביתא ('gazelle'). Apart from the good needlewoman of Acts 9:36-41, no other specific Jewish examples are known. According to two passages in the Jerusalem Talmud, however, both Tabitha and its male counterpart Tabi functioned as generic slave-names in the house of Gamaliel II.[176] Hard Diasporan examples of the names are also lacking but it is possible that the Flavia Tabita mentioned in the 1st century (AD) Roman inscription, *CIL* VI, 35310, was a Jewess. Her name suggests that she could well have been brought by the Flavians to Rome as a slave after the First Jewish War and subsequently manumitted by them. The findspot of the memorial she set up to her freedman husband (near the Porta Portuensis[177]) points in the same direction. Rome's largest Jewish cemetery was in that very area.

3. *Greek*

Alexander (Ἀλέξανδρος). Not a common name among 1st-century Palestinian Jews despite its earlier popularity there in aristocratic

---

[170] *E.g.* Puech, no. 41; F. Vitto in *Rev. Bib.* 79 (1972) 575; Naveh, 'Givat ha-Mivtar', 36-37. In Josephus, we come across another two examples. See *BJ* 2.418 and 469.
[171] Referred to at *BJ* 2.616; *Ant.* 19.299 and elsewhere.
[172] *BJ* 2.520.
[173] *BE* 89 (1976) no. 798 (Antibes); *DF*, no. 60 (formerly *CIJ* II, no. 830; Dura).
[174] *IGLS* V, no. 2212—Σαμσιγεραμος ὁ καὶ Σείλας.
[175] *IGLS* V, no. 2561.
[176] *y.Nid.* 1.5 49b and 2.1 49d. See J. Neusner, *The Talmud in the Land of Israel*, vol. 34—*Horayot and Niddah* (Chicago, 1982) 160 and 175.
[177] Details in *CIL ad loc.*

circles.[178] Most of the (1st-century) individuals of the name mentioned by Josephus belong to the royal family[179] and all but one of those occurring on the Jerusalem ossuaries came from the Diaspora[180] (his name appears in the hypocoristic form אלכשה—*i.e.* Alexa[s]).[181] The 2nd and 3rd centuries saw no increase in the popularity of the name: Murabba'at has produced only one example (at *DJD*, no. 103 there is an Alexas) and Beth She'arim no more than the letters ΑΛΕ, restored tentatively by Lifshitz as 'Αλε[ξάνδρου?].[182] In the Diaspora, its fortunes were mixed. In 1st-century Egypt and Cyrene there is only a scattering of cases[183] and in Greece[184] and Asia Minor[185] not many at any time. But among the Jews of (3rd-century) Rome, it was very common.[186] The reason probably is the overall popularity of the name there—it is among the most frequently attested of all Greek names in that city.[187]

Andrew ('Ανδρέας)—'manly'. Not a popular name with Jews anywhere in Roman imperial times. 1st-century Palestine has produced only a tiny number of examples—in addition to the Apostle himself (no. 7 above), only two other Andrews are known—both from the ossuaries. In each case the rare, variant form of the name—*viz.* 'Ανδροῦς—is used.[188] In contemporary Diasporan material the name does not appear and later evidence provides only one example—at Beroea in Macedonia an Andreas, son of Paregorios, is attested.[189] Equally sparse are instances of analogous names. Note, however, in our 1st-century sources two attestations of Andronicus ('man-

---

[178]Josephus mentions several Jewish ambassadors of the 2nd century called Alexander: Loeb index, *s.v.* Alexander, nos. 12-15.
[179]See Alexander, nos. 8-11 and Alexas, nos. 2-4.
[180]*CIJ* II, no. 1256 (now Horbury-Noy, no. 153)—Jew of Alexandria; Avigad, 'Kidron Valley', 9-11—Jew of Cyrenaica; *CIJ* II, no. 1284—Jew of Capua.
[181]See Sukenik, 'Jewish Tomb', 127.
[182]*BS* II, no. 83.
[183]*CPJ* III, 168-9; Lüderitz, 217.
[184]Only one example: *CIJ* I^2, no. 694b.
[185]A few have cropped up in Phrygia and Cilicia. See *CIJ* II, nos. 764, 770 and 776 (Phrygia); nos. 786 and 791 (Cilicia).
[186]*CIJ* I^2, nos. 84 (father and son), 85 (father and son), 92, 140, 210, 219, 370 and 501. *Cf.* no. 284—Alexus.
[187]H. Solin, *Die griechische Personennamen in Rom; ein Namenbuch* I (Berlin and New York, 1982) 186-94—540 examples! Only Eros and Hermes are attested more often.
[188]*CIJ* II, no. 1272b; Puech, no. 41. On the form, see Puech *ad loc.*
[189]*CIJ* I^2, no. 694a.

conquering')—one at Rome (the individual in question probably came from Palestine[190]), the other in Cyrenaica.[191]

Berenice (βερνίκη)—a Macedonian name meaning 'bringer of victory' (the Greek form is Φερενίκη). In 1st-century Palestine, it was largely confined to the royal family. Besides the three Herodian Berenices mentioned by Josephus,[192] only one other Jewess of that name is known—the βερνίκη/בניקי of ossuary inscription *CIJ* II, no. 1366. Among Diasporan Jews the name was not much used. Predictably it appears in 1st-century Cyrenaica.[193] The name enjoyed a general popularity there, Ptolemy III's wife, Berenice II, having come from those parts.[194] The name appears also in *CIJ* I², no. 461 (Rome) but the reading— ([Bere?]nice)—is rather doubtful.

Herod (Ἡρώδης)—from Greek ἥρως (hero).[195] In 1st-century Palestine, a name found mainly in the ruling family—besides the Herod of Acts ch. 12, another seven princes with the name are mentioned in Josephus[196] and an eighth implied.[197] The only other contemporary examples mentioned by him are confined to the pro-Roman ruling clique of Tiberias in Galilee.[198] In later Palestinian sources, the name is attested only very occasionally. Beth She'arim has produced one example and the synagogue at Capernaum another.[199] Among Diasporan Jews the name is not found,[200] despite its widespread use by Gentiles in the Graeco-Roman world.[201]

Philip (Φίλιππος)—'lover of horses'. A well-established, even if not especially popular, name among 1st-century Palestinian Jews. (It

---

190 Rom. 16:7.

191 Lüderitz, no. 52c.

192 Loeb index, *s.v.* Berenice, nos. 1-3. Note that no. 2 is the same person as the Berenice of Acts.

193 *BJ* 7.445; Lüderitz, no. 4.

194 Lüderitz, no. 4, comm. *ad loc.*

195 Pape-Benseler, *s.v.* Herodes.

196 Loeb index, *s.v.* Herod, nos. 2-3 and 5-9.

197 In *C. Ap.* 1.51. All the other men listed there belong to the House of Herod.

198 Loeb index, *s.v.* Herod, nos. 11-13.

199 *BS* II, no. 56; *DF*, no. 75 (formerly *CIJ* II, no. 983)—both of 3rd-century date.

200 One could read ['H]ροδίων, though, in *CIJ* I², no. 173. For a 1st-century Palestinian Jew with this name at Rome, see Rom. 16:11.

201 For examples from the Roman imperial period, see *CIJ* I², no. 52* (Rome); *SEG* 33 (1983) no. 952 (Ephesus); 34 (1984) no. 136 (Athens); 35 (1985) no. 930B (Chios); 39 (1989) no. 1565 (Abila in Syria).

had entered their onomastikon at least as early as the 2nd century BC.)[202] Besides the Apostle himself (no. 35 above), the other known bearers of the name are (1) Herod's son, the tetrarch of the Ituraean provinces, (2) a Jewish War hero from Ruma in Galilee and (3) Agrippa II's commander-in-chief, Philip the son of Iacimus.[203] Another possible candidate is the Evangelist of Acts 21:8 (see Appendix). Later Palestinian examples are yet to be found. In the Diaspora the name occurs sporadically from the 1st century onwards. The earliest examples are from Egypt,[204] Cyrenaica[205] and Puteoli,[206] the latter mainly from Rome.[207]

Theudas (Θευδᾶς)—shortened form of Theodotus, the Greek equivalent of Jonathan ('given by God'). Not much attested among 1st-century Palestinian Jews. Since the rabble rouser Theudas, referred to by Josephus at *Ant*.20.97-98, is probably the same man as the rebel leader Theudas of Acts 5:36,[208] we are left with only one other contemporary example—the תודוס of ossuary inscription *CIJ* II, no. 1255. The name does appear occasionally, however, in other guises—Theodotus, for example, is attested both at Jerusalem[209] and Jericho[210] and Theodotion, its diminutive, sometimes contracted to Theudion, is found twice in Josephus[211] and three times on the ossuaries.[212] In later Palestine these names are even rarer—Murabba'at and Beth She'arim have produced only one apiece.[213] In the Diaspora, Theudas itself is not

[202]*Ant.* 14.248.
[203]Josephus, Loeb index, *s.v.* Philip, nos. 6-8.
[204]Horbury-Noy, no. 70 (formerly *CIJ* II, no. 1494); *CPJ* II, no. 192.
[205]Lüderitz, no. 55f. The example in Appendix 14a is very doubtful.
[206]*CIJ* I^2, no. 561 (now Noy, no. 23). Noy is unnecessarily cautious about the Jewishness of this individual.
[207]*CIJ* I^2, no. 334; *SEG* 26 (1976-1977) no. 1157. For a possible Cilician example and the name in general in Jewish circles, see the present author in *ZPE* 92 (1992) 249-50.
[208]For a contrary view, however, see Marshall, *Acts of the Apostles*, comm. *ad loc.* and F.F. Bruce, *The Acts of the Apostles* (3rd edn.; Grand Rapids, Michigan and Leicester, England, 1990) 176.
[209]*DF*, no. 79 (formerly *CIJ* II, no. 1404)—a synagogue inscription.
[210]See Hachlili, 'Goliath Family' (*cit.* n. 13) 33 and 46-47, where it is interpreted as the servile name of the Jew Nath[an]el.
[211]*Ant.* 17.70-73 and 20.14.
[212]*CIJ* II, nos. 1265, 1266a and 1270 for תדיון, תדטיון and Θεοδοτίωνος. *Cf.* Theodore at *CIJ* II, no. 1237.
[213]Possibly at *DJD*, no. 10, l. 4 if טיון[...] is restored as תדטיון (Theodotion). Certainly at *BS* II, no. 128 (a Theodotus).

attested epigraphically but its analogues do appear. Θεοδοῦς is found (once) in 1st-century Egypt[214] and with contemporary Jews in Cyrene Theodotus was a firm favourite.[215] Elsewhere, these names are not much in evidence. Solitary examples of Theodotus occur both at Rome and Aphrodisias, but none of the shorter forms is attested.[216]

4. Latin

Agrippa (Ἀγρίππας). Roman cognomen, most famously borne by the right-hand man and son-in-law of the emperor Augustus—*viz.* Marcus Vipsanius Agrippa. Used frequently by the Herods to signal their close relationship with the Roman imperial family. Besides the Agrippa of Acts (Agrippa II), three other scions of Herod the Great were so called[217] and a fourth went by the name Agrippinus.[218] Among their admirers too the name occasionally crops up. Josephus' son Simonides, for instance, was additionally called Agrippa (ὁ καὶ Ἀγρίππας ἐπικληθείς),[219] presumably as a compliment to Agrippa II—the historian's patron at the time.[220] Elsewhere in Jewish society, the name is rarely attested. A solitary example has been found at Beth She'arim[221] and one Agrippinus at Rome.[222]

Drusilla (Δρουσίλλα). Name of the favourite sister of the emperor Gaius (Caligula), whence its appearance in the royal family of Judaea—the father of the Drusilla mentioned in Acts (no. 12 above) and Josephus[223] (*i.e.* Agrippa I) was Caligula's friend and client. No other Jewesses of the name are known.

---

[214]*CPJ* II, no. 421, l. 188.
[215]Lüderitz, 221. Although Theodotus was exceedingly common in Ptolemaic Egypt, there are very few examples (only *CPJ* II, nos. 173 and 261) from the 1st century AD.
[216]*CIJ* I^2, no. 358; RT, 101. For a Theodotus from Seleucia in Isauria buried at Jaffa, see *CIJ* II, no. 882.
[217]Agrippa I, king of Judaea (AD 41-44); a grandson of the same (*Ant.* 20.143-4) and a son of Aristobulus and Salome (*Ant.* 18.137).
[218]Another grandson of Agrippa I (*Ant.* 20.147)!
[219]*Vita* 427.
[220]T. Rajak, *Josephus* (London, 1983) 164.
[221]*BS* II, no. 195.
[222]*CIJ* I^2, no. 322. For this name in the wider community there, see I. Kajanto, *The Latin Cognomina* (Helsinki, 1965) 175.
[223]*Ant.* 20.141.

III. Second Names

1.*Aramaic*

Barnabas (βαρνάβας)—the nickname given by the Apostles to their Cypriot fellow worker Joseph, under the impression, apparently, that it meant 'son of consolation'.[224] On etymological grounds that has proved hard to justify,[225] and the name is now generally recognised to be a pagan theophoric, meaning 'son of Nabu/Nebo'.[226] Although Barnabas is a rarity in the Jewish onomastikon—the only instance, apart from our Barnabas, is a 1st-century (AD) βαρνάβις at Edfu in Egypt[227]—among other semites it is very common (as a first name), and a wide variety of forms and spellings is attested. Besides Βαρνάβας, Βαρνάβους, Βαρνέβους,[228] Βαρναβίων,[229] and ברנבו,[230] hypocoristic Βαρναῖος is also found,[231] on occasion contracted to Βᾶρνας.[232] At Rome, these shortened forms occur with great frequency,[233] brought there presumably by slaves from Syria.[234]

Barsabbas (Βαρσαβ(β)ᾶς). Attested twice in Acts, in connection with two different members of the early Christian community (nos. 24 and 29), it is best seen, not as a patronymic (as Sukenik, *inter alios*, thought),[235] but a nickname meaning 'son of the Sabbath' (*i.e.* born on the Sabbath).[236] Although Barsabbas itself is otherwise unattested, many (first) names do occur, both in Palestine and the Diaspora, whose purpose was identical—*viz.* to indicate an individual's Sabbath birth.

224Acts 4:36.
225But see S. Brock, 'ΒΑΡΝΑΒΑΣ: ΥΙΟΣ ΠΑΡΑΚΛΗΣΕΩΣ', *JTS* NS 25 (1974) 93-98 on how the false, popular etymology might have arisen.
226For this and other names associated with the Babylonian god Nabu/Nebo, the son of Marduk, see C. Bradford Welles in A. Perkins (ed.), *The Excavations of Dura-Europos, Final Report V, Part I* (New York, 1959) 61-63.
227*CPJ* II, no. 331.
228All found at Dura. See Bradford Welles in *Yale Classical Studies* 14 (1955) 203.
229See H. Wuthnow, *Die semitischen Menschennamen in griechischen Inschriften und Papyri des vorderen Orients* (Leipzig, 1930) 34.
230Cadbury, 'Semitic Personal Names', 47, citing an inscription from Palmyra, dated AD 114.
231*IGLS* V, nos. 2372 and 2510 (Emesa); VII, no. 4016 (Arad).
232*IGLS* IV, no. 1378. On the name in general, see now O. Masson, 'Quelques noms sémitiques en transcription grecque à Délos et à Rhénée', in *Hommages à A. Dupont-Sommer* (Paris, 1972) 62-63.
233See Solin, *Juden und Syrer*, 637.
234For various servile examples at Rome, Solin, *op. cit.*, 677. *Cf.* Cic. *Ad Att.* 14.19.1.

On the Jerusalem ossuaries, we find only two—שבי, the hypocoristic of שבתי,[237] and ΣΑΒΑΤΙΣ,[238] each attested just once. But in the Diaspora, a plethora of Sabbath-names occurs, some of them borne by a large number of individuals. Commonest are Σαββαταῖος (Σαββαθαῖος), Εὐσαββάθιος (Εὐσαμβάθιος, Εὐσανβάθιος) and Σαβ(β)ατίς, the preponderant forms in Egypt, Asia Minor and at Rome respectively.[239] But the undeclined Hebrew שבתי was not without its followers and in our earliest[240] and latest[241] documents is the only version of the name to occur. Gentiles also sometimes adopted these names, as a result of contact with Jewish culture. And it is one of these, a soldier from Antioch mentioned in a 3rd-century document at Dura, whose name—Βαρσαββάθας—comes closest to the form found in Acts.[242] Although nearly all the Sabbath-names mentioned above functioned as first rather than second names, there are occasional examples of the latter usage. A Μόνιμος ὁ καὶ Εὐσαββάτις is attested at Rome[243] and at Edfu a Jesus/Sambathion.[244]

Caiaphas (Καϊάφας)—the second name (ἐπίκλησις), according to Josephus, of the High Priest Joseph,[245] who succeeded Simon, son of Camith *c.* AD 18.[246] One of several derogatory nicknames given by the Jews to their priests[247] (this one is thought by some to have been derived ultimately from קוף—monkey),[248] in due course it seems to have been adopted by Caiaphas' descendants as their family name.[249]

---

[235]'Earliest Records', 365. The language of Acts at 1:23 (Ἰωσὴφ τὸν καλούμενον Βαρσαβ(β)ᾶν) and 15:22 (Ἰούδαν τὸν καλούμενον Βαρσαββᾶν) is against that interpretation. The verbs καλέω or ἐπικαλέω regularly mark the use of a second (*i.e.* additional) name. See, for instance, Acts 4:36 (Joseph called Barnabas); 12:12 and 25 (John called Mark), 13:1 (Simeon called Niger). For the patronymic, only the simple genitive is used. See Acts 1:13 (*bis*).

[236]On this, see Cadbury, 'Semitic Personal Names', 48-50—still the best treatment.

[237]*CIJ* II, no. 1243.

[238]Avigad, 'Kidron Valley', 5-6.

[239]*CPJ* III, 189-91 for Egypt; for Asia Minor, RT, 100 (Aphrodisias); *DF*, no. 32 (Hylarrima—Caria); *CIJ* II, nos. 788 and 790 (Corycus); for Rome, see *CIJ* I^2, nos. 155-157, 391, 394-5, 397 and 470.

[240]See A. Cowley, *Aramaic Papyri of the Fifth Century B.C.* (Oxford, 1923) 192, no. 81, l. 3 (Elephantine).

[241]See Noy, no. 126 (formerly *CIJ* I^2, no. 622)—6th-7th century Taranto.

[242]See A. Perkins, *Dura-Europos, Final Report V, Part I*, no. 46.

[243]*CIJ* I^2, no. 379.

[244]For this man, see, *inter al.*, *CPJ* II, nos. 220, 298 and 311.

[245]*Ant.* 18.95—Ἰώσηπον τὸν Καϊάφαν ἐπικαλούμενον.

[246]*Ant.* 18.35. On its Aramaic derivation (Qayyapha), see W. Horbury, 'The "Caiaphas" ossuaries and Joseph Caiaphas', *PEQ* 126 (1994) 37.

Thomas (Θωμᾶς)—from the Aramaic word תאומא, meaning 'twin'. Best seen as a nickname in the Gospels and Acts. Besides the strong, early tradition that the Apostle's formal name was Judas,[250] there is no good evidence that Thomas itself was used by 1st-century Jews as a first name. That only comes much later—*viz.* in a Palestinian synagogue inscription dated roughly to the 6th or 7th century.[251] By that time, Thomas had come to be used widely as a first name, primarily because of its Christian associations.[252] In the Diaspora, the name is not known. The Thomas Benaiah of Dura, thought by Frey and others to have been a Jewish painter working for a Palmyrene patron,[253] is better seen as a Gentile architect.[254]

2. *Greek*

Dorcas (Δορκάς)—'gazelle'. Although this is sometimes taken as the signum (additional name) of Tabitha, the good needlewoman of Joppa,[255] the language of Acts does not support that interpretation. Luke merely comments at 9:36 that Dorcas (a common name in the Graeco-Roman world of his day)[256] is the Greek equivalent of (Aramaic) Tabitha. Among Palestinian Jews, the name is not certainly attested[257] and in the Diaspora it is very rare. To date, Cyrenaica has produced the only examples (two) and one of them is open to doubt![258]

---

[247]Another was Cantheras—from the Greek κάνθαρος—meaning (1) dung-beetle and (2) drinking cup. For the phenomenon in general, see Hachlili, 'Names and Nicknames', 199.

[248]*E.g.* Hachlili, *ibid.* For other explanations, however, see Horbury, 'Caiaphas', 40.

[249]Tosefta, *Yev.* 1:10. On the general phenomenon of nicknames, even unflattering ones, turning into family names, see Naveh, 'Nameless People', 117, especially n. 22.

[250]*Interpreter's Dictionary of the Bible*, *s.v.* Thomas.

[251]Cited by A. Strobel, 'Ein Grabstein aus römischer Zeit in Mukawir', *Rev. Bib.* 95 (1988) 94 n. 6.

[252]Among the many recently published examples, note *SEG* 35 (1985) no. 1485 (Antioch); 36 (1986) no. 1185 (Galatia); 37 (1987) no. 1028 (Bithynia); 38 (1988) no. 1632 (Palestine); 39 (1989) no. 1613 (Syria); 40 (1990) no. 849 (Italy).

[253]*CIJ* II, no. 825 for Frey; note also Schürer (revised) III, 10.

[254]So, correctly, Milik, 'Le couvercle de Bethphagé' (cit. n. 14) 82 n. 1.

[255]As, for instance, by G. Mayer, *Die jüdische Frau in der hellenistisch-römischen Antike* (Kohlhammer, 1987) no. 769.

[256]For examples, see *New Docs.* IV, 177-8; Fraser-Matthews I, *s. v.* Δόρκας and Solin, *Griechische Personennamen*, 1047-8.

Peter (Πέτρος) Originally not a name in its own right but simply the Greek word used to translate the Apostle Sim(e)on's Aramaic nickname, Kepha (כיפא), meaning 'rock'.[259] Although Peter did develop eventually into a personal name, which came to be used widely by Christians,[260] there is no evidence that the Jews themselves ever made it part of their onomastikon. In Jewish inscriptions from the Graeco-Roman world, the name appears only once and then as no more than the baptismal name of a Jew who had converted to Christianity.[261]

3. *Latin*

Justus (Ἰοῦστος)—'just man'—an alternative nickname for Joseph, also called Barsabbas (no. 24 above). Formulated possibly in the Graeco-Roman environment of Tiberias,[262] it corresponds exactly to Hebrew הצדיק—one of several honorific nicknames to be found in the Palestinian Jewish onomastikon.[263] In 1st-century Palestine, no other instances are known of Justus as a second name,[264] and even as a first it is far from common.[265] The only Justus known from the ossuaries was a Diasporan Jew,[266] and of the three mentioned by Josephus, one was actually born, named and reared in Rome[267] (he was Josephus' second son).[268] The later evidence from Palestine suggests

[257]Ilan, 194, no. 37, has read the name at *BJ* 4.145, where Josephus writes of the Zealot hit-man, John, Δορκάδος οὗτος ἐκαλεῖτο παῖς κατὰ τὴν ἐπιχώριον γλῶσσαν. Others, however, have taken to these words to refer to John's patronymic—*viz.* בר צביא. For discussion, see Bagatti-Milik, 88.

[258]Lüderitz, no. 46g—Δορκ[άς?]; Appendix 7—Δόρκα.

[259]Jn. 1:42.

[260]For some Cilician examples, see *MAMA* III, nos. 659-64.

[261]For Petrus, formerly Papario, son of Olympius the Jew, see Noy, no. 8 (5th century).

[262]A Galilaean background for Joseph Barsabbas is implied in Acts 1:21-22. Tiberias in Galilee is the only place in Palestine where the name Justus is securely attested—Josephus, Loeb index, *s.v.* Justus.

[263]For this and analogous nicknames—*e.g.* 'the modest', see Hachlili, 'Names and Nicknames', 198.

[264]The background of Jesus Justus, Paul's co-worker (Col. 4:11), is unknown.

[265]As is Zadok, its Hebrew equivalent. The only example in Josephus occurs at *Ant.* 18.4.

[266]*CIJ* II, no. 1233a.

[267]*Vita* 5.

[268]*Vita* 5 and 427.

no great increase in the popularity of the name. At Murabba'at it is unattested. Beth She'arim and Jaffa have produced just three examples apiece,[269] not all of them Palestinian Jews,[270] and Capernaum only one.[271] In the Diaspora, the picture is rather different. At Rome, the name was enormously popular,[272] largely, one suspects, because it was so prevalent in the wider community.[273] And there is a scattering of examples from other parts of the empire—*e.g.* Greece, Gaul and Asia Minor.[274] Among the Jews of Egypt and Cyrene, however, the name was scarcely used. The only certain case so far attested is an Alexandrian Jew, buried at Jaffa.[275]

Mark (Μάρκος) The second name of John, Barnabas' cousin and missionary-assistant (no. 22 above). The circumstances in which he acquired this *epiklesis*—a name not otherwise known among Palestinian Jews—is not known,[276] but probably it was during his travels abroad. The Gentiles he was seeking to convert would have found Mark a far easier name to cope with than the outlandish and unfamiliar Yehohanan.[277] In the Diasporan onomastikon Mark occurs with fair frequency, not as a name on its own,[278] but only as the praenomen of Jews who had acquired the Roman citizenship.[279]

---

[269] *BS* II, nos. 125, 127 and 190. For Jaffa, see *CIJ* II, nos. 928, 929 and 946.
[270] *CIJ* II, no. 928 (now Horbury-Noy, no. 148).
[271] *DF*, no. 75 (formerly *CIJ* II, no. 983).
[272] See, for instance, *CIJ* I^2, nos. 13, 125, 224, 245, 252, 357-359.
[273] See Kajanto, *Latin Cognomina*, 252 for over 600 examples.
[274] *CIJ* I^2, no. 721a (Greece); *BE* 89 (1976) no. 798 (Gaul); for Asia Minor, see L. Robert in *Hellenica* 11-12 (1960) 260-2.
[275] See n. 270 above.
[276] For discussion of John Mark's second name, see *New Docs.* I, 95.
[277] See above, nn. 66 and 67, for the rare Diasporan instances of this name. Many Diasporan second names are of this 'user-friendly' variety—the most well-known being Paul and Silvanus, the missionary names of Saul and Silas respectively. Among the many other examples in our sources, note *CIJ* I^2, nos. 108 and 140 (Rome); RT, 5—'b', ll. 20, 28 and 30 (Aphrodisias).
[278] As such, it is found only in Cyrenaica. See Lüderitz, nos. 33d and 67d and f.
[279] See, for instance, Lüderitz, no. 71, l. 5 (Berenice); *CIJ* I^2, nos. 284 (Rome) and 776 (Hierapolis).

IV. General Character of the Palestinian Jewish Onomastikon

Now that the individual name-profiles have been completed, it is time to return to the general questions raised in the introduction—*viz.* were the names borne by Palestinian Jews in Acts significantly different either from those current in the contemporary Diaspora or those favoured by their descendants in Palestine in the 2nd and 3rd centuries? If so, what does that tell us about the mental outlook of 1st-century Palestinian Jews?

That there were considerable differences between the onomastic usages of 1st-century Palestinian Jews and those of their brethren in the contemporary Diaspora is the conclusion that must surely be drawn from the evidence presented above. Not only are the in-group nicknames found in Palestine largely absent in the Diaspora but, more often than not, first names common in the one turn out to be rare or even unattested in the other (only Jesus, Joseph and Simon occur frequently in both). Some of the reasons for these differences are not hard to deduce. Take the nicknames. In Palestine, they were a virtual necessity because so many people tended to have the same first name.[280] In the brief list of Jews given at the start of this study, for instance, there occur three cases of Joseph and no less than four each of Judas, Simon and John. And it is in their ranks, not among the men with rare names like Agabus, Gamaliel and Menahem, that all the second names discussed above are found. But for Diasporan Jews, such as those of 1st-century Egypt and Cyrene, such a need hardly ever arose. Centuries of habitation in a multi-ethnic environment had led to (a) a great reduction in the practices of papponymy and patronymy[281] and (b) the widespread adoption of Gentile names. In the onomastikon of Jewish Edfu, for instance, Egyptian, Greek, Latin and general semitic elements are all to be found.[282] The result of such eclecticism was to eliminate almost entirely the need for in-group nicknames. The fourteen Edfu stemmata published by Tcherikover[283] show an

[280]On this, see now Naveh, 'Nameless People', 116-7.

[281]For the rare examples of papponymy at Edfu, see *CPJ* II, 118. For the infrequent use of patronymy among the Cyrenaican Jews, see the Berenice donor list (*DF*, no. 100).

[282]*CPJ* II, 116.

[283]*CPJ* II, 117.

amazing range of names, even within individual families. Palestinian-style nicknames are not wholly absent but they are exceedingly rare.[284]

But what of the first names? Why is there so little correspondence between the Palestinian and Diasporan onomastika in this regard too? It certainly was not because of lack of contact between the Jews of Palestine and those in the Diaspora.[285] And it cannot be because there was a general aversion among Diasporan Jews to Hebrew names. We have seen that in the onomastika of both Egypt and Cyrene there is a clear Hebrew element. It is just that the names that comprise that element tend to be different from those in vogue in Palestine. With the Jews of Egypt, Jacob, for instance, was a regular favourite. Yet in 1st-century Palestine, that name, in common with other patriarchal names, was hardly used. How are we to account for such differences?

If we focus upon the names that dominate the 1st-century Palestinian Jewish onomastikon, we are struck immediately by the Hasmonaean associations of so many of them.[286] Take Salomezion, for instance, unquestionably the most popular woman's name of the day,[287] for all its absence from Acts.[288] It had not been used by Jews at all until it had entered their onomastikon with Alexander Jannaeus' queen, the Pharisees' darling, Alexandra Salomezion.[289] The name Mary (Miriam) has a similar history. For all its antiquity, there is not much evidence of its use by Palestinian Jews until it was borne by Herod's popular Hasmonaean wife, the (in Jewish eyes) martyred Mariamme. From then on, there was an explosion in its popularity.[290] On the male side, note that Judas, Simon, John, Eleazar and Mattathias all have Hasmonaean connections: these names belonged to the five members of the dynasty who had done the most to throw off the yoke of the Seleucids and secure political independence for Israel.[291] It is these associations, I suggest, that made these names so popular in Palestine and, conversely, so little used in the Diaspora. Palestinian

---

[284]For Theodotus-Niger and Jesus-Sambathion, see stemmata nos. 1 and 5, *ibid.*

[285]Among the many pieces of evidence for contact between Egypt/Cyrenaica and Palestine, note Acts 2:10; Mk. 15:21; *Ant.* 18.159-60; Avigad, 'Kidron Valley', *passim.*

[286]The point is observed by Ilan, 'Women's Names', 192, but not developed there. For a more detailed treatment, see the same author, 'The Names of the Hasmoneans (*sic*) in the Second Temple Period', *Eretz Israel* 19 (1987) 238-41 (in Heb.).

[287]See n. 5 above.

[288]In its abbreviated form, Salome, however, it does appear in the Gospels at Mk. 16:1.

[289]Schürer (revised) I, 229-32.

[290]Ilan, 'Women's Names', 191-2.

Jews of the procuratorial period still had to come to terms with direct Gentile rule (recently re-imposed by Rome)[292] and still thought (mistakenly) that a fight for political independence was winnable. Hence the First Jewish War (AD 66-73). But centuries of living under the Ptolemies had inured the Jews of Egypt and Cyrene to the idea of permanent control by others. With the struggle for independence in Palestine they consequently had nothing to do[293] and towards the war refugees who ended up in their midst in AD 73 they were decidedly hostile.[294] To people such as these, names like Judas and John, Eleazar and Salomezion with their patriotic overtones will have meant very little. When they wanted Hebrew names for their children, as they did occasionally, it was to the distant past, not contemporary Palestine, that they turned. Hence the distinctive patriarchal/matriarchal element in the Jewish onomastikon of both Egypt and Cyrenaica. In the latter, Sarah, a name barely attested in 1st-century Palestine, ranks among the most popular of all the women's names.[295]

But it is not just differences between the names borne by 1st-century Palestinian and Diasporan Jews that our evidence has shown up. Clear shifts within the Palestinian onomastikon itself over the first three centuries AD have been indicated too. Take the names borne by the Herods, their immediate entourage and, on occasion, their fellow travellers—*e.g.*, Agrippa, Alexander, Berenice and Herod itself. Never very widespread even under the Herods, they virtually dropped out of use altogether once the dynasty had been suppressed by Rome and it was no longer expedient for anyone to adopt them. As for the Hasmonaean names, here too there is clear evidence of a waning in popularity. In the papyri from the Murabba'at caves, most of which date to the period of the second Jewish uprising against Rome (AD 132-135), all are still in regular use. Simon crops up the most often (it was, of course, Bar Kokhba's personal name). Eleazar and Judas, John and Matthew are all attested and Mariamme (Mary) and Salome(zion) the most frequently mentioned women's names.[296] Only one non-Hasmo-

[291]For the beginnings of the Hasmonaean dynasty, see A.H.M. Jones, *The Herods of Judaea* (Oxford, 1938) 7-10. For Eleazar's heroic self-sacrifice at the battle of Beth Zacharia, see B. Bar-Kochva, *Judas Maccabaeus: The Jewish Struggle against the Seleucids* (Cambridge, 1989) ch. 13.

[292]Smallwood, *Jews under Roman Rule*, 199-200.

[293]See n. 2 above.

[294]*BJ* 7.409-19. For discussion, see *CPJ* I, 79-80.

[295]For examples, see Lüderitz, 225.

[296]Ilan, 'Women's Names', 195-9, *s.vv.* Johanna, Mariamme, Salome (Salomezion) and Shappira.

naean name enters into serious competition with them—the ever-popular Joseph. Patriarchal names scarcely figure. But the evidence from Beth She'arim in Galilee, which dates mainly from the high point of the Patriarchate, shows a complete reversal of this situation. Hasmonaean names now form a distinct minority. Judas, Simon, John and Mary still occur, but in far from overwhelming numbers. For Matthew there is but a single attestation. Eleazar and Salome(zion) do not appear at all. In popularity they have now been overtaken by more traditional names—*viz.* Jacob, Isaac, Sarah and Samuel[297]—names which were hardly in evidence in the 1st and early 2nd centuries. This onomastic change is revolutionary and it is hard not to connect it with the better documented changes that had taken place in the political sphere—the abandonment by almost everyone of all hopes of political independence, the wearied acceptance of Roman rule for the indefinite future and the determination to salvage and cling to as much as was possible of the Jewish heritage.[298]

I am not, of course, suggesting that choice of a name was simply a matter of political attitude. Family traditions clearly entered into the picture too. In the Goliath family from 1st-century Jericho, for instance, the name Yehoezer crops up seven times over three generations.[299] And in the ossuary inscriptions from Jerusalem relating to the Qallon family (also 1st-century) a small number of names (*e.g.*, Joseph, Simon, Yoezer) recur repeatedly.[300] Social status and cultural orientation were not unimportant either. Greek names tended to be the preserve of the rich and well-educated. Among the heavily Aramaised peasantry of Galilee they are not much found, the Apostles Andrew and Philip notwithstanding. But the general patterning of the evidence studied here—and there is a great deal of it—is best explained on the assumption that political factors often did exert a considerable, even if largely unconscious, influence on name-choice. If I am right in this, we must view the high incidence of Hasmonaean names both in Acts and our other 1st-century sources as no coincidence. It points to the broad sympathies of the mass of Palestinian Jews in the first decades of direct Roman rule—sympathies which made them prepared to risk everything in AD 66 in a Maccabaean-style fight for freedom.

---

[297]See name index at *BS* II, 227-8.
[298]Avi-Yonah, *Jews of Palestine*, chs. I-III.
[299]Hachlili, 'Goliath family', 54 and 66.
[300]*CIJ* II, nos. 1350-5.

Appendix: Palestinian Jews in Acts—the Doubtful Cases

Under consideration here are those nine individuals for whom a Palestinian Jewish origin either has been claimed or deemed possible. Only in two or perhaps three cases (Aeneas, Philip and possibly Nicanor) does the onomastic evidence suggest that this is likely. Of the remainder, most probably came from the Diaspora. Two (Rhoda and Tertullus) may not even have been Jews at all.

Aeneas—the paralytic cured and converted by Peter (Acts 9:33-35). Certainly he was Palestinian—he was a long-time resident of Lydda/Diospolis[301]—and quite possibly Jewish. The name Aeneas had entered the Palestinian Jewish onomastikon early—it first[302] occurs in the reign of Hyrcanus I (135/4-104 BC)—and was still part of it at the time of the First Jewish War (AD 66-73).[303] It continued in use among Palestinian Jews until at least the 4th century AD.[304] The name was also current in the Diaspora. Note *CPJ* I no. 24.23 (Trikomia, Fayum—174 BC), for a Ptolemaic example and Trebilco, *Jewish Communities*, 70-71, for a probable case from Acroenus in the Roman province of Asia.

Nicanor ('man-conquering')—one of the Seven (Acts 6:5). On the evidence available, it is marginally more likely that this man came from the Diaspora than Palestine. While there are no contemporary Palestinian Nicanors, 1st-century Jews of that name are known from Egypt[305] and Cyrene.[306] Note, however, that names either very similar or directly comparable to Nicanor are found in the 1st-century Palestinian Jewish onomastikon. Both Nicandros and Nicolaus[307] occur on the Jerusalem ossuaries, Josephus mentions a Nicomedes[308] and in John 3:1-10 we meet the Pharisee Nicodemus.

---

301 Acts 9:33.

302 *Ant.* 14.248.

303 *BJ* 5.326-8.

304 *CIJ* II, no. 1209 from Touba, south of the Dead Sea.

305 *CIJ* II, nos. 1256 and 1491 (now Horbury-Noy, nos. 153 and 67), from Alexandria and Leontopolis respectively.

306 Lüderitz, no. 7a, l. 28.

307 *CIJ* II, nos. 1273 (Nicandros) and 1279 (Nicolaus)—the authenticity of the latter has been doubted, however.

308 *BJ* 2.451.

Parmenas ('remaining true')—one of the Seven (Acts 6:5). The language of Acts implies that he was a Jew rather than a proselyte. The name itself and particularly the ending -ας suggests he must have come originally from a Doric-speaking Diasporan community.[309] Although the name is found occasionally in non-Jewish contexts,[310] there are no other Jewish examples.

Prochoros ('leader of the dance')—one of the Seven (Acts 6:5). A rare name, found apparently only here.[311] A Diasporan rather than a Palestinian origin is more likely for this Jew. While names with pagan cultic associations are common among Greek-speaking Diasporan Jews,[312] those in Palestine itself tended to avoid them.

Rhoda ('rose')—the servant (παιδίσκη) of the mother of John Mark (Acts 12:13). Although a Jewish identity is often assumed for this young woman,[313] it is more likely that she was, in origin at least, a Gentile slave. By the time of Acts, her name had become well established in the servile onomastikon of the Graeco-Roman world.[314] Besides Rhoda itself, Rhodia, Rhodion, Rhodope and Rhodopis are to be noted as slave names.[315] 'Rose' names, however, were not taken up by Jews until a very much later date and then only occasionally—5th/6th-century Venosa in Italy has produced a Rosa[316] and late 6th-century Antinoopolis in Egypt a Rhosune.[317]

Stephanos ('crown')—one of the Seven (Acts 6:5). Probably a Diasporan Jew. Although the name is very common in the Greek-speaking world,[318] it is rarely found in Palestine[319] and as yet to be

309Such as one of the towns of Cyrene. For names ending in -ας from there, note, for instance, Lüderitz, nos. 13d (Εὐκλείδας) and 36 (Ἀπελλᾶς). For a Cyrenaican ΑΡΡΙΣΤΟΒΟΛΑ (*sic*!) buried at Jerusalem, see Avigad, 'Kidron valley', 5.

310Fraser-Matthews I, *s.v.* Παρμένης.

311Pape-Benseler, *s.v.* Πρόχορος.

312*CPJ* I, 29.

313Most recently by Mayer, *Die jüdische Frau*, no. 465 and Ilan, 'Women's Names', no. 155.

314See L.C. Reilly, *Slaves in Ancient Greece—Slaves from Greek manumission inscriptions* (Chicago, 1978) nos. 2412-6 and Solin, *Griechische Personennamen*, 1104. *Cf. New Docs.* IV, 178.

315Reilly, nos. 2417-26.

316Noy, no. 85 (formerly *CIJ* I², no. 607).

317*CPJ* III, no. 511, l. 4.

318Fraser-Matthews I, *s.v.* Στέφανος and Solin, *Griechische Personennamen*, 1182-1186.

attested among Palestinian Jews. In the Diaspora itself, occurrences are few (because the name had become a favourite with Christians?) and fairly late. The only absolutely certain case is *CIJ* I^2, no. 405 (Rome, 3rd century) but the name could be read also in *CIJ* I^2, no. 404—a damaged graffito (the only decipherable letters are ΣΤΕΦ), possibly of the same date, from the same catacomb.[320]

Tertullus (diminutive of Tertius—'third')—advocate for the Sanhedrin in the hearing against Paul (Acts 24:1.ff.). Although a Jewish identity has been claimed for this man,[321] proof is yet to be found. The language of Acts is ambiguous[322] and the name itself does not appear in the Jewish onomastikon.[323]

Timon—one of the Seven (Acts 6:5). Whether this man was a Greek-speaking Palestinian Jew or from the Diaspora must remain open. There are no other Jewish examples of this common Greek name.

Philippos—the Evangelist and one of the Seven (Acts 21:8), to be distinguished from Philip the Apostle of Acts 1:13.[324] Although a Diasporan origin is sometimes claimed for this man, it is quite likely that he was a hellenised Jew from Palestine itself. (At Acts 21:8, we find him residing at Caesarea.) As shown in the main body of the text, Philip had become well established in the Palestinian Jewish onomastikon by the 1st century AD.[325]

---

[319]Josephus mentions a slave of the Emperor Claudius there called Stephanus. See *BJ* 2.228 and *Ant.* 20.113.

[320]Whether the Aur(elius) Stephanus mentioned in Noy, no. 9 (formerly *CIJ* I^2, no. 642—Pola, 3rd-5th centuries), was a Jew at all is very uncertain.

[321]Most recently at RT, 110.

[322]See K. Lake and H.J. Cadbury in F.J. Foakes Jackson and K. Lake (eds.), *The Beginnings of Christianity*, IV (London, 1933) 297.

[323]For a Godfearer of the name, see RT, 110 (Aphrodisias).

[324]See I.H. Marshall, *Acts of the Apostles*, comm. on Acts 6:1-7.

[325] I would like to thank Prof. J.A. Crook of St John's College, Cambridge for reading and pruning the original draft of this chapter.

Abbreviations

The following abbreviations are used throughout this chapter:

Bagatti-Milik = B. Bagatti and J.T. Milik, *Gli scavi del 'Dominus Flevit'* I, La necropoli del periodo romano (Jerusalem, 1958).

BS II = M. Schwabe and B. Lifshitz, *Beth She'arim* II—*The Greek Inscriptions* (Jerusalem, 1967).

BS III = N. Avigad, *Beth She'arim* III—*Catacombs 12-23* (New Brunswick, N.J., 1976).

CIJ I^2 = J.B. Frey, *Corpus Inscriptionum Iudaicarum* I (Rome, 1936), reprinted with a prolegomenon by B. Lifshitz (New York, 1975).

CIJ II = J.B. Frey, *Corpus Inscriptionum Iudaicarum* II (Rome, 1952).

CIL = *Corpus Inscriptionum Latinarum.*

CPJ = V.A. Tcherikover, A. Fuks and M. Stern, *Corpus Papyrorum Judaicarum* I-III (Cambridge, Mass., 1957-1964).

DF = B. Lifshitz, *Donateurs et Fondateurs dans les synagogues juives* (Paris, 1967).

DJD = P. Benoit, J.T. Milik and R. de Vaux, *Discoveries in the Judaean Desert* II—*Les Grottes de Murabba'at* (Oxford, 1961).

Fraser-Matthews I = P.M. Fraser and E. Matthews (eds.), *A Lexicon of Greek Personal Names* I (Oxford, 1987).

Horbury-Noy = W. Horbury and D. Noy, *Jewish Inscriptions of Graeco-Roman Egypt* (Cambridge, 1992).

IGLS = *Inscriptions grecques et latines de la Syrie.*

Lüderitz = G. Lüderitz, *Corpus jüdischer Zeugnisse aus der Cyrenaika* (Wiesbaden, 1983).

New Docs. = G.H.R. Horsley, *New Documents Illustrating Early Christianity* I-VI (Macquarie University, 1981-1992).

Noy = D. Noy, *Jewish Inscriptions of Western Europe* I (Cambridge, 1993).

Pape-Benseler = W. Pape and G. Benseler, *Wörterbuch der griechischen Eigennamen* (3rd edn.; Braunschweig, 1911).

SEG = *Supplementum Epigraphicum Graecum.*

RT = J. Reynolds and R. Tannenbaum, *Jews and Godfearers at Aphrodisias* (Cambridge, 1987).

Schürer (revised) = E. Schürer, *The History of the Jewish People in the Age of Jesus Christ* I-III, revised by G. Vermes, F. Millar, M. Black and M. Goodman (Edinburgh, 1973-1987).

CHAPTER 5

CHIEF PRIESTS, SADDUCEES, PHARISEES AND SANHEDRIN IN ACTS

Steve Mason

Summary

It is no longer possible to cite a body of historical knowledge about the Jewish leaders as an external guide to interpreting Acts. Rather, historical reconstruction must await patient reading of Luke-Acts, Josephus, and other relevant narratives. In his effort to write a plausible history, 'Luke' distinguishes the powerful, Jerusalem-centred, Sadducean chief priests from the Pharisees, who are popular and influential teachers. Although Jesus faces lethal opposition only from the chief priests, Jewish opposition gradually consolidates behind the chief priests against the church. The priest Josephus has an entirely different perspective, but he shares many of Luke's assumptions. *This agreement is important for historical reconstruction of the groups.*

It may seem odd at the end of the 20th century that one should venture upon a new study of the Jewish leaders in Acts. Acts and every other 1st-century source that mentions these groups have been known for nearly two millennia. If the object is to compare the portrayal in Acts with what is known historically about the chief priests, Sadducees, Pharisees, and Sanhedrin, has this not been done many times already? Remarkably, it is only within the last decade that scholars have begun seriously to study the function of the Jewish leaders in the narrative of Acts. And it is no longer (or not yet) possible to speak of 'what we know' historically about the Jewish leaders.

These two phenomena are related, for the new focus on the roles of Jewish leaders in particular texts results from the same intellectual forces that brought down the house of cards that formerly passed for historical knowledge. To be sure, intensive scholarly energy on our theme, following the rise of critical history and the emancipation of European Jews, produced great manuals of historical knowledge about the New Testament *Umwelt*. But since the turn of the century, broad intellectual movements exposing the problems of bias, perspective, context, construction, particularity, otherness, and diversity have filtered through the academy.[1] These general intellectual tendencies have been catalysed by particular advances: Jacob Neusner's reappraisal of the Rabbinic corpus, which provided much of the fuel for old constructions of the Jewish leaders, shows that this literature makes a coherent statement about its time of composition, not about the 1st century.[2] Archaeological discoveries, the recovery of lost writings, and the reappraisal of known texts have further helped to overturn the first critical syntheses, which tended to cobble together a monolithic system of thought from bits and pieces in a variety of sources.[3] The hallmark of our time is a profound historical agnosticism.[4]

---

[1]H.C. Kee, *Knowing the Truth: A Sociological Approach to New Testament Interpretation* (Minneapolis: Fortress, 1989) 1-64.

[2]J. Neusner, *The Rabbinic Traditions about the Pharisees before 70* (3 vols.; Leiden: E.J. Brill, 1971) III: 234-8.

[3]*Cf.* M. Smith, 'Palestinian Judaism in the First Century', in M. Davis (ed.), *Israel: Its Role in Civilization* (New York: JTSA, 1956); Neusner, *Rabbinic Traditions*, III, 320-368; R.A. Kraft and G.W.E. Nickelsburg (eds.), *Early Judaism and its Modern Interpreters* (Atlanta: Scholars Press, 1986) 1-30; G.G. Porton, 'Diversity in Post-Biblical Judaism', in Kraft and Nickelsburg, 57-80.

[4]S. Mason, 'The Problem of the Pharisees in Modern Scholarship', in J. Neusner (ed.), *Historical and Literary Studies* (Approaches to Ancient Judaism NS, vol. 3; 1993) 103-40.

This dissolution of reliable historical knowledge has rendered it all the more urgent to understand what is in each particular text. Since we do not possess the past itself, but only a few stories and physical remains from it, we should first try to understand what we have, rather than what we lack. So New Testament scholars have begun to return to the texts for their own sake, not merely as *sources* for patchwork historical reconstructions, and they have been greatly assisted by a new *rapprochement* with literary criticism.[5] They have begun to read the Gospels and Acts more curiously, with attention to rhetoric[6], plot and character, implied readers, narrators, and authors.[7] So we have seen a spate of studies on the Jewish leaders not as historical figures but as *literary characters*: in Matthew,[8] Mark,[9] Luke-Acts,[10] Josephus,[11] and Rabbinic literature.[12]

The new concern with texts as coherent stories does not preclude historical questioning. But it does mean that historical questions should not be asked too quickly, as they were before.[13] History can no longer be done positivistically, by looking at discrete statements in various authors and asking whether these statements are right or wrong as expressions of fact. Evidence only has meaning in context, as part of someone's story. If we do not know what it means in context,

---

[5]N. Petersen, *Literary Criticism for New Testament Critics* (Philadelphia: Fortress Press, 1978).

[6]G.A. Kennedy, *New Testament Interpretation through Rhetorical Criticism* (Chapel Hill: University of North Carolina, 1984).

[7]E.P. Sanders and M. Davies, *Studying the Synoptic Gospels* (London: SCM, 1989) 224-251.

[8]D.R.A. Hare, *The Theme of Jewish Persecution of Christians in the Gospel According to St. Matthew* (SNTSMS 6; Cambridge: CUP, 1967); S. van Tilborg, *The Jewish Leaders in Matthew* (Leiden: E.J. Brill, 1972).

[9]M.J. Cook, *Mark's Treatment of the Jewish Leaders* (NovTSup 51; Leiden: E.J. Brill, 1978).

[10]J. Ziesler, 'Luke and the Pharisees', *NTS* 25 (1978-79) 146-57; R.L. Brawley, *Luke-Acts and the Jews: Conflict, Apology, and Conciliation* (SBLMS 33; Atlanta: Scholars Press, 1987); J.T. Sanders, *The Jews in Luke-Acts* (Philadelphia: Fortress Press, 1987); R.P. Carroll, 'Luke's Portrayal of the Pharisees', *CBQ* 50 (1988) 604-21; J.A. Darr, *On Character Building: The Reader and the Rhetoric of Characterization in Luke-Acts* (LCBI; Louisville: Westminster/John Knox, 1992).

[11]G. Baumbach, 'The Sadducees in Josephus', in L.H. Feldman and G. Hata (eds.), *Josephus, the Bible, and History* (Detroit: Wayne State Press, 1989) 173-95; C. Thoma, 'The High Priesthood in the Judgment of Josephus' in Feldman and Hata (eds.), *Josephus*, 196-215; S. Mason, *Flavius Josephus on the Pharisees: A Composition-Critical Study* (SPB 39; Leiden: E.J. Brill, 1991).

[12]Neusner, *Rabbinic Traditions*.

[13]Neusner, *Rabbinic Traditions*, III, 320-68.

we cannot use it for historical purposes. In the wake of the collapse of old constructions of the Jewish leadership groups, every new historical hypothesis must demonstrate a grasp of the stories from the period, show how an author chose to use the leaders in particular roles, and state how this particular historical reconstruction plausibly explains these many uses: if hypothesis X is right, then authors A, B, C, and D came to their views of the matter in this way.[14] The modern reconstruction will not be the same as any ancient story. But it must plausibly show how the ancient stories—the evidence to be explained—came into being.

These considerations make the following study of the Jewish leaders in Acts quite different from what one might have come up with even fifty years ago, in spite of the fact that the 'evidence' has remained constant. First, the author of Acts wrote the work as a sequel to the Gospel of Luke, so interpreters of Acts can only engage the story properly by first examining the Gospel. We cannot pull out Gamaliel's speech or some other episode as somehow reflective of Luke's community, but must start at the beginning and deal with the whole story. Second, we cannot assume any historical knowledge about the groups in question as an external referent. And since an original historical investigation would require prior analysis of all relevant texts, it is beyond our scope. Jacob Neusner,[15] Ellis Rivkin,[16] and Anthony Saldarini[17] have all tried their hands at historical reconstructions of the Pharisees (or several leadership groups[18]) in the new way—*after* first interpreting each relevant source in its own world—and they are to be applauded for realising what is required. Still, none of their proposals yet commands sufficient support to serve as a secure body of knowledge. Strangely, the two most recent reconstructions of the Jewish groups,[19] while recognising the negative implications of Neusner's work, do not seem to see the need to explain the ancient stories in any comprehensive way.[20]

---

[14]S. Mason, *Flavius Josephus on the Pharisees*, 1-17.

[15]J. Neusner, *From Politics to Piety: The Emergence of Pharisaic Judaism* (Englewood Cliffs, NJ: Prentice-Hall, 1973).

[16]E. Rivkin, *A Hidden Revolution* (Nashville: Abingdon, 1978)

[17]A.J. Saldarini, *Pharisees, Scribes and Sadducees in Palestinian Society: A Sociological Approach* (Wilmington: Michael Glazier, 1988).

[18]Saldarini, *Pharisees*.

[19]E.P. Sanders, *Judaism: Practice & Belief 63 BCE – 66 CE* (Philadelphia: TPI, 1992) 317-490; L.L. Grabbe, *Judaism from Cyrus to Hadrian*, 2 vols. (Minneapolis: Fortress Press, 1992) II, 463-554.

Instead of comparing Acts with 'history', which we do not have, I propose to compare it with the only contemporary Jewish narratives that mention these Jewish leaders: the writings of Flavius Josephus. Luke-Acts is arguably the most important early Christian statement on the Jewish leaders, because of its unparalleled size and historical self-conception, and the Josephan corpus is without question the most important non-Christian witness. By formulating interpretations of the Jewish leaders in these two narrative sets, I hope to offer something of a *prolegomenon* to historical reconstruction.

The secondary literature on Luke, Acts, Josephus, and each of the Jewish groups is so vast that responsible interaction would have produced a multi-volume book rather than an article. In the available space I can only summarise three recent and comprehensive interpretations of the Jewish leaders in Luke-Acts, before proceeding with my own analysis of the primary texts. Parenthetical notes indicate studies that I have found unusually helpful, whether I agree with them or not.

I. The State of the Question

In 1987 Robert L. Brawley[21] and Jack T. Sanders[22] published the first two comprehensive studies of the Jewish leaders in Acts. Each knew the other's work in progress, but they came to quite different assessments of Luke's overall purpose and of his use of the Jewish leaders. Five years later, John A. Darr[23] tried to refine their efforts with closer attention to narratological method. The common concern of all three to identify the literary function of Jewish leadership groups in Luke-Acts marks an advance over previous work and provides a useful starting point.

---

[20]This judgement requires justification, which I hope to provide in a volume with A.J. Saldarini on *Pharisees in Context* (Approaches to Ancient Judaism NS, USFSHJ; Atlanta: Scholars Press). The following study will already make clear, however, what is not adequately explained by Sanders and Grabbe.

[21]Brawley, *Luke-Acts and the Jews*.

[22]J.T. Sanders, *The Jews in Luke-Acts*.

[23]Darr, *On Character Building*.

1. *Jack T. Sanders*

Sanders' interpretation of Luke's social context follows that of Robert Maddox[24]: this Gentile Christian community faces an identity crisis caused by the competing claims of Judaism to the same texts and tradition. Luke and his readers share a Pauline outlook.[25] The legitimacy of the young church's interpretation of scripture with reference to Christ is challenged by the established Jewish community and by Jewish Christians who call for Torah observance.[26] Luke's response is to show that the Jewish people is misguided, that it has both rejected God and been rejected by God. Gentile inclusion is now divinely authorised; non-Christian Jews and Jewish Christians who seek to remain observant have been written off by God.[27]

Sanders arrives at these conclusions after considering first how the main leadership groups and Jerusalem function in Luke-Acts (chs. 1-2). With the exception of two incidental references to High Priests (Lk. 3:1; Acts 19:14), the chief priests and elders along with their associated scribes are consistently hostile to Jesus and the young church.[28] The attitude of these leaders provides one important reference point for Luke's view of the Jews. Luke even implies that it was Jews who executed Jesus; here and elsewhere he imagines Jewish soldiers administered by the chief priests.[29] The four Herods in Luke-Acts also persecute Jesus' group (John the Baptist, Jesus, James) when behaving as Jews; when acting as secular leaders, however, they tend to acquit (Jesus and Paul[30]). Jerusalem functions as the '*locus classicus* of hostility to God, to his purposes, to his messengers'.[31] Luke normally uses the term Sanhedrin (συνέδριον) for a place, the 'courtroom' of the Jewish council, though he can also use it of the assembled body.[32]

Acknowledging the apparent ambivalence of Luke-Acts toward the Jewish people, who sometimes support Jesus and the church but sometimes oppose them, Sanders proposes that one look first at the speeches to determine Luke's fundamental view. There he finds a

---

[24]R. Maddox, *The Purpose of Luke-Acts* (Edinburgh: T. & T. Clark, 1982).
[25]J.T. Sanders, *The Jews in Luke-Acts*, 316-7.
[26]*Ibid.*, 130, 314.
[27]*Ibid.*, 54, 110-1, 317.
[28]*Ibid.*, 20.
[29]*Ibid.*, 9-12.
[30]*Ibid.*, 20-2.
[31]*Ibid.*, 26.
[32]*Ibid.*, 4-5.

consistent portrait: 'the Jews are and always have been wilfully ignorant of the purposes and plans of God expressed in their familiar scriptures...'. This view is 'repeated over and over in every possible way *ad nauseam*'.[33] Jesus' keynote sermon in Nazareth (Lk. 4:16-27) and Paul's final assessment (Acts 28:25-28) serve to frame the other speeches as declarations of Jewish rejection. Although there was a time in which the prospect of repentance and salvation was duly offered, by Stephen's speech in Acts 7 repentance is no longer an option.[34] If one then interprets the Jews' narrative actions in light of the speeches one finds that, in spite of early support for Jesus and the church, ultimately 'the Jews have *become* what they from the first *were*'[35]: intransigent opponents of the divine will who are rejected by God.[36]

With this portrait of the Jewish leaders and people in hand, Sanders turns to the Pharisees. The problem is that they appear quite friendly to Jesus throughout the Gospel, with their dinner invitations, warning to flee Herod Antipas, and absence from the passion narrative.[37] Most of their disputes concern the proper interpretation of the Law.[38] In Acts, the Pharisees remain basically friendly, as the speech of Gamaliel and their siding with Paul in the Sanhedrin indicate; strangely, the only obstructionist Pharisees are the Christian Pharisees of Acts 15:5, who insist that Gentile Christians be circumcised and observe Torah, and whose views Luke rejects.[39]

Sanders finds in this episode the key to Luke's use of the Pharisees. In the Gospel and here in Acts, 'Pharisees' stand for those Jewish Christians who dismiss Gentile Christianity (and Luke's community) as illegitimate; Luke's stories about Jesus' eating with sinners and Sabbath freedom are meant to confront those Jewish Christians.[40] The Pharisees/Jewish-Christians appear to desire Jesus' company, but they do not understand him or his programme. They are therefore the hypocrites whose leaven must be avoided, and Luke dismisses them along with non-Christian Jews.[41] But Luke also uses the friendly non-Christian Pharisees of Acts, Gamaliel and the others on the council, to

---

[33]*Ibid.*, 63.
[34]*Ibid.*, 54-5.
[35]*Ibid.*, 81.
[36]*Ibid.*, 81-3.
[37]*Ibid.*, 85-8.
[38]*Ibid.*, 90-1.
[39]*Ibid.*, 94-5.
[40]*Ibid.*, 95.
[41]*Ibid.*, 110-1.

'underscore the linkage between Christianity and the ancestral Israelite religion'.[42] Thus, Pharisees fulfil two roles in Luke's effort to exclude Judaism from Christianity: they represent Christians who do not see the implications of Jesus' coming for Judaism (in Pauline terms) and they serve as sort of official Jewish greeters and guarantors of the Christian movement.[43]

Sanders devotes nearly half of his book[44] to a linear reading of Luke-Acts in order to justify his thematic analysis *in situ*.

2. *Robert L. Brawley*

Brawley agrees with Sanders that Luke-Acts comes from a Pauline church, but the rest of his analysis is diametrically opposite. Far from providing a rationale for the severance of Christianity from Judaism, Brawley's Luke seeks to reunite Pauline Christianity with Judaism, to draw 'authentic Jews toward Christianity and authentic Christians toward Judaism'.[45] This *rapprochement* requires the rehabilitation of Paul, which is the main burden of Acts. In the face of Jewish and Jewish-Christian criticism, Paul must be shown a faithful Jew, in direct continuity with the unimpeachably Jewish Peter.[46] In Brawley's view, Jewish repentance and salvation remain options through to the very end of Acts; even Acts 28 claims that some of the Roman Jews were 'persuaded' by Paul (Acts 28:24).[47]

In support of his thesis, Brawley takes a minimalist approach to the text. That is, whereas most scholars have seen particular figures and situations as paradigmatic of the Jewish/Christian problem at Luke's time of writing, Brawley insists that they be confined to their plain sense. Thus, the rejection at Nazareth does not foreshadow *universal* Jewish rejection, but reflects only the rejection of some people at one place and one time.[48] Acts does not show a steady movement away from Jerusalem to the ends of the earth, because there is a constant return to Jerusalem throughout.[49] Acts 1:8 ('to the ends of the

[42]*Ibid.*, 97.
[43]*Ibid.*, 112.
[44]*Ibid.*, 156-299.
[45]Brawley, *Luke-Acts and the Jews*, 159.
[46]*Ibid.*, 42-3; 66-7.
[47]*Ibid.*, 141.
[48]*Ibid.*, 26.
[49]*Ibid.*, 36.

earth') remains unfulfilled in the text itself. Unlike Paul's own letters, Luke-Acts knows of no Pauline Gentile mission; Paul has a *Diaspora* mission, which includes Jews and Gentiles, and he puts more effort into the Jewish mission.[50] Most important, the 'architectonic' structure of Acts highlights not the spread of *Christianity*, but the parallel between Peter (chs. 1-12) and Paul (chs. 13-28).[51] The many standard legitimation techniques of hellenistic literature used by Luke confirm that Luke is out to defend Paul.[52]

How do the Jewish leaders fit into Luke's agenda? Like many others,[53] Brawley is impressed by the friendliness of the Pharisees in Luke-Acts—a disposition that confounds the form-critical staple that hostility to the Pharisees increases as the synoptic tradition develops.[54] Although Luke is critical of their character, tosses in a stock slander (Lk. 16:14), and takes over some negative comments from his sources, he has a marked concern to present the Pharisees as 'respected and authoritative representatives of Judaism who can hover close to the edge of Christianity. Moreover, Luke likely expects some of his readers to identify favourably with the Pharisees, and he uses them as a point of contact...'.[55] Brawley notes Luke's assumption that the Pharisees are the most eminent Jewish group, to which he finds parallels in Josephus and Rabbinic literature.[56]

By contrast, the Sadducees are inauthentic representatives of Israel, who are unmasked by the Pharisee Gamaliel, 'the genuine Jew on the verge of affirming Christianity'.[57] Brawley parallels Gamaliel's speech, which implicitly makes the Sadducees 'God-fighters' for their determination to expunge Christianity, with Josephus' portrait of the Sadducees as rejecting divine intervention in human affairs.[58] He suggests that Josephus and the Rabbis exaggerate when they claim that the Pharisees dominate the Sadducees in public life (*cf.* Josephus, *Ant.* 18.17), proposing rather that the Sadducees controlled the Sanhedrin through most of the 1st century, though they must have accommodated the Pharisees somewhat.[59]

---

[50]*Ibid.*, 49.
[51]*Ibid.*, 42-3.
[52]*Ibid.*, 51-67.
[53]*Cf.* Ziesler, 'Luke and the Pharisees', 146-57.
[54]Brawley, *Luke-Acts and the Jews*, 85-6.
[55]*Ibid.*, 84.
[56]*Ibid.*, 95-6.
[57]*Ibid.*, 97-8.
[58]*Ibid.*, 117.
[59]*Ibid.*, 113.

Most closely allied with the Sadducees in Luke-Acts are the chief priests, the leading antagonists of Jesus and the church.[60] Luke distinguishes ordinary priests, such as the Baptist's father Zechariah (*cf.* also Acts 6:7), from these wealthy aristocrats.[61] Jerusalem and the Temple, which Luke sees as interchangeable, are important for him not primarily as the *locus* of opposition to God (*pace* Sanders) but as the navel of the earth, the meeting point between heaven and earth.[62]

As for the Jewish people, Brawley disagrees with Sanders' claim that their response can be categorised as univocal rejection. He finds two responses, depending upon whether they act on their own or are led by the chief priests. In the former case they repent, and repentance remains a live option through the end of Acts (28:24). There is no final repudiation of the Jews in Acts.

3. *John A. Darr*

Darr's work brings the question of Luke's characters to a new plane of sophistication. He seeks to develop 'a reader-response (or pragmatic) model attuned to the Greco-Roman literary culture of the first century'.[63] Of the Jewish groups, Darr discusses only the Pharisees; yet his crucial methodological observations warrant mention here.

Against both formalist and reader-oriented literary theory, Darr holds that the meaning of texts is produced by the dialogue between text and reader. When a text is read, it becomes a literary 'work'. Texts necessarily assume some knowledge on the part of readers because they leave all sorts of gaps to be filled in. The reader's extratextual resources—here, knowledge of Greek language, ancient Mediterranean cultural scripts, classical literature, literary conventions and reading rules, and common historical and geographical data—are indispensable to the operation of the work, a symbiosis of author and reader. The first-time reader is tractable, open to change in light of new information as the narrative progresses. She or he 'builds characters' with each new engagement. The reader does not compare Luke-Acts with Mark or Q, but tries to create a coherent view from the text itself. Critical interpretation of Luke-Acts, therefore, requires the scholarly

---

[60]*Ibid.*, 111.
[61]*Ibid.*, 110-1.
[62]*Ibid.*, 127-30.
[63]Darr, *On Character Building*, 14.

reconstruction not of the text's historical community but of the most plausible dialogue between text and reader.

How does Darr read the Pharisees of Luke-Acts? First, he criticises the studies of Sanders and Brawley for atomising the narrative in redactional-critical fashion: they try to isolate what is characteristically Lukan by comparing Luke with his sources and by valuing the end of the story more highly than the beginning.[64] Over against his sources, and especially in Acts, Luke seems to present the Pharisees positively. Darr contends, however, that a linear reading of the text creates a much more complex picture of these characters. They provide a 'paradigm of imperceptiveness', ironically *observing* Jesus and his followers but failing to *perceive* their significance.[65] In Luke's rhetorical world, characters are graded according to their level of perception; of all the *dramatis personae,* the reader is persuaded to reject the faulty attitudes of the Pharisees. They 'become *caricatures of a morality to be avoided,* for it blinds and deafens one to God'.[66]

To fill out this reading, Darr walks through each major episode involving the Pharisees. Luke encourages the reader to think of them from the beginning (Lk. 5:17) as a homogenous group, each of whose members knows what the others know.[67] Collectively, they criticise Jesus because of their failure to perceive (Lk. 5:22).[68] The opening conflict stories of Luke 5-6 establish a contrast between two models of response to Jesus—that of the unrepentant Pharisees and that of the repentant sinner—which will operate throughout the Gospel.[69] The Pharisees grumble against Jesus[70] and reject God's purpose.[71] Whereas many scholars have found redeeming value in the Pharisees' three dinner invitations to Jesus, Darr contends that Luke deliberately confounds the reader's expectations of a *symposium* in these stories by silencing Jesus' Pharisaic companions, emphasising their unworthiness to share narrative space with him.[72] Their warning to flee Herod Antipas (Lk. 13:31) Darr interprets as an expression of nefarious motives, because they have themselves plotted against Jesus (11:53-54)

---

[64]*Ibid.*, 86-9.
[65]*Ibid.*, 86-7.
[66]*Ibid.*, 92; emphasis original.
[67]*Ibid.*, 93.
[68]*Ibid.*, 94.
[69]*Ibid.*, 95, 102.
[70]*Ibid.*, 96.
[71]*Ibid.*, 100.
[72]*Ibid.*, 103, 106.

and the narrative has not prepared the reader for any friendliness on their part.[73] In the famous 'kingdom of heaven' saying (Lk. 17:20-21) Darr finds Jesus denouncing not heavenly signs but the Pharisees' practice of 'observing' without perceiving (*cf.* παρατηρέω in 6:7; 14:2). The final episodes of the Pharisee and toll-collector (Lk. 18:9-14) and the triumphal entry (19:39) confirm the Pharisees in their collective role as imperceptive, arrogant, 'unmarked graves' full of internal filth.[74]

Although Acts omits any strong criticism of the Pharisees, Darr proposes that the reader who knows the Gospel must interpret Acts' Pharisees in a 'highly ironical' way.[75] Thus, Luke's claim that Gamaliel was 'well respected by the people' is no compliment, given the fickleness of the people.[76] He and the council free Peter only out of fear, not because of justice.[77] And the implicit contrast between Gamaliel and council-member Joseph of Arimathaea (Lk. 23:50) does not help Gamaliel's image: 'the Pharisaic leader suffers in comparison with the Arimathean'.[78] The council's actions are tragically ironic, 'sadly misguided, presumptuous, even ludicrous'.[79] Gamaliel reinforces the readers' perception of Pharisees as seeing but not perceiving.[80] The Pharisaic believers who precipitate the apostolic conference (Acts 15:5) are clearly on the wrong side of God's plan.[81] And Paul's 'Pharisaic defence' (Acts 23:1-10; 26:4-5) is a clever *ad hoc* strategy suited to his situation before the Sanhedrin, which no more reveals his true thinking than does his appeal to Greek philosophy when on trial in Athens (Acts 17:22).[82]

Thus, Darr finds in Luke-Acts a consistent portrayal of the Pharisees as dramatic representatives of attitudes not to be followed.

[73]*Ibid.*, 106.
[74]*Ibid.*, 114-5.
[75]*Ibid.*, 116.
[76]*Ibid.*, 116.
[77]*Ibid.*, 117.
[78]*Ibid.*, 118.
[79]*Ibid.*, 119.
[80]*Ibid.*, 120.
[81]*Ibid.*, 121.
[82]*Ibid.*, 124.

II. Luke-Acts: An Interpretation of the Story

It has become commonplace to observe that the interpretation of parts requires constant attention to the whole, and *vice versa*. My interpretation of the chief priests, Sadducees, Pharisees, and Sanhedrin differs from those mentioned in part because I have a different conception of parts and whole. Before considering the particular passages of interest to us, therefore, I should sketch an interpretation of the larger story.

Whenever a Greek or Latin text contains a prologue, we should pay careful attention to it because that was the place, at the very opening of the roll, where the author was expected to reveal something germane about the aim and scope of the work.[83] In spite of its brevity, the prologue to Luke-Acts contains the standard features found in historical prefaces:[84] importance of the subject, weakness of previous treatments, unique credentials of the author, author's efforts to secure the truth, and the author's thesis. Thus:

> Since many people have taken it upon themselves (ἐπεχείρησαν) to draw up an account of the events that have been fulfilled among us, even as those who from the outset were eyewitnesses and attendants of the word passed them down to us, it seemed only fitting that I, who have investigated everything precisely (ἀκριβῶς) from the start, should write in an orderly manner (καθεξῆς) for you, most excellent Theophilus, so that you might know the reliable foundation (τὴν ἀσφάλειαν) of the things that you have been taught.

Since Luke bases his eagerness to write on the fact that others have already written, he must find their work defective.[85] Elsewhere in Luke-Acts the verb ἐπιχειρέω, which he uses of the earlier works, has the sense of futile, misguided, or presumptuous effort (Acts 9:29; 19:13). Luke promises that he will demonstrate 'the reliable foundation' (ἀσφάλεια) of what Theophilus has learned. The three occurrences of the cognate adjective ἀσφαλής in Luke-Acts (Acts 21:34; 22:30; 25:26) refer to sorting out the truth in the midst of *competing claims*; this parallels the common use of the term in both historical work and philosophical quests for truth (Plutarch, *Superstition* 171 E; Justin, *Dial.* 8.1).

[83]D. Earl, 'Prologue-form in Ancient Historiography' in *ANRW* I.2.D (1972) 842-56 (856).

[84]A.J. Toynbee, *Greek Historical Thought: from Homer to the Age of Heraclitus* (New York: New American Library, 1952) 29-97.

[85]G.E. Sterling, *Historiography and Self-Definition: Josephus, Luke-Acts and Apologetic Historiography* (NovTSup 44; Leiden: E.J. Brill, 1992) 343-5.

Luke says, in effect: 'you have heard various accounts; now I shall tell you what really happened.' His story is meant to outshine his predecessors'.

How so? Because only Luke has researched everything 'with precision', only he is in a position to write 'in an orderly manner'. The adverb καθεξῆς appears five times in Luke-Acts (also Lk. 8:1; Acts 3:24; 11:4; 18:23), but nowhere else in the New Testament. We conclude that he intends *orderly progression* to be the distinguishing feature of his narrative.[86]

Luke's concern with proper sequence operates at many levels. Most obviously, his unique inclusion of a second volume dealing with the young church allows him to make distinctions unavailable to other Gospel writers. Whereas they tend to present Jesus himself in cosmic conflict with Judaism, making him overturn the Jewish dietary laws (Mk. 7:19), speak of the 'church' (Mt. 16:18; 18:17), or openly discuss his identity (Jn. 3:11-21 *etc.*), only Luke's Gospel can afford to leave Jesus wholly within the Jewish world because it awaits a second volume. Luke postpones until then the cancellation of dietary laws (Acts 10:14; 11:9), use of church language (Acts 5:11; 7:38 *etc.*), and open discussion of Jesus' identity until after the resurrection (2:36; 4:11 *etc.*). Luke's treatment of the Baptist and his students in their relationship to Jesus' group is likewise distinguished by development (Lk. 3:2-22; 7:18-23; Acts 19:1-7).

His concern with sequence also functions at a basic stylistic level.[87] It becomes clear first in the abrupt shift at Luke 1:5 from the business-like historical prologue to the scene with Zechariah in the Jerusalem Temple. Luke sets the stage with authentic 'period language' that creates an old-fashioned atmosphere, filled with angelic appearances, where actors spontaneously break into poetic verse. Throughout the entire two-volume work he will quietly adjust his language to suit the scene, from synagogues to governor's courts to a shipwreck.

Corresponding to Luke's dynamic style is his constantly evolving narrative. The golden prehistory of the birth narratives, in which people spontaneously break into verse, establishes the conditions of irony by having incontrovertible authorities declare who Jesus is—the descendant of David and Son of God, who will restore Israel's

---

[86]L.T. Johnson, 'Luke-Acts, Book of' in *ABD* (1992) vol. IV, 404-20 (405).

[87]J.M. Dawsey, *The Lukan Voice: Confusion and Irony in the Gospel of Luke* (Macon: Mercer, 1986) 1-41.

glory and defeat its enemies (Lk. 1:32-33, 69-70)—in advance of the story. In 3:1, however, Luke retreats to a 'real' world in which Jesus' identity is not yet an issue of open debate. This is a fairly stable environment in which he spends his time helping the poor, the sick, and the sinners. When Jesus arrives in cold and barren Jerusalem, the situation quickly deteriorates. He is arrested, beaten, paraded before Herod Antipas, bitterly denounced by the Jerusalem leaders, and executed. This intense suffering and conflict, though vividly described, occupies a relatively short section of the story (chs. 19-23).

Jesus' resurrection recaptures the air of peace (Lk. 24:36) and hope. But the story has taken a decisive turn, for his identity is now clear from scripture (Lk. 24:26-27, 44-47). References to Jesus in Acts maintain this two-stage scenario: he *was* a righteous teacher, healer, and prophet, whom God declared or made Messiah by resurrection (Acts 2:36; 10:38; 13:27-31). The days of ambiguity are now over: it is imperative to repent and trust in Jesus for forgiveness of sins, for outside of him there is no salvation (Acts 4:12). A succession of divine revelations to Jesus' followers is matched by their increasing separation from Judaism: the conflict leading to Stephen's death, on (false) charges of attacking fundamental Jewish institutions; Peter's reluctant mission to the Gentile Cornelius, in which God declares the Jewish dietary laws null and void (Acts 10:14; 11:9); and the divine decision, finally ratified by the apostles, to admit Gentiles without requiring that they adopt Jewish cultural markers (15:12-29).

The remainder of the book (chs. 13-28) portrays the exploits of the recent convert Paul. We cannot infer from this focus (against Brawley) that the rehabilitation of Paul was Luke's major concern. The narrowing of group history to the characterisation of individual lives was a well-established strategy, which allowed writers to develop psychological motives and build rounded characters.[88] Paul was an obvious choice for one who wished to describe the separation of Christianity from Judaism.

Luke's constantly evolving narrative makes the identification of his 'theology' hazardous.[89] In view of these constant shifts, it is important to notice where the story ends. We find in Acts 28 that the Jews have proven unresponsive, so 'this salvation' has gone out to the

---

[88]So Feldman has been able to study Josephus' biblical paraphrase as the history of key figures; many of his studies on this theme are listed in L.H. Feldman, *Jew and Gentile in Antiquity: Attitudes and Interactions from Alexander to Justinian* (Princeton: Princeton UP, 1993) 594-6.

[89]Johnson, 'Luke-Acts', 405.

Gentiles (28:25-28). For some time now, Luke has begun to speak of 'the Jews' without qualification as opponents of the Christians (12:3, 11; 14:4-5), even while allowing that many Jews believed (13:43; 14:4). By the end of Acts the reader has come to associate the term 'Jew' with unbelief and opposition. This is where Mark and John *begin* Jesus' story, but Luke delays hardened opposition until the end. Only *his* readers will know that it was not always so.

It is surprising that the dynamic qualities of Luke-Acts, which have been well known for so long (Dibelius), have had relatively little impact on studies of Luke's overall aim or his presentation of the Jewish leaders, which usually posit a static view of some kind. I conclude from the preface and the story itself, however, that these obvious shifts are the point: over against other Christian authors, Luke sees himself charting a *gradual development* of Christianity from Jewish roots. He writes as a historian, seeking to correct accounts that confused Jesus before and after the resurrection. This is the 'reliable foundation' that he offers Theophilus. We need not suppose, then, that his Pharisees or other Jewish leaders have any direct correspondence to figures known to his readers (Jewish Christians [J. T. Sanders], examples of poor attitudes and hypocrisy [Darr]); he uses these figures because he thinks that they were important in Jesus' career. The plausibility of Luke's story is, of course, a separate issue from the observation that he does mean to provide a sequential account.

Critics have identified many other themes in Luke-Acts. For our examination of the Jewish leadership, one is particularly germane: Jesus appears as a philosopher,[90] and his students as a school of Jewish philosophy.[91] Even though Luke does not call Jesus a philosopher or Christianity a philosophy, it is not a daring thesis that he assumes the category. Our identification turns on the author's and readers' shared extratextual resources: if these characters behave as philosophers were known to behave, then the reader will have perceived them as philosophers.

Recall that 1st-century 'philosophy' was not primarily a matter of abstract reasoning. Philosophers of all stripes called for a simple lifestyle, free of conventional worries. Over against the entrenched class

[90]C.H. Talbert, *Literary Patterns, Theological Themes and the Genre of Luke-Acts* (SBLMS 20; Missoula: Scholars Press, 1974) 89-98; Brawley, *Luke-Acts and the Jews*, 56-62.

[91]S. Mason, 'Greco-Roman, Jewish, and Christian Philosophies', in J. Neusner (ed.), *Religious and Theological Studies* (Approaches to Ancient Judaism NS, vol. IV; 1993) 1-28.

system, they railed against the prestige of birth and especially against wealth and luxury (Seneca, *Ep.* 17, 108.9-12). They promised true happiness (εὐδαιμονία) only to those who lived the philosophical life—advocated by their school.[92] Against the pervasive rhetorical tradition, they demanded that words and actions accord, that one really *be* what one *seemed* to be; thus, hypocrisy or false living was a primary target of their preaching (Seneca, *Ep.* 20.2). They disavowed philosophers who taught ineffective clichés or pointless abstractions, and above all those who asked for money. Epictetus complained bitterly about philosophers unworthy of the name, who delighted in abstract reasoning. He insisted that true philosophy was a cure for the soul. It required that the 'sick' person first realise his illness and then seek help (*Diss.* 2.9; 19; 3.21.30-38; Seneca, *Ep.* 15.1). The acid tests of effective philosophy were παρρησία, the ability to speak the truth no matter what the consequences, and contempt of death.[93]

Many aristocrats acquired a broad knowledge of philosophical issues during their tertiary education,[94] but it was generally understood that they should hold themselves apart from serious commitment to a particular school. Real commitment to the philosophical life, such as Epictetus demanded of his audiences and Lucian delighted in satirising, required virtual 'conversion' (μετάνοια, ἐπιστροφή) to a counter-cultural lifestyle (βίος).[95] This might involve a change in dress, diet, and demeanour (Seneca, *Ep.* 5.2; 14.4). Serious pursuit of philosophy, therefore, required a degree of detachment from public affairs (Quintilian, *Inst.* 11.1.35; 12.2.7; Seneca, *Ep.* 7-8; Lucian, *Nigr.* 3-37), though such retirement was unbecoming to Roman nobility (Seneca, *Ep.* 108.22; Tacitus, *Agr.* 4.3). In Rome itself, philosophy had long provided a home to vestigial republican sentiments, and these affiliations only complicated the philosophers' ambiguous social position.[96] Opposition between zealous philosophers and rulers was proverbial (Epictetus, *Diss.* 1.29.10; Dio Cassius 65.12.1-2; 13.1).

---

[92]H.-F. Weiss, 'Pharisäismus und Hellenismus: Zur Darstellung des Judentums im Geschichtswerk des jüdischen Historikers Flavius Josephus', *OLZ* 74 (1979) 421-33 (427-9).

[93]R. MacMullen, *Enemies of the Roman Order: Treason, Unrest, and Alienation in the Roman Empire* (New York: Routledge, 1992) 63-9.

[94]H.I. Marrou, *A History of Education in Antiquity*, tr. G. Lamb (Madison: University of Wisconsin Press, 1956) 206-16.

[95]A.D. Nock, *Conversion: The Old and the New in Religion from Alexander the Great to Augustine of Hippo* (Oxford: OUP, 1933) 173.

[96]MacMullen, *Enemies of the Roman Order*, 46-94.

So, while the philosophers of bygone ages were esteemed in public imagination and a certain philosophical literacy was *de rigeur* in polite society, the figure of the philosopher as gadfly, endlessly attacking social convention, was repulsive to those who had a stake in the *status quo*.

Luke does not need to call his characters philosophers for the 1st-century reader to understand their philosophical overtones. John the Baptist leads an extremely simple life, repudiates the privileges of birth from Abraham, demands a change of thinking (μετάνοια), and calls for ethical behaviour (Lk. 3:2-14). Before long, his fearless speech lands him in trouble with an ostensibly powerful ruler—in reality, a 'reed shaken by the wind' who prefers soft clothing and comfort (3:19-20; 7:24-5). And the established philosophers of the day are impervious to his teaching. These images were familiar to Luke's readers: whatever else he was, John was a Jewish philosopher. Josephus presents him in somewhat the same way (*Ant.* 18.116-9).

Similarly, notwithstanding Jesus' classically Jewish, messianic, and prophetic identifications in Luke-Acts, he appears in 1st-century Galilee as a philosopher, a teacher who gathers students. In spite of humble origins among the poor, this teacher is quickly recognised for his effectiveness. Other teachers respect and consult him, though he is critical of them and prefers to teach among the socially undesirable fringe groups. For them, his message has a powerful ethical thrust. He demands that the wealthy erase time-honoured social distinctions and include the outcasts in their own lives. He requires that his own followers leave their homes and sell their goods. This ascetic behaviour is necessary if they are to be effective 'salt'—a metaphor, like that of the gadfly, which emphasises their counter-cultural role. He is frank in his criticism of the established philosophers for being ineffective: hypocrites, lovers of money, irrelevant logic-choppers, concerned with outward appearance and not reality.

Luke's Jesus and his students, by contrast, provide effective teaching, always accompanied by deeds, a combination that preserves them from the philosopher's biggest pitfall: hypocrisy.[97] For Luke, Jesus is a physician in Epictetus' sense: his words and those of his followers pierce the heart of the hearer and bring about a conversion (μετάνοια). Like Socrates, Jesus is brought to trial for causing an

[97]Healing and exorcism were not incompatible with a philosopher's vocation; see Josephus, *Ant.* 8.41-4; Philostratus, *Life of Apollonius of Tyana* 4.20.45.

upheaval in the society of his day. He faces death with perfect equanimity.

In Acts the philosophical overtones are even more striking. Like the Pythagoreans and the Jewish Essenes, the early Christians practise communal ownership. They speak out before crowds and authorities with perfect freedom (παρρησία). Following Jesus' example, Stephen faces death without fear, even asking forgiveness for his judges. In Athens, Luke's Paul has no qualms about ranging Christianity alongside Stoicism and Epicureanism. Paul is a model of Christian effectiveness when, by his composure in the face of death, he saves his shipmates from drowning and casually shakes off a deadly snake. These are the marks of a true philosopher. The Pharisees, Sadducees, and Christians (Nazarenes) are described as αἱρέσεις, a term normally used of philosophical schools.[98]

Admittedly, many of Luke's categories—prophet, Holy Spirit, Messiah, scripture—do not fit the typical language of the *Greek* philosophical schools. Yet Philo and Josephus are instructive here, for they present Judaism as a philosophical culture while also preserving its biblical connections (Josephus, *Ant.* 1.25). Josephus portrays Abraham, Moses, Solomon, Daniel, and other Jewish figures as great philosophers, and claims that the Greek philosophers borrowed from Moses. This does not prevent him from talking simultaneously about the laws, the priesthood and Temple, or prophecy. In the same way, Luke's evocation of philosophical themes does not compromise his much-discussed biblical motifs.[99]

III. Chief Priests, Sadducees, Pharisees and Sanhedrin in Luke-Acts

With this background in view, we turn to the particular passages in Luke-Acts that mention chief priests, Sadducees, Sanhedrin, and Pharisees.

---

[98] Mason, *Flavius Josephus on the Pharisees*, 128.

[99] *Cf.* now C.A. Evans and J.A. Sanders, *Luke and Scripture: The Function of Sacred Tradition in Luke-Acts* (Minneapolis: Fortress, 1993).

1. In Luke

(1) Pharisees

Unlike Mark (12:13) and Matthew (3:7; 16:6; 21:45 *etc.*), the Gospel of Luke keeps the Pharisees quite separate from the Sadducees and the chief priests, who appear only in Jerusalem. The Pharisees operate in the broad expanse of Jesus' work among the common people before that final conflict. No doubt, this distinction reflects Luke's concern for correct order.

We first meet the Pharisees when Jesus has summoned a circle of his own students. The reader sees, first, that the Pharisees are coupled with teachers of the law (νομοδιδάσκαλοι), or perhaps that they *are* teachers of the law if this construction is epexegetical.[100] Luke uses νομοδιδάσκαλος only here in the Gospel, substituting 'scribes' or 'their scribes' hereafter (5:30); this suggests that he uses the descriptive term to help explain who the Pharisees were at their first appearance. The reader learns further that they have a broad base in the Jewish world: they have come from 'every village of Galilee and Judaea and Jerusalem' to observe the new teacher (Lk. 5:17). They appear, therefore, as established teachers, who assume the responsibility to scrutinise other teachers. No other teachers will surface outside of Jerusalem.

Tension builds quickly when Jesus declares a paralytic forgiven. The scribes and Pharisees first accuse him of 'blasphemy' (5:21)—not a technical charge in Luke, but generally improper speech (*cf.* Lk. 22:65; 23:39; Acts 13:45; 18:6). The tension is resolved for the moment when Jesus demonstrates his virtue by curing the man, at which point 'ecstasy seized them all and they glorified God' (Lk. 5:26).

Another problem follows, however, when Jesus associates with toll collectors and sinners, whom, it now appears, the Pharisees consider unworthy associates for a teacher (5:30). Jesus' response to this challenge seems important for understanding Luke's view of the Pharisees: 'Those who are well have no need of a physician, but rather those who are ill; not for the righteous have I come, but to call the sinners to a change of thinking' (5:31-32). In context, this saying implies that the Pharisees and their associates—the healthy and the righteous—do not need what Jesus has to offer. Jesus does not yet condemn the Pharisees, but clearly distinguishes his aims from theirs.

---

[100]The only other occurrence of the word is in Acts 5:34, where Gamaliel is called both a Pharisee and a νομοδιδάσκαλος.

Three further controversies show significant differences between Jesus and the Pharisees, and indicate that he is an enigma to them. But the issues remain unresolved as far as the reader knows. The Pharisees ask why his students do not fast, as do their own and the Baptist's (5:33); they ask why his students pluck grain on the Sabbath, when this is 'not permitted' (6:2), though his counter-argument from scripture suggests that this action *is* permitted (6:3); and they watch to see if they can accuse him for curing a man on the Sabbath (6:7), but his combination of cure and argument confounds them. Luke ends this block of five conflicts with the remark that the Pharisees were thoroughly discomfited; they were 'filled with incomprehension, and discussed with one another what they should do in the case of Jesus' (6:11). Their mission of inspection has failed to give them a basis for judging the new teacher; so the reader awaits the sequel.

We next encounter Pharisees after Jesus has lauded John the Baptist's work. Here Luke interjects that, whereas the people and the toll collectors gladly accepted John's immersion, the Pharisees and 'lawyers' (or 'legists' [J.T. Sanders], for νομικοί) set aside the will of God by refusing immersion (7:30). This aside, important because it reliably conveys the author's view, is the strongest note of condemnation so far: it is not only that the recognised Jewish teachers have different aims from Jesus, but at least in their response to John's teaching they are out of step with God's will.

Luke's criticism is soon followed, however, by a leading Pharisee's invitation to Jesus to join him for dinner (7:36). This odd juxtaposition sets in motion a pattern that will continue throughout the Gospel. Jesus will criticise the Pharisees at every opportunity, but they nonetheless continue to treat him as a respected colleague. Their cooperation with this gadfly who never stops challenging them reinforces Luke's picture of the Pharisees as obtuse: they simply do not understand the criticism.

The Pharisee who invites Jesus appears as a man of substance, since the guests 'recline' for dinner; the house in view was not the typically cramped apartment of a town dweller but a residence large enough to accommodate couches for eating. That the woman should hear of Jesus' meal at the Pharisee's house while she was in town, and that she should know where to find it (Lk. 7:37) confirms that this was an affair of high society on the local scene. Simon the Pharisee is among the relatively few comfortable residents of Galilee.

Although hosts might invite a wide range of guests, from prospective patrons to their own clients, Jesus appears in this story at least as a fellow teacher, perhaps a guest of honour, who might be invited to discourse after dinner for entertainment (Martial 11.52).[101] Simon's unspoken shock at Jesus' behaviour in acknowledging the sinful woman[102] indicates that he expected something else, that he had viewed Jesus as a worthy colleague. This surprise would be perfectly intelligible to the reader in view of the erotic connotations of the woman's action, and the traditional associations of women who attended banquets.[103] Jesus' vehement response to Simon, in which he points out the host's failings in contrast to the woman's self-effacing love, is left unanswered by the Pharisee (7:44-47). In the light of Jesus' previous encounters with Pharisees, we should probably put this down to Simon's utter perplexity, which the reader might well share. The last we hear of him is that Simon addresses Jesus respectfully and seems willing to take correction from him (7:40). If he was a poor host, the reader also sees that Jesus is not a typical honoured guest, consorting with a woman and publicly accusing the host. Luke's story is much more sophisticated than simple castigation of the Pharisees or exaltation of Jesus.

Pharisees do not appear again explicitly until Jesus has worked a good deal more among the people, when another Pharisee invites him to dine (Lk. 11:37). Since Luke has closely associated Pharisees and legists, however, we should note that it was a legist who tested Jesus' knowledge by asking him what he must do 'to inherit eternal life', and then, 'Who is my neighbour?' (10:25). The former question shows that he accepts the notion of an afterlife, as do Jesus, the Pharisees, and the people. He also 'seeks to justify himself' (10:29), which is typical behaviour of the Pharisees in Luke.

In the second meal scene, a Pharisee invites Jesus to a luncheon—or perhaps simply to 'dine' (ἀριστάω). Luke's variation of the language at least indicates that we are dealing with a common occurrence in Jesus' life. Again, the guests recline (ἀναπίπτω) in comfortable circumstances (11:37). Here too the Pharisee is surprised at this teacher's behaviour, and Jesus responds with a customarily stinging attack. Luke says that, 'when the Pharisee saw it, he was amazed that he [Jesus] was not first immersed [οὐ. . . ἐβαπτίσθη] before the meal' (11:38). Within the narrative world, of course, Luke's choice of word is

---

[101]P. Veyne, *A History of Private Life*, vol. I: *From Pagan Rome to Byzantium* (Cambridge, MA: Belknap/Harvard UP, 1987) 188-9.
[102]K.E. Corley, *Private Women, Public Meals: Social Conflict in the Synoptic Tradition* (Peabody: Hendrickson, 1993) 63, 124.
[103]*Ibid.*, 24-79.

significant: the reader has already learned that the Pharisees were not immersed by John, a serious violation of divine will (7:30); yet here they criticise Jesus for not being immersed before dinner, a routine issue that exposes their pettiness.

But what should Luke's readers have understood by this *immersion* that Jesus failed to perform? Commentators often imagine that, because the Pharisees were involved, and Mark mentions Pharisaic hand-washing (Mk. 7:3), Luke also refers here to 'ceremonial hand-washing'.[104] This conclusion seems strained, however, in view of what the passage actually says: the word βαπτίζω connotes drenching or immersion, and there is no reference to hands. Jesus goes on to talk about washing the inside and the outside, where the inside clearly has to do with human motives (11:39-41). Therefore, the issue seems to be the inside and outside of the *person*, not hands. And the implicit comparison with John's immersion only strengthens this sense of washing the whole body.

Now, it was common enough for a host to invite a dinner guest to visit the baths with him before the meal, thus providing a whole afternoon and evening of activity (Martial, 11.52). I submit that all of the narrative clues so far about the Pharisees' comfortable circumstances would incline the reader to understand the charge thus: a well-to-do Pharisee host is offended at Jesus' declining a friendly invitation to bathe before dinner. That much would be intelligible to any Mediterranean reader. In addition, some readers perhaps knew that in Jewish culture full immersion was required to remove common kinds of impurity (Lv. 15:16-27). If so, Luke may be suggesting that the Pharisee was scandalised at Jesus' failure to take advantage of his private immersion pool before eating. Though immersion before dinner was not mandated in scripture, and we do not know to what extent it was a Pharisaic norm, the assumption may simply be that most teachers would be happy for the chance to purify themselves as often as possible.[105] In any case, the issue seems to be a full immersion.

The ensuing discussion contains three woes against the Pharisees and three against their colleagues the legists, who are also present. Under the general charge of being concerned with external convention rather than thoughts and attitudes—the eternal complaint of the philosopher—Jesus accuses the Pharisees specifically of worrying

---

[104]P.F. Esler, *Community and Gospel in Luke-Acts: The Social and Political Motivations of Lucan Theology* (Cambridge: CUP, 1987) 122; Darr, *On Character Building*, 103.
[105]E.P. Sanders, *Judaism: Practice & Belief 63 BCE – 66 CE*, 217-30.

about tithing herbs while neglecting important issues of justice, and of loving honours (11:41-43). Most interestingly, he describes the Pharisees as 'indistinct memorials [or tombstones], which pedestrians walk all over without knowing' (11:44). This image is quite different from Matthew's *whitewashed* tombs (Mt. 23:27). It seems from Matthew's note that Jews marked tombs so that pedestrians could avoid corpse uncleanness[106]; as reputedly exact teachers, the Pharisees would presumably be among the more careful in this respect. Jesus' charge would then mean: while the Pharisees worry about marking other graves, they fail to mark *themselves* out as places to be avoided! (*Cf.* the similar association of them with leaven to be avoided at 12:1.) Without such knowledge of Pharisaic custom, the reader might simply infer that they, in contrast to Jesus and his students, fail to distinguish themselves from society as a whole; they are ineffective set pieces like the sophists of Greek culture.

This biting dinner speech offends (ὑβρίζω) the legists as well, but their respectful complaint ('Teacher...') only invites Jesus to turn on them with even sharper invective (11:45). Rather than helping people, he alleges, they burden them with unreasonable tasks; they block the path to knowledge (γνῶσις) and do not find it themselves. Their obstructionist behaviour leads them to oppose true prophets and apostles—the name that Jesus has given a few of his leading students (6:13)—just as their counterparts in biblical history did (11:47-51). There is a considerable overlap between the 'false prophets' or court prophets of biblical history and the sophists of Greek culture. While Luke's explicit language puts the Pharisees in continuity with these biblical predecessors, the 1st-century Greek reader could not avoid associating them with sophists.

The close relationship between Pharisees and legists is confirmed by Luke's closing remark, that when Jesus had left the house, they together began 'to bear a serious grudge, and to draw him out with questions concerning many other matters, laying an ambush to trap him with something that might come from his mouth' (11:53-54). Rather than taking the criticism to heart and examining whether they might actually change their ways, the offended philosophical élite simply look for ways to show up this new teacher. Their opposition is nothing like the chief priests' later effort to kill Jesus; it is at the level of academic debate between 'safe' philosophers who have long secured

---

[106]E.P. Sanders, *Judaism: Practice & Belief 63 BCE – 66 CE*, 72.

an established place in the *status quo* and a small group of upstarts who challenge that order.

This conflict is developed in the following paragraph. Jesus' teaching and healing draw 'tens of thousands of people', for they find real help from him. But he warns them *not* to seek help from the Pharisees: 'Watch out for the leaven of the Pharisees, which is pretence!' (12:1). Seeking out leaven was a basic Jewish custom for the Passover season, quite possibly familiar to Luke's readers from scripture (Ex. 13:6-8). As recognised teachers, the Pharisees themselves would presumably have given guidelines for ensuring that all leaven was scrupulously removed. Jesus' warning is again sarcastic: the Pharisees are the leaven that one needs to worry about! That he bothers to warn the people about the Pharisees agrees with many other indications in the story that the people generally considered the Pharisees *their* teachers. Jesus presents his own more effective teaching as an alternative to their established way.

The Pharisees' offence at Jesus' criticism does not, surprisingly, lead to hatred: Luke presents their motivation as the normal human psychology of affront and envy. For soon after, when push comes to shove, some Pharisees come to warn Jesus that Herod Antipas 'wants to kill' him (13:31). This notice out of the blue seems important for maintaining the reader's perspective on the relationships among the characters. Jesus has been in almost daily contact with the Pharisees, yet in spite of his regular and sharp criticism, the only revenge that they are either interested in or capable of is the satisfaction that might be found in embarrassing him on the basis of some teaching or other. Herod Antipas operates on the quite different plane of raw power. He has already imprisoned and executed the Baptist (3:19-20; 9:9) and now wishes to kill Jesus. The reader understands that such major political figures have a different scale of values and means at their disposal. Jesus' students and the Pharisees are, comparatively speaking, in the same boat here. They both live and function among the common people. Herod is most closely matched by the Jerusalem authorities, who actually control some machinery of government. There is no good reason to see the Pharisees' warning as duplicitous (against Darr); all of the contextual indicators point the other way.

In particular, the following paragraph has Jesus invited yet a third time to dine with 'one of the leading Pharisees', this time at a Sabbath meal (14:1). Again, it is a lavish affair with a large number of guests and many couches, typically arranged in order of honour. Again, the philosopher Jesus proceeds to challenge the whole banquet etiquette of his fellow guests (*cf. e.g.* Lucian, *Symp.* 8-9), by proposing that those eager to sit at the most honoured places—closest to the host—go first to the least desirable couches, from which they may be summoned (14:7-11). Then again, they may not be summoned—a large risk for those concerned about their image, but not a concern to those who truly know themselves! These are precisely the sorts of social conventions exposed by true philosophy (Lucian, *Nigr.* 3-37).

An even more devastating critique of dinner culture comes when Jesus discusses whom to invite (14:12-14). His insistence that hosts not invite their friends, brothers, relatives, or rich neighbours, who might repay them with a reciprocating invitation, was as radical as his coming demand that potential students abandon their homes. Hosts might invite some humble folk to dinner out of patronal obligation, perhaps feeding them less expensive fare than the others. But it was widely accepted that one should seek out equals and more distinguished guests, and that one might justifiably be offended if they accepted another invitation instead (Pliny, *Ep.* 1.15). Jesus' criticism would only make sense if he too had been invited as a respectable teacher. In the 1st-century Mediterranean context, his insistence that hosts seek out as dinner guests 'the poor, the disabled, the lame, and the blind' was no less peculiar than it would be today. Although the Christian reader will side with Jesus, Luke is evidently not presenting the Pharisees as evil, only as insensitive to the magnitude of human need and unwilling to take the extreme steps needed to become effective 'salt' (see below).

How did the Pharisees respond? We learn first that they were still watching Jesus carefully when he came to the house (14:1). Either *en route* or soon after his arrival, a man with dropsy confronted him. Jesus, after challenging the Pharisees on the question of Sabbath cures (14:3), cured the man with a touch and dismissed him (14:4)—apparently indicating that the man was not part of the banquet. The Pharisees' response is ambiguously stated: 'they were incapable of answering back to these things' (14:6). Did he, then, win them over? At least, he dominated the rest of the dinner-time discussion. And when he made his observations about inviting the disabled to dinner, one of his fellow diners enthusiastically agreed that future reward was vastly more desirable than present repayment (14:15).

By this point, the reader has acquired a fairly well rounded picture of Luke's Pharisees. They are much more complex than simply 'friends' or 'enemies' of Jesus. A complex of further encounters in chapters 14-18 solidifies the reader's understanding of the Pharisees.

The first provides a striking contrast between Jesus' way and the Pharisees'. He makes frightfully clear the conditions of becoming *his* student (14:25-35): utter disdain for the most basic social categories (father, mother, wife, children, brothers, sisters, one's own self), 'carrying one's own cross'—a vivid image of suffering in the 1st-century Mediterranean—and abandoning *all* of one's possessions (14:33). Only so can one become effective salt, not the kind of salt that has become useless (μωρανθῇ)—like the Pharisees (14:34-35)! On hearing Jesus' itemisation of student requirements, the Pharisees grumbled, while characteristically missing the point of this ascetic regimen, that he included among his pupils toll collectors and sinners, the most unworthy sorts of people. This complaint confirms their assumption that he is a fellow teacher, for if they were rabid opponents like Herod Antipas and later the chief priests, they would not care what sort of students he chose.

The whole complex of parables in 15:3-16:13 comes in response to the Pharisees' grumblings; at the end (16:14) they have been 'listening to all these things'. Without detailed analysis here, we observe that the first three parables have a common and simple point, namely: there will be more celebration over the lost who are found than over the ones who have always been safe. These parables are transparent allegories. The ninety-nine sheep who stay on the path are equated with the 'righteous who have no need of rethinking' (15:7), whereas both the lost sheep and the lost coin are interpreted as the sinner who has a change of mind (15:7, 10). The Pharisees are the older son (ὁ πρεσβύτερος), who served the father for countless years and never once transgressed his commandment (οὐδέποτε ἐντολήν παρῆλθον), while the son who associated with *harlots* is celebrated (15:29-31). The father generously allows that the older son has always been cherished, and has always had access to everything of the father's (15:32). All of this confirms that the Pharisees are the safe, righteous, and healthy, who do not need Jesus' teaching, though in other contexts he finds them culpable for having squandered their privileged position.

When, at the conclusion of the final parable of the group, Jesus declares that one cannot serve God and mammon, 'the Pharisees, being lovers of money (φιλάργυροι), turned up their noses at him' (16:14). The charge of loving money was a stock accusation of some philosophers against others from at least the time of Socrates (Diogenes Laertius 6.56).[107] It fits so precisely with the image of the Pharisees that Luke and the reader have been building so far, as complacent sophists who hold lavish banquets among their friends, that the reader might wonder at Luke's failure to launch this attack before now.

Similarly, Jesus' following words reprise all of the previous Pharisee stories: 'you are those who justify yourselves before people, but God knows your hearts; for what is exalted by people is an abomination before God' (16:15). This observation sums up the Pharisees' place in the whole scheme of 'high and low, honour and shame, internal and external, truth and convention, reality and appearance', which runs as a subtext throughout the Gospel of Luke, and which was of paramount concern to ethical philosophers of Luke's time. The Pharisees have entirely lost their credibility by allying themselves uncritically with the wrong sides of these pairs.

Jesus' most compassionate statement to the Pharisees comes when they inquire of him, still the respected teacher, 'when the kingdom of God comes' (17:20). In responding that 'the kingdom of God is *within you*' (17:22), Jesus is declaring that the Pharisees have the kingdom in themselves, as the 'older brother' with heaven's resources at their disposal, as the righteous and healthy of society; but as we have seen time and again, they squander their potential. They are not the ones to do it. Their preoccupation with appearance and self-justification is exposed once more in the parable of the Pharisee and the toll collector (18:9-14). Here, Pharisees typify those who 'are persuaded that they themselves are righteous and vilify everyone else' (18:9).

The utter incomprehension of the Pharisees is illustrated again by their final scene in the Gospel. Standing with Jesus at the eastern approach to the Temple, they heard the large crowd of joyful students praising God and citing Ps. 118:26:[108] 'blessed is the king who comes in the name of the Lord' (19:38). Some of the Pharisees among the crowd said, 'Teacher, admonish your students'. They still call him teacher, but they do not understand his programme or the momentous events unfolding before them.

(2) Chief Priests, Sadducees and Sanhedrin

Chief priests, Sadducees and Sanhedrin are closely related in the Gospel, appearing only in the climactic Jerusalem narrative (Lk. 19:45-

[107]Brawley, *Luke-Acts and the Jews*, 61, 86.

[108]*Cf.* J.A. Sanders, 'A Hermeneutic Fabric: Psalm 118 in Luke's Entrance Narrative' in Evans and Sanders, *Luke and Scripture*, 140-53.

24:53). Luke's reference to the serving High Priest(s) (ἀρχιερεύς) at Luke 3:1 is simply a chronological marker. In Luke 9:22, shortly before the travel narrative, he has Jesus predict that the Son of Man will be tried and killed by the 'elders and chief priests and scribes'. This points ahead to the Jerusalem narrative. The other thirteen occurrences of ἀρχιερεύς, along with every occurrence of Sadducee (Σαδδουκαῖος; once) and Sanhedrin (συνέδριον; once), come in the Jerusalem story.

These basic narrative facts already begin to shape the reader's evaluation of the chief priests, Sanhedrin, and Sadducees. They stand in stark contrast to the only other significant Jewish leaders in this narrative, the Pharisees. In Jerusalem, there is no more debating over modes of Sabbath observance or association with sinners, but only lethal conflict. Unlike the Pharisees, the Temple-based leadership controls a police force, and it can execute its will immediately.

Jesus' 'passion predictions' do not dominate the story here as they do in Mark. The two predictions after 9:22 (9:43-45; 18:31-34) mention only 'men' and 'Gentiles' rather than the Temple leadership, as Jesus' killers. Since the Pharisees themselves do not plot Jesus' death (contrast Mk. 3:6), and since Luke includes much special material of a general ethical nature in the body of the work, the effect of the passion predictions on the reader is to create *dissonance*: Why must Jesus die, when he is doing so much good, and getting along so well with other teachers who respect him? The opening statement of the travel narrative (9:51) and the lament over Jerusalem (13:33-35) confirm that things will be *different* there.

This difference is closely related to the theme of reversal that runs through the entire Gospel. Jesus set out to bring good news to the poor, sick, and sinners, but this message is bad news for the rich, the powerful, and the self-satisfied righteous. Since the bulk of his career has been among the common people, he has mainly spoken good news and hope. Jerusalem is different because it represents the seat of power in Jewish life, the home of the central Jewish government (even the Roman governor and Galilean tetrarch are there), and the economic heart of Jewish society. Whereas Jesus has been bringing good news to the deprived, he will now confront the powerful with bad news (*cf.* Lk. 6:20-26).

Once Jesus arrives at the gates of Jerusalem, there is no more leisure for general ethical observations. From the eastern gate he predicts the city's destruction because it remains oblivious to the time of its 'inspection' (19:44). As soon as he enters the Temple, he drives out the merchants and begins to teach (19:45). Within two sentences of describing his entry, the narrator brings us face to face with the authorities we have vaguely expected all through the story: 'the chief priests and the scribes, even the highest ranking of the people, sought to kill him' (19:47). Jesus' life has taken a decisive turn; this is no longer the world of the common people and Pharisees. For Luke's readers, who understand the Romans' ruthless intolerance of upheaval in the provinces, and who possibly also know that the Jerusalem Temple was a regular scene of trouble (*cf.* Josephus *BJ* 2.43, 224), the Temple incident would suffice to make the chief priests' actions plausible. It is not clear that Luke means to *condemn* the Jerusalem leadership. His portrayal seems more resigned: they were completely blind to Jesus' significance, and acted as one might have expected of them.

Chapter 20, immediately following this announcement of the chief priests' aims, comprises six conflict stories. It is worth comparing these with the earlier controversies involving the Pharisees and the ordinary people in Luke 5-6. There, the issues were academic and nothing came of them. Now, however, the chief priests, who have already decided to kill Jesus, are in his audience (20:1). Their first question goes to the heart of the matter: Who are you, that you should teach here (20:2)? It is not *what* Jesus teaches in the Temple that causes problems, for we are told only that he was teaching (19:47; 20:1); that activity is the point of the controversy. Jesus' authority had never been a serious issue in his dealings with the Pharisees: they did wonder about his forgiveness of sins at their first encounter (Lk. 5:26), but he temporarily convinced them by his actions; their later surprise at his actions came precisely because they accepted him as a fellow-teacher. Here, the chief priests assume an exclusive right to teach in the Temple, and so they want to know what he is doing here. Since they have determined to kill him, and are not likely to be persuaded by any answer, their question is sarcastic.

Jesus answers enigmatically, but then boldly relates an allegory that challenges *their* legitimacy. In failing to recognise his mission, he says, they are like wicked tenant farmers who have abandoned their accountability to the vineyard owner and so dismiss or kill his messengers, even his son. With this provocation, the 'scribes and chief priests sought to lay hands on him at that moment' (20:19). But in contrast to Jesus, who speaks fearlessly though he lacks any protection from visible authority, these well-armed and seemingly powerful figures are actually powerless to execute their wishes because 'they feared the people' (20:19).

To protect their image from further damage, these weak authorities must engage in subterfuge: withdrawing from the scene, they send in spies who pretend (ὑποκρίνομαι) to be decent (δίκαιος) people (20:20), just as the chief priests themselves pretend to be divinely ordained rulers. These spies blatantly lie, claiming that they accept Jesus' teaching as from God (20:21). Once again, Jesus represents the philosophical ideal of absolute integrity and fearlessness over against the sham of the social structure. With perfect composure, he sees through the chief priests' machinations (20:23). The chief priests and their spies, since they are paralysed by fear of their own people, hope to frame Jesus by finding something that will persuade the Roman governor to take action (20:21).[109] Contrary to plan, however, the spies themselves are both intimidated by the people and amazed at Jesus' answer to their question (20:26).

Enter the Sadducees, for their only scene in the Gospel. They are 'one-trick ponies', whose sole noteworthy characteristic is that they say 'there is no resurrection' (20:27). In doing so, they seem to represent the empty theology of the Jerusalem establishment who, like the rich man of Luke 16:25, already have their consolation. The Sadducees present a clever conundrum to Jesus, but Jesus, who has always assumed the resurrection in his earlier teaching, in agreement with the people and the Pharisees, has no difficulty exposing the silliness of the question (for Luke). The witless Sadducees are reduced to silence, after conceding, 'Teacher, you spoke well' (20:39). This failure of the Jerusalem establishment to convict Jesus by his words only focuses attention more closely on the chief priests' motives. Why, then, *do* they wish to kill him?

Jesus now takes the offensive, driving home the theme of reversal by exposing the (alleged) greed of the Temple authorities. He asserts that the scribes like to 'devour widows' houses' and then cover up their rapacity with a façade of piety (προφάσις; 20:47). He illustrates this with the example of a poor widow who is just then depositing two small coins in the Temple treasury, while the rich deposit their large gifts (21:1-3). Although Jesus simply remarks on the relative abundance of the widow's gift, without explicitly condemning the Temple authorities (21:4), the context seems to convey Jesus' general criticism of the Temple's financial affairs. He proceeds immediately to predict the destruction of the whole Temple edifice, in response to those who

---

[109]In supposing that the governor would be present in Jerusalem, Luke seems here to anticipate his later note that the feast of Passover was near; 22:1.

are naively impressed by its superficial beauty and votive offerings (21:5-6).

Following this prediction, we are reminded that, whereas the people are eager to hear Jesus' teaching (21:38), the chief priests and scribes are looking for a way to kill him, though they fear the people (22:2). They find their means in Judas (22:4-5). After Jesus' final meal, a crowd of 'chief priests and captains of the Temple and elders' (22:52) comes secretly to arrest him on the Mount of Olives. Once again, Jesus fearlessly exposes their cowardice. This apparent small triumph of the authorities represents the reign of darkness (22:52-53).

From the Mount of Olives Jesus is ushered to the very heart of the Jerusalem establishment, the residence of the High Priest (22:54). After being held overnight, 'the senate (πρεσβυτέριον)[110] of the people convened, chief priests and also scribes, and they led him into their council chamber (συνέδριον)' (22:66). Inasmuch as this *synedrion* is distinguished from the persons involved as a place to which one can go, we conclude with Sanders that Luke uses the term here of a building or room. Unlike the other Gospels, Luke does not place this trial by Jewish authorities in the High Priest's house. Perhaps he knows that trials were conducted in a special chamber.

Interestingly enough, although Luke seems to assume that the High Priest led the πρεσβυτέριον, since Jesus goes from the High Priest's house to the court (and *cf.* Acts 5:17, 21; 7:1; 23:2), nothing is said of the High Priest himself during Jesus' trial. All of the council's statements are collective (Lk. 22:67; 23:2, 10, 13), though the other Gospels put the same words in the High Priest's mouth (*e.g.* Mk. 14:61, 63). Perhaps Luke intends to broaden the blame for Jesus' death to the whole chief-priestly college. He may think that chief-priestly cliques were more central to the operation of the senate than any particular High Priest.

Although Luke is not explicit here, he seems to suggest that Pilate handed Jesus over to soldiers under the chief priests' control: 'Jesus he handed over (παρέδωκεν) to their will' (23:25).[111] We hear no more of the chief priests by name, but the context suggests that they are the principal members of 'the rulers' (οἱ ἄρχοντες) who ridicule Jesus on the cross (23:35). Nothing in the narrative so far has prepared us for the notice in Luke 23:50-52 that a 'good and righteous' member of the

[110]This is the only occurrence of the word in Luke, though it appears also in Acts 22:5 as a term for the council.
[111]J.T. Sanders, *The Jews in Luke-Acts*, 9-12.

council (βουλευτής), who was awaiting the kingdom of God (a Pharisee?), should ask to give Jesus a proper burial. Luke's claim that Joseph of Arimathea had not consented to the council's decision highlights his earlier rhetorical exaggeration in making the *whole* council responsible (23:1).

We conclude that the chief priests function in the Gospel of Luke as the embodiment of the powerful who have bad news awaiting them (Lk. 6:24-26). Whereas Jesus has been very successful among the people, in spite of his constantly criticising the Pharisees, his encounter with the supremely hypocritical chief priests brings him immediately into fatal conflict. They want him executed on *any* charge because he challenges their authority by assuming a teaching role in the Temple. They hold the city and the Temple in their hands, and they have police at their disposal. But they are paradigms of pretence, worried about appearances, weak and fearful in spite of their instruments of power, while the apparently powerless Jesus confronts them with perfect composure. The chief priests are the driving force in the Jewish council led by the High Priest, and they meet in a συνέδριον. The Sadducees are flat characters in Luke, vaguely associated with the Jerusalem leadership.

2. *In Acts*

We have considered the Gospel of Luke at some length because it provides the indispensable literary context for the Book of Acts. We have seen that a great deal changes in Acts, following the death and resurrection of Jesus. It is in many ways a new world, for Jesus' identity as Messiah is now openly declared by his apostles. Still, the story remains based in Jerusalem and the chief priests, Sadducees, Sanhedrin, and Pharisees continue to play important secondary roles that build upon their earlier roles in Jesus' career. Because the Pharisees often appear together with the others in Acts, it will be unnecessary to treat the leadership groups under separate heads.

Since this story begins in Jerusalem, the reader of the Gospel knows enough to anticipate some trouble for Jesus' followers from the very group that executed Jesus himself. That opposition is not long in coming. Jesus' followers explode upon the scene when they receive power from heaven, which enables them to proclaim Jesus' resurrection boldly and to confirm their teaching with spectacular cures. They quickly attract 3,000 followers to their group, who sell their possessions and join this counter-cultural school initiated by Jesus (Acts 2:1-47). One of their cures involved a lame man who used to sit begging by one of the Temple gates, where the only help he had ever received from Jewish leaders and passers-by was in the form of charitable donations. His healing at the hands of Peter and John caused a commotion in Solomon's portico, at which they began to proclaim Jesus' resurrection, the need for a change of mind, and trust in this new revelation from God (3:11-26).

It comes as no surprise to the reader that, 'the priests, the commander (στρατηγός) of the Temple (guard) and the Sadducees came upon them, greatly exercised on account of their teaching the people, and their proclaiming in Jesus the resurrection of the dead' (4:1-2). There are two issues here: (a) that Jesus' students are teaching the people without authorisation in the Temple area, and (b) that they are talking about resurrection in the case of Jesus. Both issues recall Jesus' experience in the Temple, where his authority to teach was questioned, and the Sadducees confronted him on the issue of resurrection. The added twist here is their teaching in Jesus' name: since his crucifixion was engineered by the chief priests, they are indignant that his students are still active. Also in keeping with the reader's expectations, these nameless figures exercise their power quickly: they arrest Peter and John and hold them over for interrogation the next day (4:3). In spite of the arrest, however, 5,000 more men believe as a result of the apostles' teaching (4:4), which underscores the leaders' helplessness in the face of divine action.

On the next day, 'the leaders and the elders and the scribes in Jerusalem' gather to try Jesus' students. Strangely, it is only now that Luke troubles to mention some names. In the opening of the main Gospel narrative he had confusingly dated the Baptist's career to the time when 'Annas was High Priest and Caiaphas' (Lk. 3:2)—confusingly, because the reader expects one High Priest's name. In the narrative of Jesus' days in Jerusalem, the serving High Priest plays no role. Yet now, in recounting the trial of Peter and John, Luke allows that among those gathered were 'Annas the High Priest, and Caiaphas and John and Alexander and as many as were of the High Priest's family' (4:6). This passage seems to confirm that Luke thinks of Annas as serving High Priest, but that only makes it more problematic in relation to Josephus' account (see below).

What the Temple-based authorities—leaders, chief priests, scribes, elders, and Sadducees—wish to know is where these men get their authority to teach (4:7). As in Jesus' case, they demand confirmation of what they already know, that they do not want these men teaching in the Temple. The apostles' reply cites the same irritating passage from Psalm 118:22 that Jesus had used in his conflict with these leaders (4:11; *cf.* Lk. 20:17). The Temple leaders quickly make the connection, realising that the apostles' remarkable boldness of speech (παρρησία), the philosopher's prized virtue, comes from their study with Jesus (4:13). Their deliberations take place in a room called a *synedrion,* which people can enter and exit (4:15).

As in the Jerusalem narrative of the Gospel, the leaders are in a political predicament. They realise their inability to deny the cure of the lame man because it is now well known to the people (4:16). Nor are they able to punish Peter and John 'because of the people' (4:21). But instead of giving even the slightest attention to what the miracle might imply about the new teaching, they stubbornly proceed with their plans to silence Jesus' group by forbidding them to teach 'on the basis of Jesus' name' (4:18). The issue here seems to be practical and political: they do not want the name of a recently crucified troublemaker perpetuated as a rallying call in the Temple area. Peter and John, for their part, are *unable* to cease speaking of what they have seen and heard (4:20). This divinely revealed teaching is inevitable, in spite of the powerful chief priests' designs.

The point is reinforced by what happened next. When the apostles continued their teaching in spite of the warning, 'the High Priest and all those with him, the school of the Sadducees then current (ἡ οὖσα αἵρεσις τῶν Σαδδουκαίων), were filled with zeal and laid hands on the apostles, and placed them in the public prison' (5:17). Once again the authorities used their visible powers to effect their goals, 'but an angel of the Lord' opened the prison doors and told the apostles to return to teaching the people in the Temple, which they did. The reader must smile as he or she sees the exalted High Priest convening 'the *synedrion* [here, the body more than the place] and the whole senate of the sons of Israel' to try the apostles again, but finding the cell guarded, locked, and empty (5:23)! Instead of asking what this might mean and pondering the divine will, the High Priest stubbornly uses the force at his disposal, the commander (στρατηγός) of the Temple guard with his officers, to arrest the apostles. Again, the commander must seize them carefully, without visible force, so as not to arouse the ire of the people (5:26). When the apostles appear before the *synedrion* (both the room and the place are suggested), they make the same point as before: they are simply obeying God (5:29). The Temple leadership is ignorant of God's will; it was responsible for killing the one whom

God himself has exalted as prince and saviour (5:31). 'Those who heard [those meeting in the *synedrion*] became infuriated and wanted to kill them' (5:33).

What comes next is a complete surprise to the reader—even more than Joseph of Arimathea's appearance after the *collective* council action against Jesus (Lk. 23:1, 51). Whereas he has consistently separated the popular Pharisees from the aristocratic Sadducean-priestly leadership of Jerusalem, Luke now introduces a Pharisee in the Sanhedrin! 'Now a certain Pharisee in the *synedrion* by the name of Gamaliel, *a teacher of the Law honoured by all the people,* stood up and ordered the men to be taken outside for a moment...' (5:34). On the one hand, this first reference to a Pharisee in Acts fits everything we remember about them from the Gospel: they are the esteemed popular teachers of Jesus' world. On the other hand, what is this Pharisee doing in the Jerusalem council led by the High Priest, which both the Gospel and Acts have thus far portrayed as a chief-priestly and Sadducean preserve? The Pharisees' presence in the council will become increasingly important as the narrative of Acts proceeds. It seems doubtful that Luke means to highlight the tension; rather, he is quietly introducing Pharisees in the council for a new rhetorical situation. This can only mean that he has always known about their presence, but suppressed that information when discussing the events related to Jesus' death. And this implies that he has a specific role for the Pharisees in his narrative, which he does not wish to confuse with the Sadducean chief priests' role.

Gamaliel's speech provides further clues about the Pharisees' perspective. It also shows Luke's concern for verisimilitude. Although the Christians would not see themselves as a faction comparable with the followers of Judas or Theudas, Gamaliel compares these groups as a councillor might plausibly do. He is the only councillor we have met who has the slightest interest in discussing the Christians' claims, and this alone sets him apart from the chief-priestly councillors, just as the Pharisees of the Gospel, who loved to debate issues, were different from the chief priests there.

This is the first occasion in which chief priests and Pharisees come into direct contact, and the result is illuminating. Against the chief priests' wish to kill the apostles, this popular teacher insists, 'Consider carefully what you are about to do to these men!' After recounting the examples of Theudas and Judas, whose movements came to nothing, he concludes, 'So also now I am saying to you, leave these men alone and let them be. For if this scheme or this effort is of human origin, it will be smashed to pieces. But if it is from God, you will not be able to smash them—lest you be found God-fighters' (5:38-39). This lone Pharisaic voice in what we had thought was a chief-priestly senate then *persuades* the others (5:39). How can this be? Luke does not explain: perhaps Gamaliel was a uniquely skilled orator, or admired by the other councillors. But the narrative indicators point in another direction, namely: the leaders are afraid of the people, and the Pharisee Gamaliel is highly respected by the people. The reader's most likely assumption, I submit, would be that Gamaliel carries disproportionate weight because he represents the popular will. His position is opposed to that of the council majority, but they defer to him because of his popular standing. As always, they must temper their own aims by considering the people; only now we learn that the people's school is represented in senate.

To conclude from Gamaliel's articulation of the narrator's own view here—Christianity cannot be stopped—that Gamaliel stands on the verge of Christian faith would be to miss Luke's narrative indicators.[112] He is no more a partisan of the Christians than he is of the other popular groups mentioned. But it is equally misguided to see him as a wicked man motivated by fear, or to contrast him with Joseph of Arimathea in Luke 23:51.[113] Why must each character be a paradigm of good or evil? Luke has a historian's concern for verisimilitude. Gamaliel appears as a shrewd popular politician, weighing popular piety against administrative needs. Like the Pharisees of the Gospel, he adopts a cautious wait-and-see approach, which does not preclude a sound flogging in the *synedrion* (5:40).

At this point, the narrative could go two ways: the presence of an influential Pharisee in the senate might portend increasing openness to Christianity on the part of the chief priests, or the Pharisees and people might increasingly assimilate to the obstructionist tradition of the senate.

The death of Stephen marks a significant shift. Up to that point, many thousands of the people have believed. Even a large number of priests have accepted the new faith (6:8). These are not chief priests, but they are linked with the Temple establishment. When Stephen begins to preach in Greek-speaking synagogues, however, his opponents instigate false witnesses who allege that he speaks against Moses, the laws, and the Temple (6:11-13). Although the reader knows the charge to be mischievous, in view of Luke's pronounced emphasis

---

[112]*Contra* Brawley, *Luke-Acts and the Jews*, 97-8.
[113]*Contra* Darr, *On Character Building*, 116-7.

thus far on Law-observance among Jesus' students, we see an ominous change now, for the false witnesses are able to stir up the *people* against Stephen (6:12). When Stephen is brought before the *synedrion*, the High Priest has broad support for his execution; there is no question of fearing the people or dealing with the Pharisees. Stephen accuses the whole people (7:51-53), and one of those who consents to Stephen's death is Saul (8:1), who turns out to be a Pharisee (26:5).

Christianity has been tarred with the accusation that it aims to overturn Jewish tradition, and this charge brings the Pharisees, who otherwise have quite different interests from the chief priests, into cooperation with them on the Christian problem. A major persecution of Christians breaks out in Jewish Palestine (8:1-3). Whereas until now the High Priest's authority has seemed limited to Jerusalem, on this issue he has public cooperation for a nation-wide disciplinary action (8:3; 9:1-2). The Temple-based opposition to Christianity is now solidifying with the apparent inclusion of Pharisees and many of the people.

Paradoxically, we soon see that there is something to the charge that Christianity overturns Jewish custom, though this was not yet true when Stephen died. In a pivotal revelation to Peter, God declares all food and all humanity *clean* (10:15, 28; 11:9). The abrogation, or drastic relativisation, of the dietary laws constitutes a massive break with even the most popular forms of Jewish observance. It is no coincidence that, of the 83 occurrences of Ἰουδαῖος in Luke-Acts, 73 come after the revelation to Peter. Only now are 'the Jews' mentioned without qualification as a body distinct from, and basically hostile to, Christians (*e.g.* 12:3, 11; 13:5, 45; 14:1; 17:5; 18:12; 22:30; 23:12, 20; 24:9). Unbelieving Jews are more and more allied with the Jerusalem leadership as a stubborn *bloc*. The apostolic council, by recognising the divine directive to admit Gentiles without circumcision (15:8-10, 28), seals the non-Jewish (or not necessarily Jewish) character of Christianity. As the Jews collectively fail to follow the successive revelations of God's will, they and the Christians appear headed toward mutual isolation.

Yet this growing momentum toward separation also highlights Luke's effort to *prevent* any final schism. While tending to speak of Jews without qualification as non-Christians, he nonetheless insists that 'many Jews' continued to trust in Jesus (13:43; 14:1; 17:4, 11-12; 18:8; 19:9; 20:20; 28:24). Everywhere Paul goes on his Mediterranean mission, even when taken to Rome in chains, he seeks out the local Jewish community to convince its membership that Jesus is their Messiah (13:5; 14:1; 16:13; 17:2-3; 28:23). He typically grounds his teaching in Jewish (biblical) history, and both he and the apostles continue to observe Jewish Law in general—notwithstanding the relativisation of the dietary laws (15:10; 18:18; 24:16-17). Luke has the proconsul Gallio in Corinth recognise that the question of Paul's faith is an internal Jewish matter (18:14-15). Even as many priests have already adopted the new faith, so also many 'from the school of the Pharisees' believe (15:5).

An essential element of Luke's strategy to unite Christianity and Judaism is his portrayal of the church as a Jewish *philosophical school* alongside the Pharisees and Sadducees. In the earlier chapters of Acts, both the Pharisees (15:5) and the Sadducees (4:17) have been called by the term associated with philosophical schools: αἱρέσεις. When Paul is arrested on his final trip to Jerusalem, his encounter with the *synedrion* (here signifying the council more than the place) affords Luke an opportunity to forge this link between Christianity and Jewish culture.

In this case, the *synedrion* is called together by the Roman tribune holding Paul. The High Priest Ananias heads the senate now (23:2). Paul claims not to know that he is the High Priest when he lets loose an insulting remark after being struck in the mouth (23:3), but his ignorance may well be feigned. Although Luke has never divulged this before, it suddenly serves his rhetorical purpose to have Paul realise that the *synedrion* is divided between Sadducees and Pharisees: 'the one section comprises Sadducees and the other Pharisees' (23:6). Paul seizes on this fact to create a diversion: he claims to be a Pharisee on trial simply because of his belief in resurrection—which, Luke reminds us, the Sadducees reject, along with angels and spirits (23:8). Paul's claim causes 'great commotion' as the two schools square off against each other, with the Pharisees conceding that Paul might indeed have heard from an angel or a spirit (23:9)!

The story is filled with irony and sarcasm. Since its main point seems to be that Paul cleverly devises a ruse to save himself, we should not put too much weight on particular items. The whole narrative of Luke-Acts has told us that Christianity is essentially different from Pharisaism, and that Jesus' resurrection is a unique case abundantly supported by evidence and divine demonstration. In light of all that has happened, the Pharisees and the Sadducees would be truly stupid to fall for Paul's claim. The author is making sport of these Jewish schools. Nevertheless, the joke has a serious side. First, the Pharisees' belief in resurrection confirms that Christianity belongs in the orbit of Jewish philosophical culture—even though resurrection might seem strange to Gentile philosophers (17:32). Secondly, the Pharisees' openness to Paul, comical though it is, recalls Gamaliel's more serious openness and the Pharisees' lost opportunities of bygone days; now, their academic debates with the Sadducees about resurrection are ludicrous, given their incomprehension of Jesus' significance. Luke's *division* of the senate into only two parties fits his narrative here, but we know that can present it otherwise in different situations; it is unclear exactly how he really perceives the council's make-up.

More clues for understanding the church's relationship to Jewish leaders are furnished by Paul's defence before Felix at Caesarea. The High Priest, *still* relying on outward human measures while blithely ignoring God's will, enlists the aid of an orator (ῥήτορος) named Tertullus. The appearance of an *orator* in the High Priest's team gives the story of the Jewish leaders a sense of closure, with no little humour. Luke's readers know that truth is not to be found in rhetoric. There had always been a stand-off between those interested in the truth, whether philosophers or historians, and orators, whose talent lay in making the worse case appear the better. And now, finally, the High Priest has employed an orator in his service—a fitting move for the 'white-washed wall' (23:3)! Tertullus' speech, typical of a servile golden mouth, reeks with obsequiousness toward this notoriously impious governor (as the readers perhaps understand).[114] Still, Luke has Tertullus call Christianity a *school* (αἵρεσις) alongside the other Jewish schools: Paul is 'a ringleader of the school of the Nazarenes' (24:5). The Christians appear as a philosophical school within Jewish culture, bearing the standard of truth against the rhetoric and sophistry of the others. They are persecuted in the same way that all truth-telling philosophers have always been persecuted by sophists.

Admittedly, Luke's Paul implicitly rejects the label of a 'school' ('the Way, which they call a school'; 24:14), but that is because for him Christianity is now the only way, and not simply one 'choice' (*cf.* αἱρέομαι). His reluctance does not stem from disagreement that Christianity belongs within Jewish culture, for he protests his fidelity to the Jewish people (24:16-18). By putting the term on Tertullus' lips, Luke can claim that Christianity is at least accepted by Jews as a one of their own schools, which identification helps to locate it socially within the Mediterranean world.

---

[114]Luke's Paul, by contrast, directly confronts Felix on issues of righteousness, self-control, and coming judgement (24:25). His brief flattery of Agrippa II at 26:3 seems intended as sharp sarcasm, in view of the presence of Agrippa's lover-sister Berenice (25:23), who serves no narrative function if not to make the reader recall their widely rumoured liaison.

That the word carries no negative connotation is shown by Paul's use of it again in his defence before Agrippa. This scene draws together many aspects of Luke's treatment of the Jewish leadership groups and so provides a fitting conclusion to our survey of Luke-Acts on this question. Paul says in part:

> All the Jews know my way of life right from my youth, which was spent from the beginning among my people and in Jerusalem; they have known me all along, if they are willing to declare it, that according to *the most precise school* of our [Jewish] piety I lived as a Pharisee (κατὰ τὴν ἀκριβεστάτην αἵρεσιν τῆς ἡμετέρας θρησκείας ἔζησα Φαρισαῖος).

So the Pharisees are, as the reader has come to suspect, the most famous and precise of the Jewish schools. At least for someone in Paul's position, not being a priest, there seem to be no stronger Jewish credentials than alliance with the Pharisees. Paul continues:

> And now it is on the basis of our forefathers' hope in the promise given by God that I stand on trial, for which hope our twelve tribes earnestly worship night and day, aspiring to grasp it. Concerning this hope I am accused by the Jews, O King. But why is it thought incredible by all of you that God raises the dead?

Thus far Paul stresses the closeness between the Christians' root claim, that Jesus was raised, and Pharisaic belief. In doing so, perhaps he recalls for the reader the whole Gospel of Luke and the early part of Acts, in which the Pharisees maintained a cautiously critical interest in the new teaching. They shared the belief of Jesus and his students in a future resurrection in which rewards and punishments would be meted out. In one of its two basic claims (the dying Messiah is a more contentious issue not raised here), Christianity stands in continuity with the views of the most exacting school. But this theoretical point of agreement has long passed by the time of Luke's Paul, as God's successive revelations were missed by most Pharisees and other Jews.

Paul goes on:

> Indeed I myself thought it necessary to put up strong opposition against the name of Jesus of Nazareth. That is what I did among the Jerusalemites: I locked up many of the holy ones in prisons, having received the authority to do so from the chief priests, and as they were being killed I cast a vote against them. And often punishing them in synagogues everywhere I tried to coerce them into repudiating [this

> name]—I was boiling over with rage to the extent that I pursued them even into other regions.

Paul recalls here his own entry into the Christian story, right at the moment when Jews as a whole began to turn against Stephen and the other Christians because of rumours that they were overturning Jewish tradition in the name of this Jesus. Saul the Pharisee was a vital part of this coherent Jewish effort led by the chief priests. The usual gulf between chief priests and Pharisees (with the people) assumed in the Gospel and as late as Gamaliel's speech had now been overcome for the sake of the Christian problem. Nevertheless, Paul goes on, God compelled this member of the Pharisaic school to accept Jesus as Messiah, and he could not disobey the heavenly revelation (24:12-19). The reader knows that some other Pharisees also believed.

Thus, on the one hand, Luke's view is that Christianity is the only proper response to God's revelations, which stand in complete continuity with the biblical heritage and promises. Nevertheless, from a social perspective, the mainstream of Jews see it as a new 'school' alongside those of the Pharisees and Sadducees. Luke's own use of 'Jews' without qualification to mean non-Christians belies this claim: the two communities are indeed separate by his day, and Christian groups are mainly Gentile. But this basic narrative assumption throws into relief Luke's efforts to plead the church's genuinely Jewish heritage: the church may be understood as the school that fearlessly proclaims the truth, though it is opposed by complacent sophists in positions of power, who are stereotypically unwilling to examine themselves or change their thinking (μετάνοια).

3. *Conclusion*

The Book of Acts, then, opens with the same impression of Jewish leaders that the Gospel had developed. After Jesus' resurrection, the Jewish *people* continue to respond faithfully to the message of Jesus' followers, accepting Jesus' messiahship in the tens of thousands. This broad popular response is predictably opposite to that of the Sadducean, Temple-based leadership, whose antagonism operates at several levels. Politically, they are upset at the continued propagation of Jesus' name. Socially, they reject the untutored apostles' ambition to teach the people in the Temple precincts. Theologically, they find the doctrine of resurrection absurd. Their comically futile attempts to stamp out the budding Christian movement in the face of divine intervention reinforce their image as powerless pretenders, always fearful of popular resentment.

Between the people and the Jerusalem leaders stand the Pharisees. They are popular teachers, widely respected for their precision (ἀκρίβεια). Only now do we learn, however, that the Pharisees are represented in the Jerusalem council. At the outset, things still look hopeful as the influential Pharisee Gamaliel is able to persuade the council that the Christians should be left alone for the time being—a view that accords with his roles as both pragmatic councillor and mediator of popular sentiment. The reader will ultimately discover that Pharisees constitute one of the two major blocs in the council, a fact suppressed by Luke to serve his earlier points, but Luke never abandons his basic assumption that the two parties represent different constituencies and views.

This essential difference of outlook between the schools intensifies the drama when, after some false reports about Stephen's teaching, the whole Jewish people begins to unite behind a bipartisan coalition on the Christian problem. The kind of basic conflict between Christians and 'the Jews' that is assumed in other Christian literature develops only now, late in the day; the gulf is widened by Christian relativisation of the dietary laws and full inclusion of uncircumcised Gentiles. Significant numbers of priests and Pharisees trust Jesus as Messiah, and pockets of Diaspora Jewry supplement their numbers, but this leaves a large residue of hardening Jewish opposition. While conceding this growing separation, Luke nonetheless tries to maintain the church's position within the orbit of Jewish culture by casting it as another *school* in addition to the Pharisees and Sadducees. In reality it is more than a school, since it alone has been faithful to successive divine revelations, but it is at least perceived as a school by other Jews.

Luke has nothing to say about the vexed question of the Jewish senate's right to inflict the death penalty. But he *assumes* throughout his narratives that the council can both condemn and execute offenders against Jewish law. The senate led by the chief priests plans to kill Jesus, the apostles, and Paul; they do kill Stephen without impediment. Their decision to have Jesus tried by Pilate, we have seen, stems not from an inability to try capital cases (*cf.* Jn. 18:31) but from their customary fear of the people (19:48; 20:6, 19). When this fear prevents them from seizing Jesus themselves, they send spies to ask him about tribute to Caesar, hoping that his answer will provide grounds for a trial by the governor (20:20). That would remove Jesus but still leave them free of popular resentment for the move. The reader concludes that they would have seized and executed Jesus had it not been for this pervasive fear.

Although we cannot offer detailed assessments of other scholarship on our theme, the foregoing interpretation of the Jewish leaders in Luke-Acts may serve as tacit confirmation of some points and disconfirmation of others in the work of Sanders, Brawley, and Darr. In my view, their common weakness is their desire to make the Pharisees a static symbol of some kind, though Luke's whole narrative seems to resist static identifications. To make sense of all the narrative indicators, one must respect Luke's avowed *historical* interest—in describing how things got to be the way they now are—and shed the old form-critical bugbear that requires each item in the story to correspond to some aspect of the reading community's life.

IV. In Josephus

We are fortunate indeed to possess the narratives of the 1st-century Jewish historian Josephus. They also discuss the Jewish leadership groups in question, but from an entirely different perspective. Whereas Luke disdains the Jerusalem establishment, Josephus is a proud member of it. Luke could never have written these words:

> What could be more beautiful or just than to have placed God as governor of the whole universe, to assign to the common priesthood the administration of the greatest affairs, and to have entrusted to the High Priest the governance of all the other priests? (*C. Ap.* 2.185)

With the aristocrat Josephus we enter a new world of values, which may be contrasted with Luke's according to the following scheme.

Luke	*Josephus*
God	God
Jesus and his Followers	The Chief Priests
The Jewish People	(Sadducees)
Pharisees	Essenes
Chief Priests (Sadducees)	(Pharisees)
	The Jewish People

Whereas Luke-Acts contains 38 references to chief priests, 6 to Sadducees, and 35 to Pharisees, Josephus has 372 references to chief priests, 13 to Sadducees, and 44 to Pharisees. His work has proportionately much more to do with priestly circles; he has far less interest than Luke in the Pharisees. This divergence of perspective comes through in all of Josephus' narratives, which we shall now consider in turn. The basic difference between Luke and Josephus should make us all the more aware of any *shared assumptions*, which should be extremely useful for historical reflection.

1. *The* Jewish War

In post-war Rome, the captured Jewish general Josephus first wrote an account of the war, to combat the anti-Jewish histories that had already appeared. Although those histories have not survived, we may infer from later Roman accounts (Tacitus, *Hist.* 5.1-13) and from Josephus' own story (*e.g. BJ* 1.2, 7-9) that they at least (a) presented the revolt as a typical expression of the rebellious Jewish national character and (b) portrayed the Roman victory as another triumph of Roman Fortune, which defeated the Jewish God. Josephus argues, by contrast, that (a) the revolt was an untypical action, engineered by a handful of power-seeking 'tyrants' who duped the masses—against the whole train of Jewish tradition, which advocated peaceful observance of the laws (*BJ* 1.9-12)—and (b) it was the all-powerful God worshipped by the Jews who used the Romans, to whom he had entrusted world power at this moment of history, to punish his people for their sins, particularly for the rebels' pollution of the Temple in Jerusalem. As a priest of the conquered nation (1.3), Josephus will offer an authoritative *Jewish* account to help alleviate post-war hostilities.

In this Temple-centred history, the chief priests play a critical role. From the beginning of the Hasmonaean story through the Herodian and subsequent periods, the reader is regularly informed about the identity of the serving High Priest (1.31, 56, 68, 109, 194 *etc.*). Josephus assumes everywhere that the High Priest and his associates are the authorised rulers of the nation. These chief priests regularly appear in epexegetical union with 'the powerful' (οἱ δυνατοί) and 'the eminent' (οἱ γνώριμοι) (2.243, 301, 316, 318, 336, 410, 422 *etc.*). These groups are often called simply 'the leaders' (οἱ ἄρχοντες) (2.237, 333, 405 [and councillors], 407 *etc.*). A 1st-century reader would quickly understand that these are the wealthiest and most educated Jews, the aristocratic leaders of society.

Occasionally they are mentioned alongside 'the council' (ἡ βουλή), which seems to be largely their preserve (2.331, 336). When this senate first appears in the narrative, Josephus mentions it casually, as if it needs no explanation that Jerusalem should have its own βουλή, as Rome and other cities had theirs (1.284, 285; 7.65, 107). The Jerusalem council, Josephus claims, had a meeting chamber—also called a βουλή here—beside the Xystus, or public meeting place (5.145; *cf.* 2.344; 4.243; 6.354). One scribe (ὁ γραμματεύς) of the council, a priest, is mentioned by name (5.532). Josephus also mentions incidentally a commander (στρατηγός) of the Temple precincts, to whom the sentries report (6.294). Interestingly, the word συνέδριον in the *War* consistently refers to an *ad hoc* official meeting; Josephus almost always speaks of its being convened (ἀθροίζω) or dissolved (διαλύω) on a single occasion (1.559, 571, 620, 640; 2.25, 81, 93; 6.342).

The significance of the chief priests for this narrative lies in the fact that they anchor the 'moderate' pacifist position over against the rebels. As the proper guardians of the Temple and its programme, they understand the importance of sustaining the Temple service at all costs, even though they too are deeply offended by the behaviour of Roman officials in Judaea. Their insistence on peace brings them into direct conflict with Josephus' rogues' gallery: Eleazar son of Yair and the Sicarii, Menahem, John of Gischala, Simon son of Giora, the Idumaeans, and the Zealots. Already during Felix's tenure as governor, in the 50's, the Sicarii murder the High Priest Jonathan (2.256). When Gessius Florus plunders the Temple and some of the Jews mock him, the chief priests intercede to alleviate Florus' anger and to maintain peace (2.301-4). When he then callously slaughters Jews in the upper market area, the chief priests implore the incensed people not to retaliate (2.316). They themselves represent the people's complaints to Agrippa, to try to have Florus removed (2.336), but continue to plead with the people not to lead them into open rebellion (2.411-6). The reader knows that the chief priests will be ineffective, however, when one of their own younger members joins the revolutionaries (2.409), and Josephus notes that 'not one of the revolutionary party would listen' to the aristocrats' pleas (2.417).

From this point onward, the chief priests and their associates become the object of deliberate and violent opposition from the rebels. Some rebels set fire to the High Priest's house along with the royal palace and public archives where debts were recorded (2.427). They murder the chief priests Ananias and Ezechias (2.441), and the Idumaeans later kill Jesus and Ananus (4.314-318). Josephus' editorial eulogy on the last two leaders makes clear his sympathy for their position: their love of the Temple and its service, their commitment to peace and national honour (4.319-25). The rebels crown their impiety by electing to the High Priesthood a simpleton from the countryside who was 'not even descended from High Priests' (4.155-7). Josephus complains throughout the narrative that his own views and those of the chief priests were unappealing to the common people, who saw hopes of political, social, economic, and religious salvation in the rebels' vain promises (*e.g.* 6.286-7; *cf.* 2.4, 427, 253-60).

Pharisees and Sadducees do not play a significant role in the main drama of *War*, appearing only in the first two volumes as part of the backdrop. This literary fact is itself important: the Pharisees, Sadducees, and Essenes represent old and, if we may use the term in this context, 'normal' Judaism—the kind that existed before the revolt. The rebels represent a radical departure from all such customary Jewish thinking.

This does not mean that Josephus himself is fond of either Pharisees or Sadducees. He introduces the Pharisees to his Gentile readers while describing the fall of the Hasmonaean house. Alexander Jannaeus' widow Alexandra offered some hope for the failing dynasty, and she did rule well in foreign affairs. But her reign was fatally marred by her superstitious deference to the Pharisees, who used her to manipulate the government for their own ends. Josephus defines the Pharisees for the reader as a group of Jews 'appearing (δοκέω) to be more pious than the others, and to interpret the laws with greater precision (ἀκριβέστερον)' (1.110). The sequel makes clear that he has little sympathy for the Pharisees' reputation; according to him, they were a substantial factor in the demise of the great Hasmonaean house (1.111-4). Nevertheless, they have entered the scene as an important part of Jewish public life.

Their next appearance confirms this impression. In his laudatory account of Herod, who exemplifies the friendly Jewish-Roman relations of bygone days, Josephus argues that Herod's downfall resulted from the schemes of his wives and sons (1.431). In this story of domestic intrigue, he mentions incidentally that one of the many crimes committed by Herod's sister-in-law was her offering of a 'reward' to the Pharisees for opposing him (1.571). We learn nothing more of this opposition here, but suppose that the Pharisees are the influential group introduced earlier in this volume. Their opposition was a considerable aggravation to Herod (it is mentioned along with his own brother's antagonism), and they fall among the troublesome characters in this section of the narrative.

The Pharisees next appear alongside Sadducees and Essenes. This passage sets up an explicit foil for the main story. After briefly mentioning Judas the Galilean, who tried to instigate a tax revolt in AD 6 and whose descendants will appear in the subsequent narrative as leaders of more contemporary insurrections, Josephus insists that this man 'was a sophist of his own private school, having nothing whatsoever in common with the others. For among the Jews *three* groups practise philosophy: on the one hand is the school of Pharisees, and on the other Sadducees; but the third, with a deserved reputation for practising the greatest solemnity, are called Essenes...' (2.118-9). Most of the following section is devoted to an enthusiastic report on the Essenes' virtues and beliefs, which stresses their discipline, political passivity, and fidelity to authorities (2.119-61; *cf.* 134, 139-42).

At the end of this exuberant description, Josephus devotes a summary paragraph to the Pharisees and Sadducees. The Pharisees, as we have come to expect, 'are reputed to interpret the laws with precision (μετ' ἀκριβείας δοκοῦντες) and hold the position (ἀπάγοντες) of the leading school (τὴν πρώτην αἵρεσιν)' (2.162). What Josephus thinks of the Pharisees' popular reputation seems clear enough from his earlier accounts, as well as from the overwhelming space given to the Essenes here in contrast to the Pharisees and Sadducees; it may be, too, that the verb ἀπάγω (lead off, away), which seems peculiar in this context, is meant to have negative connotations.

For the rest, Josephus contrasts the Pharisees and Sadducees on certain philosophical positions: the Pharisees credit human actions to 'Fate and God' in some way and expect rewards and punishments for souls after death, while the Sadducees remove God from the sphere of human action, stress free will, and reject the notion of *post-mortem* reward and punishment (2.163-5). Besides that, the Pharisees cultivate unity of thought among themselves and the community at large (τὸ κοινόν), while the Sadducees are rude even toward their own members (2.166). This notice fits with the Pharisees' status as the 'leading school', though the reader remains in the dark about the Sadducees' constituency. Who could afford such rudeness? Josephus does not care to elaborate. His point here is that the Jews have three old and established schools, represented most admirably by the Essenes, and that the sophist Judas initiated a brash innovation when he called for revolt.

The Sadducees will not appear again in the *War*. Nor will the 'Essenes' under that precise name, though Josephus will mention that John the 'Essaios' (apparently from the same group) entered the conflict on much the same terms as he did (2.567; 3.11). The Pharisees make one more brief but telling appearance, when their 'most eminent' members join forces with the chief priests and powerful ones to dissuade the people from revolt (2.411). This casual notice reflects Josephus' continued assumption that the Pharisees are the most prominent of the 'schools', since Sadducees and Essenes are not mentioned here, but the reader is left to speculate on their exact social status. The prominent Pharisees are no more able than the chief priests and their associates to stem the revolutionary tide. In this struggle for the hearts and minds of the people, the Pharisees appear on the leaders' side over against the rebels, but this whole coalition is sadly unable to divert the nation from ruin.

2. *The* Jewish Antiquities, Life, *and* Against Apion

We may treat together Josephus' *magnum opus*, the *Antiquities*, and his autobiography, the *Life*, which he wrote as an appendix to the longer work. In concluding this survey, I shall also include a note on Josephus' last known composition, the *Against Apion*, which mentions only the priesthood.

The preface to *Antiquities* identifies it as a sequel to the *War* (*Ant*. 1.1-4), but in a somewhat different rhetorical context. Rather than writing primarily to refute false accounts, Josephus now addresses those who, like Ptolemy Philadelphus and his patron Epaphroditus, are 'eager' to learn of Jewish antiquity and culture (1.9-10). Outside of his writings there is abundant evidence that some Romans at the end of the 1st century were attracted in varying degrees to Jewish culture.[115] For such an audience Josephus describes Judaism as the noblest and 'most philosophical' way of life ever devised, far superior to the readers' own unreasonable native mythologies (1.18-26). Only the laws of Moses bring what is most sought after by the philosophical schools: happiness (εὐδαιμονία) (1.14, 20). On the basis of these laws, God rewards virtue and punishes crime with perfect consistency. Josephus' presentation of Judaism as an *effective* system in contrast to

[115]H.J. Leon, *The Jews of Ancient Rome* (Philadelphia: JPSA, 1960) 10-35.

all others provides an interesting parallel to Luke's portrayal of Christian teaching as uniquely effective.

Josephus' autobiography is mainly devoted to the six-month period of his command in the Galilee. He is responding to a work by Justus of Tiberias that has challenged his own account of his actions as commander (*Vita* 40, 336).

As in the *War*, the chief priests are visible everywhere in the narrative of *Antiquities/Life*. In the preface Josephus takes as his model the High Priest Eleazar, who consented to the translation of Jewish scripture into Greek (1.11-2): Eleazar appears as the authorised leader of the nation. In summarising the measures revealed to Moses at Sinai, Josephus details the High Priest's clothing and its cosmic significance (3.159-87) and describes the appointment of Aaron as the first supreme priest (3.188-92). Stones on the High Priest's clothing used to shine, he says, to indicate God's presence with his people (3.214).[116] When Moses had finished receiving the laws, he consigned them to the priests for safeguarding: the High Priest and his subordinates administer the Jewish laws (4.304).

As he wends his way through the biblical era and down to his own day, Josephus again identifies the reigning High Priest at each period (4.152; 5.318; 6.122, 242 *etc.*; 10.150-2; 11.73, 90, 121, 158, 297, 300, 306 *etc.*). At the end of the book, moreover, he recapitulates the entire high-priestly succession (διαδοχή; 20.261) from Aaron through the period following Archelaus' removal (20.224-51). In casting Judaism as a philosophical culture founded by Moses and the High Priests as 'successors', Josephus recalls the language of the philosophical schools, which typically traced a list of true successors who preserved the teachings of the founding philosopher intact (Diogenes Laertius 6.13, 19; Seneca, *Ep*. 40.3).[117]

Josephus differs from Luke on the identity of the serving High Priest at the time of Jesus and his first followers. He has Annas I as High Priest in the period AD 6-15, and Caiaphas as his fourth successor (*Ant*. 18.34-35, 95), whose tenure from AD 18-37 would cover the period of Jesus' death and the church's origin (*cf*. Mt. 26:57). Although Luke implies that Annas was the serving High Priest then, Josephus can be almost equally confusing when he calls an individual 'High Priest' long after his term of office (*BJ* 2.441; *Ant*. 20.205; *Vita* 193); but unlike Luke, he usually provides enough context to clarify the

[116]Thoma, 'The High Priesthood in the Judgment of Josephus', 196-9.
[117]Mason, *Flavius Josephus on the Pharisees*, 235-9.

matter. According to Josephus, Annas was a particularly distinguished High Priest, whose five sons all subsequently served in the office (*Ant.* 20.197-8); his family was thus a major force in chief-priestly circles through the whole period from AD 6 to 70. So it is conceivable that a later writer could also see him as the power behind the office even in Caiaphas' time, though one would have expected Luke to be clearer in Luke 3:2. Luke concurs with Josephus that Ananias was High Priest during Paul's Jerusalem trial (*Ant.* 20.103, 131; Acts 23:2).

The new rhetorical situation in *Antiquities* dictates a somewhat different use of the High Priests as characters over against *War*. Now, in keeping with his theme, Josephus must distinguish good and bad actions of High Priests. The errant High Priests include the greedy and mean-spirited Onias, who brought the nation to the brink of disaster in the Ptolemaic period (12.58), and the later Hasmonaean High Priests who fell dramatically from their ancestors' glory through their selfish intrigues (13.300-19, 431-2). But the most striking examples of transgressors are those whom Josephus had praised effusively in the *War*, when he was using them as foils to the rebel leaders. In *Antiquities* the moderate Ananus is accused of injustice for convening the Jewish council without the Roman governor's permission (20.199), and King Agrippa II deposes him for this reason (20.200-203). This same chief priest accepts bribes to have Josephus ousted from command of the Galilee (*Vita* 193, 196). And on the eve of the revolt the former High Priest Ananias (also praised in *War*) has his servants rob the poorer priests of their tithes, leaving them to starve to death (20.206-7). These actions, together with Ananias' use of bribery to maintain his power (20.213), are a major cause of subsequent divine punishment (20.214, *cf.* 218).

As in the *War*, Josephus assumes that the High Priest heads a council or senate. Moses tells the people that such an aristocracy (ἀριστοκρατία), rather than a monarchy, is the best possible constitution (4.223).[118] When the people later implore Samuel to appoint a king, he is deeply upset because, being a righteous man, he hates kingship and is 'strongly committed to aristocracy' (6.36). Josephus alters the biblical narrative of Joshua's time to make the great commander consult the High Priest and his senate (γερουσία) (5.15, 43, 55). Interpreting the cycles of sin depicted in Judges, Josephus asserts that 'The aristocracy was falling into corruption: no longer did they appoint the senates or the leadership formerly legislated', which failure resulted in

[118]Thoma, 'The High Priesthood in the Judgment of Josephus', 201.

discord and, ultimately, civil war (5.135). When the Jews return from captivity, they live under a government that is 'aristocratic, with the rule of the few' (ἀριστοκρατικὴ μετ' ὀλιγαρχίας) (11.111). A letter from Antiochus III mentions the Jewish senate as the governing body (12.138, 142), and Jonathan the Hasmonaean writes as High Priest, on behalf of 'the senate and body of priests' (13.166, 169). Although the later Hasmonaean princes create a monarchy (11.111), and so begin the decline of the dynasty (13.301), the Roman Gabinius restores the *aristokratia* when he sets up regional councils in Jewish territory (14.91). The emperor Claudius again writes to the 'rulers, council, and people of Jerusalem' (20.11). This body judges at least some capital cases (*Ant.* 14.167; 20.200-202).

Josephus makes much of the fact that Herod and Archelaus altered tradition by appointing 'insignificant persons' (ἄσημοι) to the High Priesthood, not those from the Hasmonaean line. With the death of Herod and Archelaus' departure, however, 'the High Priests were entrusted with the leadership of the nation' (ἡ προστασία τοὺς ἔθνους; 20.251). These notices confirm that for him the nation is properly an aristocracy, and that Herod's rule was an aberration. This view may explain the virtual disappearance of the council led by the High Priest during Herod's reign.

Outside of Herod's reign, the term συνέδριον in *Antiquities* often means the regular Jewish senate led by the High Priest. This usage begins when Gabinius establishes five *synedria* of which Jerusalem is the first (14.91). That the Jerusalem *synedrion* was continuous with the older senate led by the High Priest (in Josephus' story) is indicated by the complaint of the Jewish leaders to the High Priest Hyrcanus II that Herod has killed bandits in Galilee without a trial before the *synedrion, as the Law requires* (14.167). Bowing to their pleas, Hyrcanus convenes the *synedrion* (14.168, 170, 171, 177-80). In this story, one of the councillors—who turns out to be a Pharisee (15.3-4), though Josephus chooses not to say so here—fruitlessly insists that Herod be punished, against the will of the majority. Paradoxically, when Herod becomes king he kills all the members of the *synedrion* except this one (or two? 14.175; 15.4). That is not the end of this council, however, for (according to one version known to Josephus) Herod later pressured it to approve the execution of the High Priest Hyrcanus (15.173). Once Herod becomes king, *Antiquities* uses *synedrion* of the *ad hoc* meetings convened by him (16.357-67; 17.46). It is not clear whether the *synedrion* that later permitted the Levites to wear linen was the standing council or another *ad hoc* group (20.216-7). But clearly, Josephus assumes that the

Jews were normally governed by a council led by the High Priest (*cf.* also *C. Ap.* 1.30; 2.185).

Early in the 60's, the High Priest Ananus' convening of a (the?) *synedrion* in the absence of a Roman governor leads to his removal (20.200, 202). Even though the council was still led by the High Priest, he did not have the power to convene it without Roman approval. Note that in Acts the Roman tribune can summon the council (Acts 22:30).

The clearest picture we get of the inner workings of *any* Jerusalem council in Josephus comes in his account of John of Gischala's attempt to have him withdrawn from the Galilee (*Vita* 189-98). Whether this body, τὸ κοινὸν τῶν Ἱεροσολυμιτῶν, was the regular senate is not immediately clear.[119] The serving High Priest, who seems to have been Matthias son of Theophilus (*Ant.* 20.223), does not surface in the proceedings; the leading figures are the *former* High Priests Ananus and Jesus. One gathers from the parallel in *War* that the rebels (mysteriously) won over those members of the ruling class that remained in Jerusalem and then appointed them leaders (*BJ* 2.556-68). Since the individuals involved were also the customary leaders of the people, however, this group appears as a makeshift war cabinet, a subset of the regular leadership (*cf.* 2.411).

In any case, our question concerns the function of τὸ κοινὸν τῶν Ἱεροσολυμιτῶν in the story of *Life*. Josephus can call this *koinon* 'the *synedrion* of Jerusalem' (*Vita* 62), or simply 'the leaders' (οἱ πρῶτοι) of the people (*Life* 28). His terms appear interchangeable. He seems to favour the expression τὸ *κοινὸν* τῶν Ἱεροσολυμιτῶν in the *Life* as a way of insisting upon the legitimacy of his military appointment, over against Justus' claims (65, 72, 190, 254, 267, 309, 341, 393): he was selected by 'the body politic of the Jerusalemites'. The *Life* gives us no reason to suppose that the war council was essentially different from the ordinary senate that governed the state under the High Priest's leadership when there was no king. Elsewhere in Josephus, τὸ κοινόν can refer to a standing council headed by the High Priest (*Ant.* 6.17; 13.366), though the meaning of the phrase is flexible.

No matter how typical this particular council was, it is significant that John reportedly tried to use his influence with Simon son of Gamaliel, a leading and respected Pharisee on the council from a 'very illustrious family', to effect his aims. In response to John's request

[119]J.J. Price, *Jerusalem under Siege: The Collapse of the Jewish State, 66-70 C.E.* (Leiden: E.J. Brill, 1992) 63-67.

Simon 'tried to persuade (ἔπειθεν) the chief priests Ananus and Jesus, son of Gamalas, and some others of their bloc (στάσις)...' (193). The situation assumed here has some parallels to what we found in Luke-Acts: chief priests and Pharisees have different constituencies and aims; the Pharisees are not the official powers but are able to sway the chief priests often enough that the Galilean considers it worthwhile trying to use Simon's influence here. Josephus claims, however, that Ananus pointed out the difficulties involved in persuading the council to take such action, since 'many of the chief priests and leaders (οἱ προεστῶτες) of the people' would testify to his ability as commander. Unfazed, the eminent Pharisee allegedly resorted to bribery in order to accomplish his goal. Finally persuaded by these underhanded means, 'Ananus and those with him' sent a delegation of three Pharisees and one other to replace Josephus (196-8). The Pharisee succeeded, one way or another.

In comparison with the chief priests, the Pharisees and Sadducees receive little attention in *Antiquities/Life*. They first appear in the time of Jonathan the Hasmonaean. Josephus interrupts his paraphrase of 1 Maccabees to say that 'at about this time' there were three philosophical schools (αἱρέσεις) among the Jews (13.171). In this summary, only the question of fate and free will is raised. Whereas *War* had presented the Pharisees and Sadducees as polar opposites on this problem, and the Essenes as a group by themselves, Josephus now places the Essenes on the pro-fate pole and shifts the Pharisees to a vague middle ground, while keeping the Sadducees at the pro-volition extreme (13.171-3). We should not make too much of the difference, since Josephus refers the reader to *War* for further clarification.

He also has a story about Pharisees and Sadducees during the time of John Hyrcanus, which he omitted from the much briefer account in *War*. There he noted only that 'large numbers' of Hyrcanus' countrymen fomented sedition because they envied the successes of his family (*BJ* 1.67). Josephus himself, however, had nothing but admiration for his great ancestor (*BJ* 1.68-9). In the more leisurely account of *Antiquities* he connects this popular opposition with Hyrcanus' abandonment of the Pharisees in favour of the Sadducean school: 'As for Hyrcanus, the envy of the Jews was aroused against him by his own successes and those of his sons; particularly hostile to him were the Pharisees.... And so great is their influence that even when they speak against a king or High Priest, they immediately gain credence' (13.288). Once again, the Pharisees appear as the vanguard of popular religious sentiment.

According to the story, the conflict arose because the Pharisees failed to specify an appropriate punishment for one who challenged Hyrcanus' right to serve as High Priest—because of a (false) rumour that his mother had been a war captive (13.290-2). Josephus' comment that the Pharisees tended toward leniency in punishment is no compliment from him: in an age of rising crime, he boasts about the perfect justice and severity of Jewish law (*Ant.* 1.14, 20-3; *C. Ap.* 2.175-8, 276-8; *cf. Ant.* 4.152-5). Josephus the narrator is as offended by this baseless insult (βλασφημία) to Hyrcanus and the Pharisees' failure to specify a fitting punishment (τῷ μέτρῳ τῆς δίκης; 13.294) as he is by the Sadducee Jonathan's exploitation of the incident (13.295-6).

Hyrcanus' departure from the Pharisees causes him to abrogate certain regulations (νόμιμα) that they had established for the people. It is this abrogation of Pharisaic laws that reportedly lies behind the popular hatred of Hyrcanus (13.296). Josephus must now pause to explain, since he has not done so elsewhere, that the Pharisees had passed on to the people 'regulations from a succession of fathers', which are not among the laws of Moses—elsewhere in Josephus, the heart and soul of Judaism. The Sadducees reject these regulations and hold only to what is written in the laws (13.297). Josephus claims that this difference was the root of 'conflicts and major differences' between the schools. But, 'whereas the Sadducees have influence among the wealthy (εὔποροι) alone, and enjoy no following at all among the populace, the Pharisees have the allegiance of the masses' (13.298).

All of this serves to justify Josephus' original connection between Pharisaic antagonism and popular opposition (13.288). The people prefer the Pharisees' laws. This passage fits well with everything else we have seen in both *War* and *Antiquities*; it also agrees with the assumptions of Luke-Acts. Note that Josephus' editorial comments here (13.288, 289, 294, 297-8) are in the present tense: he is interpreting the story according to his own experience of public affairs. His evaluation of the Pharisees is clear enough, for he praises John Hyrcanus' accomplishments in spite of popular/Pharisaic 'envy'. Moreover, his own view of scripture, that Moses' written laws are the all-sufficient code of Jewish life (*e.g. C. Ap.* 1.6-29; 2.164-189), leads one to conclude that he would side with the Sadducees *on this question*. Although he recognises Pharisaic regulations as something extra, he does not appeal to them in his many discussions of Jewish laws elsewhere. Yet he is no Sadducee.

That the Jewish leaders of Josephus' story were not free to impose their own legal views, but were typically concerned to maintain popular favour, is confirmed by what follows. Alexander Jannaeus provokes a serious civil war because of the perception that he has violated Jewish custom—partly, again, by holding the High Priesthood when his mother had been a captive (13.372-6). He ends up killing more than 50,000 of his own subjects. The aristocrat Josephus, while viewing the whole affair as unfortunate, takes some effort to justify Alexander's behaviour (13.372, 381-2).

When Alexander lies dying, however, his wife Alexandra—no longer the gullible woman of *War*—bitterly complains that he is going to leave her with a hostile nation (13.399). His recommended solution, interestingly enough, is that she invite the Pharisees back into power, for they will quickly bring the nation over to her side (13.400). Indeed, 'these men had so much influence with their fellow-Jews that they could injure those whom they hated and help those to whom they were friendly; for they had the complete confidence of the masses...' (13.401-2). Only now do we learn that Alexander's conflicts with the people resulted from his harsh treatment of the Pharisees (13.402, 410), the unnamed popular leaders of the Alexander narrative. Josephus assumes the connection between people and Pharisees that he has elsewhere spelled out. Alexandra goes along with the plan and, just as Alexander predicted, the Pharisees quickly turn the nation in her favour (13.405-6). She gives the Pharisees complete control of domestic policy and re-establishes their special regulations (13.408). So ends the popular unrest that had plagued John Hyrcanus and (especially) Alexander.

One might suppose that Josephus is pleased by the cessation of hostility, but he is no democrat. Rather, he sides with the aristocratic victims of Alexandra's popular regime, led by the vigorous Aristobulus, who should have been given the rule (13.408-18). Although the Pharisees are not legitimate rulers, they take advantage of their power to slaughter their opponents and 'play drunken games' with the Hasmonaean house (13.409-11, 426). In his closing reflection, Josephus severely criticises Alexandra for having secured her short-term prosperity by an alliance with the Pharisees, at the expense of the long-term welfare of the ruling family: she should have let her sons rule (13.430-2; *cf.* 417). The priestly aristocrat Josephus regrets the Pharisees' great influence with the people.[120]

The next significant story involving the Pharisees comes in Josephus' narrative of Herod's reign. Herod is nearing the end of his life, increasingly beset by fears and sickness caused by his many transgressions of the laws (according to *Antiquities*). A group of women in his court causes him particular difficulties. Further, 'There was also a certain faction of Jewish people greatly priding itself on its extreme precision in the national heritage and the laws, pretending [to observe] those things that pleased the Deity; the bloc of women was led by them, called Pharisees' (17.41). These Pharisees, like their forebears under Hyrcanus and Alexander, are intent on 'fighting and injuring' the king (17.41; *cf.* 13.288, 401). From a social point of view, it is striking that they seem to have such easy access to Herod's court; they obviously have great influence for some reason.

Elaborating upon his notice in *BJ* 1.571, Josephus claims that when more than 6,000 of these men refused an oath of loyalty to Caesar and Herod, their fine was paid by Herod's sister-in-law (17.42). In return, they misused their famous spiritual abilities to promise her that she and her husband would become rulers after Herod had been removed by God (17.43). When Herod discovered the plot, he put to death those who had believed 'what the Pharisee said' (17.44). The whole story is very hostile toward the Pharisees, but it fits well with Josephus' characteristic portrayal of them as popular pretenders to expertise in the laws, for whom he has no sympathy.

Finally, when Josephus comes to describe Judas' census revolt, as in *War* he contrasts Judas' 'school', here φιλοσοφία, with the three established φιλοσοφίαι among the Jews (18.9-10). He elaborates greatly on the unprecedented character of Judas' innovation, which would ultimately lead to the destruction of God's Temple (18.8). Once again, Josephus' beloved Essenes receive the highest praise as exemplary Jews (18.18-22), and once again the Pharisees and Sadducees are contrasted more or less as opposites (18.12-17).

Josephus makes five basic statements here about the Pharisees: they tend to simplicity of life, rejecting softness or luxury (18.12); they observe a special tradition and revere their elders (18.12); they attribute everything to Fate and God, although they also work out a cooperation with human volition (18.13); and they believe in rewards and punishments after death for immortal souls (18.14). 'As it happens', Josephus claims, these views make them extremely influential (πιθανώτατοι) among the people, such that 'of prayers and sacred

---

[120]S. Mason, 'Josephus on the Pharisees Reconsidered: A Critique of Smith/ Neusner', *SR* 17 (1988) 455-69; against M. Smith, 'Palestinian Judaism in the First Century', 76.

rites, whatever is considered divine happens to be conducted according to their interpretation. This much of their influence the cities have demonstrated, in both manner of life and discourse, by their pursuit of [or adherence to] the way that prevails over all' (18.15).

He draws attention to the Pharisees' influence with the people yet *again* when he describes the Sadducees. Their philosophical views are given succinctly: they hold that the soul perishes along with the body, and they reject all 'additional work/creation' (μεταποίησις) outside the laws, even reckoning it a virtue to dispute with 'the teachers of wisdom which they pursue' (18.16). What Josephus mainly wants to say about the Sadducees is that: 'This teaching has been made known to a few men only. Though these are of the very highest rank, nothing is actually done by them according to their programme. For whenever they assume some position of leadership, they accordingly defer to what the Pharisee says—albeit unwillingly and by compulsion—since otherwise they would not be tolerated by the masses' (18.17).

These descriptions of the Pharisees and Sadducees elaborate considerably on the accounts in *War*, partly because the intervening narrative has made certain points clear; for example, the Pharisees have a special extrabiblical tradition, a broad popular base, and a controlling hold on the common manner of observance, whereas the Sadducees have only a small base among (not even coextensive with) the aristocracy. This is not a matter of the Pharisees' *control*; rather, their views are the most popular, and their popular support gives them inevitable clout with the rulers. In public office (ὁπότε ἐπ' ἀρχας παρέλθοιεν), Sadducees must bow to the popular will, which means reluctantly following the Pharisees' agenda. Josephus' history of the Hasmonaeans from John Hyrcanus to Alexandra copiously illustrates his claim. Herod also faced serious problems because of the Pharisees. Josephus will show their influence again when he describes John's effort to have him removed. He writes not as an advocate of Pharisaic influence, but as a resigned commentator from the aristocratic side, who sees the pretensions of this popular school as a consistently inimical force in Jewish history. Although John Hyrcanus, Aristobulus I, and Alexander Jannaeus tried to maintain their distance from the Pharisees, those rulers could not hold out against the people's demands, and so the Pharisees' influence continues to dominate the religious scene. In view of the attention that Josephus has given to this temporary abandonment of Pharisaic laws, their reconstitution, and the current power of the Pharisees, the reader might be expected to infer that the Pharisaic regulations (whatever they were!) have remained in force to his own day.

The only remaining reference to Sadducees in *Antiquities* concerns the High Priest Ananus, whose convening of a *synedrion* to have James executed is attributed by Josephus to his Sadducean school allegiance. The Sadducees, Josephus asserts, are savage (ὠμοὶ) in punishment compared with other Jews (20.199), and this action greatly offended those who were most fair-minded and precise in the laws. They acted quickly to have the High Priest removed from office (20.201-2). Josephus does not clarify who these others were, but if they included Pharisees as many commentators think,[121] then (a) we have a striking case of Pharisees' exerting their influence to have a sitting High Priest removed, but (b) Josephus chooses not to disclose their Pharisaic identity while praising their action. Perhaps he does not wish to leave the impression that he likes Pharisees, even as he suppressed Samaias' Pharisaic allegiance when he recounted that councillor's courageous action in the *synedrion* (14.172; *cf.* 15.3-4).

Josephus' *Against Apion* offers a brief, systematic rebuttal of Judaism's literary defamers along with a positive statement of the culture's principles. The priesthood and its leadership play an important role as guardians of this peerless heritage. The Jews' ancestors put in charge of their records 'the most excellent men (οἱ ἄριστοι)', namely, priests (1.30; *cf. Vita* 1). In Jewish culture, the greatest precautions are taken to ensure that the priestly *aristoi* remain ancestrally pure (1.31). Jewish records, accordingly, contain the names of their High Priests in succession through 2,000 years (1.36). In his famous discussion of the Jewish 'theocracy' (2.165), Josephus further celebrates the priests' care for the laws: 'this responsibility included the precise administration of the Law and of the other pursuits of everyday life; the priests were charged with supervision of all affairs, the settlement of legal disputes, and the punishment of those condemned' (2.187). His emphasis on the condemnation of criminals reflects his view that only the Jewish laws deal effectively with crime (2.276-8; *cf. Ant.* 1.20-22). The priests, supervised by the High Priest (2.185), are the agents of this uniquely effective system.

---

[121]*E.g.* G. Baumbach, 'The Sadducees in Josephus', 185; E.P. Sanders, *Judaism: Practice & Belief 63 BCE – 66 CE*, 419.

V. General Conclusions

In Acts we have the second volume of a work that seeks to chart the development of Jesus' followers from a movement within Judaism to a largely Gentile group rejected by most Jews. To sketch and to justify this development, Luke makes extensive use of certain Jewish groups—the chief priests, Sadducees, Pharisees, and *synedrion*—as background characters. Our aim has been to understand how these groups function in the story of Luke-Acts. Although we have an ultimately historical interest, that history does not exist anywhere in advance. We can only try to recreate the history once we understand the evidence that needs explaining, of which Luke-Acts is a significant part. Luke's contemporary, Josephus, wrote the only non-Christian narratives of the time that mention the groups in question. So, instead of trying to compare Luke-Acts with 'history', I have included an analysis of Josephus' narratives as a way of throwing Luke's portrayal into relief.

Luke and Josephus present radically different viewpoints. For the Christian author, Jesus brought his divinely authorised teaching to the common people, and especially to the outcasts among them. In doing so, he had to contend with the Pharisees, who completely dominated popular piety outside of Jerusalem. Jesus was severely critical of these established teachers for forfeiting their responsibilities by failing to help the people. They were the salt that had lost its flavour, righteous guardians of conventional piety who were blind to the people's needs and Jesus' effectiveness. He, by contrast, summoned a group of students who lived heroically counter-cultural lives while bringing real help to the masses. The Pharisees, though often alarmed at Jesus' actions, remained cautiously open to this popular teacher.

When he came to Jerusalem, however, he encountered an altogether different group of leaders: the aristocratic, Sadducean, God-denying chief priests, with their executive council and police force. Their immediate opposition to Jesus was intended to be lethal, though Luke makes fun of their impotence. They finally managed to arrest and to execute Jesus, with unacknowledged supernatural intervention. The Jerusalem establishment was very far indeed from God's will. These lofty authorities lived in constant fear of popular sentiment, to which they regularly acceded.

In Acts, the story has fundamentally changed as a result of Jesus' resurrection, which makes acceptance of his messiahship a divine requirement. At the outset, the common people support the new teaching in large numbers and the Pharisees continue their role as cautious observers. With the circumstances that lead to Stephen's death, however, the Pharisees (who now appear in the Jerusalem council itself!) and the people close ranks with the chief priests, to present a more or less galvanised Jewish opposition, in spite of cross-overs through the remaining narrative. While acknowledging this growing separation, Luke insists that the Christians only did what was required by God, and that they have by no means abandoned the Jewish heritage. The Jews view the 'Nazarenes' as a philosophical school alongside the Pharisees and Sadducees. As a self-conscious historian, Luke has tried to correct the pictures of the Jewish leaders in the other Christian texts known to him.

Josephus, in marked contrast to Luke, is an enthusiastic spokesman for the Jewish aristocracy. He believes that the laws delivered to Moses by God are the finest in the world; the priestly *aristoi* led by the chief priests are the authorised guardians of this cosmic treasure. He looks on the common people with a combination of pity and contempt because they are vulnerable to whatever self-appointed leaders come along, who often create serious problems for the duly established leadership. In the *War*, this tension plays itself out in the struggle between the chief priests and the rebel leaders for the people's hearts and minds; Josephus admits that the chief priests failed. In the *Antiquities*, which deals with Judaism in more stable times, the Pharisees are the people's troublesome advocates, though they are not as bad as the rebel leaders. Josephus' later works elaborate his portrait of the chief priests as guardians of the nation's glorious tradition, even while conceding that some chief priests have brought God's punishment on the people (*Antiquities*).

The basic divergence of religious perspective between Luke and Josephus makes their agreement in basic assumptions remarkable. This coincidence may be summarised as follows:

(1) The chief priests were the traditional Jewish aristocracy, who had supreme control of national affairs from their base in Jerusalem. They were the highest Jewish authorities in the land when there was no king, exercising control over the Temple service, promulgating the laws, and trying cases. They typically ruled by means of a council or senate headed by the serving High Priest, which had a designated meeting place in or near the Temple precinct. Neither author claims that this council had always ruled on the same terms, but both assume conciliar aristocratic rule as the norm. The council envisioned need not

fit the old picture of an independent, representative parliament,[122] but Luke and Josephus both assume that it was a regular body with an executive function. The chief priests had security or police forces at their disposal, tried capital cases, and executed offenders. In spite of their visible authority, however, the chief priests always had to be concerned about popular sentiment, often mediated by the Pharisees, which frequently hampered their own programme. We note, incidentally, that most ancient ruling bodies were profoundly concerned to conciliate the people, even in Rome, the centre of world power.[123]

(2) Luke and Josephus describe more of what the Sadducees did not think than what they did think. For both, they were a philosophical school holding sceptical views. They had a tiny base in the aristocracy, including at least some members of the family of Ananus (Annas), though Luke estimates Sadducean influence in chief-priestly circles more highly than Josephus. According to both writers, Sadducees denied life after death and consequently the notion of *post-mortem* rewards and punishments. Their rejection of the Pharisees' special traditions along with their different social status led to the ongoing conflicts that Luke and Josephus describe. Luke's claim that the Sadducees recognised 'neither angel nor spirit' (Acts 23:8) would fit broadly with their rejection of immortality and non-biblical tradition if the reference is to a more elaborate, extrabiblical angelology and demonology accepted by the Pharisees. If Luke indicates a categorical rejection of ἄγγελοι, even those of the Pentateuch itself, his claim stands alone. Both authors lack any sympathy for Sadducean positions.

(3) Luke and Josephus understand the Pharisees as a philosophical school occupying a middle ground between the chief-priestly aristocracy and the masses. Their roots were with the people, among whom they enjoyed a long-standing reputation for precision in the laws and great piety. Their influence does not appear as authoritative control, but arises from shared aspirations, an important part of which was the hope for resurrection and judgement. The common people (Luke: largely outside of Jerusalem) had little to do with chief priests, but treated the Pharisees as authorised teachers. Yet the most eminent Pharisees, those from distinguished families such as Gamaliel's family, held positions in the senate. Because they were perceived to represent popular opinion, they were often (Josephus: routinely) able to sway

[122]Thus far M. Goodman, *The Ruling Class of Judaea: The Origins of the Jewish Revolt against Rome A.D. 66-70* (Cambridge: CUP, 1987) 113-8; E.P. Sanders, *Judaism: Practice & Belief 63 BCE – 66 CE*, 472-81.

[123]Macmullen, *Enemies of the Roman Order*, 172-3.

the council's decisions, though both authors suggest that they constituted a minority in the council. In the face of certain popular leaders, such as militants and charismatics who precipitated the revolt (in Josephus) or Jesus of Nazareth (in Luke), even the Pharisees failed to maintain the people's complete confidence.

These agreements are striking even if, as I think likely, Luke was familiar with the later volumes of Josephus' *Antiquities*.[124] Whether he knew Josephus' work or not, Luke's account of Jesus' relationship with the Pharisees and chief priests is independent, reflecting assumptions that he acquired from elsewhere. It is important for historical consideration that these agreements are in matters *assumed* by Luke and Josephus: neither author is interested in the Pharisees, Sadducees, or Sanhedrin in and of themselves; they use these figures as part of the understood 'furniture' of 1st-century Palestine. Far from inflating the Pharisees' influence out of a desire to support them, for example, both authors assume it in order to *complain* about it. This must be explained by scholars who wish to argue that historically the Pharisees enjoyed no such influence. Similarly, their shared assumption that the High Priest ordinarily headed a council must be explained by those[125] who do not think that there was such a regular body.

This summary of agreements between Luke and Josephus is not yet history. My goal has been to help *prepare* for historical reasoning about the Jewish leadership groups by clarifying their functions in two of the most important narrative collections on the issue. Historical hypotheses must account for these and all other relevant stories. Unfortunately, even some recent reconstructions of the Jewish leadership groups do not show how the hypotheses advocated would explain the narratives as we have them—on *any* comprehensive interpretation of the narratives. Paradoxically, nearly two thousand years after the chief priests, Sadducees, Pharisees, and Sanhedrin flourished, we await satisfactory explanations of their lives and times.

---

[124]S. Mason, *Josephus and the New Testament* (Peabody, MA: Hendrickson, 1992) 185-229.

[125]M. Goodman, *The Ruling Class of Judaea*; E.P. Sanders, *Judaism: Practice & Belief 63 BCE – 66 CE*, above.

CHAPTER 6

SYNAGOGUES IN JERUSALEM

Rainer Riesner

Summary

The picture of Palestinian synagogues in Luke-Acts is not anachronistic, but corroborated by other literary, epigraphical and archaeological sources. A very important piece of evidence is the Theodotus inscription from Jerusalem. Despite some recent doubts it has to be dated to a time prior to AD 70. The inscription shows the existence of a synagogue building and gives invaluable insights into the function and organisation of a Second Temple synagogue. The identification of the Theodotus synagogue, a synagogue of Alexandrians in the Rabbinic literature and the 'synagogue of the Freedmen' in Acts 6:9 remains a serious possibility.

I. The Pre-70 Synagogue

1. Modern controversy

For the Rabbis the synagogue was established as early as the time of Abraham.[1] Today we know that the synagogue, here understood as a building or room used for regular Jewish worship, is a hellenistic institution. Though it may have some roots in religious gatherings as far back as the Babylonian exile, it emerged in the creative 3rd and 2nd centuries BC. According to the majority view the synagogue was widespread by the 1st century AD, both in the Diaspora and in the land of Israel.[2] However, some are more sceptical. In a recent article, H.C. Kee wrote of the finds at Masada and Herodium, identified by the majority as synagogues from the 1st century AD: 'There is no evidence that they were structures designed for religious purposes, much less that the routines attested for 2nd-century and later synagogues were practised there'.[3] Following J. Neusner's research on the Mishna[4] Kee concludes for the 1st century AD: 'From his analysis of the literary evidence, there emerge no hints of liturgical formulae, of institutional organisation, of

---

[1]*Cf.* Strack-Billerbeck II, 740.

[2]For the current state of research, *cf.* W. Schrage, 'συναγωγή', *TDNT* VII (1971) 798-841; J. Gutmann (ed.), *The Synagogue: Studies in Origins, Archaeology and Architecture* (New York, 1975); S. Safrai, 'The Synagogue', in S. Safrai and M. Stern, (eds.), *The Jewish People in the First Century II: Historical Geography, Political History, Social, Cultural and Religious Life and Institutions* (CRINT I/2; Assen and Amsterdam, 1976) 908-44; E. Schürer, *The History of the Jewish People in the Age of Jesus Christ*, rev. and ed. G. Vermes, F. Millar, M. Black (Edinburgh, 1979) II, 423-54; J. Gutmann (ed.), *Ancient Synagogues. The State of Research* (Chico, 1981); L.I. Levine (ed.), *Ancient Synagogues Revealed* (Jerusalem, 1981); E. M. Meyers and J. F. Strange, *Archaeology, the Rabbis and Early Christianity* (London, 1981) 140-54; M.J.S. Chiat, *Handbook of Synagogue Architecture* (Chico, 1982); L.I. Levine (ed.), *The Synagogue in Late Antiquity* (Philadelphia, 1987); R. Riesner, *Jesus als Lehrer: Eine Untersuchung zum Ursprung der Evangelien-Überlieferung* (3rd edn.; Tübingen, 1988) 123-53; R. Riesner, 'Synagoge', in *Das Grosse Bibellexikon* (2nd edn.; Wuppertal and Giessen, 1990) III, 1507-12; Z. Ilan, *Ancient Synagogues in Israel* [Hebrew] (Ministry of Defence of Israel, 1991); E.M. Meyers, 'Synagogue', in *Anchor Bible Dictionary* (New York, 1992) VI, 251-60; L.I. Levine, 'Synagogues', in M. Stern, (ed.) *The New Encyclopedia of Archaeological Excavations in the Holy Land* (Jerusalem and New York, 1993) IV, 1421-4.

[3]'The Transformation of the Synagogue After 70 C.E.: Its Import for Early Christianity', *NTS* 36 (1990) 1-24 (8). The same views can be found in H.C. Kee, 'Early Christianity in the Galilee: Reassessing the Evidence from the Gospels', in L.I. Levine, *The Galilee in Late Antiquity* (Cambridge, Mass./London, 1992) 3-22 (3-14).

[4]*Formative Judaism: Religious, Historical and Literary Studies* (Chico, 1982) 75-83.

formal programmes or patterns of instruction, just as from the archaeological side there is no evidence of stylised architectural settings for group worship'.[5]

Professor Kee applies this opinion to the New Testament, especially to the Lukan writings: 'Throughout Acts, the author depicts Paul and his associates as entering the synagogues in order to preach and teach—apparently presupposing the formal patterns of synagogue practice which seem to have developed only in the post-70 or even early 2nd century period. Thus we apparently have in Luke-Acts the later forms of synagogal worship read back into the time of Jesus.'[6] R.E. Oster, responding to Kee, rejected the view that the Lukan picture of 1st-century synagogues is anachronistic and produced in support of his case a wide range of literary, epigraphical and archaeological evidence.[7] In what follows, only one terminological question and one archaeological problem of the Kee-Oster discussion will be touched. Then, we shall ask in more detail about the literary and archaeological evidence of pre-70 synagogues in Jerusalem in order to compare it with the picture of Palestinian synagogues in Luke-Acts.

2. *Terminology and history*

In Professor Kee's answer to R.E. Oster it becomes clear that his main argument concerns terminological changes pointing in his opinion to deep historical changes.[8] Kee cites 'the persuasive evidence adduced by Martin Hengel concerning the term προσευχή as the standard designation for Jewish gathering-places in the centuries before and after the turn of the era'.[9] This is not quite an appropriate description of Professor Hengel's position. He showed that προσευχή *in the Diaspora* was the original and until the 1st century AD the normal designation of Jewish places of worship.[10] According to Professor Hengel the *Palestinian* places of worship, originating in the Maccabean time, were always called בית הכנסת and in Greek translation συναγωγή to avoid any

---

[5]'The Transformation', 13.
[6]*Ibid.*, 18.
[7]'Supposed Anachronism in Luke-Acts' Use of ΣΥΝΑΓΩΓΗ: A Rejoinder to H.C. Kee', *NTS* 39 (1993) 178-208.
[8]'The Changing Meaning of Synagogue: A Response to Richard Oster', *NTS* 40 (1994) 281-3. My thanks are due to Professor Kee for sending me the manuscript of this article.
[9]'The Changing Meaning', 281.

concurrence with the Jerusalem Temple, which in Isaiah 56:7 is called בית התפילה.[11] Professor Kee is critical of R.E. Oster for failing 'to take into account adequately the range of connotations that συναγωγή has in the pre-70 CE Jewish literature'.[12] But Oster's point was not to deny that συναγωγή can mean something other than a synagogue building, but rather that in the 1st century AD it could also mean this. Oster[13] rightly refers to an inscription of AD 56 where even in a Diaspora setting (Berenice [Benghazi] in Cyrenaica) συναγωγή is used both for the gathered community and the architectural structure where the community meets (*SEG* XVII, no. 16).[14]

It cannot be denied that Philo once calls a Jewish place of worship συναγωγή (*Quod omnis probus liber sit* 81). Kee comments on this: 'The process of change of terminology for places of Jewish study and worship has begun'.[15] This remark somewhat obscures the fact that a Diaspora author writing around AD 40 can use συναγωγή for a synagogue building. So there is no reason to accuse Luke of anachronism if he uses the term in the same way. Furthermore, Philo's choice of words seems to be better explained by the geographical differentiation introduced by Hengel. As a Diaspora author Philo normally writes προσευχή, but in the one case where he is clearly describing a Palestinian (namely Essene) place of worship he uses συναγωγή. The wording leaves open the possibility that Philo is not only giving terminological information about the Essenes, but also referring to the common designation in Palestine.

Professor Kee writes: 'In Josephus προσευχή is the standard term for the gathering place of Jews [*Ant.* 14.258; *Vita* 2.276;[16] 280.3; 293.4; *C. Ap.* 2.10], while συναγωγή is used for collecting books and gathering water [*Ant.* 1.10; 15.346]. But writing as he is around and after the turn of the 2nd century, Josephus also occasionally uses συναγωγή to refer to the gathering places of pious Jews [*Ant.* 19.300-5; *BJ* 2.289; 7.44]'.[17]

---

[10]'Proseuche und Synagoge. Jüdische Gemeinde, Gotteshaus und Gottesdienst in der Diaspora und in Palästina', in G. Jeremias, H.W. Kuhn and H. Stegemann, (eds.), *Tradition und Glaube: Das frühe Christentum in seiner Umwelt* (K.G. Kuhn FS; Göttingen, 1971) 157-83 (now in J. Gutman, *The Synagogue*, 27-54).

[11]In J. Gutmann, *The Synagogue*, 47.

[12]'The Changing Meaning', 281.

[13]'Supposed Anachronism', 187-8

[14]*Cf.* also G. Lüderitz, *Corpus jüdischer Zeugnisse aus der Cyrenaika* (Wiesbaden, 1983) no. 72.

[15]'The Changing Meaning', 282.

[16]The references come from the footnotes (nos. 10-12) of Professor Kee's article. Here the reference should read *Vita* 277.

This presentation of Josephus' evidence is problematic in more ways than one:

(1) One should start with a proper chronology.[18] The Jewish historian was born in AD 37 (*Vita* 5). Whether he survived to the 2nd century nobody knows. The *Jewish Antiquities* were completed in AD 93/94 (*Ant.* 20.267) and the *Vita* apparently was an appendix to this work. The *Jewish War* is commonly dated before AD 79 and the *Against Apion* by some to around AD 95. With this widely accepted dating of *Jewish War* we come nearer to AD 70 than to the turn of the 1st century, and we have to remember that Josephus writes as a native Palestinian Jew and as an eyewitness.[19]

(2) As in all statistics one has to look closely at the details. Of six occurrences of προσευχή in Josephus,[20] three concern the synagogue of Tiberias (*Vita* 277, 280, 293), one a synagogue in Halicarnassus (*Ant.* 14.258), another refers generally to prayer houses as a Mosaic custom (*C. Ap.* 2.10) and once the word is used in its original meaning for 'prayer' (*BJ* 5.388). There are eight uses of the word συναγωγή,[21] two meaning something other than assembly or assembly room (see above). Twice Josephus calls the place of worship in Caesarea Maritima a συναγωγή (*BJ* 2.285, 289), once that in Antiochia/Orontes (*BJ* 7.44), three times that at Dora (*Ant.* 19.300, 305 [*bis*]). According to Professor Kee, this makes five προσευχαί against six συναγωγαί. It is difficult to see how this proves that 'in Josephus προσευχή is the standard term for the gathering place of Jews'.[22]

(3) Josephus testifies to the geographical factor in the distribution of terminology. The Diaspora synagogue in Halicarnassus is called προσευχή, whereas the Palestinian/Syrian buildings in Caesarea, Dora and

---

[17]'The Changing Meaning', 282.
[18]*Cf.* E. Schürer (rev. and ed. G. Vermes, F. Millar and M. Black), *The History of the Jewish People in the Age of Jesus Christ* (Edinburgh, 1973) I 47-8. 53-5; T. Rajak, *Josephus, The Historian and His Society* (Philadelphia, 1983) 237-8. A few dissenting voices are discussed by L.H. Feldman, *Josephus and Modern Scholarship (1937-1980)* (Berlin and New York, 1984) 378-84.
[19]*Cf.* now M. Hadas-Lebel, *Flavius Josephus: Eyewitness to Rome's First-Century Conquest of Judea* (ET; New York and Toronto, 1993).
[20]K.H. Rengstorf (ed.), *A Complete Concordance to Flavius Josephus* (Leiden, 1979) III, 557.
[21]*Ibid.* (1983) IV, 106
[22]'The Changing Meaning', 282.

Antioch are called συναγωγή. An apparent exception is the synagogue of Tiberias. The city was a new foundation by Herod Antipas with a very mixed population and a totally hellenized organisation.[23] This socio-historical background may explain the Diaspora terminology.[24] Another reason could be the architectural appearance of the building. It was not only very big (*Vita* 277 *cf. m.'Erub.* 10:10), but could have consisted of a double stoa (*Midr. Pss.* 93:8 [ed. Buber 416]) like the famous synagogue in Alexandria (*t. Sukk.* 4:6//). The latest work on the terminological question by F. Hüttenmeister also concludes that geography is the main factor in the distribution of terminology and that it is illegitimate to conclude that the terminological variation points to a substantial difference in function.[25]

3. *Archaeological finds in Palestine*

According to Professor Kee it is true for the Land of Israel that 'The earliest identifiable synagogues are from the late 4th century C.E., although none are dated for certain before the 6th century'.[26] In an article by E.M. Meyers, endorsed by Kee,[27] it is suggested that 'The 3rd-century building [at Nabratein in Galilee] with six columns, destroyed in a 306 C.E. earthquake, housed a fixed Torah shrine, good portions of which were preserved intact'.[28] Under this synagogue was found a broadhouse building, dating to the 2nd century AD. An inscription from Kisjon (*CIJ* II no. 972) dating to the time of Septimus Severus (193-211) may belong to a synagogue. In the second half of the 2nd century Palestinian Judaism could have recovered so far from the disaster of the Bar Kokhba war as to be able to erect synagogue buildings with special architectural features in Galilee. In the same article Meyers writes: 'Thus far only three synagogue buildings within Israel/Palestine have been securely dated to the Second Temple period: Gamla, Masada and Herodium'.[29] In this he formulates at least

---

[23]*Cf.* E. Schürer, *The History of the Jewish People*, I, 342-3.
[24]*Cf.* M. Hengel in J. Gutmann, *The Synagogue*, 47.
[25]'"Synagogue" und "Proseuche" bei Josephus und in anderen antiken Quellen', in D.A. Koch and H. Lichtenberger (eds.), *Begegnungen zwischen Christentum und Judentum in Antike und Mittelalter* (H. Schreckenberg FS; Göttingen, 1993) 163-81.
[26]'The Transformation', 10.
[27]'The Changing Meaning', 281.
[28]*Anchor Bible Dictionary* VI, 275.
[29]*Ibid.*, 255.

the majority view. The identification of these three synagogues is not merely 'wishful thinking' on the part of the excavators.[30] There are features that show a religious character, while others connect the three buildings together and make them comparable with later synagogue architecture. We can give only a very short summary.[31]

Adjacent to all three buildings equipped with stone benches surrounding the walls were ritual baths. The Masada and Herodium buildings and even that at Gamla seem to be oriented towards Jerusalem. At Masada, fragments of two scrolls (Deuteronomy and Ezekiel) were carefully buried, and in another corner of the room an ostracon referring to the priestly tithe was found. The Gamla synagogue may show the remains of a raised platform (βῆμα) and even a niche for the Torah scrolls.[32] The building was decorated with six-petalled rosettes and date palms which could have a religious meaning. Connected to the main hall of the synagogue by a window was another room also equipped with benches. In the opinion of one of the excavators it was 'probably a study room'.[33] At Masada also one palatial building (Palace XIII) may have been altered to a school room by the rebels.[34] Since several ostraca with the Hebrew alphabet were found at Herodium,[35] some sort of school is even possible there.

The Herodium and Masada synagogues were built by Jewish rebels prior to AD 70. At Masada there was possibly a synagogue at an earlier date, when the fortress was rebuilt by Herod the Great. The Gamla building always served as a public edifice, dating probably from the 1st century BC. This early date should not be surprising. In the middle of that century, as R. Deines has demonstrated, a major change took place in Palestine, indicated by the growing use of

---

[30]J. Gutmann, 'Prolegomenon', in *The Synagogue*, IX-XXIX (XI), quoted with approval by Kee, 'The Transformation', 10.

[31]*Cf.* Y. Yadin, 'The Synagogue at Masada', in L.I. Levine, *Ancient Synagogues Revealed*, 19-23; G. Foerster, 'The Synagogues at Masada and Herodium', *ibid.*, 24-9; S. Gutman, 'The Synagogue at Gamla', *ibid.*, 30-4; Z. Maoz, 'The Synagogue of Gamla and the Typology of Second Temple Synagogues', *ibid.*, 35-41; S. Gutman, 'Gamala', in *The New Encyclopedia of Archaeological Excavations in the Holy Land*, II 459-63 (460-2); E. Netzer, 'Masada', *ibid.*, III 973-85 (981-3).

[32]*Cf.* Z. Maoz, 'A Synagogue from the Time of the Second Temple', *Israel—Land and Nature* 3 (1978) 138-42 (142).

[33]S. Gutman, *The New Encyclopedia of Archaeological Excavations in the Holy Land* II, 461-2.

[34]*Cf.* Y. Yadin, 'Masada', in *Encyclopedia of Archaeological Excavations in the Holy Land* (Jerusalem, 1977) III, 793-816 (795).

[35]*Cf.* E. Testa, *Herodion: I graffiti e gli ostraca* (Jerusalem, 1972) 77-82.

ossuaries and stone vessels, both items intimately connected with Pharisaic belief and *halakha*.[36] In the First Jewish War Gamla was one of the two last strongholds of the Zealots (Jos. *BJ* 4.11-54; 4.62-83; *cf.* *BJ* 7.304-406; *Ant*. 18.4-10; 18.23-5). This, together with the building activities of the rebels at Masada and Herodium, contrary to the opinion of Neusner and Kee, speaks for a considerable influence of Pharisaism in the spread of synagogues in Palestine.

The archaeological evidence shows both sides. There is diversity even between the architecture of the three Second Temple synagogues.[37] Nevertheless, some features are already common. One or two of the buildings were originally in secular use. This points to a reason why we know so few remains of synagogues from the time before AD 70. Many if not most of these synagogues might have been slightly adjusted rooms in private houses or public buildings. This was already stressed by B. Schwank[38] as early as 1955 and is now strongly (perhaps one-sidedly) emphasised by L.M. White.[39] How carefully negative evidence should be weighed is shown in the case of Sepphoris, however. Although a Jewish presence is amply attested for Roman and Byzantine times, and the Jerusalem Talmud (*y. Kil.* 32b) speaks of eighteen synagogues, none has been discovered in the ambitious excavations until now.[40] Early this century a Greek inscription (*CIJ* II no. 991), not *in situ*, and a mosaic pavement containing a dedicatory inscription were found, which may belong to synagogues.[41]

In former times scholars were in danger of reading back too uncritically the developed synagogue system of the Talmudic literature wherever a προσευχή or συναγωγή was mentioned in pre-70 sources. But we should also not do the opposite and hyper-critically deny that without the developed system a synagogue-like structure or something called a synagogue prior to AD 70 can ever be a synagogue. L.I. Levine gave a very nuanced picture showing all the diversity, but he began his seminal article with the programmatic statement: 'By the

[36] *Jüdische Steingefäße und pharisäische Frömmigkeit. Ein archäologischer Beitrag zum Verständnis von Joh 2,6 und der jüdischen Reinheitshalacha zur Zeit Jesu* (Tübingen, 1993) esp. 3-11.

[37] *Cf.* M.J.S. Chiat, 'First-Century Synagogue Architecture: Methodological Problems', in J. Gutmann, *Ancient Synagogues*, 49-58.

[38] 'Qualis erat forma synagogarum Novi Testamenti?', *VD* 33 (1955) 267-79.

[39] *Building God's House in the Roman World: Architectural Adaptation among Pagans, Jews and Christians* (Baltimore and London, 1990) 60-101.

[40] *Cf.* Z. Weiss, 'Sepphoris', in *The New Encyclopedia of Archaeological Excavations in the Holy Land* IV, 1324-8.

[41] *Cf.* M.J.S. Chiat, *Handbook of Synagogue Architecture*, 83-4.

end of the Second Temple period the synagogue had become a central institution in Jewish life. It could be found everywhere, in Israel and in the Diaspora, east and west, in cities as well as in villages. The synagogue filled a wide variety of functions within the Jewish community and had become by the 1st century a recognised symbol of Jewish presence'.[42]

II. Pre-70 Synagogues in Jerusalem: Literary Sources

1. *Philo and Josephus*

No Jerusalem synagogue is mentioned either by Philo of Alexandria or by Flavius Josephus. One cannot build an argument on this silence. Since Josephus mentions for Syria/Palestine pre-70 synagogues in Caesarea Maritima (*BJ* 2.285), Dora/Phoenicia (*Ant.* 19.305) and Tiberias (*Vita* 280), his silence about Jerusalem must be considered purely accidental. Once more, in view of the nature of our sources, we are warned against any rash *argumentum e silentio.*

2. *New Testament*

Besides Luke-Acts the oldest possible literary source for a direct hint of synagogues in Jerusalem is the Gospel of John. In a hearing before the former High Priest Annas the following words of Jesus, defending himself, are reported: 'I have spoken openly to the world; I have always taught in synagogues (ἐν συναγωγῇ) and in the Temple [where all Jews come together]; I have said nothing secretly' (Jn. 18:20). The juxtaposition of Temple and synagogue shows that not only synagogal gatherings are in view but also buildings. Apparently, these are thought to be located in Jerusalem where Jesus speaks. Of course, it is highly disputed to what extent John gives us at least in substance the words of Jesus.[43] Clearly the words in square brackets cannot be part of the *ipsissima verba*, but are a comment by the evangelist. On the other hand there is a partial parallel in Mark 14:30. According to the evidence of P[52], the Fourth Gospel is a testimony at least for around

[42]'The Second Temple Synagogue: The Formative Years', in *The Synagogue in Late Antiquity*, 7-31 (7).
[43]R.E. Brown, *The Gospel according to John XIII-XXI* (AB 29A; London, 1971) 826 leaves open the possibility of some historical substance.

AD 125. If John were describing only the situation of this time, he would at least be presupposing synagogues in Jerusalem before the Bar Kokhba war (AD 132-135). But since John shows a remarkable knowledge of the topography of 1st-century Jerusalem,[44] we should be prepared to find genuine knowledge of the existence of synagogues in Jerusalem around AD 30, even if the evangelist formulated Jesus' answer to Annas.

3. *Rabbinic literature*

F. Hüttenmeister has collected all the Rabbinic traditions about synagogues in Jerusalem.[45] Many of these traditions can be suspected to have anachronistic traits. Of course, nobody believes today that as early as the time of Solomon (*Pesiqta de Rab Kahana* 26.2 [ed. Mandelbaum 386]) or Nebuchadnezzar (*y. Meg.* 73d [29-32]) one could find synagogues in Jerusalem. However, sometimes the anachronistic picture is only a creation of later scholarship. As A. Edersheim[46] already saw, there is no compelling reason why the Rabbinic literature should presuppose a Temple synagogue.[47] Even some modern authors are considering the numbers of Jerusalem synagogues according to the Talmudic tradition.[48] However, the numbers differ between 480 (*y. Ketub.* 73d [32-5]), 460 (*y. Ketub.* 35c [61-4]) and 394 (*b. Ketub.* 105a), and from a Rabbinic commentary on the Song of Songs (*Cant. Rab.* 5.12.2) we learn that at least the number 480 was created by a complicated *gematria*.[49]

To take the Rabbinic notices at face value would be as uncritical as to deny *a priori* that some traditions can take us back to the time before AD 70.[50] There is at least one tradition that deserves serious consideration. The Tosefta reports a tradition of Rabbi Yehuda the

---

[44]*Cf.* B. Schwank, 'Ortskenntnisse im vierten Evangelium?', *Erbe und Auftrag* 57 (1981) 427-42; J. Genot-Bismuth, *Jérusalem ressuscitée. La Bible hébraïque et l'évangile de Jean à l'épreuve de l'archéologie nouvelle* (Paris, 1992).

[45]*Die antiken Synagogen in Israel I: Die jüdischen Synagogen, Lehrhäuser und Gerichtshöfe* (Wiesbaden, 1977), 192-210.

[46]*The Life and Times of Jesus the Messiah* (3rd edn.; London, 1886) I, 246; II, 742-3.

[47]*Cf.* S.B. Hoenig, 'The Suppositious Temple-Synagogue', *JQR* 54 (1963/64) 115-31 (repr. in J. Gutmann, *The Synagogues*, 55-71).

[48]B. Lifshitz, 'Jérusalem sous la domination Romaine' (*ANRW* II, 8; Berlin and New York, 1977) 444-89 (456); H. Shanks, *Judaism in Stone: The Archaeology of Ancient Synagogues* (New York and Washington, 1979) 20-1.

[49]*Cf.* F. Hüttenmeister, *Die antiken Synagogen in Israel*, I 206-7.

Prince, the compiler of the Mishna at the end of the 2nd century AD. According to this tradition Rabbi Eleazar son of Rabbi Zadoq 'bought the synagogue of the Alexandrians (בית הכנסת של אלכסנדרים), who were in Jerusalem and used it for his own purposes' (*t. Meg.* 3.6 [224]). The tradition seems to be old since the Mishna forbids selling a synagogue for private interests (*m. Meg.* 3:1). The words 'who were in Jerusalem' are lacking in the parallel account in the Jerusalem Talmud (*y. Meg.* 73d [39-41]); but they appear in the version in the Babylonian Talmud (*b. Meg.* 26a). Another hint of an older tradition is the concrete name of the synagogue. But here the parallel account in *b. Meg.* 26a creates a problem. It mentions a 'synagogue of the טורסיים. This can either mean people from the Cilician city of Tarsus[51] or a kind of metal worker, attested also as members of the great synagogue in Alexandria (*t. Sukk.* 4.6). If one tries to combine the two different name traditions, there are two possibilities. Either the *torissim* were Alexandrian metal workers or the synagogue was owned by Alexandrians and Tarsians together.[52]

Another question is the date of the incident, if indeed it is historical. Rabbi Eleazar ben Rabbi Zadoq flourished around AD 100.[53] This would bring us to the time after the destruction of Jerusalem in AD 70. One could speculate whether Rabbi Eleazar as a private individual had been able to buy the synagogue because it lay in ruins and there was no congregation in existence to rebuild it. Such a scenario would fit the situation between the two Jewish wars. Furthermore, it is interesting that the Talmudic versions know that a private society owned the synagogue of the Alexandrians (*y. Meg.* 73d [41]) and/or Tarsians (*b. Meg.* 26a). As M. Hengel observed: 'Behind the whole account there is a clear denigration by the Rabbinic scholars of these alien private synagogues'.[54] This also can point to a time prior to the more established Rabbinate of the 2nd and 3rd centuries AD, when synagogues became more 'official' institutions.

---

50 A reasonable methodology is outlined by S. Safrai, 'Talmudic Literature as an Historical Source for the Second Temple Period', *Mishkhan* 17/18 (1992/93) 121-37.

51 So A. Neubauer, *La Géographie du Talmud* (Paris, 1868) 315.

52 One can exclude the possibility that *b. Meg.* 26a reflects another incident (*cf.* Strack-Billerbeck II, 664).

53 *Cf.* Strack-Billerbeck V/VI, 250-1.

54 'Between Jesus and Paul', in *Between Jesus and Paul. Studies in the Earliest History of Christianity* (London, 1983) 1-29, 133-56 (17).

4. *Patristic sources*

When visiting Jerusalem in AD 333 an anonymous pilgrim from Bordeaux, who was possibly of Jewish-Christian origin,[55] also climbed up to the southwestern hill then called Zion. He saw there not only the place where King David had his palace, but also a synagogue: '*Et septem synagogae, quae illic fuerunt, una tantum remansit, reliquiae autem arantur et seminantur, sicut Isaias propheta dixit* [Is. 1:8; *cf.* Mic. 3:12]' (*Itinerarium* 16 [ed. Geyer 22]). At the end of the 4th century, Bishop Epiphanius of Salamis spoke also of seven synagogues on Mount Zion (*De mensuris et ponderibus* 14 [PG 43.260-2]). He also mentioned that one survived to the time of Constantine the Great, who died in AD 337. This synagogue, according to Epiphanius, together with the 'little Church of the Apostles' stood even when Hadrian visited Jerusalem before the outbreak of the Bar Kokhba revolt. The combination of the two sources and the archaeological evidence of the so-called Tomb of David (see below III.3) is disputed. Either the synagogue was a Jewish one which was closed under Constantine or the Bordeaux pilgrim saw a Jewish Christian synagogue which Epiphanius called a church. In any case Epiphanius presupposed Jewish synagogues standing on Mount Zion before AD 130. For this he could have followed older sources.[56]

Excursus I: An Essene Quarter in Jerusalem?

In his famous description of the walls of Jerusalem, Flavius Josephus mentions a 'Gate of the Essenes' (*BJ* 5.145). It stood on the south-western hill of the city where the so-called 'first wall' changed from a north-south to a west-east direction.[57] This gate was discovered in 1894/95 by the English archaeologist F.J. Bliss.[58] It was re-excavated and dated to the early Herodian period recently by B. Pixner, D. Chen and S. Margalit.[59] Apparently, J.B. Lightfoot was the first to suggest

---

[55]*Cf.* H. Donner, *Pilgerfahrt ins Heilige Land. Die ältesten Berichte christlicher Palästinapilger (4.-7. Jahrhundert)* (Stuttgart, 1979) 41-2.

[56]One possibility is the 2nd-century Jewish Christian historian Hegesippus.

[57]*Cf.* R. Riesner, 'Josephus' "Gate of the Essenes" in Modern Discussion', *ZDPV* 105 (1989) 105-9.

[58]*Excavations at Jerusalem* (London, 1898) 16-20, 322-4.

[59]'Mount Zion: The "Gate of the Essenes" Re-excavated', *ZDPV* 105 (1989) 85-95 and plates 6-16.

that this gate received its name from an Essene quarter nearby.[60] The same opinion was expressed by no less a scholar than E. Schürer.[61] In recent years Pixner has written extensively about this quarter,[62] for which he thinks there is additional archaeological evidence and certain hints in the Qumran scrolls (esp. 11QTemple 46:13-6 and 3Q15). A number of scholars have responded positively to his arguments and have also stressed the relevance of this theory for New Testament studies.[63] If there was an Essene quarter in Jerusalem it must have had its 'synagogue' (*cf.* Philo, *Quod omnis probus liber sit* 81), which is called 'house of prostration' (בית השתחות) in the Damascus Document (CD 11:22).[64] In Qumran the biggest room (Locus 77), where the congregation obviously took its communal meals, seems to have served as this kind of synagogue.[65] Near the western wall, which faces Jerusalem, there was a raised platform.[66] So the room seems to be oriented towards the Holy City, and the platform reminds one of the later synagogal *bema*. The archaeological evidence in Qumran could suggest that some features of synagogues such as the orientation began to emerge

---

[60]*Saint Paul's Epistles to the Colossians and to Philemon* (London, 1875) 94 n. 2.

[61]*Geschichte des Jüdischen Volkes im Zeitalter Jesu Christi* (4th edn.; Leipzig, 1907) II, 657-8 n. 5. *Cf.* E. Schürer, *The History of the Jewish People in the Age of Jesus Christ* (rev. edn.; Edinburgh, 1979) II, 563 n. 5.

[62]Summaries in 'The History of the "Essene Gate" Area', *ZDPV* 105 (1989) 96-104; 'Archäologische Beobachtungen zum Jerusalemer Essener-Viertel und zur Urgemeinde', in B. Mayer (ed.) *Christen und Christliches in Qumran?* (Regensburg, 1992) 89-113; 'Das Essener-Quartier in Jerusalem', in *Wege des Messias und Stätten der Urkirche. Jesus und das Judenchristentum im Licht neuer archäologischer Erkenntnisse*, ed. R. Riesner (2nd edn.; Giessen, 1994) 180-207.

[63]*E.g.* S. Medala, 'Le camp des Esséniens de Jérusalem à la lumière des recentes recherches archéologiques', *Folia Orientalia* 25 (1989) 67-74; J. Finegan, *The Archaeology of the New Testament* (Princeton, 1992) 218-20; M. Delcor, 'A propos de l'emplacement de la porte des Esséniens selon Josèphe et de ses implications historiques, essénienne et chrétienne', in Z.J. Kapera, *Intertestamental Essays* (J.T. Milik FS; Krákow, 1992) 25-44; R. Riesner, 'Jesus, the Primitive Community, and the Essene Quarter of Jerusalem', in J.H. Charlesworth (ed.), *Jesus and the Dead Sea Scrolls* (New York, 1993) 198-234; O. Betz and R. Riesner, *Jesus, Qumran and the Vatican: Clarifications* (London and New York, 1994) 141-56, 187-90. *Cf.* also B.J. Capper, 'The Palestinian Cultural Context of Earliest Christian Community of Goods' in this volume.

[64]*Cf.* A. Steudel, 'The Houses of Prostration *CD* XI, 21-XII, 1—Duplicates of the Temple', *RQ* 16 (1993) 49-68. The בית מועד in the War Scroll (1QM 3:4) is also interesting.

[65]*Cf.* R. Riesner, *Jesus als Lehrer*, 135-6.

[66]*Cf.* R. de Vaux, *Archaeology and the Dead Sea Scrolls* (Oxford, 1973) 11.

prior to the break between Essenes and Pharisees in the middle of the 2nd century BC.

III. Pre-70 Synagogues in Jerusalem: Archaeological Evidence

1. A prayer room at Shuafat?

In 1991 the Israeli archaeologist A. Onn discovered near Shuafat, an Arab quarter just north of Jerusalem, a fortified agricultural settlement from the 2nd century BC.[67] At the beginning of the 1st century BC one underground room was altered in a remarkable way. Stone benches were built along its walls. By means of a niche in the front wall the room seems to be oriented towards Jerusalem. In front of the door to the room, there was created an open courtyard also ringed with benches. Ritual baths from the same period were found nearby. After the great earthquake of 31 BC (Jos. *Ant.* 15.121-47) the settlement was abandoned. With benches, *mikva'ot* and the orientation, we have three possible elements for a synagogue. Indeed, A. Onn identified the room as a synagogue, while his colleague Z. Greenhut spoke more cautiously of a 'prayer room'. In view of the 1st-century BC date of the Gamla synagogue this seems not *a priori* impossible. The building complex, measuring 50 x 50 metres, is to be preserved as an archaeological garden in the middle of a new quarter for orthodox Jews. The discovery was not very widely noticed,[68] although it led to controversy among Israeli archaeologists. Since no official report has yet appeared, one must await further discussion.[69]

2. The Theodotus inscription

a. The find

In the years 1913-14 the French scholar R. Weill undertook excavations on the southern part of the southeast hill of Old Jerusalem in search of

---

[67]*Cf.* A. Rabinovich, 'Oldest Jewish prayer room discovered on Shuafat ridge', *Jerusalem Post* (International Edition) 17.8.1991, 7.

[68]*Cf.* R. Riesner, 'Neue Funde in Israel', *BK* 46 (1991) 181-3 (183).

[69]A short, preliminary report will appear in *Hadashot Arkheologiyot* 101 (1994), (information by Zevi Greenhut, Israel Antiquities Authority).

the City of David and the royal necropolis. For such an early dig the campaign is very well documented.[70] One rather spectacular find was a nearly completely preserved Greek dedicatory inscription of a synagogue. The tablet is made from limestone and measures *c.* 75 cm in length and 41 cm in breadth. The inscription was discovered in December 1913 and the find announced on 29 May 1914.[71] The discovery could only be widely noticed and discussed after the end of the First World War.[72] The inscription was published in 1920[73] and is kept in the Rockefeller Museum in East Jerusalem (Inv. no. S 842). The ten lines of the inscription (*CIJ* II, no. 1404 [333]; *SEG* VIII, no. 170 [25]) read:

Θεόδοτος Οὐεττηνοῦ ἱερεὺς καὶ
ἀρχισυνάγωγος, υἱὸς ἀρχισυν[αγώ]-
γ[ο]υ, υἱωνὸς ἀρχισυν[α]γώγου, ᾠκο-
4 δόμησε τὴν συναγωγ[ὴ]ν εἰς ἀ̣ν̣[άγ]νω-
σ[ιν] νόμου καὶ εἰς [δ]ιδαχὴν ἐντολῶν, καὶ
τὸν ξενῶνα κα[ὶ τὰ] δώματα καὶ τὰ χρη-
σ[τ]ήρια τῶν ὑδάτων εἰς κατάλυμα τοῖ-
8 ς [χ]ρῄζουσιν ἀπὸ τῆς ξέ[ν]ης, ἣν ἐθεμε-
λ[ίω]σαν οἱ πατέρες [α]ὐτοῦ καὶ οἱ πρε-
σ[β]ύτεροι καὶ Σιμων[ί]δης.

Theodotus (son) of Vettenus, priest and
archisynagogos, son of an archisynagogos, grandson of an archisynagogos, con-
4 structed the synagogue for the rea-
ding of the law and the teaching of the commandments and
the guest-room and the (upper?) chambers and the installations of water for a hostelry for tho-
8 se needing (them) from abroad, which was founded by his fathers and the el-

[70]*La Cité de David. Compte rendu des fouilles executées, à Jérusalem, sur le site de la ville primitive. Campagne de 1913-1914* (Paris, 1920), I (Texte), II (Planches).

[71]*CRAIBL* (Paris, 1914) 333-4. The same text by L. Dorez was reproduced in *Revue critique d'histoire et de littérature* 1 (1914) 500 and *RB* 12 (1915) 280.

[72]Bibliographies, supplementing each other, can be found in F. Hüttenmeister, *Die antiken Synagogen in Israel* I, 192-4, 525; K. Bieberstein and H. Bloedhorn, *Jerusalem. Grundzüge der Baugeschichte vom Chalkolithikum bis zur Frühzeit der osmanischen Herrschaft* (Wiesbaden, 1994) III 117-8. There should be added M. Hengel, in *Between Jesus and Paul*, 117-8, 148; L.L. Grabbe, 'Synagogues in Pre-70 Palestine: A Re-Assessment', *JTS* 39 (1988) 401-10 (406-7); B.W.W. Dombrowski, '*SYNAGOGE* in Acts 6:9', in Z.J. Kapera (ed.), *Intertestamental Essays*, 53-65.

[73]R. Weill, *La Cité de David* I, 30 (text and translation) II, Plate XXV A (photograph).

ders and Simonides

Today the inscription is commonly dated before AD 70. The statement by L.I. Levine is typical: 'The earliest evidence for a synagogue building in Israel is the Theodotus inscription from Jerusalem which indicates the existence of such an institution at the end of the 1st century BCE.'[74] However, H.C. Kee questioned this dating and opted originally for the end of the 2nd century or the 3rd century AD.[75] Recently, he concluded that it 'dates from no earlier than the 4th century, and therefore provides evidence that fits well the sketch of development of the synagogue set forth' by him.[76] Since the Theodotus inscription is highly esteemed as precious information about the organisation and function of the synagogue in Second Temple times, but its date is regularly more assumed than argued, this question will be discussed in some detail.

b. The date

(1) *Palaeography*: The famous epigrapher C. Clermont-Ganneau compared the Theodotus inscription with the inscription prohibiting pagans from entering the inner part of the Herodian Temple (*CIJ* II, no. 1400) which he had found in 1871.[77] Clermont-Ganneau judged both inscriptions contemporary, the Theodotus inscription even slightly earlier,[78] in any case before AD 70. L.H. Vincent compared two other inscriptions from the early 2nd century AD and thought one should not be too dogmatic on the palaeographical dating, although he accepted on general considerations a date prior to AD 70.[79] In a special study of inscriptions of the early Imperial age M. Holleau subscribed to Clermont-Ganneau's date. Holleau wrote that the form of the *epsilon* 'suffirait à prouver qu'il est impossible de faire descendre cette inscription, comme on l'a témérairement proposé, jusqu'au IIe siècle de l'Empire, et qu'elle n'est point ou est à peine postérieure au

[74] In *The Synagogue in Late Antiquity*, 10.

[75] 'The Transformation', 8.

[76] 'The Changing Meaning', 282-3.

[77] *Une stèle du Temple de Jérusalem* (Paris, 1872).

[78] 'Découverte à Jérusalem d'une synagogue de l'époque Hérodienne', *Syria* 1 (1920) 190-7 (192-3). A summary appeared a little earlier in *CRAIBL* (Paris, 1920) 187-8 and in 'Une synagogue de l'époque Hérodienne à Jérusalem', *Revue Bleue* 58 (1920) 509-10.

[79] 'Découverte de la "Synagogue des Affranchis" à Jérusalem', *RB* 30 (1921) 247-77 (262-7). Without arguments, N.A. Bees, *BNGJ* 2 (1921) 259 opted for a Trajanic date.

commencement de notre ère'.[80] This judgement was accepted in the edition of the inscription in the *Supplementum Epigraphicum Graecum* (VIII, 1937, 25) and by J.B. Frey in the *Corpus Inscriptionum Judaicarum* (II, 1952, 333). It seems that no author assigned it to a time later than the early 2nd century AD on palaeographical arguments. Those few modern authors like J. Simons,[81] E.R. Goodenough[82] and M.J.S. Chiat[83] who touched on the question of palaeography opted for a date prior to AD 70. Important is the fragment of a dedicatory inscription recently found near the southern wall of the Temple area and dating from the twentieth year of Herod the Great (18/17 BC).[84] Its irregular letters are unlike the fine letters of Clermont-Ganneau's (official) warning inscription but comparable to the (private) Theodotos inscription. Even pondering the evidence very cautiously one can say: Palaeographically nothing suggests a Byzantine date, the 2nd century AD is not impossible, but the 1st century AD is more probable. In any case the early Imperial age is preferable.[85]

(2) *Archaeological context*: Concerning the inscription Kee is wrong in assuming that 'the archaeologists initially assigned it [to] the second half of the 2nd century C.E.'[86] As early as the first announcement the inscription was dated to the 1st century AD.[87] In his official report R. Weill referred to the opinion of L.H. Vincent, dating the inscription to the time between AD 70 and the Bar Kokhba War.[88] This was only a first guess and was abandoned immediately by Vincent.[89] Weill followed the epigraphical analysis of C. Clermont-Ganneau and closed his discussion of the inscription with the words: 'Concluons donc que notre Théodotos et son oeuvre sont antérieurs à la date de 70, à considérer comme un *terminus ad quem* infranchissable'.[90] Kee's impression

---

[80]'Une inscription trouvée à Brousse', *BCH* 48 (1924) 1-57 (6 n. 2).
[81]*Jerusalem in the Old Testament: Researches and Theories* (Leiden, 1952) 76.
[82]*Jewish Symbols in the Greco-Roman Period XII: Summary and Conclusions* (New York, 1965) 41.
[83]*Handbook of Synagogue Architecture*, 202.
[84]*Cf.* B. Isaac, 'A Donation for Herod's Temple', *IEJ* 33 (1983) 86-92.
[85]*Cf.* H. Lietzmann, 'Eine Synagogen-Inschrift aus Jerusalem', *ZNW* 20 (1921) 171-3 (172-3).
[86]'The Transformation', 8.
[87]*CRAIBL*, 333-4: '...l'inscription dédicatoire d'une fondation "pour les étrangers", créée vers le milieu du 1er siècle est en langue grecque'.
[88]*La Cité de David* I, 32-3.
[89]*Cf.* G.M. FitzGerald, 'Notes on Recent Discoveries', *PEFQS* 53 (1921) 175-86 (178 n. 2).

might have been created by another passage of the excavation report. Weill identified sparse remains of a building, near where the inscription was found, as remains of the synagogue mentioned. He was doubtful whether these remains should be assigned to a period after the whole area was quarried for the erecting of *Aelia Capitolina* (after AD 135), but he left open the possibility that parts were anterior to this time and came even from the Theodotus synagogue.[91]

Before the big excavation programme in the City of David (1978-85), M. Avi-Yonah could write about the architectural fragments and installations found near the inscription: 'The meagre remains, however, do not allow a reconstruction of the building which was dated to the Second Temple period only on the strength of the inscription found there'.[92] Y. Shiloh's excavation shed more light on this question. In the immediately neighbouring areas B, D^1, D^2 and E^2 nothing was found that dated later than the Herodian period.[93] This is corroborated by the finds in Weill's area. The five oil lamps he found in his excavation[94] are clearly Herodian. Shiloh summarised the results of his excavation up to 1982 concerning the period after AD 70: 'With the destruction of Jerusalem, at the end of Stratum 6, the hill of the City of David was neglected. The structures of the 'Lower City' on its ridge, and the supporting walls on its slopes, collapsed and tumbled down. The eastern slope for its entire length became covered with a layer of debris several metres thick. This debris included many finds from Stratum 6, carried down from the buildings at the top of the slope. They have been defined by us as a separate stratum, Stratum 5, which also contains almost nothing later than 70 CE'.[95]

This picture is confirmed by more recent syntheses: 'The deposition of debris along the eastern slope [of the City of David] in this period [after AD 70] inhibited construction there and determined its modern-day appearance from that time on', write J.M. Cahill and D. Tarler.[96] H. Geva concludes: 'A summary of the finds indicates that for most of the Roman period [after AD 70] the City of David remained

---

[90]*La Cité de David* I, 34.
[91]*Ibid.* I, 9.
[92]'Jerusalem', *Encyclopedia of Archaeological Excavations in the Holy Land* (Jerusalem, 1976) II, 579-627 (610).
[93]*Excavations at the City of David I (1978-1982)* (Jerusalem, 1984) 6-10.
[94]*La Cité de David* II, Pl. XXVI.
[95]*Excavations at the City of David I*, 30.
[96]'Excavations Directed by Yigael Shiloh at the City of David, 1978-1985', in H. Geva (ed.), *Ancient Jerusalem Revealed* (Jerusalem, 1994) 31-45 (42).

largely outside the built-up municipal area of Aelia Capitolina, serving mainly as a source for building stones'.[97] The remains of the heavy quarrying had already been found by R. Weill[98] and were later dated by K.M. Kenyon to the time of *Aelia Capitolina*.[99] In the Byzantine period there was no building activity in the whole area where the Theodotus inscription was found.[100]

T. Reinach thought that the inscription must have been brought from some hellenistic city.[101] But this suggestion originated only in the unwarranted assumption that in the holy city of Jerusalem there would have been no Torah teaching in Greek. Moreover, the inscription is made of the local limestone. The archaeological surroundings[102] strongly suggest that the inscription was found near the original place of the synagogue building. Nearby were three basins already identified by R. Weill through the measurements and the steps leading down as baths.[103] Today we can identify them even more precisely as Jewish ritual baths (*miqva'ot*). A little basin nearby could have served as *'ozar ser'a'*, a storage pool to lead additional flowing water into the *miqve'*, as is required by Mishnaic legislation (*m. Miqv.* 1:7; 3:1-2; 4:4). The inscription itself mentions water installations, undoubtedly for ritual purposes. Near the bathing installation were found remains of a building, two to three layers of large limestone blocks very well worked ('bien appareillées')[104] and remains of a pavement of big paving stones. Walls and pavement lay directly on the rock. The inscription was found in a cistern together with other well-worked ('bien taillés') building stones and some parts of columns. Most of these stones were deposited in a rather orderly fashion ('deposé avec un certain ordre'), as if to store them for re-use. Some of the stones were decorated with rosettes and simple geometrical designs,[105] as we

---

97 'Jerusalem: The Roman Period', in *The New Encyclopedia of Archaeological Excavations in the Holy Land*, II 758-67 (766).

98 *La Cité de David* I, 193-4.

99 *Digging Up Jerusalem* (London, 1974) 31-2, 263-4.

100 Only near the Byzantine church at the Siloam Pool (*cf.* John 9:7) were found some remains of adjacent buildings.

101 'L' inscription de Théodotos', *RÉJ* 71 (1920) 46-56 (55-6).

102 Unfortunately, today the site is very neglected. It serves as a garbage dump for nearby houses of the village of Silwan. On my regular visits between 1978 and 1993 I have been sad to see that damage has been done even to the sparse remains of buildings and installations.

103 *La Cité de David* I, 9.

104 These and the following citations from *ibid.*, I 9.

105 *Ibid.*, II Pl. XXV B.

know now from the synagogue of Gamla (see I.3 above). All this taken together makes it very probable that we have here the remains of the synagogue mentioned in the Theodotus inscription, as Weill had thought.[106]

(3) *Internal evidence*: The inscription is written in Greek, but shows some Semitisms.[107] Nothing can be deduced from the language for chronology. From the 1st to 4th centuries AD we know synagogue inscriptions from Palestine in Greek, Aramaic and Hebrew.[108] There were some attempts to identify the persons mentioned in the inscription.[109] More widely known became the suggestion of C. Clermont-Ganneau.[110] He points to a certain Vettienus, who acted as an agent in purchasing a lodge for Cicero in 49 BC. Since he is called by Cicero a *monetalis* (*cf. Ad Att.* 10.5.2; 11.5; 15.13.5), Clermont-Ganneau thought—not without a certain bias—he must have been a Jew[111] taken prisoner by Pompey in 63 BC and later set free (*cf.* Philo. *Leg. ad Gai.* 155). Clermont-Ganneau identified Cicero's Vettienus with the Vettenus of the inscription and thought that as a freedman he took over the name of the *gens Vettia*.[112] Theodotus as his son and a Roman citizen had enough possessions and influence to build the synagogue complex. This identification, too, remains speculative. The best part of it is the suggestion that the Latin name Οὐεττήνος may point to a *libertinus*.[113]

(4) *Historical circumstances*: The 4th century AD suggested by Kee as the time of the Theodotus inscription is most improbable. Although in the

[106]*Ibid.* I, 9. So also recently H. Geva, in *The New Encyclopedia of Archaeological Excavations in the Holy Land* II, 723. Many authors even do not realise that architectural remains have been found *in situ*. *Cf. e.g.* E.R. Goodenough, *Jewish Symbols* I, 179.

[107]*Cf.* L.H. Vincent, *RB* 30 (1921) 257. There is an interesting translation to Hebrew in Z. Ilan, *Ancient Synagogues in Israel*, 243.

[108]*Cf.* J. Naveh, 'Ancient Synagogue Inscriptions', in L.I. Levine, *Ancient Synagogues Revealed*, 133-9.

[109]S. Klein, *Jüdisch-Palästinisches Corpus Inscriptionum* (Vienna/Berlin, 1920 [Hildesheim, 1971]) 101-4; A. Marmorstein, 'The Inscription of Theodotos', *PEFQS* 53 (1921) 23-8; L.H. Vincent, *RB* 30 (1921) 260-1 (abandoned by himself).

[110]*Syria* 1 (1920) 196-7.

[111]This has rightly been criticised already by T. Reinach, *RÉJ* 71 (1920) 53-4.

[112]Accepted by M. Schwabe, 'Hak-ketubot hay-yavaniyyot shel yerushalayim', in *Sefer Yerushalayim* (Jerusalem, 1956) 349-68 (362-5); rejected by E. Gabba, *Iscrizioni Greche e Latine per lo studio della Bibbia* (Rome, 1958) 80-1.

[113]Accepted recently as a possibility, *e.g.*, by C.K. Barrett and C.J. Thornton, *Texte zur Umwelt des Neuen Testaments* (2nd edn.; Tübingen, 1991) 61-2.

time of Constantine the Great there were flourishing Jewish communities in Galilee, the Emperor reinforced the decrees banishing the Jews from Jerusalem.[114] The construction of a synagogue in the holy city would have been possible under Julian the Apostate, but the three years of his reign (361-3) were too short to cover the three generations between the foundation and the re-building of the synagogue. After the Bar Kokhba War (132-5), Hadrian banned the Jews from Jerusalem (Eusebius, *Hist. Eccl.* 4.6:3-4). It is possible or even probable that from the lenient reign of Antoninus Pius (138-61) the restrictions were reduced and some Jews could settle in Jerusalem.[115] This appears to be evidenced by some Rabbinical texts[116] and possibly by some Jewish tombs of the time of *Aelia Capitolina*.[117] But in this period the Jews would have been only a precariously tolerated minority. This was not the time to erect a large synagogue complex with accommodation for many pilgrims and to commemorate this event in a monumental inscription. A. Deissmann[118] and others[119] were wrong to believe that the Jews were banned from Jerusalem as early as AD 70 and that one must therefore date the inscription before 70. Already A. Schlatter demonstrated that between AD 70 and 132 there was a presence of Jews and Jewish Christians in the holy city.[120] So this period is a theoretical possibility.

However, the historical possibilities are radically reduced by the archaeological facts. We have no evidence that the area where the Theodotus inscription had been found was inhabited after AD 70. This is confirmed by the epigraphical analysis suggesting a date in the early Imperial age. Apart from Kee, the last scholar to opt for a date later than AD 70 was I. Press.[121] He connected the building with the activity

---

[114] *Cf. Itinerarium Burdigalense* 16; Jerome, *In Soph.* 1.15-6.

[115] *Cf.* E.M. Smallwood, *The Jews and the Roman Rule from Pompey to Diocletian: A study in political relations* (2nd edn.; Leiden, 1981) 499-500.

[116] *Cf.* S. Safrai, 'The Holy Community in Jerusalem', *ScrHier* 23 (1972) 62-78.

[117] *Cf.* G. Barkay, 'Excavations at Ketef Hinnom in Jerusalem', in H. Geva (ed.), *Ancient Jerusalem Revealed*, 85-106 (91-2); A. Kloner, 'The Cave of the Birds—A Painted Tomb of the Mount of Olives', *ibid.*, 306-10.

[118] *Light from the Ancient East* (ET; New York, 1927) 441. K. Galling, 'Archäologischer Jahresbericht', *ZDPV* (1927) 298-319 (315 n. 5) rightly criticised A. Deissmann, whereas Kee, 'The Changing Meaning', 282 n. 13, wrongly assumes that Deissmann was responsible for the introduction of the pre-70 dating.

[119] So *e.g.* P. Thomsen, 'Die lateinischen und griechischen Inschriften der Stadt Jerusalem', *ZDPV* 44 (1921) 90-168 (143-4).

[120] *Die Kirche Jerusalems vom Jahre 70-130* (Stuttgart, 1898). *Cf.* R. Riesner, 'Adolf Schlatter und die Geschichte der Judenchristen Jerusalems', in K. Bockmühl (ed.), *Die Aktualität der Theologie Adolf Schlatters* (Giessen, 1988) 34-70.

of Rabbi Eleazar (see II.3 above), and this brought him to the time around AD 100. But if one wishes to connect this Rabbi with the Theodotus synagogue, one could also speculate that the careful collection of the synagogue remains (including the Theodotus inscription) was his work. Be this as it may, in any case there is no ground for rejecting the present consensus that the Theodotus inscription comes from a time before AD 70.[122]

c. The meaning

Since the foundation by his grandfather and the re-building (apparently as enlargement) by Theodotus were separated by two generations, the synagogue must have existed at the turn of the era. This means that at the time of Jesus and the early Christian community in Jerusalem there stood on the southeastern hill a rather large synagogue complex. It comprised not only rooms for service (the reading of the Law) and school (the teaching of the commandments) but also ritual baths and accommodation for pilgrims. The δώματα might have been upper-rooms,[123] which are called ὑπερῷα in the synagogue inscription from Stobi in Dalmatia (*CIJ* I, no. 694) dating from the 3rd century AD.[124] Judging from the architectural remains the synagogue displayed certain elegance and wealth. With the ἀρχισυνάγωγος and a body of πρέσβύτεροι the inscription 'does imply a sort of council which formed the founding body'.[125] Another important deduction was formulated by J.N. Sevenster: 'This inscription proves irrefutably that, even in the 1st century AD, a precise boundary line could not be drawn between a hellenised Jewry, as in Egypt for example, and a completely non-hellenised Jewry in Palestine'.[126]

---

[121]*A Topographical-Historical Encyclopedia of Palestine [Hebrew]* (Jerusalem, 1948) II, 414-5.

[122]*Cf.* recently L. Roth-Gerson, *The Greek Inscriptions from the Synagogues in Eretz-Israel* [Hebrew] (Jerusalem, 1987) 76-86 (end of 1st century BC or beginning of 1st century AD); Z. Ilan, *Ancient Synagogues in Israel*, 243-4; H. Geva, *The New Encyclopedia of Archaeological Excavations in the Holy Land* II, 723.

[123]Suggested first by A. Marmorstein, *PEFQS* 53 (1921) 27. B. Lifshitz, *Donateurs et fondateurs dans les synagogues Juives* (Paris, 1967) 71, thinks of the οἶκοι in the Stobi inscription.

[124]*Cf.* M. Hengel, 'Die Synagogeninschrift von Stobi', in J. Gutmann, *The Synagogue*, 110-48.

[125]B.J. Brooten, *Women Leaders in the Ancient Synagogue* (Chico, 1982) 25.

[126]*Do You Know Greek? How Much Greek Could the First Jewish Christians Have Known?* (Leiden, 1968) 133-4.

3. *The so-called Tomb of David*

On Jerusalem's southwestern hill under the Gothic Cenacle, where Christian tradition locates Jesus' last supper, there are older walls. Many Jews and Muslims and even some Christians venerate between these walls the tomb of king David. This tradition is not attested earlier than the 10th century (*Vita SS. Helenae et Constantini* [ed. Baldi 495-6]) and is certainly erroneous, since the old necropolis of the Israelite kings was located on the southeastern hill.[127] In 1949, after a Jordanian mortar attack, the Israeli archaeologist J. Pinkerfeld during repair work could make some observations.[128] He dated the southern, eastern and northern wall of the so-called Tomb of David to late Roman times. Because he thought that an apse in the northern wall, *c.* 1.90 m above the original ground level, was oriented towards the Temple, he identified the room as a synagogue.[129] Since one of the graffiti, belonging to the oldest phase of the building, alludes to Jesus, B. Bagatti thought of a Jewish-Christian synagogue.[130] For J.E. Taylor the walls belong only to the southern part of the 4th-5th century Byzantine basilica *'Hagia Sion'*.[131] There is much controversy over how the archaeological evidence should be related to those sources mentioning a synagogue and/or church on Mount Zion before the first third of the 4th century AD (see II.4 above). On the whole there is more to be said for a pre-Byzantine date for the walls and a synagogue-like shape for the building.[132] But we should hope that peace in the Middle East will also open up the possibility of a thorough archaeological examination.

---

[127]*Cf.* B. Pixner, 'Die apostolische Synagoge auf dem Zion' in *Wege des Messias und Stätten der Urkirche*, 287-326 (290-4).

[128]'David's Tomb. Notes on the History of the Building', *Louis M. Rabinowitz Fund for the exploration of Ancient Synagogues Bulletin* 3 (1960) 41-3 (posthumously edited by M. Avi-Yonah).

[129]In this Pinkerfeld was followed by J.W. Hirschberg, 'The Remains of an Ancient Synagogue on Mount Zion' in Y. Yadin, *Jerusalem Revealed* (Jerusalem, 1975) 116-7, although this scholar dated the building to the time of Julian the Apostate (361-3). As a matter of fact the niche is not oriented towards the Temple but rather towards the Holy Sepulchre.

[130]*The Church from the Circumcision* (ET; Jerusalem, 1971) 116-22.

[131]*Christians and the Holy Places: The Myth of Jewish-Christian Origins* (Cambridge, 1993) 213-7.

[132]*Cf.* R. Riesner, 'Abendmahlstradition und Kirchbauten auf dem Sion' (forthcoming).

IV. Palestinian Synagogues in Luke-Acts

1. *The synagogue at Nazareth (Luke 4:16-28)*

A synagogue in Jesus' home town is already mentioned in Mark's Gospel (Mk. 6:2//Mt. 13:54), which the majority of scholars date around AD 70. It is disputed how far the Byzantine sources can bring us back in respect to the location of this synagogue.[133] Some architectural remains that may go back to a synagogue building cannot be dated safely since they were found out of a sure stratigraphical context.[134] Nevertheless, the hints in the Gospels of a synagogue building in Nazareth are accepted by modern Israeli scholars as reliable evidence for a time prior to AD 70.[135]

Kee suspected that Luke created a redactional expansion of Mark's text full of anachronisms.[136] But there is much to be said for the view that Luke used a supplementary tradition.[137] As Oster[138] pointed out, there is nothing anachronistic in holy scriptures kept in the synagogue (Lk. 4:17; *cf.* Jos. *Ant.* 16.164), Jesus standing to read and sitting to teach (Lk. 4:16, 20; *cf.* Philo, *Spec. Leg.* 2.62) or a synagogue attendant called ὑπερήτης (Lk. 4:20; *cf. CPJ* I, no. 138). Nor need it be anachronistic that Jesus 'finds' the appropriate place of the scripture reading (Lk. 4:17). Either Jesus could choose it freely for his own purpose, or Luke 4:16ff. may presuppose that Jesus began his public career in a jubilee year.[139] As the Melchizedek fragment from Qumran shows, the quoted passage of Isaiah 61:1-2 was connected with this date (11QMelch 2:16, 19f.) already in the 1st century AD and not only in later Rabbinic tradition.[140] A synagogue reading from the prophets is first attested explicitly by Luke, but one recalls the Ezekiel scroll buried in the Masada

---

[133]*Cf.* C. Kopp, *The Holy Places of the Gospels* (ET; Edinburgh, 1963) 55; R. Riesner, 'Nazareth', in *Das Grosse Bibellexikon* (2nd edn.; Wuppertal and Giessen, 1990) II, 1031-7 (1033-4).

[134]*Cf.* B. Bagatti, *Excavations in Nazareth* (ET; Jerusalem, 1969) I, 233-4; S.J. Saller, *Second Revised Catalogue of the Ancient Synagogues of the Holy Land* (Jerusalem, 1972) 70-1.

[135]*E.g.* L.I. Levine, in *The Synagogue in Late Antiquity*, 18.

[136]'The Transformation', 18.

[137]*Cf.* J. Nolland, *Luke 1-9:20* (Dallas, 1989) 192-4.

[138]'Supposed Anachronisms', 201-2.

[139]*Cf.* R. Riesner, *Die Frühzeit des Apostels Paulus. Studien zur Chronologie, Missionsstrategie und Theologie* (Tübingen, 1994) 38-40.

[140]For this see C. Perrot, *La lecture de la Bible. Les anciennes lectures, palestiniennes du Shabbat et des fêtes* (Hildesheim, 1973) 193-4.

synagogue (see above, II.3). We should be grateful that in this text we have 'our oldest and most detailed description of what took place in the early synagogue'.[141]

2. *The centurion's synagogue at Capernaum (Luke 7:1-10)*

This synagogue, too, is attested in Mark's Gospel (Mk. 1:21,29), this time in a collection of traditions possibly going back to Peter.[142] In the Q-tradition about the healing of the centurion's servant at Capernaum (Mt. 8:5-13//Lk. 7:1-10) only Luke has a double sending of messengers (Lk. 7:3, 6) and the Jews of the village begging: 'He is worthy to have you do this for him, for he loves our nation, and he built us our synagogue' (Lk. 7:4-5). The clear reference to a synagogue as a building makes Kee once more suspicious of anachronism.[143] Other scholars, too, think of a redactional expansion by Luke, portraying the centurion as a benevolent Godfearer.[144] But this is not the only possible explanation.[145] Matthew generally shortens miracle stories, and the absence of the friendly picture of the Capernaum Jews would fit his strongly polemical setting.

Perhaps archaeology also has something to contribute. The splendid limestone synagogue visible today in Capernaum is to be dated to the end of the 4th century AD.[146] But underneath the assembly hall lies a basalt building of the same ground plan. By means of the ceramics below the walls that earlier building was dated by S. Loffreda to the 3rd century AD. Exactly under the central nave of the two later buildings is located a pavement of basalt stones dating back to the 1st century AD. According to Loffreda we have here the remains of the centurion's synagogue. Nearby, but separated by an uninhabited piece of land, V. Tsaferis found other houses of the 1st century AD.[147] They were built in a better fashion than the houses of the main settlement,

---

[141]C.A. Evans, *Luke* (Peabody, 1990) 73.
[142]*Cf.* J. Jeremias, *New Testament Theology I: The Proclamation of Jesus*, tr. J. Bowden (London, 1971) 91.
[143]The Transformation', 17.
[144]*Cf.* recently R.A.J. Gagnon, 'Luke's Motives for Redaction in the Account of the Double Delegation in Luke 7:1-10', *NovT* 36 (1994) 122-45.
[145]*Cf.* I.H. Marshall, *The Gospel of Luke* (Exeter, 1978) 277-8.
[146]*Cf.* S. Loffreda, 'Le sinagoghe di Cafarnao', *BeO* 26 (1984) 103-14; *Recovering Capharnaum* (Jerusalem, 1985) 43-9.
[147]*Cf.* V. Tsaferis and M. Peleg, 'Kefar Nahum', *Excavations and Surveys in Israel* 4 (1986) 59.

and one of them was a typical Roman bathhouse. We may think of the centurion living here, separated as a pagan mercenary (*cf.* Lk. 7:6) from the Jewish village.[148]

3. *Many synagogues in Jerusalem (Acts 24:12)*

In his long apologetic speech on the steps of the Antonia fortress, the apostle Paul is reported to have said about his last visit to Jerusalem: 'They did not find me disputing with anyone or stirring up a crowd, either in the Temple or in the synagogues (ἐν ταῖς συναγωγαῖς), or in the city' (Acts 24:12). Obviously, Paul is speaking of synagogue buildings in comparison with the Temple and not only of synagogue congregations. For our question it is not very relevant how far this speech is a Lukan composition. That there were many synagogues in the holy city is *a priori* likely in light of the population numbers.[149] Jerusalem was not some provincial city, but a hellenistic metropolis. Furthermore, it is probable that Luke speaks as a visitor to the city. The we-passages in Acts (including Acts 20:5ff.) are better understood as the personal reminiscences of a companion of Paul than as mere literary creations.[150] Indeed, Luke in his double work shows a remarkable knowledge of Jerusalem and its vicinity, whereas he had no specific knowledge about Galilee.[151]

4. *The Synagogue of the Freedmen (Acts 6:9)*

In Acts 6:9 we read: 'Then some of those who belonged to the synagogue of the Freedmen (as it was called), and of the Cyrenians, and the Alexandrians, and of those from Cilicia and Asia, arose and disputed with Stephen' (*RSV*). It is not much disputed that Λιβερτῖνοι transliterates the Latin *libertini* and refers to former slaves that had been set free.[152] It is a more vexed question how many synagogues are mentioned. Every possibility between one and five has been defended.[153] But 'more probably one synagogue only is intended: 'the

---

[148]*Cf.* R. Riesner, 'Kapernaum', in *Das Grosse Bibellexikon* II, 764-8 (765).
[149]*Cf.* W. Reinhardt, 'The Population size of Jerusalem and the Numerical Growth of the Jerusalem Church' in this volume.
[150]*Cf.* C.J. Thornton, *Der Zeuge des Zeugen, Lukas als Historiker der Paulusreisen* (Tübingen, 1991).
[151]*Cf.* M. Hengel, 'The Geography of Palestine in Acts' in this volume.

Synagogue of the Freedmen, comprising both Cyrenaeans and Alexandrians and those from Cilicia and Asia' (καὶ Κυρηναίων καὶ Ἀλεξανδρέων and τῶν ἀπὸ Κιλικίας καὶ Ἀσίας being together, not separately, epexegetic of Λιβερτίνων)'.[154] This grammatical explanation could be strengthened by the possibility that Rabbinic sources refer to the same synagogue as one of the Alexandrians and the Tarsians (see above, II.3).

Already Weill,[155] Clermont-Ganneau[156] and Vincent[157] identified the 'synagogue of the Freedmen' with the synagogue mentioned in the Theodotus inscription. They found support from scholars such as G. Dalman,[158] J. Jeremias[159] and E.R. Goodenough.[160] Even a modern scholar such as M. Hengel is attracted to this identification,[161] and, indeed, it remains a serious possibility. The Theodotus inscription testifies to a Greek-speaking synagogue community, as was the synagogue of the Freedmen. Vettenus in the inscription could have been a *libertinus*, and thus not necessarily from Rome.[162] The building in the City of David seems to have been not too small, something we would expect for a synagogue housing several groups with different origins. Stephen is called Ἑλληνιστής (Acts 6:1) and he disputed with the members of the synagogue of the Freedmen (Acts 6:9). Later Paul, who was a native of Tarsus in Cilicia (Acts 22:3) and a Roman citizen, had

---

[152]*Cf.* H. Strathmann, *TDNT* IV, 265-6. An exception is B.W.W. Dombrowski, in Z.J. Kapera (ed.), *Intertestamental Essays*, 53-65. He thinks the text is corrupt (for which there is no manuscript evidence) and should read (as compared with Qumran texts) as the 'congregation of evil-doers'. This comes near to the translation of the *KJV*.

[153]*Cf.* K. Lake and H.J. Cadbury, *The Beginnings of Christianity I: The Acts of the Apostles. IV: English Translation and Commentary* (London, 1934) 66-7; G. Schneider, *Die Apostelgeschichte* (Freiburg, 1980) 435; R. Pesch, *Die Apostelgeschichte (Apg 1-12)* (Zurich and Neukirchen/Vluyn, 1986) 236-7.

[154]F.F. Bruce, *The Acts of the Apostles*, 187. *Cf.* also C.J. Hemer, *The Book of Acts in the Setting of Hellenistic History*, ed. C.J. Gempf (Tübingen, 1989) 176; L.T. Johnson, *The Acts of the Apostles* (Collegeville, 1992) 108.

[155]*La Cité de David* I, 32-4.

[156]*Syria* 1 (1920) 196.

[157]*RB* 30 (1921) 276-7.

[158]'Die Ausgrabungen von Raymond Weill in der Davidsstadt', *ZDPV* 45 (1922) 22-31 (30).

[159]*Jerusalem in the Time of Jesus*, tr. F.H. and C.H. Cave (London, 1969) 65-6.

[160]*Jewish Symbols* XII, 41.

[161]*The Pre-Christian Paul* (London and Philadelphia, 1991) 68-9.

[162]So Schürer, *The History of the Jewish People* II, 428 n. 8. There was a large settlement of freedmen in Rome (Philo, *Leg. ad Gai.* 155-7; Tac. *Ann.* 2.85). *Cf.* E. Schürer, *ibid.* (London, 1986) III/1, 132-3.

an argument with Ἑλληνισταί (Acts 9:29). It is tempting to conclude that both Stephen and Paul belonged originally to the hellenistic synagogue of the Freedmen. The Theodotus synagogue attracted pilgrims from abroad. If it is identified with the synagogue of the Freedmen, the Jewish hellenists may have feared that the new messianic belief could be spread through converted members to the whole Diaspora. This may further explain the zeal of Saul to persecute the Christian hellenists (Acts 7:58-8:3).

5. *The* **hyperôon** *(Acts 1:13), a Jewish-Christian synagogue?*

After the ascension, according to Acts 1:13, the disciples gathered in 'the upper room' (τὸ ὑπερῷον) somewhere in Jerusalem. The use of the definite article suggests that Luke has in view a specific room.[163] This would not be astonishing if, indeed, he had been a visitor to Jerusalem. The word ὑπερῷον is unique to Luke; it is used by no other New Testament author. Of the three other occurrences, one refers to an upper room in Troas where a Sunday service was held with breaking of bread and preaching in the light of many lamps (Acts 20:8). The two other occurrences refer to an upper room in Lydda where Tabitha, who had been living in some kind of a widow community, was put on the bier (Acts 9:37, 39).[164] Upper rooms (ὑπερῷα) are mentioned in the Stobi inscription as part of a synagogue building (see above, III.2). Upper rooms appear also in the Rabbinic literature as a preferred meeting place of teachers.[165] It seems that the upper room at Jerusalem where a rather large community met (*cf.* Acts 1:15) was in the eyes of Luke some kind of Christian synagogue. There are respectable arguments that the local tradition of the first meeting-place of the primitive community was handed down to the Byzantine period when the mighty basilica of *Hagia Sion* was erected.[166] The oldest walls of the so-called Tomb of David (see above, III.3) underneath the traditional

[163]*Cf.* F. Mussner, *Apostelgeschichte* (2nd. edn.; Würzburg, 1988) 18.

[164]*Cf.* R. Riesner, *Formen gemeinsamen Lebens im Neuen Testament und heute* (2nd edn.; Giessen, 1984) 24-5.

[165]*Cf.* Strack-Billerbeck II, 594-5.

[166]*Cf.* R. Riesner, 'Das Jerusalemer Essenerviertel und die Urgemeinde. Josephus, Bellum Judaicum V 145; 11QMiqdasch 46, 13-16; Apostelgeschichte 1-6 und die Archäologie' (*ANRW* II.26.2; Berlin and New York, 1995) (forthcoming). For the continuity of the local tradition the presence of a Gentile Christian community in *Aelia* could also guarantee this continuity. *Cf.* J. Murphy-O'Connor, 'The Cenacle and Community: The Topographical Background of Acts 2:44-45', in this volume.

Cenacle could belong to a pre-Byzantine assembly building marking the place where the original Upper Room once stood.[167]

Excursus II: The synagogue in James 2:2-3

In the Epistle of James we read the following admonition: 'For if a man with gold rings and in fine clothing εἰσέλθῃ εἰς συναγωγὴν, and a poor man in shabby clothing also comes in (εἰσέλθῃ), and you look at the one who wears the fine clothing and say, 'Please sit here' (σὺ κάθου ὧδε καλῶς), while you say to the poor man 'Stand there' (σὺ στῆθι ἐκεῖ) or κάθου ὑπὸ τὸ ὑποπόδιόν μου' (Jas. 2:2-3). L. Rost took this as proof of a Jewish-Christian synagogue building, comparing the description with the early Galilean synagogues.[168] We know today that none of these is earlier than the 3rd century AD.[169] Nevertheless, not only the Christian assembly but a definite room is in view. Where the author refers to the Christian community he speaks of the ἐκκλησία (Jas. 5:14), not of a συναγωγή. There is a fixed seating order. Apparently the leader of the service stands or sits on a raised place. This cannot be merely a stool, but presupposes ascending benches[170] or a raised platform. Next to the leaders' position are sitting places. One part of the room is free for standing. It would not be astonishing that a Jewish-Christian writer such as James could call an assembling room for the congregation a synagogue. We know through Epiphanius of Salamis that even in the 4th century AD Jewish Christians in contrast to the Gentile Christians called their meeting places synagogues (*Pan.* 30.18.2 [GCS 25.357]).

James 2:2-3 had an interesting '*Wirkungsgeschichte*'. The same seating order was followed in the 3rd century in developed house churches (*Didasc. Apost.* II, 57:1-58:6) and then in the 4th century in

---

[167]If the upper room (ἀνάγαιον) where Jesus held his last Passover meal (Mk. 14:15//Lk. 22:12) is to be identified with the upper room of Acts 1:13, as seems probable (F.F. Bruce, *The Acts of the Apostles*, 3rd edn. [Grand Rapids, 1990] 105), it is interesting to note that Jesus asks for a κατάλυμα (Mk. 14:14//Lk. 22:11), a word also mentioned in the Theodotus inscription as part of a synagogue (see above, III.3a).

[168]'Archäologische Bemerkungen zu einer Stelle des Jakobusbriefes (Jak. 2,2f)', *PJB* 29 (1933) 53-66.

[169]*Cf.* G. Foerster, 'The Ancient Synagogues of Galilee', in L.I. Levine, *The Galilee in Late Antiquity*, 289-319; L.I. Levine, *The New Encyclopedia of Archaeological Excavations in the Holy Land*, IV 1422.

[170]*Cf.* B. Schwank, *Erbe und Auftrag* 49 (1973) 414-5 (review of F. Mussner, *Der Jakobusbrief*, 2nd edn. [Freiburg, 1967]).

those longitudinal buildings (*Const. Apost.* II, 58:6) which preceded or were contemporary with the first Constantinian basilicas. P. Maser tends to think that these literary sources show that the Constantinian basilica was not a *creatio ex nihilo*, but had one of its roots in synagogal buildings of a basilical form.[171] In the 4th century Ambrosiaster, who might have stood in Jewish Christian tradition,[172] seems to suggest such an architectural history: 'The great synhedrion which survives in the synagogue and in the church made it as an institution, that in all religious assemblies people should be sitting, the nobler ones on stools, those who are after them on benches, the rest on mats, which are spread out on the floor' (*In Epist. 1 ad Cor.* 12:1-2 [*PL* 17.258]). This text allows one to ask if James 2:2-3 also has in view two kinds of seats: honorary places (stools at the *hypopodion*?) and normal places (benches under the *hypopodion*?),

The introductory questions about the Letter of James are hotly disputed. In the opinion of this writer the balance of arguments favours a pre-70 date and an origin in circles around James, the brother of the Lord.[173] The most recent commentary by G.M. Stulac[174] even defends a dating before the so-called Apostolic council (Acts 15) in about AD 48. If the Letter of James originated in such a setting it testifies to Jewish Christian and consequently also to Jewish synagogues before AD 70 in Judaea and/or Jerusalem. This would be all the more interesting since the Jesus tradition in James shows a certain resemblance to Luke's special tradition in the Gospel.[175] This special tradition seems to go back to conservative Jewish Christians gathered around James and his followers in the leadership of the *Hebraioi* (*cf.* Acts 6:1) in Jerusalem.[176]

---

[171]'Synagoge und Ekklesia. Erwägungen zur Frühgeschichte des Kirchenbaus', in D.A. Koch and H. Lichtenberger (eds.), *Begegnungen zwischen Christentum und Judentum in Antike und Mittelalter*, 271-92 (also in *Kairos* 32/33 [1990/91] 9-26).

[172]Ambrosiaster, a name given by Erasmus to an unknown author of the time of Pope Damasus (366-84), had an excellent knowledge of Judaism and was remarkably friendly towards the Jews. *Cf.* A. Stuiber, 'Ambrosiaster', *TRE* II (1978) 356-62 (359). Some authors have thought that he was a converted Jew. *Cf.* A. Souter, *A Study of Ambrosiaster* (Nendeln, 1967 [Cambridge, 1905]).

[173]*Cf.* F. Mussner, *Der Jakobusbrief* (5th edn.; Freiburg, 1987) 1-23, 237-40.

[174]*James* (Downers Grove and Leicester, 1993) 13-7.

[175]*Cf.* P.H. Davids, *The Epistle of James* (Exeter, 1982) 47-50.

V. Conclusion

There is nothing anachronistic in Luke's and the other evangelists' picture that there were many synagogues in Galilee and in Jerusalem. Many of the details given by Luke are corroborated by other literary, epigraphical and archaeological sources. The fact that Jesus and his first followers started their mission in the ambience of the synagogue cannot be overestimated. The synagogue was a comparatively intellectual milieu. This has a bearing on the question of the transmission and reliability of the Gospel tradition.[177] The process of translating this tradition began not far away in the Diaspora, but in the bilingual situation of Greek-speaking synagogues in Jerusalem. The structure of synagogue congregations was one of the models for organising Christian communities.[178] Possibly, even the style of early church buildings, including symbols and art,[179] was influenced by synagogue architecture. From the synagogue the early Christian service inherited the central position given to reading and expounding the holy scriptures.[180] This feature made Judaism and Christianity unlike all other cults in antiquity.

Addendum

A major event in synagogue research has been the publication of the first part of a composite volume, *Ancient Synagogues, Historical Analysis and Archaeological Discovery*, edited by D. Urman and P.V.M. Flesher in November 1994 (Studia Post-Biblica 47/1; Leiden). Three of the articles are most interesting for our question. D.E. Groh ('The Stratigraphic

[176]*Cf.* R. Riesner, 'Prägung und Herkunft der lukanischen Sonderüberlieferung', *TB* 24 (1993) 228-48 (summarised in 'Luke's Special Tradition and the Question of a Hebrew Gospel Source', *Mishkhan* 20 [1994] 44-51); 'James's Speech (Acts 15:13-21), Simeon's Hymn (Luke 2:29-32), and Luke's Sources', in J.B. Green and M. Turner (eds.), *Jesus of Nazareth: Lord and Christ. Essays on the Historical Jesus and New Testament Christology* (I.H. Marshall FS; Grand Rapids and Carlisle, 1994) 263-78.

[177]*Cf.* R. Riesner, 'Jesus as Teacher', in H. Wansbrough (ed.), *Jesus and the Oral Gospel Tradition* (Sheffield, 1991) 185-210.

[178]*Cf.* R.S. Neal, *Synagogue and Church: The Model of the Jewish Synagogue in the Formation of First-Century Christianity* (PhD thesis; Forth Worth, 1988).

[179]*Cf.* K. Schubert, 'Die jüdische Wurzel der frühchristlichen Kunst', *Kairos* 32/33 (1990/91) 1-8.

[180]*Cf.* J.T. Burtchaell, *From Synagogue to Church: Public Services and Offices in the earliest Christian Communities* (Cambridge, 1992).

Chronology of the Galilean Synagogue from the Early Roman Period Through the Early Byzantine Period' [*c.* AD 420], *ibid.* 51-69) accepts not only the Gamla building as a Galilean pre-70 synagogue but also the little structure in Migdal (*ibid.* 58-60), the Magdala of New Testament times (*cf.* Mk. 14:40 *et passim*). Groh further identifies the oldest broad house structure at Nabratein (see above, I.3), dating to the earlier 2nd century AD, as a synagogue (*ibid.* 60). It provides our first indisputable example of a permanent set of *bemahs* on the Jerusalem wall.

P.V.M. Flesher accepts Gamla as a pre-70 synagogue, but is doubtful in the cases of Masada and Herodium ('Palestinian Synagogues before 70 C.E. A Review of the Evidence', *ibid.* 27-39). These doubts are connected with his assumption that there were no synagogues in Judaea as long as the Temple was standing. Flesher accepts Acts 6:9 as a historical hint to a Second Temple synagogue in Jerusalem, but thinks it is an exception to the rule because it was found by Diaspora Jews. A sure date of the Theodotus inscription is not possible according to Flesher, and even the 3rd or 4th century AD cannot be excluded (*ibid.* 33 n. 21). His discussion of the historical problems is all too short, however, the handling of the archaeological data insufficient and the question of palaeography not even touched.

A new point of view is introduced by R. Reich ('The Synagogue and the *miqweh* in Eretz-Israel in the Second Temple, Mishnaic, and Talmudic Periods', *ibid.* 289-97). He ends his article: 'next to each of the synagogues dating to the Second Temple period [Gamla, Masada, Herodium, Theodotus synagogue], archaeologists found a *miqweh*... Since several score excavated ancient synagogues are known from all over the country, while only a handful of them are related to *miqwaot*, we may conclude that in the period of Mishna and Talmud there is no apparent linkage between these two institutions' (*ibid.*, 297). One of the reasons for this linkage before AD 70 might have been the holding of sacred meals in synagogues. Out of his great experience Reich confirms that the water installations near to the spot where the Theodotus inscription has been found were indeed *miqvaot* (*ibid.*, 291-2). One of the two basins measures 6.20 to 8.20 m. which places this *miqveh* among the largest in Jerusalem. This might be an indication that it served a community and not a private household. If one connects the water installations mentioned in the inscription (ll. 6-7) and the archaeological remains of *miqvaot* nearby we have another indication for a pre-70 date of the Theodotus synagogue.

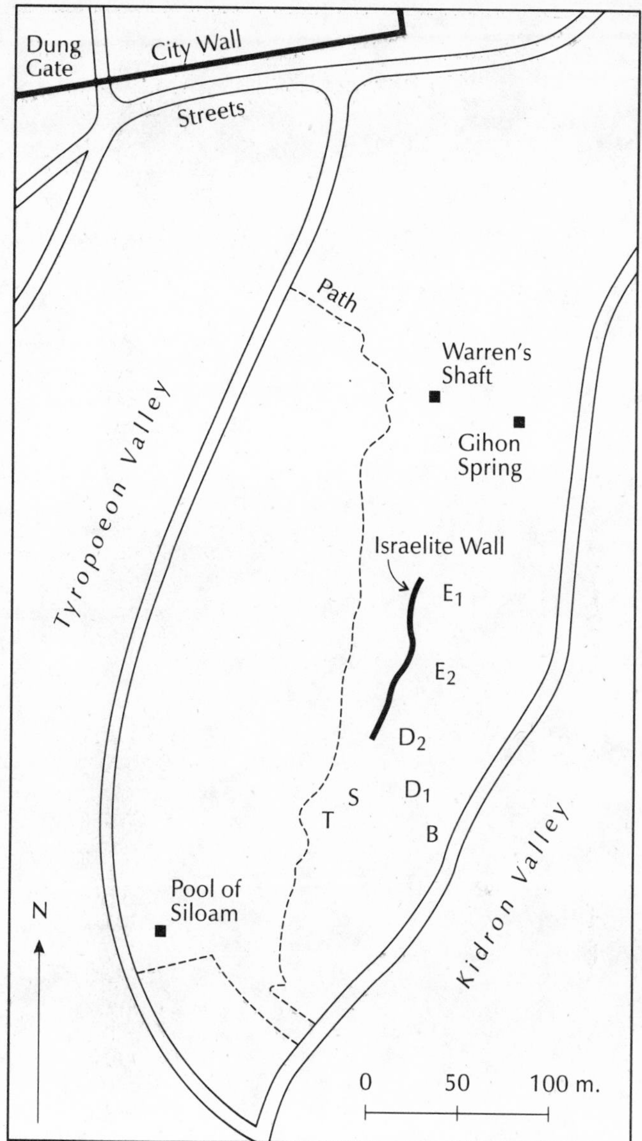

Jerusalem — City of David

T = Cistern where Theodotos inscription was found by R. Weill (1913)

S = Sparse building remains (well, ritual baths)
belonging probably to a synagogue

B, D_1, D_2, E_1, E_2 = excavation areas (Y. Shiloh, 1948-85)

CHAPTER 7

THE COMPOSITION OF THE JERUSALEM CHURCH

David A. Fiensy

Summary

Jerusalem in the 1st century AD was a moderate-sized urban centre with a socially and culturally pluralistic population. Typical of ancient cities, it was composed of the very rich, the craftsmen, and the destitute, among others. Further, this city had a substantial element of Greek-speaking Jews. Although the sources, especially the book of Acts, give only hints about the make-up of the Jerusalem church, the indications are that nearly all levels of society were represented. The church seems to have been a microcosm of the city.

Studies on the theology and practice of the Jerusalem church are legion.[1] These studies usually point out that early Christianity was closely tied to Judaism, practised some kind of voluntary communism, had the Twelve apostles and later the Seven as leaders and, of course, proclaimed Jesus as the Messiah.

This undertaking will examine the composition of the primitive Christian community. What sort of people were these sociologically and culturally? Did the Christian movement, the 'Way', attract only the poor or other classes as well? Were these people culturally diverse?

We shall maintain below that although the early Jerusalem church was entirely Jewish, it was nonetheless socially and culturally pluralistic. Indeed, the primitive church reflected to a great extent the rich diversity of Jerusalem itself, the 'most illustrious city in the east'.[2] A city of 60,000 or more inhabitants,[3] Jerusalem in the early Roman period contained the fabulously rich as well as the unbearably poor. Further, most of the inhabitants were probably Palestinian natives but the city also had a sizeable minority of Jews from the Diaspora (and of course some Gentiles as well).

Jerusalem is described by Josephus as mainly consisting of two parts: the Lower City and the Upper City. The Lower City, also called the Acra (*BJ* 5.253), consisted of the Ophel, the City of David, and the Tyropoeon Valley. The Upper City was on the hill now called Mt. Zion (*BJ* 2.422). Josephus also writes of an area just north of the Lower and Upper Cities which he calls New Town (*BJ* 2.530; 5.331). By the time of the war in AD 66 this last area was encompassed by the third north wall. But within most of our time frame (AD 30-66) only a small part of that suburb was enclosed—by the second north wall.[4] Finally, the

[1]See *e.g.* F.J. Foakes Jackson and K. Lake, *The Beginnings of Christianity* (Grand Rapids: Baker, 1979) I, 300-420; L. Cerfaux, 'La première communauté chrétienne à Jérusalem (Act., II, 41-V, 42)', *Ephemerides Theologicae Lovanienses* (1939) 5-31; W.L. Blevins, 'The Early Church: Acts 1-5', *Review and Expositor* 71 (1974) 463-74.

[2]Pliny, *N. H.* 5.70.

[3]This figure is in line with the estimates of J. Wilkinson, 'Ancient Jerusalem, Its Water Supply and Population', *PEQ* 106 (1974) 33-51; M. Broshi, 'Estimating the Population of Ancient Jerusalem', *BARev* IV, 2 (1978) 10-15; P. King, 'Jerusalem', in D.N. Freedman (ed.), *The Anchor Bible Dictionary* (New York: Doubleday, 1992) III, 753; B. Mazar, *The Mountain of the Lord* (Garden City, NY: Doubleday, 1975) 210; and N. Avigad, 'Jerusalem' in E. Stern (ed.), *New Encyclopaedia of Archaeological Excavations in the Holy Land* (New York: Simon and Schuster, 1993) II, 721. Wilkinson estimates that at the time of Herod the Great there were 36,280 residents and in the time of Agrippa II there were 76,130. Broshi estimates 40,000 residents for Herod's time and 80,000 just before the war. See also the chapter by W. Reinhardt in this volume.

Temple mount formed one of the significant districts of ancient Jerusalem.

I. The Social Groups in Jerusalem

L. Finkelstein[5] has sketched the social situation in Jerusalem which when informed by the sociologically sensitive work of G. Sjoberg[6] can serve as a model for us.

The upper class lived mainly in the Upper City and consisted of the Temple nobility and the lay nobility. Most of these, even the wealthy priests, were probably large estate owners though some may have been wealthy merchants.

Literary and archaeological sources[7] have identified many medium to large estates[8] in Judaea and even around Jerusalem itself. Since large landowners tended in antiquity to live in the city as absentee landlords and leave the administration of their estates to bailiffs, these land holdings may well have belonged to the members of the Jerusalem upper class.

The sources certainly testify that wealthy families lived in Jerusalem before the first Jewish war. The rabbinic sources tell of three wealthy men, Naqdimon ben Gorion, Ben Kalba Shabua and Ben Tzitzit, who lived in Jerusalem before and during the first Jewish war. They were allegedly capable of supplying Jerusalem for twenty-one years. One of them could supply wheat and barley, one oil and wine and the third, wood. These men were either large estate owners whose

---

[4]See the maps in *e.g.* J. Wilkinson, *Jerusalem as Jesus Knew It* (London: Thames and Hudson, 1978) 62, 64; and Avigad, 'Jerusalem' in Stern (ed.), *New Encyclopedia*, II, 718.

[5]Finkelstein, *The Pharisees* (Philadelphia: Jewish Publication Society of America, 1962) I, 4.

[6]G. Sjoberg, *The Preindustrial City* (Glencoe, IL: The Free Press, 1960) 118-33.

[7]See S. Applebaum, 'The Problem of the Roman Villa in Eretz Israel' *Eretz Israel* 19 (1987) 1-5; *idem*, 'The Roman Villa in Judaea: A Problem', in Applebaum, *Judaea in Hellenistic and Roman Times* (Leiden: Brill, 1989); *idem*, 'Judaea as a Roman Province: The Countryside as a Political and Economic Factor', *ANRW* II.8 (1977) 355-96; D.A. Fiensy, *The Social History of Palestine in the Herodian Period* (New York: Mellen, 1991) 21-73.

[8]See H. Dohr, *Die italischen Guthöfe nach den Schriften Catos und Varros* (Cologne: PhD, 1965) and K.D. White, *Roman Farming* (London: Thames and Hudson, 1970) 385-87, for the categories of small, medium and large estates in antiquity.

estates produced these crops or merchants. Even allowing for obvious exaggerations, the three must have possessed great wealth.[9]

The rabbinic sources also allude to other wealthy landowners who resided in or near Jerusalem during this time. Hyrcanus, father of Eleazar the famous student of Yohanan ben Zakkai, was a wealthy man who owned lands near Jerusalem.[10] Elisha ben Abuya was descended from a wealthy landowner who lived in Jerusalem before AD 66.[11] Rabbi Dosa ben Harkinas was an elderly and wealthy scholar during the time of the school of Jamnia (AD 70-125). A. Büchler argued that he must have, therefore, lived in Jerusalem before the war and that he had been able to maintain his wealth even in the aftermath of the destruction of Jerusalem.[12]

Probably the most significant class of wealthy landowners was the group of aristocratic priests, especially the High Priestly families. M. Stern[13] suggests that the statement of Hecataeus (Diodorus Siculus 40.3.7) that Moses gave the priests a larger share of land than other Israelites reflects the social situation in Palestine in the Second Temple period. Certainly Hecataeus did not base this observation on the Old Testament since, according to the Law (Dt. 10:9; 12:12; 18:1; Nu. 18:24), the priests and Levites did not own land. As Stern also notes, it is doubtful that the priests could have become wealthy from the tithes alone since the Mishnah indicates that many peasants did not always pay them (see *m. Dem.*).

At any rate a number of priestly families were quite wealthy. The most obvious example is the family of Josephus. He states that he has come from a wealthy and influential priestly family of the Hasmo-

---

[9] *B. Giṭ.* 56a and *Lam. Rab.* I.31. The latter source gives the names of four men. See Applebaum, 'Economic Life in Palestine', in S. Safrai and M. Stern (eds.), *The Jewish People in the First Century* (Assen/Amsterdam: Van Gorcum, 1976) I.2, 659. See J. Jeremias, *Jerusalem in the Time of Jesus* (ET; Philadelphia: Fortress, 1962) 95f., 226. See also *ʾAbot R. Nat.* Rec A 6, Rec B 13, *Eccles. Rab.* 7.12 and *Gen. Rab.* 42.1 for the same three men called here the 'great ones of Israel'. Compare also H. Kreissig, 'Die Landwirtschaftliche Situation in Palästina vor dem Judäischen Krieg', *Acta Antiqua* 17 (1969) 234.

[10] *ʾAbot R. Nat.* Rec A 6; *Gen. Rab.* 42.1; *Pirqe R. El.* I; and S. Mendelsohn, 'Eliezer ben Hyrcanus', in I. Singer (ed.), *Jewish Encyclopedia* (New York: Funk and Wagnalls, 1903); and A. Büchler, *The Economic Conditions of Judea after the Destruction of the Second Temple* (London: Oxford, 1912) 40.

[11] *Y. Ḥag.* 2.1.; *Eccles. Rab.* 7.18. See Büchler, *Economic Conditions*, 14, and Jeremias, *Jerusalem*, 92.

[12] *B. Yebam.* 16a for R. Dosa and Büchler, *Economic Conditions*, 40.

[13] M. Stern, 'Aspects of Jewish Society: The Priesthood and Other Classes', in S. Safrai and M. Stern (eds.), *Jewish People*, I.2, 586f.

naean line (*Vita* 1f.; *Ant.* 16.187) and that he owned lands near Jerusalem (probably just west of the city) before the war (*Vita* 422). Since, according to his autobiography, he is never seen residing on his farm, we can assume that he had a bailiff to oversee his tenants or slaves and that he lived for the most part in Jerusalem.

Other priests, especially the High Priests, were also wealthy. Ananias son of Nebedaeus (High Priest in AD 48) was wealthy enough to pay bribes to Albinus the Procurator and the current High Priest, Jesus son of Damascus, so that he could continue a campaign of extortion against both the peasants and poorer priests (*Ant.* 20.205-7) to extract forcibly the tithes for himself and his servants.[14]

Wealth was especially prominent in the main High Priestly families, that is, the houses of Boethus, Hanan, Phiabi and Kathros (Kadros).[15] The Talmud represents these families as powerful and ruthless:

> Woe is me because of the house of Boethus, woe is me because of their staves!
> Woe is me because of the house of Hanin, woe is me because of their whisperings!
> Woe is me because of the house of Kathros, woe is me because of their pens!
> Woe is me because of the house of Ishmail the son of Phabi, woe is me because of their fists.
> For they are High Priests and their sons are (Temple) treasurers and their sons-in-law are trustees and their servants beat the people with staves.[16]

That these priestly houses were wealthy can hardly be doubted. The wealth of the house of Boethus, for example, was legendary (*b. Giṭ.* 56a; *b. Yebam.* 61a), as was that of the house of Phabi (*b. Yoma* 35b).

---

[14]See Stern, 'Aspects of Jewish Society', 586f. and E.M. Smallwood, 'High Priests and Politics in Roman Palestine', *JTS* 13 (1962) 27.

[15]See Stern, 'Aspects of Jewish Society', 605-9; Smallwood, 'High Priests', 14-34. Stern wants to add the house of Kimchi to these other four families. Jeremias, *Jerusalem*, 194 maintained that the fourth great High Priestly house was Kamaith instead of Kathros and that Kathros was a branch of Boethus.

[16]*B. Pesaḥ.* 57a. Translation in I. Epstein (ed.), *The Babylonian Talmud* (London: Soncino, 1948). See the notes on this passage also in Epstein. The whisperings represent secret meetings to devise oppressive measures. The pens write evil decrees. See the list in Appendix A of Smallwood, 'High Priests', 31f. of the High Priests in the Herodian period and the families to which they belonged. This same lament appears in *t. Menaḥ.* 13.21.

Annas and Caiaphas of the house of Hanan apparently owned large mansions.[17] Some of their riches may have been acquired by extortion and violence, but such practices could not produce sustained wealth. They must have owned lands in Judaea and perhaps elsewhere which brought them such large fortunes.[18]

The rabbinic sources also refer to several priests who lived between the two Jewish rebellions who were wealthy. That priests should have maintained their wealth even after the war is not surprising. As Büchler maintained, Josephus indicates that many priests quickly capitulated to the Romans and so were allowed to keep their lands (*BJ* 6.115).[19] The most celebrated of these wealthy priests was Eleazar ben Harsom, who allegedly owned 1,000 villages.[20] Mentioned alongside ben Harsom is Eleazar ben Azariah, also of priestly descent, who possessed extraordinary wealth.[21] Also to be included in this list is Rabbi Tarfon, a wealthy sage who as a young man had participated as a priest in the Temple ritual. R. Tarfon owned an estate in Galilee and may also have owned land near Joppa.[22]

Thus the literary evidence indicates that a wealthy, aristocratic class lived in Jerusalem in the 1st century AD, many of whom, but not all, belonged to the influential priestly families. In this context we must add the testimony of Josephus. He writes of a significant group of wealthy citizens living in the Upper City of Jerusalem at the outbreak of the war who became the targets of the Sicarii and other revolutionary factions (*BJ* 2.428, 652; 4.140f.). Here Herod had built a palace, and Agrippa II and several chief priests had mansions there (*BJ* 1.402; 2.422, 426, 428). In this district is also the traditional location of Caiaphas' house.[23]

---

[17]Jeremias, *Jerusalem*, 96. See Jn. 18:15, 18; Mk. 14:53.

[18]See Jeremias, *Jerusalem*, 108; and Stern, 'Aspects of Jewish Society', 586f. M. Goodman, *State and Society in Roman Galilee, A.D. 132-212* (Totowa, NJ: Rowman and Allenheld, 1983) 33 also doubts that priests could have grown wealthy on even unearned tithes.

[19]A. Büchler, 'Die Schauplätze des Bar-Kochbakrieges', *JQR* 16 (1904) 191.

[20]See *b. Yoma* 35b; *b. Qidd.* 49b; *b. Shabb.* 54b; and *b. Beṣa* 23a.

[21]See *b. Qidd.* 49b; *b. Shabb.* 54b; *b. Beṣa* 23a. He traced his lineage back to Ezra, *b. Ber.* 27b and *y. Yebam.* 1.3. See S. Mendelsohn, 'Eleazar ben Azariah', in Singer (ed.), *Jewish Encyclopedia*.

[22]*Y. Shebu.* 4.2; *b. Ned.* 62a; *Eccles. Rab.* 3.11; *b. Qidd.* 71a; *y. Yoma* 3.7; *t. Ḥag.* 3.36. See S. Oscher, 'Tarfon', in Singer (ed.), *Jewish Encyclopedia*; and L. Finkelstein, 'The Pharisees: Their Origin and their Philosophy', *HTR* 22 (1929) 190. For lands near Joppa see the tomb inscription of Tarfon's son in J.B. Frey, *CIJ* (Rome: Pontificio Istituto di Archeologia Cristiana, 1952) II, no. 892.

The archaeological excavations of the Jewish quarter of Jerusalem confirm the impression we get from the literary sources that a significant wealthy class resided in Jerusalem before the war. The excavation team of N. Avigad[24] discovered in the Upper City large mansions owned obviously by very rich people. The 'Herodian house' from the 1st century BC, the 'Palatial Mansion' from the 1st century AD, and the 'Burnt House'[25] from the 1st century AD are architectural testimony of this class. But just as interesting for our purposes are not only the huge mansions but the rows of slightly more modest houses which still, according to Avigad, 'belonged to upper class families'.[26] These houses are not only distinguished by their size from other houses of the same period, but by their furnishings and decorations. The costly pottery, the wine imported from Italy, the elaborate frescoes and floor mosaics and the many water installations, among other items, point to the wealth of the occupants. That these people were Jewish is evident from the *mikvaot* found in many of the houses. This evidence, then, fits hand-in-glove with the literary evidence.

The lower classes consisted of the poorer priests and Levites, the small merchants, the craftsmen, and the unskilled labourers.[27] The lower-class priests, divided into twenty-four weekly courses (*Ant.* 7.365), lived in villages throughout Judaea and Galilee.[28] But many priests resided in Jerusalem. The priests in Jerusalem at the time of Nehemiah numbered 1,192 (Ne. 11:10-14; but *cf.* 1 Ch. 9:13).[29] E.P.

---

[23]See M. Broshi, 'Excavations in the House of Caiaphas, Mt. Zion', in Y. Yadin (ed.), *Jerusalem Revealed* (Jerusalem: Israel Exploration Society, 1975) 57f.; J. Wilkinson, *Jerusalem as Jesus Knew It* (London: Thames and Hudson, 1978) 133-6, 166 for Caiaphas' house. For Herod's palace see D. Bahat and M. Broshi, 'Excavations in the Armenian Garden', in Yadin (ed.), *Jerusalem Revealed*, 55.

[24]N. Avigad, *Discovering Jerusalem* (Oxford: Basil Blackwell, 1980) 83-137; and *idem*, 'How the Wealthy Lived in Herodian Jerusalem', *BARev* 2 (1976) 22-35.

[25]The Burnt House apparently, from an inscription found in it, belonged to a member of the house of Kathros, the priestly family listed above. See Avigad, 'The Burnt House Captures a Moment in Time', *BARev* 9 (1983) 66-72.

[26]Avigad, *Discovering Jerusalem*, 95.

[27]*Cf.* Finkelstein, *The Pharisees*, I, 4 and Sjoberg, *The Preindustrial City*, 121-125. Finkelstein actually lists both a middle class and a lower class, but most sociologists would be reluctant to identify a true middle class until the industrial age.

[28]See R. Hachlili, 'The Goliath Family in Jericho; Funerary Inscriptions from a First Century A.D. Jewish Monumental Tomb', *BASOR* 235 (1979) 31-65 (on a priestly family in Jericho); *b. Ber.* 44a; *b. Ta'an* 27a; *t. Yebam.* 1.10; Lk. 1:39; *t. Soṭa* 13.8; *Ant.* 17.66; and M. Stern, 'Aspects of Jewish Society', 584.

[29]See Stern, 'Aspects of Jewish Society', 595 who notes that Hecataeus writes of 1,500 priests, evidently referring to priests of Jerusalem (*C. Ap.* 1.188).

Sanders surmises reasonably from this figure in Nehemiah's time that by the 1st century AD there were probably 'a few thousand priests and Levites' in Jerusalem.[30]

The poorer priests worked at a trade such as stone cutting, the sale of oil, or in agriculture.[31] Sanders' contention that many priests were scribes, teachers of the law and judges has some support also (Sir. 45:17; *Vita* 9.196-8; *C. Ap.* 2.187).[32]

Priests also received tithes, at least theoretically, but it is difficult to know how much income they actually received from them.[33] Not all peasants paid the tithes (*m. Dem.*; Philo, *Spec. Leg.* 1.153-5). Further, the more powerful and wealthier priests on occasion seem to have robbed the poorer ones of their dues. In the time of Agrippa II, the High Priestly families sent their slaves to claim forcibly the tithes while the poorer priests went hungry (*Ant.* 20.179-81; *cf. b. Pesaḥ.* 57a). This text from Josephus may hint at ongoing class animosity between the wealthier and poorer priests.

Likewise Levites formed a subgroup in the lower class. They were considered beneath the ordinary priests in station. In the main they must have been of rather modest means. Stern remarked on the relative lack of references to Levites in the Second Temple sources.[34] Nehemiah 11:18 gives the number of Levites as 460 in his day, less than half his figure for priests. We may assume that the same proportion existed in the 1st century AD.

Jeremias conjectured that the Levites' two subgroups, the singers and the servants or doorkeepers were of unequal rank (*b. ʿArak.* 11b; *Ant.* 20.216-8). The singers were, he maintained, considered to be higher in social standing. Each desired in the time of Agrippa II to be given greater honours.[35] This is an interesting suggestion, although the evidence is slight.

---

[30]E.P. Sanders, *Judaism: Practice and Belief 63 B.C.E.-66 C.E.* (London: SCM, 1992) 170. Jeremias, *Jerusalem*, 200 estimated that the total number of priests in Palestine was 7,200 and the total number of Levites was 9,600. Sanders (78) accepts that Josephus' (*C. Ap.* 2.108) total figure of 20,000 for the priests and Levites in Palestine is probably close to correct. See J.B. Frey, *CIJ* II, nos. 1221, 1317, and 1400 and J. Naveh, 'A New Tomb Inscription from Giv'at Hamivtar', in Yadin (ed.), *Jerusalem Revealed*, 73 for inscriptions in Jerusalem referring to priests.

[31]See Stern, 'Aspects of Jewish Society', 586f. who cites *t. Yoma* 1.6; *t. Beṣa* 3.8 and Hecataeus (Diodorus Siculus 40.3.7).

[32]Sanders, *Judaism*, 170-2. Jeremias also pointed out these roles for priests. See *Jerusalem*, 207, 234.

[33]Stern, 'Aspects of Jewish Society', 585f.

[34]*Ibid.*, 597.

Apparently Levites like priests found employment as scribes or craftsmen. One of the Temple singers, Joshua ben Hananiah, for example, was a nailsmith.[36]

The lower class also included craftsmen and small merchants. One of the main sources of income was the Temple, which required bakers, weavers, goldsmiths, washers, merchants of ointments and money changers.[37] Further, the Temple was still in the process of being built. This labour force employed a large number of carpenters and stone masons. Josephus reported that when the Temple was completed in the procuratorship of Albinus (AD 62-64), it put 18,000 workers out of a job (*Ant.* 20.219). Thus the Temple required a large force of craftsmen throughout most of the 1st century AD.

But in addition there were markets both in the Upper and Lower Cities where wares were sold (*BJ* 2.305, 315). Jerusalem was famous for jewellery, spinning, weaving, dyeing, tailoring, shoemaking, perfume and incense but also produced oil, pottery, ossuaries, stoneware and woodwork.[38] In the Lower City was the Tyropoeon Valley with a main street running through it lined by shops on both sides of the street. The name suggests that a cheese market stood there,[39] but we should expect that other goods were found there as well. Archaeologists have found remains of the street, its large drain, and some shops from Robinson's Arch next to the Temple all the way south along Tyropoeon street.[40]

In addition there was a market centre in the New Town district, north of the first wall. The Mishnah refers to a weavers' and wool-dealers' market in Jerusalem (*m. ʿErub.* 10:9; *m. ʿEd.* 1:3). Josephus writes that metal workers, tailors, fullers, wool dealers, and timber

---

[35]Jeremias, *Jerusalem*, 212f. But see the note in L.H. Feldman, *Josephus* (Cambridge, MA: Harvard University, 1981) X, 117, who maintains that the doorkeepers were the upper rank of Levites. The Levites were, like the priests, divided into 24 weekly courses and thus served in the Temple about twice a year (*Ant.* 7.366f.).

[36]See Jeremias, *Jerusalem*, 234.

[37]See M. Avi-Yonah, *The Holy Land* (Grand Rapids: Baker, 1977) 194 and his references. The tomb of an artisan family that worked on the Temple has been found. See J. Naveh, 'The Ossuary Inscriptions from Givat Ha-Mivtar', *IEJ* 20 (1970) 33-37.

[38]See B. Mazar, *The Mountain of the Lord* (Garden City, NY: Doubleday, 1975) 210; Jeremias, *Jerusalem*, 4-9 and their citations.

[39]Its name in Greek means 'Valley of the cheese makers', but Avi-Yonah suggests it is a corruption of some unrecognisable Hebrew term. See *The Holy Land*, 193.

[40]F.J. Bliss and A.C. Dickie, *Excavations at Jerusalem* (London: Palestine Exploration Fund, 1878) 133; Mazar, *The Mountain of the Lord*, 205f.; M. Ben-Dov, *In the Shadow of the Temple* (New York: Harper and Row, 1985) 114.

merchants had a market in the New Town district (*BJ* 2.530; 5.147, 331; *cf. Lam. Rab.* 1.1).

Also in the lower class were the unskilled day labourers. Labourers could work in the fields or olive groves around Jerusalem ploughing, weeding, harvesting, threshing, picking fruit and doing other seasonal jobs.[41] Most often the labourer worked as a burden bearer who carried wood, reeds, harvested crops, and other kinds of burdens. Some even carried around other people.[42] Many unskilled labourers were watchmen. They were paid to watch over animals, fields of crops, children, the sick, corpses, and the city gates.[43] But labourers also performed functions such as bathhouse attendants, messengers, manure gatherers, and thorn gatherers.[44]

The unskilled worker was apparently paid on average one denarius per day.[45] But many were certainly paid less. Hillel worked as a wood cutter in Jerusalem, earning one half denarius a day (*b. Yoma* 35b). Another poor man of Jerusalem made a living by trapping doves and lived on about one fourth denarius a day (*Lev. Rab.* 1.17).

We should expect that most of the craftsmen and small merchants lived near the Tyropoeon market and thus in the Lower City or in the less populated New Town. Archaeologists have discovered the ruins of some houses in the Lower City. M. Ben-Dov describes the area in the Lower City known as the City of David as 'slums' and terms it 'run -down'.[46]

The City of David (the southern part of the Ophel spur) was of course the oldest inhabited area in Jerusalem. Even in the hellenistic period the evidence is that most residents lived there. Only in the 1st century BC did people begin moving up the slope towards the Upper City.[47] Thus most of the lower class lived in the older district of the city.

---

[41]*T. Maʿas* 2.13, 15; *t. B. Meṣ.* 7.5f.; *m. B. Meṣ.* 7:5, 7:4, 7:7, 6:1, 8:8; *m. Peʾa* 5:5. See S. Krauss, *Talmudische Archäologie* (Hildesheim: Georg Olms, 1966) II, 105; and M. Goodman, *State and Society in Roman Galilee, A.D. 132-212* (Totowa, NJ: Rowman and Allenheld, 1983) 39.

[42]*T. B. Meṣ.* 7.4; *m. B. Meṣ.* 6:1 and Krauss, *Talmudische Archäologie*, II, 105.

[43]See *m. B. Meṣ.* 7:8f.; *m. B. Qam.* 8:1; *m. Shebu.* 8:1; and Krauss, *Talmudische Archäologie*, II, 106.

[44]See Krauss, *Talmudische Archäologie*, II, 106.

[45]See Mt. 20:2, 9, 13; Tob. 5:14; *y. Sheb.* 8.4; *b. B. Bat.* 87a; *b. ʿAbod. Zar.* 62a and A. Ben-David, *Talmudische Ökonomie* (Hildesheim: Georg Olms, 1974) 66 and D. Sperber, 'Costs of Living in Roman Palestine I', *Journal of the Economic and Social History of the Orient* 8 (1965) 248-71.

[46]Ben-Dov, *In the Shadow of the Temple*, 155. *Cf.* Finkelstein, *The Pharisees*, I, 14.

As we shall see below, however, Jews from the Diaspora and proselytes were also drawn to this area.

At the very bottom of the social and economic scale was the 'submerged' class or the class of 'outcasts'. This class included slaves, beggars, those from unapproved occupations, the diseased, and those from questionable births.[48]

According to the Talmud, the occupations which were scorned included prostitutes, dung collectors, donkey drivers, gamblers, sailors, tanners, peddlers, herdsmen and usurers.[49]

Those groups inferior to the common people due to heredity would have included mainly those born illegitimately. *M. Qidd.* 4:1 lists a hierarchy of births ranging from priests to the lowly four: bastards, Gibeonites, those that must be silent when reproached about their origins, and foundlings.[50] Bastards were those born of an incestuous union (as defined by Lv. 18 and 20). A bastard could not 'enter the congregation of the Lord' (Dt. 23:3). That is, he could not marry an Israelite.[51] The Gibeonite was supposedly a descendant of the Gibeonites whom Joshua made to become Temple slaves (Jos. 9:27) and they were also excluded from the Israelite community as far as intermarriage was concerned (*b. Yebam.* 78b).[52] Those that must be silent when reproached about their origins were those that did not know who their father was (*m. Qidd.* 4:2).[53] The foundling is a child taken up from the street whose father and mother are unknown (*m. Qidd.* 4:2).[54]

With regard to the diseased we should think especially of the lepers who seem to have abounded in Palestine.[55] Such people were declared unclean by a priest (Lv. 13:11, 25) and had to remain apart

---

47Y. Shiloh, *Excavations at the City of David I, 1978-1982* (Jerusalem: Hebrew University, 1984) 30.

48Finkelstein, *Pharisees*, I, 4 used the term 'submerged', and Sjoberg, *Preindustrial City*, 133 used the designation 'outcasts'. See also Fiensy, *Social History*, 164-7.

49Lk. 7:37-39, Mt. 21:31; *m. Qidd.* 4:14, *m. Ketub.* 7:10, *m. Sanh.* 3:3; *b. Qidd.* 82a, *b. Sanh.* 25b; and Jeremias, *Jerusalem*, 303-12.

50The translation of these terms is by H. Danby, *The Mishnah* (Oxford: Oxford University, 1933). *Cf.* also m. Horayoth 3:7f.

51See L.N.D. Dembitz, 'Bastard', in Singer (ed.), *Jewish Encyclopedia*.

52See M. Jastrow, *A Dictionary of the Targumim, the Talmud Babli and Yerushalmi, and the Midrashic Literature* (New York: Judaica, 1975).

53See *ibid*.

54See *ibid*. *B. Baba Metzia* 87a says a man should not marry a foundling.

55Mk. 1:40; 14:3, Lk. 17:12; *m. Meg.* 1:7; *m. Mo'ed Qaṭ.* 3:1; *m. Soṭa* 1:5; *m. Zebaḥ.* 14:3; *LAB* 13:3; Apocryphal Syriac Psalm 155. The word seems to have been generally used for infectious skin diseases. See Lv. 13.

from everyone else crying out from a distance 'Unclean!' (Lv. 13:45f.). Lepers lived then a life of social ostracism.

Beggars also appear frequently in 1st-century Palestine. They are lame (Acts 3:2; Jn. 5:3; *m. Shabb.* 6:8; Lk. 16:20) or blind (Jn. 9:1; Mt. 21:14; Mk. 10:46) and sit along the roadside in the country (Mk. 10:46) or along the streets and alleys in the city (Lk. 14:21). Jeremias suggested that beggars were especially numerous in the Temple precincts.[56]

Slaves in Jerusalem were mostly domestics of the wealthy. A Jew could become a slave as punishment for stealing, out of poverty or from indebtedness. The Hebrew slaves would presumably be liberated in the Sabbatical year. Gentile slaves or 'Canaanites' were slaves for life. Jeremias and Krauss note that slaves were sold on a special platform in Jerusalem.[57]

The royal courts of the Herodian family had many domestic slaves (*BJ* 1.511, 673; *Ant.* 17.199). The High Priests also had numerous slaves (Mk. 14:4-7; Jn. 18:18, 26; *Ant.* 20.181, 206f.). Thus the wealthy elites could own scores or even hundreds of slaves which served as household servants, body guards, eunuchs in the harem (*BJ* 1.511; *m. Yebam.* 8:4) and other purposes. But other well-to-do residents could also own a few slaves (*cf. m. ʿEd.* 5:6) such as the physician of Jerusalem (*m. Rosh Hash.* 1:7) or Mary the mother of John Mark (Acts 12:13).

In the ancient cities the submerged class, especially the destitute, the beggars, and the terribly ill, usually lived on the outskirts of the city.[58] The farther one was from the centre socially and economically, the farther one lived also from the centre geographically. Thus the wealthy lived mainly in the Upper City, the lower class in the Lower City and the New Town, and the outcasts lived on the fringes of the city if indeed they had residences at all.

We must say a word about the role of women. Women for the most part shared the social status of their husbands. In one case, however, a rich woman bought the High Priesthood for her future

---

[56]Jeremias, *Jerusalem*, 116f.

[57]See Ben-David, *Talmudische Ökonomie*, 70; Jeremias, *Jerusalem*, 312, 36; Krauss, *Talmudische Archäologie*, II, 362.

[58]See G. Sjoberg, 'The Preindustrial City', in J.M. Potter, M.N. Diaz, and G.M. Foster (eds.), *Peasant Society: A Reader* (Boston: Little, Brown and Company, 1967) 15-24; R. MacMullen, *Roman Social Relations* (New Haven, CN: Yale University, 1974) 48-87; and R.L. Rohrbaugh, 'The Pre-Industrial City in Luke-Acts: Urban Social Relations' in J.H. Nehrey (ed.), *The Social World of Luke-Acts* (Peabody, MA: Hendrickson, 1991) 125-49.

husband (*m. Yebam.* 6:4; *b. Yebam.* 61a; *Ant.* 20.213). Thus sometimes the husband shared the social status of the wife.

By most accounts, women in the patriarchal Palestinian Jewish society lived according to strict rules of modesty and retirement.[59] Jeremias could write: 'Eastern women take no part in *public life*'. It is true that they were sensitive about being veiled in public or at least about having their hair tied up on top of the head (Su. 32; *m. Shabb.* 6:5; *m. Ketub.* 2:1; *m. Soṭa* 1:5; *m. B. Qam.* 8:6). Men were admonished in the Talmud not to talk much with women (*m. ᾿Abot* 1:5; *cf. m. Qidd.* 4:12; *b. Ber.* 43b). Women of means apparently were kept in seclusion, seldom venturing into public (Philo, *Spec. Leg.* 3:169; *Flacc.* 89; 4 Mac. 18:7). Women were for the most part under the power of either a father or a husband (*C. Ap.* 2.201; *m. Ketub.* 4:4). And of course one can certainly find misogynist statements in the literature (*BJ* 2.121; Philo, *Hypoth.* 11.14; *LAE* 18.1).

Yet some caution is in order in interpreting this evidence. In the first place, there was a Hasmonaean queen, Alexandra (*Ant.* 13.405-431), who ruled from 76-67 BC. She obviously had a public life and wielded power. Further, many of the Herodian women do not at all seem shy and retiring—for example, Herod's mother-in-law, also named Alexandra, and the infamous Salome (*Ant.* 15.42-45; Mk. 6:2). The women of the High Priestly house of Boethus flaunted their wealth in public (*Lam. Rab.* 1.50; *cf. b. Giṭ.* 56a). Women of wealth then could be quite the opposite of the stereotype we encounter in some of the sources.

But the women of the lower class probably did not usually fit the stereotype either. Common sense would indicate that they could not be cloistered away from the public but had to work beside their husbands producing and selling their wares (*m. Ketub.* 9:4).[60] Since

---

[59]See Jeremias, *Jerusalem*, 359-62; H.L. Strack and P. Billerbeck, *Kommentar zum Neuen Testament aus Talmud und Midrasch* (Munich: C.H. Beck, 1963) III, 427-36; B. Witherington III, 'Women, New Testament', in D.N. Freedman (ed.), *The Anchor Bible Dictionary*, VI, 957f.; E. Stagg and F. Stagg, *Women in the World of Jesus* (Philadelphia: Westminster, 1978) 15-54; L. Swidler, *Women in Judaism: The Status of Women in Formative Judaism* (Metuchen, NJ: Scarecrow Press, 1976) 114-25, 167-73.

[60]Jeremias makes this point (*Jerusalem*, 362). See also the interesting work of A. Prost in A. Prost and G. Vincent (eds.), *A History of Private Life* (ET; Cambridge, MA: Harvard University, 1991) 9-16 who points out that craftsmen from antiquity to fairly recent times opened their homes to the public. These were usually only one-room residences. Thus women—who also helped produce the goods—could not have remained secluded. On the use of residences as workshops in ancient cities see also R. MacMullen, *Roman Social Relations*, 48-87.

most of them lived in one-room houses that doubled as workshops, the life of the retiring and pampered élites was impossible.

The Talmud (*b. Giṭ.* 90a) quotes a saying from a Palestinian sage which illustrates this point. The sage, R. Meir, indicates there are three types of men. One keeps his wife locked away; one allows her to converse with male relatives; the third, a base fellow, allows his wife to go out with her hair down and spin in the streets. Thus women often lived in tension with the stereotype.

The documents relating to a Jewish woman named Babatha (dating to the early 2nd century AD) are informative. They are, it is true, from a period later than our primary focus and do not pertain explicitly to Jerusalem, but surely nonetheless provide insight into the role and status of women. The documents indicate that Babatha managed a considerable agricultural business yet needed a male representative in her contacts with authorities.[61]

Therefore we would conclude that although this society was very patriarchal, we should not read too literally the statements of the Talmud and other sources. The practical necessities of living demanded that women often exceed customary expectations in public life and independence.

Thus Jerusalem in our period of consideration (30-66 AD) was inhabited by a population varied in its socio-economic composition. The wealthier class tended to live in the Upper City and the lower class in the Lower City or the burgeoning New Town. Many in the submerged class were probably homeless and wandered the streets and alleys begging or otherwise lived on the outskirts of the city.

II. The Socio-Economic Composition of the Jerusalem Church

The Jerusalem church was probably fairly representative of the city's population. There were well-to-do members, though one cannot say they were among the wealthy élite. Simon of Cyrene owned a farm in the vicinity of Jerusalem (Mk. 15:21). Barnabas sold his lands (in Judaea or in Cyprus? See Acts 4:36f.) and gave the proceeds to the poor. Ananias and Sapphira (Acts 5:1) also possessed lands. We cannot

---

[61]On the Babatha collection see B. Isaac, 'The Babatha Archive: A Review Article', *IEJ* 42 (1992) 62-75 and M. Broshi, 'Agriculture and Economy in Roman Palestine: Seven Notes on the Babatha Archive', *IEJ* 42 (1992) 230-40.

be certain that the 'fields' referred to in these texts were medium-sized estates or larger, but the sale of the property in the cases of Barnabas and especially Ananias (whose lands are called κτῆμα) seem to have involved a not inconsiderable sum of money. Therefore, we would suggest that the latter two landowners, Ananias and Barnabas, owned medium-sized estates.[62] In addition, Mary, mother of John Mark, owned a house large enough to serve as a place of assembly for the primitive church and owned at least one domestic slave (Acts 12:12-17). She, like her kinsman, Barnabas (Col. 4:10), was wealthy. Manaen, the foster-brother of Herod Antipas (Acts 13:1), became later a leader in the church at Antioch. He was obviously from Palestine and probably a sometime resident of Jerusalem. Finally, one of Jesus' close disciples may also have been wealthy. Levi the tax collector (Mk. 2:13-17) may have been rich since he could give a banquet in which many people reclined at their meal. Such a banquet suggests a large house. Certainly tax collectors could become quite wealthy (see Lk. 19:1-10; *BJ* 2.287).

The lower class was certainly represented as well in the Jerusalem church. The occupation of some of Jesus' twelve disciples is reported in the Gospels. James and John's father, Zebedee, was the owner of a somewhat prosperous fishing business in Galilee which could employ day labourers. Whether James and John still lived *in absentia* by this income or were entirely supported by the gifts of others we cannot know.[63] Peter and Andrew had also been fishermen (Mk. 1:16). Jesus' brother, James, one of the pillars of the Jerusalem church (Gal. 1:19; 2:9; 1 Cor 15:7; Acts 15:13-21; 21:17-25; *Ant.* 20.200), was presumably a carpenter by trade like Jesus (Mk. 6:3). We would reasonably expect that most of the members of the Jerusalem church were craftsmen or small merchants, but the sources do not clearly indicate this.

---

[62]H. Kreissig, 'Die Landwirtschaftliche Situation in Palästina vor dem Judäischen Krieg', 223, argued that these men owned large estates. S. Applebaum, 'Economic Life in Palestine', in S. Safrai and M. Stern (eds.), *The Jewish People in the First Century*, I.2, 259, urges caution in assuming too much from these examples. Jeremias, *Jerusalem*, 96, maintained that Joseph of Arimathea (Mk. 15:42) also was a large estate owner.

[63]See Mk. 1:19f. On fishing in Galilee see W.H. Wuellner, *The Meaning of Fishers of Men* (Philadelphia: Westminster, 1967) 45-63; H. Hoehner, *Herod Antipas* (Cambridge: Cambridge University, 1972) 67; K.W. Clark, 'Sea of Galilee', in G.A. Buttrick, *The Interpreter's Dictionary of the Bible* (Nashville: Abingdon, 1962) II, 348-350; S. Freyne, 'Sea of Galilee', in D.N. Freedman (ed.), *The Anchor Bible Dictionary*, II, 899-901.

The text of Acts (6:7) does state that 'A great number of the priests were obedient to the faith'. These were not of course from the High Priestly family since the latter actively persecuted the church (Acts 4:1-21; 5:17-42). Some have alleged that these priests were Essene priests and thus not from those serving in the Temple.[64] There were probably Essenes living in Jerusalem since one of the gates at the southwest of the city was called by Josephus the Essene Gate (*BJ* 5.145) and Josephus may even refer to the Essene latrines.[65] It is also true that one of the traditional locations of the Upper Room (Acts 1:13) is in the general vicinity of the Essene Gate.[66] Yet we do not know for sure that the Jerusalem Essenes had priests like those at Qumran (*e.g.* see 1QS 1.18). The simplest conclusion is that some of the ordinary Temple priests—who numbered in Jerusalem perhaps 2,000—became members of the Jerusalem church.

We have reference to at least one Levite among the Christian community: Joseph Barnabas (Acts 4:36) who was named above as possibly a wealth member. Since Barnabas was a Levite, his kinsman, John Mark (Col. 4:10), was evidently one as well. Mark's mother, Mary, was a also a woman of some means as we indicated above. Since Barnabas was a native of Cyprus, however, he may not have served in one of the twenty-four courses in the Temple.

The submerged class was also a part of the Jerusalem church. One would assume that the beggars and diseased people healed by Jesus (Jn. 5:1-14; 9:1-12) or the apostles (Acts 3:1-10; 5:12-16) became members of the church. In addition to the impoverished widows (Acts

---

[64]See O. Cullmann, 'The Significance of the Qumran Texts for Research into the Beginning of Christianity', *JBL* 74 (1955) 213-26; reprinted in K. Stendahl (ed.), *The Scrolls and the New Testament* (New York: Harper and Brothers, 1957) 18-32. See the rebuttal of this view in G. Schneider, *Die Apostelgeschichte* (Freiburg: Herder, 1980) 430; and E. Haenchen, *The Acts of the Apostles* (Oxford: Basil Blackwell, 1971) 269.

[65]See *BJ* 5.145 the 'Bethso'; and 1QM 7:6-7; 11QTemple 46; and Y. Yadin, 'The Gate of the Essenes and the Temple Scroll', in Yadin (ed.), *Jerusalem Revealed*, 90f. The Essene Gate would be south of where the present Zion Gate stands. Yadin maintained that the latrines were west of the Hippicus tower (the modern Jaffa Gate). Others affirm that the latrines were near the American Institute of Holy Land Studies on the southwest point of Mt. Zion. See R.M. Mackowski, S.J., *Jerusalem, City of Jesus* (Grand Rapids: Eerdmans, 1980) 64.

[66]See Mackowski, S.J., *Jerusalem, City of Jesus*, 143f.; and Wilkinson, *Jerusalem*, 168f. On the other hand, one of the traditional sites of the Upper Room is near the possible location of Caiaphas' house. Does this mean then that the primitive Christians were Sadducees? To argue from geographical proximity seems very tenuous. See the map in Mackowski and in D. Bahat, *The Illustrated Atlas of Jerusalem* (New York: Simon and Schuster, 1990) 55.

6:1) there must have been other destitute persons cared for by the church (Acts 2:44f.; 4:34). These texts, which admittedly tend to be utopian in style, give the impression that the church assisted a considerable proletariat. We read nothing in Acts about church members of unapproved occupations and questionable births, though we might expect that Jesus' overtures to such people were continued by his disciples (Mk. 2:13-17; Lk. 15:1f.). Likewise, only Rhoda (Acts 12:13) appears in our sources as a servile member of the church, but there must have been others.

Women played a significant role in the Jerusalem Christian community. They were of course a prominent part of Jesus' ministry.[67] In the Upper Room before Pentecost Mary mother of Jesus and other unnamed women[68] were part of the praying community (Acts 1:14). Women were among the first converts (Acts 5:14), and they were persecuted by Saul of Tarsus (Acts 8:3; 9:1f.; 22:4f.).[69] Sapphira, wife of Ananias, a wealthy member of the church, was condemned along with her husband for lying about their donation (Acts 5:1-11). That she was named alongside her husband probably indicates that she was a woman of influence. Another wealthy woman, Mary, mother of John Mark (Acts 12:12), used her house for the assembly of the believers. Thus in the church as well as in urban society in general certain women of wealth and influence could play prominent roles.

What is striking about our main source for early Jerusalem Christianity—the book of Acts—is that so little is said about socio-economic class distinctions. The wealthy are hardly noticed at all except for a few cases of extraordinary generosity. We cannot document that any of the High Priestly family or any of the governing élite were members of the earliest church. The lower class has the fewest references, although one could speculate that they had the largest representation. The submerged class enters the story only to indicate that the church is caring for them. The central figures are those that perform ministries of some kind, whether they come from the upper or

---

67See B. Witherington III, *Women and the Genesis of Christianity* (Cambridge: Cambridge University, 1990) 88-112; L.F. Massey, *Women and the New Testament* (Jefferson, NC: McFarland, 1989) 7-27.

68G. Lüdemann suggests these women were the apostles' wives. See *Early Christianity According to the Traditions in Acts*, tr. J. Bowden (ET; London: SCM, 1989) 27. F.F. Bruce maintained that they were women who had followed Jesus from Galilee (Lk. 8:2f.). See *Commentary on the Book of Acts* (Grand Rapids: Eerdmans, 1983) 44.

69See L. Swidler, *Biblical Affirmations of Women* (Philadelphia: Westminster, 1979) 291f.

lower class. One should stop short of concluding that class went unnoticed in this religious community, but the traditions we have certainly de-emphasise it.

Second, we should note, however, that all the classes were represented. Neither the wealthy nor the impoverished were excluded. Earliest Christianity was not a movement within one socio-economic class, but from the beginning, was as pluralistic as the city of Jerusalem itself. The observation made by G. Theissen and others about the Pauline churches is also true for the Jerusalem church. Christianity was no proletarian movement. It appealed to a broad spectrum of classes.[70]

III. The Cultural Groups Among Jerusalem's Jews

The predominantly Jewish city of Jerusalem was bicultural. Most of the residents spoke and understood only Aramaic; some were bilingual; still others could probably speak only Greek.

Certainly the mother tongue of most Palestinian Jews was Aramaic: 'The prominence of Aramaic at every level as the main language of Palestinian Jewry is now solidly backed by evidence...'.[71] Even in Jerusalem Aramaic was predominant. The ossuary inscriptions in Jerusalem are mostly in a Jewish script.[72] The native languages tended to remain strong even under the cultural assault of Greek in the eastern part of the empire and Latin in the west.

Yet many, especially the educated and merchants, did learn Greek either out of an interest in Greek literature, a desire to appear sophisticated, or for business reasons. The incursion of the Greek language and culture into Jewish Palestinian society is quite evident

---

[70]G. Theissen, *The Social Setting of Pauline Christianity*, tr. J.H. Schütz (ET; Philadelphia: Fortress, 1982) 69. See also W.A. Meeks, *The First Urban Christians* (New Haven and London: Yale University, 1983) 73; and A.J. Malherbe, *Social Aspects of Early Christianity* (Baton Rouge and London: Louisiana State University, 1977) 31.

[71]E. Schürer, G. Vermes, F. Millar and M. Black, *The History of the Jewish People in the Age of Jesus Christ* (Edinburgh: T. & T. Clark, 1973-87) II, 26. The same was true for most parts of the empire. Native languages persisted as dominant for centuries in North Africa, Britain, Gaul and Spain. See M. Rostovtzeff, *Social and Economic History of the Roman Empire*, rev. P.M. Fraser (Oxford: Clarendon, 1957) 193; A.H.M. Jones, *The Greek City from Alexander to Justinian* (Oxford: Clarendon, 1940) 291f.; P. Brunt, *Social Conflicts in the Roman Republic* (New York: Norton, 1971) 170-72.

[72]See Frey, *CIJ* II, 244-339.

on many fronts. Coins were minted in Palestine with Greek inscriptions; the Hebrew and Aramaic languages adopted numerous Greek loan words; many Palestinian Jews had Greek names; the architecture of the residences and the pottery show Greek influences; the government—as far back as Herod the Great—was Hellenized; there was a gymnasium; and numerous inscriptions, papyri and ostraca in Greek have been found.[73] N. Avigad writes from his experience excavating the houses of the wealthy: 'The pursuit of things Hellenistic was then not uncommon in Jerusalem, particularly among the Hellenistic nobility'.[74] The same pursuit existed in most cities and towns in the eastern empire.[75] To be Greek to some extent was highly desired by the wealthy.

But others were Greek culturally because they grew up in Greek centres of the Diaspora. Even their tomb and ossuary inscriptions were chiselled in Greek. Hengel reports on an ongoing project of collecting all the known epitaphs from Jerusalem. So far, of all the ossuaries with inscriptions (many ossuaries are not inscribed), the Greek inscriptions make up 39% of the total. Most of the rest are in a semitic language only, but some are bilingual. Hengel concludes that those people inscribed their ossuaries in Greek whose family used Greek as the vernacular. Thus he suggests (conservatively) that the Greek-speaking population of Jerusalem was 10% to 20% of the total population.[76] Based on our figure for the total population of Jerusalem (60,000 residents) the Greek-speaking Jews numbered 6,000 to 12,000.

There is evidence that many if not most of these Jews grew up in the Diaspora. There are ossuary and epitaph inscriptions in Greek of a man called Africanus Furius, of Justus the Chalcidian, of Nicanor from Alexandria, of Maria wife of Alexander from Capua, of Rabbi Samuel from Phrygia, of Anin from Scythopolis[77] and possibly of a family from Cyrenaica.[78]

P. Thomsen maintained that at least some of these were brought to Jerusalem after their deaths to be buried in the holy city.[79] This

---

[73]See M. Hengel, *The Hellenization of Judaea in the First Century After Christ* (ET; London: SCM, and Philadelphia: Trinity, 1989) 8, 9, 12; G. Mussies, 'Greek in Palestine and the Diaspora', in S. Safrai and M. Stern, *The Jewish People in the First Century*, I.2, 1040-64; S. Krauss, *Lehnwörter* (Hildesheim: Georg Olms, 1964); J. Jeremias, *Jerusalem*, 74; N. Avigad, *Discovering Jerusalem*, 83, 120; J. Fitzmyer, *A Wandering Aramean* (Chico, CA: Scholars Press, 1979) 35.

[74]Avigad, *Discovering Jerusalem*, 120.

[75]See *e.g.* N. Lewis, *Life in Egypt Under Roman Rule* (Oxford: Clarendon, 1983) 39.

[76]Hengel, *Hellenization of Judaea*, 10. L.Y. Rahmani is managing this project.

[77]See Frey, *CIJ* II, nos. 1226, 1227, 1233, 1256, 1284, 1372, 1373, 1374, 1414.

suggestion is certainly possible. We know for sure of at least one case of this.[80] Yet we have plenty of literary evidence of Jerusalem residents from the Diaspora. Ananel the priest came from Babylonia (*Ant.* 15.22, 34, 39-51), and Boethus the priest came from Alexandria (*Ant.* 15.319-22; 17.78, 339; 18.3; 19.297f.). The New Testament refers to other Jerusalem residents that came from the Diaspora: Simon of Cyrene (Mk. 15:21), Barnabas of Cyprus (Acts 4:36), Nicolas a proselyte from Antioch (Acts 6:5). One ossuary inscription seems to state clearly that a family has immigrated to Jerusalem: 'The bones of those who immigrated...the house of Izates' (in Greek).[81]

There were also proselytes in Jerusalem, former non-Jews who had grown up in Greek culture. One of the Seven in Acts was Nicolas the proselyte from Antioch (Acts 6:5). The ossuaries tell of others: 'Judas, son of Laganio, the proselyte' (in Greek).[82] In addition, the royal family of Adiabene, which had converted to Judaism, had palaces and tombs in Jerusalem. Queen Helena, her son Menobazus, and Grapte, another relative, had residences (*BJ* 4.567; 5.55, 119, 252f.; 6.355; *Ant.* 20.17-37, 75-80). These palaces were located in the lower city not far from the Siloam pool. B. Mazar believes that a large building excavated on the southeast edge of the Ophel was one of these palaces. He suggests that this area was the popular place of residence for the highly-placed Jewish proselytes from abroad.[83]

Therefore, we conclude that a considerable number of Diaspora Jews had immigrated to Jerusalem by the 1st century AD. As Hengel maintains, we have to assume an independent, Jewish-hellenistic culture in Jerusalem. Jerusalem was the 'most important centre of the Greek language in Jewish Palestine...'.[84]

---

[78]See N. Avigad, 'A Depository of Inscribed Ossuaries in the Kidron Valley', *IEJ* 12 (1962) 112; J.N. Sevenster, *Do You Know Greek?* (Leiden: Brill, 1968) 147; M. Hengel, *Between Jesus and Paul*, tr. J. Bowden (ET; London: SCM Press, 1983) 17.

[79]P. Thomsen, 'Die lateinischen und griechischen Inschriften der Stadt Jerusalem', *ZDPV* 44 (1921) 116. See Sevenster's discussion, *Do You Know Greek?*, 146f.

[80]See the Abba inscription in which the deceased boasts of bringing back the bones of Mattathiah to be buried in Jerusalem. Yet Abba also illustrates the other position. He was born in Jerusalem, had gone into exile in Babylonia, and had returned. See J. Naveh, 'A New Tomb Inscription from Giv'at Hamivtar', in Yadin (ed.), *Jerusalem Revealed*, 73.

[81]Frey, *CIJ* II, no. 1230.

[82]Frey, *CIJ* II, no. 1385. But see also no. 1386: 'Maria the fervent proselyte' (in Hebrew).

[83]B. Mazar, 'Herodian Jerusalem in the Light of Excavations South and South-West of the Temple Mount', *IEJ* 28 (1978) 230-337; *idem*, *The Mountain of the Lord*, 213; and M. Ben-Dov, *In the Shadow of the Temple*, 155.

In addition to the residents of Jerusalem that spoke Greek, there were thousands from the Diaspora that came to the feasts. Estimates vary as to the number of pilgrims that came to Passover and the other feasts. J. Jeremias concluded that 125,000 pilgrims arrived on average at Passover. E.P. Sanders arrived at the figure of 300,000 to 500,000. Of these tens of thousands were from the Diaspora and the rest from Palestine.[85] If we assume that 30,000 of the pilgrims were from the Greek-speaking Diaspora, then we have at various times of the year an even larger number of Greek-speaking Jews in Jerusalem.

These pilgrims had to stay somewhere, and it appears that they stayed in community centres built especially for them. Archaeologists have discovered several buildings south of the Temple mount with a large number of rooms, ritual baths and many cisterns.[86] There was also an inscription found that indicated that one Paris, a Jew from Rhodes, had donated a pavement in the vicinity evidently for a community centre for pilgrims.[87]

The most significant inscription, the Theodotus Greek inscription, was found in the City of David. Theodotus, the ruler of the synagogue, donated a building for studying Torah and included guest rooms to house pilgrims and ritual baths to prepare them to enter the Temple.[88] Thus pilgrims were housed in the synagogue. This Theodotus, since he calls himself in the inscription the 'son of Vettenus' (a Roman name), is believed by many to be a freedman. He would have been freed and granted citizenship by the help of someone from the Roman *gens Vettena*. Thus there is speculation that this synagogue is the 'synagogue of the freedmen' alluded to in Acts 6:9.[89]

Acts 6:9 may be referring to no less than five synagogues: one for the freedmen, one for the people from Cyrenaica, one for Alexandrians, one for those from Cilicia and one for those from Asia. The synagogue of the Alexandrians is referred to in the rabbinic sources (*t.*

---

[84]Hengel, *The Hellenization of Judaea*, 9, 11.

[85]See Jeremias, *Jerusalem*, 83; Sanders, *Judaism*, 127f.

[86]Mazar, 'Herodian Jerusalem', 236; Ben-Dov, *In the Shadow of the Temple*, 153f.

[87]B. Isaac, 'A Donation for Herod's Temple in Jerusalem', *IEJ* 33 (1983) 86-92; and Ben-Dov, *In the Shadow of the Temple*, 155.

[88]The text is in Frey, *CIJ* II, no. 1404; and A. Deissmann, *Light from the Ancient East*, tr. L.R.M. Strachan (ET; Grand Rapids: Baker, 1965) 439-40. A text and translation are also found in Hengel, *Between Jesus and Paul*, 17, 148. See also Hengel, *Hellenization*, 13.

[89]See Hengel, *Between Jesus and Paul*, 18. But contrast Deissmann, *Light*, 441. Compare the Goliath family in Jericho. One of them was a freedman who returned to Palestine after many years. See R. Hachlili, 'The Goliath Family', 33.

Meg. 3.6; *y. Meg.* 3.73) and possibly a synagogue for people from Tarsus is named (*b. Meg.* 26a).[90] The Talmudic assertion that there were 390 synagogues in Jerusalem (*b. Ketub.* 105a) may be an exaggeration, but certainly one should assume that a great many of them existed before the war. A substantial percentage of these synagogues must have been for Greek-speaking Jews (*cf.* Acts 24:12).[91]

Thus the Lower City, especially the City of David and the Ophel, was the locus for Greek-speaking Jews. The noble proselytes had palaces there; evidence of hospices for pilgrims from the Diaspora was found there in two inscriptions; one of these hospices was connected to a synagogue for Greek-speaking Jews; archaeologists have uncovered what could be guest rooms.

IV. Cultural Diversity in the Jerusalem Church

The Jerusalem church was distinguished by its two groups: the Hebrews and the hellenists (Acts 6:1). The traditional view since John Chrysostom was that these groups were differentiated by language. The former group spoke a semitic language and the latter group spoke Greek (*Homilies* 11, 14, 21). Various other views have been advanced, mainly that the hellenists were Gentile Christians,[92] that the hellenists were related to the Qumran Essenes,[93] that the Hebrews were Essenes,[94] and other suggestions.[95]

---

[90]See Strack and Billerbeck, *Kommentar*, II, 663 and Jeremias, *Jerusalem*, 5, 66. H. Conzelmann, *Acts of the Apostles*, tr. J. Lumberg, A.T. Kraabel and D.H. Juel (ET; Philadelphia: Fortress, 1987) 47 maintains that there is only one synagogue in mind in Acts 6:9 as did F.F. Bruce, *Commentary on the Book of Acts*, 133. On the other hand, I.H. Marshall, *The Acts of the Apostles* (Grand Rapids: Eerdmans, 1980) 129, and E. Haenchen, *Acts*, 271, maintain that there are two synagogues in view.

[91]*Cf. y. Meg.* 3.1 which gives 480 synagogues for Jerusalem. H. Shanks, *Judaism in Stone* (Jerusalem: Steimatzky, 1979) 20, is not so sure the Talmudic numbers are exaggerations. The example of Rome may be useful. At least eleven different synagogue communities can be identified, according to Hengel. The members of each were distinguished by nationality, profession and the like (*Between Jesus and Paul*, 14f.). See also G. Lüdemann, *Early Christianity According to the Traditions in Acts*, 83.

[92]See H.J. Cadbury, 'The Hellenists', in F.J. Foakes Jackson and K. Lake, *The Beginnings of Christianity* (Grand Rapids: Baker, 1979) V, 59-74.

[93]Cullmann, 'The Significance of Qumran', in Stendahl (ed.), *The Scrolls and the New Testament*, 29: 'I do not assert that these Hellenists were former Essenes (which is not impossible) but that they came from a kind of Judaism close to this group'. See Haenchen, *Acts*, 260f. and M. Black, *The Scrolls and Christian Origins* (Chico, CA: Scholars Press, 1961) 76f., for a rebuttal of Cullmann.

Yet since C.F.D. Moule's important article,[96] a consensus has been building in favour of the traditional view of Chrysostom. This view has been strongly supported by Hengel, C.C. Hill and others.[97] Moule concluded that the hellenists were 'Jews who spoke *only* Greek' and the Hebrews were those 'who, while able to speak Greek, knew a Semitic language also'.[98] As Hill remarks, the second part of this conclusion may be suspect—it is doubtful that most 'Hebrews' could speak Greek, although surely some could—but Moule's language-based distinction between the two groups is surely correct.[99] Thus the Jerusalem church had two factions separated by language and culture.

The Hebrews were of Palestinian origin. Some of them had possibly been pilgrims for the feast of Pentecost and had remained after conversion, but we should expect that most of them were inhabitants of Jerusalem.

Likewise the hellenists could have been in part pilgrims from the Diaspora. The simplest explanation, however, is that most of them came from the ranks of the Greek-speaking Jews of Jerusalem who lived and worshipped in the Lower City, especially in the City of David. This location contrasts with the traditional sites of the Upper Room, both of which are in the Upper City.

Thus we should see at least three locations for the activity of the Jerusalem church: the Upper Room in the Upper City, the hellenistic synagogues in the Lower City, and of course the Temple. The evidence indicates that sociologically and culturally the church was quite diverse.

The Jerusalem church, almost from the very beginning if not actually from Pentecost on, was culturally pluralistic. One cannot

---

[94]Black, *The Scrolls and Christian Origins*, 77.

[95]Hengel lists twelve views (*Between Jesus and Paul*, 4-6). See also the bibliography given in F.F. Bruce, *New Testament History* (New York: Doubleday, 1969) 219 n. 1.

[96]Moule, 'Once More, Who Were the Hellenists?', *ExpTim* 70 (1958-59) 100-102.

[97]Hengel, *Between Jesus and Paul*, 8-11, and C.C. Hill, *Hellenists and Hebrews* (Minneapolis: Fortress, 1992) 22-24. In addition see J. Fitzmyer, *A Wandering Aramean*, 123; H. Conzelmann, *Acts*, 45; H. Lietzmann, *A History of the Early Church*, tr. B.L. Woolf (ET: Cleveland/New York: World Publishing, 1961) 70; A.F. Loisy, *The Birth of the Christian Religion*, tr. L.P. Jacks (ET; New Hyde Park, NY: University Books, 1962) 113; E. Larsen, 'Die Hellenisten und die Urgemeinde', *NTS* 33 (1987) 205-25; G. Schneider, *Die Apostelgeschichte*, 406; R. Pesch, *Die Apostelgeschichte* (Zurich: Benziger, 1986) 227; F.F. Bruce, *Acts*, 128; I.H. Marshall, *Acts*, 125f.; E. Haenchen, *Acts*, 260.

[98]Moule, 'Once More, Who Were the Hellenists?', 100.

[99]Hill, *Hebrews and Hellenists*, 23.

speak of an Aramaic stage followed by a hellenistic Jewish stage.[100] These 'stages' were always contemporaneous. The two subcultures within the early church—the Aramaic and the Greek—were two springs flowing from the same source and in turn nourishing together the subsequent Gentile Christianity.

Likewise one cannot determine that a portion of the New Testament (*e.g.* a pericope of the Gospels) originated outside Palestine because of 'hellenistic' influences.[101] To consider Palestine and earliest Christianity only in terms of the Aramaic culture is now quite impossible.

---

[100]See *e.g.* S. Schultz, *Q Die Spruchquelle der Evangelisten* (Zurich: Theologischer Verlag, 1992) 57-184, who posits these stages for the hypothetical source Q.

[101]See *e.g.* R. Bultmann, *History of the Synoptic Tradition*, tr. J. Marsh (ET; Oxford: Basil Blackwell, 1963) 48, 299, who made decisions of provenance based on such considerations.

CHAPTER 8

THE POPULATION SIZE OF JERUSALEM AND THE NUMERICAL GROWTH OF THE JERUSALEM CHURCH

Wolfgang Reinhardt

Summary

The main argument against the historical credibility of Luke's figures for the size of the first Jerusalem church, according to most major commentaries on Acts, has been their alleged incompatibility with the (assumed) size of the population of Jerusalem at the time of Jesus (no more than 25-30,000 according to the now old works of Jeremias, which most contemporary authors still rely on). Several more recent investigations show far higher figures. On testing the criteria used in these studies, the question of density of population turns out to be decisive. Referring to demographic studies on ancient cities and considering many factors affecting the density of population in Jerusalem at a time of great prosperity, most arguments lead to the conclusion that 1st-century Jerusalem must have had many more inhabitants than is usually assumed. A figure of 60,000 to 120,000 seems realistic, and even the higher end of this scale not impossible for the 30s of the 1st century. In the wider context of the subject of the numbers given by Luke in Acts 2:41; 4:4, the question is discussed whether pilgrims to the feast of Pentecost might be included and what is known about the numbers of pilgrims. Other factors in the remarkable growth of the Jerusalem church are only mentioned. But the dominant argument against the historical plausibility of Luke's figures—the alleged small population of Jerusalem at the time—can no longer be considered valid.

I. Questioning the Figures' Reliability

In the recent commentaries and monographs in German, one encounters an almost unanimous consensus on the figures given in Acts for the Jerusalem church (Acts 2:41; 4:4; *cf.* 21:20). The 3,000 (Acts 2:41) are dismissed in offhand notes with, 'Of course the number cannot be historically verified,'[1] 'of course an unreal figure, which can in no way be brought into accordance with the actual situation,'[2] a 'greatly exaggerated figure,'[3] and that the figures cited 'served only to illustrate the miraculous working of the Holy Spirit in the early church.'[4] 'If the Pentecost sermon was written by Luke himself, then this also answers the question as to the historical aspect of this sermon's enormous success.'[5] 'The exaggerations in ancient calculation are well known'.[6] The mass conversion itself is an 'improbable fiction.'[7] 'In the quiet life of the primitive community there were no mass assemblies such as Luke places at the outset of the Christian mission, therefore no conflicts with the Sadducees arising from them.'[8]

When reasons are given, they are the following:

---

[1]H. Conzelmann, *Acts of the Apostles*, tr. J. Limburg, A.T. Kraabel and D.H. Juel (Philadelphia, 1987) 22 on 2:41.

[2]J. Roloff, *Die Apostelgeschichte* (NTD 5; Göttingen, 1985) 63.

[3]W. Schmithals, *Die Apostelgeschichte des Lukas* (ZBK NT 3,2; Zürich, 1982) 38, also on 4:4: 'exaggeratedly high'.

[4]Similarly in many of the most recent works, *e.g.* T. Söding, 'Widerspruch und Leidensnachfolge. Neutestamentliche Gemeinden im Konflikt mit der paganen Gesellschaft', *MThZ* 41 (1990) 140 n. 14: the figures are 'known to be statistically useless; they would be much too high; at this time, Jerusalem had around 20,000 inhabitants.'

[5]A. Weiser, *Die Apostelgeschi*chte (ÖTK 5/1 and 2; Gütersloh and Würzburg, 1981/85) 96.

[6]Haenchen, *The Acts of the Apostles*, tr. B. Noble and G. Shinn (Oxford, 1971) 608-9 on Acts 21:20.

[7]A. Loisy, *Les Actes des Apôtres* (Frankfurt am Main, 1973) 213; similarly and completely without argument, L. Brun, 'Etwa 3000 Seelen Act 2,41', *ZNW* 14 (1913) 95.

[8]Haenchen, *Acts*, 258.

(1) Most frequent is reference to these figures' incompatibility with the size of the Jerusalem population in the time of Jesus. It is striking in this connection that the critics only adduce the population count given by J. Jeremias, who arrived at 25-30,000 inhabitants in an essay in 1943, later in his book, *Jerusalem in the Time of Jesus*[9], taking first a figure of 55,000, which, however, in a note in the second edition of 1958, he reduced again to 25-30,000.[10] This extremely low estimate is now still used as a basis by many commentators, decades later, to draw the conclusion: 'accordingly after Peter's second sermon one-fifth or one-sixth of them would have become Christians. This shows that the figure of five thousand possesses not statistical but symbolic value.'[11] Even in the relatively recent article on Jerusalem in the *TRE*, these old figures still continue to exercise an influence, the writer arriving at 20,000 (!) within the town walls and 5-10,000 inhabitants outside.[12]
(2) Together with this predominant argument, other reasons occur only very rarely (almost exclusively in Haenchen): the difficulty of addressing 3,000 people in the open air without a microphone,[13] the question whether a mass baptism was possible in Jerusalem at that time,[14] and the problem that such a mass movement would have resulted in official intervention.[15]
(3) The fact that the large figures would have coincided with Luke's fundamental theological intent to demonstrate the divine blessing on the church[16] is no argument against historical reliability, since an

[9]J. Jeremias, *Jerusalem in the Time of Jesus*, tr. F.H. and C.H. Cave (London, 1969) from the German *Jerusalem zur Zeit Jesu* (3rd edn.; Göttingen, 1962).
[10]*Jerusalem*, in the 'Additional Note', p. 84.
[11]Haenchen, *Acts*, 215 n. 2; similarly referring to Jeremias: E. Lohse, 'Σιών, B and C', *ThWNT* VII, 322; G. Lohfink, *Die Sammlung Israels. Eine Untersuchung zur lukanischen Ekklesiologie*, StANT 39 (Munich, 1975) 52; E. Otto, *Jerusalem—die Geschichte der Heiligen Stadt. Von den Anfängen bis zur Kreuzfahrerzeit*, UB 310 (Stuttgart *etc.*, 1980) 148 n. 146.
[12]J.K. Elliott, 'Jerusalem II. Neues Testament', *TRE* 16 (1987) 609; similarly Söding (see n. 4 above).
[13]Haenchen, *Acts*, 188.
[14]*Ibid.*, 184-185: this question, he notes, misses the point; also G. Schneider, *Die Apostelgeschichte*, HThK V/1-2 (Freiburg *etc.*, 1980/82) 279, considers it 'futile to speculate whether a mass baptism, such as the narrator reports it, was technically possible.'
[15]Haenchen, *Acts*, 184-185; G. Schille, *Die Apostelgeschichte des Lukas*, ThHK V (Berlin, 1983) 132, believes that the whole Temple guard would have been powerless against the at least one thousand newcomers, in contrast to which the apostles were dismissed for fear of the people.
[16]Haenchen, *Acts*, 189; P. Zingg, *Das Wachsen der Kirche. Beiträge zur Frage der lukanischen Redaktion und Theologie*, OBO 3 (Freiburg and Göttingen, 1974) 176.

historically correct figure can also be easily fitted into the wider theological context. The strictly historical question must therefore be asked, whether the counter-arguments adduced are valid. Since these arguments refer almost exclusively to the size of the population of Jerusalem, this question will be given particular consideration.

II. The Size of the Population of Jerusalem in the Time of the Earliest Church

1. The basis for Jeremias' calculations

Since Jeremias' figures still exercise a very great influence today, they will be examined first. In his book, *Jerusalem in the Time of Jesus*, he arrived at the figure of 55,000 inhabitants. In doing this, he began with two different figures for the area inside the west, south and east sides of the pre-Agrippan walls (= 2,575 m) and the third wall (which Agrippa I had begun to build): if it were the same as the present northern wall, one would arrive at an additional 2,025 m; if Josephus' figure is to be believed, 3,530 m.[17] This adds up to the town being either 4,600 m or 6,105 m across and having an area of 1,322,000 m^2 or 2,329,000 m^2. On the basis of the population density of contemporary (20th century) Palestine, of one person to *c.* 30 m^2, Jeremias assumes a slightly denser population for the first century of one person to 25 m^2. Thus he arrives at a figure for the population of ancient Jerusalem of 'about 55,000 to 95,000' (p. 83 n. 24). In later editions, in an 'Additional Note', he expresses the reservation that the figures he had given are too high: 'Jerusalem in the time of Jesus will have had around 25-30,000 inhabitants'.

He gives the argument for this in his later essay, 'Die Einwohnerzahl Jerusalems zur Zeit Jesu' (1943). He first describes the figures in Josephus and the Talmud on the size of Jerusalem as 'extreme exaggeration' (p. 25). The 120,000 of Hecateus of Abdera as well as the 70,000 in Rev. 11:13 (10 x 7,000), which might refer to Jerusalem, stand, he says, under the suspicion that popular round figures (7 and 12) were used to express completeness (pp. 26-27). The only way to check would be by knowing the town area. The town wall had in the time of Jesus a length of 3,600 m and enclosed an area of 830,000 m^2. After

[17]In the later essay, he identifies the 'third wall' with that which lies far in the north and has been uncovered particularly by Sukenik and Mayer (p. 29, *cf.* n.1).

subtracting the uninhabited public areas, there remained within the town walls only around 660,000 m^2 of living space. A further condition is the assumption that the population density in the time of Jesus corresponded to the density of settlement 60 years before Jeremias' work, that is, one person to 35 m^2. This would give him a figure of 20,000 inhabitants. Finally, he assumes for the area outside of both town walls (particularly north of the Temple) a settlement of more than 5,000, but maximum 10,000 people. Thus he comes to the (very tentative) result: 'the population of Jerusalem in the time of Jesus consisted of around 25,000-30,000 inhabitants' (p. 31).

However, since Jeremias' time many more recent calculations have been made.

2. *More recent calculations of the population figure*

These have appeared especially on the basis of new archaeological discoveries, as have some special investigations which seem, however, to have gone completely unnoticed by most Acts commentators. The following overview (Table 1), which also lists some older works, gives an impression of the various estimates, which are almost all higher—and some significantly so—than that of Jeremias.

It is, of course, not enough just to register the different figures and draw the conclusion that the size of the Jerusalem population was therefore probably significantly higher. The criteria and methods of the investigations must also be compared and evaluated.

The most common method is calculation by means of the product of area and density.

Table 1: Figures for the Jerusalem Population

Author	*Population and period*	*Method*
Avi-Yonah[18]	120,000 pre-AD 70	Number of graves, 100 BC-AD 135
Avi-Yonah[19]	90-100,000	
Avi-Yonah[20]	120,000	
Beloch[21]	*c.* 100,000	Ancient sources, pop. density x area

[18]M. Avi-Yonah, Critical review of P.B. Bagatti and J.T. Milik, *Gli scavi del 'Dominus flevit.' Parte I: La necropoli del periodo romano*, PSBF 13 (Jerusalem, 1958), in *IEJ* 11 (1961) 91-94 (93).

[19]M. Avi-Yonah, *Jerusalem through the Ages* (1963).

[20]M. Avi-Yonah, 'Jerusalem', in *EJ*, 1397.

Ben-David[22]	80-110,000 (126,000) under Herod	1) residential units x persons, 2) area x density
Ben-Dov[23]	150-200,000 under 2nd Temple	Construction method, prosperity
Broshi[24]	82,500 in AD 66 38,500 in 4 BC	Density x area
Broshi[25]	80,000 just pre-AD 66 40,000 in 4 BC	Density x area
Cornfeld[26]	80-200,000	
Daniel-Rops[27]	≤150,000 (50-150,000)	Area incr.; projection to time of Jesus
Elliott[28]	25-30,000	Obviously based on Jeremias
Har-El[29]	200,000 end 2nd Temple	Area
Jeremias[30]	55,000: 'too high', instead 25-30,000	Area x density
Jeremias[31]	20,000 (within walls) –30,000 (also outside)	Area x density
Maier[32]	50,000 (x 3 at festivals)	
Mazar[33]	120,000 max., ≤100,000?	Area (tentatively), water supply *etc.*
McCown[34]	100,000	Projection back from mod. demographic investigations
Michel /Bauernfeind[35]	70-80,000	Area x density

[21]J. Beloch, *Die Bevölkerung der griechisch-römischen Welt (Historische Beiträge zur Bevölkerungslehre. Erster Teil)* (Leipzig, 1886) 248.

[22]A. Ben-David, *Talmudische Ökonomie, Die Wirtschaft des jüdischen Palästina zur Zeit der Mischna und des Talmud*, I (Hildesheim/New York, 1974) 57.

[23]M. Ben-Dov, *In the Shadow of the Temple. The Discovery of Ancient Jerusalem* (Jerusalem, 1985) 75.

[24]M. Broshi, 'La population de L'ancienne Jérusalem', *RB* 82 (1975) 5-14 (13).

[25]M. Broshi, 'Estimating the Population of Ancient Jerusalem', *BARev* IV,2 (1978) 10-15.

[26]G. Cornfeld, *Josephus, The Jewish War* (Grand Rapids, 1982) 170.

[27]H. Daniel-Rops, *La Vie Quotidienne en Palestine au Temps de Jésus* (Paris, 1961).

[28]Elliott, 'Jerusalem', 609.

[29]M. Har-El, *This is Jerusalem* (Jerusalem, 1977) 68.

[30]Jeremias, *Jerusalem*, 84.

[31]J. Jeremias, 'Die Einwohnerzahl Jerusalems zur Zeit Jesu', *ZDPV* 66 (1943) 24-31 (31).

[32]P.L. Maier, *First Christians: Pentecost and the Spread of Christianity* (New York, *etc.*, 1976) 22.

[33]B. Mazar, *Der Berg des Herrn. Neue Ausgrabungen in Jerusalem* (Tel Aviv, 1975; Bergisch Gladbach, 1979), 190 (= *The Mountain of the Lord—Excavating in Jerusalem* [ET; New York, 1975]).

[34]C.C. McCown, 'The Density of Population in Ancient Palestine', *JBL* 66 (1947) 425-36 (436).

[35]O. Michel and O. Bauernfeind, *De bello Judaico. Der jüdische Krieg. Zweisprachige Ausgabe der sieben Bücher* Vols. 1-3 (Darmstadt, 1959-69, ^{3}1982) II.2.208, exc. XVII.

Neumann[36]	1-2 million in 'heyday'	Josephus (incl. those under siege)
Otto[37]	*c.* 50,000? *c.* 40,000 under Herod *c.* 60,000 pre-AD 70	Dependent on Jeremias.
Riesner[38]	*c.* 50,000 (or more)	
Scheckenhofer[39]	*c.* 120,000 (150,000 around AD 66)	Synagogue figure, area x density, proj. back by growth quota, water supply
Schick[40]	200-250,000	Area x density, corrected figures from Josephus
Wilkinson[41]	>70,000 70,398 under Herod the Great	Water supply: daily usage

3. *Area*

The area within the first two walls can be calculated relatively reliably. Even figures for the Temple area and other uninhabited areas show a relatively high level of agreement. It is, however, more difficult to ascertain how many inhabitants lived outside the two walls and in the suburbs. It now seems certain that Jerusalem had expanded far beyond the walls in the time of the first church.[42]

---

[36]B. Neumann, *Die Heilige Stadt und deren Bewohner in ihren naturhistorischen, culturgeschichtlichen, socialen und medizinischen Verhältnissen* (Hamburg, 1877) 213.
[37]Otto, *Jerusalem*, 148.
[38]R. Riesner, 'Jerusalem', in H. Burckhardt, *etc.* (ed.), *Das grosse Bibellexikon* II, 661-77 (671).
[39]J. Scheckenhofer, *Die Bevölkerung Palästinas um die Wende der Zeiten. Versuch einer Statistik* (Munich, 1978) 26-31.
[40]C. Schick, 'Studien über die Einwohnerzahl des alten Jerusalem', *ZDPV* 4 (1881) 211-21.
[41]J. Wilkinson, 'Ancient Jerusalem, Its Water Supply and Population', *PEFQS* 106 (1974) 33-51 (49).
[42]*Cf.* Josephus, *BJ* 5.148f.: 'The population, uniting to the hill the district north of the Temple, had encroached so far that even a fourth hill was surrounded with houses. This hill, which is called Bezetha....' See as early as Jeremias, 'Einwohnerzahl', 28; in more detail, E. Vogt, 'Das Wachstum des alten Stadtgebietes von Jerusalem', *Bib* 48 (1967) 350: Expansion 'both towards the south and towards the north. Particularly on the hill Bezatha north of the Temple, there developed a new quarter, whilst the area north of the suburb and the upper town was only 'sparsely' populated (*BJ* 5.260) and probably mostly planted with gardens. The entire northern extension was called "Newtown" and Bezatha was one—albeit the most important—part of it.'

Table 2: Calculations of the inhabited area

Beloch[43]	112 hectares (=1,120,000 m^2)
Ben-David[44]	Herodian: 1.02 km^2 minus 0.136 = 0.88 km^2 Under both Agrippas: 1.8 km^2 (with Hecker and Avi-Yonah)
Broshi[45]	Until 4 BC: 915 minus 144 dunam for the Temple mount: 770,000 m^2 (shortly before AD 66: 1750 minus 145 dunam = 1.56 km^2) *(corresponds to the figures in the later essay:* 'Herod the Great [*c.* 4 BC] 230' acres, minus 36 acres for the Temple area. 'Before the destruction of the Second Temple' [*c.* AD 66] 450 acres)
Chaplin[46]	*c.* 720 acres (for AD 70) minus half for public buildings: 360 acres = 1.457 km^2
Har-El[47]	2 km^2 minus 144 dunam Temple area = 1,800 dunam = 1.8 km^2
Jeremias[48]	830,000 m^2 minus uninhabited areas = 660,000 m^2 plus the settlement outside with *c.* 5-10,000 inhabitants
Kenyon[49]	(under Herod: 140 acres = *c.* 57 hectares) (under Agrippa I: 310 acres = *c.* 1.25 km^2)
Mazar[50]	1.25 km^2 (or a little more, shortly before Agrippa I)
Scheckenhofer[51]	82 hectares minus 27 hectares uninhabited area = 550,000 m^2 (towards the end of the Herodian period)
Schick[52]	60 square stadia = 1.94 km^2
Wilkinson[53]	(until the death of Herod: 615,000 m^2), Agrippa: 0.895 km^2

Commentary on Table 2

For the town area in the time of the earliest Christian church, one must include not only the area within the first two walls but also a consider-

[43]Beloch, *Bevölkerung*, 248.
[44]Ben-David, *Ökonomie*, 52 and 55.
[45]Broshi, 'La Population', 13; 'Estimating', 13f.
[46]'Note on the Population of Jerusalem during the Siege of Titus', *Athenaeum* 23/2 (1878) 255-6.
[47]Har-El, *Jerusalem*, 46, 68.
[48]Jeremias, 'Einwohnerzahl', 27-31.
[49]Kenyon, *Jerusalem*, 193f.
[50]Mazar, *Berg*, 189.
[51]Scheckenhofer, *Bevölkerung*, 26f.
[52]Schick, 'Studien', 215f.
[53]Wilkinson, 'Jerusalem', 50.

able settlement beyond the western and northern sections of the second wall:[54] 'The population of Jerusalem increased so much in the first century AD that "the town, overflowing with inhabitants, had gradually crept beyond the ramparts,"[55] both towards the south and towards the north.'[56] The residential areas north of the Temple in the so-called 'Newtown' (Beth-Zeta = Bezetha) were unprotected until the time of Agrippa I, when a further wall (the 'third wall')[57] was built around it.

It must also be borne in mind that, at the times of the great pilgrimage feasts, when the number of people could be tripled or quadrupled by the pilgrims, religious law allowed for the town area to be officially extended.[58] Thus Bethphage, for example, from where Jesus had the donkey brought for his entry into Jerusalem, was considered by the Rabbis as the farthest district of Jerusalem.[59]

4. *The population density of Jerusalem in the time of Jesus*

a) Arguments against the density factor assumed by Jeremias

The main error in Jeremias' calculation is probably the low estimate of the town's population density (1:35, *i.e.* one person to 35m^2; in the essay). Michel/Bauernfeind in an excursus on the 'population of Jerusalem excluding pilgrims and aliens' consider his estimate too low and propose 'a ratio of at least 1:25.'[60] They base it on the small size of

---

[54]Mazar, *Berg*, 189; Jeremias, 'Einwohnerzahl', 28: 'that the settlement area of the town had already in Jesus' day extended far beyond the second north wall'; Broshi, 'Estimating', 10: 'Jerusalem developed considerably towards the north and the north-west…'.

[55]Josephus, *BJ* 5.148.

[56]Vogt, 'Wachstum', 350.

[57]The most recent archaeological results speak for identifiying the third wall with the most northern wall already discovered by Sukenik and Mayer; *cf.* G. Schmitt, 'Die dritte Mauer Jerusalems', *ZDPV* 97 (1981) 153-70; S. Ben-Arieh and E. Netzer, 'Excavations along the 'Third Wall' of Jerusalem', *IEJ* 24 (1974) 97-107; Riesner, 'Jerusalem', 670; now H.-P. Kuhnen, *Palästina in griechisch-römischer Zeit* (with contributions by Leo Mildenberg and Robert Wenning; Handbuch der Archäologie. Vorderasien II,2; Munich, 1990) 137: 'Against Hennessy and others, it must be remembered that a fortification from the time of Agrippa I under the Damascus gate had not yet been discovered.'

[58]Riesner, *Jerusalem*, 671.

[59]*idem*, 'Betfage', *GBL* I, 196.

[60]*Bell.* II,2, p. 208.

ancient houses (with reference to *Sifre Dt.* 229; *m. B. Bat.* 6:4; and G. Dalman[61]) and come to the conclusion that: 'Taking uninhabited (Temple area) and less densely settled areas (such as Bezetha) into consideration, one arrives at a population figure of 70-80,000.'[62] They also refer to figures by G.H. Schubert, *Reise in das Morgenland*, vol. 2 (1839) 555-56, and considerations by C. Schick.

b) Schick's argument

Schick's arguments deserve renewed consideration, since they are superior to some more recent rash calculations. In his *Studien über die Einwohnerzahl des alten Jerusalem* (1881), he explains why Jerusalem combines relatively restricted living space with a high population density: 'The special advantage of a mountain town is that it has more contact with the air and the light....thus there is no disadvantage in a mountain town being rather more densely populated than one situated in the plain' (p. 212). Against Ferguson's older estimate of just 25,000 inhabitants,[63] he cites the following reasons for the high population densities in antiquity: (1) The defence line was to be kept as short as possible by means of as small as possible an extent of the walls. (2) As much as possible of the inner space was to be used for habitations. (3) 'The streets were simply alleys, not only narrow, but often also built over and therefore often dark passageways.' (4) 'The oriental needs little room in any case, since he possesses so few household items; one room is adequate for a whole family. In short, everything was so arranged that the town, even with relatively restricted spatial extension, could contain a far greater number of people than might seem possible using conventional standards' (p. 221). These views should also be considered as we look at a more recent influential basis for calculation.

c) The density factor according to Broshi

In his earlier essay of 1975, 'La Population de L'ancienne Jérusalem', M. Broshi first rightly establishes that most work on ancient Jerusalem brushes over this question (p. 5). He then advances two main sources for the answer to the question. The first is the ancient literature, the

[61]G. Dalman, *Arbeit und Sitte in Palästina*, vols. I-VII (Gütersloh, 1928-42) VI, 66.
[62]Michel/Bauernfeind, *ibid.*, 208.
[63]J. Ferguson, *The Ancient Topography of Jerusalem* (London, 1847) 50ff.

figures in which are however mostly unreliable—Josephus, for example, whose figures are usually accurate, is, Broshi claims, nevertheless not very realistic in the population figures. The more reliable method is archaeology. Broshi considers attempts to specify the population of Jerusalem on the basis of the water supply (*e.g.* with Wilkinson, *cf.* below) senseless, since one cannot specify the average water consumption in a particular region in antiquity. The only reliable method, according to Broshi, is calculating the population from the product of a city's area and population density.

In estimating the area, he follows Avi-Yonah's reconstruction for Jerusalem under Herod the Great and arrives at 915 dunam (1 dunam = 1,000 m^2) minus 145 dunam for the areas of public use, *i.e.* 770 dunam. For the subsequent period, he considers the great expansion of the city to the north and northwest and arrives at a built-up area of 1560 dunam (1,705 minus 145) shortly before the destruction of Jerusalem (pp. 10-11, 13). He puts the second factor, the population density, at 40-50 persons per dunam. For this, he cites comparable estimates of ancient cities, *e.g.* that an average of 5 houses per dunam was assumed for some Mesopotamian cities (p. 6). If a house accommodated 6-10 persons, then one would arrive at an average of 40 persons per dunam (p. 6). He adds that the old parts of modern oriental cities also have a population density of 40-50 persons per dunam. Broshi thus assumes an identical population density for the ancient cities and the modern old-towns in the orient.[64] Hence he arrives at a population size of 38,500 at the end of the Herodian period and 82,500 shortly before the destruction of the Temple. For the time of Jesus and the earliest church, an average should then be put at around 60,000 inhabitants. His later essay, 'Estimating the Population of Ancient Jerusalem' (1975) presents no new results, only rounded figures: 40,000 at the end of the Herodian period, 80,000 before the destruction of the second Temple. This also gives a figure of around 60,000 at the time of the first Christians.

Even if Broshi's calculation (like those of Byatt, McCown and Wilkinson) offers new perspectives as against Jeremias, reservations must still be held about his estimation of the population density of Jerusalem.

---

[64]'The similarity in density between ancient cities and modern old-towns is not surprising, since construction methods have changed little in the course of the ages and the ancient cities, just as modern old-towns, tend towards maximum density' (p. 7).

d) Variation in population density with time and in various places

Particularly Broshi's assumption that the population density of modern old-towns has not changed significantly from ancient cities has suffered criticism. In his literature review on the population of Palestine and Jerusalem in connection with Josephus, Feldman opposes Broshi's criticism of the high population figures in Josephus and modern researchers, with a demonstration that the population density has not been so constant as Broshi assumes. In connection with the discussion of McCown's essay on population density (*cf.* Table 1), he notes 'that not all of western Palestine had an equal density of population..., and that to assert that Palestine was then not more productive than it is today is to disregard the evidence of the Talmud, as it is to assume that the standard of living of people then was what it is today.'[65] This also addresses the factor of productivity, which must be reconsidered in connection with the question of the 'carrying capacity'.

Demography knows many variables which influence the reconstruction of demographic parameters from settlement data, and some demographers warn against levelling-out the density coefficients at different places,[66] refer to the normal fluctuations in ground-area size for identical family units,[67] and particularly to the high degree of flexibility that exists in human population density, such that different settlement types cannot be compared.[68] This is what Frankfort (whom Broshi most often cites) does, however, obviously corresponding to a tendency to generalise, which can also be observed at other points in his work and which then easily claims authoritative validity.[69] The *growth rates* of a civilisation also fluctuate greatly at various times; they can increase enormously during the rise of civilisations and in times of economic prosperity.[70]

With reference to Palestine, Shiloh asks, after first appearing to agree with Broshi's density coefficient of 40-50 persons as an upper limit, whether we can really rely on the assumption that there has been

---

[65]*Josephus*, 369.

[66]F.A. Hassan, 'Demographic Archaeology', in M.B. Schiffer (ed.), *Advances in Archaeological Method and Theory*, I (New York, 1978) 49-103 (59), referring to Cook and Heizer, who, he says, show that towns in California with areas as different as 370 and 9200 m^2 have the same average settlement of 30 persons.

[67]S. LeBlanc, 'An Addition to Naroll's Suggested Floor Area and Settlement Population Relationship', *American Antiquity* 36 (1971) 210-1.

[68]S.E. Casselberry, 'Further Refinement of Formulae for Determining Population from Floor Area', *World Archaeology* 6,1 (1974) 112-22 (117, 119).

no essential change in the circumstances of towns in the Near East from ancient times to the present day: 'can the same density coefficient be applied to a town such as Jerusalem over the whole span of its existence?'[71] This is exactly the question that is to be answered with Wilkinson in the negative: he assumes that the population density rose from 37 to 115 persons per dunam before the Jewish War, but then sank dramatically after AD 70.[72]

e) The varying population density in modern Jerusalem

Even if one considers present-day Jerusalem, significant variations in population density can be observed. The density varies greatly according to the respective type of settlement. Thus, for example, the population density in the Arab residential districts with their relatively rural lifestyle (except in the old city!) is much less than in the government-built houses in the Jewish quarter with a more western lifestyle.[73] On the other hand, in the old city, the Muslim quarter has the highest population density.[74] When considering the modern old city, it must be remembered that space for religious institutions (land and buildings of religious communities) occupies almost 50%.[75] Nevertheless, there are residential areas in the old city with a density over

---

[69]*Cf.* H. Frankfort, 'Town Planning in Ancient Mesopotamia', *Town Planning Review* 21 (1950) 98-115 (103f.); Broshi, *Estimating*, 10; *Population*, 6; in another context, P. Matthiae criticises Frankfort's tendency to unhistorical generalisation (after previously having praised him as one of the great personalities of Middle East research). He is responsible 'for an authoritative synthesis in which were taken up and codified some of the most antihistorical judgements on the artistic civilisation of Syria...', and 'he identified a succession of external influences as the very rhythm of Syria's history, instead of seeking to define the particularities of artistic style in each individual centre at a given period' (P. Matthiae, *Ebla: An Empire Rediscovered* [London, 1980] 6).

[70]*Cf.* Hassan, 'Demographic Archaeology', 69 with a view to the late period of Uruk up to the late dynastic period of Mesopotamia; C.T. Young Jr., 'Population Densities and Early Mesopotamian Urbanism', in Ucko *etc.* (eds.) *Man, Settlement and Urbanism. Proceedings of a Meeting of Research Seminar in Archaeology and Related Subjects held at the Institute of Archaeology, London University* (London, 1972) 827-842, shows the various interdependent factors in greater Mesopotamia of population growth, new water supply systems, colonisation, productivity, conflicts with other population groups and concentration in towns.

[71]*Population*, 26; in n. 6 with express reference to Broshi's calculation of the size of the Jerusalem population.

[72]*Jerusalem*, 50.

[73]M. Safdie, *The Harvard Jerusalem Studio. Urban Design for the Holy City* (Cambridge, Mass. and London, 1986) 58.

(sometimes significantly over) 50 persons per dunam (abbreviated to p/d in the following)[76] and in the centre of the Muslim quarter, 140 p/d.[77] This alone questions Broshi's claim that the population density at the time of the second Temple cannot have risen above 50 p/d and that the population density of Jerusalem in the time of Herod can under no circumstances have been double that in today's old city, *i.e.* according to Wilkinson's calculation 114 p/d, or 84 p/d in the time of Herod Agrippa.[78] (Thus one could assume around 100 p/d for the time of Jesus.) There are a number of additional factors to consider for Jerusalem at that time, which suggest a population density higher than the average for the modern old city.

f) The level of development of Jerusalem in its heyday

Jerusalem in the Augustan period cannot be compared with Palestinian settlements at the beginning of the nineteenth century. K. Kenyon notes that the first half of the first century was a period of great prosperity: 'The enormous amount of material shows how closely built-up the area was, and one can certainly deduce a prosperous and fully inhabited city.'[79]

The links between economic upturn, increasing floods of pilgrims to Jerusalem and a high population density in much of the city is also referred to by Ben-Dov, who had excavated remains of domestic dwellings on the slopes of the western hill and in the north of the city of David:

> Their buildings were constructed very close together, reminding us again that Jerusalem in the Second Temple period was both a heavily populated and highly prosperous city with an economy nourished by

[74]According to the *Statistical Yearbook* of Jerusalem for 1988, for subquarter 64 (Muslim quarter) it was 41.6 persons per dunam (including Temple area!), while it was only 17.0 persons per dunam in the spaciously built Jewish quarter; *cf.* also the density diagram in Safdie, *Harvard*, 105 and in A. Sharon (ed.), *Planning Jerusalem. The Old City and its Environs* (Jerusalem, 1983) 116.
[75]Sharon (ed.), *Planning Jerusalem*, 144 on 'Existing Land Use'.
[76]*Cf.* the more precise listing on the residential districts of the old-town in the *Statistical Yearbook*, p. 35f.: the density in the Muslim quarter varies from 48.4 p/d in the Eastern part to 70.7 p/d in the southern part (area and population count are given in each case in the quarters nos. 641 to 643).
[77]Sharon (ed.), *Planning Jerusalem*, 117.
[78]In Broshi, *Population*, 13 n. 28; the figure '86' is presumably a printing error, in Wilkinson, 50, it is 84 per 1,000 m^2 in the time of Agrippa.
[79]*Digging up Jerusalem* (London/Tonbridge, [2]1974) 237.

> a steady traffic of pilgrims and a burgeoning network of commercial ties. ...The lively trade in real estate for building purposes, particularly in the areas closest to the Temple Mount, made it necessary to exploit every patch of land to the utmost. ...shops were even built into the piers of Robinson's Arch and Wilson's Arch. The residential quarters that began near the commercial center adjoining the Temple Mount extended southward and westward, growing into densely built neighbourhoods. In essence the streets were no more than narrow alleys that threaded their way between the houses—when, indeed, these buildings did not actually touch up against each other or share common walls... .[80]

Mazar considers it very difficult to put precise figures on the population size, but believes that one must 'be amazed at the most unusual population density in a city of less than two square kilometres at the peak of its development, even if one also includes a number of suburban settlements outside the city walls.'[81]

The archaeological finds are supported by the testimony of Josephus, who often refers to the narrow alleys (οἱ στενωποί) between the houses in Jerusalem, which were then built very closely together (*BJ* 2.306, 329; 3.303; 5.331). And in the description of Jerusalem's topography, he refers to the houses as 'closely pressed-together' (ἐπάλληλοι...αἱ οἰκίαι: *BJ* 5.136). This is especially true of the lower town, the densely built-up slopes of the upper town and the market quarter.[82] One element is the multi-storey construction of houses.

g) The multi-storey form of construction in Jerusalem as in other cities of the Roman Empire

De Geus has shown in his investigations[83] that in the archaeological reconstruction of ancient cities it is usually only the horizontal aspect that is considered. He comes to the conclusion that Israeli houses had more than just one floor, and adduces the following observations in his support: (1) The Assyrian palace reliefs, the only representations of ancient cities from the middle eastern iron age, stress the vertical aspect of the city. (2) The houses were often built on the city walls (*cf.*

---

[80]Ben-Dov, *Shadow*, 149; similarly Mazar, *Berg*, 208.
[81]*Berg*, 189.
[82]Ben-Dov, *Shadow*, 149-50; Mazar, *Berg*, 206ff.
[83]The following summarises his essay, C.H.J. de Geus, 'The Profile of an Israelite city', *BA* 49 (1986) 224-7; de Geus himself refers here to his larger investigation, *De Israelische Stad* (Kampen, 1984).

Jos. 2:15; 1 Sa. 19:12). (3) The walls were often integrated into the circle of houses running immediately behind them (especially the 'casemate' type). (4) The traditional reconstruction of the Israelite four-room house should not deceive us into thinking that it had only one storey, as it is portrayed in many reconstruction drawings. (5) The presence of stone roof supports and double rows of columns for storage rooms would not have been necessary in single-storey construction. (6) The earlier objection that the weight-bearing capacity of clay bricks was too low for multi-storey construction has now been refuted.

In our context, De Geus' concluding note is particularly interesting: 'The additional storeys on private dwellings would have allowed for greater population densities within city walls, explaining how it was possible for such large numbers of people to reside within an Israelite city.'[84]

McKay refers to the construction of several storeys in Augustan times: Strabo reports that in his time 'the inhabitants of Babylon reacted to the population pressure with the construction of multi-storey houses using vault technology and that multi-storey houses can also be found in Tyre and Arad.'[85] Strabo says of Tyre 'that the houses here, as is said, have many storeys, even more than in Rome' (ἐνταῦθα δὲ φασι πολυστέγους τὰς οἰκίας ὥστε καὶ τῶν ἐν Ῥώμῃ μᾶλλον).

Byatt considers it very probable that multi-storey houses were built in Jerusalem as in Hippo and Tyre:[86] Josephus himself (*BJ* 2.504) compares the method of construction of houses in the Galilean Chabulon with that of Tyre, Sidon and Berytus. Ben-Dov explains that vault technology made possible the construction of multi-storey houses; 'indeed, many of Jerusalem's houses in that period rose to a height of two or three storeys, which was a boon for coping with the pressures of a burgeoning population.'[87] Broshi, in his report on the excavations on Mount Zion, takes the houses as having consisted certainly of two storeys and some even of three.[88] Thus the indications of extremely

---

[84]*Ibid.*, 227.

[85]A.G. McKay, *Römische Häuser, Villen und Paläste* (Ger. tr.; Edition Antike Welt; Feldmeilen, 1980) 157 n. 296 referring to Strabo 16.1.5 (for Babylon), 16.2.23 (for Tyre) and 16.2.13 (for Arad); also Pomponius, *Mela* 12.7.6 for the high houses of Aradus.

[86]*Josephus*, 57: 'This alludes to their several storeys, and G.A. Smith mentions the "high stacked houses of Hippo." It is quite likely that such houses were built in Jerusalem' (referring to G.A. Smith, *The Historical Geography of the Holy Land* [[25]1931] 460).

[87]*Shadow*, 150.

[88]*Excavations*, 58.

closely-packed building and a multi-storey method of construction should warn us against estimating the population density too low.

The question arises, however, whether there are reliable figures for the population size and density or demographic calculations for comparable ancient cities, especially since Broshi has maintained that the density coefficient of 50 p/d has never been exceeded in any ancient city or in any modern old-town.

h) The population density of ancient cities

As a counter-argument, let us first consider Byatt, who questions Jeremias' estimate of the population of Jerusalem ('160 persons per acre'), amongst other reasons, on the basis of a town in the Negev:

> Although an extreme contrast, the population of Khalasah in the Negev is illustrative of the dense population possible in those times. Dr Nelson Glueck wrote, "It is estimated that some twenty thousand people may have lived in the hundreds of stone houses which were jammed into its roughly rectangular area of approximately 110 by 630 yards." This means more than 1,300 persons per acre. A figure of one-third this amount, say 400 persons to the acre, seems reasonable when other considerations are reviewed.[89]

This means around 100 p/d. Unfortunately we learn neither from him nor from N. Glueck how he arrives at these figures.

For Ebla, the excavators of Tell Madikh have, on the basis of a text, estimated a population of 260,000 inhabitants in an area of 560 dunam in the early bronze age,[90] giving a density of 464 p/d![91] Even if this enormous figure should refer to the 'greater Ebla,'[92] there is still a lot speaking for a large and very dense population. Matthiae, the other leading excavator from Ebla, writes that the area around Tell Mardikh was in ancient times incomparably more fruitful than today and that it was still full of water at the beginning of this century.[93] The Mardikh region was quite densely settled in the early bronze age due to

---

[89]Byatt, *Josephus*, 57 with reference to N. Glueck, *Rivers in the Desert. An Exploration of the Negev. An Adventure in Archaeology* (London, 1959) 258f.

[90]G. Pettinato, 'The Royal Archives of Tell Mardikh-Ebla', *BA* 39 (1976) 44-52 (44, 47).

[91]Y. Shiloh, 'The Population of Iron Age Palestine in the Light of a Sample Analysis of Urban Plans, Areas and Population Density', *BASOR* 239 (1980) 25-35 (26).

[92]Pettinato, *Archives*, 47.

[93]*Ebla*, 219.

geographical and ecological conditions which were not dissimilar to those which massed together the village-dwellers of Sumeria's Uruk period into the first great city concentrations.[94]

With the aid of modern demographic methods, attempts have been made to estimate the population of Dura-Europos and Ugarit. E. Will has attempted to calculate the size of the population of Dura-Europos as the product of the number of residential units (600) and an average fixed figure per residential unit (max. 10, probably a little less), so that he arrives at a total figure of 5-6,000 inhabitants.[95] With reference to the population density, he offers no figures, but his claim should be noted that Dura-Europos has to be considered a small town in comparison with the large cities of Antioch and Seleucia, whilst Aleppo and Damascus are to be counted among the medium-sized cities.[96]

For Ugarit, W.R. Garr has produced a more comprehensive demographic investigation based on: (1) epigraphic data (on the composition and size of the average family); (2) archaeological data (allocations for public buildings and accommodation units, average room size, distribution of space within the city) and (3) formulae for estimating the population (from ethnographic studies).[97] Most interesting in our context are the formulae for the number of persons per given area. Naroll's formula[98] states that one tenth of the living space corresponds to the figure for the population. LeBlanc[99] refined this formula, applying it only to roofed space (which is, however, often hard to distinguish on the basis of archaeological research). Adams attempted for Mesopotamia a direct relation of area and number of persons. In his various publications, his figures fluctuated from 200 to 100 persons per hectare,[100] that is, 20 to 10 p/d. It must be borne in mind, however, that these ratios have been obtained for Mesopota-

---

[94]*Ibid.*

[95]*La Population*, 320.

[96]*Ibid.*, 321.

[97]W.R. Garr, 'A Population Estimate of Ancient Ugarit', *BASOR* 266 (1987) 31-43; *cf.* the summary of methods (p. 31); the results of a) and b) in summary: the average household in Ugarit had 5.25 persons; the area was 20 hectares, the relation of public to private buildings was 1:3, most rooms were in the grouping of 5-10 m^2, less than 50% of the space was used as living space.

[98]R. Naroll, 'Floor Area and Settlement Population', *American Antiquity* 27 (1962) 587-9; in Garr, 'Population Estimate', 39 with the note that this formula, which was originally derived from prehistoric settlements, seemed also to be applicable to middle-eastern villages, as Kramer attempted to show in various publications.

[99]'Addition'.

mian villages with low population density and low water supplies.[101] Thus this ratio can scarcely be used for densely populated Palestinian cities.

5. *The specification of the population of Jerusalem from various approaches*

One example of the attempt to specify the population of Jerusalem from various approaches and thus to have also a relative mutual check is the work of Scheckenhofer. He also establishes that Jerusalem in antiquity was densely populated and had narrow alleys.[102] As a minimum height of construction, he cites one and a half to two storeys:

> A construction site in a residential area can on average not have exceeded 100 m^2. This would then give 5500 houses, two thirds of which would have accommodated families with servants and the rest two families each. The size of a family can be set at seven persons. This gives a population of 58,000, to which then have to be added the inhabitants of the public areas (garrison of the Antonium, king's body-guard, court staff, priesthood, administrators, all in all certainly several thousand). If we estimate a total population in the time of Herod of 70,000 inhabitants, this cannot be far from the truth.[103]

From another approach, he calculates back from the accepted minimum size of Jerusalem at the start of the Jewish War, assuming a constant population growth of 'on average half a percent' per year.[104] Thus, at the end of Herod's reign, Jerusalem was a large city of 100,000 inhabitants. At the time of the first Jerusalem church, it would then have had *c.* 120,000 inhabitants.

A further significant attempt to specify the population of Jerusalem from various sides has been undertaken by Ben-David. In the context of a thorough examination of the size of the Jewish population in the Roman Empire and in Palestine,[105] he then looks at the towns

[100]In Garr 38f., on the publications of R.M. Adams 1965 (Land Behind Baghdad. A History of Settlements in the Diyala Plains [Chicago]), 1972, 1981.

[101]'The revised estimate took into account "low population densities, poorly drained terrain and relatively limited governmental or landlord-imposed restraints"': Garr, 38 with reference to Adams and Nissen (1972) 29.

[102]*Bevölkerung*, 27.

[103]*Ibid.*

[104]*Ibid.*, 30.

and particularly at Jerusalem. Looking at the areas, he first gives an overview of the greatly varying figures of ancient authors on the length of the town walls, which are reproduced here, together with the areas that result:

60 stadia (Strabo)	7.79 km^2
50 stadia (Hecateus of Abdera)	5.41 km^2
40 stadia (Timochares, biographer of Antiochus IV)	3.4 km^2
30 stadia (Josephus)	2.25 km^2
27 stadia (Xenophon the topographer)	1.55 km^2

Modern archaeologists would also find it difficult to specify the area of Jerusalem at a particular time, especially since it grew by 40-50 times from the small mountain town of David to the Herodian metropolis.[106] In a table, Ben-David compares the calculations of Galling, Hecker and Avi-Yonah. This gives for Jerusalem under:

the Hasmonaeans and Herod the Great:	74 - 98 - 86 ha.
both Agrippas:	134 - 180 - 180 ha.[107]

For his own investigations, Ben-David begins with the results of Avi-Yonah, which give a medium value and 'are anyway supported by two relatively credible sources.'[108] Herodian Jerusalem would thus have a walled area of 1.02 km^2, leaving 884,000 m^2 after deduction of the Temple area. If one assumes that 60% of this actually accommodated domestic buildings, this would then give 530,000 m^2 of pure living space.

From this basis, Ben-David comes to similar results by two paths. On the one hand, he asks after the *number of residential units*. According to the Mishnah, a small house was supposed to have a floor area of 3 x 4 m, a large house 4 x 5 m, a hall 5 x 5 m.[109] If one begins with the above cited (already greatly reduced) 'pure living space' and accepts that these 'houses'—'similarly to the simple single-storey Arab houses of today—consisted of just one room, a "hall" of 25 m^2, then 21,000 such halls, wall to wall, would have covered this residential area.'[110] According to the number of people which one assumes per room, one

---

[105]*Ökonomie*, 41ff.
[106]*Ibid.*, 55.
[107]*Ibid.*
[108]*Ibid.*
[109]*Ibid.*, 57 with reference to *m. B. Bat.* 6:4.
[110]*Ibid.*, though very many of the Arab houses in the modern Jerusalem are multi-storey.

arrives at, for 4 people 84,000, for 5 people, 105,000, for 6 people (which Ben-David considers most probable), 126,000. [111]

By another path he arrives at a remarkably similar result. Like Jeremias and Hecker,[112] he assumes the population density of modern Jerusalem, but more helpfully takes as his yardstick the Jewish quarter of the old city, in which, according to Vilnay, 15,000 people lived in 1895. 'Since the Jewish quarter had an area of 102,000 m^2, this number of inhabitants equals a density of 147,000/km^2.'[113] The area assumed for the Herodian period would then have accommodated 130,000 people. Considering the fact that a high percentage was deducted for gardens, streets and palaces, and the northern areas of the city were not so densely populated, 'the final estimate of 90-110,000 inhabitants for Jerusalem in its heyday [seems] appropriate.'[114] One cannot assume that this figure was significantly exceeded at any time in antiquity, 'since a natural limit lay simply in the scarcity of water, which often enough afflicted Jerusalem.'[115] Nevertheless, under these circumstances, on the basis of a constant population growth also in the time after Herod, for the time of the first Christian church, a still higher figure can be taken, so that one arrives again at the figure of around 130,000 inhabitants, as do Ben-David (from the first approach on), Scheckenhofer and Avi-Yonah (*cf.* above, Table 1).

The approximate population size of Jerusalem in the time of Jesus can also be calculated from the following factors:

6. *Water supply*

In his study, 'Ancient Jerusalem: Its Water Supply and Population' (1974), Wilkinson takes as his basis an average private water consump-

---

[111]*Ibid.*; the average *family size* was in Talmudic times much higher and 'not comparable with that of western industrial countries, since despite the probably high infant and child mortality rate, a family of that time had between six and nine members, as is clear from the sources' (45 with examples).

[112]On Jeremias, *cf.* above; M. Hecker, 'The Growth of Jerusalem in the Israelite Period' (Hebrew), in *Jehuda and Jerusalem* (1957) 177-9.

[113]Ben-David, *Ökonomie*, 57; he also shows the difference from the old city of Jerusalem in 1968, when 25,000 people lived in an area of 450,000 m^2, which corresponds to a population density of 55,000/km^2 (n. 257).

[114]*Ibid.*, 57; this view is in principle also that of Avi-Yonah; for his figure of 100,000 in Jerusalem's heyday, he cites the source: 'Bevölkerung,' *Enzykl. Bild*, vol. I, p. 146 (n. 258, not n. 257, as in the text).

[115]Ben-David, *loc. cit.*, 57.

tion of 40 litres per person per day in ancient Jerusalem, half of which came from private cisterns and the rest from the public water supply.[116] He considers Byatt's population figure of 220,000 for Jerusalem and its environs much too high, since water consumption would then have stood at the improbably low rate of less than 10 litres per person per day, assuming that the majority of the population lived within the city walls.[117] By taking as a basis the public water supply systems and a daily consumption of 20 litres per person per day from these supplies, he arrives at a result of over 70,000 inhabitants after Herod the Great and before Herod Agrippa.[118] But it can be questioned whether water consumption might not in fact have been lower than Wilkinson assumes. A consumption of 4.5 litres per day has been estimated for Samaria.[119] For Arad, N. Rosenan has calculated 2-3 litres daily, assuming that the climate in the Negev during the early bronze age was scarcely different from today's.[120]

7. *Annual population growth*

Scheckenhofer believes that the figures given by ancient writers (see below) for the situation at the beginning of the siege of Jerusalem, though they need some reduction, nevertheless offer a basis for back-projections: 'Though the city in times of emergency could offer refuge to only 400,000 people, this assumes a minimum size, which can hardly have lain below 150,000.'[121] By subtracting half a percent per year, he arrives at an initial core of 110,000 inhabitants (*i.e.* at the end of the Herodian period).

8. *The reliability of ancient authors' figures*

This should be subjected to a new, less prejudiced examination. The figures of Josephus and Tacitus (see below) for the festival pilgrims and refugees shortly before the start of the Jewish War are almost

---

[116] *Loc. cit.*, 47f.
[117] *Ibid.*, 50.
[118] *Ibid.*
[119] G.M. Crowfoot, K.M. Kenyon and E.L. Sukenik, *The Buildings at Samaria* (Palestine Exploration Fund, 1942) 4; in Shiloh, *Population*, 27.
[120] N. 14.
[121] *Ibid.*

always dismissed as completely unreliable and hugely exaggerated. In contrast, Baron notes that these figures are 'not quite so out of line as they appear at first glance. Jerusalem's population before the siege had been swelled by countless numbers of pilgrims from all over the Dispersion and refugees from the provinces previously occupied by the Roman legions.'[122] Feldman notes, in the light of Josephus' figure of 2.5 million pilgrims at passover, which has been viewed as a confusion with the total Jewish population of the country:[123] 'Josephus' figure may indicate that Jews in Palestine and elsewhere took seriously the obligation to go to Jerusalem for pilgrimage festivals.'[124] This leads us to another important aspect:

III. The Number of Pilgrims in Jerusalem at the Great Feasts, Especially Pentecost

1. *The significance of this question for the present discussion*

The importance of this problem for the present discussion results from the fact that the growth of the earliest church is mentioned in connection with the feast of Pentecost. Hence a large number of pilgrims may have been among those who 'were added' after Peter's sermon (2:41) and may also have been among those who stayed several days in Jerusalem and heard of the miracle in the Temple and the further preaching of the apostles (3:1-4:4). It might be objected that the number of those who converted at Pentecost refers exclusively to inhabitants of Jerusalem, because the κατοικοῦντες of Acts 2:5 can only describe permanent inhabitants of the city. One can reply to this, however, with Marshall's argument that, although the verb usually has the sense of 'permanent residents', the hearers of the Pentecost sermon were 'not necessarily all permanent residents in Jerusalem...for the same verb is used in 2:9 of one section of this people and describes them as residing in Mesopotamia.'[125] He refutes the objection that the newly-formed Christian church in Jerusalem would have shrunk very quickly to a smaller size, if it had consisted largely of pilgrims: 'But Luke says

[122]*Population*, 871.
[123]So Avi-Yonah, *The Holy Land from the Persian to the Arab Conquests (536 B.C. to A.D. 640): A Historical Geography* (Grand Rapids, 1966) 219f. after L.H. Feldman, *Josephus and Modern Scholarship* (Berlin, 1984) 369.
[124]Feldman, *ibid*.

nothing about the proportions of visitors and residents.'[126] This does not rule out the possibility, however, that at least the circle of those who were 'added' in the beginning may have consisted to a significant extent of pilgrims. Therefore the question of the number of festival pilgrims, particularly to the Feast of Weeks, is important here.

2. *The number of pilgrims to Jerusalem according to the sources*

Philo speaks of countless people going up to the Temple from many thousands of cities for each festival:

> Μυρίοι γὰρ ἀπὸ μυρίων ὅσων πόλεων, οἱ μὲν διὰ γῆς, οἱ δὲ διὰ θαλάττης, ἐξ ἀνατολῆς καὶ δύσεως καὶ ἄρκτου καὶ μεσημβρίας καθ' ἑκάστην ἑορτὴν εις τὸ ἱεπὸν καταίρουσιν (*Spec. Leg.* 1:69).

Josephus gives the total number of those who died in the siege as 1,100,000 people and adds: 'Of these the greater number were of Jewish blood, but not natives of the place [Jerusalem]' (*BJ* 6.420). If one adds the 97,000 prisoners taken in the course of the war, one arrives at a total of 1,200,000 participants in the passover, who had been 'suddenly enveloped in the war' (*BJ* 6.421). He had, of course, to face the question how such a large number of people could find space in Jerusalem, and so continues: 'That the city could contain so many is clear from the count taken under Cestius. For he, being anxious to convince Nero, who held the nation in contempt, of the city's strength, instructed the chief priests, if by any means possible, to take a census of the population' (*BJ* 6.422). This census was probably taken by indirect counting at the sacrifice, as mentioned also in rabbinic writings, since direct counting was not allowed.[127] Josephus then mentions a passover shortly before the siege of Jerusalem at which 255,600 sacrificial animals were counted, going on to make the calculation himself, 'allowing an average of ten diners to each victim', and obtaining a

---

[125]I.H. Marshall, 'The Significance of Pentecost', *SJT* 30 (1977) 347-69 (357). See also the discussion of this expression in the third chapter of the author's dissertation: 'Das Wachstum des Gottesvolkes: Sprachliche, theologische und historische Untersuchungen zum "Wachsen der Kirche" im lukanischen Doppelwerk auf dem Hintergrund des Alten Testaments und mit einem Ausblick in die frühpatristische Literatur' (Kirchliche Hochschule, Wuppertal, 1992; pending publication in abbreviated form) I.C.2.b.

[126]*Ibid.*

[127]*Cf.* Michel/Bauernfeind, *De bello Judaico* II.2.215 n. 250.

figure of 2,700,000 participants (*BJ* 6.425). Finally, Tacitus claims that in 70 AD, 600,000 people were besieged in Jerusalem (*Hist.* 5.13 [3]). These figures are considered hugely exaggerated by most commentators.[128]

3. *More recent attempts to ascertain the number of pilgrims*

Jeremias made his own attempt to calculate the number of participants in a festival by trying to work out the amount of space in the Temple which the three divisions needed for the slaughter. After a detailed calculation, which began with the assumption 'that in Jesus' time the Passover victims were always slain in the Temple and not in private houses,'[129] he arrives at the result that around 18,000 passover animals could be slaughtered. Then an average table of ten participants per sacrificial animal would give a figure of 180,000 participants in the festival, from whom (as Jeremias himself agreed) the 55,000 inhabitants of Jerusalem have to be deducted. Thus one would arrive at 125,000 festival pilgrims.[130]

Safrai has criticised Jeremias' calculation on two counts: on the one hand, for assuming too much space for the sacrificial area, and, on the other, for taking a too low multiplication factor of ten. In *Lam. Rab.* 1.1, two rabbis accept meal groups of 'forty, fifty or even a hundred people.' 'Both Talmuds have retained the expression, "an olive of passover and Hallel, until the roof falls in," which means that the number of participants in a passover meal was so far above ten that there was only an olive-size piece of sacrificial meat for each individual.'[131] But Safrai sees 'no possibility even of approximating the number of festival guests.'[132]

There is, however, one fact that can take us further, which Byatt referred to when he exposed the contradictions in Jeremias' figures on

---

[128]Jeremias, *Jerusalem*, 78: 'These four sources give, without exception, such fantastic figures that we cannot regard them as historically accurate.' Beloch, *Bevölkerung*, saw in Josephus' figure of 2.7 million participants in the festival 'only a proof of Josephus' tendency to brag' (246). But Beloch's anti-Semitism must be remembered: 'Whether it has been a matter of persecutions of Jews or of satisfaction of their own vanity, Jews have always been full of it' (246).

[129]*Jerusalem*, 78.

[130]*Ibid.*, 83.

[131]S. Safrai, *Die Wallfahrt im Zeitalter des Zweiten Tempels* (Forschungen zum jüdisch-christlichen Dialog 3; Neukirchen-Vluyn, 1981) 97.

[132]*Ibid.*

the pilgrims: at other points Jeremias speaks of the enormous increase in visitors,[133] indeed that three times a year the entire Jewish population of the world streamed to the Temple.[134] Even if one puts the number of Jews in the Roman Empire at just five million,[135] a pilgrimage of 125,000 for each of the three feasts would mean each person going only once in every 14 years.[136] A more realistic figure might be around a million pilgrims to the three festivals. This result by Byatt is supported by Menashe Har-El in an archaeological investigation into streets and fortifications of Jerusalem and Judaea:

> As the population of Jerusalem itself grew so did the settlements in the mountains together with the road network serving them. The pilgrim's route also converged on Jerusalem, and in the period of the Second Temple approximately one million pilgrims from all over the country, as well as the Diaspora, made the journey on feast days three times a year. The roads were so full that during the month of Ader the authorities would repair them and prepare the reservoirs for the pilgrims with their cattle and carts.[137]

The need to accommodate so many people demanded the voluntary cooperation of the population, the construction of emergency accommodation of every kind, but also accommodation outside the city,[138] including in tents all around the city.

Of particular interest in the context of this study is one further aspect:

4. The number of pilgrims to the Feast of Weeks and the duration of their stay in the city

Safrai stresses that pilgrimage to all three festivals was obligatory. The idea that the passover festival attracted the most pilgrims is, he notes, not supported by the sources. 'From the writings of Josephus[139] and

---

[133]*Ibid.*, 58, 73.
[134]*Ibid.*, 75.
[135]S.W. Baron, 'Population', in *EJ* 13 (1971) 866-903 (871) gives the number of Jews shortly before the fall of Jerusalem as over 8 million, of whom not more than 2.35-2.5 million lived in Palestine.
[136]*Josephus*, 57 n. 47.
[137]M. Har-El, 'Jerusalem and Judea. Roads and Fortifications', *BA* 44 (1981) 8-19 (13).
[138]Safrai, *Wallfahrt*,161; *cf, e.g.* Josephus, *BJ* 2.10.

the New Testament [*cf.* Acts 2:5ff.; 20:16; 21:27], we often hear that, especially at the Feast of Weeks, countless pilgrims came to Jerusalem. On the other hand, we do not have any evidence that the number of guests at the Feast of Weeks was less than at the other two festivals.'[140] Though the Feast of Weeks lasted only a day according to biblical prescription (Lv. 23:21), it was permitted to bring the appropriate offerings for a further seven days thereafter.[141] 'Some festival customs also suggest that it was considered a duty to stay in Jerusalem for the entire festival week.'[142]

IV. Conclusion

It has not been possible within the scope of this work to examine all the factors involved in assessing Luke's figures for Jesus' first followers after Pentecost in Jerusalem. Limitation to the question of the population of Jerusalem (along with the number of festival pilgrims) is, however, justified and fruitful enough, since the argument which appeals to what is supposedly such a low population figure for Jerusalem in the time of Jesus is by far the most often used. Let us then summarise the results:
(1) There is no reasonable ground for believing that Jerusalem in the time of Jesus' activity and of the earliest church had only 20-35,000 inhabitants, as is still claimed in even the most recent treatments on the basis of Jeremias' calculations.
(2) The primary error in these figures is the too low estimate of the population density in the Jerusalem of that time. As has been shown, much evidence suggests that Jerusalem was extremely densely populated at that time; the density may have averaged over 50 persons per 1,000 m^2.
(3) An exact calculation of the population appears impossible at present. A figure of 60,000 is a conceivable lower limit, though it is more probable that the figure was up to 100-120,000 inhabitants in the forties.

---

[139]*Cf. BJ* 2.42-3: 'On the arrival of Pentecost...a countless multitude flocked in from Galilee, from Idumaea, from Jericho, and from Peraea beyond the Jordan.'
[140]*Wallfahrt*.
[141]Rabbinic references in Safrai, 45; the Book of Jubilees also assumes that the Feast of Weeks lasted longer than one day.
[142]Safrai, *Wallfahrt*, 259.

(4) In the Lukan figures of 'about 3,000' who believed and were baptised (Acts 2:41) or the 5,000 to which the 'number of the men' rose (Acts 4:4), one cannot, for the reasons given, rule out the idea that pilgrims, staying in Jerusalem for a few days for the Feast of Weeks, were included. If one still assumes several thousand locals joining the Jesus movement, this does not appear improbable.

(5) Apart from the 'theological' factors, especially the powerful working of the Spirit and of the word empowered by him, and the attracting power of the church as the eschatological people of God, 'non-theological' factors—just as very clearly later in the growth of the church in the Roman Empire[143]—can also be identified, which promoted the great growth of the Jesus movement before and after Easter. Some sociological (socio-economic, socio-ecological, socio-political and socio-cultural) factors which proved advantageous for the Jesus movement and Christianity have already been named by Theissen.[144] He refers in particular to the following factors:[145] (a) social uprooting (by socio-economic pressure as a consequence of disasters, over-population, the concentration of wealth and competing systems of taxation); (b) the opposition between city and countryside (between hellenistic city-republics and the Jewish metropolis or settled areas of land and impassable mountains and deserts); (c) socio-political tensions in Palestine due to the critical tension between claimed theocracy and factual aristocracy (a feeding-ground for radically theocratic movements); (d) the identity crisis in Judaism ('When a nation ascribes to itself a privileged role among all nations, but is in danger of subjection to a political and cultural superpower, it must find itself in a difficult identity crisis'[146]). Here there are some points of real importance also with respect to the growth of the earliest churches, touching on a wide field of future research.[147]

---

[143]These factors are listed in the final chapter of the author's doctoral dissertation (see above, n. 125).

[144]G. Theissen, *Soziologie der Jesusbewegung, Ein Beitrag zur Entstehungsgeschichte des Urchristentums* (KT 35; Munich, [5]1988; first in TEH 194, 1977) 33ff.; *cf.* also the reception by Tidball, 'The Growth of the Jesus Movement', in *idem*, *An Introduction to the Sociology of the New Testament* (Exeter, 1983), 41ff., esp. 46-50: 'Factors which aided the Growth of the Movement'.

[145]Here following the summary by R. Pesch, 'Voraussetzungen und Anfänge der urchristlichen Theologie', in K. Kertelge (ed.), *Mission im Neuen Testament* (QD 93; Freiburg, *etc.*, 1982) 11-70 (18-19).

[146]Theissen, 88; Pesch, *Voraussetzungen*, refers to the link between 'identity crisis' and 'mission' in van der Leeuw, *Phänomenologie der Religion* (Tübingen, 1933) 579-80.

(6) Since there is also no convincing theological interpretation of the figures 'about 3,000' and '(about) 5,000,'[148] one will instead have to accept that Luke was dependent on a reliable transmission of these figures. The fact that he formed the style and composition of the growth figures (on the basis of traditions) needs to be differentiated from the historical question of the credibility of the source figures as to the number of people who came to faith after the Pentecost event.

Thus critical research, in contradiction to predominant (largely uncritical) opinion, arrives at the conclusion that the Lukan figures need not be unhistorical at all and can in fact be dependent on reliable tradition.[149]

---

[147]Pesch sees in Theissen's analysis of the factors 'many clues and suggestions which merit discussion (also correction), for better locating the circumstances of early Christian mission in the perspective and context of the history of the first century AD' (*ibid.*, 19).

[148]Brun, in a note as early as 1913 (L. Brun, 'Etwa 3000 Seelen Act 2,41', *ZNW* 14 [1913] 94-96), saw the figure 3,000 in the context of the giving of the law on Sinai and the detail in Ex. 32:28 (LXX), καὶ ἔπεσαν ἐκ τοῦ λαοῦ ἐν ἐκείνῃ ἡμέρᾳ εἰς τρισχιλίους ἄνδρας and concludes, 'the figure agrees, the emphasis on the significant day agrees and the content presents a striking antithesis, which can hardly be coincidental, but could very well be intended. In the time of the old giving of the law up to 3,000 men killed on one day by the LORD...on the day of the new pouring out of the Spirit, about 3,000 souls rescued from the perverted generation...' (*Seelen*, 95f.). This parallel is, however, in fact very vague and the linguistic agreements slight—one could just as well construe a link with the feeding of the 3,000 (*cf.* F.F. Bruce, 'The Church of Jerusalem in the Acts of the Apostles', *BJRL* 67 [1984-85] 641-61 [643] on Acts 4:4 and Mk. 6:44). Thus Pesch is right in establishing, 'since a particular symbolic sense of the figure cannot be identified and since one can also not speak of a Lukan fiction, which just expresses the blessing resting on the mission of the early Church, it only remains to consider whether the proto-Lukan tradition knew of large initial successes of the early Christian mission at the Passover festival (among Jerusalemites and festival pilgrims, from Galilee, for example, who had already come into contact with Jesus' message)' (R. Pesch, *Die Apostelgeschichte* I (EKK; Neukirchen-Vluyn/Zurich: Neukirchener Verlag/ Benziger Verlag, 1986).

[149]This chapter is an English translation (by Andrew Warren) of chapter 4 of the author's doctoral dissertation: 'Das Wachstum des Gottesvolkes: Sprachliche, theologische und historische Untersuchungen zum "Wachsen der Kirche" im lukanischen Doppelwerk auf dem Hintergrund des Alten Testaments und mit einem Ausblick in die frühpatristische Literatur' (Kirchliche Hochschule, Wuppertal, 1992).

CHAPTER 9

JEWISH PRAYER LITERATURE AND THE JERUSALEM CHURCH IN ACTS

Daniel K. Falk

Summary

This chapter compares descriptions of the prayers of Jerusalem Christians in Acts with the picture of Jewish prayer gathered from other sources, paying particular attention to the place and times for prayer. Luke's portrayal is consistent with the silence in pre-70 Jewish evidence with regard to the synagogue as a place for daily prayer, but instead emphasising such assembly in the Temple. Luke also does not contradict the finding that Jewish prayer in the Second Temple period followed two patterns: sunrise and sunset, based on the course of the sun, and morning and afternoon, based on the Temple sacrifices. There is little evidence to suggest that Luke's picture contains elements from post-70 developments in Jewish and Christian worship.

I. Introduction

Scholars have long noted that the Gospel of Luke provides more information on prayer than any of the other Gospels, and that this special interest continues in Acts. The two volumes include eleven prayer texts and numerous narrative descriptions of prayer. Much modern literature discusses this material with regard to Luke's theology of prayer. The prayers themselves are viewed as primarily Lukan creations, and the placing of the narrative descriptions at key points in the life of Jesus and the early Christians is taken to indicate concerns of the evangelist, such as a desire to show that prayer is the means by which God guides salvation history.[1]

Yet, despite the fact that Luke-Acts is an important primary source for the historical reconstruction of Jewish and Christian worship in the 1st century, much less attention has been paid to assessing the compatibility of Luke's picture with what is known from other sources. The following are perhaps the most important of the questions still unresolved concerning Jewish prayer in the late Second Temple period on which Luke's evidence has a bearing: (1) Was there prayer in synagogues?; (2) What daily times of prayer were observed by Jews and Christians?; (3) To what extent did Jerusalem Christians continue in the prayer practices customary among Jews?; and (4) Did the church adopt developments in Jewish prayer subsequent to the recognition of Christians as a distinctive group, in particular, innovations introduced after AD 70?

In what follows, Acts is examined as a source for reconstructing the worship of the Jerusalem church in the context of Palestinian Jewish practice. The issue is immediately complicated by the uncertain dating of Acts. Apart from the possible use of earlier sources, the majority of scholars date the final redaction of Acts later than AD 70, and thus subsequent to the destruction of the Temple—an event which is widely held to have been the single most formative factor in the development of the Jewish liturgy. Talmudic sources ascribe radical liturgical reforms to the decades following its destruction, under the leadership of Rabban Gamaliel II. In this period, the times of worship are said to have been formalised, and the Benediction of the *Minim* is said to have been added to the central daily prayer known as the Eighteen Benedictions (=*Amidah*). According to E. Fleischer, the very idea of prayer as a religious obligation was Gamaliel's distinctive inno-

[1]*E.g.* F. Plymale, *The Prayer Texts of Luke-Acts* (New York: Peter Lang, 1991).

vation.[2] How much, then, was Luke's portrayal of worship influenced by Jewish liturgical reform after the destruction of the Temple? Such influence could have come indirectly, through the impact of developing Jewish usage on Christian worship at the time when Acts was composed, or directly, through the evangelist's own knowledge of contemporary Jewish prayer. This question will be taken into account below, and is addressed in the light of evidence for places and times for prayer.

With regard to Acts, attention will concentrate on passages relating to Jerusalem. Narrative accounts of prayer describe its use in the Upper Room (1:12-4), in daily life (2:41-7), at the Temple (3:1; 22:17), as an apostolic function (6:1-7), and in homes (12:5, 12). Texts of prayers appear in the contexts of deciding Judas' replacement (1:24-5), requesting boldness to speak (4:23-31), and Stephen's death (7:59-60). Also, of indirect relevance are the descriptions of religious activities in the Temple, synagogue and homes (2:1-4; 4:32-7; 5:12-6; 6:8-9; 9:26-31; 24:11-2), as well as Cornelius' and Peter's prayers in Caesarea and Joppa (10:1-10, 30; 24:11-2).

II. Lukan Evidence for Jewish and Christian Worship

It must be noted first of all that in the second volume of his work, Luke never actually shows non-Christian Jews at prayer. Only Jesus' followers and would-be followers (Cornelius) pray in Acts. This should caution us against over-emphasis on arguments from silence. In Acts, Luke is not interested in informing us about Jewish prayer, but rather about the life of the early Christians. This does not, however, exclude the possibility that the Jerusalem Christians shared in the prayer practices of their fellow Jews, and that Luke along the way provides some useful information in this regard. In particular, Luke's concern to highlight the early Christians' faithfulness to their Jewish roots means that he is careful to note particularly Jewish aspects of their worship.

Acts portrays Palestinian Christians praying in only two specified venues: the Temple (Acts 3:1; 22:17; perhaps 2:42, 46-7?) and homes (Acts 4:24-31; 12:5, 12; perhaps 1:14, 24-5?).[3] Strikingly absent is

---

[2]E. Fleischer, 'On the Beginnings of Obligatory Jewish Prayer' (Hebrew), *Tarbiz* 59 (1990) 397-441 (426-7).

[3]The latter passage does not state that the prayer took place in the Upper Room.

any reference to prayer in Palestinian synagogues, despite their importance in both the Gospel and Acts. Thus Luke mentions synagogues in Jerusalem (Acts 6:9; 24:12), although he does not describe activities in them. On the other hand, he portrays the communal use of Galilean synagogues consistently with his notices of the synagogues of Galatia, Asia Minor, and Macedonia and Achaia: regular activities include Sabbath assembly, reading of Torah and the Prophets, preaching and debate.[4] One should not assume from silence that Luke knew of no prayer in synagogues, but he certainly does not portray this as the central activity. Further strengthening this impression is the observation that although Luke portrays Christians as continuing to frequent synagogues, particularly in the early period (Acts 6:9; 22:19), he mentions only homes and the Temple in his summaries of the communal worship and prayer of the Christian community, never synagogues.

According to Luke, the first Jerusalem Christians continued their devotion to the Temple and its service (Acts 21:15-26) and maintained a distinctive presence there with preaching (Acts 5:20-21, 42) and regular assembly in Solomon's portico (Acts 3:11; 5:12-13) so that even many priests believed (Acts 6:7).[5] The Temple was for them a place of regular prayer (Lk. 24:52; Acts 22:17). Acts 3:1 says specifically that Peter and John went up to the Temple at the hour of prayer, which Luke reveals was at the ninth hour, although, admittedly, it does not state that they went with the intention of praying. Following hard on the heels of Acts 2:41-47, however, the visit to the Temple at the hour of prayer is intended as an example of the early Christians' devotion to prayer (2:42).

It is not immediately clear what is meant in Acts 2:42 by 'they devoted themselves to the apostles' teaching and to the fellowship, to the breaking of bread and to the prayers'. Salzmann disagrees with Jeremias' suggestion that the four activities listed describe 'a sequence of an early Christian service' (=instruction, Agape [κοινωνία], Eucha-

---

[4]Lk. 4:16-28; 4:31-37; 6:6-11; 13:10-17; Acts 13:14-44; 14:1; 17:1-4; 17:10-11; 17:17; 18:4; 18:19; 18:26; 19:8.

[5]*Cf.* C. K. Barrett, 'Attitudes to the Temple in the Acts of the Apostles', in W. Horbury (ed.), *Templum Amicitiae: Essays on the Second Temple Presented to Ernst Bammel* (JSNT Supplement Series 48; Sheffield: Sheffield Academic Press, 1991) 345-367, for the two attitudes toward the Temple which Luke allowed to stand in Acts. The view that the first Christians continued to frequent the Temple occurs in both his source material and the summaries of his composition. See his summary of the relevant passages in Acts.

rist [breaking of bread], and psalms and prayers) which took place in homes. Salzmann offers the following grounds: (1) the order, where prayers follow the Eucharist, is not what one would expect; (2) this theory provides no satisfactory explanation for the plural ταῖς προσευχαῖς in a list of singular members; (3) κοινωνία is defined in vv. 44-5; and (4) one would expect a καί between each member if it described an order of worship.[6] He thinks, rather, that 42a is a unity describing briefly the teaching and life of the Christians, followed by a two-part description of their liturgical life covering both venues for worship. The breaking of bread took place in the homes, while 'the prayers' signifies the observance of times of prayer in the Temple.[7]

If Cadbury was right about the relationship of the summaries, comparison with Acts 5:12-4 seems to indicate that Acts 2:46a and 47a both primarily concern the Temple:[8]

Acts 2:46-7	Acts 5:12-4
(46a) καθ' ἡμέραν τε προσκαρτεροῦντες ὁμοθυμαδὸν ἐν τῷ ἱερῷ,	(12b) καὶ ἦσαν ὁμοθυμαδὸν ἅπαντες ἐν τῇ στοᾷ Σολομῶντος
(46b) κλῶντές τε κατ' οἶκον ἄρτον, μετελάμβανον τροφῆς ἐν ἀγαλλιάσει καὶ ἀφελότητι καρδίας	
(47a) αἰνοῦντες τὸν θεὸν καὶ ἔχοντες χάριν πρὸς ὅλον τὸν λαόν.	(13b) ἀλλ' ἐμεγάλυνεν αὐτοὺς ὁ λαός
(47b) ὁ δὲ κύριος προσετίθει τοὺς σῳζομένους καθ' ἡμέραν ἐπὶ τὸ αὐτό.	(14) μᾶλλον δὲ προσετίθεντο πιστεύοντες τῷ κυρίῳ, πλήθη ἀνδρῶν τε καὶ γυναικῶν

[6]J. C. Salzmann, *Lehren und Ermahnen: zur Geschichte des christlichen Wortgottesdienstes in den ersten drei Jahrhunderten* (WUNT, 2nd series, 59; Tübingen: J.C.B. Mohr [Paul Siebeck], 1993) 32-4. *Cf.* J. Jeremias, *The Prayers of Jesus*, tr. J. Bowden, C. Burchard, J. Reumann (Philadelphia: Fortress, 1967) 79; *The Eucharistic Words of Jesus* (The New Testament Library; London: SCM, 1966) 119-20. This has also been rejected by E. Haenchen, *The Acts of the Apostles*, 14th edn., tr. B. Noble, G. Shinn and H. Anderson, rev. R. McL. Wilson (Oxford: Blackwell, 1971) 191.

[7]Salzmann, *Lehren und Ermahnen*, 32-4.

[8]H. J. Cadbury, 'The Summaries in Acts' in F.J. Foakes Jackson and K. Lake (eds.), *The Beginnings of Christianity*, Part 1, *The Acts of the Apostles* (London: Macmillan, 1920-1933) 5:392-402 (= *Beginnings*).

That is, Acts 2:46-7 is essentially an expanded form of the summary concerning the Christian presence in the Temple which appears in 5:12-14. It describes Christian activity more generally by adding a reference to the other sphere, the home (2:46b).[9] This gives a neat form to the summary, introducing the two spheres of activity by participial phrases and then expanding on each beginning with the main verb and further participles in the following manner:[10]

καθ' ἡμέραν

A τε προσκαρτεροῦντες ὁμοθυμαδὸν ἐν τῷ ἱερῷ,
B κλῶντές τε κατ' οἶκον ἄρτον,
B′ μετελάμβανον τροφῆς ἐν ἀγαλλιάσει καὶ ἀφελότητι καρδίας
A′ αἰνοῦντες τὸν θεὸν καὶ ἔχοντες χάριν πρὸς ὅλον τὸν λαόν.

Of course they praised God and prayed in the homes as well, but it is particularly their presence in the Temple which wins them favour before the people, and so it is likely that 2:47a refers above all to Temple prayer. This is supported by the conclusion of Luke's Gospel which states that on returning to Jerusalem, 'they were continually in the Temple blessing God' (Lk. 24:53).[11] Both the Temple and home assembly are described as daily occurrences, then—the former for prayer and the latter for sharing food. Acts 3:1 follows with an immediate example of gathering at the Temple for prayer, indicating that what is meant by 'they were continually together in the Temple'[12] is that Christians met at the Temple not by coincidence or because they were always loitering there, but because they assembled at particular hours of prayer.[13] Bradshaw is thus correct that 'devoting themselves...to the prayers' (προσκαρτεροῦντες . . . ταῖς προσευχαῖς; Acts

[9]With Barrett, 'Attitudes to the Temple', 347, this should not be considered independent Christian meeting-houses, but rather family settings.

[10]O. Bauernfeind, *Kommentar und Studien zur Apostelgeschichte*, ed. V. Metelmann, intro. M. Hengel (WUNT 22; Tübingen: J.C.B. Mohr [Paul Siebeck], 1980) 58, also suggested a chiastic structure for this passage. B. Reicke, *Diakonie, Festfreude und Zelos: in Verbindung mit der altchristlichen Agapenfeier* (Uppsala: A.-B. Lundequistska, 1951) 25, finds a similar chiastic structure in 2:42.

[11]It is possible that the variant of Codex Bezae and the majority of Old Latin witnesses, which read αἰνοῦντες instead of εὐλογοῦντες, widely attested in conflated readings as early as the 5th century, was due to recognition of the link between Luke 24:53 and Acts 2:46-47.

[12]For this use of προσκαρτερέω ἐν see Sus. (Θ) 6; *TDNT* III, 618.

[13]*Cf.* B. Reicke, *Glaube und Leben der Urgemeinde* (ATANT 32; 1957) 61; W.O.E. Oesterley, *The Jewish Background of the Christian Liturgy* (Oxford: Clarendon Press, 1925) 94.

2:42) 'most naturally suggests the observance of a fixed pattern of prayers',[14] although below I will question his particular reconstruction. Perhaps Acts 1:14 should also be considered. Even though the only location mentioned in this context is the Upper Room, it is possible, on comparison with Luke 24:53, that προσκαρτεροῦντες ὁμοθυμαδὸν τῇ προσευχῇ ('they devoted themselves with one accord to prayer')[15] refers particularly to prayers in the Temple, since both passages intend to describe the activities of Jesus' followers on returning to Jerusalem. Further, this summary is parallel to that in Acts 2:42 and 2:46. In Acts 6:4, the apostles describe their ministry as one devoted to prayer and the ministry of the word (ἡμεῖς δὲ τῇ προσευχῇ καὶ τῇ διακονίᾳ τοῦ λόγου προσκαρτερήσομεν). Although no venue is specified, it is likely that this too pertains primarily to the dedication to keeping the hours of prayer in the Temple, where the apostles also preached.

This scenario of Christian prayer at the Temple is consistent with that of Jewish prayer found in Luke's Gospel. The Temple is depicted as a regular place of prayer (Lk. 2:36-38; 18:10), and crowds of people gather at the Temple at the hour of incense to pray (Lk. 1:10), which could indicate either the same time of prayer as Acts 3:1, or the morning incense offering.[16]

Luke likewise presents the home as an important place of prayer for the Christian community. Here it was that the church expressed their distinctive devotion to Jesus, particularly in breaking bread together (Acts 2:46; 20:7f.). Only here does Luke recount prayers (Acts 4:24-31; perhaps 1:24-25).[17] Although these cannot be trusted to represent the actual wording of the prayers spoken, it is apparent that both of these are occasion-specific, that is, they appear to be *ad hoc* prayers (for the choice of a replacement for Judas; in response to the release of

---

[14]P. Bradshaw, *Daily Prayer in the Early Church: A Study of the Origin and Early Development of the Divine Office* (Alcuin Club Collections 63; London: Alcuin Club/ SPCK, 1981) 23. *Cf.* Jeremias, *Prayers*, 79; P.T. O'Brien, 'Prayer in Luke-Acts', *TynBul* 24 (1973) 122.

[15]The suggestion by K. Lake and H. J. Cadbury, *Beginnings*, 4:10, followed by C.W. Dugmore, *The Influence of the Synagogue Upon the Divine Office*, 2nd edn. (London, 1964) 7, that τῇ προσευχῇ refers to a place of prayer is unlikely in the light of other occurrences of the phrase (Acts 2:42; 6:4; Rom. 12:12; and Col. 4:2).

[16]See below, p. 297.

[17]One may infer from Acts 1:13 and 2:2, and the nature of the activity, that the disciples prayed for the election of Judas' replacement (Acts 1:24-5) in the upper room, but this is not certain. It could have taken place in Solomon's portico where they held assemblies and preached.

Peter and John). Nevertheless, Luke wants the reader to believe that these were prayed collectively by the entire group, but provides no hint as to how he thinks this was accomplished. It is possible that he has in mind one person speaking the prayer while others affirm with 'Amen', or that the account summarises the tone of a prayer meeting at which many prayed singly. The only other instance of prayer in Jerusalem homes where the content is provided is also occasion-specific (Acts 12:5, 12, for Peter's release from prison). Outside Jerusalem, however, there is prayer in homes which more closely resembles prayer at the Temple. At Caesarea, Cornelius prays continually (διὰ παντός),[18] and in particular at the ninth hour (Acts 10:3), understood as a time of prayer (Acts 10:30). His prayers, seemingly regular and not specific to an occasion, are interrupted by a vision in which an angel compares his prayers to sacrifice.[19] This, then, seems to be the counterpart to prayer at the Temple at this time for one living away from Jerusalem, and it is significant that in this case, at least, it occurs at his home and not a synagogue.[20] Peter in Joppa similarly prays at home, again seemingly as a regular practice and without a specific occasion, but this is at the sixth hour. The specific mention of the time favours the possibility that Luke understood that this was a regular time for prayer, but there are no definite indicators of this in the text, and commentators have disagreed. It is certainly tantalizing to consider the reference to 'third hour' in Acts 2:15 as indicating a regular time of prayer in which the disciples were engaged on the day of Pentecost,[21] and to compare these three times of prayer mentioned in Acts to prayers at the third, sixth and ninth hour attested in the church from the 3rd century by the Apostolic Tradition, Tertullian, Origen, and Cyprian.[22] However, prayer is not specifically mentioned in Acts 2:15, and it is impossible to prove from Acts whether the third

---

[18]*Cf.* Lake and Cadbury, *Beginnings*, 4:113.

[19]The wording ἀνέβησαν εἰς μνημόσυνον ἔμπροσθεν τοῦ θεοῦ is reminiscent of descriptions of burnt offerings in the LXX (*e.g.* Lv. 2:2; *cf.* Lake and Cadbury, *Beginnings*, 4:113).

[20]As a God-fearer, he would have had access to synagogues; E. Schürer, *The History of the Jewish People in the Age of Jesus Christ*, rev. edn. by G. Vermes, F. Millar, M. Black (Edinburgh: T & T Clark, 1973-1987) 3/1:162.

[21]The note that they were sitting does not necessarily favour the setting of a private house (*pace* Bruce, *Acts*, 114), since sitting was the usual posture of teachers and dignitaries (C. Schneider, *TDNT*, III,442-3), and 'they' may refer to the apostles who commonly taught in the temple (*cf.* W. Horbury, 'The Twelve and the Phylarchs', *NTS* 32 (1986) 503-27 (522).

[22]Dugmore, *Influence*, 66ff.

and sixth hours were considered by Luke to be regular times of prayer among Jews or Christians.[23] It is certainly possible that Luke, and perhaps other Christians, considered it appropriate to accompany with prayer the publicly-sounded hours which were associated with significant events in Jesus' passion.

Luke's idea of the content and formal structure of prayer as seen in the texts which he provides is compatible with Jewish prayer developments in the Second Temple period. All three of the prayer texts in Acts are addressed in the second person. Acts 4:24-31 addresses God directly (δέσποτα, σὺ) and continues with an expanded invocation of a type common among Jewish prayers: 'the one who made heaven and earth and the sea and everything which is in them'. A similar use of this formula from Exodus 20:11 in Psalm 146:6 and expanded in Nehemiah's prayer (Ne. 9:6) suggests this had become an established Jewish liturgical formula.[24] The direct address + appellative expanded by a participial clause to introduce a prayer seems to be a development of the Second Temple period, on the analogy of the history of the *berakah* (benediction) forms.[25] The closest analogies from the Hebrew Bible are (1) the common use of כי אתה יהוה or ואתה יהוה expanded by various verbal or adjectival phrases as a motive clause in the middle or at the end of prayers (*e.g.* Ps. 86:5, 15, 17), and (2) the late *berakah* form which opens a prayer with ברוך אתה יהוה greatly expanded by further appellatives but not a verbal clause (1 Ch. 29:10). The form in Acts 4:24 stands much closer, but probably prior in type, to the full liturgical *berakah* which later Rabbis promoted as the standard: ברוך אתה יהוה followed by additional appellatives and a participial clause. Various forms in the Dead Sea Scrolls reflect a similar stage of development to Acts 4:24.

In summary, we must conclude that the picture that Luke allows us of prayer in the early Christian community in Jerusalem is very incomplete. Nothing is said in Acts about the use of the Lord's Prayer, and there is little evidence concerning grace at meals or Eucharistic prayers, although we must imagine that these took place as well.[26] All of these are attested in liturgical use in Syria before the end of the century, and perhaps before AD 70.[27] Likewise, Luke mentions nothing about recital of the *Shema*. The lack of specific mention of the Lord's Prayer should caution against assuming from silence that the

[23]*Cf.* Dugmore, *Influence*, 64-5.

[24]*Cf.* F.F. Bruce, *The Book of the Acts*, rev. edn. (NICNT; Grand Rapids: Eerdmans, 1988) 156.

[25]J. Heinemann, *Prayer in the Talmud: Forms and Patterns* (Studia Judaica 9; Berlin: Walter De Gruyter, 1977) 82ff.

Shema was not recited. Jesus' quotation of Dt. 6:5 in all three Gospels indicates familiarity with the *Shema*.[28]

However, the credible style of the prayer Luke records suggests contact with pre-70 Judaism,[29] and evidence for the use of sources in Luke's account of the Jerusalem church encourages confidence in his accuracy, even if Acts is dated late.[30] We can thus reasonably conclude that prayer focused on two institutions: the Temple and the home. In the Temple, they met regularly at the time of the afternoon sacrifice (and probably morning sacrifice) for prayer with other Jews, assembled in Solomon's portico, and preached and healed. The prayers were probably general Jewish public praise and petition. In their homes, they broke bread together and engaged in occasion-specific and group-specific prayer. The home, then, was the centre of the distinctively 'Christian' elements added to their Jewish worship focused on the Temple, but they would probably also carry on grace at meals and recital of the *Shema* morning and evening as was customary among Jews. There is abundant evidence that Christians fully participated in synagogue communal gatherings, although there is silence concerning prayer in synagogues. No indication is given whether synagogue gatherings for corporate services were held more frequently than weekly. At least the ninth hour of the day was observed as a regular time for prayer, in the Temple if in Jerusalem, and at home if elsewhere, in accord with common Jewish practice. It is possible, but not definite, that the third and sixth hours were also observed as times of prayer. Nothing is indicated about prayers at morning/sunrise and evening/sunset.

---

[26]It is impossible to imagine that the first Christians departed from Jewish custom and Jesus' consistent practice of saying grace before breaking bread and over wine. Paul certainly followed it (Acts 27:35). For bibliography and discussions on these prayers see C. Jones, G. Wainwright, E. Yarnold, and P. Bradshaw (eds.), *The Study of Liturgy*, rev. edn. (London: SPCK, 1992) and P. Bradshaw, *The Search for the Origins of Christian Worship* (London: SPCK, 1992).

[27]*Didache* 8.

[28]Jeremias' argument (*Prayers*, 73-4, 79-81) that it had ceased to be used in the Christian community by the time of the composition of the Synoptics because of the divergence in textual forms is not convincing. Liturgical items often exist in varying forms from the earliest periods.

[29]See above, p. 275.

[30]See *e.g.* Salzmann, *Lehren und Ermahnen*, 32-33.

III. Pre-70 Jewish Worship from Other Sources

Evidence for Jewish worship prior to the destruction of the Temple agrees substantially with the picture of Acts in two primary matters: (1) the synagogue is not a place particularly devoted to prayer but rather to reading and the study of Scripture, and (2) crowds of people did gather at the Temple at the time of the sacrifice for prayer, or if away from Jerusalem, prayed at the time of sacrifice facing Jerusalem. At this point, we leave the direct consideration of Acts for a time, in order to consider other evidence for the place and time of prayer in pre-70 Jewish worship.

1. The synagogue and prayer

Much secondary literature assumes that already by the 1st century, Jews in Palestine as well as the Diaspora assembled daily in synagogues for services including regular, communal prayer and Scripture reading. However, there is little evidence to back up the assumption of daily, communal prayer in synagogues at this time, and few studies reckon with the probable differences which pertained in Jerusalem.

(1) Literary evidence

Philo, Josephus, the New Testament, and even Rabbinic literature are unanimous in focusing on the reading and study of Scripture as the primary activity of synagogues prior to AD 70.[31] In 1st-century sources, there is no mention of prayer in Palestinian synagogues apart from two exceptions.[32] In the one case, Matthew 6:5 assumes the practice of public prayer in synagogues. However, the nature of Jesus' rebuke implies that it is ostentatious individual prayer performed in public which is under criticism.[33] It does not necessarily confirm or

[31]See S. Zeitlin, 'The Tefillah, the Shemonah Esreh: an Historical Study of the First Canonization of the Hebrew Liturgy', *JQR* 54 (1963-4) 208-49; L. I. Levine, 'The Second Temple Synagogue: The Formative Years' in L. I. Levine (ed.), *The Synagogue in Late Antiquity* (Philadelphia: ASOR, 1987) 16-7.

[32]In fact, synagogues are not mentioned at all in writings of the Hasmonaean or pre-Hasmonaean period, especially Eccl., Tob., Jdt, Ps.-Aristeas, and 1 and 2 Mac. where mention would be expected. The synagogue in Palestine may have been a young institution in Jesus' day, L. Grabbe, 'Synagogues in pre-70 Palestine', *JTS* 39 (1988) 401-410.

deny that legitimate corporate prayer might take place there. In the other case, Josephus, *Vita* 290-5, describes Josephus praying in a *proseuche* in Tiberias: 'We were proceeding with the ordinary service and engaged in prayer, when Jesus rose and began to question me...'.[34] Three observations are important in assessing the significance of this witness. First, it takes place during the week on a specially-called public fast. Thus, the customary prayer service (τὰ νόμιμα ποιούντων καὶ πρὸς εὐχὰς τραπομένων) is that of a public fast-day, and does not evidence daily assemblies for prayer. Indeed, the preceding day, Sunday, the people had also assembled at the *proseuche* at the same hour of the day, 7 *a.m.*, but the gathering was by special arrangement using the *proseuche* in the capacity of a secular meeting place rather than a regular assembly for prayer. In fact, Josephus notes that the men had no idea why they were being assembled (*Vita* 280). Nevertheless, this passage does show that there were customary observances on public fast-days which included prayer.[35] Second, it must be noted that this occurs in Galilee, and third, in a building called a *proseuche*. We have no such statement concerning Jerusalem, or even Judaean, synagogues, although if it were a customary practice, perhaps silence would not be unusual.

Although there has been considerable debate as to the relation between *proseuche* and synagogue, it is certain that at least in many of the instances attested from as early as the 3rd century BC,[36] *proseuche* is a building for assembly.[37] Besides the name, which is the same as the Greek word for prayer, the case for prayer being a central activity in *proseuchai* can be strengthened by three other considerations:
(1) In their joy at hearing of the arrest of Flaccus, the Jews ran to the beach in the morning to sing and pray because their *proseuche* had been taken from them (Philo, *In Flacc*, 122), implying that they would other-

---

[33]R. T. Beckwith, *Daily and Weekly Worship: Jewish to Christian*, 2nd edn. (Alcuin/ GROW Liturgical Study 1; Bramcote: Grove Books, 1989) 12.

[34]On this passage, see E. P. Sanders, *Jewish Law From Jesus to the Mishnah* (London: SCM, 1990) 73-4; *cf. Judaism: Practice and Belief 63 BCE-66 CE* (London: SCM, 1992) 199. He appears not to notice that this particular meeting was for a specifically called public fast, and so considers it possible that the 'customary service' was what may ordinarily have been said at home.

[35]*Cf.*Heinemann, *Prayer*, 108-11; *m. Ta'an.* 2:2-4.

[36]For a convenient summary of most of the primary evidence, see Schürer, *History*, II,425, 439 n. 61.

[37]There are references to the appurtenances of a *proseuche*, a gate, the water supply, a wide range of activities taking place inside *proseuchai*, the construction and destruction of *proseuchai*.

wise have prayed there. The reason they went to the beach as an alternative is presumably because of the importance of water for washing in relation to prayer,[38] and there is evidence that *proseuchai* tended to be either located near a body of water or supplied with water.[39]
(2) Philo, *In Flacc.* 48 claims that one of the purposes of a *proseuche* is to honour benefactors. This seems to be confirmed by the inscriptions which dedicate various *proseuchai* to rulers, but it probably included praying for the well-being of the ruler. The purpose of the dedication seems to be to pledge good faith with a ruler to pray for him. It is possible that in this way the *proseuchai* were to fulfil the function of the sacrifices and prayer at the Jerusalem Temple for the foreign ruler.[40]
(3) One may infer from the customary practice of prayer in the Tiberias *proseuche* on public fasts (see above, p. 277f.) that this understanding of the *proseuche* as an appropriate place for prayer would have extended at least to some degree to regular Sabbath gatherings for the reading of Scripture, and even have inspired some prayer on weekdays.

However, it does not necessarily follow that prayer was a central feature of daily *proseuche* activity at this time, since most sources never mention prayer and seem to envisage a rather general-purpose place of assembly.[41] Nor is it wise to assume that *proseuche* represented a uniform institution with identical practice everywhere.

Although the wide variety of names for places of assembly[42] cautions against the view that *proseuche* and synagogue represent completely different institutions,[43] there are several reasons for remaining very cautious about assuming prayer in Jerusalem synagogues on the analogy of prayer in *proseuchai*.

---

[38]*Cf. Ep. Arist.* 305-6 and Josephus, *Ant.* 12.106.

[39]Josephus, *Ant.* 14.258; the building in Delos (1st century BC) identified as a synagogue/*proseuche* is located by the sea, as are those of Aegina, Miletus and Capernaum; Acts 16:13; *CPJ*, no. 134; the Theodotus inscription; *CPJ*, no. 432. *Cf.* E.L. Sukenik, *Ancient Synagogues in Palestine and Greece* (Schweich Lectures 1930; London: Oxford University Press, 1934) 49f.; Lake and Cadbury, *Beginnings*, IV,191; Haenchen, *Acts*, 494.

[40]*Cf.* Ezr. 6:10; 1 Mac. 7:33; Bar. 1:10-12; Philo, *Gaius* 317, 356; Josephus, *C. Ap.* 2.76; *BJ* 2.197, 409. That is, the *proseuchai* functioned as external indicators of the loyalty of a Jewish community in the Diaspora to a ruler *in lieu* of being able to offer sacrifices for him.

[41]*E.g.* Josephus, *Vita* 277ff.

[42]See the chart in R.E. Oster, 'Supposed Anachronism in Luke-Acts' Use of ΣΥΝΑΓΩΓΗ: A Rejoinder to H.C. Kee', *NTS* 39 (1993) 186, for a listing of other co-referents.

(1) In the light of the diverse functions of *proseuchai,* argument from the name to prayer as a central feature is not as conclusive as it might appear.
(2) As Levine has noted, the use of different terms may reflect a different function or ritual, in addition to the geographical /chronological distinction which Hengel has championed.[44] Levine's suggestion that prayer came to be a part of assemblies in the Diaspora while in Jerusalem prayer focused on the Temple is plausible, but it should be extended to allow that in Galilee and perhaps even in Judaea prayer came to have some place in synagogue gatherings.
(3) The Theodotus inscription[45] omits any mention of prayer in its list of synagogue activities. This is admittedly an argument from silence.
(4) However, the silence concerning prayer in any pre-70 building called synagogue in Palestine is striking in comparison to the abundant testimony to the Temple as a House of Prayer where prayer has a prominent place in the proceedings. S. Hoenig has effectively dispelled the conjecture of the existence of a synagogue in the Temple precincts for such prayer.[46]
(5) In Jerusalem, the status of the Temple as a place of prayer could have been a sufficient deterrent from giving prayer a central role in local synagogues.[47]
(6) The *proseuche* dedications suggest that this institution is intended to fulfil some Temple functions, such as demonstrating loyalty to rulers, and it may be that even the name *proseuche* recalls the function of the Temple as a place of prayer.[48]
(7) In contrast to many scholars who simply assume that prayer was a central feature of the *ma'amadot* services, Levine correctly notes that the

---

[43]For the view that synagogues were essentially secular buildings of assembly until the destruction of the Temple, and of completely different origin than the *proseuche*, see *e.g.* S. Zeitlin, 'The Origin of the Synagogue', repr. in J. Gutmann (ed.), *The Synagogue: Studies in Origins, Archaeology and Architecture* (New York: KTAV, 1975) 14-26.
[44]Levine, 'The Second Temple Synagogue', 21; M. Hengel, 'Proseuche und Synagoge. Jüdische Gemeinde, Gotteshaus und Gottesdienst in der Diaspora und in Palästina', repr. in J. Gutmann (ed.), *The Synagogue*, 27-54.
[45]See below, p. 281.
[46]S. Hoenig, 'The Suppositious Temple-Synagogue', repr. in Gutmann (ed.), *The Synagogue*, 55-71.
[47]*Cf.* Grabbe, 'Synagogues in Pre-70 Palestine', 403; M. Goodman, *State and Society in Roman Galilee, A.D. 132-212* (Totawa, New Jersey: Rowman & Allanheld, 1983) 86; Levine, 'The Second Temple Synagogue', 22.

sources indicate only that these lay representatives met at the time of the sacrifice to read Scripture.[49] There is no mention of prayer.

(2) Epigraphic evidence

No synagogue inscription has yet been found which mentions prayer as a feature of synagogue activity. Although this is an argument from silence and must be used with caution, the Theodotus inscription purports to describe the purpose of a Jerusalem synagogue, but conspicuously fails to mention prayer:

> Theodotus, the son of Vettenos, priest and *archisynagogos*, son of an *archisynagogos* and grandson of an *archisynagogos*, built the synagogue for reading of the law and for teaching of the commandments, and the hostel, chambers, and the water installations for a lodging for them that need it from abroad, which his fathers and the elders and Simonides founded. (*CIJ* 1404)[50]

(3) Architecture

It is by no means certain that any pre-70 synagogues can be identified.[51] However, two conclusions are clear on the basis of those which have been proposed:[52] (1) they lacked a distinctive architecture, appearing to have been adapted from domestic or public structures, perhaps for use as all-purpose communal buildings, and (2) they lacked uniform orientation towards Jerusalem as is characteristic of later synagogues.[53] Also, the focus of these earliest Palestinian synagogues is towards the centre, with seating on all four sides, rather than towards one side as in later synagogues.[54] Since there is no biblical precedent for orientation with regard to reading as there is with prayer

---

[48]This may be reflected in the growing understanding of the Temple as a 'House of Prayer'. In the Hebrew Bible, the Temple is called a House of Prayer (בבית תפלתי) only in Is. 56:7, but the LXX adds two references by the alteration of Is. 60:7 (ὁ οἶκος τῆς προσευχῆς μου), and an allusion to Solomon's prayer in 1 Mac. 7:37: εἶναι οἶκον προσευχῇ.

[49]Levine, 'The Second Temple Synagogue', 17.

[50]For the probable pre-70 dating, see A. Deissmann, *Light from the Ancient East: The New Testament Illustrated by Recently Discovered Texts of the Graeco-Roman World*, 4th edn., tr. L.R.M. Strachan (London: Hodder & Stoughton, 1927) 441. H.F. Kee's recent arguments against this position are not as convincing in proving his proposed date in the 3rd or 4th century as they are in showing that the pre-70 dating is much less certain than scholars often assume.*Cf.* n. 51.

(*e.g.* 1 Ki. 8:44//2 Ch. 6:34; 1 Ki. 8:48//2 Ch. 6:38; Ps. 5:7; Dn. 6:10), it is possible that the change was due to the rise of the importance of prayer in synagogues some time after the destruction of the Temple.[55] Although synagogue experts now almost unanimously reject chronological typologies of synagogue design, it is still clear that there is a striking difference between those buildings considered to be 1st-century synagogues in Palestine and the Galilean synagogues of the 3rd and 4th centuries, evidenced primarily in increased size, the introduction of external and internal ornamentation, Torah niches and raised platforms.[56] 1st-century synagogues in Palestine were functional and plain.[57] It is plausible that this change accompanied a

---

[51]H.C. Kee argues that before AD 70, the term 'synagogue' refers to a (sporadic, informal) gathering of people in private homes or public buildings, and not an architecturally distinct building. *Cf.* Kee, 'The Transformation of the Synagogue After 70 C.E.: Its Import for Early Christianity', *NTS* 36 (1990) 1-24 and the response by Oster, 'Supposed Anachronism', 187-90. Although he is correct to stress the distinction between the use of the term 'synagogue' as an assembly and its use for a meeting place or building, the evidence for 'synagogue' as a distinct building prior to AD 70 is stronger than he admits. He ignores the strongest witness, which is the dated Berenice inscription (AD 55/56), where a synagogue (= congregation) agrees to record the names of donors for the repair of their synagogue (= building), *cf.* G. Lüderitz, *Corpus jüdischer Zeugnisse aus der Cyrenaika* (Wiesbaden: Dr. Ludwig Reichert, 1983) no. 72, p. 155-8. Other instances which he dismisses too readily can only be listed here: Philo, *Every Good Man*, 81 (Essenes); Josephus, *BJ* 2.285-91 (rented plot; entrance; desecration of the place); 7:43-4 (brass votive offerings stored in the synagogue); *Ant.* 19.299-305; and Luke 7:15, which Kee suggests is a later anachronism.

[52]These are Herodium, Masada, Gamla and perhaps Magdala for Palestine, *cf.* Delos for the diaspora. See the articles conveniently collected in J. Gutmann (ed.), *Ancient Synagogues: The State of Research* (Brown Judaic Studies 22; Chico, California: Scholars Press, 1981); L. Levine (ed.), *Ancient Synagogues Revealed* (Jerusalem: Israel Exploration Society, 1981); L. Levine (ed.), *The Synagogue in Late Antiquity*.

[53]*Cf.* A. R. Seager, 'Ancient Synagogue Architecture: An Overview', and M. Chiat, 'First-Century Synagogue Architecture: Methodological Problems', both in Gutmann (ed.), *Ancient Synagogues*, 39-47 and 49-60; Levine, *The Second Temple Synagogue*, 11-12, 19.

[54]Fleischer, *Beginnings of Obligatory Jewish Prayer*, 408; Z. Ma'oz, 'The Synagogue of Gamla and the Typology of Second-Temple Synagogues', in Levine (ed.), *Ancient Synagogues Revealed*, 35-41 (40). Ma'oz suggests from the design of the Gamla synagogue that prayer was an organised activity in it, but this is only a conjecture.

[55]*Cf.* Levine, 'The Second Temple Synagogue', 19; N. Avigad, 'The 'Galilean' Synagogue and Its Predecessors', in Levine (ed.), *Ancient Synagogues Revealed*, 42-4 (44).

[56]On the difficulties in dating synagogues, and descriptions of features, see the articles in J. Gutmann (ed.), *The Synagogue*; and Levine (ed.), *Ancient Synagogues Revealed*.

change in attitude towards the synagogue *vis-à-vis* the now destroyed Temple.[58] Zahavy makes the valid point that the diversity in the earliest synagogue architecture and art probably reflects on the practice in synagogues at that time as well.[59]

(4) Rabbinic Evidence on Synagogues and Prayer.

Even well into the Rabbinic period, there is still no source which sets out from the beginning to give a full description of a synagogue service, and not until the 9th century is the first prayer book attested. Therefore, one must be cautious about arguments from silence. Still, the earliest Rabbis express little interest in the synagogue with regard to prayer, seem to assume that prayer was not limited to a particular *locus* such as the synagogue,[60] and primarily discuss prayer as an individual activity.[61] Of the handful of rulings on prayer attributed to pre-70 Rabbis (*i.e.* the Houses), there is not a single one which discusses prayer in a synagogue.[62] Establishing the synagogue as the place of prayer recital seems rather to be the special concern of Amoraic scholars primarily of the latter half of the 3rd century AD.[63] This is asserted by statements that a man's prayer is only heard by God when he prays in the synagogue (*b. Ber.* 6a; *tannaitic* authority); that the God of Abraham is the helper of those who establish a fixed place for their prayer (*b. Ber.* 6b); and that whoever does not pray in a syna-

---

[57]J. F. Strange, 'Archaeology and the Religion of Judaism in Palestine', *ANRW* II/19.1, 646-85 (656-8).

[58]It seems that the decoration is consciously intended to mimic the Temple, as in the triple door façades compared with the triple portals of the eastern Huldah gates in the Temple and depictions of Temple implements on mosaic floors; *cf.* Strange, 'Archaeology', 664.

[59]Tz. Zahavy, *Studies in Jewish Prayer* (Lanham: University Press of America, 1990) 49.

[60]Zahavy, *Jewish Prayer*, 49ff.

[61]Sanders, Jewish Law, 73.

[62]See the chart in J. Neusner, *The Rabbinic Traditions About the Pharisees Before 70* (Leiden: E. J. Brill, 1971) 2:344-53. The *Shema* is recited at home, grace at meals and the *Hallel* in the home, the *locus* of festival prayers is unstated. *Cf.* S. Safrai, 'Gathering in the Synagogues on Festivals, Sabbaths and Weekdays', in R. Hachlili (ed.), *Ancient Synagogues in Israel* (BAR International Series 499; Oxford: BAR, 1989) 7-15 (7).

[63]Zahavy, *Jewish Prayer*, 86. None of this material is directly related to the Mishnah's concern for the time of recital and the framework of blessings; see J. Neusner, *The Talmud of Babylonia: An American translation* (=*TBA*), *Tractate Berakhot* (Chico, California: Scholars, 1984) I,79.

gogue if one is available is called a bad neighbour (*b. Ber.* 8a). Accompanying this is an effort to link the *Amidah* and *Shema*, prayers originally from the Temple and home respectively.

(5) Conclusion

Therefore, one can only infer that prayer probably had some part of synagogue gatherings in pre-70 Jerusalem.[64] The only direct evidence concerns prayer on public fasts held in a Galilean *proseuche*, while in Jerusalem, no sources contradict the impression that public fasts focused on the Temple rather than synagogues. However, it is difficult to imagine that such use of *proseuchai* for prayer in the Diaspora did not affect Jerusalem Sabbath assemblies, particularly through the influence of pilgrims and in light of the close connections between Judaea and the Diaspora. It is probable that benedictions were recited in connection with the reading of Scripture[65] in the Synagogue as well as the Temple, on the precedent of Nehemiah 8:6, where Ezra recites a blessing and the people respond 'Amen, Amen' before the reading of the Law. Also, the presence of Torah scrolls and a Torah ark in synagogues, and the degree of reverence in which these were held, may have made it a natural place to pray.[66] Safrai argues plausibly from Rabbinic evidence that a series of seven benedictions was recited after the Torah reading on Sabbath and festival synagogue assemblies during Temple times.[67] Certain individuals and devout groups may have used synagogues throughout the week as well for their individual supplications. Many references to assemblies for prayer,[68]

---

[64]This inferential argument is made most effectively and succinctly by W. Horbury, 'Women in the Synagogue' in W.D. Davies, L. Finkelstein and J. Sturdy (eds.), *The Cambridge History of Judaism*, vol. 3 (Cambridge: University Press, forthcoming). I am gratefully indebted to him for the use of a preliminary draft, particularly in the following paragraph.

[65]*Cf.* Heinemann, *Prayer in the Talmud*, 227f.

[66]*Cf.* Josephus, *Ant.* 16.164.

[67]Safrai, 'Gathering in the Synagogues', 12. *Cf.* the prayer at the *Therapeutae* Pentecost festival (Philo, *De Vita Cont.* 64-89).

[68]*E.g.* the following listed by Horbury: 1 Ki. 8:44, 48; Je. 29:7, 12; Bar. 3:6-7; Philo, *Flacc.* 121; Josephus, *Ant.* 14.258, 260-1. The interpretation of 'pure offerings' made in every place in Mal. 1:11 as a reference to Jewish prayers, reflected in the Targum (see further K. J. Cathcart and R. P. Gordon, *The Targum of the Minor Prophets* [The Aramaic Bible 14; Edinbugh: T. & T. Clark, 1989] 231 n. 26) and Justin Martyr, *Dial.* 117, likely derives from before AD 70. For responsive forms of prayer, see *e.g.* 11QPs^a 145; 2 Mac. 1:23-4).

sometimes specifying orientation towards the Temple and at the time of the sacrifices,[69] may allow that even in Jerusalem some gathered in synagogues for communal prayer, as dictated by personal preference and circumstances. Common prayer in homes among early Christians may also lean in this direction. This must be acknowledged as inference, however. The incomplete evidence available points to the conclusion that prior to its destruction, the Temple was the place of prayer in Jerusalem, and the synagogue was primarily for the reading and study of Scripture and not for daily, public prayer services.[70]

2. *Prayer at the Temple*

Although no one will deny that people did pray in the Temple, much of the secondary literature seems to minimise the importance of the Temple in favour of the synagogue, which is viewed as the true focus of prayer activity, often under a scheme of opposition between the Temple as an exclusivist institution and the synagogue as a lay institution.[71] The evidence, however, consistently points towards the Temple as far as prayer is concerned in the Second Temple period.[72] In contrast to the synagogue, numerous sources depict the Second Temple as a focus for prayer (Is. 56:7; *cf.* Mk. 11:17//), not only the place at which people prayed (1 Ki. 8:33; Ps. 5; 3 Mac. 2:1, 10; Eccl. 50:16-21; Lk. 1:10), but also a direction to pray towards (1 Ki. 8:29-30, 35, 38, 43, 44; Ps. 5; Dn. 6:10). Further, a significant amount of prayer during the Second Temple period is performed at times related to the sacrificial service in the Temple, even when one is distant from Jerusalem (*e.g.* Dn. 9:21; Ezr. 9:5; Jdt 9:1; Acts 10:30; *cf.* Greek Life of Adam and Eve 7:2; 17:1). The indications which are available as to the use of the great collections of psalms from the period point towards liturgical recitation focused on the Temple, either by the Temple singers or by people on festival pilgrimages or offering a sacrifice.[73] The likelihood that much of the Psalter owes its present form to use and adaptation in dispersion

---

[69]See next paragraph.

[70]*Cf.* S. Reif, *Judaism and Hebrew Prayer: New Perspectives on Jewish Liturgical History* (Cambridge: University Press, 1993) 46, 72-5.

[71]*E.g.* Y. Kaufmann, *The Religion of Israel* (Hebrew; Tel-Aviv, 1976) 476, speaks of the 'holy silence' of the service and the Temple as the 'kingdom of silence'; *Cf.* E. Bickerman, *From Ezra to the Last of the Maccabees: The Historical Foundations of Post-Biblical Judaism* (New York: Schocken Books, 1962) 178.

[72]Reif, *Judaism and Hebrew Prayer*, 38-42, 46.

communities does not negate the important connection between the Temple and the Psalms.[74] Even if the *Songs of the Sabbath Sacrifice* found at Qumran and Masada were composed and used by a separatist group away from the Temple, their imagery is Temple-based and their function explicitly related to the Temple daily whole-offerings.[75]

In order to gain a perspective of the great diversity of Temple prayers, they can be categorised according to the functionaries involved, type of prayer, *locus* of prayer, occasion and time, motivation and method of recitation.[76] Such classification seems very useful, but it is not usually adopted in discussions of prayer in the Second Temple period.[77]

(1) Priestly Prayer

(a) Public priestly prayer, occasion-specific petition (for deliverance), in the Temple, at a non-regular occasion of national crisis. The recital is corporate and seemingly spontaneous: 2 Maccabees 14:34-36 (includes wording of the prayer); Judith 4:14-15 (in connection with the daily sacrifices); cf. 2 Maccabees 3:15.

(b) Daily, public priestly prayers, of general interest, at the Temple. *M. Tamid* 5:1 describes the public, liturgical recitation performed by the priests daily after the slaughter but before the incense offering of the morning Temple service (supposedly at the Chamber of Hewn Stone) as an established institution:

---

[73]Perhaps by those who had been unable to bring a sacrifice, S.J.D. Cohen, *From the Maccabees to the Mishnah, Library of Early Christianity* (Philadelphia: Westminster, 1987), 64-5. For the cultic origin and use of the canonical Psalms, *cf.* S. Mowinckel, *The Psalms in Israel's Worship*, tr. D.R. Ap-Thomas (Oxford: Blackwell, 1962).

[74]Particularly important is the influence of the Levitical singers. See E.S. Gerstenberger, *Psalms. Part 1. With an Introduction to Cultic Poetry* (The Forms of OT Literature 14; Grand Rapids: Eerdmans, 1988) 21-2, 27-8; and G. Wanke, 'Prophecy and Psalms in the Persian Period', in *The Cambridge History of Judaism* (Cambridge: Cambridge University Press, 1984) I,162-88 (184-6).

[75]C. A. Newsom, 'Sectually Explicit Literature from Qumran', in W. Propp, B. Halpern, D. N. Freedman (eds.), *The Hebrew Bible and its Interpreters* (Winona Lake, Indiana: Eisenbrauns, 1990) 179ff. now thinks they were not of sectarian authorship, but they were used at Qumran. *Cf.* C. A. Newsom, *Songs of the Sabbath Sacrifice, a Critical Edition* (Harvard Semitic Studies 27; Atlanta: Scholars Press, 1985).

[76]See Heinemann, *Prayer in the Talmud*, 123-55 for examination of the talmudic witnesses to Temple prayer.

[77]See J. Maier, 'Kult und Liturgie der Qumrangemeinde', *RevQ* 14 (1990) 543-86, for a preliminary classification of Qumran prayers.

> The officer said to them, 'Recite a Benediction!' They recited a Benediction, and recited the Ten Commandments, the Shema' [Dt. 6:4-9], the 'And it will come to pass if you will obey' [Dt. 11:13-21], and the 'And the Lord spoke to Moses' [Nu. 15:37-41]. They pronounced three Benedictions with the people: 'True and sure', and '[Temple] Service', and the Priestly Blessing; and on the Sabbath they pronounced a further Benediction for the outgoing Course of priests.

Although it cannot be confirmed from Second Temple sources that the Decalogue and the *Shema* were actually recited by priests in the Temple, it is plausible in the light of corroborating evidence for the combination of the Decalogue with the *Shema* for liturgical purposes in the Nash papyrus, a couple of liturgical compilations from Qumran (so-called 4QDeut^{j,n}),[78] 1QS 10, and numerous *tefillin* at Qumran.[79]

The three specified benedictions seem to relate to the first one after the *Shema* in the prayerbook and two of the Eighteen Benedictions,[80] but the original formulation of this passage is disputed,[81] along with the identity of the unspecified benediction.[82] A number of scholars insist that benedictions were not even joined to the recital of the *Shema* during Temple times, but some suggestive pieces of evidence may indicate that they were. Josephus' allusion to the *Shema* as thanksgiving (*Ant.* 4.212) seems inappropriate unless the *Shema* was accompanied with benedictions, since the *Shema* passages are neither thanksgiving nor prayer by themselves but recital of a confession. Further, Josephus referred to this daily prayer as acknowledging 'before God the bounties which He has bestowed on them through their deliverance from the land of Egypt', which is the theme of the benediction immediately following the *Shema* in the Rabbinic liturgy, and it is this same benediction which *m. Tamid* 5:1 states the priests in the Temple recited with the *Shema*.[83] The fact, then, that Josephus

---

[78]See M. Weinfeld, 'Grace After Meals in Qumran', *JBL* 111 (1992) 427-40.

[79]*Cf.* G. Vermes, 'Pre-Mishnaic Jewish Worship and the Phylacteries from the Dead Sea', *VT* 9 (1959) 65-72; Y. Yadin, *Tefillin from Qumran* (Jerusalem, 1969); Schürer, *History*, II,479-81; R. S. Fagen, 'Phylacteries', *ABD*, V,368-71.

[80]A. Idelsohn, *Jewish Liturgy and its Development* (New York: Henry Holt, 1932) 22.

[81]Fleischer, *Beginnings of Obligatory Jewish Prayer*, 420.

[82]*B. Ber.* 11b; *y. Ber.* 1.8 (ET 1.4), 3c, ll. 26-41.

[83]*Cf.* R. Hammer, 'What Did They Bless? A study of Mishnah Tamid 5.1', *JQR* 81 (1991) 305-323; R. Kimelman, 'The Shema and its Blessings: The Realization of God's Kingship', in Levine (ed.), *The Synagogue in Late Antiquity*, 74; also W. Horbury, 'Ezekiel Tragicus 106: δωρήματα', *VT* 36 (1986) 41, who reasons that Josephus refers to an early form of the *Ge'ullah* benediction by the phrase 'they are to acknowledge to God the gifts bestowed upon them'.

combines them and attributes them to Mosaic injunction suggests that by this time it was an established custom to accompany the recital of the *Shema* with other prayers or benedictions. This is further supported by column ten of the Community Rule (1QS) where reference to the recital of the *Shema* and Decalogue[84] is immediately preceded by a benediction concerning the luminaries and the themes of blessing and singing praise to God among the Holy Ones, which are in common with the first benediction preceding the *Shema* in the Rabbinic liturgy (*Yoṣer*).[85]

It is not possible to determine the nature of the recitation mentioned in *m. Tamid* 5:1, but it is possible that the priests here recited in the Temple what most others would have recited at home, or with those who assembled that early at the Temple. This is earlier than and separate from the prayers of the people in connection with the offering of the incense itself.

Philo, *Spec. Leg.* 1:167 does not give details other than to indicate that prayers and thanksgivings are regularly offered by priests (εὐξόμενοι ἢ εὐχαριστήσοντες) near the altar; *cf. m. Tamid* 7:2.

(c) Public, liturgical prayer performed individually by the High Priest on the Day of Atonement. *M. Yoma* 7:1 describes an elaborate ceremony of reading Scripture and the recital of eight benedictions by the High Priest in the Temple on the Day of Atonement as a regular institution.[86] Three of the benedictions share the same topic as in the *Amidah*: for the Temple service, thanksgiving, forgiveness. Perhaps here also should be placed Philo, *Spec. Leg.* 3.131. Although Philo claims that the High Priest offers prayers and sacrifices daily (εὐχὰς δὲ καὶ θυσίας τελῶν καθ' ἑκάστην ἡμέραν) on behalf of the nation, Zeitlin notes that this could not actually have been daily since the High Priest seldom performed sacrifices other than on festivals and the Day of Atonement.[87]

---

[84]'With the arrival of day and night, I will enter into the covenant of God; And with the going forth of evening and morning, I will recite his laws... . As soon as I stretch out my hand or my foot, I will bless His name. As soon as (I) go out or come in, to sit down or rise up, and while I recline on my couch, I will cry out to Him.'

[85]M. Weinfeld, 'Traces of Kedushat Yotzer and Pesukey De-Zimra in the Qumran Literature and in Ben-Sira' (Hebrew), *Tarbiz* 45 (1976) 15-26; and 'Grace After Meals', also finds reflections of the *Yotzer* benediction in Eccl. and 11QPs[a], but these rest on scant linguistic parallels.

[86]*Cf. m. Sotah* 7:7; *t. Yom.* 3.18. Heinemann, *Prayer in the Talmud*, 127ff. thinks that this is a very ancient series of benedictions, along with the similar benedictions for recital after the *haftarah* reading, *Soferim* 13:10.

(d) Private prayer of the High Priest on emerging from the Holy of Holies on the Day of Atonement (*m. Yoma* 5:1).

(2) Temple singers

All of these prayers are corporate, public, statutory liturgies performed by professionals with particular wording of general interest.

(a) Regular daily hymns and psalms of praise and thanksgiving in the Temple at the time of the drink offering accompanied by music (Eccl. 50:16-19; *m. Tamid* 7:3; *cf.* 1 Ch. 15-16, 25; Eccl. 47:9; Ps. 100 = thank offering?).

(b) Regular hymns and psalms at festivals during the time of the sacrifice, accompanied by music (1 Mac. 4:52-59; 2 Mac. 1:18, 23-30; Eccl. 47:10; *m. Sukk.* 5:4). The *Hallel* was probably chanted responsorily with the congregation at festivals while sacrifices were being offered.[88]

(c) General corporate petition led by the Temple liturgists at festivals, involving all the people in some type of participatory recital. 2 Mac. 1:23-29[89] specifies an entire model (τὸν τρόπον ἔχουσα τοῦτον) of a general petitionary prayer recited responsively by all the people during the time of sacrifice, led by one of the Temple liturgists.[90] The prayer itself includes numerous themes in common with the *Amidah*, particularly the first two benedictions,[91] but also the seventh, ninth, tenth, eleventh and seventeenth. It must be acknowledged that these themes are biblical, but the grouping together of them in a way unprecedented in the biblical prayers suggests the existing practice of series of benedictions similar to the *Amidah*.[92] Followed by hymns by the Temple singers, it purports to have been used at the dedication of the

---

[87]Zeitlin, 'Tefillah', 220.
[88]Heinemann, *Prayer in the Talmud*, 125.
[89]Even if this passage is not Judaean in origin, it is important as showing what could be envisaged as a plausible representation of what took place in the temple.
[90]*Cf.* J. A. Goldstein, *II Maccabees* (The Anchor Bible 41A; Garden City: Doubleday, 1983) 177-8, for a discussion of the participants.
[91]Goldstein, *II Maccabees*, 178.
[92]*Cf.* Heinemann *Prayer in the Talmud*, 37-69; and E. Bickerman, 'The Civic Prayer for Jerusalem', *HTR* 55 (1962) 163-85.

Temple under Nehemiah, but functions as a model for the institutionalised (*cf.* 1:18) celebration of *Hanukkah*.

Baruch 1:10-3:8 specifies two prayers to be recited in the Temple at feasts and appointed seasons, seemingly at the time of the sacrifices (*cf.* 1:10): a civic prayer for the well-being of the ruler (Nebuchadnezzar) and a communal confession. This is a statutory, institutionalised, corporate and liturgical recitation with particular wording, but a text is provided only for the latter prayer. The details which are provided resemble most closely the type of prayer in 2 Mac. 1:23-29, particularly if Bickerman is correct that the *Amidah* developed from an ancient civic prayer for the well-being of the city.[93]

Heinemann thinks that the series of benedictions for the New Year (*m. Rosh. Hash.* 4:5) must have originated in the Temple, and argues that various supplicatory litanies (*e.g.* the *Hoshanoth* and *Selichoth*) originated in religious processions in the Temple on festival and fast days which involved the responsorial participation of the people.[94]

(d) General hymns and psalms of praise and thanksgiving (from the Davidic Psalter; *cf.* 1 Esd. 5:60) accompanied by music at non-regular cultic events such as Temple/altar dedications (2 Ch. 5:12-14; 29:20-30; Ezr. 3:10-13; 1 Esd. 5:59-65; 1 Mac. 4:52-58; 2 Mac. 1:23-30). Ezra 3:11 indicates the responsive refrain 'for he is good, for his steadfast love endures for ever towards Israel', suggesting the responsive participation of the people.

(3) Lay prayer.

(a) Lay representative occasion-specific prayer. Solomon's petition (1 Ki. 8:23-53) for God to answer prayer was performed in the Temple in front of the altar during the time of sacrifice in connection with a non-regular cultic occasion (dedication of the Temple), probably as a non-statutory institution in a public liturgical setting by an individual representative.

(b) Private, individual lay prayer in the Temple. This is occasion-specific petition concerning individual matters (Ps. 141; Eccl. 51:13-14; Lk. 18:9-13; *cf.* Hannah's prayer at the Shiloh 'Temple': 1 Sa. 1:9-13) or concerning community or national crises (1 Ki. 8:31-32, 37-40; 8:41-43).

---

[93]Bickerman, 'The Civic Prayer'.

[94]Heinemann, *Prayer in the Talmud*, 128, 139-55.

(c) Public, corporate, lay, occasion-specific petition for forgiveness and deliverance, at or towards the Temple, in times of communal or national disaster, repentance or battle (1 Ki. 8:33-40, 44-53; Jdt. 4:8-15). In both cases, it seems that one should imagine this prayer as spontaneously motivated and as free, but it is also possible that Solomon's prayer points to the post-exilic ideal of regular, institutionalised, communal prayers of repentance with customary wordings.

(d) Public, lay, non-occasion-specific prayer in connection with the Temple service as a customary institution. Few hints are given as to the content and nature of the prayers. Sometimes the texts suggest praise, other times petition, and sometimes both as separate components, one accompanied with prostration. It is also difficult to determine whether the prayers were performed corporately or individually, and as a liturgical or free recital. Such prayer does occur within a liturgical complex in connection with the sacrificial service and the singing of the Temple singers on both regular and non-regular occasions.

(i) Daily. Ecclesiasticus 50:16-21 (*cf. m. Tamid* 7:3-4)[95] indicates that at the time of the libation after the sacrifice when the priests shout and blast on the trumpets, the people prostrate themselves and worship (להשתחוות, προσκυνῆσαι), and they pray while the singers praise God.[96] Josephus, *Contra Apionem* 2.193-98 describes a general civic prayer for the peace of the community as well as personal petitions (*cf.* 1 Mac. 12:11), and Luke 1:10 indicates the time of incense as a time when the people gather at the Temple to pray.

(ii) Festivals. Both *Hanukkah* (1 Mac. 4:59) and Booths (*m. Sukk.* 5:4) are specifically attested. The latter passage describes the songs and praises of pious men facing the Temple during the lighting of the

---

[95]Despite slight differences, there is no question that *m. Tamid* 7:3-4 is essentially accurate and in agreement with the description in Eccl. 50. *Cf.* F. Fearghail, 'Sir. 50,5-21: Yom Kippur or the Daily Whole-offering?', *Biblica* 59 (1978) 301-31; and A. Di Lella in P. W. Skehan, *The Wisdom of Ben Sira* (The Anchor Bible; New York: Doubleday, 1987) 551.

[96]For various interpretations of the nature of this prayer, *cf.* K. Kohler, 'The Origin and Composition of the Eighteen Benedictions', repr. in J. J. Petuchowski (ed.), *Contributions to the Scientific Study of Jewish Liturgy* (New York: KTAV, 1970) 52-90; Idelsohn, *Jewish Liturgy*, 110; M. R. Lehmann, 'A Re-interpretation of 4Q Dibre Ham-me'oroth', *RevQ* 5 (1964) 106; E. Bickerman, *The Jews in the Greek Age* (Cambridge, MA: Harvard University Press, 1990) 136-7, 280. Also *cf.* the Hebrew Cairo Geniza text and the Greek text.

golden candlesticks at the festival of Booths. This was part of a corporate liturgy involving Temple singers.

(iii) Temple dedication as a non-regular occasion: 2 Chronicles 29:28-30; Ezra 3:10-13; 1 Esdras 5:59-65; 1 Maccabees 4:52-58. The people worship at the same time as the sacrifices are being offered, but it is not certain whether these are conducted prayers as a corporate recital, or individual prayers of a crowd.

(e) Regular, daily, lay public prayer in the Temple, not in specific connection with the sacrificial service but rather in relation to the course of the sun, since it is to be offered morning, noon and evening. 2 Enoch 51:4 indicates a prayer of general praise to God as creator, but there is no indication whether there was particular wording, nor whether it was performed corporately or individually or as a liturgical or a free recital. It is endorsed as a good practice. Daniel's thrice daily prayer in the direction of the Temple reflects the same, perhaps pious minority custom. Perhaps it is a way of indicating an ideal of constant prayer in the Temple (*cf.* Lk. 2:37).

It is not accurate to speak of any of these types of Temple prayer as obligatory, if by that is meant a written statute demanding compliance at the threat of punishment. However, it is possible to speak of prayer patterns which have become institutionalised either by custom or by official endorsement. The liturgical singing of the Temple singers is the latter, while the lay prayers at the time of the sacrifice are the former. Custom often has the binding force of statute. That the prayers of the people are an established institution is attested by the importance of their mention when describing the Temple ritual (*e.g.* Eccl. 50, *m. Tamid* 5:1). The evidence as evaluated here suggests that public prayer was a significant factor in the Second Temple, despite those who have minimised it.[97] Further, it seems probable in the light of this that the influence flowed from the Temple to the synagogue rather than *vice versa*, at least within Palestine. It certainly seems plausible that prayer developed more rapidly in the Diaspora, particularly given the use of the term *proseuche* for a place of assembly, as well as Galilee, but even here the lack of evidence is surprising, and there is nothing approaching the emphasis one finds on prayer as a central institution in the Temple. The wide range of prayer attested in relation to the Temple in a great number of sources makes the expression 'house of prayer' for it a fitting description.

---

[97] *E.g.* Bickerman, *Jews in the Greek Age*, 136-9, 241-2, 279-81.

3. *Prayer at Home*

Prayer in the home is not as debatable an issue as prayer in the Temple and synagogue, and the data are scarce, so it cannot command detailed attention here. Grace at meals must certainly be considered one of the most important features of prayer at home, particularly for its impact on Christian daily practice as well as the Lord's Supper.[98] The *Shema* was recited on rising and retiring as a widespread custom. The Sabbath welcome and closing ceremonies *Kiddush* and *Havdalah* were originally performed at home. In the light of debate concerning them by the Houses of Shammai and Hillel, these probably had a pre-Christian origin.[99] Liturgical prayers and the *Hallel* on festivals would have been a common feature, as would numerous free and spontaneous prayers concerning private issues.

4. *Times of prayer*

The investigation of Jewish and Christian times of prayer in the 1st century is hindered by conflicting patterns of prayer in the sources: a twice daily recital morning and evening, thrice daily morning, noon and evening; and thrice daily morning, afternoon and evening. When one adds to this the more complex patterns of Christian prayer in the second, third and fourth centuries where the third, sixth and ninth hours are standard in addition to morning, evening and midnight, there is great confusion. Many scholars assume that the synagogue system described in Rabbinic literature, which included recitation of the *Shema* and *Amidah* in the morning, the *Amidah* in the afternoon, and both again in the evening, was already in operation throughout the 1st century. Dugmore in some ways pioneered the modern search for the origins to the Christian hours of prayer in Judaism.[100] He argued that the Rabbinic cycle of prayer was a conflation of two earlier patterns of daily prayer: *Shema* at sunrise and sunset, and then *Amidah* morning and evening at the times of sacrifice (after the time for the evening sacrifice was changed from twilight to the ninth hour). The pattern of the 3rd, 6th and 9th hours was not a Jewish pattern. Christianity continued the pattern of sunrise and sunset prayer from Judaism, but

[98]Oesterley, *Jewish Background*, 91-5; Jeremias, *Eucharistic Words*, 109. *Cf.* Schürer, *History* II,482 n. 99.
[99]Oesterley, *Jewish Background*, 79ff.
[100]Dugmore, *Influence*, 59-70; *cf.* Bradshaw, *Search for the Origins*, 185.

then added the 3rd, 6th and 9th hours because these were hours which were called out publicly in the Roman world. To this fivefold pattern were later added midnight, cock-crow, prime and compline.

Beckwith and Bradshaw both rightly criticise Dugmore's assumption of a daily cycle of public prayer in the synagogue, but both of them also miss the importance of the Temple as a place for daily public prayer.[101] Beckwith suggests on the authority of Daniel 6:10 and Psalm 55:17 that there was an ancient pattern of daily, individual prayer morning, noon and evening, in relation to the course of the sun. The daily Temple sacrifices took place in the morning at the fourth hour and in the evening at sunset. On Sabbaths, an additional sacrifice was offered. Consequently, the public synagogue services, which were held only weekly on Sabbaths, reflected a conflation of the individual daily prayer times and the Temple sacrifices with four services: morning, additional prayer (no set time), noon and evening. The noon hour became redundant when the morning prayer was linked with the morning sacrifice (fourth hour) and by the 1st century was dropped. At the same time, however, the evening sacrifice was moved to the mid-afternoon. The evening hour still survived because of recital of the *Shema*. Since these developments also affected daily individual prayer, in the 1st century weekly public synagogue services were morning, additional, afternoon and evening, and each day individuals privately recited the *Shema* morning and evening and the *Amidah* morning, afternoon and evening.

This reconstruction is attractive for the problems it seems to explain,[102] but it has problems of its own. For prayer at the fourth hour, he relies on the statement of *m.'Eduyyot* 6:1 that the morning daily whole-offering was offered at the fourth hour, when in fact the morning prayer would have accompanied the incense offering some time earlier in the morning activities which began at dawn (*cf. m. Tamid*). Also against this theory is that Christians didn't pick up the Additional service. Most significantly for the purposes of this study, however, is the problem of how this routine could have been

---

[101]Note that Bradshaw, *Search for the Origins*, 15, deliberately omits consideration of the Temple!

[102]His view in many ways is an attempt to deal with the fundamental problem of the theory of an original pattern of thrice daily prayer morning, ninth hour and sunset, which is that the only early sources which refer to thrice-daily prayer mention morning, noon and evening. For this theory, see O. Holtzmann, 'Die täglichen Gebetsstunden im Judentum und Urchristentum', *ZNW* 12 (1911) 90-107; Schürer, *History* II,303 n. 40.

employed in Jerusalem while the Temple still stood. Who was at the Temple on the Sabbath if there were four services that day in the synagogue at the time of the sacrifices?

Bradshaw proposed that the earliest Christians inherited a cycle of Jewish daily prayer morning, noon and evening, plus midnight, dating at least from the mid-1st century BC.[103] It was originally influenced by the movements of the sun, later to be linked with Temple sacrifices. He later modified his view on the basis of the work of his doctoral student L.E. Phillips (1989), who agrees that the earliest pattern of Christian daily prayer was morning, noon, evening and night, but argues that in some places this was based on the course of the sun, while in others, on the Temple service and/or the passion of Christ, giving the four times of prayer at the third, sixth, and ninth hours plus night.[104] The latter is that attested in the Apostolic Tradition and in Alexandria. A conflation of the two patterns led to the five hours of 3rd-century Africa.

This theory may work with later Christian evidence, but it lacks evidence from Jewish sources. 1QS 10:1-3a and 1QH 12:4-7 do not attest four times of prayer as Bradshaw supposes, but only two. Apart from these passages, he admits he has no evidence for the midnight prayer, but finds the pattern of morning, noon and evening attested in Daniel 6:10;[105] Psalm 55:17; 2 Enoch 51:4; Epiphanius, *Adv. Haer.* 29:9; and his reconstructed pattern of Christian prayer. Concerning Daniel, he asserts that this must have been a widely held practice, otherwise why would it have been mentioned?[106] This is poor logic, since the point of the passage is to stress Daniel's exceptional piety. Psalm 55, as Bradshaw admits, may be a poetic way of indicating continual prayer. Although a pre-70 Alexandrian date and provenance have been asserted by some for 2 Enoch, both issues have been widely debated and there is no confidence that these identifications are reliable.[107] Therefore, the fact that it contains a unique reference to prayer in the Temple morning, noon and evening carries little weight without

---

[103]Bradshaw, *Daily Prayer*, 1-11.

[104]Bradshaw, *Search for the Origins*, 190ff.; *cf.* P.T. O'Brien, 'Prayer in Luke-Acts', *TynBul* 24 (1973) 122, who argues that the early Christians added noon and midnight to the regular Jewish hours of prayer.

[105]Although Dn. 6:10 does not specify any time element, the fact that 9:21 indicates sacrifice in the evening (כעת מנחת ערב) makes clear that the middle prayer time cannot have been at the ninth hour.

[106]Bradshaw, *Search For the Origins*, 8.

[107]*Cf.* Andersen, '2 Enoch', in J. H. Charlesworth (ed.), *The Old Testament Pseudepigrapha* (=OTP; Garden City: Doubleday, 1983-5) I,94-7.

further corroboration. It is unlikely that noon was a widely practised time of assembly for prayer in Temple times. Epiphanius is likewise not a reliable witness, as Bradshaw confesses: middle of the day could loosely refer to 3 p.m. Although he is able to marshall a convincing argument for Christian prayer morning, noon, evening and midnight, this cannot be demonstrated for the 1st century, and this cannot be traced back to Second Temple Judaism.

By far the majority of sources on times of prayer for the Second Temple period witness either just morning prayer or twice-daily prayer, morning and evening, in relation to the course of the sun.[108] Of those sources which represent twice-daily prayer, morning and evening, those which are specific indicate that this is private, individual, lay recital of the *Shema* at home on rising and retiring.[109] Both *Epistle of Aristeas* 158-60 and Josephus, *Ant.* 4.212-3 discuss this in the context of *tefillin* and *mezuzot* as a Mosaic ordinance which should be followed by all. This recital included the Decalogue along with a small collection of passages including Deuteronomy 6:4ff. and probably some blessings, both at Qumran and elsewhere.[110] Apart from indications of the *Shema*, prayer at sunrise and sunset is attested both at Qumran (1QS 10:1-3; 1QH 12:4-7; 1QM 14:12-14) and among the *Therapeutae* (Philo, *De Vita Cont.* 27-28). One other text from Qumran (4Q503), of uncertain provenance (no sectarian indications), provides prayers to be recited at sunrise and sunset.

More passages testify to private, individual prayer in the morning, particularly on waking: Psalm 57:8-9; 88:13; Psalms of Solomon 3:1f.; 6:4f.; Sibylline Oracles 3:591-3 (while still in bed); *Testament of Joseph* 3:6; *Epistle of Aristeas* 305-6 (first hour); Wisdom 16:28. The latter passage places emphasis on this as a practice which should be followed by all: 'in order to make it known that one ought (δεῖ) to rise before the sun to give you thanks, and to petition you at the dawning of the light.' Ecclesiasticus 39:5 describes individual private confession of sin early in the morning as a regular practice of the scribe. Prayer before sunrise is also a practice of the Essenes according to Josephus, *BJ* 2.128, but here it is distinctly a communal gathering. The Qumran text *Dibre Hame'orot* (4Q504-6), of uncertain provenance, also

---

[108]Ps. 119, which claims a practice of prayer seven times a day (v. 164), including midnight (v. 62) and before dawn (v. 147), is probably to be taken as an expression of continual prayer rather than a common pattern.

[109]Besides the other sources mentioned in this section, Mt. 23:5 and Mk. 12:28-34 may also attest to regular recital of the *Shema*.

[110]See above, p. 287.

provides a series of communal petitions for weekday mornings.[111] Two main types of patterns arise out of this: private prayer before sunrise, or at least early morning, and communal morning prayers. It is very likely that the first group, particularly those which stress prayer on rising, reflect recital of the *Shema*, probably accompanied with the Decalogue and blessings or other prayers. The second category may reflect the particular practice of isolated groups. Sanders comments that 'it is noteworthy that the discussions in the Mishnah and Tosefta of saying the *Shema* and praying for the most part presuppose that these are individual activities.'[112]

Besides prayers regulated according to the course of the sun, morning and evening, several sources indicate prayers regulated by the Temple service. The time of the evening sacrifice changed some time during the hellenistic period from twilight to mid-afternoon.[113] Thus Ezra 9:5; Daniel 9:21; Psalm 141:2 and Judith 9:1 indicate prayer at the time of the evening sacrifice, while Acts 3:1 and 10:30 indicate prayer at the ninth hour, the time of the afternoon sacrifice according to the later practice. Ecclesiasticus 50:16-21; Luke 1:10; and Josephus, *C. Ap.* 2.193-98 attest prayer at the time of the incense offering generally, but this could be morning or afternoon, since incense was offered twice daily: before the morning sacrifice and after the evening (afternoon) sacrifice, so that the incense offerings framed the daily Temple service. Psalm 5:3, 7 and Luke 21:38 probably assume prayer in the Temple at the time of the morning sacrifice.[114]

In the end, Dugmore's confident assertion that in 1st-century Judaism 'daily attendance at the public worship of the community would be the practice of every devout Jew' is not as far off the mark as Bradshaw imagines,[115] even if it requires significant revision. This

---

[111]E. Chazon, *A Liturgical Document from Qumran and its Implications: 'Words of the Luminaries' (4QDibHam)* (unpublished PhD Thesis; Hebrew University, 1991) 57, thinks that the title *Dibre Hame'orot* (Words of the Luminaries) relates to the liturgical function of the prayers. She conjectures that it might refer to recital at the transition of luminaries in morning and evening. However, only one prayer for each weekday is provided, and unless they recited the same prayer both morning and evening, I think it more likely that they were just morning prayers.

[112]E. P. Sanders, *Jewish Law*, 73.

[113]*Cf.* Josephus, *Ant.* 14.65; *m. Pesah* 5:1. The change may have been due to a re-interpretation of the phrase 'between the evenings', as attested in Jub. 49:1, 10-12; *cf.* R. H. Charles, *The Apocrypha and Pseudepigrapha of the Old Testament in English* (Oxford: Clarendon, 1913) II,80; Schürer, *History*, II,300-303.

[114]*Cf. m. Tamid* 5:1 and 7:3-4.

[115]Bradshaw, *Search for the Origins*, 24.

daily, public prayer would pertain to Jerusalem alone rather than every large town as Dugmore envisioned, and to the Temple rather than the synagogue. Further, although a crowd gathered every day establishing a pattern, it is doubtful whether 'every devout Jew' attended every day. Outside Jerusalem, the evidence is difficult to assess and far outside the scope of this study, but as suggested earlier, one may infer that some individual and group prayer took place in Galilean and Diaspora synagogues even during the week.

IV. Acts and the Jewish Heritage of Pre-70 Christian Worship

I have attempted to describe the evidence for the prayer practices of Jerusalem Christians derived from the Book of Acts, as well as that which may be gathered from other sources concerning the probable practices of Jerusalem Jews. How do the two compare? They are in substantial agreement in the following elements: (1) the Temple and the home are regarded as places of prayer; (2) the Temple is a particular focus for public prayer; (3) prayer at the time of the sacrifice is a common pattern; (4) there is silence concerning the synagogue as a place of regular, public prayer; (5) the style of prayer is similar. In other words, the framework of Christian prayer as portrayed by Luke in terms of locations, times, and content is Jewish, and authentic to the pre-70 period. Luke's silence concerning the *Shema* and prayer in relation to the course of the sun is not determinative in light of his selectivity. On the other hand, the Christian prayer in homes which he describes is communal, and expresses the distinctive identity of the Christian community. It is reasonable to conclude that the early Christians in Jerusalem substantially retained their heritage of Jewish prayer, and the distinctively Christian elements were primarily additions.[116] Therefore, where it corresponds to other sources, Acts may be used as corroborative evidence for Jewish prayer practice at the end of the Second Temple period.

Returning to the four questions raised in the introduction above, we may evaluate the results of this investigation. First, although there

[116]Some scholars wrongly downplay the influence of Temple and synagogue worship on early Christianity, with apparent apologetic intent, as *e.g.* D.G. Delling, *Worship in the New Testament*, tr. Percy Scott (London: Darton, Longman and Todd, 1962) and F. Hahn, *The Worship of the Early Church*, tr. D.E. Green, ed. with intro. J. Reumann (Philadelphia: Fortress, 1973).

are good reasons to infer some public prayer in synagogues on fast days and Sabbath assemblies, and perhaps some individual and group prayer on weekdays, this study has thrown doubt on the existence of a prominent cycle of daily public prayer services in Palestinian synagogues while the Temple stood, especially in Jerusalem. On the other hand, assembly at the Temple for prayer at the time of the daily sacrifice was prominent enough that when one described what happened at the Temple service, this gathering of the people was an important element. It is probably this factor which enabled the Christian community to maintain a distinctive presence: they habitually assembled for prayer at one or possibly both of the times of sacrifice. At least in Jerusalem, then, the early patterns of prayer among Jewish Christians owed more to the Temple and home than to the synagogue.[117] Thus they did have a pattern for daily public prayer (contra Bradshaw), but primarily in the Temple, rather than the synagogue (contra Dugmore).

Second, we may also conclude that Christianity did not inherit from 1st-century Judaism a single threefold pattern of prayer morning, noon and night, nor a fourfold pattern including midnight. Rather, the Jewish heritage behind Christian prayer had two distinct patterns: one related to the course of the sun, and the other according to the times of the Temple sacrifice.[118] However, there was no central regulation of prayer at this time, and we probably have to reckon with local and personal variations in actual practices, although of course, the outspoken pious would encourage a maximal approach.[119] That this was the case is suggested by the effort of Yavnean Rabbis to delimit appropriate times for prayer, but even then they allowed considerable variation. The same pertains to where people prayed, as again indicated by the even later Rabbinic effort to centralise prayer in the synagogue.

Morning and evening, or more specifically, daybreak and sunset, are natural times for any people to pray, but among Jews it was primarily linked with the command to declare God's unity upon rising and retiring, and seems to have been widely practised at home. Recital of the *Shema* was central to this time of prayer, probably accompanied

---

[117]*Cf.* Zeitlin, 'Tefillah', 237. Oesterley, *Jewish Background*, 96, seems to recognise to some degree that in Jerusalem the Temple was more important for Christian worship, and the synagogue elsewhere, but he still assumes a regular, public synagogue liturgy with the *Amidah* recited thrice daily.

[118]Does Ezk. 8:16 reflect a conflict between the two patterns?

[119]*Cf.* Reif, *Judaism and Hebrew Prayer*, 66; Gerstenberger, *Psalms*, 21-2.

with the Decalogue and a blessing concerning the creation of light, and perhaps other personal prayer.

It also seemed appropriate to many to pray at the time of the sacrifice, at the Temple or towards it from the home or synagogue, either in public or in private. Here, petition seemed particularly appropriate (*cf.* 1 Ki. 8), especially for the well-being of the community, along with praise, and it is plausible that the *Amidah* may have developed from this type of Temple prayer. It is possible, as Zahavy has tried to demonstrate, that the two types of prayer were promoted by competing groups: the *Amidah* by the priests and the *Shema* by the scribes.[120] 3rd-century Rabbis encouraged the joining of these to produce a single pattern of thrice-daily prayer morning, afternoon and evening. This is seen in R. Yohanan's approval of the ancient pious group known as the *watikin*,[121] who made a practice of finishing their recital of the *Shema* with sunrise so that they could follow the final benediction of the *Shema* immediately with the *Amidah* shortly after dawn (*b. Ber.* 9b). This passage assumes a system of two separate traditions of prayer as has been argued here: prayer at home at sunrise (and sunset), and early morning (and afternoon/evening) prayer in connection with the Temple service.

Third, although we cannot determine the degree to which the earliest Christians innovated with these patterns of Jewish prayer, it seems that for the most part they remained faithful to Jewish prayer practices. Luke notes something special about the Christians' observance of prayer when he refers to their devotion to αἱ προσευχαί, but the prayers are probably the Jewish prayer times rather than exclusively Christian prayers. In this light, it is probable, but by no means certain, that the early Jerusalem Christians recited the *Shema* at home privately, as well as petitions with other Jews in the Temple. Resemblances to the *Amidah* which appear in some of the church orders of the 3rd and 4th centuries (*e.g.* the seventh book of the Apostolic Constitutions) are not likely due to this, but to later borrowing from the synagogue.

Fourth, although it seems probable that Christians did adopt later developments in Jewish prayer, there is no indication that Luke's portrayal of prayer practices is influenced by post-70 Jewish liturgical reform, such as the growing importance of the synagogue as a place of prayer, the unified thrice-daily pattern of prayer, or the Rabbinic

---

[120]Zahavy, *Jewish Prayer*.

[121]These are often considered as a group from Hasmonaean times, and some identify them with the Essenes.

standard form of prayer. The one possibly late feature is the mention of the third and sixth hours, which Luke may have understood as regular times of prayer. However, if so, this was a Christian rather than a Jewish development, based on the publicly sounded hours.[122, 123]

[122]Dugmore, *Influence*, 66-67; R. Taft, *The Liturgy of the Hours in East and West* (Collegeville, 1986) 19. That stages in Jesus' death were marked by the public hours also seems to have given special significance to the third, sixth and ninth hours among Christians. Note that even after the other hours had become established as regular times for Christian prayer, morning and evening prayer still maintained their priority. *Cf.* Tertullian, Chrysostom, Cassian; *cf.* Taft, *Liturgy of the Hours*, 18.

[123]Special thanks to Dr. William Horbury, Andrew Clark and Philip Kern, who graciously read and commented on this article. Thanks also to those who listened to this paper read at the University of Cambridge Divinity Faculty New Testament Seminar, 25th October 1994, and offered stimulating discussion.

CHAPTER 10

THE CENACLE—TOPOGRAPHICAL SETTING FOR ACTS 2:44-45

Jerome Murphy-O'Connor, OP

Summary

Textual and archaeological data suggest the existence of a Christian building on Mount Zion in the 2nd century. The difficulty of access and the proximity of suspicious Roman sentries preclude invention of a Christian holy place at that period. The tradition of veneration must go back to the 1st century when highly idealistic Christians shared a common life in the home of a wealthy believer in the most affluent quarter of Jerusalem.

It is not really surprising that there has been no serious discussion of the authenticity of the Cenacle, a rather dilapidated building outside the south wall of the Old City of Jerusalem, where the Upper Room of Pentecost and the Last Supper rises above the Tomb of David.

According to the Old Testament, David was buried in the City of David (1 Ki. 2:10), which is identified with the city of the Jebusites on the Ophel Ridge (2 Sa. 5:6-9). The two great shafts running horizontally into the bed rock, which were discovered by Raymond Weill in 1913-14,[1] were immediately identified as the royal tombs, an identification which has been accepted by some[2] but rejected by others.[3] Throughout the whole Byzantine period the tomb of David was located in Bethlehem.[4] 4th and 5th-century lectionaries reveal that in those centuries a memorial service for David and James the brother of the Lord, founders of the old and new Jerusalem respectively, was celebrated in the Church of Mount Zion on December 25 (subsequently December 26). The liturgical memorial eventually gave rise to physical memorials, namely tombs, that of James in the Armenian cathedral and David beneath the Cenacle.[5]

If the foundations are so insecure, what chance of authenticity can the Upper Room have? Its features are so specifically Lusignan gothic that it can only have been constructed by craftsmen from Cyprus recruited by the Franciscans, when they returned as Guardians of the Holy Land in 1335. A papal bull of Clement VI dated 21 November 1342 notes the construction on this site of a monastery for twelve religious.[6]

Nothing visible, therefore, has the slightest claim to authenticity. Does this mean that the site is totally devoid of interest? I think not. On the contrary, it throws new light on the circumstances of the first Christian community in Jerusalem. After discussing the archaeological and textual evidence for the existence of a 2nd-century Christian

---

[1] *La Cité de David. Compte rendu des fouilles exécutées à Jérusalem sur le site de la ville primitive. Campagne de 1913-1914* (Paris: Geuthner, 1920).

[2] L.-H. Vincent, 'La Cité de David d'après les fouilles de 1913-1914', *RB* 30 (1921) 419; B. Mazar, *The Mountain of the Lord* (Garden City: Doubleday, 1975) 183-85.

[3] K. Kenyon, *Jerusalem. Excavating 3000 Years of History* (New York: McGraw-Hill, 1967) 188; D. Ussishkin, *The Village of Silwan. The Necropolis from the Period of the Judean Kingdom* (Jerusalem: Israel Exploration Society and Yad Izhak Ben-Zwi, 1993) 299.

[4] J. Wilkinson, *Jerusalem Pilgrims before the Crusades* (Jerusalem: Ariel, 1977) 151.

[5] O. Limor, 'The Origins of a Tradition. King David's Tomb on Mount Sion', *Traditio* 44 (1988) 453-62.

[6] L.-H. Vincent and F.-M. Abel, *Jérusalem nouvelle* (Paris: Gabalda, 1922) 423, 465.

building on Mount Zion, I shall argue that the determination of the strong Christian community in Aelia Capitolina to maintain contact with the site, despite severe obstacles, betrays an attachment to the place which is explicable only in terms of the importance the site had in the 1st century, when the quarter was the home of the most affluent residents of the city.

I. A 2nd-Century Church on Mount Zion

After a century and a half of persecution the Muslims finally took possession of the Cenacle and transformed it into a mosque in 1524.[7] The heavy fighting around the Zion Gate in the spring of 1948 forced the Arabs to leave, and after the truce was signed they were not permitted to return. The site was then right on the frontier with Jordan, and they were considered a security risk to Israel. It was some time before the situation stabilised and Orthodox Jews moved in. The interval was put to good use by J. Pinkerfeld, who in 1951 conducted the only excavation on the site. It is fortunate that he had produced a preliminary report before he was killed in the terrorist attack on the Archaeological Convention of 1956 at Ramat Rahel, but it is regrettable that the site has never been fully published.[8] Instead of digging out unpublished material J. W. Hirschberg offers no more than a bland summary of Pinkerfeld.[9] It is equally deplorable that the latter approached his investigation with the mistaken conviction that the building was a synagogue oriented to the Temple by a niche in the north wall.[10]

About 12 cms beneath the present floor of the burial chamber Pinkerfeld found the floor corresponding to the Crusader sarcophagus. The next floor appeared 48 cms deeper. It was 'a coloured mosaic decorated with geometric designs characteristic of the late Roman or early Byzantine period'.[11] Ten cms below that was a further floor, 'quite possibly the remains of a stone pavement', but it too might have been mosaic.[12] The sketchy character of this information will escape no

---

[7]Vincent and Abel, *Jérusalem nouvelle*, 471.

[8]J. Pinkerfeld, '"David's Tomb'. Notes on the History of the Building. Preliminary Report', *Louis Rabinowitz Fund for the Exploration of Ancient Synagogues. Bulletin III* (Jerusalem: Hebrew University/Department of Antiquities, 1960) 41-43.

[9]'The Remains of an Ancient Synagogue on Mount Sion', in Y. Yadin (ed.), *Jerusalem Revealed. Archaeology in the Holy City 1968-1974* (Jerusalem: Israel Exploration Society, 1975) 116-17.

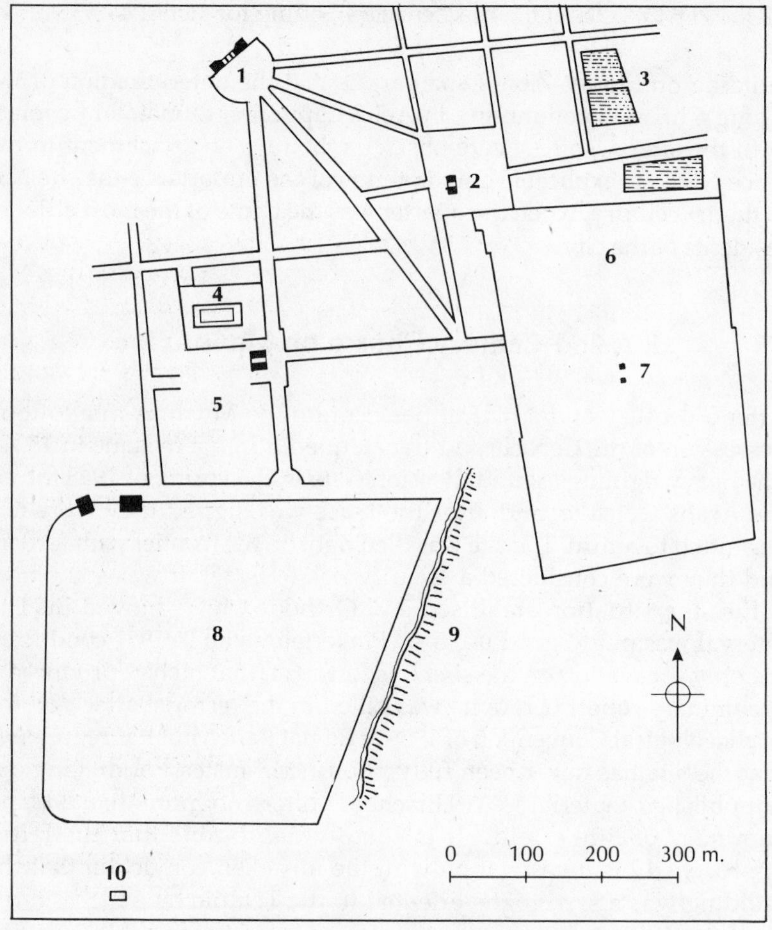

Aelia Capitolina

1. Monumental Gate
2. Eastern Forum with Triumphal Arch
3. Temple of Aesclepius
4. Capitoline Temple
5. Western Forum with Triumphal Arch
6. Temple Mount
7. Statue of Hadrian and Antoninus
8. Camp of the Tenth Legion
9. Escarpment
10. The Little Church of God

one. Nonetheless one important conclusion can be drawn. There was a building on this site in the late Roman period, *i.e.* in the 2nd or 3rd century AD.

The three groups of Greek graffiti on plaster of the earliest period passed through the hands of Professors Schwabe and Lifshitz before being given to the Franciscans where they were interpreted by E. Testa. He read the most specific as 'Oh, Jesus, that I may live, O Lord of the autocrat'.[13] As one might have expected, such a bizarre reading is refused by E. Puech, who nonetheless finds a mention of Jesus and insists that the context is Christian.[14]

Writing in 394 Epiphanius of Salamis noted that when the emperor Hadrian visited Jerusalem in 130 he found the city in ruins

> except for a few houses, and the little church of God (καὶ τῆς τοῦ θεοῦ ἐκκλησίας μικρᾶς) on the spot where the disciples went to the upper room on their return from the Mount of Olives after the Ascension of the Redeemer. It was built there, namely on Zion, which escaped the destruction, and the houses around Zion and seven synagogues (συναγωγαί) which remained isolated in Zion like huts, one of which survived into the time of bishop Maximos and of the emperor Constantine, like a shanty in a vineyard, as the Scripture says [Is. 1:8].[15]

---

[10]Pinkerfeld's assertion that 'the niche pointed north with an eastern deviation of several degrees, *i.e.* exactly towards the Temple Mount' ('David's Tomb', 41) is incorrect. B. Pixner, 'Die apostolische Synagoge auf dem Zion' in R. Riesner (ed.),*Wege des Messias und Stätten der Urkirche. Jesus und das Judenchristentum im Licht neuer archäologischer Erkenntnisse* (Giessen/Basel: Brunnen, 1991) 293, 298, is closer to reality in claiming that the niche is directed towards the Holy Sepulchre but produces no parallels to prove intention. Moreover, the architectural parallel to the niche which Pinkerfeld offers is that of the synagogue at Eshtemoa, which is dated to the 4th century AD. A synagogue on Mt Zion at that period is inconceivable, and orienting niches are not attested in 1st-century synagogues (*e.g.* Gamla, Masada). On the whole issue see J. Wilkinson, 'Orientation, Jewish and Christian', *PEQ* 116 (1984) 16-30.

[11]'David's Tomb', 42.

[12]'David's Tomb', 43.

[13]B. Bagatti, *The Church from the Circumcision. History and Archaeology of the Judaeo-Christians* (Jerusalem: Franciscan Press, 1971) 121.

[14]'La synagogue judéo-chrétienne du Mont Sion', *Le Monde de la Bible*, n. 57 (Jan.-Feb. 1989) 19.

[15]*De mensuris et ponderibus* 14; *PG* 43.261; *cf.* J. E. Dean, *Epiphanius' Treatise on Weights and Measures, the Syriac Version* (Chicago: University Press, 1935) 30.

Despite his name, which he only acquired in 367 when he was consecrated Metropolitan of Salamis, Epiphanius was a Palestinian who had been born in 315 in Eleutheropolis (today Bet Guvrin) of Christian parents, and who directed a monastery there for over thirty years. His contacts with Jerusalem must have been frequent, which makes him an eyewitness of the situation in Jerusalem at the beginning of the Byzantine period. That his information in fact stems from this period rather than his later visit in 393 is suggested by his slightly older contemporary the Bordeaux Pilgrim, who arrived in Jerusalem in 333. Regarding Mount Zion he wrote,

> 'Inside Zion, within the wall, you can see where David had his palace. Seven synagogues were there, but only one is left—the rest have been "ploughed and sown" as was said by the prophet Isaiah [1:8].'[16]

The identical reference to Is. 1:8 makes it certain that Epiphanius and the Pilgrim drew on precisely the same local tradition, which mentioned the survival of a single synagogue into the third decade of the 4th century. When taken at face value this is highly improbable. After the second Jewish revolt (132-35), Hadrian decreed the city and territory of Jerusalem to be off-limits for all Jews.[17] The decree has been reconstructed by M. Avi-Yonah, 'It is forbidden for all circumcized persons to enter or stay within the territory of Aelia Capitolina; any person contravening this prohibition shall be put to death'.[18] There is no evidence that this edict was subsequently rescinded. On the contrary, the exception mentioned by both Origen[19] and the Bordeaux Pilgrim[20] attests that it was in force in the 3rd and 4th centuries. Even if individual Jews occasionally took the risk of living in Jerusalem,[21] it is impossible that there should have been a functioning synagogue.

---

[16]Translation by J. Wilkinson, *Egeria's Travels to the Holy Land* (rev. edn.; Jerusalem: Ariel/Warminster: Aris and Phillips, 1981) 157-58.

[17]Eusebius, *Church History*, 4.6.3.

[18]*The Jews of Palestine. A Political History from the Bar Kokba War to the Arab Conquest* (Oxford: Clarendon, 1976) 50-51.

[19]'O Jew, when you come to Jerusalem ... do not weep as you do now "after the fashion of infants." Do not lament... .When you see the altar abandoned I do not wish that you should suffer. When you do not find priests, I do not wish that you should dispair ...' (*Homélies sur Josué. Jesu Nave*, XVII, 1; SC 71, 373). This text is dated to 249-50.

[20]'There is a pierced stone which the Jews come and anoint each year. They mourn and rend their garments and depart.'(Wilkinson, *Egeria's Travels*, 157).

[21]M. Avi-Yonah, *The Jews of Palestine*, 76.

A European visitor, such as the Bordeaux Pilgrim, who recognised the religious character of the building but found it alien to his religious experience, might be forgiven for thinking it a synagogue rather than a church of indigenous Christians.[22] A native like Epiphanius, however, could not have made this sort of mistake. Another explanation must be sought.

A strange feature of Epiphanius' report is its repetitiousness. Although the passage is very short, the second part duplicates the first. It opens by recalling the survival of a few houses and the little church of God, and concludes by evoking the survival of a few houses and a single synagogue. There are two mentions of Zion in close proximity. It would appear that the author has combined two slightly different descriptions of the same locality, one reflecting Palestinian and the other Diaspora language. Alternatively, Epiphanius might have given his own interpretation—'little church of God' implies that he knew greater churches—to a report from another source. In either case the church and the synagogue would be one and the same building but looked at from two different perspectives, which reflect the change introduced by the legalisation of Christianity. The edifice had not been built as a church; it was a Jewish Christian place of assembly which in fact served as a church.[23] Now the point of mentioning that the synagogue survived into the time of Maximos becomes evident. It was during his episcopate (335-49) that the first church on Mount Zion was consecrated some time before 348, when Cyril of Jerusalem speaks of the Upper Church of the Apostles.[24] Evidently it was well known in the 4th century that an earlier building had been transformed, because Egeria casually notes that 'it has now been altered into a church'.[25] The absence of any synagogue in 370 was noted by Optatus of Milevis.[26]

---

[22]So rightly P.W.L. Walker, *Holy City, Holy Places? Christian Attitudes to Jerusalem and the Holy Land in the Fourth Century* (Oxford: Clarendon, 1990) 286, 290.
[23]I find implausible Bagatti's suggestion that 'there were two separate rooms: one for the celebration of the Eucharist on the upper floor, and one on the lower floor for ritual prayers. The first represented the church, the second the synagogue' (*The Church from the Circumcision*, 118).
[24]*Catechetical Lectures*, 16:4.
[25]Wilkinson, *Egeria's Travels*, 141.
[26]*De schismate Donatistarum* 3.2.

II. The Christian Community of Aelia Capitolina

When correctly understood, therefore, both Epiphanius and the Bordeaux Pilgrim assert the existence of a Christian church on Mount Zion from the 2nd to the 4th century. Is this credible? Two conditions must be fulfilled for an affirmative answer to be plausible: (a) the continuous presence in Aelia Capitolina of Christians (b) whose public activity was uncircumscribed. That both these conditions were in fact met can be demonstrated from Eusebius.

The fact that Christians used the messianic name Bar Kokhba, which was invented by Rabbi Akiba for Bar Kosiba the leader of the second Jewish revolt (AD 132-35),[27] suggests that they had come under pressure to accept his leadership, something, of course, they could not do, having accepted Jesus as the Christ. Writing only 20 years after the event, Justin, in fact, reported that Bar Kokhba had attempted to force Christians to deny that Jesus was the Messiah.[28]

The fact of having been persecuted by the rebels was probably what saved the Jewish Christian survivors when Hadrian expelled the Jews from the territory of Aelia Capitolina in AD 135. The impression given by Eusebius that the church of Aelia was composed exclusively of believers of Gentile origins is too neat to be historical.[29] Where did the members of this Gentile church suddenly spring from? With the benefit of hindsight Eusebius simplifies a complex process. The new members who joined the surviving Jewish Christians were all Gentiles and inevitably changed the character of the church, particularly since the Jewish institutions and practices, which had reminded pre-Hadrianic believers of their roots, no longer existed.

The continuity implicit in this peaceful transition is reflected in the unbroken succession of bishops from the time of Hadrian to the early 4th century.[30] The substantial accuracy of this list cannot be impugned.[31] The character of the Christian presence is illustrated by the figure of Alexander. While a bishop in Cappadocia he had already

---

[27]Eusebius, *Church History*, 4:6.2; see Schürer, *History of the Jewish People*, I,543 n. 130.

[28]*1 Apologia* 31.6, which is quoted by Eusebius, *Church History*, 4.8. For a contemporary hint of this persecution in the *Apocalypse of Peter*, see R. Bauckham, 'The Two Fig Tree Parables in the *Apocalypse of Peter*', *JBL* 104 (1985) 269-87, especially 285-86.

[29]*Church History* 4.6; 5.12.

[30]*Church History* 5.12. (from Hadrian to the early 3rd century); 6.10-11; 6.39; 7.14; 7.32 (to the early 4th century).

been imprisoned for the faith.[32] He made a pilgrimage to Jerusalem in 212, where, against his will, he was forced to become the auxiliary of the aged bishop of Narcissus, whom he succeeded. One of the achievements of his long episcopate of 39 years was the construction of the library of Aelia, which was used by Eusebius,[33] and most probably by Julius Africanus.[34] This library should be understood as an institution of the city rather than as a purely ecclesiastical library, although a concern for theological resources may have been its primary motivation. It was a time when cities felt that they owed themselves libraries, and the initiative of citizens was welcomed.[35]

The foundation of such an institution by Christians in Jerusalem manifests the strength and vitality of the church there. It certainly was not an isolated beleagured community. It had regular contacts with neighbouring churches, whose heads supervised the selection of bishops.[36] Visitors from abroad may have been numerous. There is no justification for thinking that Eusebius' mention of Melito, Origen, and Alexander implies that they were the only visitors to the Holy City.[37] Their scholarship and/or office demanded the attention of a church historian. Many other visitors were too insignificant to be mentioned by name in his wide-ranging story. Some may have stayed and provided the community with new blood.

Prior to the 3rd century persecution of Christians was conditioned by local factors, notably the attitude of the local governor. The consequences of the favour shown Christians by Alexander Severus (222-35) could hardly have been forseen. Subsequently the stance of the emperor became critical and a cyclical policy developed. If one emperor tolerated Christianity, his successor repressed it.[38] Such

---

[31]The only problematic point is *Church History* 5.12, which claims to list 15 bishops but in fact mentions only 13. As R. Bauckham points out, however, 'the names of Maximus and Antoninus can be supplied, after Capito, from Eusebius' *Chronicon*' (*Jude and the Relatives of Jesus in the Early Church* [Edinburgh: Clark, 1990] 71 n. 79).

[32]Eusebius, *Church History* 6.11.5.

[33]*Church History* 6.20.1.

[34]POxy. III, 412; see J.R. Villefond, *Les 'Cestes' de Julius Africanus. Etude sur l'ensemble des fragments avec édition, traduction et commentaires* (Firenze: Sansoni/ Paris: Didier, 1970) 278, 288-91.

[35]C. Wendel, 'Bibliothek', *Reallexikon für Antike und Christentum*, II,231-74; F. Granger, 'Julius Africanus and the Library of the Pantheon', *JTS* 34 (1933) 157-61.

[36]Eusebius, *Church History* 6.10-11.

[37]As J.E. Taylor attempts to suggest (*Christians and the Holy Places. The Myth of Jewish-Christian Origins* [Oxford: Clarendon, 1993] 307-13).

[38]H. Chadwick, *The Early Church* (London: Penguin, 1974) 117.

swings were unfortunate for the flourishing Jerusalem church, because Philip the Arabian (244-49)—Eusebius 'had reason to believe' he was a Christian[39]—was succeeded by Decius (249-51), who initiated the first systematic persecution of Christians. It would have been impossible for the imperial representative in Palestine not to have summoned bishop Alexander of Jerusalem to Caesarea to put him to the test. Alexander refused to sacrifice but, before he could be put to the torture, he died in prison in 251.[40] It is not known if commissioners were sent to Jerusalem to check the certificates of those who had sacrificed to the gods.[41] J. E. Taylor deduces a climate of fear from the fact that the throne of James was not kept in one place.[42] According to Eusebius, 'the brethren look after it in turn'.[43] However, this may mean no more than that each successive bishop kept it in his residence.

In 261 the rescript of the emperor Gallienus (253-68) guaranteed Christians the freedom to practice their faith.[44] In the 40 years which followed, the menace to the church came from within.[45] None of these divisive theological controversies, however, appears to have touched the church of Jerusalem. The impact on Jerusalem of the great 10-year persecution unleashed by Diocletian in 303 is not documented. One might assume that the community contributed its share both of the great number of renegades in Palestine and of those who deliberately provoked the authorities in order to obtain the martyr's crown.[46] It is certain that the church survived to transmit its traditions.

---

[39]*Church History* 6.34. His conclusion is universally rejected.

[40]Eusebius, *Church History* 6.39.2-3.

[41]As elsewhere, the authorities in Caesarea would have had their hands full with local believers. 'Only prominent Christians were pursued, but there was no effective prison service where they could be detained for long periods. For the rest, the authorities, overwhelmed by their apparent success, were content to let matters be. In both Carthage and Alexandria there is evidence that about a score of confessors were imprisoned for obduracy, and there were some executions, but on the whole surprisingly little force had to be used' (W.H.C. Frend, *The Early Church* [Philadelphia: Fortress, 1982] 99).

[42]*Christians and the Holy Places*, 209.

[43]*Church History* 7.19.

[44]Eusebius, *Church History* 7.13.

[45]Eusebius, *Church History* 8.1.7.

[46]According to Frend only 44 were executed in Palestine, and a further 46 died in exile (*The Early Church*, 120).

III. The Camp of the Tenth Legion

The next step in the argument is to highlight the significance of the location on Mount Zion of the little church of God. It was cut off from the city by the camp of the Tenth Legion.

One of the most significant discoveries made by N. Avigad in the Jewish Quarter was the southern portion of the Cardo Maximus of Aelia. Even though at first debated, his dating of the foundation of this section of the main street to the 6th century is now accepted.[47] The Hadrianic Cardo Maximus of Aelia terminated somewhere in the area of the present David Street. If it did not go further south it can only be because the line of its extension was blocked by the camp of the Tenth Legion *Fretensis*.

It is known from Josephus that Titus established the legion in the area of the palace of Herod the Great:

> Caesar gave orders that they should now demolish the entire city and temple, but should leave as many of the towers standing as were of the greatest eminence, that is, Phasaelus, and Hippicus, and Mariamne, and so much of the wall as enclosed the city on the west side. This wall was spared in order to afford a camp for such as were to be the garrison.' (*BJ* 7:1-2)

This report suggests that three towers of the palace constituted the northwest corner of the legion camp. At this time the west wall of Herodian Jerusalem followed the curve of the Hinnom valley to the east, but it is most improbable that all its length was utilised by the legion.[48] The Madaba Map shows an interior east-west wall on approximately the line of the present south wall of the Old City. The simplest explanation of its origins is that on the west it represents the south wall of the legion camp, which was subsequently prolonged to the east to join the Temple mount when the legion was definitively withdrawn by

---

47 *Discovering Jerusalem* (Nashville: Nelson, 1983) 225-26.

48 *Pace* H. Geva, 'The Camp of the Tenth Legion in Jerusalem: An Archaeological Reconsideration', *IEJ* 34 (1984) 247, 249. His study, which is essentially an argument from silence, is internally contradictory in that he assigns far too great a space to far too few soldiers. In addition he ignores Epiphanius and the Bordeaux Pilgrim.

Diocletian (284-305).[49] Only at that time did Aelia need or acquire a wall.[50]

The line of the eastern wall of the legion camp is more difficult to determine. The average size of a permanent Roman legion camp housing 6,000 men was 50 acres.[51] In order to come anywhere near this dimension the camp of the Tenth Legion would have had to go as far east as the escarpment of the Tyropoeon valley, which, moreover, would have offered the same defensive advantage as the Hinnom valley on the west.[52]

Since the residential area of Aelia Capitolina was north of the legion camp, the Christians of Aelia Capitolina would have had to go round the legion camp either on the east or on the west in order to reach the little church on Mount Zion.

The former route would have been extremely difficult, if not impossible. In order to defend the Temple the Zealots demolished the bridge crossing the Tyropoeon. B. Mazar cites the early homiletic Midrash *Ekha Rabbati* 4.7, 'Said Rabbi Abba bar-Cahana: The aqueduct which came from Etam was destroyed one day by the Sicarii'.[53] The huge mass of debris which this dumped on the road below was increased to a height of almost fifteen meters when the Romans pushed out the external walls projecting above the platform of the Temple.[54] The slope to the west up to the escarpment was a mass of loose stones from the ruined buildings. To scramble through this scree would have been both laborious and dangerous. Conditions might

---

[49]Excavations on this line near Zion Gate have not brought to light any traces of the Roman wall; see M. Broshi and Y. Tsafrir, 'Excavations at the Zion Gate', *IEJ* 27 (1977) 34-36.

[50]The aqueduct coming from the north and still visible west of Herod's Gate was taken out of commission only at the beginning of the 4th century, when the ditch containing the present road was cut; see L.-H. Vincent, 'Encore la troisième enceinte de Jérusalem', *RB* 54 (1947) 104.

[51]See in general E. Saglio, 'Castra', in C. Daremberg and E. Saglio (eds.), *Dictionnaire des antiquités grecques et romaines* (Paris: Hachette, 1899) I,940-59; A. von Domaszewski, 'Castra', in G. Wissowa (ed.), *Paulys Realencyclopädie der classischen Altertumswissenschaft* (Stuttgart: Metzler, 1899) III,1762-69.

[52]In this respect (but not in others) the plan given by Vincent and Abel (*Jérusalem nouvelle*, Planche 1) is more accurate than those proposed by D. Bahat (*Carta's Historical Atlas of Jerusalem. An Illustrated Survey* [Jerusalem: Carta, 1983] 35) and K. Prag (*Jerusalem* [London: Black, 1989] 31). An intermediate position is taken by J. Wilkinson, 'Jerusalem under Rome and Byzantium 63 BC-637 AD', in K.J. Asali (ed.), *Jerusalem in History* [London: Scorpion, 1989] 91).

[53]*The Mountain of the Lord* (Garden City: Doubleday, 1975) 221.

[54]*The Mountain of the Lord*, 217.

have improved to the southeast but not by much. The area immediately south of the Temple Mount was resettled only in the 4th century.

The alternative route around the western side of Aelia offered other difficulties. It would have been much easier physically, the only difficulty being the rather steep eastern slope of the Hinnom valley. The danger came from Roman sentries. The Mount Zion segment of the south wall of the legion camp was one of its weakest points because unprotected by a valley. In consequence it was guarded more securely. Between the two great revolts there were moments of high tension, possibly in 86, certainly in 115,[55] when Christians assembling on Mount Zion would have been seen as a threat, and severely questioned.

The relationship between the legion camp and the city changed after Septimius Severus permitted soldiers to marry on active service. They lived with their families in the city, and came to work in the camp.[56] At precisely this moment, however, the governor of Palestine was based in Jerusalem.[57] One cannot imagine that the discipline of the camp was relaxed. Even when the centre of power shifted to Caesarea, the security of the legion camp remained a major concern in the 3rd century as the situation on the eastern frontier of the empire deteriorated. No commander could afford to relax surveillance of Mount Zion. At this stage the problem for Christians would have come from bored sentries. Then as now their most common form of amusement was harassing passers-by.

Such difficulties make it impossible that Jerusalem Christians should have invented a holy place on Mount Zion in the 2nd century. If, despite all obstacles, they maintained contact with a site there, it must have been of extreme importance to them. This means that veneration of the site must be pushed back into the 1st century and prior to the fall of Jerusalem.

Although Joan Taylor admits this possibility, she is more impressed by the fact that Eusebius never mentions a Christian site on the southwest hill.[58] The flimsiness of the argument from silence needs no emphasis. Peter Walker, in fact, interprets it quite differently,

---

[55]E. Schürer, *The History of the Jewish People in the Age of Jesus Christ (175 BC-AD 135)* (Edinburgh: Clark, 1973) I,514-18.

[56]E. Cagnat, 'Légion', in in C. Daremberg and E. Saglio (eds.), *Dictionnaire des antiquités grecques et romaines* (Paris: Hachette, 1899) III,1064.

[57]Vincent and Abel, *Jérusalem nouvelle*, 891-92.

[58]*Christians and the Holy Places*, 212.

namely, as a manifestation of historical scepticism and scholarly ambivalence on the part of the great churchman.[59]

IV. Flight from Jerusalem?

The credibility of 2nd and 3rd-century identification of a site considered important in the 1st century depends on a constant Christian presence in the Holy City in the period marked by the two great Jewish revolts. Otherwise transmission of the tradition becomes problematic. Eusebius documents two serious objections. Before the First Revolt the Jerusalem church fled to Pella and never returned. After the Second Revolt an entirely Gentile community replaced the Jewish Christians.

With respect to the Pella story Eusebius contradicts himself. According to his *Church History* the believers departed from Jerusalem and 'dwelt in one of the cities of Perea which they call Pella' (3.5.3). Yet in his *Proof of the Gospel* he asserts, 'Until the time of the siege by Hadrian there was an extremely significant Church of Christ at Jerusalem, which consisted of Jews' (3.5.108). We have a choice between permanent departure and perfect continuity, and opinion is deeply divided. The traditional view, which accepts the historicity of the flight, has been defended most recently by V.S. Balabanski[60] and attacked by G. Lüdemann.[61] The latter makes the more convincing case. The three allusions to the flight by Epiphanius[62] depend on Eusebius, whose probable source is Aristo of Pella. The possibility of special pleading diminishes the credibility of Aristo's late and lone voice. Moreover, Pella is improbable as a city of refuge.[63]

If there was no flight to Pella, did the Christian community remain in Jerusalem for the duration of the siege? By the spring of AD 68 only the rich could buy their way out of Jerusalem; others who attempted to leave were cut down.[64] Those who escaped the year

---

[59]*Holy City, Holy Places?*, 290.

[60]*Eschatology in the Making: Mark, Matthew and the Didache* (Ph.D. Dissertation, University of Melbourne, 1993) 96-127.

[61]*Opposition to Paul in Jewish Christianity* (Minneapolis: Fortress, 1989) 200-11.

[62]*Panarion* 29.7.7; 30.2.7; *De mensuris et ponderis* 15.

[63]A Gentile city which had been laid waste by Alexander Jannaeus (Josephus, *BJ* 1.1104), and again by Jews at the beginning of the First Revolt (*BJ* 2.458), would have had little sympathy for Jewish Christian refugees. The case of Gerasa (*BJ* 2.480) proves nothing; there is no question of its accepting the enemy as refugees.

[64]Josephus, *BJ* 4.377-79.

before must have been very farsighted. Did Christians belong to this group? Eusebius mentions 'an oracle given by revelation' which warned the church.[65] Just such an oracle appears as one of Mark's sources in ch. 13. As reconstructed by Balabanski it reads, 'When you see him, the abomination of desolation, standing where he ought not to be—let the reader understand—then flee to the mountains... .But pray that it does not happen in winter' (vv. 14-18).[66] She also establishes a most plausible *Sitz im Leben* for the oracle, namely, the struggle of the Zealots to wrest power from the high-priestly families, and in particular their campaign to change the procedure by which high priests were appointed.[67] This goal they achieved by the nomination by lot of Phanias in the winter of AD 67.[68] That would have been the sign for believers to seek safety elsewhere. That the oracle survived to be incorporated in Mark's Gospel would suggest that it was heeded by at least some of the Christians in Jerusalem.

To be safe they did not have to go as far as Pella. Anywhere 10 to 20 km north of Jerusalem—the region to which Jesus had retired when he was in danger (Jn. 11:54)—would have provided adequate security. Vespasian had left the hill country north of the city untouched until the early summer of AD 69.[69] By that time Judeans would have acquired a very precise idea of the operational tactics of the legions, and it would have been relatively easy for Christians to evade danger by moving to the edge of the desert. The Romans attacked only where resistance was offered. The believers could have returned to the ruins of Jerusalem before the end of AD 70, *i.e.* after an absence of little more than 18 months.

[65]*Church History* 3.5.3.

[66]*Eschatology in the Making*, 87. I doubt that 'to the mountains' belonged to the original form of the oracle; it is lowland language and inappropriate for Jerusalemites living on the mountain of the Lord.

[67]*Eschatology in the Making*, 121-25.

[68]Josephus, *BJ* 4.147-57. Ananus commented, 'How wonderful it would have been if I had died before seeing the house of God full of countless abominations' (*BJ* 4.163). See also S. Sowers, 'The Circumstances and Recollection of the Pella Flight', *TZ* 26 (1970) 318-19.

[69]Josephus, *BJ* 4.550-51.

V. The Quality of Life in 1st-Century Mount Zion

Having established that there was a constant Christian presence in Jerusalem to carry the tradition from the 1st to the 2nd century, the next question is: What event in the life of Jesus or the early church was associated with Mount Zion?

Epiphanius, as we have seen, simply identifies the site of the little church of God as the residence of the disciples in Jerusalem (Acts 1:13). A certain plausibility accrues to this assertion because of its very modesty. More significant spiritual associations appear only much later. Pentecost (Acts 2:1-4) is first localised there in the 4th century,[70] and early in the next century it becomes the place of the Last Supper.[71] A debate about the name of the owner of the building began very early. In the 5th and 6th centuries at least three candidates had their partisans, John/Mark, Mary, and James.[72] Such speculation, however, is pointless, since no definitive answer will ever be possible. It is more fruitful to ask if the location of the building says anything about the social status of the owner.

Although Wilkinson's street layout has only the slightest evidence to recommend it,[73] he is certainly correct in supposing that the western hill was extensively remodelled when Herod the Great, about 24 BC, built his palace there.[74] Whereas previously the houses of the wealthy clustered around the Hasmonaean palace,[75] now those who could afford it erected their mansions in the vicinity of the new royal seat. The palace of Agrippa and Berenice, which was burnt by the rebels in 66, is to be identified with the Hasmonaean palace.[76] The palace of Ananias, the high priest (47-59), burnt on the same occasion, has not been located. He was not from the four great high-priestly families. Thus he did not have a traditional residence. Newcomers to

---

[70]Cyril of Jerusalem, *Catechetical Lectures*, 16:4; *Egeria*, 43:3.

[71]The earliest hint is provided by the content of the readings (1 Cor. 11:23-32; Mk. 14:1-26) assigned by the Old Armenian Lectionary; see Wilkinson, *Egeria's Travels*, 267.

[72]For details see J. Wilkinson, *Jerusalem Pilgrims before the Crusades* (Jerusalem: Ariel, 1977) 171-72.

[73]'Jerusalem under Rome and Byzantium', 81.

[74]Josephus, *BJ* 1.402; 5.156-83.

[75]The hints given by Josephus (*BJ* 2.344; 6.325; *Ant.* 20.189-96) place this palace in the vicinity of the residences excavated by Avigad (*Discovering Jerusalem*, 83-139). See the reconstruction by Leen Ritmeyer in J. Pritchard (ed.), *The Times Atlas of the Bible* (London: Times Books, 1987) 166-67.

[76]Josephus, *BJ* 2.426; *Ant.* 20.189-90.

office hive closely to the centre of power, and so, if he built, it is likely to have been further up the hill in the vicinity of the new palace.

Certainly that is the area where the earliest Byzantine tradition locates the palace of the High Priest Caiaphas (18-36).[77] From the Bordeaux Pilgrim we learn only that it was a ruin on Mount Zion.[78] Writing sometime before 518 Theodosius is much more precise in his *The Topography of Jerusalem*, 'From Holy Zion to the House of Caiaphas which is now the Church of St Peter it is about 50 paces'.[79] Abel understands *passus* in the Roman sense of 1.5 metres; hence the distance was about 75 metres,[80] almost exactly the distance between today's Cenacle and the Armenian Monastery of St Saviour which enshrines a house of Caiaphas.

Mosaic floors, one with the geometric patterns typical of the 5th century,[81] and a well-constructed apse oriented to the east,[82] came to light in the courtyard of the Armenian Monastery of St Saviour, between the Cenacle and the present south wall of the Old City. Whether these represent traces of St Peter's Church is no more certain than that the Herodian material brought to light by Broshi on the same site belongs to the palace of Caiphas. This, however, is less important than the character of the structures. Following the earthquake of 31 BC[83] the area was rebuilt of two and possibly three-storey buildings with barrel vaulted cisterns. Some rooms were decorated with *fresco secco* murals depicting birds, trees, stylised tendrils, garlands and architectural elements, which, according to Broshi, 'leave no doubt that this quarter was occupied by the more affluent residents of Jerusalem'.[84]

If the building which subsequently became known as 'the little church of God' was located in a wealthy quarter of the city, its owner must have had significant financial resources. Curiously Taylor

---

77*A priori* the top of the ridge is a much more probable site for a palace than the site half way down the eastern slope, now occupied by St. Peter in Gallicantu, which is defended by E. Power, 'Eglise de Pierre et maison de Caiphe', in L. Pirot (ed.), *Dictionnaire de la Bible. Supplément* (Paris: Letouzey, 1934) II,691-756.

78Wilkinson, *Egeria's Travels*, 157.

79Wilkinson, *Jerusalem Pilgrims*, 60; *cf.* also 60 and maps 18 and 21.

80Vincent and Abel, *Jérusalem nouvelle*, 485.

81M. Broshi, 'Excavations on Mount Zion, 1971-72. Preliminary Report', *IEJ* 26 (1976) 86. For better illustrations see his 'Excavations in the House of Caiaphas, Mount Zion', in Y. Yadin (ed.) *Jerusalem Revealed*, 57-60.

82Vincent and Abel, *Jérusalem nouvelle*, 489, 499.

83Josephus, *Ant.* 15.121-22.

84Broshi, 'Excavations on Mount Zion', 83-84.

considers this a decisive objection to the validity of the tradition; 'the socio-economic character of this part of Jerusalem would make it very unlikely that Christians had their main centre in this quarter. The early Christians were not an upper-class movement'.[85] Upper-class is anachronistic in this context. It is preferable to speak of individuals with disposable income because the economics of the Jesus movement demanded patrons. Peter and Andrew were not poor men; they had partners and employees (Lk. 5:5-10; Mk. 1:20). Joanna, the wife of Herod's steward (Lk. 8:3), and the other women who subsidised Jesus (Mk. 15:41), must have had surplus wealth. It is no accident that the first believers in Corinth—Crispus (1 Cor. 1:14), Gaius (1 Cor. 1:14; Rom. 16:23) and Stephanas (1 Cor. 1:16; 16:15)—were all well-established figures with the ability to provide facilities for Paul and his converts, as was Phoebe in Cenchreae (Rom. 16:1-2). Why should not Jesus have made a convert among this type of person during his extensive ministry in Jerusalem?

The highly idealistic common life (Acts 2:44-45) revealed by the most primitive source of the Acts of the Apostles[86] necessarily presupposes a spacious house and a generous host. It was the lifestyle of Jesus' immediate companions (Mt. 19:27), whose internal financial organisation (Jn. 12:6; 13:29) was primed by gifts from female supporters (Lk. 8:1-3). This may point to Mary as the owner of the house (Acts 12:12-17a). How many might have been involved no one can say, but such fervor is unlikely to have been shared by a great number.

This lifestyle cannot have lasted very long, because at a later stage, represented by Acts 4:32, 34-35,[87] we find that idealism has been tempered by practicality. A lived ideal has been transformed into Platonic theory.[88] The church has grown. There is no longer any question of living together, nor of complete community of goods. The apostles act as the channel between the haves and the have nots. That the same edifice which once housed a community should now have become an administrative centre would not have diminished its value in the eyes of believers. Through good times and bad the little church

---

[85]*Christians and the Holy Places*, 208, *cf.* 219.

[86]M.-É. Boismard and A. Lamouille, *Les Actes des deux apôtres*. II. *Le Sens des récits* (Paris: Gabalda, 1990) 31-32.

[87]Boismard and Lamouille, *Les Actes des deux apôtres*, II,159-63.

[88]On the influence of Plato (*Republic*, 3.416d; 5.462c) see L. Cerfaux, 'La première communauté chrétienne à Jérusalem (Act., II, 41-V,42)', *ETL* 16 (1939) 26-28.

of God was cherished as the first assembly-place of the church in Jerusalem.[89]

[89]Earlier versions of this paper were delivered in the New Testament Archaeology seminar at the Annual Meeting of the Society for New Testament Studies, held at the University of Chicago in August 1993, and published in M.D. Coogan, J.C. Exum and L.E. Stager (eds.), *Scripture and other Artifacts: In Honor of Philip J. King* (Louisville, Ky: Westminster/John Knox Press, 1994). The permission of Westminster/John Knox Press to publish here is gratefully acknowledged. I am indebted to David Myres for the drawing of Aelia Capitolina.

CHAPTER 11

THE PALESTINIAN CULTURAL CONTEXT OF EARLIEST CHRISTIAN COMMUNITY OF GOODS

Brian Capper

Summary

Luke's account of the community of goods of the earliest community in Jerusalem is clearly idealised with popular philosophical catchphrases. However, instances of formal community of property were a feature of Palestinian Jewish culture, and had persisted for approaching two centuries amongst the sect of the Essenes prior to the events which Luke purports to describe. Features of Luke's account suggest linguistic usages and organisational forms employed in the legislation for Essene community of goods revealed in the Rule of the Community discovered in Qumran cave 1. Other elements of Luke's account are illuminated by the practicalities of Essene property-sharing arrangements revealed in the accounts of the Essenes given by Philo and Josephus. These clues point to the probable Palestinian origins of the tradition and suggest that a group within the earliest Jerusalem Church practised formal property-sharing. Luke's portrayal of earliest Christian community of goods can be taken seriously as a historical account.

I. Introduction

Luke claims at Acts 2:44 and 4:32 that the earliest church in Jerusalem had 'all things common'. This 'community of goods' involved the sale of property and the surrender of the money thus raised to the apostles (2:44-45; 4:32–5:11), daily meal-fellowship in homes (2:46), and a process of 'daily distribution' (6:1) by which the material needs of the underprivileged such as widows in the community (6:1-6) and indeed of all (2:45; 4:35) seem to have been met. The critical consensus is almost universally against seeing any historical phenomenon of actual, organised property-sharing behind Luke's account.[1] This negative historical judgement of the Acts account persists despite awareness that community of goods was widely practised in 1st-century Palestine, in those Essene communities which fully shared their property. The following are the principal arguments raised against the claim of Acts that the earliest Christian community had 'all things common'.

(1) Acts 2:44 and 4:32 reflect the language of Greek philosophising about the ideal society. The usage 'all things common', πάντα (or ἅπαντα) κοινά (*cf.* 2:44 εἶχον πάντα κοινά, *cf.* 4:32 ἦν αὐτοῖς ἅπαντα κοινά) is found in Plato's *Republic*, a Utopian scheme,[2] and in other literature which emphasises the philosophical ideal; it is found, for example, in praise of the tribal economy of the primitive Scythians or in connection with the renunciation of the ideal philosopher.[3] D.L. Mealand notes that the phrase 'no one called anything ... his own' at Acts 4:32 (οὐδὲ εἷς τι ... ἔλεγεν ἴδιον εἶναι) recalls the usage 'to call nothing one's own',

---

[1]*Cf.* M. del Verme, *Communione e condivisione dei beni. Chiesa primitiva e giudaismo esseno-qumranico a confronte* (Morcelliana: Brescia, 1977); L.T. Johnson, *The Literary Function of Possessions in Luke-Acts* (Missoula: Scholars Press, 1977) 1–12, 162–3, 183-190, and *Sharing Possessions. Mandate and Symbol of Faith* (Philadelphia: Fortress, 1981) 21–3; B.H. Mönning, *Die Darstellung des urchristlichen Kommunismus nach der Apostelgeschichte des Lukas* (PhD thesis; Göttingen, 1978); L. Schottroff and W. Stegemann, 'Die konkrete Sozialutopie des Lukas', *Jesus von Nazareth: Hoffnung der Armen* (Stuttgart: Kohlhammer, 1978) 149–53; D.P. Seccombe, *Possessions and the Poor in Luke-Acts* (Linz, 1982) 199–214; M. Hengel, *Property and Riches in the Early Church* (London: SCM, 1974) 31-4; H.J. Klauck, 'Gütergemeinschaft in der klassischen Antike, in Qumran und im neuen Testament', *RQ* 11 (1982–85) 47–79; J.A. Fitzmyer, 'Jewish Christianity in Acts in Light of the Qumran Scrolls', in L.E. Keck and J.L. Martyn (eds.),*Studies in Luke-Acts* (Nashville, 1966) 230–57.

[2]D.L. Mealand, 'Community of Goods and Utopian Allusions in Acts II–IV', *JTS* 28 (1977) 96–7.

frequently found in Plato's *Republic* and other writings in conjunction with the 'all things common' *topos*.[4] A Greek proverb about friendship, 'friends have all things in common' (κοινὰ τὰ (τῶν) φίλων), is preserved from antiquity with extraordinary frequency.[5] It is found in conjunction with another proverb, 'friends are one soul' (μία ψυχή) in a line of Aristotle's *Nichomachian Ethics*.[6] The combination of the phrases 'all things common' and 'one heart and soul' at Acts 4:32 is remarkably similar. Luke seems intent to suggest that the life of the earliest community in Jerusalem realised the vaunted Greek ideal of friendship.[7]

It is therefore clear that Luke presents the early Christians in Jerusalem in the dress of Greek thinking about ideal political organisation, or a state of detachment from possessions realised by the ideally pious. This is often taken as an indication that Luke is *idealising* events of lesser magnitude into a formal sharing of property, and that the historical reality was only some occasional events of charitable generosity.

---

[3]*E.g.* Plato, *Crit.* §110D; *Resp.* 3.22 §416D; 5.10 §462C (also §463B–C, E); *Legg.* 5 §737C, *Resp.* 5 §464D; Philo, *Hyp.* 11.4 on the property-sharing Essenes; Arrian, *Epict.* 3.24 §68; Iamblichus, *Vit. Pyth.* 18 §30, 30 §167; Aristophanes, *Ekk.* §§590–595; Aelius Aristides, *Pan. in Cyz.* 24; Lucian, *On Salaried Posts in Great Houses* §§19-20.

[4]*Op. cit.*, 97. Mealand cites Plato *Crit.* §110D; *Resp.* 3.22 §416D, 5 §464D, 8 §543B; *Tim.* §18B. Also Euripides, *And.* 376; Euhemerus in Diod. Sic. 5.45.5; Iamblichus, *Vit. Pyth.* 30 §168.

[5]Euripides *And.* 377, *Ph.* 244, Or. 735; Plato, *Phaedr.* 279C, *Lys.* 207C, *Resp.* 424A, 449C, *Legg.* 5.739C; Aristotle, *Pol.* 2.2.1263A, *Eth. Eum.* 1237B, 1238A, *Eth. Nic.* 8.9.1159B, 9.8.1168B; Diogenes Laertius 4.53, 6.37, 6.72, 8.10, 10.11; Libanius, *Ep.* 327.3.2, 1209.4.4, 1236.3.4, 1504.1.6, 1537.5.2; Iamblichus *Vit. Pyth.* 6 §32, 19 §92; Porphyry, *Vit. Pyth.* 33; Lucian, *On Salaried Posts in Great Houses*, §§24-25; Aelius Aristides, *Pan. in Cyz.* 24; Menander, in *Menandri Sententiae*, ed. S. Jaekel (Leipzig, 1964), 534, in *Menandri quae supersunt*, ed. A. Koerte and A. Thierfelder (Leipzig, 1959) 10.1; Terence, *Adelph.* 803–4; Plutarch, *De frat. am.* 20.490E; Philo, *De Abr.* 235; Seneca, *Ep.* 6.2–3; Martial, *Ep.* 2.43.1, 16; Dio Chrysostom 3.111, 37.7; Plutarch, *Flatt.* 65A, *Quaest. Conv.* 644C, 743E, *Amatores* 767D; *Praec. geren. rep.* 807B, *Non posse suav. viv. sec. Epic.* 1102F; Appian, *Bella Civilia* 5.3.19; Sextus, *Sentences* (ed. H. Chadwick) Nr. 228; Athenaeus, *Deipn.* 1.14.10 (=1.8A); Eustathius, *Comm.* Il. 2.184.12, 2.817.13, 3.456.17, 3.465.29, 3.473.8, 3.566.14; Clement of Alexandria, *Protrept.* 12.122.3; Cicero, *De off.* 1.16.51, *Laws* 1.12.34; Schol. to Plato, *Phaedr.* 297C; Photius, *Lexicon*, κοινόω; Plutarch, *Non posse suav. viv. sec. Epic.* 1102F; Seneca, *De benef.* 7.4.1; Philo,*Vit. Mos.* 1.156–159, *cf. Sobr.* 56–57; Dio Chrysostom, 3.104ff.

[6]9.8.2 §1116B.

[7]*Cf.* A.C. Mitchell, 'The Social Function of Friendship in Acts 2:44-47 and 4:32-37', *JBL* 111 (1992) 255-72.

(2) Peter's challenge to Ananias and Sapphira, who have failed to hand in the full price obtained from the sale of their property, at Acts 5:4, includes the rhetorical questions 'While it remained (unsold) did it not remain yours, and after it was sold, did it not remain in your power?' This is taken to indicate that their donation of property was voluntarily undertaken. It is argued that since they were under no complusion to make the sale, there can have been no formally organised community of property. That Acts remembers only one other example of major property-surrender, that of Barnabas (4:36-37), is thought to indicate that such events were rare. The rare occurrence of large-scale donations of property to the community is taken to weigh against the existence of formal property-sharing arrangements.

(3) In Acts 6:1-6 care for widows was at issue. This underprivileged group remained identifiable and permanently dependent upon the community, in need as it were of a perpetual 'dole'. Hence, it is argued, there was no common ownership of property, merely a structure which provided care for the indigent. The widows of the 'hellenists' complain that they are being 'overlooked' (6:1). This is sometimes taken to imply that organisation of the community was rudimentary, suggesting that no well-organised community of property existed, but only badly run charity.

(4) Property-sharing on a determined model such as Acts seems to imply does not recur in the New Testament period, and does not reappear until the birth of monasticism (late 3rd century AD). Hence it is unlikely that it was ever a feature of earliest Christianity.

An argument occasionally raised *in favour* of finding an important kernel of historical truth in Luke's claim that the early church in Jerusalem had 'all things common' is the testimony of the Fourth Gospel that Jesus' party of travelling disciples lived from a common purse, administered by Judas.[8] Might not they simply have preserved this mode of life, and opened it to those who desired to join them, in Jerusalem? It is possible that property-sharing was from the day of Pentecost effectively limited to an 'inner group' within the community, the disciples and those who joined them in their common purse, or that over time it became limited to this inner group although at the beginning there was a serious attempt to include all believers. The

[8]Jn. 12:6; 13:29.

Galilean travelling party's habit of living from a common purse may even have been opened to those converted on the day of Pentecost without carefully laid plans about what should follow.

An argument in favour of Luke's account rarely given the weight it deserves derives simply from the existence of community of goods as an established feature of 1st-century Palestinian culture, amongst those Essene communities which shared their property communally. Scholarly comparisons of Essene practice and the Acts account of Christian community of goods have almost universally found the phenomena vastly different and quite unrelated. The net result is to grant one set of sources credence, but to throw the other (the claims of Acts) largely to the wind. This outcome has a certain historical implausibility. Since two sets of sources seem to attribute the same practice to two Jewish sects which existed at the same time, in the same small country of Palestine, the balance of probability is in favour of some kind of connection between them. Otherwise we must attribute to mere coincidence that Luke portrays the earliest Christians in Jerusalem operating a practice common in their environment. It is well known that there is also a high degree of idealisation of the Essenes in Philo and Josephus. If Essene community of goods survives this aspect of the sources but Christian community of property does not, are the sources being treated even-handedly? Although we have no knowledge of the actual practice of community of goods in this period anywhere else in this ancient world, despite much philosophical lauding of the ideal, we have *two* claimed instances of it in our sources for early 1st-century Palestine. Can the consensus be correct to hold them quite apart?

II. Community of Goods as a Feature of Palestinian Culture

As is well known, Philo, Pliny the Elder and Josephus all attribute a communal lifestyle to the sect of the Essenes.[9] Our information about this practice was substantially augmented by the discovery of the *Rule of the Community* (1QS) from cave 1 at Qumran, which contains the legislation which governed the practice of community of goods. Amongst the Dead Sea scrolls were also discovered fragments[10] of the

[9]Philo, *That every good man is free* 75-91; *Hypothetica* 1-18; Pliny the Elder, *Natural History* 5.17.4 §73; Josephus, *BJ* 2.119-161; *Ant.* 18.18-22.
[10]From cave 4 (4Q266-273), cave 5 (5Q12) and cave 6 (6Q15).

Damascus Document (CD), already known since its discovery in 1896 in the Cairo Geniza, which legislates a looser form of social organisation. Despite recent objections to the 'Essene' character of the Dead Sea Scrolls, this treatment will allow the designation 'Essene' to the *Rule*, while conceding that the term may have denoted a broad movement containing a complexity of groupings rather than a monolithic entity.[11]

The legislation governing community of property in the *Rule of the Community* consists of a description of a complex entry procedure (1QS 6:13-23[12]) and a rule concerning lies in regard to matters of property which follows in lines 24-25. The entrance procedure was phased: an initial examination was followed by a period of testing (possibly a year, 1QS 6:13-15), after which a second examination took place followed by a further year of testing (6:15-17). During the period of testing up to this point, which might be termed the 'postulancy', the candidate for entry did not surrender his property to the community. On successful completion the candidate was allowed to eat the pure food of the community but not to touch the community's drink. The candidate was also allowed to surrender his property on a provisional basis and to enter a final year of testing, which could be termed the 'novitiate':

> ... the many shall enquire about his affairs according to his intelligence and deeds in the Law, and if the lot go forth for him to approach the company of the community on the authority of the men of their covenant, they shall commit both his property and his income into the hand of the man who is acting as Overseer. He shall enter it to the man's credit in the account with the possessions of the Many but he must not spend it on the Many. (1QS 6:18-20)

The candidate's surrender of property was therefore always made on a provisional basis at first. The candidate proceeds to full membership and full participation in the common purse—'mixing' his property—on successful completion of the novitiate year:

---

[11]L.H. Schiffman's identification of the authors of the scrolls as Sadducees, 'The Sadducean Origins of the Dead Sea Scroll Sect', in H. Shanks (ed.), *Understanding the Dead Sea Scrolls* (New York: Random House, 1992) 35-49, is considered one-sided by J.C. Vanderkam, *The Dead Sea Scrolls Today* (Grand Rapids: Eerdmans, 1994) 71-98 and O. Betz and R. Riesner, *Jesus, Qumran and the Vatican* (London: SCM, 1994) 36-49. Betz and Riesner expose the weaknesses in the views of R. Eisenman (69-82) and B. Thiering (99-113); *cf.* also E.M. Cook, *Solving the Mysteries of the Dead Sea Scrolls* (Carlisle: Paternoster, 1994) 82-151.

[12]*Cf.* Josephus, *BJ* 2.137–42.

> ... if it be his destiny, according to the judgement of the Congregation, to enter the Community, then shall he be inscribed among his brethren in the order of his rank for the Law, and for justice, and for the pure Meal; his property shall be mixed and he shall offer his counsel and judgement to the Community. (1QS 6:21-23)

The provisional surrender of property is to be explained as a social necessity if community of property is to be successfully established. It enables the candidate to experience what life in community of goods means in practice with a minimum of risk. Should the candidate find himself unable to carry out his intent to live without property in practice, he can simply receive back his property and leave. Were he to make full surrender of property immediately on seeking to enter the community, his first misgivings would precipitate a process of increasing anxiety, since he has already fully committed himself to the community. The community would have greater difficulty, even if it so desired, in returning his property, since it had already entered the communal economy. How much should be returned? The provisional surrender procedure offers maximum protection to both the candidate and the community, thereby in fact giving the greatest chance of the candidate's easy progress into full membership.

The procedure of provisional surrender of property is also found in the hellenistic accounts of the reputed community of goods of the Pythagorean community, at Croton in Magna Graecia, in the 6th century BC. Specific mention is made of the return of the candidate's funds, should he not proceed to full membership.[13] On this point the Pythagorean sources illuminate the Essene procedure. The question of 'Pythagorean influence' upon the Essenes has often been posed, but similarities between the Essenes and the Pythagoreans[14] are insufficient to justify the assertion that the Jewish sect consciously modelled itself upon this Greek philosophy.[15] The similar entrance procedure probably evolved independently as the only practical means of achieving integration of new candidates into a property-sharing community. In fact, such procedures are usually found wherever elective human communities attempt to construct communality of property without coercion. Close parallels, probably also developed independently out of the same social necessities, are found in Christian monasticism[16] and in at least one Anabaptist property-sharing group.[17]

While the additional information which the *Rule of the Community* provides will be essential to the case here presented, we must avoid an unhelpful tendency which its discovery has introduced into the debate concerning possible similarity between the practice of community of goods in Essenism and earliest Christianity. The discovery of this document amongst others in the caves by the site of the Essene settlement at Qumran has sometimes led commentators to assume that Essene community of goods was limited to the Qumran site, and always had a monastic, completely isolated ethos. As is readily apparent from both Philo and Josephus, Essene communities which practised full property-sharing were distributed amongst the towns and villages of Palestine.[18] The *Rule of the Community* itself assumes that it legislates for small communities.[19] Focus on the desert site at Qumran alone in the portrayal of Essene community of property gives an incorrect impression of its ethos. At the desert site, Essene

---

[13]Iamblichus, *Vit. Pyth.* 17 §72: 'After this, he ordered those who came to him to observe a quinquennial silence.... During this (probationary) time, however, the property of each was disposed of in common, and was committed to the care of those appointed for this purpose.... And with respect to these (probationers), those who appeared worthy to participate of his dogmas, from the judgment he had formed of them from their life and the modesty of their behaviour, after the quinquennial silence, then became 'esoterics'.... But if they were rejected, they received back the double of the wealth which they brought, and a tomb was raised for them as if they were dead...'. Iamblichus in another passage says that the candidate received his property back 'and more' (καὶ πλείονα, 30 §168), and again that the disciples 'drove him out of the auditory, loading him with a great quantity of gold and silver' (17 §74). *Cf.* Hippolytus, *Ref. omn. haer.* 1.2: 'on being released, he was permitted to associate with the rest, and remained as a disciple, and took his meals along with them; if otherwise, however, he received back his property, and was rejected.' The likelihood of an historical community of goods amongst the original disciples of Pythagoras is not great; *cf.* J.A. Philip, *Pythagoras and Early Pythagoreanism* (Toronto, 1966) 25ff, 185ff. Neopythagoreanism was influenced in its portrayal of Pythagoras' school at Croton by the Platonic ideal state; *cf.* R. von Pöhlmann, *Geschichte der sozialen Frage und des Sozialismus in der antiken Welt* (München, 1912) II, 611. However, the process of provisional surrender implies actual experience of community of property, probably in Neopythagoreanism.

[14]Demonstrable are only community of goods, reverence for the sun, white garments, and emphasis on ritual purity.

[15]*Cf.* M. Hengel, *Judentum und Hellenismus* (Tübingen: Mohr, ^{2}1973) 448–53.

[16]*Cf. The Code of Canon Law in English Translation* (Canon Law Society of Great Britain and Northern Ireland, 1983) 116–7.

[17]*Cf.*R. Friedmann (ed.), *Andreas Ehrenpreis. An Epistle on Brotherly Community* (New York: Plough, 1978) 59-62.

[18]Josephus, *BJ* 2.124; Philo, *Hypothetica* 11.1. At *Every good man is free* 12 §76 Philo has the Essenes living in villages but avoiding the towns (= cities), but he is here imposing the literary topos of flight from cities as evil places; *cf.* Plato, *Laws* 677B (no cities in the primaeval age); Dio Chrysostom 7.7, 59; Tibullus, *Elegies* 1.51ff. *Cf.* Philo, *De vit. cont.* 19; *De Abr.* 23; *De decal.* 2; *De prov.* in Eusebius, *Praep. ev.* 8.14.12.

community of property undoubtedly involved a high degree of social isolation and may even have involved a sophisticated system of common production on land owned and irrigated by the community. Concerning the Essene community of Qumran, scholars may be right to speak of Essene 'exile', and to employ, as they often do, the terms 'monks', 'monastery' and 'monastic'. However, at most two hundred souls could live at Qumran,[20] although as we know the Essene movement numbered some four thousand.[21] Life at the desert site, therefore, although the most striking manifestation of Essene community of goods,[22] involved a physical isolation from the surrounding populace which the Essene life in community of property did not always involve.

A revealing passage in one of Philo's accounts actually shows how property-sharing Essenes in the settlements distributed throughout Palestine had daily contact with outsiders through their work, which typically took them *outside* their communities. They recreated their common life each day by a process of sharing their wages in the evening, at their return from work, for the common meal. After explaining that the Essenes hold property in common, and what kinds of work they undertake each day, such as farming, shepherding, beekeeping and crafts (*Hypothetica* 11.4–9), Philo describes their evening gathering:

> Each member, when he has received the wages of these so different occupations, gives it to one person who has been appointed as treasurer. He takes it and at once buys what is necessary and provides food in abundance and anything else which human life requires. Thus having each day a common life and a common table they are content with the same conditions, lovers of frugality who shun expensive luxury as a disease of both body and soul. (*Hypothetica* 11.10–11)[23]

This daily round was the process by which property was shared in the distributed Essene communities on an ongoing basis, after individuals

[19]1QS 6:3-4 enjoins, 'And in every place where there are ten men of the Council of the Community there shall not lack a priest among them.' Regulations for entry into the community with full surrender of property begin at 6:13-14: 'Every man from Israel who volunteers to join the Council of the Community…'. Hence those who had made full surrender of their goods to the community could live in communities of males numbering as little as ten.

[20]*Cf.* R. de Vaux, *Archaeology and the Dead Sea Scrolls* (London, 1973) 86.

[21]Philo, *That every good man is free* 75; Josephus, *Ant.* 18.20.

[22]Hence Pliny the Elder limits not merely Essene community of goods but the whole Essene movement to the site by the Dead Sea.

had made the required property-surrender on joining the order. The daily handing-in of wages was complementary to the major act of property-surrender which each member made only once, in the course the lengthy entrance-procedure (1QS 6:13-23). Craftsmen and day-labourers pursue their own occupations during the day, but are required each evening to hand over their earnings to the community. This 'double' structure in the Essene system of property-sharing has been missed by commentators. It is also implied in the (otherwise quite curious) legislation of the *Rule of the Community*, where the novice's 'property *and earnings* shall be caused to approach into the hand of the man who has the oversight of the earnings of the Many' (1QS 6:19f.),[24] and community members are exhorted to abandon 'wealth *and earnings*' (הון ועמל כפים, 9:22).[25] The mention of 'earnings' in the *Rule of the Community* makes it plain that the daily collection of wages was usual for Essene community of property. If production was communalised at the Qumran site, the daily collection of wages would not have occurred; strictly, however, the mention of 'earnings' in 1QS may have something to do with why so many coins were found there.[26] As property-sharing Essenes usually worked outside their communities, the absence of complete social insulation from the surrounding population implies that it is inappropriate to apply the term 'monasticism' to Essenism anywhere except at the desert site.

The *Damascus Document* mentions women and children and legislates that a tax of two days' pay per month be raised for the support of orphans and widows.[27] This looser social form was appar-

---

[23]Translation F.H. Colson, *Philo* IX (Loeb Classical Library, 1941) 441, but reading at the beginning of this passage ἕκαστος as 'each member' rather than 'each branch', a deduction of common production which the text does not support. G. Vermes and M.D. Goodman, *The Essenes according to the Classical Sources* (Sheffield: JSOT Press, 1989) 29, similarly translate: 'When each man receives his salary for these different trades…'.

[24]יקרבו גם את הונו ואת מלאכתו אל יד האיש המבקר על מלאכת הרבים. Here we follow E. Lohse's translation of מלאכה as 'Einkünfte' ('earnings'), *Die Texte aus Qumran. Hebräisch und Deutsch* (München: Kösel-Verlag, [2]1971) 25. This seems preferable to Leaney's translation 'possessions'; *The Rule of Qumran and its Meaning* (London: SCM, 1966) 190.

[25]Lit. 'property and work of the hands.' G. Vermes, *The Dead Sea Scrolls in English* (Harmondsworth: Penguin, [2]1975) 88, translates 'wealth and earnings'.

[26]*Cf.* R. de Vaux, *Archaeology and the Dead Sea Scrolls*, 18-19; 22-23, 34, 37, 44. Level Ib (*c.* 135-4 BC), 166 coins; Level II (*c.* AD 6-68) 270. Against the view of C. Rabin, *Qumran Studies* (Oxford, 1957), that 1QS legislates not for community of property but for a closed trading circle, see D.L. Mealand, 'Community of Goods at Qumran', *TZ* 31(1975) 129-39.

ently more suited to married communities. The discovery of this document in the Qumran caves probably alone indicates that the communities for which it legislates were an accepted part of the movement, which included the celibate male communities for which 1QS legislates. The combination of marrying and celibate communities within the Essene movement is confirmed by Josephus, who notes a 'second order' of marrying Essenes,[28] of which the *Damascus Document* clearly gives us an internal view. It is worth noting that Josephus, as an outside observer, does not note any difference between the property arrangements of the two types of Essene community. When he states that this order 'while at one with the rest in its mode of life, customs, and regulations, differs from them in its views of marriage,'[29] he appears to think that the difference of view on marriage was the only actual difference between the social forms of the two types of Essene community. This may suggest that the social pattern of the *Damascus Document* married communities often approached in character aspects of the life of the 1QS communities, for example with frequent communal meals for adults, and a willingness for mutual support to extend if necessary beyond the regulated tax for the support of widows and orphans.

Commentators who contrast a 'monastic' settlement at Qumran with 'married' Essene communities throughout Palestine oversimplify the reality of Essene community of goods. The Essene movement knew, distributed throughout Palestine, both celibate, fully property-sharing communities and married communities with more limited formal mutual support. Particular towns and villages will have known linked communities of both types.[30] This gives us a very important insight into the ethos of the Palestinian practice of community of goods. It was not promoted as the only valid lifestyle by those who lived after the fashion of the *Rule of the Community*. Rather, it was a form of life appropriate only to a section of the Essene movement, the 'Council of the Community.'[31] Community of goods was therefore

[27]CD 14:13

[28]*BJ* 2.160–1.

[29]*BJ* 2.161.

[30]In social terms those undergoing the complex and lengthy entrance procedure into 1QS-type communities may have stood somewhere in between.

[31]*Cf.* above, n. 19. The twelve men and three priests who comprise the 'Council of the Community' in 1QS 8 were probably the original founding group whose life in community of property was extended to others as the group was later expanded; *cf.* E.F. Sutcliffe, 'The First Fifteen Members of the Qumran Community', *JSS* 4(1959) 134-8.

conventionally practised in Palestine on the understanding that it was a way of life appropriate to a part, in particular the superior part, of a religious movement, but not to all.[32]

The foundation at Qumran can be dated to around 150–135 BC,[33] a date supported by the probable identification of the 'Teacher of Righteousness' as the Zadokite High Priest who presided from 159 to 152 BC, when he was ejected by Jonathan Maccabaeus.[34] Community of goods had therefore been a feature of Palestinian culture, progressively becoming more and more widespread amongst the sect of the Essenes, for almost two centuries at the time of the events of property-sharing in the early church of Jerusalem which Luke describes in Acts. It is possible that other conventicle-type groups existed with similar practices apart from those known to us as Essenes; did the disciples of John the Baptist, for example, keep a common purse, as had Jesus' party of travelling disciples?[35]

The long establishment of Essene community of goods and its widespread distribution amongst the towns and villages of Palestine mean that its processes of administration must have been commonly understood. It could hardly be otherwise with an impressive and distinctive social form which must have frequently attracted attention and discussion. Any religious group within Palestine with a mind to try, any group which thought the exercise meaningful, could have reasonably easily imitated Essene community of property.[36] Both Philo and Josephus present the Essenes as the supreme example of Jewish piety; their currency was surely high in Palestine. Since the issue of wealth and poverty was a theme of Jesus' teaching, his disciples must

---

[32]It may be that older Essene males from *Damascus Document* communities passed over, after raising families, to the celibate lifestyle of the 1QS communities.

[33]*Cf.* R. de Vaux, *Archaeology and the Dead Sea Scrolls*, 116-7; G. Vermes, *The Dead Sea Scrolls. Qumran in Perspective*, 151.

[34]*Cf.* H. Stegemann, *Die Entstehung der Qumrangemeinde* (Bonn, 1971) 224. The 'intersacerdotium' (159–152 BC) of Josephus, *Ant.* 20.237 is probably a fiction, since it is inconceivable that the Day of Atonement, at which a High Priest had to officiate, had not been celebrated in this period. The name of the Teacher was excised from the records. Other plausible views of the identification of the Teacher of Righteousness would not affect the argument here; *cf.* G. Vermes, *The Dead Sea Scrolls. Qumran in Perspective*, 147–56 and 161; J.H. Charlesworth, 'The Origin and Subsequent History of the Authors of the Dead Sea Scrolls', *RQ* 10(1980) 213–33.

[35]*Cf.* above, n. 8.

[36]While the Essenes may have been secretive about their doctrines, those who failed the entrance procedure in 1QS at least would have made its character known. There was no advantage to the Essenes in obscuring the fairness with which they would treat potential recruits to their property-sharing communities.

have discussed and weighed the Essene lifestyle. Did they attempt to imitate it in Jerusalem? Such is certainly possible, if only as an attempt to prolong the common purse which Jesus' travelling disciples had kept with him prior to the crucifixion. We must be prepared to follow seriously any hints in the account of Acts 2–6 that earliest Christian community of goods employed analogous procedures to Essene community of goods. In the following it will be argued that there are, in fact, a sufficient number of close terminological and administrative parallels between the Acts account and our sources on Essene community of goods to suggest that the property-sharing which took place in the earliest Christian community was substantially similar to Essene community of goods, and was probably modelled upon Essene practice.

III. The 'Summary' Statements of Acts 2:44-45 and 4:32, 34

Walter Bauer's immense familiarity with the nuances of Greek literature led him to argue in his 1924 article on the Essenes in the Pauly-Wissowa *Real-Enzyclopädie* that, since the descriptions of Essene community of goods in Philo and Josephus draw heavily upon Greek Utopian *topoi*, no Essene communities ever actually practised community of property.[37] Since the publication of the *Rule of the Community* from Qumran, which gives from an internal view, as we have seen, the legislation which governed Essene property-sharing, his argument has not been re-employed.[38] The method of attempting to discern historical reality simply by removing Greek commonplaces and seeing what remains has proved too crude in the case of Essene community of goods. However, as we have seen above, it is still applied to the case of the early Christian community of goods recounted in Acts. The method proves inadequate because community of goods, though rare in actual practice, was so lauded an ideal in the ancient world.[39] Any writer who sought to commend to his audience a group who had actu-

---

[37]W. Pauly *et al.* (eds.), *Real-Enzyclopädie der klassischen Altertumswissenschaft. Neue Bearbeitung* (Stuttgart, 1893ff.), *Supplement* IV (1924) 386-430, repr. in his *Gesammelte Aufsätze und Kleine Schriften*, ed. G. Strecker (Tübingen, 1967) 1-59.

[38]Only S. Segert, 'Die Gütergemeinschaft der Essener', *A. Salach oblata* (Prague: 1955) 66-73, discussed Bauer's position, which he found untenable in the light of 1QS.

[39]*Cf.* above and M. Wacht, 'Gütergemeinschaft', in T. Klauser *et al.* (eds.), *Reallexikon für Antike und Christentum* XIII (Stuttgart, 1982-84) 47–79.

ally instituted formal property-sharing arrangements would naturally have included in his account the rhetorical elements associated with the theme.[40]

In fact, a phrase in Acts 2:44 suggests that there was ancient, originally semitic source-material behind the assertion that the early believers 'had all things common'. The verse begins 'All those who believed *were together* (ἦσαν ἐπὶ τὸ αὐτὸ) and had all things in common (καὶ εἶχον παντα κοινά)'. The Dead Sea Scrolls employ the Hebrew adverb 'together' (יַחַד) as a substantive to indicate 'the community'. Max Wilcox observed that ἦσαν ἐπὶ τὸ αὐτὸ at Acts 2:44 reflects the semitic idiom 'to be to the together' (לִהְיוֹת לַיַּחַד) found in the *Rule of the Community* from Qumran.[41] The 'together' was for the Essenes a technical term designating the Essene *community*. It therefore appears that the Greek phrase 'all things common' was supplied (possibly prior to Luke's receipt of the tradition) as an epexegesis to explain a phrase (ἦσαν ἐπὶ τὸ αὐτὸ) which could not carry in Greek the technical significance which it had earlier had in a semitic source—that all who believed belonged to a יַחַד, a social grouping which included within its organisation formal community of goods arrangements. In this regard it is important to observe that John Chrysostom found the Greek phrase ἦσαν ἐπὶ τὸ αὐτὸ at Acts 2:44 awkward, which shows that it was not natural Greek, and deduced that it must refer on to the following phrase about community of goods.[42] B.W.W. Dombrowski has demonstrated that the designation יַחַד at Qumran probably began as an attempt to render into Hebrew the Greek term τὸ κοινόν.[43] Hence in Acts 2:44 the idiom has almost come full circle, being explained with a phrase which included the adjective κοινός.

Wilcox also showed that the idiom 'to add together' which at Acts 2:47 designates the process of expansion of the community (προσετίθει ... ἐπὶ τὸ αὐτό) reflects the Qumran idiom לְהוֹסִיף לַיַּחַד. Matthew

---

[40]This merely reveals rhetorical training. Libanius, John Chrysostom's teacher, supplied rhetorical exercises on the theme of denunciation of wealth; *Or.* 6–8, *cf. Progymn.* 9.5.

[41]M. Wilcox, *The Semitisms of Acts* (Oxford, 1965) 93-100.

[42]'And they speedily came, ἐπὶ τὸ αὐτὸ, to the same thing in common, even to the imparting to all'; *John Chrysostom. Homilies on the Acts of the Apostles*, tr. J. Walker and R. Sheppard, rev. with notes on the text H. Browne (Library of the Fathers; Oxford, 1851), Homily VII on Acts 2:44; *cf.* Homily XI on Acts 4:32, pp. 101-2 and 155-6.

[43]'היחד in 1QS and τὸ κοινόν. An instance of Early Greek and Jewish Synthesis', *HTR* 59 (1966) 293-307; further M. Weinfeld, *The Organisational Pattern and the Penal Code of the Qumran Sect* (Göttingen: Vandenhoeck & Ruprecht, 1986) 13-14.

Black approved Wilcox's analysis.[44] The appearance of this obviously semitic material, related elsewhere to the property-sharing Essenes, in a context in Acts related to community of goods strongly suggests the antiquity and historicity of the tradition of Acts 2:44 that the earliest church in Jerusalem practised community of goods.

These semitic idioms do not reappear in the second notice on community of goods in Acts 4:32 and 34, where 'idealising' in terms of the Greek commonplaces is stronger. H. J. Cadbury deduced from a comparison of 'summary' material in Luke's Gospel with its probable sources in Mark that Luke has a tendency to use summary-type material from his sources more than once, in order to give a more flowing narrative. Cadbury observed that when Luke does this, the first use of the material is closer to its original wording, but its second use, while varying wording for stylistic reasons, gives the original position in Luke's source.[45] That Acts 2:44 and 47 give instances of more semitic language, but Acts 4:32 and 34 a more stylised version of events, suggests that Luke has employed the same working method with his sources on the community of goods in Acts. From this we may deduce that the essential content of Acts 2:44-45, a statement about the יחד and a note that many believers sold their possessions, are closest to the pre-Lukan tradition behind Acts 4:32 and 34 and probably originated 'in that position' with either the story of Barnabas' property-donation, or that of Ananias and Sapphira, since these follow at 4:36–5:11.

IV. Barnabas, Ananias, and Sapphira: Acts 4:36–5:11

If Acts 5:4 indicates that the donation of property by Ananias and Sapphira was seen by Peter as voluntary, this may not actually contradict the existence of formal community of property within the earliest church in Jerusalem. Community of property can be both voluntary and formally organised, as in, for example, Christian monasticism. This verse may suggest that there existed within the community of believers an inner group which practised community of property, but that the practice did not extend to all. Ananias and Sapphira were under no compulsion to enter this inner group, but if they wanted to,

---

[44]M. Black, *An Aramaic Approach to the Gospels and Acts* (Oxford, ^{3}1967) 10.
[45]H.J. Cadbury, 'The summaries in Acts', in F.J. Foakes Jackson and K. Lake, *The Beginnings of Christianity* V (London, 1933) 392-402.

they had to obey its rules, which they signally failed to do by withholding some of their property.[46]

However, we have to ask more closely after the precise intent of Peter's question. As we have found a technical idiom involving the יחד terminology, elsewhere found in the *Rule of the Community*, in the note on community of goods at Acts 2:44, we must ask whether the procedures which appear in that document are not relevant for understanding this technical-sounding assertion of Peter about the status of Ananias' and Sapphira's property. As we have seen, joining an Essene property-sharing community involved a complex entry procedure in the course of which property was only surrendered on a provisional basis at first. This mechanism, designed to ensure the smooth running of the common purse, would have been fully explained to candidates for entry before they decided to hand their property over to the community. It would have been explained to them that, after handing in their property, it remained theirs for a year until their decision and permission to fully join the community. It passed into the keeping (physical control) of the community, but not into the community's possession (ownership).

The Essene novice, therefore, who secreted away some of his property expressed a grave distrust of the community and went through an acted lie as he surrendered his property, since all understood him to be surrendering the full amount. *Culturally, the meaning of a property-surrender ritual in 1st-century Palestine was that the candidate handed in all assets, and was known by all to be doing this, although the property remained fully his until a later date.* The holy trust of the moment, the essence of the ritual, revolved around the fact that although he was handing his property over, it still remained his, and would be returned to him at his request if he decided that the life in community of goods was not for him. *If an Essene novice was found to have withheld some of his property, the rhetorical challenge to him would stress the point that was uppermost in the minds of all those present, that his property was still regarded as entirely his own by the community, so that there was absolutely no need for him to have retained a part of it for his own security.* His security

[46]J. Schmitt, 'Contribution à l'étude de la discipline penitentielle dans l'église primitive', in A. Dupont-Sommer (ed.), *Les Manuscrits de la Mer Morte. Colloque de Strasbourg 1955* (Paris, 1957), 93-109, and E. Trocmé, *Le 'Livre des Actes' et l'histoire* (Paris, 1957) 196ff., both suggested that an 'inner group' structure helped understand the problems of the Ananias and Sapphira story. *Cf.* C. Grappe, *D'un Temple à l'autre* (Paris, 1992) 58-59. Schmitt, Grappe and Trocmé suggest that the 'young men' of Acts 5:6 and 10 may be novices.

was ensured by the community, who would exercise the holy trust of holding his property in his name alone until he finally joined the community completely, or departed. The rhetorical challenge to him could be formulated so as to stress that at the ritual of handing in his property, no change in its ownership occurred. *It was as much his after handing it in as it had been before.*

At Acts 5:4 Peter says that Ananias' property was 'his' before it was sold, and after sale 'in his power'. This may reflect exactly the same complex process as was employed in the Essene property-sharing community. The first phrase, 'When it remained, did it not remain yours...? (οὐχὶ μένον σοὶ ἔμενεν)' may refer to the period of initial training, the postulancy, during which the candidate's property remained fully in his control, outside the community's control, and was probably not liquidated. When Peter proceeds to ask '... and after it was sold, did it no remain in your power?' (καὶ πραθὲν ἐν τῇ σῇ ἐξουσίᾳ ὑπῆρχεν;) he may be referring to the unchanged status of Ananias' property in the 'novitiate' phase. He emphasises that, although Ananias had now liquidated his property and handed it over to the community, it remains as much his own, although no longer physically in his control. He must trust the community to keep it for him. The overall point of the two rhetorical questions is to say that nothing has changed; the property still belongs to Ananias.

In support of this reading of Acts 5:4, it may be pointed out that in both of the other claimed instances of actual community of goods in the ancient world, amongst the Essenes and in the accounts of Pythagoras, we find a phased entrance procedure involving only provisional initial surrender of property. The use of this progressive procedure is probably the only way to implement community of goods without a high degree of coercion and anxiety, since divesting oneself of one's property is so large and life-changing an act. Where we find the operation of community of goods, as Acts claims for the early Jerusalem community, we should *expect* to find this complex entrance procedure. Essene organisation was known throughout Palestine and available to serve as a model. At Acts 2:44 and 47 technical idioms using the יחד term, which designates precisely the community form which employed a phased entrance procedure, may be deduced behind Luke's Greek. The balance of probabilities is therefore on the side of assuming that such a procedure may have existed in the early Christian community. The texts become more intelligible on this assumption, which is thereby proved correct.[47] A regulation governing lies in matters of property follows immediately after the description of the Essene process at 1QS 6:24-25:

> If one of them has lied deliberately, he shall be excluded from the pure Meal of the Congregation for one year and shall do penance with respect to one quarter of his food.

Though the fate of the lying Essene novice was not so disastrous as that of Ananias and Sapphira, Peter calls Ananias' action a lie against the Holy Spirit and to God (5:4). The similarity between the two texts again shows that 1QS 6 illuminates the legal and cultural context of Acts 5:4.

It is argued that since the only other account of property-surrender which Acts relates is that of Barnabas (4:36-37), such events were rare. This may be correct, but does not necessarily speak against the existence of community of goods. Those who sought to join the property-sharing arrangements will still have required accommodation, and will have retained their own premises, but made them available for the community's use; at Acts 2:46 we see the community 'breaking bread from house to house'. To accommodate such meetings the community needed to retain its usable accommodation rather than dispose of it. It is most likely that major events of the sale and surrender of real estate would only occur when a member had property which could not be usefully employed. This would apply to those who had property surplus to their needs which could not serve the community in any way. If only those who had surplus property sold up and laid the proceeds at the apostles' feet, only a limited number of these property donations will have occurred. When Luke writes that 'as many as were owners of *houses and lands* sold them' (4:34) he seems to have wealthier members of the community in view. Poorer converts will not have been expected to sell their land and livelihood, but rather to work it and put the proceeds at the service of the community.

Barnabas is said to have been from Cyprus (4:36). The 'field' (4:37) of which he disposed may have been located there. Or, it may be that as someone entering upon special service for the community he had no further use for agricultural land. He soon appears in the important roles of introducing Paul to the Jerusalem apostles (9:27) and as the community's delegate to investigate the conversion of Gentiles at Antioch (11:22). These events may suggest that at the time of his prop-

---

[47]For further discussion *cf.* B.J. Capper, 'The Interpretation of Acts 5.4', *JSNT* 19 (1983) 117-31; 'In der Hand des Ananias. Erwägungen zu 1QS VI,20 und der urchristlichen Gütergemeinschaft', *RQ* 12(1986) 223-36.

erty donation he was being seconded to the leading class of the community.

Luke only had need, from a literary point of view, of one positive example to set against the negative example of Ananias and Sapphira. The presence of only one other example does not imply that Luke could not have named more. He may have had literary reasons for choosing Barnabas as his example. He has a *penchant* for giving an introduction to some of his characters before they arrive on stage in their major roles. Philip and Stephen are introduced in the election of the Seven (6:5) before Stephen's long speech and martyrdom (6:8–8:1) and Philip's evangelistic activity (8:4-40). Paul is introduced as the young man at whose feet the coats of Stephen's murderers were laid (7:58; 8:1) before his persecution of the church, conversion, and subsequent preaching (9:1-30). Similarly, the reader learns something of Barnabas in the present notice before his appearance in the important role of introducing Paul to the apostles at 9:27. Barnabas is singled out as Luke's example because of the later significant role that he would play, rather than because he achieved a reputation merely through selling his field.

V. Influence from an 'Essene Quarter' on Mount Zion?

How is it that technical processes and terminology known to us from 1QS seem to illuminate the Acts account of earliest Christian community of goods? Did the early Christians merely imitate Essene processes, or was there actually a conduit of direct Essene influence on the nascent Christian church? Some evidence does suggest that a group formerly linked with the Qumran Essenes may have lived in closest proximity to the first community of Jesus' disciples in Jerusalem and entered the community in significant numbers. Bargil Pixner has since 1976 argued that in New Testament times there was an 'Essene Quarter' in Jerusalem, on the southwest hill, known since the 1st century AD as 'Zion'.[48] The site which he delineates for the Essene settlement is immediately adjacent to the Cenacle church, the tradi-

[48]B. Pixner, *An Essene Quarter on Mount Zion? Studia Hierosolymitana* I, *Collectio Major* 22 (Jerusalem, 1976) 245–84, also reprinted separately; 'The History of the "Essene Gate" Area', *ZDPV* 105 (1989) 96-104; *Wege des Messias und Stätten der Urkirche*, ed. R. Riesner (Gießen/Basel: Brunnen, [2]1994) 180–207, 327–34. Dr. Riesner has kindly allowed the author to read his own 'Das Jerusalemer Essenerquartier und die Urgemeinde', forthcoming in *ANRW* II,26.2.

tional site of the 'upper room', where the events of Pentecost and the community of goods which immediately followed apparently took place.

As we have seen, both Josephus and Philo imply that the Essenes had settlements in every significant centre of population in Palestine. The sanctity of the holy city certainly suggests that, were the Essenes ever able to overcome their tension with the Jerusalem Temple-establishment we might expect to find Essenes there. The *Damascus Document* prescribes chastity for the male Essene while in the city.[49] Josephus refers to a 'gate of the Essenes' in Jerusalem, in the southwestern corner of the city wall on the southwest hill.[50] Rainer Riesner has noted that both J.B. Lightfoot[51] and E. Schürer[52] thought the name of the 'Gate of the Essenes' indicated an Essene settlement within the city behind it.[53] The line of the 1st-century southern wall of Jerusalem was traced by F.J. Bliss in 1894. In the section of the wall which ran northwest–southeast across the southwest extremity of the hill, as the wall turned the corner of the city, Bliss uncovered the successively laid thresholds of an ancient gate.[54] The location corresponds to Josephus' description. B. Pixner, D. Chen, and S. Margalit have uncovered afresh these thresholds. A variety of dating techniques show that they are a later addition to a Hasmonaean wall and date from the early Herodian period.[55]

---

[49]CD 12:1; *cf.* R. Riesner, 'Essener und Urkirche in Jerusalem', *BK* 40 (1985) 73.
[50]*BJ* 5.145.
[51]*Colossians and Philemon* (London, 1875) 94.
[52]*A History of the Jewish People in the Time of Jesus Christ* (Edinburgh, 1901) II.2, 215 n. 16.
[53]*Cf.* R. Riesner, *BK* 40 (1985) 70, and 'Das Jerusalemer Essenerviertel. Antwort auf einige Einwände', *Intertestamental Essays in honour of Józef Tadeusz Milik*, ed. Zdzislaw J. Kapera (Kraków: Enigma Press, 1992) 179-86, 179, and 180-2 against other explanations of the gate's name. The naming of the gates of Jerusalem after groups which live in the immediate vicinity of the gate within the wall is attested in other periods of the city's history. Until 1967 the nearby gate into the old city was known since the 19th century as *Bab el Maghreb* because of a settlement of Muslims from the Maghreb in North Africa, who established themselves just inside the wall; *cf.* B. Meistermann, *New Guide to the Holy Land* (London, 1923), 213. At the time of the crusades, David's Gate (*i.e.* the Zion Gate) in the southwest corner of the city became known as the 'Pisans' Gate, named after the 12th-century crusaders from Pisa who later established their settlement behind it; *cf.* the woodcut of Jerusalem in 1492 reproduced in M. Avi-Yonah, *A History of the Holy Land* (London, *c.* 1969) 231.
[54]*Cf.* F.J. Bliss and A.C. Dickie, *Excavations at Jerusalem 1894–1897* (London, 1897) 16-20, 26-28.

Confirmation that the Essene Gate was related to a community of Jerusalem Essenes comes from Josephus' information that, starting from Herod's tower Hippicus to the north, the wall first ran south, and 'descended through the place called *Bethso* (Βηθσώ) to the gate of the Essenes', before turning east. B. Pixner points out that J. Schwartz long ago deduced that Βηθσώ reflects the Aramaic בת צואה, indicating a sanitary facility,[56] an interpretation followed by G. Dalman.[57] As B. Pixner points out, the interpretation of Schwartz is strongly supported by a passage of the Temple Scroll from Qumran. Y. Yadin has argued for a connection with a prescription relating to the plan for the ideal organisation of the Temple and Jerusalem.[58] The passage prescribes the construction of a 'place of the hand outside the city' consisting of 'buildings (בָּתִּים)' for the disposal of waste (צוֹאָה, 11QTemple 46:13–16).[59] Josephus' phrase evokes a picture of an Essene community intensely concerned for the sanctity of the Holy City, who dwell within the walls but attend to sanitary requirements outside the boundary of the city. We are reminded of Josephus' description of the Essenes' scrupulous sanitary procedures.[60] A terrace lies outside the wall, a little

---

[55]On the dating of the remains of the Essene gate see B. Pixner, D. Chen and S. Margalit, 'Mount Zion: The "Gate of the Essenes" Re-excavated', *ZDPV* 105 (1989) 85-95; metrological researches are helpful in dating the lowermost threshold; it measures 2.66 metres wide, nine standard Roman feet (of 0.2957 metres), or six standard Roman cubits, showing that the gate cannot have been an original part of the Hasmonaean wall (87); pottery below the paving slabs within the gate is 'first century', Herodian in character, not later than 70 AD (87). B. Pixner, 'The History of the Essene Gate Area', *ZDPV* 105 (1989) 96-104, notes that Professor B. Mazar observed that the excellent workmanship of limestone slabs which line a channel which passes below the gate points to the workmen of Herod the Great (97). Pixner also points out (98) that the pottery below the paving slabs may be later than the gate itself, since Agrippa II undertook street paving operations to employ the workmen left jobless by completion of work on the Temple; Josephus *Ant.* 20.22. On the identification of Josephus' "Essene Gate" with the recently re-excavated gate see R. Riesner, 'Josephus' "Gate of the Essenes" in Modern Discussion', *ZDPV* 105 (1989) 105-9.

[56]B. Pixner, *An Essene Quarter on Mount Zion*, 256; J. Schwartz, *Crops of the Holy Land* (Jerusalem, 1900) 335. R. Riesner, *Bibel und Kirche* 40, 2 (1985) 71, points also to J. Schwartz *Das Heilige Land nach seiner ehemaligen und jetzigen geographischen Beschaffenheit*, ed. I. Schwartz (Frankfurt a. M., 1852) 206, Hebrew original text, הארץ תבואת (Jerusalem, 1845) 334.

[57]G. Dalman, *Jerusalem und Sein Gelände* (Gütersloh, 1930) 307.

[58]Y. Yadin, 'The Gate of the Essenes and the Temple Scroll', in his *Jerusalem Revealed. Archaeology in the Holy City 1968–1974* (Jerusalem, 1976) 90–91.

[59]On the interpretation of this passage see section II.3 of R. Riesner, 'Das Jerusalemer Essenerquartier und die Urgemeinde', forthcoming in *ANRW* II,26. 2.

[60]Josephus, *BJ* 2.147–149.

back along the wall to the northwest from the gate, below the scarp on which the wall rests at this point. In 1875 C. Conder took various cuttings in the rock of the scarp above the terrace to indicate a roofed construction outside the wall, built on the terrace.[61] He suggested that the construction had been a stable. This roofed establishment can now be seen to have been the *Bethso*. Pixner notes a number of cisterns and ritual baths hewn in the rock within the wall, which he suggests define the perimeter of the area of the Essene Quarter.[62]

Excavations at Qumran show that the site of the monastic 'head-quarters' of Essenism there was uninhabited from around 40–37 BC to somewhere between 4 BC and AD 6.[63] The presence of (rare) coins of Antigonus (40–37 BC) demonstrate that the previous phase of occupation persisted into Antigonus' reign. The timing of the abandonment of the Qumran site closely coincides with the archaeological evidence dating the construction of the Essene Gate to the early Herodian period. This strongly suggests that during their absence from the desert site, the Essenes of Qumran moved to Jerusalem and established their quarter on the southwest hill.

The period of abandonment of the Qumran site corresponds with the reigns of Herod the Great (36-4 BC) and his son Archelaus (4 BC - AD 6). The reason for the reoccupation of the site seems to have been the arrival of direct Roman rule in AD 6, after which, as the *War Scroll* shows, Essenism tends in a Zealot direction.[64] The wily Herod appears to have exploited inner-Jewish rivalries to his own advantage. He had to assert himself against the Hasmonaean dynasty, which he had deposed. The reason for the establishment at the Qumran site had been the Maccabaean seizure of the High Priesthood from the Teacher of Righteousness. Herod therefore seems to have turned to the prestigious Essenes of Qumran as a bulwark against popular support for the Hasmonaeans. In doing this he placed his finger on the Hasmonaeans' point of weakness, their illegitimacy, as non-Zadokites, as High Priests. According to Josephus, Herod 'held the Essenes in great honour, and thought higher of them than their mortal nature required'. The reason was supposedly the prophecy, by an Essene prophet called Menahem, of Herod's future rise to power, while the

---

[61]C. Conder, 'The Rock Scarp of Zion', *PEFQS* (1875) 81–89, see 84; *cf.* R. Riesner, *Bibel und Kirche* 40, 2 (1985) 72.

[62]B. Pixner, 'Unravelling the Copper Scroll Code. A Study of the Topography of 3Q15', *RQ* 11 (1983–86) 323–67.

[63]*Cf.* R. de Vaux, *Archaeology of the Dead Sea Scrolls*, 21–34.

[64]*Cf.* J.T. Milik, *Ten Years of Discovery in the Wilderness of Judaea* (London, 1959) 94-8.

king was yet a boy. When Herod was 'at the height of his power' he called Menahem for an audience to thank him, and 'held, from that time on, the Essenes in high esteem'.[65] The Essenes were a group whose long-standing opposition to the Hasmonaeans gave them common cause with Herod against the Hasmonaeans.[66] We can also surmise, on the basis of the Temple Scroll from Qumran, that the possibility of gaining influence in Herod's marvellous reconstruction of the Temple would prove extremely attractive to Essenes formerly grouped around Qumran. Some Essenes may have considered it the Temple hoped for in the *Temple Scroll*.[67] The alliance of the Essenes with Herod's house seems to have broken down under his son Archelaus. According to Josephus, the Essene prophet Simon interpreted a dream of Archelaus as pointing to his limited reign and final downfall.[68] The story points to the passing of Essene favour from the Herodian dynasty,[69] and is consistent with the archaeological evidence for the resettlement of the Qumran site during Archelaus' reign. It is hardly surprising that the Essenes did not succeed in sustaining an alliance with Archelaus, the most brutal and unloved of the Herods.[70]

The so-called 'David's Tomb', the oldest part of the Cenacle church, traditional site of the 'upper room' (Mk. 14:15; Acts 1:13; 2:1 ὑπερῷον; Lk. 22:12 ἀνάγαιον μέγα), lies about one hundred and seventy five metres to the north from the Essene gate, and has been thought to represent part of a pre-AD 70 Jewish-Christian synagogue.[71] It is, however, more likely to represent a corner-fragment of the 'Church of Holy Sion' (*Hagia Sion*), constructed around AD 340.[72] This Church extended eastward from 'David's Tomb' some one hundred metres, into the area which B. Pixner suggests was occupied by the Essene

---

[65]Josephus, *Ant.* 15.372–379.

[66]E. Bammel, 'Sadduzäer und Sadokiden', *ETL* 55 (1979) 107–15.

[67]R. Riesner, 'Das Jerusalemer Essenerviertel. Antwort auf einige Einwände', *Intertestamental Essays in honour of Józef Tadeusz Milik*, ed. Zdzislaw J. Kapera (Kraków: Enigma Press, 1992) 179-86, points to the theory of M. Delcor ('Is the Temple Scroll Source of the Herodian Temple?', in G.J. Brooke, *Temple Scroll Studies* [Sheffield: JSOT Press, 1989] 67–90) that the Temple Scroll influenced the design of the Herodian Temple.

[68]Josephus, *BJ* 2.113; *Ant.* 17.345–8.

[69]*Cf.* O. Betz, *Offenbarung und Schrifterforschung in der Qumransekte* (Tübingen, 1960) 99–109.

[70]*Cf.* Josephus, *Ant.* 17.342; *BJ* 2.111.

[71]J.W. Hirschberg, 'The Remains of an Ancient Synagogue on Mount Zion', in Y. Yadin (ed.), *Jerusalem Revealed* (Jerusalem, 1976) 116–7.

[72]*Cf.* J. Wilkerson, *Jerusalem as Jesus Knew It* (London, 1978) 170–1 .

Quarter. The centre of Hagia Sion lies roughly on the perimeter of this area. William Sanday[73] judged the patristic tradition of the site very positively:

> ...I believe that of all the most sacred sites it is the one that has the strongest evidence in its favour. Indeed, the evidence for it appears to me so strong that, for my own part, I think that I should be prepared to give it an unqualified adhesion.

The most important patristic testimony to the site comes from Epiphanius of Salamis, who came from Palestine, and who wrote (*c.* AD 392) that Hadrian found a small Jewish-Christian church on the site on his tour of the East in AD 130:[74]

> 'He found the whole city razed to the ground and the Temple of God trodden under foot, with the exception of a few buildings and of the little church of God, on the site where the disciples returning after the ascension of the Saviour from Olivet, had gone up to the upper room, for there it had been built, that is to say in the quarter of Zion...'.

Epiphanius' reference to the church is incidental to the context, which speaks for its authenticity; the purpose of the passage is to introduce Aquila as a translator of the scriptures. Hadrian undertook a tour of the East as a result of illness, which led to the foundation of Aelia Capitolina, with which Aquila was involved, on the razed site Jerusalem. Any writer who sought to give an account of Aquila would have to turn to ancient tradition, and Epiphanius' long and rambling account, typical of his style, appears to excerpt an earlier work which is recognisably a church-historical chronicle. The source appears to have centred on events in Jerusalem, so it is most likely a Palestinian chronicle. Epiphanius is known to cite Hegesippus elsewhere.[75] Hegesippus' anti-heretical chronicle represented virtually the standard work on the Jerusalem church, as can be seen from Eusebius' frequent dependence on him for information about Jerusalem Christianity.[76]

---

[73]W. Sanday, *Sacred Sites of the Gospels* (Oxford, 1903) 77–78.

[74]Epiphanius, *De mens. et pond.* 14. The Bordeaux Pilgrim gives a picture of the southwest hill in AD 333, prior to the construction of Hagia Sion, largely confirming Epiphanius, though he identifies the sole building as one of the seven synagogues which tradition has it once existed on the site, a tradition which Epiphanius also mentions in this context. *Cf. e.g.* H. Donner, *Pilgerfahrt ins Heilige Land* (Stuttgart, 1979) 57–8.

[75]T. Zahn, *Forschungen zur Geschichte des neutestamentlichen Kanons* (Leipzig, 1900) VI, 258, 261–2.

Hegesippus had dedicated his life to the refutation of heresy by an investigation of the traditions of the church in each of its major centres, as preserved by the established episcopate in each place,[77] compiling a succession list of bishops for Rome,[78] and certainly making the succession in Jerusalem clear in his history of the Jerusalem church, a record which Epiphanius uses.[79] Epiphanius' portrayal of Aquila in the present passage seems to echo his approach. The discipline of the church is the guiding principle. Aquila, an apostate from the Jerusalem community, went astray because of a perverse interest in astrology. Though the 'teachers' rebuked him for his error, eventually he had to be expelled.[80] This approach is certainly not unique to Hegesippus, but the account of Hadrian's arrival in Jerusalem most likely stems from his work, the *vade mecum* on heresy and the Jerusalem church. Hegesippus lived *c.* AD 115–85, and was a youth in Palestine at the time of Hadrian's visit.[81] After his travels he maintained intimate contact with the Jerusalem Church,[82] collecting the local tradition[83] and even using Jewish oral tradition.[84] Hegesippus would be a reliable witness for local tradition concerning the site of the upper room around AD 130.

The annalist Eutychius, patriarch of Alexandria in the 10th century, claims that Jewish Christians returned to Jerusalem in the fourth year of Vespasian (AD 72–73) following the destruction of Jerusalem in AD 70. Rainer Riesner points out that the date of this apparent return makes some sense, suggesting as it does normalisation of relations after the last resistance of the Zealots, at Masada, was put down in this year.[85] Eutychius associates the return with the building of a

---

[76]*Cf.* Eusebius, *Hist. Eccl.* 2.23.4–19; 3.11–12; 3.20.1–2; 3.32; 4.22.

[77]Eusebius, *Hist. Eccl* . 4.22.1–3.

[78]Eusebius, *Hist. Eccl.* 4.22.3. Epiphanius found his Roman bishop-list in 'certain memoirs' (*Haer.* 27.6), which are certainly those of Hegesippus; *cf.* J.B. Lightfoot, *Apostolic Fathers* I, S. Clement of Rome I (London 1890) 328–32, and Zahn, *Forschungen*,VI, 258–61.

[79]Epiphanius, *Haer.* 66.20; *cf.* Zahn, *Forschungen*, VI, 290.

[80]Epiphanius, *De mens. et pond.* 15.

[81]He had experienced the catastrophe of the Bar-Kokhba revolt personally, *cf.* Eusebius, *Hist. Eccl* . 4.8.1–4 and Zahn, *Forschungen*, VI, 250–4.

[82]He refers to it as *the* church; Eusebius, *Hist. Eccl.* 4.22.4–5.

[83]Eusebius, *Hist. Eccl.* 4.22.8.

[84]Hegesippus brought the name of Panther—unwittingly, from Jewish polemic against the virgin birth—into association with the family of Jesus, thus becoming an undesirable author; *cf.* Zahn, *Forschungen*, VI, 262, further 266–9. Epiphanius may intentionally avoid naming his source.

[85]R. Riesner, *BK* 40 (1985) 68.

church and the election of Simon bar-Clopas.[86] Eutychius at least gives a plausible explanation of the origin of the church that was to be found on the site in AD 130. J.E. Taylor has recently objected that the early Christians, in her view of low social level, are unlikely to have had a centre on the southwest hill, adjacent to the 'Belgravia' of the prestigious High Priestly houses.[87] However, the Fourth Gospel witnesses that the unnamed 'disciple whom Jesus loved', probably the host at the last supper,[88] and therefore probably the individual in whose house the 'Upper Room' was located, was 'known (γνωστός) to the High Priest' (18:15, 16); γνωστός has occasionally been taken to imply that the disciple was a kinsman of the High Priest, a meaning which the adjective can definitely carry.[89] B. Pixner has pointed out in objection to Taylor, that as well as a region of grand housing, there is an area of poorer dwellings on the southwest hill.[90] All evidence combined suggests that the Jerusalem Christians, only some of whom were drawn from the wealthier classes in Jerusalem, nevertheless gained a foothold on the hill (and indeed survived in the city generally) through the support of some wealthier patrons. The patristic tradition of the site is remarkably consistent with the New Testament and archaeological evidence.

The early Christian historians assume that from Simon's time onwards until the founding of Aelia Capitolina there was a Jewish-Christian presence in Jerusalem. Eusebius says that it was recorded 'that there was a very important Christian church in Jerusalem, administered by Jews, which existed until the siege of the city under Hadrian'.[91] Elsewhere he appears to know of the resettlement of Jews in Jerusalem by the time of Bar-Kokhba.[92] Adolf Schlatter argued the

---

[86]'Then the Christians, fleeing from the Jews, crossed the Jordan, and there established their seat. When they heard that Titus had destroyed the rebellious Jews, they returned to Jerusalem, nominating their second bishop Simon bar-Clopas. Clopas was the brother of Joseph who brought up our Lord Jesus Christ. This happened in the fourth year of Vespasian'; Eutychius, *Annales* 343.

[87]J.E. Taylor, *Christians and the Holy Places* (Oxford: Clarendon, 1993) 208, 218, 219.

[88]D.E.H. Whiteley, 'Was John written by a Sadducee?', *ANRW* II, 25.3, 2481–2505 (2494). The argument of Whiteley's whole piece suggests that this Jerusalem disciple had close connections with the High Priestly aristocracy.

[89]*Cf.* C.K. Barrett, *The Gospel According to St.John* (London: SPCK, [2]1978), 526.

[90]B. Pixner, *Wege des Messias und Stätten der Urkirche* (ed. R. Riesner; Gießen/Basel: Brunnen, [2]1994) 402-7.

[91]Eusebius, *Dem. ev.* 3.5 §124d. He probably has writers like Hegesippus and Julius Africanus in mind.

[92]Eusebius, *Dem. ev.* 6.18 §§285–96.

case for a resettlement of Jerusalem between the two wars with Rome, though his evidence, mainly Rabbinic, is not always convincing.[93] B. Lifshitz assumes with older opinion that Jerusalem lay in ruins till the foundation of Aelia Capitolina.[94] However, there are a number of quite believable Rabbinic references to pilgrim-visits of scholars to Jerusalem, to mourn the Temple, during the period.[95] The environs of the city also remained a treasured final resting place for Jews.[96] For the reliability of local memory we need not think of wholesale resettlement, merely of an ongoing attachment to the Holy City amongst Jewish Christians, which led to continuous contact with the city area, the erection of makeshift shelters, and some commemorative salvage of important sites. This is very much the picture which Epiphanius gives us, and makes his notice that the site of the Upper Room was remembered credible. As the probable site of the central premises of the Christian community in Jerusalem throughout the period c. AD 33–67, the Upper Room is the most likely pre-AD 70 Christian site of all to have been remembered. Jewish Christians, mourning the destruction of the city with their fellow-Jews, probably preserved the knowledge of the former site of their own centre, replete as it must have been with important memories.

Thus the major Essene community of Qumran relocated itself until about AD 6 to a site in the immediate vicinity of that probably used later on by the early church in Jerusalem from *c.* AD 30. In all probability some kind of Essene presence continued to that time on the site of the Jerusalem Essene Quarter, probably a group which chose to remain because it preferred to hold on to a connection won with the Temple and the High Priestly establishment. This group may have represented a quietist strand unwilling to return to the desert and the sharpening opposition of Qumran to the Jerusalem establishment. While Qumran Essenism now headed in the direction of the Zealots,[97]

93A. Schlatter, *Synagoge und Kirche bis zum BarKochba-Aufstand* (Stuttgart, 1966) 69–86.

94B. Lifshitz, 'Jérusalem sous la Domination Romaine', *ANRW* II, 8, 444–489.

95*b. Mak.* 24b; *Ber.* 3a; *y. Ḥag.* 2.77b (59), *cf. Ec. Rab.* 7.8. Further Schlatter, *op. cit.*, 73-78. Commenting on the phrase 'deeds of loving-kindness' in *'Abot* 1.2, Rabbi Nathan (*'Abot R. Nat.*, version A chapter 4) says: '"Woe to us!" Rabbi Joshua cried, "that this, the place where the iniquities of Israel were atoned for, is laid waste!" "My son," Rabban Yohanan said to him, "be not grieved; we have another atonement as effective at this. And what is it? It is acts of loving-kindness, as it is said, For I desire mercy and not sacrifice."'

96*M. Ṣem.* 10; *cf.* A. Büchler, *The Economic Conditions of Judaea after the Destruction of the Second Temple* (London, 1912) 17.

this group took a more independent course. It is entirely possible that this group of Essenes responded first to the preaching of John the Baptist, then to that of Jesus and his disciples, and passed into the Christian church.[98] If this happened, it will have provided a direct conduit for the transmission of the language and regulations of 1QS into the first church of Jerusalem.

VI. The 'Daily Ministry' of Acts 6:1-6

At Acts 6:1 a dispute over economic arrangements arises between the 'hellenists' (Ἑλληνισταί) and the 'Hebrews' (Ἑβραῖοι)within the growing community. The widows of the 'hellenists' were being 'neglected' or 'overlooked' (παρεθεωροῦντο) in the 'daily distribution' (διακονία καθημερινή). As may be deduced from the responsibilities of the financial officers visible in 1QS and, for example, the process of collection and distribution described by Philo at *Hypothetica* 11.4-11, community of goods in its Palestinian cultural context did not mean that all had direct access to funds and resources, but rather that resources were controlled by a limited number of officers. Hence mention of an 'underprivileged group' does not contradict organised community of goods. Elderly widows will have been a distinct group in, say, the community of the 'Hebrews' because they had right to receive resources without bringing any daily financial contribution from work outside the community.

Commentators frequently cite certain instances of organised care for the poor attested in Rabbinic literature[99] as analogous to the process of 'daily distribution' mentioned amongst the early Christians at Acts 6:1. The Rabbinic system was based on the synagogue, whose 'receivers of alms' (גבאי צדקה) administered a 'weekly money-chest' (קופה, lit. 'basket'), from which the local resident poor received money

---

[97]*Cf.* above, n. 64.

[98]Jesus' disciples were directed to find the room where they were to prepare the Last Supper by meeting and following a man carrying water who would aproach them (Mk. 14:13; Lk. 22:11). Carrying water was normally the work of the women-folk of the household. The man may have carried water because as a celibate he belonged to a community without women. It may have been a feature of Jerusalem life that if men were spotted carrying water, they were associated with the ascetic conventicle on the southwest hill. If this was not Jesus' reason, we must assume that a man walked in the direction of the disciples carrying a jar of water in order to be recognised by them, a rather contrived signal.

for the purchase of a week's meals (fourteen) each Friday, when the alms-collectors made their rounds to the houses of the district to collect money. A daily collection of food was also taken, in the 'tray' (תמחוי), for distribution to those poor in immediate need. Poor travelling through could receive food from the 'tray', but money from the 'basket' was restricted to the better-known resident poor.

This system is hardly close to Luke's description in Acts. The continual neglect of the hellenistic widows (παρεθεωροῦντο, 6:1, imperfect), suggests that *resident* poor seek to avoid being neglected in a *daily* distribution. In the Rabbinic system they would receive a weekly dole, not daily food. The information given in two phrases, the 'daily ministry' (6:1) and the apostles' refusal to 'serve at tables' (6:2) shows that the widows are provided for in the context of *daily meal fellowship* (*cf.* Acts 2:46). This is a fundamental difference between the Rabbinic and Christian systems, suggesting that the Rabbinic system has little to tell us about the ethos of the 'daily distribution' of Acts 6:1. Care for the poor of the community was always associated with table-fellowship in early Christianity;[100] a continuation of Jesus' characteristic meal-fellowship with 'tax-collectors and sinners'.

Jeremias[101] argues that the Rabbinic 'basket' and 'tray', which are well attested only for the 2nd century, operated in pre-AD 70 Jerusalem. G.F. Moore is cautious about an early dating of the Rabbinic system, noting that there are only 'scanty intimations' of it before the Hadrianic war, and nothing from the 1st century.[102] D. Seccombe has shown that Jeremias' evidence for the early dating carries no weight[103] and lists some evidence against. Accounts of the relief organised in two pre-70 famines make no mention of such a system.[104] Begging poor are frequent in the Gospels,[105] where the attitude towards begging is much more positive than in later times, when the system of poor-care made begging suspect.[106] The origins of the Rabbinic system are later, in the troubled times following the destruction of AD 70.

---

[99]On the system *cf.* S. Krauss, *Talmudische Archäologie*, III (Leipzig, 1912), 66–74; G.F. Moore, *Judaism*, II (Cambridge Mass., 1927), 174–8; H.L. Strack and P. Billerbeck, *Kommentar zum Neuen Testament aus Talmud und Midrasch* I (München, 1922) 387–91. *Cf.* K. Lake and H.J. Cadbury, *The Beginnings of Christianity* IV (London, 1933) 64; E. Haenchen, *The Acts of the Apostles* (Oxford: Blackwell, 1971) 261–2; C.S.C. Williams, *The Acts of the Apostles* (London: Black, 1957) 96; G. Schille, *Apostelgeschichte* (Berlin, ^{2}1984) 168; A. Strobel, 'Armenpfleger um des Friedens willen', *ZNW* 63 (1972) 271–76.

[100]*Cf.* 1 Cor. 11.17–34; *Epistle to Diognetus* 5; Justin, *Apol.* 1.13 and 67.

[101]*Jerusalem in the Time of Jesus* (London, 1969) 131–4.

[102]*Judaism* II, 175.

The Essene system of daily meal-fellowship with collection of wages and distribution noted above (Philo *Hypoth.* 11.4-11) is much closer to the 'daily ministry' of Acts 6:1 than the usually cited Rabbinic system. The early Jerusalem Christians broke bread and took food with each other on a *daily* basis (καθ' ἡμέραν ... κλῶντές τε κατ' οἶκον ἄρτον, μετελάμβανον τροφῆς, Acts 2:46). On this occasion distribution is made so that all believers receive 'according as any had *need*' (καθότι ἄν τις χρείαν εἶχεν, 2:45; 4:35). Acts 6:2 mentions *tables* (διακονεῖν τραπέζαις) in regard to these meals. Each of these elements appears in Philo's description of the daily Essene process:

> 'He (the treasurer) takes these (wages) and at once buys *what is necessary* (τἀπιτήδεια = τὰ ἐπιτήδεια) and provides food in abundance and anything else which human life *requires* (ὁ ἀνθρωπος βίος χρειώδης). Thus having *each day* (καθ' ἑκάστην ἡμεραν) a common life and a common *table* (ὁμοτράδεζοι, *cf.* 11:12 τράπεζα) they are content with the same conditions, lovers of frugality who shun expensive luxury as a disease of both body and soul.' (*Hypoth.* 11:10–11)

It might be objected that Luke connects distribution only with the sale and surrender of property (2:45, 4:34-35), and does not mention any collection of wages. However, the association of selling and distribution is formulaic, already laid down in Jesus' command to the rich man to 'sell all and give to the poor'.[107] Furthermore, Luke has based his summary material on the dramatic events of the sale and surrender of property which tradition recorded, and may not have heard of the less noticeable process of daily collection. Hippolytus, when describing *Essene* community of goods, makes the same, incor-

---

[103]'Was there organised charity in Jerusalem before the Christians?' *JTS* 29 (1978) 140–3. *M. Ketub.* 13:1–2 is about a claim on the estate of a woman's deceased husband, not on the community. Provision of a Passover meal for the poor from the 'tray' in *m. Pesaḥ* 10:1 is probably not pre–AD 70, since it is written as a prescription (imperatives), whereas *Pesaḥ* 5.1(ff.), describing the proceedings of the Passover at the Temple, is written in the perfect tense. The 'Chamber of secrets' in the Temple, *m. Sheqal.* 5:6, where the pious left alms for the poor, is a charitable institution of some kind, but is not similar to the 'basket' or 'tray'. G.F. Moore, *Judaism* II, 174, thought that the earliest notices date to just prior to the Hadrianic war.

[104]The grain distributions of Herod and Helena; Josephus, *Ant.* 15.299–316, 20.51–53.

[105]*Cf.* Lk. 18:35; Acts 3:2–10.

[106]The beggar is despised in Rabbinic teaching; *B. Bat.* 9a.

[107]Mk. 10:17–31 and parallels; Lk. 12:33.

rectly exclusive association of sale of property with the distributive process, though the Essenes did not simply live off their capital:

> No one amongst them, however, enjoys a greater amount of riches than another. For a regulation with them is, that an individual coming forward (to join) the sect must sell his possessions, and present (the price of them) to the community. And on receiving (the money) the head (of the order) distributes it to all according to their necessities. Thus there is no one among them in distress. (*Ref.* 9.14)[108]

Before we can understand the relation of the dispute of Acts 6:1-6 to the community of goods, we must first gain a picture of the social relations between the 'hellenists' and 'Hebrews'. The distinction between these two groups was probably linguistic in the first instance. All Jews in Palestine in the New Testament period would know at least some Greek, the *lingua franca* of the eastern Mediterranean since Alexander's conquests. The 'hellenists' were probably those Jews who knew *only* Greek, but no Aramaic or Hebrew.[109] These Greek-speaking Jews appear to have been a part of the synagogue communities with clear links with the Diaspora which appear at 6:9. We may therefore assume also a degree of cultural divergence from the community of the 'Hebrews', although this point should not be unduly stressed in view of the increasing appreciation of the penetration of Greek culture in Palestinian Judaism.[110] The 'hellenists' probably found participation in the (Aramaic) worship of the original disciple-group difficult, and started to develop as a more independent community, based in their own synagogues. Hence they rapidly came into conflict with those in the Greek-speaking synagogues who did not share their views, and a persecution resulted (6:9-8:3) which scattered them from Jerusalem (8:4). The apostles and by implication the community of 'Hebrews', Aramaic-speaking Christians, were able to remain in Jerusalem (8:1).

The solution to the dispute over care for the hellenists' widows was the appointment of seven officers (6:5). All Seven have Greek names and appear to be drawn from the hellenist community alone.[111] This implies that the solution to the dispute was *not* the integration of the 'hellenist' widows *into* the 'daily distribution' of the 'Hebrew'

---

[108]Translation by J. H. MacMahon, *Ante-Nicene Christian Library* (Edinburgh, 1870) I, 353.

[109]*Cf.* M. Hengel, *Between Jesus and Paul* (London: SCM, 1983) 1-29, 133–56; C.F.D. Moule, 'Once More, who were the Hellenists', *ExpTim* 70(1958–59) 100–102.

[110]*Cf.* especially M. Hengel, *Jews, Greeks and Barbarians* (London: SCM, 1980).

[111]One of their number, Nicolaus, is called a 'proselyte of Antioch'; Nicolaus (6:7).

congregation, but rather the establishment of officers to organise care within the hellenist community itself, which clearly had no arrangements of any kind for the care of its poor. They probably instituted a looser form of care based on charitable giving alone. With this move community of goods was left behind as something sometimes found within Palestinian Christianity, but not found in the wider church to which most of the New Testament writings bear witness.

The churches of the Pauline mission attest an interest in mutual support, without formal community of goods. Paul's mission was based on Antioch; we have no evidence that community of goods arrangements were ever instituted in Antioch as they had been in Jerusalem. The founding of the church at Antioch was the work of believers driven out from Jerusalem (Acts 11:19-21). Acts specifically states that these preachers were originally from Cyprus and Cyrene; they were probably hellenists driven out of the Greek-speaking synagogues such as those of Acts 6:9 (*cf.* the naming of Cyrene and Alexandria). Thus the social form instituted by the hellenists in response to the difficulties of Acts 6:1-6 is probably that observable at Antioch and in the Pauline mission. The 'hellenists' had probably never themselves been a part of the community of goods arrangements of the Hebrew group; their communities had grown separately from the start in the Greek-speaking synagogues. They faced the issue of caring for their poor with the looser structure based on charitable giving which became the pattern for later Christianity. The dispute over economic arrangements in Acts 6:1-6 is thus a record of the point at which community of goods was programmed out of the social form of the developing wider church.

While traditionally the model for the deacons of later Christianity, it appears that the Seven were really leaders for the separately developing community of hellenist believers. One of their number, Stephen, 'did great signs and wonders' (6:8) and encountered opposition over his public teaching (6:10-14). Clearly, his duties were not limited to the administration of care for the poor. Similarly, another of their number, Philip, when the hellenist Christians were scattered from Jerusalem, evangelised amongst the Samaritans (8:4-24). The Seven, therefore, were leaders of the hellenist community with responsibility both for teaching and care of the poor. In this combination of roles they appear very close to the 'Guardian' or *Mebaqqer* figure of the *Damascus Document*, who combines in himself teaching responsibilities with the duty to care for widows and orphans, including the raising of a tax for their support.[112]

As we have noted above, the ethos of community of goods in its Palestinian cultural context was as a practice appropriate for the leading section of a community of common belief, but not for all. Full property-sharing communities regulated by the *Rule of the Community* were linked with the partially property-sharing communites of the *Damascus Document*. The Christian community appears to have developed an analogous two-level structure. In creating a looser social form, the hellenists probably had a Palestinian model, and acted with the full approval of the Jerusalem apostles. The secondary communities which they created were the Christian counterpart to the Essene *Damascus Document* communities, in which the overseer ensured that the poor received succour, but in which community of goods was not practised. We hear of no regulated tax in the communities of the hellenists, but the two-level structure in the different sects gives the analogy point. The hellenist communities probably organised charitable care for the poor as it is found in later Christianity. They also probably began the practice of occasional, rather than daily, fellowship meals, also the pattern of later Christianity. This looser social form could not sustain community of goods, which as we have seen depended on the *daily* gathering and sharing of all members of the community. In Jerusalem, comunity of goods extended over a section of the community of the 'Hebrews'. It was not binding on the whole group, and was probably not reproduced amongst the hellenists while in Jerusalem, and certainly not in the hellenist community at Antioch and beyond in the Pauline mission.

VII. Conclusions

The Christian church considered for centuries that Luke's evocative picture of community of goods was realised in the 'angelic life' of monasticism.[113] Some Anabaptist groups at the Reformation and since have taken it as a realisable ideal for all Christians.[114] The very nega-

[112]CD 13:7–14:2; *cf.* W. Staerk, *Die jüdische Gemeinde des Neuen Bundes in Damaskus* (Gütersloh, 1922) 32.

[113]*Cf.* L. T. Johnson, *The Literary Function of Possessions in Luke-Acts* (Missoula: Scholars Press, 1977) 1 and n. 3.

[114]*Cf.* H.-D. Plümper, *Die Gütergemeinschaft bei den Täufern des 16. Jh.* (Göppingen, 1972); R. Friedmann, 'The Christian Communism of the Hutterite Brethren', *ARG* 46 (1955) 196–209; V. Peters, *All Things Common. The Hutterian Way of Life* (Minneapolis, 1965).

tive consensus of present-day scholarship against the historicity of the community of goods of Acts 2–6 arose partly in opposition to the sharpest Anabaptist positions, but principally as a reaction to the Christian precedent which socialist thinkers over the last hundred and fifty years have found in these passages for their views on the organisation of the state.[115] The pervasive effects of this reaction have combined with the frequent negative assessment of Acts as an historical source to deny the key new evidence made available through the publication of the *Rule of the Community* from Qumran the illuminating role which it deserves.

The Essene יַחַד terminology of the *Rule of the Community* provides close linguistic parallels to the difficult phrases employing ἐπὶ τὸ αὐτό at Acts 2:44 and 2:47. It is possible to understand Peter's challenge to the incomplete property surrender of Ananias and Sapphira at Acts 5:4 against the background of the Essene procedure of the provisional surrender of property (1QS 6:20),which is linked to a similar-sounding rule governing lies in matters of property (1QS 6:24-25). Patristic tradition and archaeological evidence combine with evidence from Josephus and the Dead Sea Scrolls to suggest that the early community in Jerusalem grew in the immediate vicinity of an Essene group occupying a site which some twenty-five years earlier had housed the Essene community of Qumran itself. This community may have provided converts to the early church who were themselves the conduit into Jerusalem Christianity of Essene language and procedures.[116] The 'daily distribution' of Acts 6:1 is much closer to the Essene process found in Philo, *Hypothetica* 11.4-11, and hinted at in the *Rule of the Community*, than to the Rabbinic analogy usually cited. Thus a cumulative case, building from a wide variety of sources and types of evidence, suggests that earliest Christian community of goods in Acts 2-6 is a historically verifiable aspect of the life of the earliest Jerusalem community, close in form to the widespread Essene practice of community of goods. Acts emerges as a source which reveals good knowledge of Palestinian cultural features of the earliest community, despite Luke's evident desire to stylise his material in a manner which appealed to those readers who shared the esteem for community of goods in Greek popular philosophy.

---

[115]Beginning with W. Weitling (1808–71), *Das Evangelium des armen Sünders* (Hamburg, 1971, reprint of [2]1846); *cf.* L. W. Countryman, *The Rich Christian in the Church of the Early Empire* (New York: Edward Mellen, 1980) 1-2.

[116]Wholesale conversion of the community is possible, but not demonstrable.

CHAPTER 12

JEWISH ACTIVITY AGAINST CHRISTIANS IN PALESTINE ACCORDING TO ACTS

Ernst Bammel

Summary

Acts gives evidence for numerous and varied measures taken against the Christians, both of a juridical and a para-juridical nature. Acts mentions them only in passing, because it plays down any animosity in the hope that the Romans might exercise a salutary influence on the Jews.

In the Acts of the Apostles, the Jewish actions against the apostles are regarded as entirely caused by their preaching Jesus' resurrection[1] or, as it is put in Christian terminology, that God has made him Lord and Saviour. There is no indication that the disciples' fellowship with Jesus or, indeed, their own activity during the lifetime of Jesus played any role in the developing hostility. While the Gospel of Peter describes the disciples as having had to take refuge because they were wanted for having attempted to burn down the temple (2:6), features of this kind are completely absent from Acts.

The passion of Jesus is viewed as caused by a deliberate action of the Jews. They condemned him (13:28)[2] and handed him over to be fixed to the cross by lawless men[3]—in 13:28 even the name of Pilate is mentioned, while 4:26 contains an allusion to Herod Antipas.[4] It is these ἄνομοι who carry out only a subsidiary activity (*cf.* esp. 2:23), while it is the Jews—this is a *unicum*—who give him a burial.[5] The most telling formula is προδόται καὶ φονεῖς (7:52), which implies that the initiative rested entirely on the Jewish side. These facts are not in dispute—there is no indication whatever that the Christian polemic is directed against an attempt on the Jewish side to shake off the responsibility.[6] It is not the trial with its data which is at issue, but the Christian claim and conviction that God's judgement is *toto coelo* different from the verdict pronounced by his earthly representative.

A new perspective is indicated by the term Ἑλληνισταί. Stephen is one of the Christian group called by that name, a group which is parallel to Jewish formations, which, although not called by that name in chapter 6, evoke this association. A band of persons who want to apprehend Paul is actually so called in 9:29.[7] The success that these antagonists of Stephen score and the eagerness to achieve the same in the case of Paul is indicative of a sharpening of the situation. Making offensive speeches against the temple (τόπος) and the law (νόμος) is the

---

[1]4:2: τὸν Ἰησοῦν ἐν τῇ ἀναστάσει τῶν νεκρῶν. This reading of D is superior to that of the standard text, which levels down the clash between the Christians and the Sadducees, the judges of Jesus, to the point of dispute between the former and the Pharisees (*cf.* 23:6).

[2]κρίναντες has this meaning at this place. D, which repeats κρίναντες, combines two versions.

[3]The term may refer to Gentiles, although this is not necessarily the case.

[4]M. Dibelius, *ZNW* 16 (1915) 123-25.

[5]For an interpretation see K. Lake, *The Historical Evidence for the Resurrection* (London, 1907) 48ff.

[6]Such attempts are sporadic and late; *cf. TRev* 1988, col. 369ff.

[7]Ephrem reads Judaei (*Beginnings*, III.414).

accusation which they level against Stephen (6:13). This certainly marks a change of direction. It is not any longer an interpretation of the past which is at stake but the precepts recommended by the Christians. Paul's preaching gave almost the same impression according to Acts 21:22; 25:8. The term Ἑλληνισταί, however, has disappeared. One gets the impression that the author, who traced the term in his 'Antiochean' source,[8] was no longer sure about its meaning and replaced it as soon as possible by Ἰουδαῖοι, which he made use of whenever hostile actions from this side are indicated.

The reference to action against Jesus for which the inhabitants of Jerusalem[9] and the ἄρχοτες are held responsible is supplemented by the remark κατὰ ἄγνοιαν. The repetition of this qualification (3:17; 13:27) makes it clear that this is a standard device on the Christian side to come to terms with the Jewish hostility: they are lacking in deeper understanding.[10] The two passages are actually christological summaries which were made use of by the compiler of the speeches of Peter/ Paul. They are one of the earliest formations of Christian literature.[11] They indicate the tendency on the Christian side to reduce the tension and to appeal to the Jews as to *melius informandis*. The author of Acts does not deviate from this.

On the other hand, the experiences of the Christian missionaries are such that the proviso is becoming obsolete. The attitude of the Jews is characterised by the word βλασφημεῖν, which means the cursing of Jesus (and the Christians): 13:45; 18:6.

The execution of Stephen is the only case of martyrdom to be narrated *in extenso*. It is, however, not the only martyrdom. References to persecution and even murder are made again and again. Paul accuses himself of having put Christians to death (22:4; *cf.* 9:1).[12] The execution of James carried out by Herod Antipas (12:2) is only part of an attempt to please the Jews and to κακῶσαί τινας τῶν ἀπὸ τῆς ἐκκλησίας (functionaries of the church?). The Jews of the Diaspora are described as having incited (13:50) people against the Christians, instigated persecution by sinister means (17:5) and actually themselves

---

8Reconstructed by J. Jeremias, *ZNW* 36 (1937) 213ff.

9This may be a reference to the Barabbas scene; Lk. 23:18ff.

10=בשגגה. The difference of the two levels of understanding in Jewish law was pointed out by D. Daube, *Sin, Ignorance and Forgiveness in the Bible* (London, 1960) T.U. 79 [1961] pp. 58ff.

11E. Stauffer, *Die Theologie des Neuen Testaments* (Stuttgart, 1941) 222f., 323ff. (ET London: SCM Press, 1955) 244-46, 339-42.

12The ἔτι in 9:1 implies a repetition of acts of persecution.

carried out harassment (14:2). They are characterised as having been propelled by zeal (an indicative term!) in this activity (13:45; 17:5). Their machinations are a standing feature on the journeys of Paul. They are, however, only mentioned in order to convince the reader that the apostle was justified in rending his garment and in turning exclusively to the Gentiles (18:6) as, indeed, the Jews themselves shake the dust into the air and pronounce him not worthy to go on living (22:22).

They actually harass Paul wherever he goes. His withdrawal from Damascus, Jerusalem (9:23-28) and, eventually, Antioch was of no avail, and even his decision to turn to the mission of the Gentiles (13:46) does not help. The enemies follow him (14:19) on his journey and even on his way back to Jerusalem (24:10). On the other hand, Paul's own appearance in synagogues is his right, especially as he represents the legitimate tradition of Israel (13:17ff.; 24:14).

The actions of the Jews are partly direct and partly indirect: they instigate others (17:5); their own involvement only becomes obvious during a riot (19:33).[13] The means of persecution are varied as well: punitive actions in local synagogues (26:11) and transportation to Jerusalem (22:5). Special ἐπιτροπαί were issued for this purpose (26:12).

A number of actions are indicated in Acts: searching of houses (8:3), ὑποβάλλειν of witnesses (6:11), flogging (22:19), taking into custody (8:3; 22:19), fettering (9:21; 22:4), forced renunciation of the faith (26:11), tormenting (26:11), stoning by witnesses (7:58f.), application of lynch justice (9:1 φόνος),[14] and the public display of agreement with such measures (8:1 συνευδοκεῖν), which is equally or possibly even more abhorrent than the rash action of a persecutor.[15]

Acts singles out Paul as instigator of the measures of persecution.[16] This is due to the biographical interest it takes in the apostle. It

---

[13]This seems to be the meaning of the difficult sentence.

[14]*Cf.* 22:4 ἄχρι θανάτου.

[15]For the evaluation of such acclamations see the material assembled by O. Michel, *Der Brief an die Römer* (Göttingen, 1978), on Rom. 1:32. *Cf.* D. von Dobschütz (see below, n. 15) 83f.

[16]Two views which cannot be reconciled easily with each other are to be found in Acts. Paul is a νεανίας according to 7:58, and a member of the Sanhedrin according to 26:10 (κατήνεγκα ψῆφον); *cf.* D. von Dobschütz, *Paulus und die jüdische Thorapolizei* (PhD thesis; Erlangen, 1968), a most informative piece of work.

does not mean that he was the only one to proceed to hostile action.[17] Nor does it mean that the Sanhedrin had to be urged on by Paul.

The harassment of the Christians was not confined to Jerusalem or Judaea but was aimed at hindering the missionary work outside Palestine, as Paul himself says.[18] This means that a repetition of actions of the kind Paul himself had carried out in his pre-Christian days is to be assumed. Paul was not only harassed by followers of James (Gal. 1:7; 2:4), but, even more serious for him, by emissaries of the Sanhedrin.

Acts does not mention the initiatives from Jerusalem. On the contrary, it gives the impression that the authorities in the capital had to be pressurised in order to act against the returning Paul. The initiative comes from the side of the Ἰουδαῖοι from Asia.[19] This appears to be a device of the author of Acts, by which he attempts to reduce the tension with the official representatives of Judaism, stresses the due reverence willingly paid by Paul to the High Priest (23:5) and even claims that he had undertaken the effort of his collection for the nation (24:17 ἔθνος), which means for metropolitan Judaism and not only for the mother church.[20]

The data of persecution are merely mentioned in Acts. Hardly any attempt is made to embellish the details and to work out a martyrological history or a hagiographical portrait of nascent Christendom.

The Jews are a divided nation. Different parties exist (23:6), and different opinions are voiced if a new issue comes to the fore (28:25 ἀσύμφωνοι κτλ.). They may act against Stephen or Paul with a concerted effort (7:57; 18:12), but they speak with different voices if it comes to crucial questions, while Paul's message is ῥῆμα ἕν (28:25). The former prove the unreliability of the Jews from a Roman point of view, whereas the latter sheds a favourable light on the Christians.

The difference of attitude is emphasised when it comes to the treatment of the Christians. The author takes pains to attribute direct action to the Sadducees (4:1; 5:17), while he hints at a different attitude on the side of the Pharisees (5:34ff.). The account of the measures taken

---

[17]Paul was accompanied by fellow-investigators on his way to Damascus (9:7ff.; 26:14). None of them is mentioned as having joined Paul later on. Did they carry on with what they had been engaged in before?

[18]1 Thes. 2:16a—still dependent on Ἰουδαίων in v. 14.

[19]21:27; 23:12; 24:19. Ἰουδαῖοι is the term which is invariably made use of in the description of those who acted against Paul and his companions.

[20]*Cf. TWNT* VI, 909, where the view is aired that the collection money was handed over by the Jerusalem church as a kind of toleration fee.

against Peter (4:18) is followed by the advice given by Gamaliel not to hinder the Christians as long as it is undecided whether God is with them or not. The same is emphasised in the report on the arrest of Paul (23:6) and may reflect the strategy of the redactor, who does not want to implicate all the Jews in anti-Christian activity. 23:9 even attributes to τινὲς τῶν γραμματέων τοῦ μέρους τῶν Φαρισαίων a statement which is entirely favourable towards Paul.

Paul's defence is reproduced at great length. He is able to make use of the different trends within Judaism (23:6). His tactic is, in part at least, successful and is appreciated by non-Jews. It sets an example for the Christians and shows them that their case is not without hope. This is especially true for the confrontation with the non-Jewish side.

It may be in keeping with this that the Jewish community in Rome is said not to have received adverse reports on Paul. It would mean that the Jerusalem authorities had considered it too risky to proceed with inquisitorial action in a case which had been taken over by the Romans. It results that ἀκωλύτως, the last word of Acts, refers to the absence of Jewish machinations rather than a Roman licence.

Acts 28:21 mentions that the Jews of Rome had not received reports detrimental to Paul nor had they been visited by persons making representations on his behalf. The former (γράμματα) may refer to instructions of the kind mentioned in 9:2. The latter could mean the same, all the more so as the letters of Acts 9:2 contained the commissioning of a person charged with a task. Still, the long-winded description in 28:21b is surprising and invites a different interpretation. Ananias and the representatives of the Sanhedrin had made their accusation against Paul in person in the procurator's residence in Caesarea ad mare. Paul had appealed to the Emperor and thereby forced his opponents to follow him to Rome or to abandon their scheme.[21] The emissary referred to in v. 21 is therefore likely to be an agent commissioned by the Sanhedrin to proceed with the accusation in the imperial court: such a person had not appeared so far, as the Jewish leaders at Rome show no hesitation in admitting. This is narrated at some length. The author must have had his reasons for reproducing this voice from

---

[21]*Cf.* O. Eger, *Rechtsgeschichtliches zum Neuen Testament* (Basel, 1919) on the edict (Aegyptische Urkunden aus den kgl. Museen zu Berlin, I [Berlin, 1898] no. 628 = L. Mitteis and U. Wilcken, *Grundzüge und Chrestomathie der Papyruskunde*, II.2 [Leipzig, 1912] 417f.; *cf.* II.1, p. 281 = S. Riccobono, *Fontes Juris Romani Antejustiniani*, I [Florence, 1941] 452-4), probably issued by Nero, according to which a trial automatically lapses if the parties have not appeared in Rome within 18 months (pp. 19f.).

outside, although it distracts from the main gist of the message given by Paul in the following verses, that salvation is offered to the Gentiles: they will listen. The willingness of the representatives of the Roman Jews to consider Paul's statement (v. 22) even contradicts Paul's accusation in the following speech that the heart of this people is hardened.[22] It is also not easily reconcilable with chapter 9: there it was Paul who had actually carried letters with incriminating contents. And it is taken for granted that this was not an isolated action but had become common practice in the meantime. Every reader of Acts must have become alerted to the hiatus. The author himself wants to point to it. This is underlined by the fact that the chief priests, who were in the habit of providing letters, had just made their representation against Paul to the Roman provincial authorities (24:1ff.). Paul mentions this to the Jewish leaders in Rome (28:19). This sharpens the issue: those who had acted against Paul recently had not continued to carry on with this so far. This is important for the view that the author wants to convey on the state of Paul's trial. The Romans had always been fair[23]—the *auctor ad Theophilum* does not miss any opportunity to drive home this point. Now, we learn, even the Jews become reluctant to proceed with further actions.[24] In the light of this the reader will certainly expect a positive outcome for Paul.[25,26]

---

[22]A different view is taken by D.W. Palmer, *Reformed Theological Review* 52 (1993) 62ff.

[23]*Cf.* P.W. Walaskay, 'And so we came to Rome' (SNTSMS 49; Cambridge, 1983) *passim*.

[24]This is a literary device. But it may be not without a historical basis. The execution of James in Jerusalem had had a significant aftermath: Ananus, the High Priest responsible for it, was deposed by the Romans because he had exceeded his powers. This may explain the temporary absence of Jewish machinations.

[25]It is true that an authority as eminent as E. Meyer claims that a negative outcome has been indicated in ch. 20 already and that ch. 28 has to be read with this in mind (*Ursprung und Anfänge des Christentums* III [Stuttgart, 1923] 56f.). It is, however, sufficient to interpret ch. 20 as foreshadowing the events of chs. 21ff., where Paul narrowly escaped an assassination. Meyer's view is taken up with variations by R.L. Fox, *Pagans and Christians* (Harmondsworth, 1986) 430.

[26]This means that the account of the hearings in Jerusalem, Caesarea and Rome is likely to have been written while Paul was still alive (*cf.* A. von Harnack's statement: 'Die Schlussverse der Apostelgeschichte, im Zusammenhang mit dem Fehlen jeder Anspielung auf das Ende des Prozesses des Paulus und auf sein Martyrium im Buch, machen es im höchsten Grade wahrscheinlich, dass das Werk geschrieben worden ist, als der Prozess des Paulus in Rom noch nicht beendet war' (*Neue Studien zur Apostelgeschichte* [Leipzig, 1911] 69)—maybe as an *aide mémoire* for his defence. Whether the earlier parts of Acts were in existence at that time already or came to be 'appended' at a later date, can be left open. It is certainly not a correct procedure to date Acts on the basis of the Gospel, as was pointed out already by M. Schneckenberger (*Ueber den Zweck der Apostelgeschichte* [Bern, 1841] 7ff.)—and forgotten since. The first sentence of Acts, which establishes the direct link with the Gospel, is a label which was superimposed, as is evidenced by the awkward construction (starting with a relative clause, no δέ after μέν), which was necessitated by the desire to incorporate elements of the earlier opening of the work.

CHAPTER 13

PAUL'S PRE-CHRISTIAN CAREER ACCORDING TO ACTS

Simon Légasse

Summary

This chapter aims to examine, from the point of view of historical criticism, the data in Acts about the life of Paul before his conversion. It deals with Paul's relations with Tarsus; his Roman citizenship; his arrival, education and academic training in Jerusalem; and his role in the persecution of Christians, the motives which provoked it and the forms it took. In this way there emerges clearly the figure of Paul as a Hellenistic Jew opposed, through religious zeal, to those members of his group who, under the aegis *of Stephen, had joined the Jesus movement.*

Albrecht Oepke[1] once compared the fate of Paul with that of Philo: the beginning and the end of the apostle's life, like those of the philosopher, are covered in obscurity. It is in order to dispel this obscurity a little that I shall examine, as a historian, the information in Acts relating to the period before the event which made Paul a Christian.

Whereas from Acts 12:25 onwards Paul occupies the central place in the work, in the early chapters he appears only sporadically, though not without purpose, *i.e.* in order to prepare the reader for the narrative which follows. The only personal feature up to 9:2 characterises him as a persecutor of Christians. However, the rest of Acts adds retrospectively several details of this period which should also be incorporated in the picture which we are endeavouring to reconstruct.

I. Born in Tarsus, Citizen of Tarsus and Rome

Of his birth at Tarsus in Cilicia[2] Paul says nothing in his letters; the information comes to us only from Acts. Clearly the author likes to refer to this origin, since he does so three times (9:11; 21:39; 22:3), to which one should add two other references to Tarsus in the same work (9:30; 11:25). None of the passages which provide us with this information offers a sufficient guarantee of historicity, given the contexts in which they are situated: the order given by God to Ananias (9:11), Paul's declaration of identity to the tribune who has arrested him (21:39) or his profession of Jewish faith before the crowd in Jerusalem (22:3). These are all passages in which the writer's own hand has been preponderantly at work. Despite this, there is general agreement today in recognising a reliable historical tradition[3] in Paul's Tarsian origin. There is little or nothing in Luke's work to call for such an origin, and while he knows, as in 21:39, how to take advantage of it in the circumstances he evokes, he is clearly much more concerned to exploit Paul's connections with Jerusalem.

---

[1]A. Oepke, 'Probleme der vorchristlichen Zeit des Paulus', *Theologische Studien und Kritiken* 105 (1933) 387; also in K.H. Rengstorf (ed.), *Das Paulusbild in der neueren deutschen Forschung*, WdF 24 (Darmstadt: Wissenschaftliche Buchgesellschaft, 1982) 424.

[2]On Tarsus and its history, see the bibliography (ancient sources and modern works) in M. Hengel (in collaboration with R. Deines), *The Pre-Christian Paul*, tr. J. Bowden (London: SCM Press, Philadelphia: Trinity Press International, 1991) 90-92 (n. 11).

To this one should add a confirmation which is of a general kind but carries weight. Although the evidence outside Acts is silent as to a Jewish presence in Tarsus, we are well informed about the Jewish colonies of Asia Minor.[4] The first traces appear already in the Bible (Joel 3:6 [MT 4:6]: Judaeans sold to the Ionians; Is. 66:19). Later, piracy, honoured on these coasts, as well as the slave trade and commerce in general, brought Jews to the region. At the end of the 3rd century BC Antiochus III settled two hundred Jewish families as military colonists in Lydia and Phrygia, granting them arable lands and vines (Josephus, *Ant.* 12.147-53). Wine and other agricultural products were imported to Palestine from Cilicia (*t. Sheb.* 5.2; *m. Ma'as.* 5:8). Acts (6:9) mentions a synagogue in Jerusalem where hellenistic Jews, including people from Cilicia and Asia, assembled.

Paul presents himself in Acts 21:39 as a citizen of Tarsus.[5] If, as is possible (see below), he left the city when still a youth, his right to citizenship cannot have come to him only from his father or his grandfather. But can this fact be historical? In Greek cities this right was granted to foreigners only with difficulty, and, despite the privileges the Jews enjoyed, these did not include political equality (ἰσοπολιτεία) with the other members of the city. Nevertheless there are examples which show that this was not impossible for Jews.[6] One can also envisage the acquisition of this right by a financial payment, a procedure which was quite common and which Augustus had to forbid to

[3]It is to this that the two notices of Acts 9:30 and 11:25 are linked. The first offers only a relatively brief contact with Gal. 1:21, which includes Syria in the purpose of the journey. On the other hand, in the second, if the no doubt schematic role of Barnabas is excluded, Paul's coming to Antioch from Tarsus can hardly attract criticism, since it is rather contrary to the 'Jerusalemite' tendency of Luke. One can see in 9:30 a result of what one reads in 11:25, from which Luke will have derived a return journey. See S. Légasse, *Paul apôtre. Essai de biographie critique* (Saint-Laurent: Fides, Paris: Cerf, 1991) 80-1, 96-7.

[4]For details see E. Schürer, *The History of the Jewish People in the Age of Jesus Christ (175 B.C.-A.D. 135)*, rev. G. Vermes, F. Millar and M. Goodman, vol. 3/1 (Edinburgh: T. & T. Clark, 1986) 17-38; S. Applebaum in S. Safrai and M. Stern *etc.*, *The Jewish People in the First Century* (Compendia Rerum Iudaicarum ad Novum Testamentum 1/2; Assen: Van Gorcum, 1976) 715-9.

[5]See the collection of evidence on the question in C.J. Hemer, *The Book of Acts in the Setting of Hellenistic History* (WUNT 49; Tübingen: Mohr [Siebeck], 1989) 122 n. 59; Hengel, *The Pre-Christian Paul*, 4-6, 98-102.

[6]According to Josephus, *Ant.* 12.119, Seleucus Nicator granted to Jews citizenship in the cities he founded, including those in Asia. See also Hemer, *loc. cit.*, for other, more debatable instances.

Athens, which was using it to replenish the city's coffers (Dio Cassius 54.7).

However, one should notice that, by contrast with Paul's Roman citizenship, the reference to his citizenship of Tarsus is isolated in Acts. Moreover, the precision which makes him a citizen of Tarsus is brought about by the mention of this city, which corrects the tribune's error in identifying Paul with the rebellious 'Egyptian.' The text lays no special emphasis on the right of citizenship itself. In this way one could suppose that the word πολίτης[7] should not be pressed, and that, divested of its politico-juridical meaning, it means only that Paul is a 'native of Tarsus.' But this meaning, as such, is not attested. Moreover, since the purpose of this declaration is to enhance Paul's standing in the eyes of the Roman officer, to see in it an indication simply of origin is to reduce its significance too much. On the contrary, everything suggests that Paul, in the author's view, presents himself as well and truly a citizen of the noble city. If one considers that this was a rare thing for the Jews, a doubt is here permitted, and Luke could well be the author of this exaggeration in the interests of his hero.

It is for the same purpose that he insists on Paul's Roman citizenship. This, like his citizenship of Tarsus, contributes to the apologetic enterprise which Luke pursues in his work. The Jew accused by members of his own people of betraying his religion and disturbing the public order is not just anybody. The zealous propagandist for Christianity possesses titles of noble status which have impressed the magistrates. Luke, who does much to show that Christianity derives from the best of Judaism, is concerned to make it clear that the Christians do not make converts only among the ἰδιῶται and the lower strata of the population. Rather less than Sergius Paulus, an illustrious convert (13:12), but more than the distinguished ladies of Pisidian Antioch (13:49) and Thessalonica (17:4), Paul should be able to impress those, such as perhaps the κράτιστος Θεόφιλος, who tended to consider Christianity a religion only fit for the common people.

However, there is now much less hesitation than in the past to admit that Paul was a Roman citizen. Although we cannot here recount the history of this institution,[8] let us establish to what extent the Jew Paul could have benefited from it.

---

[7]In LXX (see Strathmann, 'πόλις, κτλ.', *TDNT* VI, 525-6) the word πολίτης (for בֶּן־עַמִּי, עֲמִית, רֵעַ) means, not citizen, but fellow-citizen or compatriot. An exception is 3 Mac. 1:22 ('citizen of Jerusalem', as in Josephus, *Ant*. 9.99). In Lk. 19:4 and Heb. 8:11 (Je. 31:34) the meaning is 'fellow-citizen'; in Lk. 15:15 the word means 'inhabitant.'

Historians are unsure how numerous Jews who were Roman citizens were in our period, but their existence is nevertheless indubitable. Despite his Idumaean origin, Antipater counted as a Jew when he received from Caesar Roman citizenship (Josephus, *Ant.* 14.137; *BJ* 1.194) which he was therefore able to transmit to his son Herod the Great. In AD 66 the governor of Judaea, Gessius Florus, had several Jews of equestrian rank flogged and crucified (*BJ* 2.308), from which can be deduced the presence of several Roman citizens at the heart of the Jerusalem aristocracy. Flavius Josephus, when he had settled in Rome, received the same dignity (*Vita* 423). As for Asia Minor, Josephus informs us that in 48 BC the consul Lucius Lentulus exempted from military service the Jews of Ephesus who were Roman citizens (*Ant.* 14.228, 234, 240). The same tolerance was practised at Delos (*Ant.* 14.231-2) and at Sardis (*Ant.* 14.235-7). Whether or not the documents quoted by Josephus (in which there are both obscurities and contradictions) are authentic, it must be admitted that in this period of the civil war, such exemption could not really harm the army of the Senate and that Lentulus, by means of a gesture in favour of a handful of Jews, wished to win the favour of their communities in Asia.

We have seen that it is only Acts which, through its references to Paul, informs us of the presence of Jews in Tarsus and, consequently, of the presence of Roman citizens among them. But is the report credible?

The objections raised to Paul's Roman citizenship are of various kinds. First, why does Paul say nothing of it in his letters? We can reply that he is also silent about everything which relates to his family and does not serve his religious interests (Phil. 3:5). Moreover, his claims to glory were clearly quite different (2 Cor. 11:21b–12:10). But among these claims does he not provide us with a reason for doubting that he was a Roman citizen? In the list of his trials, he reports that he has been 'flogged (ῥαβδίζειν) three times.' The expression designates a typically Roman punishment administered with a rod by 'lictors' (ῥαβδοῦχοι: Acts 16:35, 38). Paul distinguishes it from the thirty-nine lashes which he received from Jews in accordance with the law (2 Cor. 11:24-25). Luke (Acts 16:22) notes that Paul and Silas received the former punish-

---

[8]See L. Wenger, 'Bürgerrecht', *RAC* II, 778-86; A.N. Sherwin-White, *The Roman Citizenship* (Oxford: Clarendon Press, [2]1973); *idem*, 'The Roman Citizenship: A Survey of its Development into a World Franchise', *ANRW* I,2 (1972) 23-58; E. Ferenczy, 'Rechtshistorische Bemerkungen zur Ausdehnung des römischen Bürgerrechts und zum ius Italicum unter dem Principat', *ANRW* II,14 (1982) 1017-58.

ment by order of the magistrates of Philippi, but stresses that this act was ordered in ignorance of the citizenship of the two prisoners (16:38). A law promulgated (probably in 198 BC) by M. Porcius Cato, after whom it was called the *lex Porcia*, forbade the flogging of Roman citizens.[9] The objection, however, is weak, because we know of several infractions of this law.[10] Besides the action of Florus already mentioned, Plutarch (*Caes*. 29.2) reports that Marcellus, when he was consul, 'had a senator of Novum Comum who had come to Rome flogged.' Anyone who has read Cicero's accusations against Verres, the governor of Sicily, guilty of having inflicted the same treatment on a certain P. Gavius, after the latter had declared loudly that he was a Roman citizen (*Verr*. 5.62-66), will not doubt that a Jew, who no doubt was not at all 'Roman' in appearance,[11] would have been more than anyone exposed to this kind of illegality. That he had suffered it three times is not exceptionally surprising, though it is difficult to judge in which circumstances.[12]

Against Paul's Roman citizenship it is also argued that holders of Roman citizenship bore three names. But this usage was frequently

[9]Livy 10.9.4-5: 'Porcia tamen lex sola pro tergo civium lata videtur: quod gravi poena, si quis verberasset necassetve civem romanum sanxit.'

[10]Not including cases of crucifixion inflicted on Romans, which was necessarily preceded by flogging: see M. Hengel, *Crucifixion*, tr. J. Bowden (London: SCM Press, 1977) 39-45 ('Crucifixion and Roman citizens').

[11]M.-F. Baslez, *Saint Paul* (Paris: Fayard, 1991) 24, remarks: 'Paul was certainly a Roman citizen, but he lacked the bearing which one normally expected to see in these privileged individuals.' However, apart from the absence of a toga, which is easily supposed, the rest of the portrait of Paul rests either on a passage of doubtful historicity in Acts (Paul would have had a 'dark complexion', since according to Acts 21:38 he could be confused with an Egyptian: *ibid.*) or on physiognomic suppositions without the least basis in the New Testament: see Légasse, *Paul*, 42-43.

[12]That Paul omitted to say that he was a Roman citizen in order to have the honour of carrying in his body 'the marks (στίγματα) of Jesus' (Gal. 6:17) (so Hengel, *The Pre-Christian Paul*, 6-7) is a debatable explanation. For if it is true that Paul accepted the thirty-nine lashes (2 Cor. 11:24) in order not to dissociate himself from those he calls his 'kinsfolk according to the flesh' (Rom. 9:3), the rods of the lictors of Rome carried no religious consequence beyond the one who endured them; on the contrary, they carried a strong risk of hindering, by inflicting serious physical harm, the apostolate of the missionary. As for envisaging, with the same author (*ibid.*), that Paul, by disclosing his citizenship, while propagating faith in a Christ crucified (by the Romans!), would have created an obstacle to his preaching, this is to attribute to the magistrates too much interest in the content of this preaching (reading the acts of the martyrs, one finds not a single imperial official concerned with this), as well as an investigation into the circumstances of the death of Jesus among people who were above all anxious about public order.

neglected among Greekspeakers, while Jews do not seem to have been especially attached to it, since, on the 500 Jewish funerary inscriptions in Rome, among which at least 10% designate Roman citizens, none is found bearing the *tria nomina.*[13] As for Christians, none of the persons named in the New Testament or in Clement of Rome is designated in this way, and the same must be said of bishops up to the 2nd century.[14] So one will not be surprised that Paul is not an exception on this point.

Finally, it is sometimes alleged that being a Roman citizen required concessions to paganism incompatible with the strict Judaism which Paul and his family professed.[15] But our sources tell us of nothing involving sacrifices to pagan gods, the imperial cult, or milder concessions. On the contrary, everything suggests that a Jew who was a Roman citizen continued to enjoy the privileges accorded to his people in that matter and that he did not run the risk of associating with hellenism on other points.

If, as we can now see, the objections to Paul's Roman citizenship have little weight, there are also, on the other hand, good arguments to show that Luke, on this point, reproduces historical tradition. Of these the most important is the legal process as it unfolds. Unless (with the rest of Acts) it is put down to pure fiction by exaggerating Luke's apologetic tendency,[16] one must admit that Luke reproduces essentially what happened at Jerusalem and then at Caesarea. Had he been a non-Roman, Paul would not have been sent to Rome to appear before Caesar at the conclusion of the local procedure, but would have been judged and sentenced or freed in Judaea by the procurator with no other complications.[17]

However, besides this argument, one should not neglect evidence which, while it does not constitute strict proof, turns out to be fully consistent with Paul's status as a Roman citizen. Thus there is the

---

[13]See G. Fuks, 'Where Have All the Freedmen Gone? On an Anomaly in the Jewish Grave Inscriptions from Rome', *JJS* 36 (1985) 25-32.

[14]The phenomenon appears only with Tertullian and Cyprian: see Hengel, *The Pre-Christian Paul*, 8 and 105 n. 69.

[15]So W. Stegemann, 'War der Apostel Paulus römischer Burger?', *ZNW* 78 (1987) 200-229 (225).

[16]W. Schmithals, *Die Apostelgeschichte des Lukas*, ZBK 3/24 (Zurich: Zwingli Verlag, 1982) 218, exceeds the rights of criticism by suggesting that Paul was arrested in Rome where he would have arrived as a free man.

[17]Hengel, *The Pre-Christian Paul* , 7-8, rightly stresses the difference between Paul and certain agitators and bandit leaders of the period, such as Eleazar the son of Dinaeus (Josephus, *Ant.* 20.161) or Jonathes (Josephus, *BJ* 7.437-50) who, though not Roman citizens, were dispatched to Rome.

fact that, in his apostolic plans, he was always concerned only with regions, provinces or colonies of the Roman empire. Or again, is it without relation to his Roman citizenship that Paul imagines Christians on earth as the citizens of a 'state' (πολιτεῦμα) in which the exalted Christ is the supreme authority (Phil. 3:20)? Similarly one can see that a Roman citizen would have been more inclined than others to include in his catechesis a passage such as Romans 13:1-7, so absolute as to obedience to the secular power, whose authority is theologically based.

According to Acts 22:26 Paul was a Roman citizen from birth. We must ask what was the origin of this situation which presupposes that Paul's parents were themselves Romans. How had they or their parents acquired this status? To this question no definitive answer can be given. However, it seems wise to avoid the hypothesis of service in the army.[18] The army derived its cohesion from the imperial cult, the sacred ensigns and the augurs. Hence the reluctance of Jews to join it and the hesitation of the authorities to enrol them. Although exceptions have been noted,[19] their number in the imperial forces must have been very small. Given that Paul presents himself as an observant Jew born of an observant family (Phil. 3:5), it must be doubted that he derived his Roman citizenship from a soldier in the Roman army. In fact the most common origin of this status for Jews outside Palestine was the manumission of Jewish slaves by masters who were themselves Roman citizens. In this case the citizenship was acquired, though with certain limitations, by the freedman after one or two generations.[20] The redemption of Jewish slaves by their fellow-Jews was considered a pious act of charity.[21]

---

[18]On the Jews and service in the Roman army, see S. Applebaum in S. Safrai and M. Stern, *etc.*, *The Jewish People in the First Century*, CRINT 1/1 (Assen: Van Gorcum, 1974) 458-60.

[19]Among others, the four thousand men, 'of a race of freed slaves', imbued with 'Egyptian and Jewish superstitions' ('sacris aegyptiis iudaicisque'), forcibly enlisted by Tiberius to fight the bandits of Sardinia (Tacitus, *Ann.* 2.85). But they could have been pagans converted to Judaism.

[20]On this usage, see Sherwin-White, *The Roman Citizenship*, 322-324; H. Chantraine, 'Zur Entstehung der Freilassung mit Bürgerrecht in Rom', *ANRW* I (1972) 59-67.

II. Paul in Jerusalem

Acts, which locates Paul's birth in Tarsus, allows him little time in that city. Speaking before Festus and Agrippa Paul recalls—what 'all the Jews' are supposed to know—his life 'from [his] early youth (ἐκ νεοτήτος ... ἀπ' ἀρχῆς) within [his] nation and in Jerusalem' (26:4). More precisely, in Paul's speech to the Jews before his arrest, when, after making profession of Judaism (ἐγώ εἰμι ἀνὴρ Ἰουδαῖος), he continues by saying that he was 'born (γεγεννημένος) in Tarsus of Cilicia,' this is a parenthesis, indeed a foil, for he goes on: 'but (δέ) I was brought up ("nurtured": ἀνατεθραμμένος) in this city (*i.e.* Jerusalem), and it was at the feet of Gamaliel that I was educated (πεπαιδευμένος) according to the exact observance of the law of our fathers' (22:3). These words, spoken 'in the Hebrew language' (22:2), recount the same stages and do so in the same terms as Stephen, speaking before the Sanhedrin, used of Moses. Willem Cornelis van Unnik[22] has shown well their stereotyped character. This tripartite formula recurs, with several variations, in a number of examples in Greek and Latin literature.

We must recognize that the author's interest is in putting his hero in contact with the holy city of Judaism as early as possible. For if the evidence of Paul himself on his past bears the marks of his break with it (Phil. 3:2-7), in Acts, conversely, it is the continuity which is highlighted. On reading Paul's speech to the Jews of Jerusalem we learn that his life, from birth up to and including his adherence to Christ, was dominated by Judaism (22:3).

Luke is the only writer who has preserved for us Paul's Hebrew name.[23] Is he also faithful to history in his reconstruction of the circumstances of Paul's childhood and youth? In Acts 23:16-22 we learn that, when Paul was taken prisoner by the Romans, a nephew of his in Jerusalem revealed the Jews' plot against Paul. This information, neutral and so of good historical value, does not contribute much to the issue

---

[21]See the declarations of *manumissio* from Panticapaeum (modern Kerch, in the Crimea) and from Gorgippia (modern Anape, on the Turman peninsula, east of the Crimea) in Schürer, *The History of the Jewish People* , vol. III,1, 36-38. For Egypt: Pap. Oxy. 1205 (*CPJ* III, no. 473, pp. 33-6), mentioning the redemption of a young Jew by Palestinian Jews (AD 291). In the liberation, at the time of the capture of Jerusalem, of certain prisoners or people who were being crucified, obtained from Titus by Josephus (*Vita* 418-21), it is not a question of redemption. In *b. Qidd.* 29ab, the subject is the redemption of the firstborn.

[22]'Tarsus or Jerusalem: The City of Paul's Youth', in W.C. van Unnik, *Sparsa Collecta I*, NovTSup 29 (Leiden: Brill, 1974) 259-320.

which concerns us, since it does not guarantee that the young man and his family were then settled in Jerusalem. Indeed, it is legitimate to remark, with Marie-Françoise Baslez,[24] that 'the intervention of the nephew takes place at the time of the feast of Pentecost, when pilgrims from all over Palestine and even from the Diaspora went up to the temple.' On the other hand, the language of Paul in his letters could be a way of approach to the duration of his residence in Tarsus. Paul handles everyday Greek with ease, showing that he had spoken it since childhood.[25] His Bible is the Septuagint. He is truly 'at home' in it,[26] and a good many of the Semitisms which are scattered about his letters derive from it. Conversely, his knowledge of Greek literature does not go beyond what could be absorbed from contact with hellenistic Jews, on whom literary clichés[27] and commonplaces of current philosophy had rubbed off, unless Paul can be compared either with Jewish-Greek literary writers of the period or with Philo. On the other hand, we know that Jerusalem at that time contained a good number of Diaspora Jews who had their own synagogues and spoke Greek.[28] So we should hesitate to reject the version of Acts which places Paul's

---

[23]A Greek form of the name of the first king of Israel, Sha'ul. In the LXX (and in Acts 13:21) the form is simply transliterated as Σαούλ. Josephus and a Jewish inscription from Apamea have Σαοῦλος. The form Σαῦλος, in Acts 7:58; 8:1, 4; 9:1, 8, 11, 22, 24; 11:25, 30; 12:25; 13:1, 2, 7, is an assimilation to the Latin name Παῦλος. On the use of this name among the Romans (it was the *cognomen* of several members of the *gens Aemilia)*, see the article 'Paulus', in *Der kleine Pauly, Lexikon des Antike*, vol. 4 (Munich: DTV, 1979) 562-68; *The Oxford Classical Dictionary* (Oxford: Clarendon Press, [3]1976) 791-2; among Jews in antiquity, see Hengel, *The Pre-Christian Paul*, 8-9. For J.A. Fitzmyer, *According to Paul: Studies in the Theology of the Apostle* (New York/Mahwah: Paulist Press, 1993) 2, Paul will have received his Latin name at birth and Saul is the *signum* or the *supernomen* attested among Jews of this period. The same author (*ibid.*, 124 n. 6) refers to an article which I have not been able to consult: M. Lambertz, 'Zur Ausbreitung des Supernomen oder Signum im römischen Reiche', *Glotta* 4 (1913) 78-143. But see also J. Juster, *Les Juifs dans l'empire romain*, vol. 2 (Paris, 1914; repr. New York: Burt Franklin, n.d.) 228-9.

[24]*Saint Paul*, 34. The dating at Pentecost, however, depends on Acts 20:16, where one notes a very Lukan touch (*cf.* also 20:6: a Jewish Passover, at Philippi!): the Paul of Acts faithfully respects the calendar of the synagogue and the Temple.

[25]On the basis of Paul's writings one cannot subscribe to this judgment of W.C. van Unnik, 'Tarsus or Jerusalem', 34: 'It can safely be said that Aramaic was his earliest and principal tongue.'

[26]Hengel, *The Pre-Christian Paul*, 37.

[27]For the use of the diatribe in particular, see S.K. Stowers, *Diatribe and Paul's Letter to the Romans*, SBLDS 57 (Chico: Scholars Press, 1981); T. Schmeller, *Paulus und die 'Diatribe'. Eine vergleichende Stilinterpretation*, *NTA* N.F. 19 (Münster: Aschendorff, 1987).

earliest education in Jerusalem rather than Tarsus. We should at least recognize that although this education could have been given in Tarsus, there is no objection to the claim that Paul received it in Jerusalem.

After the rudiments came, at least if we believe the evidence of Acts (22:3), the academy. This is in agreement with what it is easy to guess from Paul's letters as to his earlier education: it was indisputably Jewish and given in a Jewish school where he was taught the religious disciplines and a thorough knowledge of Scripture (Paul *quotes* the Old Testament over ninety times[29]). There he was prepared for proceeding to the higher level of Rabbinic studies. These required knowledge of Hebrew,[30] which it is not difficult to presuppose in a fervent Jew,[31] a Pharisee moreover (see below), though his speaking of Greek would not prevent him from entering the school: we know that the hellenistic Jews of Palestine were never ostracized by the local Rabbis; later, in the

[28]The term 'hellenist' (Acts 6:1; 9:29) indisputably refers to language: see the complete documentation in M. Hengel, *Between Jesus and Paul*, tr. J. Bowden (London: SCM Press, 1983) 4-11. On Diaspora Jews in Jerusalem, see Hengel, *The Pre-Christian Paul*, 54-62. On their synagogues (Acts 6:9), see S. Légasse, *Stephanos. Histoire et discours d'Étienne dans les Actes des apôtres*, LD 147 (Paris: Cerf, 1992) 197-200.

[29]Everywhere (among the certainly authentic letters) except in 1 Thessalonians, Philippians and Philemon, where there are no explicit Old Testament citations.

[30]One should add the local Aramaic (this is the meaning of τῇ Ἑβραΐδι διαλέκτῳ in Acts 21:40; 22:2; 26:14; *cf.* also Jn. 5:2; 19:17, 20; Rev. 9:11; 16:16; Josephus, *BJ* 6.96; *Ant.* 18.228). If Paul's stay in Arabia (Gal. 1:17) was, as it is reasonable to suppose, already of a missionary nature, he would have been able to make himself understood to the Nabataeans who inhabited the area and, although Arabs, spoke a variety of Aramaic.

[31]One hesitates to appeal here to Paul's declarations in 2 Cor. 11:22 and Phil. 3:5, for although the word ἑβραῖος can designate Semitic-speaking Palestinian Jews to differentiate them from Greek-speaking Diaspora Jews (Philo, *Conf. Ling.* 68, 129; *Mut. Nom.* 71), it can also include all Jews (Eusebius, *Hist. Eccl.* 2.4.2; 4.18.6). Moreover, nothing requires us to distinguish between the three categories of adversary whom Paul lists in 2 Cor. 11:22; on the contrary, 'Hebrew', 'Israelite' and 'descendant of Abraham' (*cf.* Rom. 11:1) say the same thing by repetition in rhetorical style. Given that the two latter expressions envisage the Jews, in the full sense and in general, whether Palestinian or of the Diaspora, the same is evidently the case for the first. For a different point of view, see, *e.g.*, Fitzmyer, *According to Paul*, 6, who stresses that knowledge of Aramaic is not in conflict with the fact that Paul spent his youth in the hellenistic world, since Aramaic 'was widely used in his day throughout Syria and Asia Minor.' But, unless one supposes that Paul's family spoke Aramaic because they were recent immigrants (see below, n. 36), it is difficult to believe that Paul could have learnt this language in a hellenistic city such as Tarsus.

2nd century, the reactions of some Rabbis against the teaching of Greek as well as the concessions made to their position (*b. Sota* 49b) show that knowledge of Greek, if not of Greek learning, had not been condemned by the authorities in Jerusalem previously.[32]

However, on this subject Paul provides us with his own guarantees when he recalls the time when he 'advanced in Judaism beyond many of my people of the same age, for I was far more zealous for the traditions of my ancestors' (Gal. 1:14). This progress must refer to a continuous improvement in the learning of the Torah in the school of the teachers who perpetuated its interpretation.[33] This kind of teaching was specifically Palestinian.[34] The fact that Paul, both according to Acts (23:6) and according to his own words (Phil. 3:5), was a Pharisee, also keeps us in Palestine. Acts specifies that his father was also a Pharisee, which implies that he had lived in Palestine until adulthood, for we know nothing of the existence of Pharisaic confraternities in the Diaspora. As far as the documents we have indicate, the movement was born in Palestine and remained there.[35] Whatever may have been

[32]On knowledge of Greek among the population of Jerusalem and Palestine, see E. Schürer, *The History of the Jewish People in the Age of Jesus Christ (175 B.C.-A.D. 135)*, rev. G. Vermes, F. Millar and M. Goodman, vol. II (Edinburgh: T. & T. Clark, 1979) 74-80.

[33]The expression 'tradition of the fathers' (αἱ πατρικαὶ παραδόσεις), Gal. 1:14, echoes Josephus, *Ant.* 13.297, where the παράδοσις τῶν πατέρῶν is applied to the rules (νομιμά) of the oral law recognized by the Pharisees but rejected by the Sadducees. Having said this, there are serious risks of anachronism in seeing Paul as an 'ordained Rabbi', because the institution as such, the rite of ordination (סְמִיכָה) and the title 'Rabbi' in all probability took shape after 70: see, among others, M. Hengel, *The Charismatic Leader and His Followers*, tr. J.C.G. Greig (Edinburgh: T. & T. Clark, 1981) 44 and n. 22. The documentation on the subject is assembled in Strack-Billerbeck II, 647-61 (on Acts 6:6). It is not irrelevant to remark, with Oepke, 'Probleme', 405, 428, that Paul, in his letters, never claims a distinction such as teacher in Judaism: it would have been easy for him to add a καὶ γραμματεύς to the Φαρισαῖος of Phil. 3:5.

[34]The exceptions prior to the Amoraim of Babylonia must be used with care, especially for the period which concerns us: see Hengel, *The Pre-Christian Paul*, 33-34.

[35]Hengel, *The Pre-Christian Paul*, 29-30, rightly criticizes the arguments to the contrary based on Mt. 23:13 and the conversion of King Izates of Adiabene, according to Josephus, *Ant.* 20.38-48.

the case with his father,[36] Paul assures us of his own Pharisaism and, consequently, of his belonging to Palestinian Judaism.[37]

That Paul, as he declares in Acts 22:3, had been a pupil of Gamaliel, *i.e.* Gamaliel I the Elder, there is no reason to deny from the point of view of chronology, since according to the Rabbinic sources this Rabbi lived before 70.[38] His intervention in favour of the Christians according to Acts 5:34-42[39] is doubtless more indebted to Luke than to historical reality. On the other hand, the information in Acts 22:3 should not be considered legendary without other evidence. After all, nothing obliged Paul to refer to it when, in his letters (2 Cor. 11:22; Gal. 1:14; Phil. 3:5-6), he listed his claims to glory from the point of view of Judaism, for the name Gamaliel would mean nothing to Gentile Christians.

However, the attempt to discover in Paul's writings the traces of a teaching which could be attributed to Gamaliel, and, through him, go back to Rabbi Hillel, Gamaliel's supposed grandfather, is fruitless.[40] What is possible is to observe in Paul's letters the influence of this kind of education. Of course, during the twenty years which separate the Damascus experience from the first writings, he was subject to other influences. Nevertheless, in his free arguments from Scripture, Paul makes use of Palestinian midrashic methods rather than developments in Jewish-Greek literature,[41] and his eschatology bears the stamp of apocalyptic views also expounded in Palestine.[42] This can be said

[36]The origin of the settlement of Paul's family in Tarsus remains obscure, and Jerome's information (*De vir. ill.* 5; *Comm. in Philem.* 23-24) does not clarify the situation. The description of his relatives as 'Hebrews' is difficult to use (see above, n. 31). It is quite possible that, by calling his father a Pharisee, the Paul of Acts obeys the author's desire to portray his hero as rooted in the strictest Judaism.

[37]Fitzmyer, *According to Paul*, strangely modifies in his second chapter the rather peremptory statements of his first chapter, where he writes (pp. 5-6) that Paul 'was not a Jew of Palestine' and that 'though Luke makes Paul assert that he was brought up in Jerusalem and educated at the feet of Gamaliel (Acts 22:3), his letters never give an indication of the influence of Palestinian Judaism, apart from some points to be discussed in chapter 2.' One can even legitimately ask if the 'some points' in question and some others do not destroy the thesis of Paul as a pure 'child of the Graeco-Roman world' (p. 6).

[38]See J. Neusner, *The Rabbinic Traditions about the Pharisees before 70*, vol. I (Leiden: Brill, 1971) 373-6.

[39]The optimistic views of J. Roloff, *Die Apostelgeschichte*, NTD 5 (Göttingen: Vandenhoeck & Ruprecht, 1981) 100-1, on the historicity of the matter are criticized by G. Lüdemann, *Early Christianity according to the Traditions in Acts*, tr. J. Bowden (London: SCM Press, 1989) 72-3. According to Lüdemann, the figure of Gamaliel would have been known to Luke in the tradition about the pre-Christian Paul to which Acts 22:3 belongs.

without erecting a wall between the two types of Judaism and remembering that Jews from the Diaspora settled in Jerusalem, with whom, as we shall see, Paul will have had more than occasional connections. But it should be added that in the course of his travels Paul, thanks to the remarkable ability of Jews to adapt, will have gained a familiarity with the hellenistic world, especially that of the cities, their institutions and customs, which would have been less apparent in his letters had he lived only in Palestine.

Although textile workers and entrepreneurs played a role in the political and social life of Tarsus,[43] it was certainly also at Jerusalem that Paul was able to learn the manual trade of which Acts (18:3; 20:34) tells us and which Paul himself (1 Cor. 4:12; *cf.* also 1 Thes. 2:9) confirms that he practised. According to Acts (18:3) Paul, like his host Aquila, was a 'tentmaker' (σκηνοποιός). Whether the tents were made of leather or goatskin or cloth, opinions differ, and we hesitate to decide the matter, while acknowledging a certain difficulty in envisaging a Pharisee exercising a despised trade like that of a weaver.[44] However that may be, such a trade was clearly compatible with the

---

[40]This is nevertheless what J. Jeremias, 'Paulus als Hillelit', in *Neotestamentica et Semitica: Studies in honour of Matthew Black* (Edinburgh: T. & T. Clark, 1969) 88-94 attempted. For the opposite view, see already M. Enslin, 'Paul and Gamaliel', *JR* 7 (1927) 360-375. Other authors, no more felicitously, attempt to attach Paul to the rival school of Shammai: K. Haacker, 'War Paulus Hillelit?', *Das Institutum Judaicum der Universität Tübingen* (1971-72) 106-20; *idem*, 'Die Berufung des Verfolgers und die Rechtfertigung des Gottlosen', *TBei* 6 (1975) 1-19; H. Hübner, 'Gal 3,10 und die Herkunft des Paulus', *KD* 19 (1973) 215-31 (228-229); *idem*, *Das Gesetz bei Paulus*, FRLANT 119 (Göttingen: Vandenhoeck & Ruprecht, [3]1982) 142-3 n. 16. On the supposed descent of Gamaliel I from Hillel via a certain Simon, see Schürer, *The History of the Jewish People*, vol. II, 367-9.

[41]Cf. Rom. 4; 5:12-20; 9-11; 1 Cor. 10:1-11; Gal. 3:6-18; 4:21-31. See Hengel, *The Pre-Christian Paul*, 47-49.

[42]On the connections between Paul and the Qumran writings in particular, see H. Braun, *Qumran und das Neue Testament*, vol. I (Tübingen: Mohr [Siebeck], 1966) 169-240; J. Murphy-O'Connor and J.H. Charlesworth (eds.), *Paul and the Dead Sea Scrolls* (New York: Crossroad, [2]1990); Fitzmyer, *According to Paul*, 18-35 (with a stimulating hypothesis on the attachment of the Qumran community to the Sadducees and rather surprising consequences for Paul's background in Palestinian Judaism). On the subject of justification especially, see E. Lohse, 'Die Gerechtigkeit Gottes in der paulinische Theologie', in L. De Lorenzi (ed.), *Battesimo e giustizia in Rom 6 e 8*, 'Benedictina': sezione biblico-ecumenica 2 (Rome: Abbazia S. Paolo fuori le mura, 1974) 13-16, 27-32.

[43]This is noted by Baslez, *Saint Paul*, 31 and 311 n. 41, who refers to Dio Chrysostom 34.21, mentioning a sort of guild of λινουργοί (textile workers) on whom the opinion of the town was divided. (On this text, see also Hengel, *The Pre-Christian Paul*, 6.)

status of a man learned in religious matters, and there is no lack of examples among the Rabbis to prove their practice and their esteem of manual work, especially since their office did not, at least in theory, carry emoluments.[45]

III. The Persecutor

Paul makes his appearance in Acts in a modest capacity. In the account of the martyrdom of Stephen he slips in,[46] so to speak, as a 'young man' (νεανίας) responsible for guarding the coats of the witnesses while they proceeded with the execution (7:58b). However, a little later we learn that Saul (so called by his Hebrew name up to 13:9) approved of the murder of Stephen (8:1a). Finally and without delay, the same Saul is presented as a formidable police officer making searches of the houses in Jerusalem in order to drag out the Christians and to throw them in prison (8:3). This process leads the reader by stages to the section of the narrative that follows. It is in fact the same persecutor who is found a little later 'breathing threats and murder[47] against the disciples of the Lord' (9:1), but in order to introduce, by contrast, the episode in which the persecutor is changed into an apostle of Christ. It is the same contrast that Paul depicts for the benefit of the Jewish crowd in Jerusalem (22:4-5) and then, at Caesarea, before Festus and Agrippa (26:10-12), when he recalls his anti-Christian activity in order to lead up to the Christophany on the Damascus road. Furthermore, the speech in Jerusalem concludes with the account of Paul's vision in the Temple, well suited to trigger the fury of his hearers. Paul there recalls the same persecution, without forgetting to go back to its very first origins: his role, already hostile to Christianity, at the time of the martyrdom of Stephen (22:19-20).

In this series of passages, besides several New Testament *hapax legomena* and quasi-*hapax legomena*,[48] there are numerous indications of Lukan redaction. There is the expression παρὰ τοὺς πόδας,[49] the word

---

[44]See J. Jeremias, *Jerusalem in the Time of Jesus*, tr. F.H. and C.H. Cave (London: SCM Press, 1969) 3.

[45]See, however, S. Légasse, 'Scribes—Nouveau Testament', in *Dictionnaire de la Bible, Supplément*, XII, col. 268. On the social consequences of this manual labour, see Légasse, *Paul*, 40-42; Hengel, *The Pre-Christian Paul*, 15-17.

[46]The resumption of the verb ἐλιθοβόλουν (7:58a, 59) indicates the insertion.

[47]On this phrase, see the philological study by P.W. van der Horst, 'Drohung und Mord schnaubend (Acta IX 1)', *NovT* 12 (1970) 257-69.

νεανίας,[50] and the use of καλούμενος to introduce a personal name or surname[51] (7:58b). In 8:1a and 22:20 the verb συνευδοκέω (also in Rom. 1:32; 1 Cor. 7:12, 13) should be compared with its use in Luke 11:48,[52] and similarly the expression 'to shed the blood' (ἐκχύννεσθαι τὸ αἷμα: 22:20) refers back to the murder of the prophets (Lk. 11:50//23:35). The 'way' (ὁδός: 9:2; 22:4), as a designation of the Christian community, is a usage peculiar to Acts (19:2, 23; 24:14, 22; *cf.* 18:25-26). Other terms and expressions indicating the hand of the author are: εἰσπορεύομαι (8:3), μαρτυρέω (22:5), πρεσβυτέριον for the Sanhedrin (22:5), ἐκεῖσε (22:5; *cf.* 21:3), ἐπίσταμαι (22:19), ἐφίστημι (22:20), ἀναιρέω (22:20; 26:10), ἐν φυλακαῖς κατακλείω (26:10; *cf.* Lk. 3:20), the future participle ἄξων (22:5) as well as the periphrastic conjugation (8:1a; 22:19, 20).[53]

To this can be added an observation which bears on the parallels between these passages: 'men and women' (8:3; 9:2; 22:4), 'to put in prison' (8:3; 22:4, 19; 26:10), 'murder' (ἀναίρεσις: 8:1a) and 'to put to death' (ἀναιρέω: 22:20; 26:10), 'the synagogues' (22:19; 26:11). These parallels are linked with a crescendo which reaches its climax in 26:10-11. First, with regard to the victims of the persecution: whereas in 8:3 and 22:4 they are described neutrally as 'men' and 'women,' in 22:19 they are 'those who believe in you,' and then, in 26:10, 'many (πολλούς) of the saints.' Similarly, with regard to the cruelties endured: according to 22:19 Paul travelled around 'the synagogues'; in 26:11 we read 'all (πάσας) the synagogues,' and we learn, moreover, that the operation took place 'often' (πολλάκις). It is only in this last passage that the imprisonment of Christians is said to have been carried out on the orders of the chief priests and that it is indicated that the purpose of the ill-treatment in the synagogues was to force the Christians to 'blaspheme.' Also to be noted is the superlative expression for Paul's state of mind in the circumstances: 'furiously enraged' (περισσῶς ἐμμαινόμενως), and, finally, the extension of the persecution 'even to

---

[48]ἀναίρεσις (8:1a), λυμαίνομα (8:3), ἐμπνέω (9:1), φυλακίζω (22:19), τιμορέω (22:5; 26:11), ἐμμαίνομαι (26:11).

[49]Apart from the summary in Mt. 15:20, it is found in the whole NT only here and in Lk. 7:38; 8:35 (add. Mk. 5:15); 8:41 (diff. Mk. 5:22); 17:16; Acts 4:35, 37 *v.l.*; 5:2; 7:58; 22:3.

[50]In the NT only in Acts 7:58b; 20:9; 23:17, 18 (*v.l.* νεανίσκος).

[51]11 times in Luke, 13 in Acts, and 3 times in Revelation.

[52]Compare also σύρω, 'to drag' (8:3), with its use in relation to two other Jewish persecutions, one suffered by Paul at Lystra (14:19), the other by Jason and some other Thessalonian Christians (17:6). This verb occurs three times in Acts and twice elsewhere in the NT, but in very different contexts (Jn. 21:28; Rev. 12:4).

[53]More than half the occurrences in the NT are in Luke-Acts.

foreign cities' (26:11). Above all, whereas in 8:3 it is only a question of arrests, in 9:1 it is 'threats and murder' which stir Paul; and then he comes to recognize that he 'persecuted this way as far as death' (ἄρχι θανάτου: 22:4), concluding with the declaration that, when Christians were put to death, this had his vote (κατήνεγκα ψῆφον: 26:10).

From all of these allusions a grave picture emerges which it is pointless to wish to tone down. Referring particularly to Acts 26:11, Philippe Menoud[54] envisaged, by way of persecution of Christians by Paul, only statements made in the synagogues against the messiahship of Jesus, with a view to persuading the newly converted Christians to deny their faith. But this is in no way inspired by Acts (nor by Paul's letters). The vocabulary of Acts, which corresponds to that of the letters, expresses, without any possibility of doubt, violent actions. The verb διώκειν is the one found in the words of reproach which Jesus addresses to Paul on the road to Damascus (9:4, 5; 22:7, 8; 26:14, 15). This verb, if one takes account of its New Testament use, especially by Luke (Lk. 11:49; 21:12),[55] cannot exclude physical violence, which, moreover, it normally includes in comparable circumstances. The same goes for the verb πορθεῖν. The author of Acts uses it when he reports that the Jews of Damascus were astonished to hear that Paul was preaching Jesus, when they recognized the man who, not long before, 'was persecuting (ὁ πορθήσας) in Jerusalem those who invoke this name' (Acts 9:21). πορθεῖν, even more clearly than διώκειν, includes violent action. Ceslau Spicq[56] sums up its usage: 'This verb, not used in the Septuagint, had, from Homer to the *koine*, the meaning: to create havoc, to ravage, to lay waste a city, to devastate an area.' The same author proposes 'to ill-treat' (French: *maltraiter*) as a translation of this verb in the New Testament.

These violent activities, according to Acts, went as far as to include the death of their victims. This is really what Paul—who breathed 'threats and murder (ἐμπνέον ἀνειλῆς καὶ φόνου[57]) against the disciples of the Lord' (9:1)—intended, and this is really what he recog-

---

[54]'Le sens du verbe πορθεῖν (Gal. 1.13,23; Act 9.21)', in *Apophoreta: Festschrift für Ernst Haenchen* (Berlin: Töpelmann, 1964) 178-86, or P. Menoud, *Jésus-Christ et la foi*, BT(N) (Neuchâtel/Paris: Delachaux & Niestlé, 1975) 40-47.

[55]See also 2 Cor. 4:9, 10-11, with 11:24-25; 2 Tim. 3:11-12; Mt. 5:12, with 23:30, 35.

[56]*Lexique théologique du Nouveau Testament* (Fribourg: Editions Universitaires/ Paris: Cerf, 1991) 1275-6, where detailed documentation can be found. One example: Josephus, *BJ* 4.534, reports that Simon ben Giora devastated the villages and towns of Idumea: there πορθεῖν is synonymous with λυμαίνεσθαι (*cf.* Acts 8:3, where the second verb implies searches, arrests and imprisonment).

nized that he had done when he declared to the crowd in Jerusalem: 'I have persecuted this way as far as death (ἄρχι θανάτου)' (22:4).[58] Not that he had himself laid hands on the Christians,[59] but, in Acts 26:10, the expression κατήνεγκα ψῆφον[60] seems to attribute to him a properly judicial function at the execution of some of them. If one doubts that Luke[61] considered Paul a member of the Sanhedrin,[62] then the needs of a dramatic climax have led him to ascribe exorbitant powers to Paul in this murderous enterprise, in order the better to show him entirely transformed by Christ at Damascus.

The persecution in Jerusalem extended, according to Acts 26:11, 'as far as the foreign cities' (εἰς τὰς ἔξω πόλεις). This is a matter both of a literary progression by comparison with the parallel passages in 9:2 and 22:5, according to which Paul went directly from Jerusalem to Damascus, and also of a transition to prepare for Paul's arrival in this 'foreign city' where the decisive event which turned his life around took place.

---

[57]Probably a hendiadys: see C. Burchard, *Der dreizehnte Zeuge. Traditions- und kompositions-geschichtliche Untersuchung zu Lukas' Darstellung der Frühzeit des Paulus* (FRLANT 103; Göttingen: Vandenhoeck & Ruprecht, 1970) 43 n. 9.

[58]The expression is related to ἕως θανάτου in the scene of the agony (Mk. 14:34 // Mt. 26:38) where the phrase echoes Jon. 4:9 and expresses a sorrow such that it threatens life itself. In the case of Paul, in Acts 22:4, it is definitely the death of the Christians which constitutes the purpose of his activities.

[59]Against E. Haenchen, *Die Apostelgeschichte* (KEK 3; Göttingen: Vandenhoeck & Ruprecht, [6]1968) 308 n. 1: 'Saul hat nach Lukas wirklich gemordet.'

[60]As such the expression καταφέρειν ψῆφον is an absolute *hapax*, but it is related to other formulae where ψῆφος ('small stone', especially for voting; by derivation: vote) is used with the simple verb φέρειν, with βάλλειν, τίθεσθαι, προστίθεσθαι, in the dative with κρίνειν, *etc.* The nuance perceived by M. Zerwick and M. Grosvenor, *A Grammatical Analysis of the Greek New Testament* (Rome: Biblical Institute Press, 1981) 444 ('when they were being [*i.e.* about to be, liable to be] killed') is not at all necessary. Nor is that of an imperfect *de conatu*, for the author certainly intends to indicate that Christians have been executed.

[61]We should not speak of Paul sitting in the Sanhedrin as a historical fact: the remark made above (n. 33) on the apostles' 'Rabbinate' applies *a fortiori* to his membership of the supreme council of the Jewish nation. Besides, as Oepke, 'Probleme', 395/418, has rightly noted, even in Acts, except for 26:10, the picture is everywhere that 'of a fanatic, not a judge'.

[62]He never presents him as such and in Acts 23:5 Paul does not recognize the High Priest: although several persons have meanwhile succeeded as head of the Sanhedrin, such lack of perspicacity is astonishing. That Paul had been, according to Acts 22:3, instructed in Rabbinic learning at the feet of Gamaliel does not imply that at the conclusion of these studies he had the right to a seat in the Sanhedrin; besides, Luke makes no connection between the two matters.

In order to go there he had to obtain letters from the High Priest so that he could take action in the synagogues against the Jews who had become Christians, 'should he find any' (9:2),[63] and bring them captive to Jerusalem to be judged. This request for direction addressed to the supreme authority of Judaism is exceptional. Everywhere else Paul is said to have acted without a mandate and to have organized the persecution of Christians on his own authority. Even for the business at Damascus the initiative was his. The whole portrays the character of the persecutor *par excellence* and, so to speak, unique, whose sole occupation is to hound the Christians. The contrast that Paul, in his letters, likes to set up between his violent opposition to nascent Christianity and his apostolic call (Gal. 1:13-6) is reinforced in Acts: the super-missionary of the Gospel began by being a super-persecutor of those who professed it—to the glory of Christ who showed himself able to effect such a transformation. Here the apologetic note, while not explicit, is no less perceptible.

If one asks what motives led Paul to conduct this anti-Christian campaign, Acts replies, like Paul himself (Phil. 3:6), by citing the 'zeal' which impelled him: it was as a 'zealot for God' (ζηλωτής ... τοῦ θεοῦ) that he conducted his persecution of the Christians. This description has biblical and traditional roots: it is a matter of the charismatic fury which impels the faithful Jew to fight for God's cause by means of violent actions against the impious members of his own people. The prototype here is Phinehas (Nu. 25:1-9) whose zeal reappears in Elijah (1/3 Ki. 19:20; *cf.* 18:40), then in Maccabaean times (1 Mac. 2:24-26). Philo provides an apologia for it.[64]

We now move to Paul's own testimony in his letters, and we must first recognize that there is substantial agreement between the letters and Acts on the subject of Paul's persecution of the Christians. In his letters Paul not only recognizes the facts but also expresses them in the same vocabulary as Luke does in Acts.

If Paul attributes to himself the last place in the apostolate, it is because, he says, 'I persecuted (ἐδίωξα) the church of God' (1 Cor. 15:9). He was a 'persecutor of the church' (διώκων τὴν ἐκκλησίαν: Phil.

---

[63]For the author of Acts, Paul does not know if a Christian community exists in Damascus. As there has not yet been any question of evangelizing this city, the writer has judged it preferable not to attribute to Paul more knowledge than the reader has: see A. Weiser, *Die Apostelgeschichte*, vol. I (ÖTKNT 5/1; Gütersloh: Mohn/Würzburg: Echter, 1981) 223.

[64]*Spec. Leg.* 2.55-57; *Vita Mos.* 1.301-4. Hengel, *The Pre-Christian Paul*, 71, compares this 'zeal' to that of present-day Islamic fundamentalism.

3:6). In Galatians we find the two verbs διώκειν and πορθεῖν, whose use in Acts we have noticed above: 'You have heard, no doubt, of my earlier life in Judaism:[65] how I persecuted (ἐδίωκον) excessively the church of God and ravaged (ἐπόρθουν) it' (1:13). Later he recalls how the churches of Judaea learned that 'the one who not long ago had been engaged in persecution (διώκων) was now preaching the faith he wished to destroy (ἐπόρθει)' (1:23).

Moreover, the letters also provide the key to this relentlessness against the Christian communities: for Paul also, it was 'zeal,' that religious ardour manifesting itself in physical violence, which determined him to act against the adherents of the new faith: κατὰ ζῆλος διώκων τὴν ἐκκλησίαν (Phil. 3:6). The one who at that time showed 'an unremitting zeal' (περισσοτέρως ζηλωτής ὑπάρχων) for the ancestral traditions[66] applied the same ardour to the eradication of the nascent church (Gal. 1:13, 14). At the most one could here make clear what is only implicit in Acts. For a Jew zeal for God is necessarily zeal for the *law* of God. Acts evidences the profound convictions of Paul on this point. He himself puts them directly in relation to the persecuting zeal which motivated him: 'as to the law, a Pharisee, as to zeal, a persecutor of the church' (Phil. 3:5-6).

According to Acts the persecution which Paul instigated and carried out was aimed not only at the arrest and imprisonment, on a large scale, of the Christians, but also at their execution. A suspicion of hyperbole arises when the reader becomes aware of the dramatic progression of the facts under the pen of the author, as has been emphasized above. This suspicion becomes certainty on reading the letters. There Paul, who nevertheless does not moderate his confessions when he speaks of his activities against the Christians, never goes so far as to say that he is responsible for the death even of one of them. If, in view of the vocabulary used,[67] one has no basis for toning down actions which were certainly violent in nature, one must admit that they did not lead to executions.[68]

---

[65]'Judaism', not only in the sense of objective membership of the Jewish people or even of the Jewish religion, but also implying subjective and practical obedience and fidelity to the law of God (as in 2 Mac. 14:38): see W. Gutbrod, ''Ισραήλ, κτλ.', in *TDNT* III, 383; R.Y.K. Fung, *The Epistle to the Galatians* (NICNT; Grand Rapids: Eerdmans, 1968) 56; Hengel, *The Pre-Christian Paul*, 41 (ἐν Ἰουδαϊσμῷ = 'in the law').

[66]The terms τῶν πατρικῶν μου παραδόσεων (Gal. 1:14) are not synonymous with Torah-νόμος. However, whether it is a matter of the Jewish tradition in general, written or oral, or of the traditions peculiar to the Pharisees and professed in the Rabbinic schools, the reference to the Torah is in any case clear.

What is conceivable is that Paul contributed to bringing Christians before the Rabbinic courts: a role of spy and informer[69] which had to bring about the dispensing of the statutory punishments in the context of the synagogue, such as Paul himself later boasts of having received (2 Cor. 11:24) and such as other Christians had to undergo (Mk. 13:9).[70]

Acts first mentions Paul's activity in Jerusalem. As for Paul, he writes that he persecuted 'the church' (Phil. 3:6), 'the church of God' (1 Cor. 15:9; Gal. 1:13). In the Pauline letters, except for Colossians and Ephesians, 'the church' and 'the church of God' always refer not to the universal church but to the local community.[71] But there is no evidence of a community which suffered from Paul's persecution other than that of Jerusalem. One can therefore easily identify this church in the anonymous formulae we have just cited.[72]

However, an objection arises from reading Galatians 1:22 where Paul writes that at the time of his first visit to Jerusalem, after his conversion, he was 'not personally known to the churches of Judaea.'

---

[67]But Paul can distinguish 'persecution' and 'sword' (Rom. 8:35); nor does he confuse 'persecutors' and murderers, when he recommends victims to pray for the former (Rom. 12:14). As for the expression καθ' ὑπερβολήν ('beyond measure', 'to an extraordinary degree': Fung, *Galatians*, 55), the intensity it includes must be evaluated according to the other information on the subject; by itself, it does not indicate that this persecution included murders.

[68]These would not be conceivable except as lynchings, as was the case of Stephen, despite the the judicial varnish with which Acts covers it, but that could not be extended to whole groups of Christians. On this question, related to the power of the Sanhedrin in capital cases, see Légasse, *Stephanos*, 207-10; *idem*, *Le procès de Jésus: L'histoire* (LD 156; Paris: Cerf, 1994) 88-94. In fact one cannot cite from the sources the name of any Christian for whose death Paul was responsible.

[69]See Oepke, 'Probleme', 395/418, 403/26.

[70]Hengel, *The Pre-Christian Paul*, 85, who admits this version of the facts, but then adds the possibility that 'some may even have suffered more serious physical hurt and *even have been killed*' (my italics), forgetting that Paul never accuses himself of having contributed to the death of a single Christian. The same author calls Paul's persecuting activity a 'pogrom' (*loc. cit.*), an inappropriate term since a pogrom implies the violent and murderous action of one group against another, indeed, in the strict sense, of non-Jews against Jews.

[71]For 'the church of God' in the singular: 1 Cor. 1:2; 10:32; 11:32; 15:9; 2 Cor. 1:1; Gal. 1:13; 1 Tim. 3:15; in the plural: 1 Cor. 11:16; 1 Thes. 2:4; 2 Thes. 1:4; 1 Tim. 3:5.

[72]Roloff, *Apostelgeschichte*, 147; 'ἐκκλησία', *EWNT* II, 1000-1002, concluding that the Jerusalem community was the first to be described in this way, in the consciousness of being the community of the last days, on the model of the Qumran community which similarly attributed this title to itself (קהל אל: 1QM 4:10; 1QS 1:25). The absence of any other specification in 1 Cor. 15:9; Gal. 1:13; Phil. 3:16, supports this interpretation.

Is Jerusalem not in Judaea? One can respond that it is here a matter of 'churches' and that in the phrase quoted the expression τῷ προσώπῳ, literally 'by face,' implies a physical presence in the communities in question, as in 1 Thessalonians 2:17; therefore that the phrase does not mean that Paul was an unknown person for the churches of Judaea. However, it is too simple to say, on the one hand, that Jerusalem is not named in the text, and, on the other hand, that the term 'Judaea' had a broad use (so frequently in Luke[73]) designating the 'country of the Jews,' Jewish Palestine, without further specifications, which in a letter written to the Galatians would in any case be superfluous.[74]

One should therefore admit that it was in Jerusalem that Paul pursued his persecuting activity against the Christians. On this point the letters confirm Acts.

Acts, for its part, can remedy a point of reticence in the letters if one can use the former with prudence in its presentation of the affair of Stephen and its consequences. Assuming that Paul, as a Diaspora Jew by origin, and a Greek speaker, would have attached himself to the hellenistic synagogues in Jerusalem, one may deduce that he would have witnessed the activity of certain of their members in favour of adherence to Jesus and his message. One cannot attribute to Paul more than an accessory role in the murder of Stephen. But, when the death of the leader did not break the movement, he will have felt himself invested with a mission of defence in the face of what he considered as serious damage to the Jewish faith: a radical calling into question of the Torah[75] through a greater and perhaps radicalized assimilation of the teachings of Jesus. From this came the persecution whose character and extent we have attempt to specify.

If the preceding deductions are correct, the persecution would have been directed only at the Christians who derived from the hellenist group, although Luke presents the flight of Christians from Jerusalem as well-nigh total (Acts 8:2), in clear contradiction of the massive police operations attributed to Paul in 8:3, as well as of the presence of a full community in Jerusalem according to 9:26. In fact those people from Jerusalem who are later found among these fugitives are Philip, a hellenist, and, in 11:19-20, people who preach to the

---

[73]Lk. 1:5; 4:44; 6:17; 23:5; Acts 2:9; 10:37.

[74]See O. Betz, ''Ιουδαία', *EWNT* II, 468-70; Hengel, *Between Jesus and Paul*, 99 (= p. 32 in the present volume); *idem*, *The Pre-Christian Paul*, 73-74.

[75]The criticism of the *Temple*, mentioned in Acts 6:13, 14, as well as the effect of a crescendo which it produces, is suspect as a harmonization of this 'trial' with that of Jesus: see Légasse, *Stephanos*, 200-1, 203-4.

Jews of the Diaspora and to the pagans. The flight, like the persecution or the threat of persecution which provoked it, would have affected only the hellenists among the Christian, or rather a certain number of them.[76] Such is the chain of events which Luke will have had at his disposal. He has blended it into an account which he wished to be open to what follows in his work.

To the persecution in Jerusalem succeeds, in Acts, the enterprise of Damascus.[77] One can be sure that it was at Damascus or near it (see below) that Paul underwent the experience that transformed his life. In Galatians 1:17, after recalling this decisive turning-point, Paul writes: 'at once I went away into Arabia, and afterwards returned to Damascus' (καὶ πάλιν ὑπέστρεψα εἰς Δαμασκόν), proof that what preceded the departure for Arabia[78] had taken place in Damascus. If Paul did not say this previously, it is perhaps because the Galatians had already been informed of it;[79] more certainly, it is because the report of Paul's apostolic call in Galatians 1:15-16 is not at all a circumstantial account and confines itself to theological statement in scriptural terms.

The existence of a Christian 'cell' within the Jewish community in Damascus[80] some two or three years after the death of Jesus meets no serious objection. Besides Acts one would rather have an additional guarantee, for the presence of Christianity in Damascus escapes the geographical scheme outlined by the author for the propagation of the Gospel (Acts 1:8). The origin of the group—Luke never speaks of a church in this connection, only of 'disciples'[81]—remains subject to

---

[76]One finds later (Acts 21:16) at Jerusalem (despite the 'western text') a Cypriot Jew, 'an early disciple', named Mnason.

[77]S. Sabugal, *Analisis exegético sobre la conversión de san Pablo. El problema teológico e histórico* (Barcelona: Herder, 1976) thinks he has avoided the historical difficulties inherent in the account of Acts by identifying Damascus with the region of Qumran, according to the Zadokite Document (CD 6:5, 11; 7:15, 19; 8:21; 19:34; 20:12), where 'Damascus', according to one interpretation, describes this region. Among the objections which can be raised against this theory the most important is that one cannot see how the author of Acts, writing after 70, and so after the destruction of the Qumran community, for the benefit of non-Palestinian, Greek-speaking and mostly Gentile Christians, would have had the idea of using a cryptogram whose meaning only the initiates of a sect which had ceased to exist could supply. For Luke and his readers, Damascus would mean Damascus. On this work, see the criticisms of M. Iglesias, *Bib* 58 (1977) 132-5; C. Bernas, *CBQ* 39 (1977) 157-8; W. Wiefel, *TLZ* 103 (1978) 185-8.

[78]See now J. Murphy-O'Connor, 'Paul in Arabia', *CBQ* 55 (1993) 732-737.

[79]So Hengel, *The Pre-Christian Paul*, 72.

[80]Damascus at that time contained a considerable proportion of Jews; Josephus, *BJ* 2.561; 7.368.

hypotheses. Although one should not rule out the hypothesis of an infiltration from Galilee, it is not fantastic to recognize in the first Christians in Damascus the fruit of a mission carried out by some hellenist fugitives, following the persecution in Jerusalem.[82] In this case Paul will have pursued his hatred for the renegades of his own group, who had propagated the new faith in the great commercial metropolis of Syria as other hellenists had done at Antioch (Acts 11:19-20).

In any case, the presence of Christians in Damascus on the eve of Paul's conversion should be considered an established fact, as should the place where this transformation of the persecutor occurred. Acts locates it not in the city of Damascus itself but on the approach to it (9:3; 22:6; *cf.* 26:12). The critical thesis[83] which supposes that, in the absence of persecutions in Jerusalem, Paul had begun to act against the Christians in Damascus is not only opposed to the information in Acts but also creates certain aporias.[84] What interest had anyone in modifying the tradition in this way? Would it not have been, for Luke in particular who is so concerned to bring out the contrast, more impressive to let the persecutor be seized by Christ in the very place of his misdeeds, in full exercise of the mission he had assumed for himself? Moreover, how, if Paul had ill-treated the Christians of Damascus, would he have been received so easily and with open arms among them, and how would he have returned at once to stay there for a period after his return from Arabia? One would have thought he would receive a welcome—to say the least—as cool as he received later at Jerusalem according to Acts 9:26.

The episode at Damascus, as it is recounted in Acts, cannot be a faithful transcription of historical fact. Without encroaching on the continuation of the three accounts of the 'conversion' and confining ourselves solely to Paul's career as a persecutor, we note that it is inconceivable that the High Priest or the Sanhedrin would have

---

[81]9:10, 19, 25. Compare, for Jerusalem, Judea, Galilee and Samaria, 8:3; 9:31.

[82]See Hengel, *The Pre-Christian Paul*, 76, for a series of good reasons for what remains only a hypothesis.

[83]See especially Haenchen, *Apostelgeschichte*, 257, for whom, on the basis especially of Gal. 1:22, this persecution belongs to the *Pauluslegende.* According to the same author, 'The Book of Acts as Source Material for the History of Early Christianity', in L.E. Keck and J.L. Martyn (ed.), *Studies in Luke-Acts: Essays presented in honor of Paul Schubert* (Nashville/New York: Abingdon Press, 1966) 258-78 (264-5), 'probably Paul ... lived in Damascus and persecuted the local Hellenistic Christian community through the means at his disposal in the local synagogue.'

[84]See Hengel, *The Pre-Christian Paul*, 75.

authorized Paul to carry out arrests at Damascus and to transfer the Christians apprehended to Jerusalem. The jurisdiction of the High Priest and the Sanhedrin would in fact have been limited to the eleven toparchies of Judaea. To save the account in Acts a case presented in the first book of Maccabees (15:15-21) has often been cited, where 'Lucius, consul of the Romans' required King Ptolemy of Egypt to deliver the Jewish rebels who had taken refuge in his country to the High Priest Simon to be punished according to the Jewish law. But, even supposing this letter is authentic,[85] it is not addressed, like the letter of which Acts speaks, to the 'synagogues' but to a local ruler by the Roman authority. The case is therefore wholly different, as are the period (the events mentioned are supposed to have occurred in 139 BC) and the political situation: whereas at the time of Paul Judaea was a Roman province administered by a Roman governor, Simon, the brother of Judas Maccabeus, was a sovereign, autochthonous vassal of the Seleucids of Antioch. Did Luke remember this passage when he filled in the *lacunae* in his tradition? One cannot affirm it, though it is possible. In any case, one cannot rely on this example to justify the intrusion of Jewish government into the province of Syria.

What facts did Luke or his tradition embellish? First, what aim did Paul pursue? If one excludes arrests such as Acts envisages, there remains, as action to be taken against the Christians, only to subject them to the punishments envisaged by Jewish law and administered in the context of the synagogues. This, as we have said above, is what happened at Jerusalem, and it is what must have happened at Damascus. But in this case Paul had no need to go to the High Priest and to request letters of recommendation from him. Besides, one of the tendencies of Acts is to make as official as possible the persecution conducted against Christians by attributing it to the highest authorities of the Jewish nation with, at their head, the High Priest.[86] So let us then leave the latter as well as the Sanhedrin out of the affair.[87] Although Paul never says that he acted under orders (but did he wish to say so?), one can envisage rather—this seems to be suggested in Acts 9:2—a request from synagogues to synagogues.[88]

---

[85]It could be a matter of an interpolation, imitating the much later letter which is quoted by Josephus, *Ant.* 14.145-8; *cf.* Haenchen, *Apostelgeschichte*, 275 n. 4.
[86]4:4; 5:17, 21, 27; 7:1; 22:5; 23:2, 4, 5; 24:1.
[87]Oepke, 'Probleme', 403/426, who does not exclude a request from Paul to the High Priest, sees it, not as a mandate to arrest officially entrusted to Paul, but a letter like the συστατικαὶ ἐπιστολαί to which 2 Cor. 3:1 refers.

IV. Conclusion

Those who have willingly read the preceding study will realise the necessity of using Acts when it is a matter of relating the life of Paul. Of course, the work is to be handled with delicacy, and this is why the professional exegete must intervene to grasp, through a composition which is far from neutral, the unfolding of the facts. Moreover, it is indispensable to compare the results obtained with the data in the letters, to the extent that they come into contact with the Lukan account. The method, which consists in wishing to construct a biography of Paul solely from the letters, and to have recourse to Acts only in a subsidiary manner once one has extracted what Paul provides—such a method is already debatable in relation to the missionary travels of the apostle (how can one disregard the itineraries outlined in Acts?); it is inapplicable to the period which precedes the Damascus event, owing to the parsimoniousness of the letters on this subject. The use of two sources with the same critical spirit (it is also necessary in approaching the letters) is, when all is said and done, essential. If no one can claim to have acquired certainty in so complex a field, one has every interest in not neglecting what can contribute to it.

---

[88]In the hypothesis according to which the Christians of Damascus originated from a dispersal of fugitives under the impact of persecution in Jerusalem, one will think of hellenistic synagogues.

CHAPTER 14

PETER AND BEN STADA IN LYDDA

Joshua Schwartz

Summary

Peter's mission took him to many regions of Palestine including Lydda, where he healed Aeneas (Acts 9:32-35) and apparently also sought out the Judaeo-Christian community. Rabbinic tradition, relating events that purportedly took place in that same city of Lydda at what could well have been the same time, tells of a certain Ben Stada who was known as a 'beguiler' (Hebrew: mesit*) who was entrapped and arrested in Lydda for his 'theological' crimes and later executed. It is our intention to show that the Peter and Ben Stada traditions should be understood in light of one another and that both should also be understood in the light of the geographical background of Lydda and the theological-legal concept of* mesit.

I. Peter in Lydda

Peter's mission took him to a number of regions and settlements in Palestine. His activities in Jerusalem were, of course, very important, as we shall see, but he also travelled. Acts 9:32 begins an extended travel sequence. Peter starts out in Lydda (Acts 9:32-35), and moves on to Joppa (Acts 9:36-43) and later to Caesarea (Acts 10:1-48).[1] Peter's short stay in Lydda will prove most important for our purposes and, therefore, we cite the relevant verses in their entirety:

> Now as Peter went here and there among them all, he came down also to the saints that lived at Lydda. There he found a man named Aeneas, who had been bedridden for eight years and was paralyzed. And Peter said to him, 'Aeneas, Jesus Christ heals you, rise and make your bed'. And all the residents of Lydda and Sharon saw him and they turned to the Lord.

These few verses are far from clear. Acts 9:31, the previous verse, would seem to imply that Peter's trip to Lydda, and subsequently to Joppa and Caesarea, was the result of the 'peace' enjoyed by the churches of Judaea, Galilee and Samaria.[2] There are scholars, though, who claim that Peter's travel episodes took place after his escape from prison in Jerusalem (Acts 12:1-19) and that only after the death of Herod Agrippa was Peter able to return to Jerusalem and explain his actions *vis-à-vis* non-Jews (Acts 11:1-18).[3] Thus, it is not clear whether Peter arrived in Lydda on an inspection or missionizing tour in a period of relative peace,[4] or whether he fled there seeking refuge. If the

[1]Although journeys are a favourite motif of Luke, it is not necessary to assume that these journeys were not genuine. See J.N. Sanders, 'Peter and Paul in Acts', *NTS* 2 (1955/56) 135.

[2]See, for instance, F. Fearghail, *The Introduction to Luke-Acts: A Study of the Role of Lk 1, 1-4, 44 in the Composition of Luke's Two-Volume Work* (Rome, 1991) 74-75. See also J. Munck, *The Anchor Bible: The Acts of the Apostles, Introduction, Translation and Notes*, rev. W.F. Albright and C.S. Mann (Garden City, NY, 1967) 89.

[3]See, for instance, W. Grundmann, 'Die Apostel zwischen Jerusalem und Antiochia', *ZNW* 39 (1940) 129ff. See also D.R. Schwartz, *Agrippa I: The Last King of Judaea* (Tübingen, 1990) 213-6.

[4]See H. Conzelmann, *A Commentary on the Acts of the Apostles* (Philadelphia, 1987) 76. Conzelmann sees Peter's trip as one of an inspection tour and not as a missionary journey. It is likely, though, that Peter would have taken advantage of his sojourn in Lydda or the other sites to engage in some missionary activity, regardless of his original reasons for arriving at this or that site. If he had arrived seeking refuge, he simply would have exercised more caution. We shall see that this too will prove to be of great importance for our study later on.

latter escape scenario is true, and we shall see that our understanding of the Rabbinic parallel would seem to indicate that such is the case, it is not clear whether Peter arrived at Lydda by chance or whether conscious design brought him there. Was it Lydda's convenient location at the intersection of many inter-urban thoroughfares which drew Peter to a city from which he could escape in a hurry,[5] or was the religious atmosphere and environment sympathetic to one "on the lam"? As we have already stated, we shall have more to say about some of these issues later on.

In spite of all the questions raised above, one thing seems to be clear: once Peter was in Lydda, he sought out the Judaeo-Christian community there.[6] Although there has been some question as to whether this particular Aeneas mentioned in Acts was already Christian at the time of his encounter with Peter and whether he derived from pagan or Jewish stock, it would seem that in spite of his rather non-Jewish name, he belonged to the small and undoubtedly close-knit Judaeo-Christian community of Lydda.[7]

The healing of Aeneas at Lydda does not seem to have been a public event, and the impression from the text is that it took place indoors, whether in Aeneas' house or in that of someone else. It is likely, therefore, that Aeneas was cured before only a select few members of the Christian community of Lydda. Thus, the supposed conversions at the end of Peter's sojourn in Lydda were not the result of a popular witnessing of events connected with the actual miracle, but rather the result of seeing Aeneas healed and participating in society (Acts 9:35). All this would appear to be somewhat strange. Peter heals through the power and name of Jesus, but he does not seem to be all that eager to publicise this. Rather, he prefers to let the results of his actions embark on their own natural course. Aeneas is healed and serves as a witness to the power of Jesus and Peter. The importance of all of this will emerge in the course of further discussion of

---

[5]On the location and geography of Lydda see Schwartz, *Lod (Lydda)*, 19-30. On the different names of the site see 15-17. For the sake of convenience, we shall use Lydda when referring to Acts and Lod when referring to Rabbinic literature.

[6]See E. Haenchen, *The Acts of the Apostles, A Commentary* (Göttingen, 1965) 338 n. 3.

[7]See Haenchen, *Acts*, 338 n. 34 (*contra* K. Lake and H.J. Cadbury, *The Beginnings of Christianity, Part I, The Acts of the Apostles* [London, 1933] 108ff.). During the Talmudic age Lydda became rather cosmopolitan, and Jews from Asia Minor and Syria made the city their home. A 'foreign' Jewish community in Lydda in the 1st century would not, therefore, be unusual. Two Jews named Aeneas are mentioned in Josephus (*BJ* 5.326; *Ant.* 14.248).

Peter's activities. In any case, apart from the healing of Aeneas, Acts describes no other activities of Peter at Lydda.

II. Ben Stada in Lod

An enigmatic Rabbinic tradition relates that a certain Ben Stada advocated some type of cult or religion outside the framework of normative Judaism. Accordingly, he was entrapped by witnesses specifically planted for that purpose, apprehended, brought before a court and executed. The events, according to this Rabbinic tradition, took place in Lod or Lydda. It is our view that this Ben Stada tradition should be seen in light of Peter's activities in Lydda, as well as in a number of other sites, and as part of the Jewish polemic against early Judaeo-Christianity. It is also our view that the Peter-Lydda tradition in Acts can be better understood in light of the religious-*halakhic* background of the Ben Stada traditions which we shall describe.

The background for the Ben Stada tradition is Mishnah (= *m.*) *Sanhedrin* 7:10:[8]

> He that beguiles others [to idolatry] (= Hebrew: הַמֵּסִית)—such is a common man (Hebrew: הֶדְיוֹט) that beguiles another common man...they may not place witnesses in hiding against any that become liable to the death penalties enjoined in the Law save in this case alone. If he spoke [after this fashion] to two, and they are such that can be witness against him, they bring him to the court and stone him.[9] If he spoke so to only one he may reply, 'I have companions that are so minded' and if the other was crafty (Hebrew: עָרוּם) and would not speak before them, witnesses may be placed in hiding behind a wall. Then he says to the other, 'Say [again] what you said to me in private' and the other speaks to him [as before]...If he retracted it shall be well with him, but if he said, 'It is our duty and it is seemly to do so', they that are behind the wall bring him to the court and stone him.

The crime of *mesit* is so serious that deception and entrapment are permitted to apprehend and punish him. We shall later on examine

[8]The translation is essentially that of H. Danby, *The Mishnah* (London, 1933) 393.
[9]Theoretically, capital cases could be tried before a court of twenty-three. Such courts were found in the major cities of Palestine, and Lydda would have been no exception to this. Realistically, however, capital cases would have been tried before the Sanhedrin in Jerusalem.

in detail many of the Rabbinic *mesit* traditions and particularly in reference to Peter and Ben Stada. For the moment, though, we cite this Mishnah as the background for the Ben Stada traditions. It is interesting to note, though, that this Mishnah deals with *mesit* in theory only and records no examples of entrapment.

Tosefta (= *t.*) *Sanhedrin* 10.11 elaborates on the entrapment procedure and cites the single example of such an occurrence recorded in all Talmudic literature:[10]

> Against all those who are liable to the death penalty in the Torah they do not hide witnesses except for the one who beguiles others to idolatry (Hebrew: הַמֵּסִית). How [do they do it]? They assemble two sages in an inside room, and he sits in an outside room and they light a candle so that they can see him. And they listen to what he says. And so did they to Ben Stada[11] in Lod. They appointed against him two sages [and in consequnce of what they heard and saw] they stoned him.

The Tosefta does not record much information regarding Ben Stada. Was he a native of Lydda or was he just passing through and entrapped there by chance? Since this is the only entrapment of a *mesit* cited in Talmudic literature, it would hardly seem likely that the Rabbis considered the events in Lydda to be mere coincidence. It is more likely that the case of Ben Stada was cited because of its magnitude and importance, implying that great preparation and care had been invested in the entrapment which, it should also be remembered, could be used only when more acceptable means were of no avail. All this would mean that according to Tosefta, Ben Stada spent a considerable time in Lod, probably not unlike Peter, although Acts is not very clear on that matter.

The Ben Stada tradition is also found in the Palestinian Talmud (= *y.*). *Y. Yebamot* 16.15d (= *y. Sanh.* 7.25c-d) states:[12]

> How is he (= מֵסִית) tricked? They hide two witnesses in the inner room and place him in the outer room. And they light a candle near him in

[10]The translation is that of J. Neusner, *The Tosefta, Neziqin* (New York, 1981) 231, with revision.

[11]MS Vienna has: 'the house (בי״ה) of Stada'. The standard printed editions of the Tosefta read: 'a certain man'. This reading reflects internal Jewish censorship seeking to obfuscate any connection between Jesus and Ben Stada. See further our discussion below.

[12]The translation is ours, with occasional reference to J. Neusner, *The Talmud of the Land of Israel, Sanhedrin and Makkot* (Chicago, 1984) 255-6.

> order that they should see him and listen to his voice. For thus they did to Ben Sitra (*sic*)[13] in Lod. They hid two sages and brought him to the court and stoned him.

Y. then asks why it was particularly necessary to see the accused in the course of the entrapment, and at the end of the discussion answers that 'he (= מֵסִית) should not run away and continue to beguile others'.[14] As long as the *mesit* was at large, he was considered to be a serious menace to society.

Babylonian Talmud (= *b.*) *Sanhedrin* 67a describes the entrapment procedure in a similar manner to the versions cited above and then adds: 'And thus they did to Ben Stada in Lod and they hung (= crucified) him on the eve of Passover. Ben Stada was Ben Pandira'.[15] *B.* adds three new elements: Passover, hanging (instead of stoning) and Ben Pandira. These elements, though, would seem to indicate a clear-cut identification of Ben Stada with Jesus, particularly since Jesus is occasionally referred to as Ben Pandira in other Rabbinic texts.[16] We shall see, though, that the matter is not so simple and that *b. Sanh.* was just not familiar with all the *personae* connected with the early history of Palestinian Christianity.

The continuation of *b. Sanh.* is more explicit:

> Rav Hisda said: The husband was Stada, the paramour Pandira. But was not the husband Pappos ben Judah? His mother's name was Stada. But his mother was Miriam a dresser of women's hair? As they say in Pumpiditha, this woman has turned away (Aramaic: *satah da*) from her husband.

According to *b.*, Ben Stada explicitly refers to Jesus, and the name itself is a derogatory reference to Mary. This version led certain scholars to conclude that the other Ben Stada traditions refer to Jesus. Others were more wary. The earlier versions of the tradition in *t.* and *y.* do not support this identification. Can the later version in *b.* as well as the obviously confused and polemical statements of a 3rd-century AD Babylonian sage serve as sufficient evidence for this identification?[17] Many scholars did not think so.[18] We shall see that the identification in *b.* is a logical outgrowth and development of the real situation

---

[13] *Y. Sanh.* has: 'Ben Sotada'.

[14] *Y. Sanh.*: 'that he should not go and beguile others with him'.

[15] This is found only in manuscript versions. Internal Jewish censorship apparently resulted in its deletion from printed editions. The translation is that of ed. Soncino.

[16] See, for example, *t. Ḥul.* 2:24 and parallels.

and dependent upon the real identification of Ben Stada and we shall also see, that identification was Peter and not Jesus.

III. Identifying Ben Stada

The various theories as to the identification of Ben Stada have been catalogued by J. Maier.[19] We shall briefly discuss these identifications and some of the problems inherent in them before discussing the Peter identification. We shall see that the key to any identification is the *mesit* mentioned above.

We have already mentioned the Jesus theory. Jewish scholars, for obvious reasons, sought to avoid this identification.[20] Some scholars, for instance, identified Ben Stada with the unnamed Egyptian 'prophet' who appeared during the time of the procurator Felix (AD 52-60), claiming to be able to destroy Jerusalem.[21] This identification has nothing to do with Lydda and, in any case, convinced no one. Recently, however, the Jesus identification has become popular again,

[17]The Rabbis, and particularly the Babylonian ones, often lacked any clear sense of chronology. Pappos ben Judah was a contemporary of the 2nd-century AD sage R. Akiva and could, therefore, have little to do with Jesus. For the Rabbis, the pun was more important than the history.

[18]See J.Z. Lauterbach, *Rabbinic Essays* (Cincinnati, 1951) 523, and the literature cited there.

[19]J. Maier, *Jesus von Nazereth in der Talmudischen Überlieferung* (Darmstadt, 1978) 204-5.

[20]See *b. Shabb.* 104b. There is another group of Ben Stada traditions which relate that Ben Stada brought magic marks from Egypt in scratches on his flesh. These traditions are in the name of the late 1st-century AD sage R. Eliezer b. Hyrcanus regarding scratching or tatooing on the Sabbath. The continuation of the tradition in manuscript version discusses the relationship of Ben Stada to Ben Pandira as well as Rav Hisda's comment, all of which we have seen already above. See also *y. Shabb.* 12.13d and *t. Shabb.* 11.15. These scholars could see no connection between these magic marks and Jesus. We shall see later on that the Ben Stada-magic traditions have nothing to do with the Ben Stada-Lod traditions.

[21]See Josephus, *Ant.* 20.169-72. On those who proposed this identification see, for instance, J. Lauterbach, *Rabbinic Essays*, 524 and S. Lieberman, *Tosefta Ki-Fshutah* (New York, 1962) III 179-80. A number of manuscripts spell the name Stada as 'Stara'. Lauterbach tried to connect this spelling to the Hebrew *seritah*. Lieberman, based also on the reading 'Stara', sought the etymology in the Greek *sōtēr*, meaning redeemer or messiah. However, the reading 'Stara' is not necessarily preferable to 'Stada' and as we have seen above, Stada was apparently the reading of *b. Sanh.*, as is evident from the pun on Stada. On the numerous forms of the name see Maier, *Jesus*, 205-6.

at least regarding some of the Ben Stada traditions.[22] However, Jesus was certainly not stoned, and in no way was he ever connected with Lydda, making it difficult to identify Jesus with Ben Stada.[23]

There have been other suggestions. Derenbourg, one of the first to reject the Jesus identification, postulated that Ben Stada was an otherwise unknown prophet at some time after the destruction of the Jerusalem Temple.[24] This view met with little acceptance. Although the literary formulation of the Ben Stada traditions certainly post-dates the destruction of the Temple, the Rabbis clearly meant to describe events taking place during the Second Temple period. Moreover, according to Derenbourg's view, the Lydda element plays no role whatsoever, which, as we have seen, is not the impression from the tradition itself.[25]

Derenbourg, almost as an afterthought, suggested another possibility. The Rabbis, in his view, may have been familiar in some form or fashion with the story of the execution of Stephen by stoning (Acts 6:8-7:60). This, according to Derenbourg, may also have accounted for some of the confusion of the Rabbis regarding Ben Stada and Jesus. Stephen, however, had nothing to do with Lydda. Derenbourg's

---

[22]See D. Rokeah, 'Ben Stara is Ben Pantera—Towards the Clarification of a Philological-Historical Problem', *Tarbiz* 39 (1970) 9-18 (Hebrew). Rokeah interprets the name as deriving from *stauros* or cross. See also M. Smith, *Jesus the Magician* (Wellingborough, [2]1985) 47, 178.

[23]2nd-century pagan and Christian writers do refer to marks on the body of Jesus and there are those scholars who claim that the Ben Stada-magic tradition mentioned above (*b. Shabb.* 104b) might well reflect this. Moreover, Mt. 2:13-21 does record the flight of the infant Jesus to Egypt. See Smith, *Jesus*, 48. However, as mentioned above, none of this can be tied to Lydda. There were also scholars who claimed that only the Ben Stada-magic tradition should be identified with Jesus. See H.L. Strack, *Jesus die Haeretiker und die Christen nach den ältesten jüdischen Angaben* (Leipzig, 1910) 28 n. 4. According to Strack, a common or similar etymology of the name or nickname might have resulted in the eventual mix-up in Rabbinic sources. Be that as it may, and whether *b. Shabb.* 104b should be identified with Jesus or not (but *cf. t. Shabb.* 11.15, the earliest form of the Ben Stada-magic tradition which does not mention Egypt), it is clear that the Ben Stada-Lod tradition is distinct and separate from the Ben Stada-magic tradition.

[24]J. Derenbourg, *Essai sur l'histoire et la géographie de la Palestine* (Paris, 1867) 471.

[25]Derenbourg's dating is based on the assumption that Ben Stada and R. Eliezer, the tradent of the Ben Stada magic traditions (see n. 20), were contemporaries. There is not much to recommend this view. Maier, *Jesus von Nazareth*, 205 tentatively suggests that the execution of Ben Stada took place, or could have taken place, with the permission of the Roman authorities. This too is rather unlikely. The same is true regarding his ultimate conclusion that the Ben Stada-Lod traditions are related to the Bar-Kochba War (AD 132-5).

assumption, though, that the Rabbis had a basic acquaintance with early Palestinian Christianity is of great importance, as we shall see later on.

In the wake of Derenbourg's rejection of the Jesus identification, other scholars sought Ben Stada in a number of other New Testament figures such as James, brother of Jesus, who was executed in AD 62,[26] or Simon Magus (Acts 8:9-24).[27] Once again, though, none of these figures has anything to do with Lydda and, therefore, there is no reason to connect them with the Ben Stada Lydda traditions.

One identification based on a New Testament figure does have a connection with Lydda. B. Königsberger was the first to identify Ben Stada with Peter,[28] who, as we saw above, certainly was associated with that city. His reasoning, however, was so convoluted and his philological analysis, the basis of his reasoning, was so preposterous that his theory was immediately ignored and promptly forgotten.[29] It is our view, however, that Königsberger stumbled onto the correct solution.

---

[26]J. Loewy, 'Die drei Jacobus', *Das Juedische Literaturblatt* 7 (4) (1878) 15. On the execution of James see Jos. *Ant.* 20.200-203 and Eusebius, *Hist. Eccl.* 2.1. Loewy was convinced that Ben Stada had to be a 'James' and, therefore, offered the alternate identifications of James the Great who was indeed put to death by Herod Agrippa (Acts 12:2) and James the Less (Mt. 10:3 *et al.*). As we stated above, none of this has anything to do with Lydda and in any case, none of these identifications were accepted by scholars. We shall see, though, that the Ben Stada traditions may describe events contemporary to the times of James the Great.

[27]R. Eisler, *Iesous basileus ou basileusas* (Heidelberg, 1928-30) I, 178; J. Schoeps, 'Simon Magus in der Haggada', *HUCA* 2 (1948) 257-74. There are certain similarities between Ben Stada and later (!) representations of Simon Magus. Thus, later tradition describes the heresiarch as a native of Gitta in Samaria going to Egypt as a young man to learn magical arts. He later returned to Palestine and founded the gnostic sect of Simonians. Later literature also refers to him as 'Stadios' or the 'Standing One', which does sound similar to Stada. Other sources state that his father was called Sotades. It is important to stress, though, that it is not even clear that Simon of Acts is identical with Simon Magus of Gitta. Once again, however, the key is Lydda. There is no reason to connect Simon of Acts or the later Simon with that site. Moreover, there is no reason why Simon of Acts would have been considered dangerous enough to have warranted the severe legal tactics described in the Ben Stada traditions.

[28]B. Königsberger, 'Miscellen aus der juedischen Alterthumskunde', *Das Juedische Literaturblatt* 20 (1891) 40.

[29]Königsberger refers to the reading Ben Patya (instead of Ben Stada) found in the 11th-century commentary of Hananel on the Ben Stada-magic Egyptian traditions (see n. 20). This reading is clearly a mistake. Königsberger, though, took this form of the name, combined it with the reading Ben Stara and came up with Ben Petra, which he explained as Petrus or Peter. The 'Ben' he interpreted as 'young'. All of this is patent nonsense.

Of all the personalities suggested by scholars to be identified with Ben Stada, the only one with a connection to Lydda was Peter and this, in our view, is one of the major elements necessary to understand both the Peter and Ben Stada traditions.

However, another major element or key to the understanding of both traditions is the *halakhic* or legal status of Ben Stada. As we have seen, Ben Stada is described in Rabbinic sources as a *mesit*, or one who entices or beguiles, and is the only example of such activity cited by name in Rabbinic literature. This is also of great importance since it is our view that many of Peter's activities may also have been those of a *mesit*. Thus, both were at Lydda and, as we shall see, both fit the *halakhic* category of *mesit*.

IV. The *Mesit* of the Rabbis

In the Ben Stada traditions mentioned above, we have seen that the crime of the *mesit* is so serious that deception and entrapment were permitted to apprehend him. This was necessary because the *mesit* was 'crafty' and capable of escaping his pursuers in order to continue to beguile others.

Rabbinic literature has more information regarding the *mesit*.[30] It is important to point out that while it is true that many of these traditions are clearly much later than the events described either in Acts or than those purportedly described in the Ben Stada traditions, it may be possible to at least learn something of the *halakhic* milieu of the *mesit* traditions. It is important also to remember that we do not have the Sadducean *halakhah* on *mesit*, nor have I been able to find any reference to this matter in the writings of the Dead Sea Sect.[31] We thus make do with Rabbinic traditions and their biblical bases.

If we return, though, to the matter of the *mesit*, it appears that entrapment was not the only exception to the rule. Thus, for example, *t. Sanh.* 7.5 (p. 426 ed. Zuckermandel) states that eunuchs, those who

---

[30]Some of these sources were collected by D. Neale, 'Was Jesus a Mesith? Public Response to Jesus and His Ministry', *TynBul* 44.1 (1993) 89-101. As we shall shortly show, it is our opinion that in view of Rabbinic tradition, Jesus was not or could not have been a *mesit*. The best collection of Rabbinic sources on this matter is found in Y.M. ben Menahem, '*Mesit* and *Mediah* and the False Prophet in the Framework of "Thou Shalt Listen Unto Him" of the True Prophet', in S.Y. Zevin (ed.), *Mazqeret: Torah Collection in Memory of Chief Rabbi I. Herzog* (Jerusalem, 1962) 124-61 (Hebrew).

are childless and those who have a reputation for being cruel are not allowed to serve as judges in capital cases since they would not tend to be merciful, an attribute that the accused, at least, would hope for in a judge. *B. Sanh.* 36b adds that regarding the *mesit* this was not the case; in fact these types of judges were to be preferred since the Bible specifically stated that 'neither shall thine eye pity him, neither shalt thou spare' (Dt. 13:9). The harsher the judge the better.

This was not the worst of it, though, for the *mesit*. Sifre Deuteronomy #89 (p. 152, ed. Finkelstein), citing Dt. 13:9, explains that one must not attempt to acquit the *mesit*, but rather must volunteer to the court any information to convict him. If he should be convicted, he is not to be returned to court again even if new information should be available. If he is acquitted, however, he should be returned to court, if possible, in order to be convicted. The rules were certainly stacked against him.

B. Sanh. 29a adds that if one was accused of a capital case and had nothing to plead, someone else must plead for the accused to secure an acquittal, if it was possible. One does not plead for a *mesit*, however. The Talmud here cites Dt. 13:9 once again, but the 3rd-century sage R. Jonathan adds an interesting aside:

> And how do we know that one does not plead for a *mesit*? From the primordial serpent. As R. Simlai said, 'there was much that the serpent could have pleaded, but he did not. And why did the Holy One Blessed be He not plead for him? Because he (= serpent) did not plead.

The image used by the two 3rd-century Rabbis is quite telling. The *mesit* is not much different than the evil serpent.[32] In the final analysis,

[31]A complete discussion of the question of the applicability of 'later' Rabbinic sources to historical research and particularly to the 1st-century AD would undoubtedly take up our allotment of space for this article. For the present see, for instance, Neale's brief comments, *TynBul* 90. Suffice it to say that caution must be exercised, but in view of the 'layered structure' of much of Rabbinic literature, the gist of even late traditions can often provide relevant background material. On questions pertaining to the penal code of the Dead Sea sect see most recently J. M. Baumgarten, 'The Cave 4 Versions of the Qumran Penal Code', *JJS* 43 (1992) 268-76. Although there does not seem to be any reference to the concept of *mesit*, there is some reference in the sect's penal code to those who deviate from their teachings. Improper use of the divine name would result in expulsion from the sect. There were also punishments for disobeying a senior, slandering, murmuring against the community and deviating from fundamentals. None of this, in spite of perhaps some superficial similarity, has anything to do with *mesit*.

the crafty serpent of the Garden of Eden could not save itself, and even though God could have done so, he chose not to.[33] The crafty *mesit* will meet the same end, and nobody will plead for him. The *mesit* had little chance in court, at least once he got there, and was accused of being a *mesit*.

The severity of all this is quite extraordinary. There were many capital offences in ancient Judaism, and not a few were connected to transgressions in matters of religion or theology.[34] What was there in particular about the *mesit* that caused all this judicial harshness?

The *mesit*, according to the Rabbis, threatened the very fabric of Jewish survival. The *mesit* preached action: 'Enticement always implies acting in error…others say that enticement always indicates deliberate action'.[35] The *mesit* preached his message only in secret[36] and often disguised it as a social encounter, preaching at a meal.[37] The *mesit* spoke in a 'low voice'[38] and preferred to preach to individuals since 'an individual does not ask outside advice and will err after him (= the *mesit*) while groups of many will seek advice and not err'.[39] A *mesit* was also usually careful to preach someone else's gospel or message, or to serve, as it were, as a 'front man' and not to preach his own veneration, since this was likely to invite ridicule.[40] A *mesit* was neither a sage, Rabbi or prophet, but rather a 'common man' (הֶדְיוֹט), someone who would not automatically be recognised.[41]

---

[32]See *Midr. Tannaim* 13:9 (66, ed. Hoffmann): 'If he should be bitten by a snake do not check up after him'.

[33]See *b. Menaḥ.* 99b. God is described as the opposite of the *mesit* who allures his fellow from life to death. God allures or entices mankind from death to life. It is important to note, therefore, that *mesit* can also be used in a positive sense. It depends on who is enticing and to what one is being enticed. See also *b. Ber.* 62b: 'The Holy One Blessed be He said to David, "You accuse me of being a *mesit?*"' (*Cf.* 1 Sa. 26:19). In *b. B. Bat.* 16a Satan manages to entice (or really finagle) God into letting Job be severely tested (*cf.* Job 2:13). Needless to say, the Rabbis had problems with this. See also *b. Ḥag.* 5a.

[34]During 'special emergencies' legal niceties were also often dispensed with. See *Sipre Dt.* #22 (p. 253, ed. Finkelstein). Simeon ben Shetah (1st century BC), for instance, executed eighty witches without observing all details of laws pertaining to capital cases. The laws of *mesit*, although they may reflect historical circumstances, as we shall see, do not fall within this specific legal or *halachic* category.

[35]*Sipre* Dt. #87 (p. 151, ed. Finkelstein; tr. p. 138, ed. Hammer).

[36]*Sipre*, *ibid*. True words of Torah were always spoken publicly.

[37]*B. Ḥul.* 4b.

[38]*Y. Sanh.* 7.25d.

[39]*B. Sanh.* 61b. See also *m. Sanh.* 7:10 above. If the *mesit* preached to two, these two were sufficient witnesses to secure his arrest and execution.

It was virtually impossible, therefore, to catch this type of dangerous character. That was why entrapment was necessary and that was why when he was finally captured he was held, according to one view, in custody until a festival and only then was he executed, to fulfill the verse in Dt. 13:12: 'and all Israel shall hear and fear'.[42] In any case, the execution, whenever it took place, was accompanied by public proclamation.[43]

V. Peter as *Mesit* and *Mesit* as Healer

As we mentioned above, it is our view that the Peter and Ben Stada traditions are related to one another. Both were associated with Lydda. Ben Stada was the classic *mesit* of early Rabbinic literature and Peter's activities in Lydda and other sites would have also made him the classic *mesit*.[44] The Ben Stada traditions are also, in our view, part of the Jewish polemic against early Judaeo-Christianity.[45] The Rabbis, it seems, had a different version of attempts to Christianise Lydda or other sites, and this version did not end happily for the Christians.[46]

It is important to stress, though, that we do not claim that *all* of Peter's activities and teachings were within the framework of *mesit*.

---

[40]*B. Sanh.* 61a-b. There is a discussion there as to whether one who preaches his own message would constitute a *mesit*. One view is that even those who might be prone to follow a *mesit* would hardly believe someone who preached his own gospel. Although this tradition is relatively late, it is hard to describe Jesus as a *mesit* in view of this.

[41]*M. Sanh.* 7:10.

[42]See *t. Sanh.* 11.7 (p. 432, ed. Zuckermandel) and parallels. The *mesit* is included among a number of other dangerous characters such as 'rebellious son', 'rebellious elder', *madiah* who are held, according to R. Akiva, for execution on a festival. R. Judah said they are executed at once, and notification is sent out immediately to the communities of the Land of Israel in order to fulfill the verse (Dt. 13:12) and serve as a future deterrent.

[43]See *b. Sanh.* 89a.

[44]See Neale, 'Was Jesus a Mesith' (see n. 30 above). Neale argues that Jesus was a *mesit* and, thus, one might also argue that Ben Stada should indeed be identified with Jesus as *b. Sanh.* 67a mistakenly does. Jesus, however, hardly corresponds to what we have seen above to be the major characteristics of the *mesit*, even bearing in mind the problematic and non-uniform nature of the Rabbinic traditions discussed above. The *mesit* survived on secrecy. If anything, Jesus might be described as the *madiah* which from the standpoint of Rabbinic literature was one who preached in public, usually with an entourage. On the public aspects of the *madiah* see H. Albeck, *Shishah Sidrei Mishnah: Seder Neziqin* (Jerusalem and Tel-Aviv, 1959) 450 (= additional notes).

This, in fact, is the very problem regarding the *mesit*. Most of Peter's public activities were probably not forbidden, at least according to a strict interpretation of Jewish law, although, as is also clear from Acts, many of them would have irritated the Jewish authorities. Peter in their view was a questionable character. It seemed to be difficult, however, clearly to catch him at anything blatantly forbidden. Those activities in which Peter crossed the line and became a *halakhic mesit* were done in a much more private milieu, as we shall now try to see.[47]

Thus, Acts 3:1-10 describes Peter curing a lame man on the Temple Mount 'in the name of Jesus Christ the Nazarene'.[48] This was undoubtedly not the type of thing that was commonly done or accepted in or around the Temple Mount area, and it was logical that a great commotion should have followed all this.[49] However, it was only when the cured man went into the Temple that people were actually aware of what had happened. The 'miracle' itself probably took place in a quiet, secluded part of the Temple Mount,[50] or so quickly that no one was aware of what had happened. This seems to prefigure the scenario of the miracle at Lydda. The healing itself is done with

---

[45]It would serve absolutely no purpose for our present study to become involved in the problems pertaining to the existence and development of Judaeo or Jewish Christianity. It is fairly safe to state that in the 1st and early 2nd centuries AD there still were Christians of Jewish origins and that the normative Jewish community would have been aware of them and opposed them. See, most recently, J.E. Taylor, *Christians and the Holy Places: The Myth of Jewish-Christian Origins* (Oxford, 1993).

[46]It is unlikely that the Rabbis actually read Acts or knew the stories exactly as recorded there, although they may have been familiar with certain books of the New Testament (see *t. Yad.* 2.13 *et al.*) and it is not, therefore, completely impossible that they knew this book. Acts certainly drew on early traditions regarding such figures as Peter and Paul, and perhaps these may have been familiar to the Rabbis. We cite Acts as the most comprehensive surviving collection of these traditions, but many of those traditions in Acts undoubtedly circulated independently and were familiar to the Rabbis in this version.

[47]It is obvious that not every Peter tradition in Acts will fit in with the *mesit* scenario. It is important once again to stress that it is not Acts *per se* which is important for our purposes, but how these traditions would have been perceived by the Rabbis.

[48]John accompanies Peter to the Temple Mount but according to Cullmann, he may be a secondary addition. See O. Cullmann, *Peter: Disciple, Apostle, Martyr: A Historical and Theological Study* (London, [2]1962) 34-35. This is important. A *mesit* operates alone. A *madiah* has an entourage or at least one compatriot. See Albeck, *Shishah Sidrei Mishnah*, 450.

[49]On the legality or halakhic position regarding such types of healing see our discussion below.

little fanfare. Peter lets the results speak for themselves, and once this has been accomplished, it is then possible to talk about them publicly.

Thus, only when knowledge of the miracle became widespread in the Temple area did Peter begin to address the crowds, and specifically crowds which had not been witness to the miracle (Acts 3:11-26). Peter chose his words carefully, and even though he stated that the lame man had been cured by the power of Jesus and that repentance could wipe out the sin of putting Jesus to death, he apparently avoided being charged with blasphemy, a capital offence. We shall shortly have much more to say on the matter of healing and in particular healing through the name of Jesus. Suffice it for the moment to say that Peter's hesitance in calling attention to the actual moment of healing was quite justified. In matters of 'sorcery', it was actions and not incantations which were the capital offence. This is not to say that the latter were permitted; the fleeting nature of words, however, just made it harder to prove a serious offence.[51] This was indeed part of the problem of catching the *mesit*: finding the correct accusatory legal balance between words and actions in public and private.

Peter's speech, however, did elicit a reaction, apparently of the Sanhedrin. Amazingly, Peter and John were arrested because they disrupted the order of the Temple Mount. Acts also adds that they were charged with having preached the resurrection of Jesus, an idea at odds with Sadducean theology which rejected resurrection.[52] It is hard to imagine, though, anyone being charged with such a crime, and the charge was probably no more than an excuse to arrest them. Both apostles, however, were released even after Peter repeated that he had healed through Jesus (Acts 4:8-12), and they both refused to promise that they would cease to teach in the name of Jesus. They had apparently not yet crossed the theoretical boundary between teaching and healing on one hand, and sorcery and blasphemy on the other.

Before we go on, though, with our discussion of the *mesit*, it is necessary briefly to discuss this theoretical boundary between teaching and healing and sorcery and blasphemy. The Sanhedrin was

---

[50]This might have been possible even at the entrance to the Beautiful Gate (Acts 3:2-3). On this gate see Th.A. Busink, *Der Tempel von Jerusalem von Salamo bis Herodes: eine Archäologisch-Historische Studie unter Berücksichtigung der West-semitischen Tempelbau, II, von Ezechiel bis Middot* (Leiden, 1980) 1185-7. On the relationship of this gate to Temple gates mentioned in Josephus and the Rabbis see J. Schwartz, 'Once More on the Nicanor Gate', *HUCA* 62 (1991) 245-83.

[51]See H. Mantel, *Studies in the History of the Sanhedrin* (Cambridge, 1965) 298.

[52]Josephus, *Ant.* 18.11-18.

obviously disturbed by the healing in the name of Jesus. Peter made no secret of it. On the contrary, he talked about it a great deal, yet avoided blatant acts of healing in public. As we shall see now, the problem was not so much the healing, in spite of its magical nature, but healing in the name of Jesus (Acts 4:30), and it was in this that Peter came perilously close to crossing the murky line between toleration and being a *mesit*. As far as the Rabbis were concerned, he probably crossed over that line.

As we just stated, though, the magical elements of healing were not *per se* the major problem. True, there was a 'science' of medicine and healing in ancient Judaism, and normative *halakhic* Judaism of that time did take a dim 'official' view of healing which deviated from that 'scientific' line.[53] It was that 'scientific line', however, which was not all that clearly defined. On one hand, the Mishnah could state that one who utters charms over a wound has no share in the world to come, even if that charm should be a pertinent biblical verse such as Exodus 15:26;[54] yet on the other hand, the Rabbis became sensitive enough to recognise that if something worked, they could not forbid it as magic or sorcery.[55]

There were, however, limits to this:

> R. Eleazar ben Damma was bitten by a snake and Jacob of Kefar Sema came to heal him in the name of Yeshua ben Pantera [= Jesus], but R. Ishmael prevented him. He declared: Ben Damma, you are forbidden. And Ben Damma replied: I will bring proof that he may heal me, but he died before he could bring proof. Declared R. Ishmael: Blessed are you Ben Damma that you left in peace without breaching the fence of the sages, for he who breaches the fence of the sages, in the end evil

53See J. Preuss, *Biblisch-talmudische Medizin: Beiträge zur Geschichte der Heilkunde und der Kultur überhaupt* (Berlin, 1923[3]).

54See, for instance, *m. Sanh.* 10:1. Cf. also *b. Sheb.* 15b on the view of the 3rd-century AD Lyddan Rabbi Joshua ben Levi, who forbade healing through the magical use of any biblical verses. Apparently, though, R. Joshua ben Levi permitted these verses to be used for 'protection' or for what in a wider sense might be called 'preventive medicine'.

55The Rabbis could not stand in the face of reality. If it worked, it was usually tolerated. See, for example, the statement of the 3rd-century AD sage R. Johanan: 'Whatever heals, does not fall in the category of the "ways of the Amorites" (= pagan magic).' We shall see, though, that this does not pertain to healing in the name of Jesus. *Cf.* J. Naveh and S. Shaked, *Magic Spells and Formulae: Aramaic Incantations of Late Antiquity* (Jerusalem, 1993) 31-39 on magic and medicine in later Judaism.

> comes upon him as it is written, 'And whoso breaketh through a fence, a serpent shall bite him'. (Ec. 10:8)[56]

Jacob of Kefar Sema, of the late 1st and early 2nd century AD, was most likely a Judaeo-Christian who sought to heal through the name of Jesus, much like Peter.[57] The Rabbis, as we have just seen, tended to be lenient in matters of medicine and healing, and Ben Damma, realizing his mortal danger, was willing to try anything. R. Ishmael refused to let him be healed through the name of Jesus. It is true that this tradition reflects ordinances instituted by the Rabbis, and it is hard to know to what extent these restrictions existed in the late Second Temple period. This, however, is not really important since, and as we shall expand upon this later, the Rabbis would have been familiar with Peter and other New Testament motifs only at the end of the 1st century AD or beginning of the 2nd century, at exactly the time when Ben Damma had his unfortunate encounter with the snake. They would have reacted to these motifs in keeping with the realities of their own time and not those of the late Second Temple period. Moreover, there were pagan claims that Christians really healed by calling upon demons, and according to these same pagan traditions, the Jews also believed this.[58]

It is important to note, though, that R. Ishmael took no action against Jacob of Kefar Sema. This is undoubtedly both because of the nebulous legal status of the healing and the little that R. Ishmael could have done in terms of concrete punishment. The Jewish community and sages were undoubtedly limited or constrained in their rights to exercise such power. At the end of the Second Temple period, however, and in spite of Roman rule, the Sanhedrin or other Jewish

[56] *T. Ḥul.* 2.22-23, *y. 'Abod. Zar.* 2.44d and *b. 'Abod. Zar.* 27b. See also *y. Shabb.* 4.14d on the *min* (= Judaeo-Christian [?]) who healed the grandson of R. Joshua ben Levi in Tiberias. The fact that Eleazar ben Damma was bitten by a snake is quite interesting. See, for instance, *Midr. Tannaim* on Dt. 13:9 (n. 32 above) on a *mesit* bitten by a snake, and see our discussion above on *b. Sanh.* 29a on the connection between the *mesit* and the primordial serpent. It is the *mesit* who represents particular danger to the framework instituted by the Rabbis.It would seem to be quite telling, therefore, that Ec. 10:8 was cited regarding the fate of one who damages or attempts to destroy that framework.

[57] *Cf.* Taylor, *Christians and Holy Places*, p. 29. Taylor has a minimalist view regarding the connection between *minim* and Judaeo-Christians, but in this case even she would seem to agree that Jacob is Christian and not just some type of magician bandying about the name of Jesus in order to heal.

[58] See D. Rokeah, *Judaism and Christianity in Pagan Polemics: Celsus, Porphyry and Julian* (Jerusalem, 1991) 50 (Hebrew).

leadership institutions still had a degree of power in these areas, as indeed one can learn even from Acts. Peter could heal, but healing in the name of Jesus may have been a different matter indeed. The matter, though, was still apparently quite new. Peter exercised caution. The healing itself was done in private, and this seemed to suit both Peter and those who sought his services (Acts 5:15). Talking about it was apparently less serious. The private nature of the healing would, however, certainly be in keeping with the *mesit* traditions we have seen so far.

The remainder of the Temple Mount healing tradition is also in keeping with what we have seen so far of the *mesit*. It is interesting to note, for instance, that according to Acts, the priests and Temple Mount functionaries considered Peter and John to be 'uneducated and common men' (Acts 4:13),[59] yet capable of bold or charismatic action. This is very close to the profile of the *mesit* we discussed above who was a *hedyot*, but beyond a doubt also quite capable. We do not claim, of course, that the Jews were familiar with all the details related by Acts, but magic and miracles did make an impression on ancient Judaism[60] and, therefore, it is likely that the basic elements of the story were known.

Peter continued to tread a thin line between 'legal' public activity and more dubious actions of a private nature. Just as Peter could heal, he could also harm. The embezzlers Ananias and his wife Sapphira died after being rebuked by Peter (Acts 5:1-11). Both of the deaths occurred, it would seem, indoors, and only before the apostles and other believers. Indeed, it would have been difficult to prove that Peter was responsible and, in any event, the matter never came to the attention of the authorities.[61]

---

[59]See Conzelmann, *A Commentary* (see n. 4) 31. This motif also appeared in the early Church Fathers.

[60]See E.E. Urbach, *The Sages, Their Concepts and Beliefs* (Jerusalem, 1975) I, 115-6; II, 730 n. 55.

[61]See J. Duncan and M. Derrett, *Studies in the New Testament*, I, *Glimpses of the Legal and Social Presuppositions of the Authors* (Leiden, 1977) 193-201. Acts is not clear exactly what the role of Peter was here. If the early Church considered itself to be a Temple community, then embezzlement was punishable by death from God. Was Peter an active agent in causing the death of Ananias or was Ananias a victim of conscience and perhaps a heart attack. The quick disposal of his body and utter lack of mourning probably increased the shock of Sapphira when she was confronted later on. Once again Peter walks a thin line. These events, in any case, stayed within the community.

Peter and the other apostles ignored the injunction of the Sanhedrin regarding healing and teaching, but did so in a manner in keeping with the delicate balance of public and private activity we have described above (Acts 5:12-16). In spite of the increasing number of believers in Jesus and the power of the apostles, no one dared join Peter and the other apostles in their meeting area in Solomon's Colonnade.[62] It was as if there was some type of agreement to avoid public contact. The same was true regarding Peter's large volume of healing. There were no direct contacts (Acts 5:15). The increasing number of believers, though, might well indicate a good deal of private contact, indicative of *mesit*-type activity.

Peter and his fellows continued to play a 'cat-and-mouse' type of game with the Sanhedrin. As a result of their renewed activity they were arrested. It is impossible to know whether they would have been tried or just held in custody until they promised to obey the Sanhedrin since they managed to escape custody, with the aid of an angel. The angel bade them to return to the Temple Mount to preach, which they did, and they were arrested once again and this time brought to trial (5:26).

Once again, Peter and his compatriots were apparently not charged with blasphemy, but rather with contempt of the previous injunction of the Sanhedrin (5:27-28). Their defence, as stated by Peter, basically consisted of slandering the Sanhedrin regarding complicity in the death of Jesus. This in itself was certainly not a capital crime,[63] although certain members of the Sanhedrin did wish to kill them (5:33). In the final event, and after a speech by the Pharisee Gamaliel who described them as fringe-element ineffectual fanatics, they were let off with a beating and a stern admonition to cease teaching in the name of Jesus.[64] They ignored the orders of the Sanhedrin, which surprisingly, at least according to Luke, did not bother them again.

---

[62]On Temple Mount geography see J. Schwartz, 'Once More on the Nicanor Gate' (see n. 50 above). Conzelmann states that in spite of the honour in which the apostles may have been held, there was also an element of fear involved. This also is not all that far removed from the background and reality of the *mesit* (and perhaps the editing process here was not as clumsy as Conzelmann thought).

[63]H. Cohn, *The Trial and Death of Jesus* (London, 1942) 247.

[64]This was not the thirty-nine stripes (Dt. 25:1-3) which were inflicted by a court of three (*m. Sanh.* 1:2) for specific crimes (*m. Mak.* 3:1-9), but a common means employed by legal and political institutions to enforce decrees. Judaeo-Christians were sometimes beaten in such a manner. See, for example, *Gn. Rab.* 7:2 (51-52, ed. Theodor-Albeck) and parallels.

This is even more surprising in view of what happened later on to Stephen after his long address to the Sanhedrin (Acts 7:1-59). However, if our interpretation of events so far has been correct, this may not be so surprising after all. Stephen, in contrast to Peter, went out of his way to go public and became embroiled in controversy. Opposition to him resulted in his being charged with blasphemy (Acts 6:8-15). Peter, as we have seen, preferred a different approach. The Sanhedrin considered him irritating and probably quite dangerous, but Peter was quite adept at obfuscation and there was never anything really tangible to accuse him of that warranted more than a beating and an admonition. This, as we remember, was quite lucky for him since if there had been real proof that he was a *mesit*, his end undoubtedly would have been similar to that of Stephen. Be all that as it may, however, if our interpretation of Ben Stada is correct, the Jewish accounts recorded one more run-in between Peter and the Sanhedrin and in this version, Peter was accused of being a *mesit* and met the fate of one.

The Sanhedrin may have given up according to Acts, but others not so restricted by legal formalities were not so complacent.[65] Acts 12, describing events that took place at the latest by the spring of AD 44, relates that Herod Agrippa I executed James, the brother of John, Peter's colleague on the Temple Mount and partner in trial before the Sanhedrin (Acts 12:1-2).[66] The account continues to state:

> And seeing that it was acceptable to the Jews, he (= Herod Agrippa) proceeded to arrest Peter too and it was the Days of unleavened bread, and he seized him (= Peter) and put him in prison...wishing after Passover to bring him out to the people. (Acts 12:3-4)

Agrippa used political power and privilege to do what normal judicial procedure could not.[67] He arrested Peter only after he was sure of popular support (Acts 12:3, 11). In spite of Peter's success in preaching

---

[65]See G. Alon, *Jews, Judaism and the Classical World* (Jerusalem, 1977) 120, who cites a tradition in *b. Sanh.* 8b, apparently at odds with *m.* and *t. Sanh.* we have discussed above regarding the *mesit*. In *b. Sanh.* 8b the *mesit* could be put to death without due process of law. Alon claims that this tradition reflects the Second Temple period and that Herod Agrippa was operating within some type of *halachic* framework. All this is unlikely, however. If a *mesit* were not entitled to due process of law in the Second Temple period, the Sanhedrin undoubtedly would have made short shrift of Peter, James and the rest from the very beginning.

[66]See, however, Cullmann, *Peter*, 34-35 (n. 48 above). John may have been a secondary addition to at least some of the Temple Mount traditions.

and healing, there were not many who were willing to express open support and to publicly defend him. This is also in keeping with the private nature of *mesit* activities. Peter may have convinced many, but he convinced them as individuals, if our interpretation is correct, and Herod Agrippa did not see this as a real threat. Peter had, though, probably irritated enough people to have aroused the suspicion and reaction of Herod Agrippa. Once again, though, Peter is saved by an angel.[68] This time, however, he did not return to preach at the Temple Mount, but left Jerusalem, at least for the time being.[69]

The sum total of Peter's actions was not very different from the general description of the *mesit* which we have seen above. The *mesit* was a 'common man' (*hedyot*) yet 'crafty', who usually operated in secret and preached to individuals, yet never his own gospel or cult. Sometimes all of this was done in an intimate social setting. He was next to impossible to catch, but if he were caught, with legal entrapment being permitted, he would be executed around the time of a festival and the execution would be accompanied by a proclamation. This, in our view, aptly describes a good deal of Peter's activities.

---

[67]See J. Blinzler, 'Rechtsgeschichtliches zur Hinrichtung des Zebedaeiden Jakobus (Apg XII,2)', *NT* 5 (1962) 191-206. It is difficult to understand why Blinzler seeks to exonorate Herod Agrippa and blame the Sanhedrin for these events. This is particularly so if our description of the legal background is correct. Blinzler claims that Peter was tried as a *madiah*—one who entices a whole city to idolatry. As we have seen above, the *madiah* operates as much as possible in public while the *mesit* prefers a more private setting for his preaching, although their activities in the final analysis may be quite similar. Stephen may have qualified as a *halachic madiah*, and perhaps even Jesus was not that far removed from this *halachic* category. If Peter had crossed that line, he would have met the same end as Stephen. See also D. Rokeah, *Judaism and Christianity in Pagan Polemics*, 15 (see n. 58 above). Rokeah argues that Peter perhaps should be considered as a 'rebellious elder'. As we have seen, though, Peter was not considered an 'elder' (Acts 4:13) and if he were a 'rebellious' one, the Sanhedrin would have made short shrift of him (*cf. m. Sanh.* 11:2).

[68]See J.W. Swain, 'Gamaliel's Speech and Caligula's Statue', *HTR* 37 (1944) 341-349. According to Swain, Agrippa simply changed his mind and decided to release Peter secretly. The guard sent to release him was confused with an angel. None of this seems very likely. See also D.F. Robinson, 'Where and When Did Peter Die', *JBL* 64 (1945) 255-67, who claims that in spite of later literary evidence to the contrary, Peter was really executed in Jerusalem at that time. The evidence and later traditions regarding Peter, however (and discussed at great length by Robinson himself), would seem to make Robinson's theory unacceptable.

[69]Acts 12:17. Peter, however, participated in the Jerusalem council described in Acts 15 (Acts 15:7-11).

VI. Peter and Ben Stada

Based on what we have seen above, Peter might have been described in *halakhic* terms as a *mesit*. Ben Stada was according to Rabbinic tradition the classical *mesit*. Both were in Lydda. The arrest of both was connected with the Jewish festival of Passover.[70] 'Ben Stada in Lod' was, in our view, part of the Rabbinic response to Peter in Lydda and its environs.

As we have stated above, we do not claim that this identification is based on actual Rabbinic knowledge or familiarity with the details of Acts. Rather, the Rabbis would have been familiar with traditions regarding a certain slippery *mesit* who had managed to perpetrate his designs without being apprehended or who, having been apprehended, managed to escape. The original traditions probably derived from Judaeo-Christian circles and were used by them to show the supposed impotency of the Sanhedrin and other Jewish institutions. The Rabbis might have actually known that the name of what they considered to be an infamous *mesit* was Peter, but this is not absolutely necessary.[71]

It is the Lydda element, though, long neglected by scholars, which enables us to see the entire affair within a local perspective. Peter's travel traditions in one or another early form were undoubtedly part of the Judaeo-Christian lore and used in their ongoing polemic with Rabbinic or normative Judaism. This was undoubtedly also so regarding Lydda. It has been suggested that the activities of Peter, although in themselves not necessarily illegal, as we have often seen, may have led to disturbances of a more widespread nature.[72] Perhaps such disturbances actually took place in Lydda after Peter's departure (or flight if he was a fugitive) and, thus, the Ben Stada tradi-

[70]As we remember, it was *b.* which added the Passover element, and it might be argued that this is simply part of *b.*'s assimilation of Ben Stada to Jesus. Since, however, the Passover element is important both in the crucifixion of Jesus and the attempted execution of Peter, it is possible that Passover in *b.* actually represents the point of transfer from Peter to Jesus. It is not likely that *b.* had knowledge of events described in Acts 12. *B.*, however, would have known of the connection of Jesus to Passover. There are, of course, minor differences between *b. Sanh.* and Acts regarding Passover. In *b.*, Ben Stada is arrested on the eve of the festival. In Acts, Peter is arrested on the festival and would not have been executed until afterwards. In both instances, though, an attempt is made not to desecrate the festival itself with an execution. See also A. Strobel, 'Passa-Symbolik und Passa-Wunder in Act. XII. 3ff.', *NTS* 4 (1957/58) 210-5.

tions represent the 'capture' of the culprit, at least in the Jewish version.

The events described in the Ben Stada traditions clearly relate to the end of the Second Temple period. The literary formulation, however, was later and the initial traditions probably date to the late 1st or early 2nd century AD, not too much unlike the case of Acts.

Lydda is also important within this time framework. Thus, it is accepted today that the centre of Jewish life at this time was not Jabneh but Lydda, and that in the post-Destruction period the Sanhedrin eventually moved to Lydda on a permanent basis, at least until shortly before the Bar-Kokhba War (AD 132).[73] It is also known that there was a good deal of tension at this time between the Jewish community and the Judaeo-Christians, many of whom were still a part of the Jewish community.[74] The Ben Stada Lydda traditions then may represent the Jewish response to Judaeo-Christian claims regarding the antiquity and primacy of the Christian community in that city.[75] It is perhaps then also no accident that one of the most anti-Christian Rabbis of the time was the Lyddan scholar R. Tarfon, who apparently even headed the Sanhedrin when it moved to Lydda.[76] The Ben Stada traditions, therefore, might be said to represent the Jewish battle against the

---

[71]Stada may be explained in terms of the Greek *stadios*, meaning 'standing firm, fast or steady'. The irony of the name, however, is that he did not stand firm but deviated (סטא in Aramaic). This could also apply to the name Peter. Peter was supposedly firm as a rock, but actually as far as his Jewish brethren were concerned, he was a deviate. Perhaps the Rabbis were familiar with Peter's nickname κηφᾶς from the Aramaic כיפא, meaning 'stone'. On other ironic interpretations of Peter's name see Mt. 16:23 and A. Strock, 'Is Matthew's Presentation of Peter Ironic?' *BTB* 17 (2) (1987) 64-9. Mediaeval Jewish tradition was familar with Peter and strangely enough, much of this Jewish material was positive. According to some of these traditions, Peter, or Simeon Kaipha as he is called here, is a Jewish sage who converts as an act of self-sacrifice in order to convince the Christians to cease persecuting Jews. After his conversion, Peter went to Rome, sat in a tower, and in some accounts then wrote synagogue poetry. See A. Jellinek, *Bet ha-Midrash* (Leipzig, 1853) V, 60-2; VI, 9-14, 155-6.

[72]See D.R. Schwartz, *Agrippa I* (see n. 3 above) 119-24.

[73] See Schwartz, *Lod (Lydda)*, 79-99.

[74]See G. Alon, *The Jews in Their Land in the Talmudic Age (70-640 C.E.)*, tr. and ed. G. Levi (Jerusalem 1980) I 294-307.

[75]According to Christian tradition, there was an uninterrupted Christian presence in Lydda from before the time of Peter and through Byzantine times with a bishop by the name of Zeno (or Zenas) in the city from as early as the time of Paul. See in detail Schwartz, *Lod (Lydda)*, 124-125. Most of these traditions, however, are late Byzantine or Crusader period idealisations. There was probably only a small Christian community in Lydda before the 4th century AD.

claims of Judaeo-Christians to the status of *Verus Israel* in a major Jewish centre. In the Jewish version, Ben Stada or Peter was obviously much less successful in his endeavours.

Ben Stada, therefore, is no longer the enigmatic figure he may have seemed to be and represents, as we have seen, a composite Rabbinic picture of Peter within the framework of some of the 1st century AD events described in Acts. Moreover, the Ben Stada traditions also allow us a glimpse into local Rabbinic tactics in their struggle against early Christianity. Ben Stada may have been the only *mesit* mentioned by name, but the *mesit* motif continued to play a role in the struggle between Jew and Christian later during the Byzantine period when the *mesit* became clearly identified with Christianity and the Judaeo-Christian polemic of that time.[77,78]

---

[76]See, for example, *t. Shabb.* 13(14).5: 'The Gospels (= Hebrew: *Ha-Gilyonim*) and the books of the *minim* are not to be saved from a fire. But they are allowed to burn where they are and the references to the Divine Name which are in them. Said R. Tarfon, "may I bury my sons, if such things come into my hands and I do not burn them, and even the references to the Divine Name which are in them. And if someone were running after me, I should go into a temple of idolatry, but I should not go into their houses (of worship). For idolaters do not recognise the Divinity in denying Him, but they recognise the Divinity and deny Him".' The translation is basically that of J. Neusner, *The Tosefta, Mo'ed* (New York, 1981) 49. R. Tarfon's earlier contemporary, R. Eliezer b. Hyrcanus, the tradent of the Ben Stada-magic traditions, also had contacts or run-ins with Judaeo-Christians, but it is not clear that this took place in Lydda. See *t. Ḥul.* 2:24 and *b. 'Abod. Zar.* 16b-17a.

[77]See, for instance, the late Byzantine midrash *Pesiq. Rab Kah.*, Piska 5, *Ha-Hodesh Ha-Zeh*, 96-97, ed. Mandelbaum (and the parallel in *Pesiq. R.* 15 [74b, ed. Ish-Shalom]): '"For lo the autumn (Hebrew: סתיו) has passed" (Ct. 2:11)—R. Azariah said: This is the evil kingdom (= Edom = Rome = Christianity) which leads people astray, as it is written, "If thy brother entice thee *etc.*" (Dt. 13:7)'. The midrash obviously plays on the similar roots of סתיו for autumn and סות to entice. *Cf. Midr. Tannaim* Dt. 13:9 (66, ed. Hoffmann): '"Neither shalt thou spare" (Dt. 13:9)—take wood and strike him with it'. The wood may refer to the Cross. The text here, however, is far from clear (*qwv kyskha 'lyv*), and consequently this last explanation must be accepted with caution.

[78]The above is a revised and expanded version of a previous study entitled, 'Ben Stada and Peter in Lydda', *JSJ* 21 (1990) 1-18. A shorter version appeared also in my book *Lod (Lydda), Israel: From its Origins through the Byzantine Period 5600 B.C.E.–640 C.E.* (*BAR* International Series 571; Oxford, 1991) 67-71, 74-77.

CHAPTER 15

JAMES AND THE JERUSALEM CHURCH

Richard Bauckham

Summary

This chapter focuses on the Jerusalem church especially in the period after the persecution by Herod Agrippa I (Acts 12:1-17), which was the point at which the Twelve ceased to be the leadership of the Jerusalem church and James the Lord's brother began to reach a position of pre-eminence in the Jerusalem church. The historicity of the portrayal of the Jerusalem church in Acts is assessed by relating it to that church's context in 1st-century Judaism and by checking it against other available evidence, so that an account which critically integrates the evidence of Acts with other evidence emerges. It is argued that the centrality of Jerusalem in the 1st-century Jewish worldview and experience provides the essential background for understanding both the way in which the leadership of the Jerusalem church was constituted and the role of the Jerusalem church in the early Christian movement. The Jerusalem church's authoritative oversight of the whole Christian mission, which was widely acknowledged, is seen most importantly in the decisions of the Jerusalem council (Acts 15). Careful study of the speech Luke attributes to James (Acts 15:13-21), in the light of Jewish exegetical practice, shows that Luke has here preserved, in summary form, the exegetical basis on which James and the Jerusalem leaders argued that Gentile believers belonged to the eschatological people of God as Gentiles, without having to become

Jews and observe the Law, but also that the Law of Moses itself makes provision for them in the form of four commandments to which alone they are obligated (the prohibitions in the apostolic decree). This authoritative ruling on the relationship of Gentile Christians to the Law of Moses was promulgated by the Jerusalem church leaders for the whole Christian movement, and evidence down to the 3rd century shows that it was very widely accepted as such. It was accepted not least by the majority of Jewish Christians. The common assumptions that the Jerusalem church under James, or at least an influential faction in it, continued to maintain that Gentile Christians must be circumcised, and that this view was held by much of later Jewish Christianity also, have no basis in the evidence. It appears that Luke's presentation of the Jerusalem council as an event which decisively affected the whole development of early Christianity by authoritatively discrediting the view that Gentile Christians must be circumcised is historically accurate. The Jerusalem church under James was not, as is often supposed, progressively marginalised as the Gentile mission developed in opposition to its allegedly conservative Jewish stance. On the contrary, the Jerusalem church remained central.

I. Introduction

This chapter is concerned with the portrayal of the Jerusalem church in Acts, with an emphasis on the later period (from AD 44 onwards) in which the pre-eminent figure in the leadership of the Jerusalem church was James the Lord's brother. This period is more or less exactly half of the whole period covered by Acts, but, because it is the period in which Luke's narrative focuses exclusively on the Pauline mission, the information Luke gives about the Jerusalem church in this period is relatively little. It can be checked against and supplemented by information from other sources, but this too is sparse and fragmentary. However, Luke does give the Jerusalem church a uniquely important role during this period: the decision of the Jerusalem council (Acts 15) is, according to Luke's account, a turning-point in the history of the early church. His account of this decision, its circumstances, its content and its influence, has been one of the most controversial issues in the study of Acts. Its historical value has been questioned in a variety of ways. Critics of Luke's account, though they differ on what actually happened, seem to agree in allowing the Jerusalem church a far less central and decisive role in actuality than in Acts. The broader question—as we shall see, much misunderstood—of the Jerusalem church's continuing attitude to the Gentile mission is also involved. In the last analysis, the key question is whether the Jerusalem church remained, during the period of James' leadership, central to the whole early Christian movement, or whether its alleged conservative Jewish stance made it marginal to the Christian movement as it was developing elsewhere. Has Luke's supposed 'Jerusalem bias' exaggerated the role of the Jerusalem church and suppressed the deep divisions between Paul and Jerusalem?[1] Has Luke himself marginalised Jerusalem by portraying Paul as successor to the Twelve and the centre shifting with him from Jerusalem to Rome?

II. Jerusalem at the Centre

Jerusalem lay at the centre of the inhabited world (the οἰκουμένη). The point would have seemed obvious to most 1st-century Jews. An ancient tradition of Jewish mythical geography located Judaea and in particular mount Zion, on which the Temple stood, at the centre of the world (see Ezk. 5:5; 38:12; Jub. 8:19;[2] 1 Enoch 26:1; Rev. 20:8-9; *b. Sanh.* 37a).[3] Whereas for the Greeks in the early period, the navel (ὀμφαλός) of the world was at Delphi, for the Jews it was at Jerusalem. This kind of locating of its own sacred centre at the centre of the world is a geographical myth found among many peoples.[4] But two facts gave the old Jewish tradition of locating the centre at Jerusalem continuing relevance for Jews in the 1st century. The first was that the best hellenistic and Roman geography gave reasonably good support to this position. Eratosthenes, Strabo and the great world map which Marcus Agrippa erected in public in Rome in the reign of Augustus[5] all place

---

[1]In terms of the history of scholarship, we are here concerned with the legacy of F.C. Baur's reconstruction of early Christian history. Baur's position has recently been revived without qualification by M. Goulder, *A Tale of Two Missions* (London: SCM Press, 1994). On the other hand, C.C. Hill, *Hellenists and Hebrews: Reappraising Division within the Earliest Church* (Minneapolis: Fortress, 1992) makes a cogent case against Baur's continuing influence across a wide spectrum of recent scholarship.

[2]For the Jubilees world map, see the reconstruction in P.S. Alexander, 'Notes on the "Imago Mundi" of the Book of Jubilees', *JJS* 33 (1982) 199-213. It is informed by the best Greek geography of its time, but uses it to interpret traditional biblical geographical information, especially the table of the nations (Gn. 10).

[3]*Cf.* the remarks on 1 Ch. 1-2 in J.M. Scott, 'Luke's Geographical Horizon', in D.W.J. Gill and C. Gempf (eds.), *The Book of Acts in Its Graeco-Roman Setting* (Grand Rapids: Eerdmans/Carlisle: Paternoster, 1994) 502-3. See also P. Hayman, 'Some Observations on Sefer Yesira: (2) The Temple at the Centre of the Universe', *JJS* 37 (1986) 176-82.

[4]*Cf.* M. Eliade, *The Myth of the Eternal Return*, tr. W.R. Trask (Bollington Series 46; Princeton: Princeton University Press, 1954) 12-7; *idem*, *Patterns in Comparative Religion*, tr. R. Sheed (London and New York: Sheed & Ward, 1958) 374-9.

Jerusalem somewhat to the west of centre on the east-west axis,[6] but everyone knew that the eastern limits of the οἰκουμένη were very uncertain. It was not difficult in 1st-century geographical terms to imagine Jerusalem at the centre on both an east-west and a north-south axis.

The second fact was the Jewish Diaspora. Students of the New Testament too readily forget that from the perspective of Jews in Judaea the eastern Diaspora was just as important as the western Diaspora. The conventional view that Jews were to be found in all the nations (reflected in Acts 2:5)[7] was, of course, something of an exaggeration, though not too much so. More important was the realistic perception that the Diaspora stretched as far east of Jerusalem as it did west, and that Jews were to be found among nations situated in all directions from Jerusalem. For residents of Jerusalem this was not just something they knew but something they experienced, since for several weeks of every year Jerusalem was packed with pilgrims from the whole of this far-flung Diaspora. To live in Jerusalem must have been to have a rather realistic sense of living at the centre of the world and in communication very nearly with the ends of the earth. Conversely, Jews all over the Diaspora looked to Jerusalem as the symbolic centre of their universe, where their God's presence was uniquely accessible in his Temple. It was the centre to which they travelled on pilgrimage if possible, to which they sent their Temple tax contributions, to which some even returned to settle, and to which, they prayed and expected, the whole Diaspora would be regathered by God in the messianic age. Geography and religious meaning were deeply interconnected in the Jewish sense of the centrality of Jerusalem in the Diaspora and the world.

James Scott has drawn attention to the way the supposed letter of King Agrippa I to the Emperor Gaius (Philo, *Leg. Gai.* 276-329) describes the Jewish Diaspora, instancing many of the countries in which Jews lived, in such a way as to place Jerusalem implicitly at the

---

[5]For maps of the world as described by Eratosthenes and Strabo and a reconstruction of Agrippa's map, see C. Nicolet, *Space, Geography, and Politics in the Early Roman Empire* (Ann Arbor: University of Michigan Press, 1991) figures 23, 26, 41.

[6]The great 2nd-century AD geographer and astronomer Claudius Ptolemy located Judaea and a group of contiguous nations at the centre of the οἰκουμένη (*Apotelesmatica* 2.3.29; 2.4.1-2); see Scott, 'Luke's Geographical Horizon', 499 n. 54.

[7]See the evidence in Scott, 'Luke's Geographical Horizon', 497 n. 48. With Acts 2:5, *cf.* especially Dt. 28:64; 30:4; 2 Mac. 2:18; 4Q448 2:3-6 ('all the congregation of your [King Jonathan's] people Israel who are in the four winds of heaven'); Ps. Sol. 9:2.

centre of the worldwide Diaspora (281-4).[8] However, although, with its failure to mention Italy or Rome, it cannot be said to adopt a Roman perspective, its Jewish perspective is a rather Mediterranean one, as we should perhaps expect from Philo of Alexandria. After a long list of many named countries bordering the eastern Mediterranean, the lands to the east of Euphrates are mentioned in very general terms (282). In this respect, Luke's list of the nations and countries from which the pilgrims attending the festival of Pentecost had come (Acts 2:9-11) provides a much more authentically *Jerusalem* perspective on the Diaspora. The order in which the names occur has perplexed interpreters.[9] In fact, if we take the trouble to plot the names on a map of the world as an ancient reader would have perceived it, we can see that Luke's list is carefully designed to depict the Jewish Diaspora with Jerusalem at its centre.

For the sake of illustration, I have used a reconstruction of the world as mapped in Strabo's *Geography*.[10] The names in Acts 2:9-11 are listed in four groups corresponding to the four points of the compass, beginning in the east and moving counterclockwise.[11] This arrangement corresponds to the way in which reference to the four points of the compass was often used to indicate the Diaspora's relationship to Jerusalem at the centre (Is. 11:12; 43:5-6; 49:12; Zc. 2:6; 4Q448 2:3-6; Ps. Sol. 11:2-3; *cf.* Bar. 4:37; 5:5; Mk. 13:27). The first group of names in the list, consisting of four names (Parthians, Medes, Elamites, residents of Mesopotamia), begins in the far east and moves in towards Judaea, which is then named. Recognizing that Judaea is in the list because it is the centre of the pattern described by the names is the key to understanding the list. The second group of names (Cappadocia, Pontus, Asia, Phrygia, Pamphylia) is of places to the north of Judaea, and follows an order which moves out from and back to Judaea, ending at

[8]Scott, 'Luke's Geographical Horizon', 495-9.

[9]The attempt of Scott, 'Luke's Geographical Horizon', 527-30, to place it in Jewish Table-of-the-Nations tradition does not help very much in this respect. That it is a *pars pro toto* list, of course, is true; that it includes many of the nations in Josephus' updated version of the Table of the Nations is hardly surprising; but neither of these observations provides a principle of selection which explains why the actual names given in the list have been selected. As for the order of names, Scott can only claim that 'Acts 2:9-11 shares the apparent lack of structure and uniformity often found in the Table-of-the-Nations tradition' (528).

[10]Based on E.H. Bunbury, *History of Ancient Geography*, vol. II (London: John Murray, 1879) map facing p. 238.

[11]For the four points of the compass in a counterclockwise movement centred on Jerusalem and beginning in the east, *cf.* 1 Enoch 26–36.

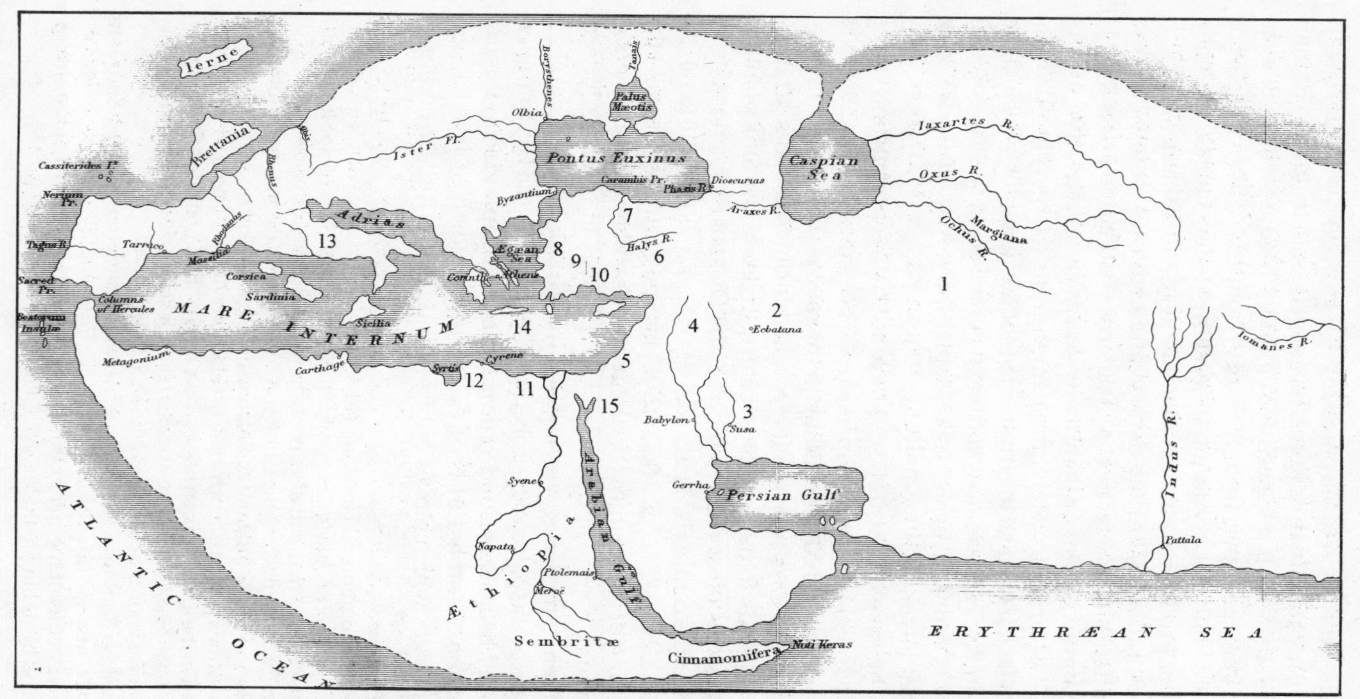

The Jewish Diaspora according to Acts 2:9 - 11 on a map of the world according to Strabo

East, Parthians (1) and Medes (2) and Elamites (3) and residents of Mesopotamia (4), *Centre,* Judaea (5), *North,* Cappadocia (6), Pontus (7) and Asia (8), Phrygia (9) and Pamphylia (10), *West,* Egypt (11) and the parts of Libya belonging to Cyrene (12), and visitors from Rome (13), both Jews and proselytes, Cretans (14) *South,* Arabs (15)

the point from which one might sail to Judaea. The third group of names (Egypt, the parts of Libya belonging to Cyrene, visitors from Rome, Cretans) moves west from Judaea through Egypt (which would most naturally in this context suggest Alexandria) and Libya to Rome, and then back to Judaea by a sea route calling at Crete. Finally, a single name (Arabs) represents the movement south from Judaea, presumably indicating Nabataea, immediately due south of Judaea,[12] but conceivably including parts of Arabia further south.[13] It is striking that Parthia and Rome, respectively the furthest points east and west in the list, are, according to ancient calculations, more or less equidistant from Jerusalem in each direction. The desire to place Jerusalem centrally may explain why, if there was a small Jewish community in Spain at this period,[14] it does not appear in the list, for no Jewish community east of Parthia could have been named to balance the geography. Similarly, including the Jewish communities on the northern shores of the Black Sea[15] would have given the impression that the Diaspora stretched further north than south. Thus, despite the conventional hyperbole of Acts 2:5, the list is informed by good knowledge of which were actually the main areas of Jewish Diaspora settlement,[16] but also controlled by the desire to place Jerusalem centrally.

[12]On Nabataea as 'Arabia' to 1st-century Jews, see J. Murphy-O'Connor, 'Paul in Arabia', *CBQ* 55 (1993) 732-3. For Jews in Nabataea in the 1st century AD, see E. Schürer, *The History of the Jewish People in the Age of Jesus Christ (175 B.C.–A.D. 135)*, revised by G. Vermes, F. Millar and M. Goodman, vol. III,1 (Edinburgh: T. & T. Clark, 1986) 17.

[13]There were Jews in the Yemen by the 4th century AD (Schürer, *History* , vol. III,1, 16), but it is not known when Jews first settled in Arabia south of Nabataea.

[14]*Cf.* Schürer, *History* , vol. III,1, 84-85.

[15]Schürer, *History* , vol. III,1, 36-38.

[16]Information on Jewish settlement in all the places named in the list, with the exception of Parthia and Elam, can be found in Schürer, *History* , vol. III,1, 3-86; and for Crete, see also now P.W. van der Horst, 'The Jews of Ancient Crete', in van der Horst, *Essays on the Jewish World of Early Christianity* (NTOA 14; Freiburg: Universitätsverlag and Göttingen: Vandenhoeck & Ruprecht, 1990) 148-65. 'Parthians' in the list cannot refer to inhabitants of the Parthian empire in general, but must refer to Parthia proper, the homeland of the Parthians, east of Media. It probably includes Hyrcania, where Artaxerxes III Ochus settled Jewish captives who were still there in the 5th century AD: see Schürer, *History* , vol. III,1, 6 and n. 12; J. Neusner, *A History of the Jews in Babylonia*, vol. I, SPB 9 (Leiden: Brill, [2]1969) 11. For Elam, see Neusner, *History*, vol. I, 10; A. Oppenheimer, *Babylonia Judaica in the Talmudic Period* (Beihefte zum Tübinger Atlas des vorderen Orients B47; Wiesbaden: Reichert, 1983) 70-9, 422-3. Apart from Is. 11:11, specific evidence of Jewish settlements is later than the 1st century AD, but it is very likely that the strong Jewish community of the Talmudic period had been established for centuries.

Interestingly, the area depicted stops short of the conventional 'ends of the earth' in each direction: India, Scythia, Spain, and Ethiopia.

Luke is adept at providing his readers with the perspective appropriate to different parts of his narrative. Just as in Luke 2:1 he assumed a Roman view of the world, with its propagandist fiction that Rome, since Augustus, ruled the whole οἰκουμένη,[17] so in Acts 2:9-11, at the beginning of his story of how the gospel was taken out into the οἰκουμένη from Jerusalem, he provides his readers with the Jewish, Jerusalem-centred geographical perspective appropriate to that story. In doing so, he acknowledges the limitations of his narrative in Acts. Clearly Paul's missionary travels, on which Luke's narrative focuses once it moves outside Palestine, carried the gospel to only one part, the northwestern part of this world defined by the Jewish Diaspora, and not at all to the ends of the earth that lie beyond the extent of the Diaspora in each direction. Luke knew that Christianity spread in all directions from Jerusalem.[18] He had his reasons for telling only part of the story, the Pauline mission as representative of the whole of the church's mission, but he makes no pretence that it was more than part of the story.[19]

In providing a Jerusalem-centred perspective for readers of Acts, Luke is certainly true to the outlook of the first Jewish Christians. The centrality of Jerusalem had a number of very important consequences for the early history of the church. In the first place, it was entirely natural that the first Christian community, which saw itself as the nucleus of the renewed Israel, reconstituted by God under the rule of

---

[17]*Cf.* Nicolet, *Space*, chapters 1-2.

[18]Therefore it is not wholly accurate to suppose that Luke is interested in the history of the Jerusalem church only as the transition from Jesus to Paul. For Luke, the Jerusalem church was foundational for the whole early Christian movement, not just for that part of it (the Pauline mission) on which the second half of his work focuses. Acts 8:27-39 is at least a pointer—the most the development of his narrative allows—in the direction of other stories besides Paul's. As the eunuch leaves Luke's story he is on his way to one of the ends of the earth.

[19]The geographical perspective of Acts 2:9-11 seems to me to throw doubt on the argument of E.E. Ellis, '"The End of the Earth" (Acts 1:8)', *Bulletin of Biblical Research* I (1991) 123-32, to the effect that the singular ἐσχάτου τῆς γῆς in Acts 1:8 refers to Spain as the goal of Paul's mission after Rome. In Acts 13:47 Luke may have Paul's mission to Spain in mind, as one instance of the Gospel reaching an end of the earth, but Acts 1:8 surely has a more universal reference. The later traditions taking Thomas *(Acts of Thomas)* or Bartholomew (Rufinus, *Hist. Eccl.* 1.9-10) to India, Andrew to Scythia (Origen, *ap.* Eusebius, *Hist. Eccl.* 3.1; *Acts of Andrew and Matthias)* and Matthew to Ethiopia (Rufinus, *Hist. Eccl.* 1.9-10) should probably be related to the idea of the gospel reaching the ends of the earth.

his Messiah and the leadership of its twelve phylarchs,[20] should have placed its headquarters in Jerusalem. Despite the silence of Acts, we need not assume that there were no Christians outside Jerusalem until persecution first scattered members of the Jerusalem church to other parts of Palestine and elsewhere (Acts 8:1, 4, 31; 11:19). Many followers of Jesus no doubt remained in Galilee. From the very beginnings of the Jerusalem church pilgrims to Jerusalem will have become believers and taken the Christian message back to their own communities in Palestine or the Diaspora. But there will never have been any question that the followers of Jesus in Jerusalem who called themselves 'the church of God' (Gal. 1:13)[21] were as central to the growing Christian movement as the Temple was to all Jews. Indeed, as we shall see below (sections III.2 and IV.2), the fact that the centrality of Jerusalem for Jews meant, fundamentally, the centrality of the Temple as the place of God's presence had a further consequence for earliest Christianity. From a very early stage the first Christians seem to have seen their own community as the messianic Temple: the place of God's eschatological presence. Though this notion of the new Temple as a community, rather than a building, in principle freed it from geographical limitations, nevertheless it was natural to locate the essential structures of the new Temple—the leaders of early Christianity—in Jerusalem. Whether the leaders of the early Christian movement were the phylarchs of the new Israel (the Twelve) (see section III.1 below) or the foundations, pillars or rampart of the new Temple (see section III.2 below) they would be associated with Jerusalem, so that the leadership of the Jerusalem church would naturally be seen as *ipso facto* the leaders of the early Christian movement. The eventual dispersal of many of the apostles (the Twelve and others)—through persecution and mission—may have modified this picture somewhat, but it is probable that the Jerusalem church under the leadership of James the Lord's brother held James to be not only the head of the Jerusalem church but also the central authoritative figure for the whole early Christian movement. Many Christians outside Jerusalem will have agreed with them.

A third implication of the centrality of Jerusalem relates to the long-standing Jewish practice of letters from the authorities in Jerusalem to the Diaspora, giving directions on cultic and other legal

[20]See W. Horbury, 'The Twelve and the Phylarchs', *NTS* 32 (1986) 503-27.
[21]On this phrase as a reference to the Jerusalem church, see S. Légasse, 'Paul's Pre-Christian Career' (in this volume).

matters.[22] This practice is probably evidenced as early as the late 5th century BC by a letter to the Jewish colony at Elephantine, giving instructions about the way that Passover and Unleavened Bread are to be observed.[23] Two letters from Jerusalem to the Jews of Egypt (143 and 124 BC) enjoining the observance of the recently instituted festival of Hanukkah are preserved in 2 Maccabees 1:1-10a,[24] while 1:10b–2:18 provides an inauthentic example of the genre, on the same subject.[25] Apparently contemporary with the early Jerusalem church is the letter to the Diaspora ascribed to Gamaliel the Elder, the early 1st-century Pharisee, declaring the intercalation of a month in that year. It is preserved with other letters of Gamaliel, on different but similar subjects, to various parts of the land of Israel (*t. Sanh.* 2.6; *y. Sanh.* 1.2; *y. Ma'as. Sh.* 5.4; *b. Sanh.* 11a).[26] Since a calendrical matter of this kind would have been the responsibility of the Temple authorities, the letter is somewhat problematic, but on the other hand there seems little reason for such a letter to have been invented[27] and good reasons for accepting the authenticity of the group of letters to which it belongs. Perhaps Gamaliel, as a Pharisaic member of the High Priest's council (*cf.* Acts 5:34), writes to Jews of Pharisaic allegiance in the Diaspora.[28] Whether or not the letter as it stands is authentic, we can be sure that

---

[22]*Cf.* I. Taatz, *Frühjüdische Briefe: Die paulinischen Briefe im Rahmen der offiziellen religiösen Briefe des Frühjudentums* (NTAC 16; Freiburg: Universitätsverlag and Göttingen: Vandenhoeck & Ruprecht, 1991). She distinguishes two types of letters from Jerusalem to the Diaspora: (1) collective, institutional letters on cultic and related matters (major examples discussed below); (2) prophetic letters of instruction (Je. 29; and the pseudepigraphal letters of Jeremiah [Ep. Je.] and Baruch [2 Bar. 77-87]). Acts 15:23-9 would correspond to (1), the letter of James (whether or not authentic) to (2).

[23]Papyrus 21 (419/18 BC) in A.E. Cowley, *Aramaic Papyri of the Fifth Century B.C.* (Oxford: Clarendon Press, 1923) 60-5. The order has the formal authority of Darius II, but comes from Hananiah, evidently a figure of importance in the Jewish administration in Jerusalem.

[24]The earlier letter is quoted in vv. 7-8.

[25]See the full discussion of these letters in J.A. Goldstein, *II Maccabees* (AB 41A; New York: Doubleday, 1983) 137-88.

[26]Translations and discussion in J. Neusner, *The Rabbinic Traditions about the Pharisees before 70*, vol. 1 (Leiden: Brill, 1971) 356-8, 360, 361, 368, 372-3. Letters of the same type are ascribed to Gamaliel's son Simeon, along with Johanan b. Zakkai (including: 'we have not begun to write to you, but our fathers used to write to your fathers'), though not in this case to the Diaspora; see Neusner, *The Rabbinic Traditions*, vol. I, 378-9.

[27]Since the letter refers to sacrificial animals and its point is to warn Diaspora Jews not to make the pilgrimage to Jerusalem a month too early, its subject-matter would not be that of later letters from the Rabbinic authorities to the Diaspora.

such letters were regularly sent,[29] as more general references to communications from the Temple authorities to the Diaspora on calendrical and other matters confirm (*m. Rosh. Hash.* 1:3-4; Acts 28:21). This tradition of direction and communication from the centre is the background to the letter in Acts 15:23-29, which communicates a major halakhic decision of the Jerusalem Christian leadership, assumed to have universal authority on such a matter, to (in this case) Gentile members of churches in the Diaspora (see section IV below).

Finally, the centrality of Jerusalem was, above all, eschatologically important. Not only was the Jewish Diaspora to be regathered to Jerusalem from all four points of the compass (*e.g.* Is. 11:12; 43:5-6), but also the Gentile nations were to come from all directions to Jerusalem to worship God and to participate in the messianic salvation (Is. 2:2-3; *cf.* Mt. 8:11; Lk. 13:29, interpreting Is. 49:12 in this sense).[30] In some texts, the returning exiles and the Gentile pilgrims form a single movement converging on Jerusalem (Is. 60:3-16; Zc. 8:20-23; Tob. 13:11-13). The early Christian community had naturally to be at this centre of God's eschatological action. Indeed, it was itself the messianic Temple in which both returning Jewish exiles and repentant Gentile nations would find God's eschatological presence. But it would probably be a mistake to imagine the earliest Christian group in Jerusalem merely waiting for these events to happen, imminent though they no doubt expected them to be. The prophecies in fact described not only the movement of Jews and Gentiles to Jerusalem, but a prior movement of the word of the Lord out from Jerusalem (Is. 2:3).[31] In the earliest period of the Jerusalem church the expectation was perhaps that through their proclamation of the gospel in Jerusalem (*cf.* Is. 40:9) its

---

[28]Neusner, *The Rabbinic Traditions*, vol. I, 358-9, suggests this, but doubts there were Pharisees in Babylonia and Media (the named destinations in *t.Sanh.* 2.6), and concludes the letter must be authentic, 'but I do not know who would have received it.' He may be too sceptical about the presence of Pharisees in the eastern Diaspora at this date; *cf.* Josephus, *Ant.* 20.43.

[29]*Cf.* P.S. Alexander, 'Epistolary Literature', in M.E. Stone (ed.), *Jewish Writings of the Second Temple Period* (CRINT 2; Assen: Van Gorcum and Philadelphia: Fortress, 1984) 581 n. 14: 'Whether or not the attributions are accurate, letters such as these were undoubtedly sent out by the religious authorities in Jerusalem, and it is very probable that the letters before us accurately reflect those letters' general formulae and style.'

[30]See the classic study of J. Jeremias, *Jesus' Promise to the Nations*, tr. S.H. Hooke (SBT 24; London: SCM Press, 1958).

[31]The light which is to shine from the city in the last days, attracting the nations to it (*e.g.* Is. 60:1-3), could also easily be understood in this sense.

sound would reach to the ends of the earth. The constant stream of pilgrims coming to Jerusalem and returning to the Diaspora would ensure this.[32] In that case, Luke provides us, in his portrayal of the first preaching of the gospel in Jerusalem to a crowd drawn from all nations under heaven (Acts 2:5-11), with a programmatic account of the earliest missionary strategy of the Jerusalem church. As apostles and others later began to take the word out from the centre, this movement of active missionary witness was easily understood within the Jerusalem-centred eschatological outlook. As this active missionary movement (which was far from only Pauline; *cf.* 1 Cor. 9:5; Rom. 15:20) developed, the Jerusalem church would naturally see itself as responsible for its oversight, as both the source and the goal of the movement. Even Paul, more independent of Jerusalem than most early Christian missionaries, knew that the word of God originated from Jerusalem (1 Cor. 14:36),[33] portrayed his own work of proclaiming the gospel as a movement out from Jerusalem as the centre (Rom. 15:19), devoted much effort to and faced personal danger for the sake of his collection for Jerusalem, which was intended to cement the fellowship of his churches with the mother-church and to symbolise the complementary movement back to the centre (Rom. 15:25-31).

The centrality of Jerusalem lost much of its meaning for most Christians after AD 70.[34] To some extent this is reflected in Acts, which portrays Jerusalem emphatically as the source of the movement that brings eschatological salvation to the ends of the earth, but hardly as the eschatological goal of this movement. Yet to a remarkable extent Luke does convey the Jerusalem-centred perspective of the early Christians. Against the background of the multifaceted centrality of Jerusalem for 1st-century Jews, Luke's concern to make clear the links between the Jerusalem church and the developing mission both within and beyond Palestine (Acts 8:14-25; 9:27; 9:32–11:18; 11:22-29; 12:25; 15:40), and his account of the Jerusalem council as the occasion when an authoritative decision was made in Jerusalem which secured and determined the future of the whole Gentile mission (Acts 15), carry much more credibility than those scholars who so readily treat them as tendentious distortions of history[35] have perceived. Luke's 'Jerusalem

---

[32]*Cf.* M. Hengel, *Between Jesus and Paul*, tr. J. Bowden (London: SCM Press, 1983) 59.
[33]Perhaps Paul here alludes to Is. 2:3.
[34]*Cf.* R. Bauckham, *Jude and the Relatives of Jesus in the Early Church* (Edinburgh: T. & T. Clark, 1990) 93-94.
[35]Probably a kind of hyper-Paulinism has influenced this judgment.

bias' is not peculiarly Luke's, but derived from the early Jerusalem church itself. We shall see this in more detail in the next two sections.

III. The Leadership of the Jerusalem Church

By the end of Luke's narrative, James the Lord's brother occupies a position of unique preeminence in the Jerusalem church (21:18). Other evidence supports this, not least the remarkable reputation of James in 2nd and 3rd-century Christian literature, when his authority was claimed by Catholic, Gnostic and Jewish Christian writers alike.[36] Some historical reality must lie behind this legendary greatness.[37] But the changes in the leadership of the Jerusalem church which led to this unique role for James and the ways in which this leadership was understood are difficult to discern. In this section we discuss, first the evidence of Acts, secondly other relevant evidence.

1. From the Twelve to James and the Elders (Acts)

Up to Acts 11:1 it is clear that 'the apostles' constitute the leadership of the Christian group in Jerusalem (see especially 2:42-43; 4:33, 35, 37; 5:1, 18, 29, 40; 6:6; 8:1, 14; 9:27; 11:1). Luke has already established in Acts 1 that 'the apostles' means the Twelve (1:13, 25-26), and this seems confirmed by his sole explicit reference to 'the Twelve' in 6:2 (*cf.* 6:6). Although Luke evidently recognised a wider use of the term 'apostles' (14:4), his normal usage refers to the Twelve. His emphasis is certainly on their role as witnesses (1:8, 22; 5:32; 10:41-42), but he also attributes to them an authoritative status in the Jerusalem church (4:35, 37; 5:2; 6:2; 9:27), though important decisions are made by the whole commu-

---

[36]See W. Pratscher, *Der Herrenbruder Jakobus und die Jakobustradition* (FRLANT 139; Göttingen: Vandenhoeck & Ruprecht, 1987) chs. 2-5; R.P. Martin, *James* (WBC 48; Waco: Word Books, 1988) xli-lxi.

[37]R.McL. Wilson, review of Pratscher, *Der Herrenbruder*, in *Bib* 70 (1989) 143, says: 'From the New Testament evidence James does not appear as the dominant figure which he was to become in later tradition.' But it should be remembered that (a) the Pauline letters are the only NT documents written during James' lifetime (except for the letters of Jude and James, if authentic, which support the prominence of James); (b) after 70 the Jerusalem church lost its role in the wider church, whose literature (represented in the canon) would be unlikely to reflect the now anachronistic dominance of James. Nevertheless the dominance of James can still be glimpsed in Galatians and Acts.

nity (1:23; 6:5; *cf.* 11:22; 15:22).[38] Among the Twelve, Peter is clearly the pre-eminent figure (see especially 1:15; 5:1-11, 15, 29), though himself subject to the apostles as a group (8:14). Outside the list of the Eleven (1:13), with the addition of Matthias (1:26), the only members of the Twelve named in Acts are Peter, John and James the brother of John (the last only in 12:2). Apart from the Seven (6:3-6), for whom Luke has no descriptive title, the apostles, identified as the Twelve, are the only category of Christian leaders who appear in Acts before 11:30. While they are not confined to Jerusalem (8:14-25; 9:32–10:48), they are permanently based there.

This is a straightforward and consistent picture which Luke maintains up to chapter 11. One reference to the apostles which is of particular importance is that in 8:1. The statement that, in the persecution of the Jerusalem church following the death of Stephen, 'all except the apostles were scattered throughout the countryside of Judaea and Samaria,' certainly appears implausible, even when allowance is made for a generalizing exaggeration. One would expect precisely the leaders of the community to be the main targets of such a persecution. But the difficulty is not really solved by supposing that the historical reality behind the text is that only the hellenists were persecuted and scattered, whereas the Hebrews, represented in the text by the apostles as their leaders, escaped persecution.[39] This explanation, which originated with F.C. Baur and has been popular ever since,[40] is an example of trying to probe the historical reality behind Luke's text before paying sufficient attention to what Luke meant by the text he wrote. Postulating a historical reality different from the text may explain what happened, but it cannot explain the text. Certainly, if Luke's source told him that only the hellenists were persecuted, we could understand that he might wish to obscure such a distinction among the Jerusalem Christians. But there are many ways in which he could have glossed over this alleged historical fact without saying precisely what 8:1 actually says: that all except the apostles were scattered.

---

[38]*Cf.* F. Scott Spencer, *The Portrait of Philip in Acts* (JSNTSS 67; Sheffield: JSOT Press, 1992) 196-8: 'throughout the book of Acts a non-hierarchical, democratic process characterizes church government in general and the appointment of ministers in particular' (198).

[39]So, recently, M. Hengel, *Acts and the History of Earliest Christianity*, tr. J. Bowden (London: SCM Press, 1979) 74-5; P. F. Esler, *Community and Gospel in Luke-Acts* (SNTSMS 57; Cambridge: Cambridge University Press, 1987) 139.

[40]For many examples of it, see Hill, *Hellenists*, 7-15.

Luke's text is not concerned to claim that the apostles escaped persecution.[41] This is not the most natural reading of the text for a reader who observes that, at other points in Acts, it is precisely the apostles who are the targets of persecution (4:1-3; 5:17-18; 12:1-19). Given that 'all' is hyperbolic (as 8:3 makes clear it must be), the real point is that, whereas many prominent members of the Jerusalem church were *permanently* dispersed to other parts of the country (*cf.* 8:40; 11:19-20), the apostles remained the leaders of the Jerusalem church. It would not be inconsistent with what the text tells us to suppose that they were imprisoned (*cf.* 8:3) but eventually released, or even that they fled from Jerusalem for safety but later returned. All that Luke maintains is that the persecution did not bring their leadership of the Jerusalem church to an end.[42] In this respect, as we shall see, he is drawing an important contrast between this persecution and the next major persecution to trouble the Jerusalem church (12:1-19).

Luke's consistent pattern of reference to the apostles as sole leaders in the Jerusalem church comes to an end in 11:1. It is noteworthy that in 11:22 it is the Jerusalem church which sends Barnabas to Antioch; the apostles are not mentioned. But since, as we have noticed, Luke does attribute major decisions, especially the selection of persons for tasks of ministry, to the whole church (1:23; 6:5), this in itself cannot suggest a change in the situation in Jerusalem. What does suggest such a change is that, when the church of Antioch sends famine relief to Jerusalem, they send it 'to the elders' (11:30).

The appearance in this verse of a term not previously used in Acts has been explained in broadly three different ways. First, the elders can be seen as a body of leaders distinct from the apostles, responsible for the financial affairs of the community and the daily material needs of the people. Either they were the same people as the Seven appointed in Acts 6:1-6[43] (apart from Stephen), or, on the assumption that these seven were no longer in Jerusalem, their successors.[44] As such they would be the appropriate people to whom to

---

[41]Surprisingly, the otherwise incisive critique of the common interpretation of Acts 8:1 in Hill, *Hellenists*, 32-40, does not question the view that Luke means to say that the apostles were not persecuted.

[42]Hill, *Hellenists*, 38-39, doubts the historicity of the persecution in Acts 8:1-3, but this issue is not important to our present argument.

[43]T.M. Lindsay, *The Church and the Ministry in the Early Centuries* (London: Hodder & Stoughton, 1902) 115-7; A.M. Farrer, 'The Ministry in the New Testament', in K.E. Kirk (ed.), *The Apostolic Ministry* (London: Hodder & Stoughton, 1946) 133-42.

[44]Bruce, *Acts*, 277.

deliver the famine relief. If this implies that they were subordinate to the apostles, Campbell's objection is justified: 'If anything is clear from a study of the word "elder" in both the Greek and Jewish context *(sic)* it is that it referred to people honoured for their seniority.'[45] However, account should be taken of Spencer's argument that Luke does not in fact represent the Seven as subordinate to the apostles either in status or in function, but understands the two groups in a non-hierarchical way as partners in ministry, undertaking complementary roles.[46]

A case for seeing the elders as a body of leaders alongside the Twelve could also be made on the basis of the pentateuchal precedent for the appointment of the Seven which Spencer, following Daube,[47] cites from Numbers 11.[48] This passage, in which Moses appoints seventy elders, together with Isaiah 24:23, which places the elders in the context of eschatological expectation, is also seen by Karrer as the basis on which the early Jerusalem church, understanding itself as the renewed Israel of the last days, developed an office of eldership.[49] In Karrer's view the elders were not only almoners (in view of the context in Nu. 11) but also interpreters of the Law for the eschatological age (*cf.* the judges of Ex. 18:13-26; Dt. 1:9-17). The former role accounts for their appearance in Acts 11:30, the latter for their conjunction with the apostles in Acts 15. This approach is especially attractive because a good case can be made for the view that, in the early Jerusalem church, the Twelve were understood as analogous to the twelve phylarchs (princes of the tribes) who play an important part in the account of Israel in the wilderness in the Torah. A major stream of Jewish interpretation evidently understood the phylarchs to be an essential element in the ideal constitution of Israel and expected their restoration in the eschatological age.[50] Just as a group of elders appears alongside the phylarchs in the pentateuchal narratives,[51] so, it could be

[45]R. A. Campbell, 'The Elders of the Jerusalem Church', *JTS* 44 (1993) 514.
[46]Spencer, *The Portrait of Philip*, 189-211.
[47]D. Daube, 'A Reform in Acts and its Models', in R. Hamerton-Kelly and R. Scroggs (ed.), *Jews, Greeks and Christians* (W.D. Davies FS; Leiden: Brill, 1976) 151-63. This precedent was already identified and discussed by Farrer, 'The Ministry', 135-39. *Cf.* also J.D. McCaughey, 'The Intention of the Author: Some Questions about the Exegesis of Acts 6:1-6', *AusBR* 7 (1959) 27-36.
[48]Spencer, *The Portrait of Philip*, 209-11. Both Daube and Spencer also refer to Ex. 18:13-26 (Moses appoints judges, not specifically called elders, though presumably drawn from the elders of 18:12) and Dt. 1:9-17 (another account of Moses' appointment of judges).
[49]M. Karrer, 'Das urchristliche Ältestenamt', *NovT* 32 (1990) 152-88.
[50]Horbury, 'The Twelve and the Phylarchs.'

argued, in the eschatological self-understanding of the early Jerusalem church, a body of elders could appropriately complement the Twelve in the leadership of the church.

The second interpretation of the elders is that of Campbell, who argues that the Twelve themselves were also known as the elders. He thinks that the composition of the Twelve gradually changed, as members of the original Twelve died or left Jerusalem and were replaced by others.[52] But the term 'elder' was used equally of original members of the Twelve and of those who took their place.[53] This means that, in choosing to call the Twelve by the later term for them—'the apostles'—up to Acts 11:1, and then preferring the term 'the elders,' Luke is not intending to indicate any change in the leadership of the Jerusalem church, but has a specific redactional purpose related to his perception of the role of the Twelve in the mission of the church. While they are effectively exercising their commission to bear witness to Jesus Christ throughout the world, Luke calls them the apostles, but when the leadership in the church's mission to the world passes to Paul and his associates, he begins to call them elders (11:30), and indicates the succession to their role by calling Barnabas and Saul apostles in 14:4, 14.[54]

One serious weakness in Campbell's case is his failure to explain the role of James. In support of his case that the Twelve as the leadership group in Jerusalem survived throughout the period covered by Acts he cites my own argument that the Jerusalem bishops list, which ostensibly lists fifteen bishops who ruled successively up to the Bar Kokhba war, can be plausibly understood as a list of three bishops (James and his two successors) and twelve elders who governed the church along with James. I had suggested that this group of twelve elders, which plausibly includes two or three of the original Twelve, was constituted, to replace the original Twelve, at a time when the original Twelve had dwindled, through death and departure, to very few.[55] Campbell modifies this argument by suggesting that members

---

[51]Campbell, 'The Elders', suggests that they may sometimes be identified with the phylarchs in the LXX, but Horbury's exhaustive study of Jewish interpretation of the references to the phylarchs provides no support for this view.

[52]For the contrary view that Luke treats the replacement of Judas by Matthias as a unique occurrence and otherwise regards the original Twelve as irreplaceable, see P.H. Menoud, 'The Additions to the Twelve Apostles According to the Book of Acts', in Menoud, *Jesus Christ and the Faith*, tr. E.M. Paul (Pittsburgh: Pickwick, 1978) 133-48.

[53]Campbell, 'The Elders', 518-9.

[54]Campbell, 'The Elders', 520-8.

of the group were replaced as they died or departed, and that the list of twelve preserved in the Jerusalem bishops list is simply the membership of the Twelve at a stage when most of the original members had been replaced.[56] However, he accepts that James himself was not a member of the Twelve, at any stage, but ruled along with the Twelve: 'the leadership of Jesus and the Twelve was followed at quite an early stage by that of his brother James and the Twelve.'[57] This seems to explain James' unique position by claiming that he succeeded to Jesus' role in relation to the Twelve. If so, it is hard to see how he could have done so at any point later than the very beginnings of the Jerusalem church. On this view, James must have been seen as pre-eminent over the Twelve from the earliest days of the church. Paul's evidence (Gal 1:18-19; 2:9) could perhaps be read as not inconsistent with this view, though it does not positively support it. However, it is demonstrably not the view presented in Acts. Up to chapter 11, it is unquestionably Peter who is pre-eminent among the leaders of the church, and Luke's first reference to James (12:17) is designed to suggest that James' rise to eminence coincided with Peter's relinquishing of permanent leadership in Jerusalem. The fact that this apparent indication that James succeeded Peter is closely linked with Luke's first reference to 'the elders' (11:30) suggests that Luke is signalling, not merely a change in the salvation-historical significance of the

---

[55]R. Bauckham, *Jude and the Relatives of Jesus in the Early Church* (Edinburgh: T. & T. Clark, 1990) 70-79, developing the argument of R. van den Broek, 'Der Brief des Jakobus an Quadratus und das Problem der judenchristliche Bischöfe von Jerusalem (Eusebius, *Hist.Eccl.* IV,5,1-3), in T. Baarda, A. Hillhorst, G.P. Luttikhuizen and A.S. van der Woude, (eds.), *Text and Testimony: Essays on New Testament and Apocryphal Literature in Honour of A.F.J. Klijn* (Kampen: Kok, 1988) 56-65. The recent discussion by F. Manns, 'La liste des premiers évêques de Jérusalem', in F. Manns and E. Alliata (eds.), *Early Christianity in Context: Monuments and Documents* (Studium Biblicum Franciscanum: Collectio Maior 38; Jerusalem: Franciscan Printing Press, 1993) 419-431, refers to my book, inaccurately, in his section on the 'Status quaestionis' (420), but Manns has apparently not read my discussion of the bishops list. He defends the view that all fifteen names were bishops in succession before 135. His comparison with the rapid succession of Jewish High Priests in the Herodian period is of little value, since the latter were political appointments, appointed and deposed by the Herods and the Roman governors for their own reasons. While nothing is impossible, it remains improbable that there were only two bishops (James and Symeon the son of Clopas) up to *c.* 100 (the earliest possible date for Symeon's martyrdom) and then thirteen in succession up to 135.

[56]Campbell, 'The Elders', 516-9.

[57]Campbell, 'The Elders', 528.

Twelve, but a change in the constitution of the Jerusalem church leadership.

Both of the interpretations of the appearance of the elders in Acts 11:30 which we have so far discussed neglect the connection which Luke establishes between this reference to the elders and the immediately succeeding narrative of the fate of two leading members of the Twelve in the persecution of Herod Agrippa I (12:1-19). This connection, we shall now show, requires the third interpretation: that Luke introduces the elders as the group which replaced the Twelve as the leaders of the Jerusalem church.

The section 12:1-24 constitutes a kind of flashback sandwiched between the reference to the mission of Barnabas and Saul from Antioch to Jerusalem (11:30) and the account of their return to Antioch after completing the mission (12:25).[58] Luke certainly does not mean that the events of 12:1-24 happened while Barnabas and Saul were in Jerusalem.[59] The introductory words 'About that time' (κατ' ἐκεῖνον δὲ καιρόν: 12:1) are vague, indicating no more than that these are relatively recent events. As Dupont observes, place tends to take precedence over chronology as a principle for organizing material in Acts.[60] Luke has taken advantage of the fact that his narrative about the church of Antioch, begun in 11:19, includes a visit by Barnabas and Saul to Jerusalem, in order to insert some traditions about the persecution of the Jerusalem church under Herod Agrippa. But this is not sufficient explanation of his procedure. These traditions could have

[58]12:25 is problematic because εἰς Ἰερουσαλήμ must be regarded as the best reading (other readings are attempts to remove the obvious difficulty it creates), and yet the context (Barnabas and Saul have been sent to Jerusalem in 11:30; the section 12:1-19 is set in Jerusalem; John Mark [12:25] is a member of the Jerusalem church [12:12]; Barnabas and Saul are back in Antioch in 13:1) requires a reference to the return of Barnabas and Saul from Jerusalem to Antioch. The exhaustive discussion of the problem by J. Dupont, *Études sur les Actes des Apôtres* (LD 45; Paris: Cerf, 1967) 217-41, argues convincingly for the translation: 'Then Paul and Barnabas, having completed their mission in Jerusalem, returned.'

[59]Against E. Haenchen, *The Acts of the Apostles*, tr. B. Noble and G. Shinn (Oxford: Blackwell, 1971) 387. On the other hand, the fact that the famine (11:28) certainly took place after the death of Herod Agrippa (12:23) does not in itself show that Luke dated the events of 12:1-24 before 11:29-30, even if we can assume that he knew the date of the famine. The decision to send famine relief to Jerusalem (11:29) was based on Agabus' *prediction* of the famine (11:28), and so the visit of Barnabas and Saul to Jerusalem could have preceded the famine, even by some years, though it would be more natural to assume that the narrative means it arrived not long before it was needed.

[60]Dupont, *Études*, 224.

been inserted between 11:18 and 11:19, appropriately completing the account of Peter's leadership of the Jerusalem church before proceeding to the events at Antioch that lead directly to the first missionary journey of Paul and Barnabas.[61] Instead, Luke has deliberately interwoven his accounts of developments in Jerusalem and developments in Antioch. His broad purpose is to emphasise the links between Jerusalem and Antioch in the developing Gentile mission (*cf.* 11:22, 27; 12:25; 13:5; 15:22, 40).[62] Within this context, one minor function of 12:1-24 is to introduce John Mark (12:12, *cf.* 25), utilising a literary technique found elsewhere in Acts, whereby a passing reference to a character prepares for his introduction as a significant figure in the narrative (*cf.* 7:28; 8:1; and 6:5; 8:5). The same could be said of the reference to James (12:17),[63] which prepares for his appearance in a major role in the narrative in chapter 15. But there is more than this involved in the reference to James, as we can see from the fact that he appears in the narrative of Acts just as Peter leaves it (12:17).

12:17 is a key verse in the development of the narrative of Acts. It marks Peter's exit from the story. The deliberately vague phrase 'to another place'[64] signals the fact that Peter's story, though unfinished, is of no further concern to the readers of Acts. Had we been told where

[61]This point is not really confronted by I.H. Marshall, 'Apg. 12—ein Schlüssel zum Verständnis der Apostelgeschichte', in C.P. Thiede (ed.), *Das Petrusbild in der neueren Forschung* (Wuppertal: Brockhaus, 1987) 192-217, who sees Acts 12:1-24 as the climax of Luke's account of the Jerusalem church. But he is correct to stress that 12:24 is the note with which Luke wishes to end his account of the Jerusalem church.

[62]These verses make the point that, although Paul never belonged to the Jerusalem church, all his early colleagues in Gentile mission—Barnabas, John Mark, Silas—came from Jerusalem.

[63]Hitherto James has appeared in Acts only as one of the unnamed brothers of Jesus in 1:14. In fact, Luke never tells his readers that James was a brother of Jesus, which he must assume to be universal Christian knowledge. A reader of Acts who did not know who James was, on reading 12:17 could only assume, incorrectly, that the reference is to James the son of Alphaeus (1:13).

[64]For the most recent argument that this was in fact Rome, see C.P. Thiede, 'Babylon, der andere Ort: Anmerkungen zu 1 Petr 5,13 und Apg 12,17', *Bib* 67 (1986) 532-8, reprinted in Thiede (ed.), *Das Petrusbild*, 221-9; *cf.* also Thiede, *Simon Peter: From Galilee to Rome* (Exeter: Paternoster, 1986) 153-6. He argues for a reference to Ezk. 12:3, where 'another place' is Babylon. The plausibility of this use of a deliberate (and extremely difficult) cryptogram for Rome depends on his view that Luke was writing before Peter's death, when Peter was again in Rome, and wanted to conceal the whereabouts of a wanted man from the authorities. For references to earlier arguments of this kind, see O. Cullmann, *Peter: Disciple—Apostle—Martyr*, tr. F.V. Filson (London: SCM Press, 1953) 37-38.

Peter went, we might have expected to encounter him there again later in the narrative. This is what happens with Saul, left at Tarsus in 9:30 until Barnabas finds him there in 11:25-26. It is what happens with Philip, left at Caesarea in 8:40 until Paul meets him there in 21:8.[65] By contrast, Peter's destination in 12:17 is unnamed because his story is not going to be resumed. It is true that he does reappear in 15:7-11, at the Jerusalem council, but he does so only in order to recall his earlier role in the conversion of Cornelius and his household, so that the council may take the lesson of these earlier events into account. This intervention integrates Peter's earlier role into the decisive step, with regard to the future of the Gentile mission, which is taken in chapter 15. Even here it is James who really advances the discussion and proposes the novel development: the provisions of the apostolic decree. After 12:17 Peter is no longer the key figure at the forefront of the Luke's story of the church's mission. The section 12:1-24 is so placed as to indicate that Peter's leading role—which has hitherto been seen both in his leadership in Jerusalem (chapters 1-5) and in his pioneering role in the mission out from Jerusalem, including the first breakthrough to the Gentiles (8:14-25; 9:32-11:18)—passes not merely to one successor, but to two: James (12:17) in Jerusalem, and Paul (13:2)[66] in the mission to the Gentiles.[67] Luke certainly does not intend, as is sometimes supposed, to denigrate the role of James and the Jerusalem leaders after chapter 12: he consistently portrays them as affirmative and enthusiastic about Paul's Gentile mission (15:4, 14-20; 21:18-20a), as well as successful in their own mission to the Jews in Judaea (12:24; 21:20b). It is not that Paul replaces the Jerusalem leaders in the way that Campbell suggests is Luke's perspective.[68] The point is rather

[65]Admittedly, this is not always the case in Acts. In 15:39 Barnabas and Mark go to Cyprus, but never reappear in Acts.

[66]At this stage of the narrative, Barnabas is still the senior partner, but the prominence given to Paul in chapter 9 has already prepared the reader for the way Paul very soon (13:13) becomes the leading figure in the narrative as Luke tells it, even before the breach with Barnabas (16:36-39) leaves him unquestionably the leader of his missionary team.

[67]The meaning is not some kind of apostolic succession in ecclesiastical office, for which Luke would have had to provide much more specific detail about the transfer of authority from Peter to James and Paul. Acts 12:17 does not portray Peter actually handing over authority to James, but uses a narrative device to suggest what happened in the course of events. Marshall, 'Apg 12', 214, correctly argues that Luke has no real interest in this kind of 'early catholic' issue. But he fails to see that Luke is concerned with succession in a broad historical sense. It is not ecclesiastical office that interests Luke, but the roles his leading characters play in the history of the Christian mission.

that in chapter 12 the narrative has reached the point where leadership at the centre in Jerusalem can no longer be combined with personal leadership in the missionary movement out from the centre. Peter, who had combined these roles, steps out of the narrative. James steps in, as the wise and statesmanlike leader at the centre, while Paul assumes the leading role in at least one movement of the gospel further and further out from the centre.[69]

However, the issue in chapter 12 is not only the succession to Peter himself. Peter has appeared in the earlier chapters of Acts not simply as an individual leader, but as the leading member of the Twelve. In 12:1-17 Luke narrates not only Peter's departure from Jerusalem, but also the martyrdom of another leading member of the Twelve, James the son of Zebedee (12:2). Perhaps the only specific traditions available to him about Herod's persecution concerned these two members of the Twelve, but he uses them to indicate that this persecution put an end to the leadership role of the Twelve as such. (The reader must notice that in 12:17 Peter does not ask the news to be given to the other apostles; he or she must presume that they too are in prison or have fled from Jerusalem.) The persecution did not hinder the advance of the gospel (12:24), but, whereas in the case of the previous persecution Luke had made a point of indicating that the leadership of the apostles in Jerusalem continued (8:1), in this case he does not. Rather, the narrative of 12:1-17 serves, among other things, to explain the appearance of 'the elders' in 11:30. The reason Barnabas and Saul deliver the famine relief to the elders is that the apostles had not survived, as a constitutional body of leaders in Jerusalem, the recent persecution by Herod Agrippa. Luke could have introduced James, along with the elders, in 11:30. But leaving reference to James to 12:17 suggests more effectively that he was to succeed to the specially pre-eminent position of Peter, while also perhaps allowing for his unique preeminence to emerge over a rather longer period than the narrative has yet reached in 11:30. In any case, Peter could not refer to 'James and the elders' in 12:17, since presumably the reconstitution of the Jerusalem leadership as a body of elders is envisaged as occurring only subsequently to Peter's departure.

---

[68]Campbell, 'The Elders', 520-8.

[69]This point is also argued by R.W. Wall, 'Successors to "the Twelve" According to Acts 12:1-17', *CBQ* 53 (1991) 628-43, though I am not persuaded by his claim that Luke creates a systematic parallel between Peter's succession to Jesus and James' succession to Peter.

Consistent with the view that 11:30 marks a stage at which the Twelve had been replaced by a body of elders, among whom, sooner or later, James attained a position of unique authority, is 21:18, where it is clear that James and the elders now constitute the Jerusalem church leadership. In that verse it is not clear whether James himself is one of the elders or not, but in any case he evidently occupies a position of distinctive importance. However, Luke's picture of transition from the apostles to the elders is complicated by chapter 15, where, in connection with the council of Jerusalem, he refers repeatedly to 'the apostles and the elders' (15:2, 4, 6, 22; 16:4; *cf.* 15:23). From 15:2, 4 it is not clear whether Luke envisages the apostles, now dispersed from Jerusalem, gathering for the council, or whether 'the apostles and the elders' are the permanent Jerusalem leadership.[70] The explanation may be that the body of elders newly constituted after Agrippa's persecution to replace the Twelve included any members of the Twelve who remained in or returned to Jerusalem. The Twelve as such no longer existed as a constitutional group, but members of the Twelve could have belonged to the new body of elders. In connection with the Jerusalem council, Luke makes this explicit by specifying 'the apostles' as well as 'the elders,' because it is important to him to give the fullest possible authority to the council's decisions, and also because he wants to indicate here the continuity between the mission of the Jerusalem church as he has described it in the early chapters of Acts and the Pauline mission to the Gentiles which is here endorsed by the Jerusalem council.

However, in addition to these points, we should also consider the opening of the letter from the Jerusalem church: Οἱ ἀπόστολοι καὶ οἱ πρεσβύτεροι ἀδελφοί (15:23). This well-attested reading (in which ἀδελφοί must be understood as in apposition to both οἱ ἀπόστολοι and οἱ πρεσβύτεροι) should probably be preferred to that which adds καὶ οἱ before ἀδελφοί.[71] Since the better reading is a form of expression

---

[70]At first sight, 15:12 (πᾶν τὸ πλῆθος) seems to suggest that the apostles and elders must be a rather large body of people, but, although the council is described in 15:6 as a meeting of the apostles and elders, it seems from 15:22 as though Luke assumes the whole Jerusalem church is also present; *cf.* πλῆθος in 4:32; 6:2, 5; 15:30. J. Fitzmyer, 'Jewish Christianity in Acts in the Light of the Qumran Scrolls', in L.E. Keck and J.L. Martyn (ed.), *Studies in Luke-Acts* (London: SPCK, 1968) 245-6, makes the interesting suggestion that the use of τὸ πλῆθος to designate the Christian community as a whole reflects an early Jewish Christian usage comparable with the use of רב, רוב and הרבים in the Qumran community.

[71]So, *e.g.*, Haenchen, *Acts*, 451 and n. 4; B.M. Metzger, *A Textual Commentary on the Greek New Testament* (Stuttgart: United Bible Societies, 1975) 436.

unparalleled in Luke-Acts, it may be that Luke here preserves the original wording of the letter.[72] Although there are certainly indications that Luke has rewritten the letter to some extent, the Lukan characteristics of the letter as a whole are by no means sufficient to show that he composed it *de novo*.[73] He probably knew a copy of the letter communicating the apostolic decree to the churches of Antioch, Syria and Cilicia,[74] which he may have abbreviated and somewhat adapted. In that case, it may be because this letter itself described its senders as 'the apostles and the elders' that Luke adopted this twofold expression to describe the Jerusalem leaders at this—but at no other—point in his narrative. If the expression was used in the letter itself, its meaning may have been a little different from the sense it acquires in the context of Acts, since 'the apostles' could have a wider meaning than in Luke's usage, where it designates the Twelve.[75] But neither in Luke's nor in the original sense need the two terms 'apostles' and 'elders' be intended as mutually exclusive. 'The apostles and the elders' could be a way of describing a body of elders some of whom were also apostles. Alternatively it could describe a group consisting of both the local Jerusalem church leadership (the elders) and a wider group of leading missionaries not all of whom were usually in Jerusalem (the apostles).

---

[72]Note the interesting parallel with 2 Mac. 1:1.

[73]A. Harnack, *Luke the Physician*, tr. J.R. Wilkinson (London: Williams & Norgate/ New York: Putnam's Sons, 1907) 219-23, argued (against T. Zahn) that Lukan vocabulary and style show the letter to be Luke's composition, but some of his evidence is dubious, such as the explanation of certain words as medical phraseology (following W.K. Hobart). There are also, as Zahn pointed out, a number of striking *hapax legomena*. Harnack's evidence seems consistent with Lukan stylistic revision of an existing document. In any case, Harnack's argument should not be treated as having settled the matter once and for all, as it is by G. Lüdemann, *Early Christianity according to the Traditions in Acts*, tr. J. Bowden (London: SCM Press, 1989) 168.
The order of the names 'Barnabas and Paul' (15:25), which Luke himself has not used since 13:2 ('Barnabas and Saul'), while using 'Paul and Barnabas' throughout the surrounding context (15:2, 12, 22, 35), is striking and rarely noticed (Haenchen, *Acts*, 452, is so far from noticing it that he misquotes the text as 'our beloved Paul and Barnabas'!), though it is not impossible that Luke aimed at verisimilitude, correctly thinking that this is how the Jerusalem leaders would have perceived the seniority.

[74]In view of the authority attached to the apostolic decree for a long period after its promulgation (see section IV.3 below), such a letter would certainly have been copied and readily available to Luke.

[75]We should not rule out the possibility that in the early Jerusalem church 'the apostles' could be used especially to designate the Twelve, as well as having a wider meaning.

We shall now assess the historical plausibility of the account of the leadership of the Jerusalem church in Acts, before turning to the most important information in other sources. There is no good reason to doubt Luke's view that the Twelve were based in Jerusalem in the early years of the church. The fact that Luke does not depict them on journeys outside Jerusalem until 8:14-25; 9:32–10:48 may be the result of his schematised presentation of the development of the Christian mission, but in fact even Galatians 1:18-19 (if it means that only one of the Twelve was to be found in Jerusalem on Paul's first visit after his conversion) does not contradict Luke's picture,[76] since by this date even Acts shows the apostles travelling outside Jerusalem. Galatians 1:17 ('I did not go up to Jerusalem to those who were apostles before me') confirms that at that time Jerusalem was the obvious place in which to find the apostles (for Paul, including, though not limited to, the Twelve). Though Luke does not give much impression of the (by his time, rather antiquated) eschatological ideas of the early community, we can take it as certain that the Twelve, the phylarchs of the eschatological Israel (Mt. 19:28; Lk. 22:29-30), would have taken up residence in Jerusalem precisely because of their and its eschatological roles.

Luke's picture of Peter succeeded, in different ways, by James and Paul is, of course, schematic. Peter did not entirely disappear from Jerusalem after Agrippa's persecution, as Luke himself acknowledges in 15:6-11, but the fact that in Galatians 2:9 James takes precedence over him supports Luke's account when it is understood as a broad indication of the course of events. Peter certainly did not pass the torch of missionary leadership over to Paul, and may well have become even more important as a travelling missionary (*cf.* 1 Cor 9:5), arguably among Gentiles as well as Jews, though our information is very little.[77] Here Luke's scheme is justified simply by his own decision—no doubt for reasons of narrative effect and information available to him, as well as his devotion to Paul—to tell the story of the Christian mission after chapter 12 as Paul's story. (As we have already noticed, he does not pretend this is the only story there is to tell.) But it is historically very

[76]As M. Hengel, *Between Jesus and Paul*, tr. J. Bowden (London: SCM Press, 1983) 60, alleges. There could, of course, have been other reasons why Paul did not meet other apostles, and it is possible his words do not mean literally that he did not even see any other apostles, but only that he did not have conversations with them.
[77]For Peter's later reputation as apostle to the Gentiles, and its probable basis in some historical fact, see R. Bauckham, 'The Martyrdom of Peter in Early Christian Literature', ANRW II,26/1 (1992) 576-577.

credible that the persecution of Agrippa I (AD 43 or 44) was the point at which the Twelve ceased to be the leadership of the Jerusalem church.[78] It would be very difficult to envisage James' rise to preeminence while the Twelve as a body were still in Jerusalem. The constitutional role of the latter must have been unchallengeable and unsurpassable within the Jerusalem church.[79] If Agrippa's persecution caused the dispersal of the Twelve, along with at least one—but perhaps more than one—martyrdom, James, already a highly respected and important figure (Gal. 1:19), would have stepped into the vacuum.

The fact that James could remain in Jerusalem when his namesake the son of Zebedee had been executed and Peter had to flee for his life should not be explained by reference to his allegedly more strict Torah-observance.[80] It is true that both Luke (Acts 11:3) and Paul (Gal. 2:11-14) refer to criticism of Peter for eating with Gentiles, but there is no evidence that this kind of laxity with regard to the Law lay behind Agrippa's persecution[81] and no evidence that James the son of Zebedee or other members of the Twelve were less strict in their Torah-observance than James. Agrippa's persecution stands in succession to earlier measures taken by the High Priests against the Twelve (4:1-3; 5:17-18), before there was any question of such neglect of the Law, and in line with the High Priest Ananus' later action against James himself (Josephus, *Ant.* 20.197-200). The reason the Twelve were targeted by

[78]It is tempting to connect this with the later tradition that, by the risen Christ's command, the Twelve remained in Jerusalem for twelve years before embarking on their mission to the rest of the world (Kerygma Petrou, *ap.* Clement of Alexandria, *Strom.* 6.5.43; Apollonius, according to Eusebius, *Hist. Eccl.* 5.18.14). Allowing for the appropriateness of the number twelve, there is a rough chronological correspondence.

[79]The idea that James was the leader of a specific group in the Jerusalem church, distinct from Peter's group, is quite dubious. It certainly cannot be supported from Acts 12:17 (against F.F. Bruce, *Men and Movements in the Primitive Church* [Exeter: Paternoster, 1979] 88). Of course, the Jerusalem church was then too large to meet in one house, and James is not present in the house to which Peter goes. But this does not mean that the Christians meeting in this house are specifically Peter's group. Most probably, Peter and the rest of the Twelve exercised general oversight over all house churches in Jerusalem. Peter's words in 12:17 refer to all the members of the Jerusalem church not present in Mary's house and name the one leader important enough to be named.

[80]*E.g.* Hengel, *Acts*, 95-97; Pratscher, *Der Herrenbruder*, 75-76.

[81]Pratscher, *Der Herrenbruder*, 74-75, suggests it did, in consequence of the apostolic conference (Gal. 2:1-10) which he dates before Agrippa's persecution. But there would in this case be no basis for distinguishing James from Peter: both had endorsed Paul's Gentile mission.

Agrippa whereas James was relatively safe must have been simply that the Twelve were recognised as the leaders of the Christian community. James was not yet sufficiently prominent to attract such attention, but became prominent precisely during and in the aftermath of the persecution. A group of elders, among whom he naturally assumed the leading role, took the place of the Twelve, and retained this position when it became clear that, even after Agrippa's death, not enough of the Twelve were returning to permanent residence in Jerusalem to make the reconstitution of the Twelve as the ruling group feasible. Whether this reconstruction of events is consistent with Galatians 2:9, as a reference to the Jerusalem leadership a few years after Agrippa's death, will be considered in the next section.

2. *From the Pillars to the Rampart (Galatians and Hegesippus)*

Paul's reference to 'James and Cephas and John, who were acknowledged to be pillars (οἱ δοκοῦντες στῦλοι εἶναι)' (Gal. 2:9)[82] is invaluable evidence of James' rise to prominence in the Jerusalem church. That Paul lists James first very probably reflects his perception of the relative importance of the three at the time of the meeting he describes.[83] If, as seems likely, his opponents in Antioch (*cf.* 2:12) and in Galatia appealed to the authority of James, as head of the Jerusalem church, Paul is not likely to have played into their hands by giving James anachronistic prominence at the time of the crucial agreement he describes in Galatians 2:9. Even though James was the eldest of the Lord's brothers and had received an individual resurrection appearance (1 Cor. 15:7), it is remarkable that he should have attained some kind of precedence over Peter and John. The only plausible explanation is that the latter were no longer permanently based in Jerusalem. This is supported by the way Paul still gives Peter preeminence in the mission to the circumcised (2:7-8), which the agreement made the responsibility of all three 'pillars' (2:9). Peter had become a travelling missionary (*cf.* also 2:11), still regarded as the foremost of the apostles in their missionary task,[84] but no longer pre-eminent among the leaders in Jerusalem. James was now the leading figure in Jerusalem.

---

[82]Whether there is irony intended in Paul's use of δοκέω here and in vv. 2, 6 is not important for our present purpose.

[83]This view is defended by D. Georgi, *Remembering the Poor: The History of Paul's Collection for Jerusalem* (Nashville: Abingdon, 1992) 168-70, against Haenchen and others.

This is all the more explicable if, as we have argued, there had recently been a period when, owing to the persecution of Herod Agrippa, those members of the Twelve who did not suffer martyrdom had had to leave Jerusalem. In the absence of any of the Twelve, James had come to be recognised as leader of the Jerusalem church. However, this raises the question whether, at the time of Galatians 2:1-10, Peter and John were now regarded as members of the ruling group in Jerusalem, subordinate to James, or whether there was now a distinction between the local church leadership (James and the elders) and the leadership of the Christian mission (the apostles, headed by the three 'pillars'). We should also note that, although all discussions of Galatians 2:9 seem to assume that there were only three 'pillars,' this is not at all a necessary conclusion. It is certainly true that, if the leaders with whom Paul met (2:2, 6) were a larger group, of whom he names only the most prominent three in v. 9, then his use of στῦλοι only in v. 9 probably shows that, of this larger group, only these three could be called 'pillars.' But Paul's meeting may have been only with the leading three of a larger group of 'pillars.' We shall return to these questions after considering the significance of the term 'pillars.'

As others have argued,[85] this term needs to be understood within the context of the early church's understanding of itself as the eschatological Temple. The pillars are key architectural features, which function to support the Temple building. If the Temple is understood as the Christian community, key leaders of the community can be designated its pillars. To grasp the significance of this usage more fully, a remarkably close parallel to the early church's use of Temple imagery is instructive. As far as we know, the Qumran community and the early Christian church were the only two Jewish groups who understood their own community as the Temple of God and applied to it scriptural prophecies of the eschatological Temple.[86] The two cases are not precisely parallel. The Qumran community did not regard themselves as *the* eschatological Temple but as a temporary substitute for the Jerusalem Temple, while the priestly ministry in the latter was, in their view, illegitimate. They expected the new Temple of the messianic age to be built in Jerusalem. The early Christian church, on the other hand, saw itself as the place of God's eschatological pres-

---

[84]But it is remarkable that in 1 Cor. 9:5, where Paul wishes to instance the best known examples of apostles who, like him, were travelling missionaries, it is the brothers of the Lord who come before Cephas.

[85]Especially C.K. Barrett, 'Paul and the "Pillar" Apostles', in J.N. Sevenster and W.C. van Unnik (eds.), *Studia Paulina* (J. de Zwaan FS; Haarlem: Bohn, 1953) 1-19.

ence, destined to supersede the Jerusalem Temple. For the time being, until God should remove the latter, they continued to worship in it, but did not expect a new Temple building.[87] Despite these differences, the way the two communities used Temple imagery to refer, not to a building, but to a community, is strikingly parallel.

At Qumran the members of the community and its leaders and officials were identified as various parts of the Temple structure. Of particular interest is the commentary on Isaiah 54:11-12 (4QpIsa[d]).[88] This passage describes the future, glorious Zion, but probably the Qumran *pesher* understands it as the Temple rather than the city. The architectural features mentioned in the text are allegorically interpreted as follows: the stones are 'all Israel' (probably the whole community, as the true Israel); the foundations are taken to refer to the founding of the community; the pinnacles are 'the twelve [men and three priests][89] who shine with the judgment of the Urim and Thummim' (the ruling group of twelve founding members of the community, here identified also with the stones on the high-priestly breastplate);[90] and the gates are 'the heads of the tribes of Israel in the la[st days].' Unfortunately the extant text breaks off before offering an interpretation of the last architectural feature of Isaiah 54:12: the wall.

Such an exegetical passage need not be evidence that such terms from the biblical text were used in other contexts. But the term 'foundation(s)' (יסוד, סוד), which seems to be used in a variety of ways—for

---

[86]For the community as Temple at Qumran, see B. Gärtner, *The Temple and the Community in the Qumran Scrolls and the New Testament* (Cambridge: Cambridge University Press, 1965) 16-46; D. Juel, *Messiah and Temple: The Trial of Jesus in the Gospel of Mark* (SBLDS 31; Missoula, Montana: Scholars Press, 1977) 159-68; H. Lichtenberger, 'Atonement and Sacrifice in the Qumran Community', in W.S. Green (ed.), *Approaches to Ancient Judaism*, vol. II (Brown Judaic Studies 9; Chico, California: Scholars Press, 1980) 159-71; G.J. Brooke, *Exegesis at Qumran: 4QFlorilegium in its Jewish Context* (JSOTSS 29; Sheffield: JSOT Press, 1985) 178-93.

[87]Expectation of an eschatological Temple other than the Christian community is remarkably absent from early Christian literature. For the early church's attitude to the Temple, see R. Bauckham, 'The Parting of the Ways: What Happened and Why', *ST* 47 (1993) 142-8.

[88]On this passage see H. Muszynski, *Fundament, Bild und Metapher in der Handschriften aus Qumran* (AnBib 61; Rome: Biblical Institute Press, 1975) 192-7; M.P. Horgan, *Pesharim: Qumran Interpretations of Biblical Books* (CBQMS 8; Washington, DC: Catholic Biblical Association of America, 1979) 126-31; J.A. Draper, 'The twelve apostles as foundation stones of the heavenly Jerusalem and the foundation of the Qumran community', *Neot* 22 (1988) 52-7.

[89]Draper supplies the lacuna from 1QS 8:1.

[90]Draper, 'The twelve apostles', 56-7. Draper argues that in 1QS 8:1 the three priests are not additional to, but included in the group of twelve (47-8).

the whole community, for a more restricted group within the community, perhaps for the Teacher of Righteousness himself[91]—appears to be an element of the Temple structure which can be used quite independently. For example: 'Whoever has murmured against "the foundation" of the community...' (1QS 7:17);[92] 'At the age of twenty-five years he may take his place among "the foundations" of the holy congregation to work in the service of the congregation' (1QSa 1:12). Here specific individuals or groups are designated, in a quite matter-of-fact context, by a term drawn from the Temple metaphor. Also of particular interest for our purposes is 4QpPs[a] 1-10/3:15-16, which refers to 'the Teacher of [Righteousness, whom] God [chose as a pillar (לעמוד). For he established him to build for him a congregation of [his chosen ones in truth].'[93] Here the Teacher of Righteousness is not only the one who builds the community as a Temple. He is also the pillar which is erected first to support the rest of the building.[94]

If Galatians 2:9 stood alone in early Christian literature, it would have to be very uncertain whether the term 'pillar' belongs to the image of the Christian community as Temple. In the ancient world, where the pillars which support a building were an essential feature of most substantial buildings, the pillar was a natural image of someone who stands firm in support of others or of an institution or ideal. It could also designate an important person or leader in a community. Such usage can be found not only in classical,[95] but also in Jewish[96] and early Christian literature.[97] However, not only is the image of the Christian community as Temple so common in early Christian literature[98] that it very plausibly goes back to early Palestinian Christianity, but also particular elements in the structure of the Temple building are used as metaphorical references to people and groups within the

---

[91]See the full study by Muszynski, *Fundament*.

[92]Muszynski, *Fundament*, 224-7, sees here a reference to the Teacher of Righteousness.

[93]See Horgan, *Pesharim*, 197-8, 219.

[94]It is possible that the words 'For he established him (הכינו)' (picking up כוננו in Ps. 37:23) allude to the pillar in Solomon's Temple called Jachin (יכין) (1 Ki. 7:21). *Cf. b. Ber.* 28b, where Johanan b. Zakkai is called 'right-hand pillar', identifying him with Jachin.

[95]Aeschylus, *Agamemnon* 897-8; Euripides, *Iphigeneia in Tauris* 57; Livy 38.51, cited by Barrett, 'Paul', 4.

[96]Sir. 36:29; 4 Mac. 17:3; Tg. Ps.-Jon. Gn. 46:28; 49:19; Ex. 15:14, 15. It is therefore not the case, as Barrett, 'Paul', 4-5 argues, that, simply because Paul's usage in Gal. 2:9 reflects the Jewish usage of the Jerusalem church, it cannot be an instance of this general metaphorical usage.

church, in ways which compare well with the usage at Qumran. Thus Christians in general are the stones of which the Temple is constructed (1 Pet. 2:5; Hermas, *Vis.* 3; *Sim.* 9; *cf.* 4QpIsa[d]); the apostles and Christian prophets are the foundation (Eph. 2:20);[99] Peter is the rock on which the Temple is built (Mt. 16:18);[100] Jesus Christ is the foundation (1 Cor. 3:11) or the cornerstone/keystone (Eph. 2:20; 1 Pet. 2:4, 6-7, alluding to Is. 28:16;[101] Ps. 118:22). We can imagine that in the early Jerusalem church the Twelve must have been identified with a key architectural feature of the messianic Temple. They cannot have been the pillars, since James the Lord's brother, not one of the Twelve, was a pillar (Gal. 2:9). Revelation 21:14 may preserve an early identification of the Twelve with the foundations (Is. 54:11). But we should notice that the use of the imagery was evidently somewhat flexible. In Revelation 3:12 Christ promises to make every Christian who is faithful as far as death a pillar in the Temple of his God.[102] But the use in Gala-

---

[97]Letter of the churches ofVienne and Lyons, *ap.* Eusebius, *Hist. Eccl.* 5.1.6; 5.1.17; Dionysius of Alexandria, *ap.* Eusebius, *Hist. Eccl.* 6.41.14; *cf.* 1 Tim. 3:15. Whether some early Christian references to apostles as pillars are examples of this general metaphorical usage or are dependent on Gal. 2:9 or preserve an independent memory of the early usage to which Gal. 2:9 refers is difficult to tell: see 1 Clem. 5:2; Questions of Bartholomew 2:7; Bodleian Coptic fragment of the Acts of Andrew.

[98]As well as passages mentioned below, see 1 Cor. 3:16-17; 2 Cor. 6:16; 1 Pet. 4:17; Heb. 13:15-16; Rev. 11:1-2; Did. 10:2; Barn. 4:11; 6:15; 16; Ignatius, *Eph.* 9:1. The frequent use of the metaphor of 'building' the Christian community should also be seen as evidence of this concept: Acts 9:31; 20:32; Rom. 14:19; 15:2, 20; 1 Cor. 8:1; 10:23; 14:3-5, 12, 17, 26; 2 Cor. 10:8; 12:19; 13:10; Gal. 2:18; Eph. 4:12, 16; Col. 2:7; 1 Thes. 5:11; Jude 20.

[99]*Cf.* Rev. 21:14, where the names of the Twelve are written on the foundation stones of the New Jerusalem. This passage, which is dependent on Isa. 54:11-12 and which also identifies the foundation stones with the jewels of the High-Priestly breastplate (21:19-20), is strikingly close to 4QpIsa[d]. *Cf.* Draper, 'The twelve apostles', 41-63. The identification of the gates with the twelve tribes (Rev. 21:12) is less striking, since it derives from Ezk. 48:30-34.

[100]*Cf.* 1QH 6:26; 7:8, where the community built by the Teacher of Righteousness (7:8-9) or by God (6:25-26) is founded on a rock, probably alluding, like Mt. 16:18, to the rock on which the Temple was built. This should be distinguished from the foundation (Is. 28:16), which is laid on the rock. In Hermas, *Sim.* 9 the rock is the Son of God. *Cf.* also Odes Sol. 22:12.

[101]This text was important at Qumran, but was understood to refer to the foundation-wall which is the community as a whole (1QH 6:26-27 [*cf.* Is. 28:17]; 7:9; 1QS 8:7).

[102]See also R.H. Wilkinson, 'The Στῦλος of Revelation 3:12 and Ancient Coronation Rites', *JBL* 107 (1988) 498-501.

tians 2:9 must refer to a group of leaders who were identified as the pillars of the messianic Temple.[103]

Pillars, though they must have been an important structural feature of the Temple building, are rarely mentioned in descriptions of either historical or eschatological Jerusalem Temples.[104] But there was probably a specific scriptural support for the idea that pillars were a key feature of the messianic Temple: Proverbs 9:1 ('Wisdom has built her house, she has hewn her seven pillars'). In favour of the possibility that this text could have been understood to refer to the Temple, we may note, first, that in Proverbs 9:1-6 Wisdom not only builds her house but also prepares and issues an invitation to a feast, which could easily be understood as a sacrificial meal, the eschatological banquet eaten in the presence of God (Is. 25:6). Moreover, there is a striking parallel between Proverbs 9:1-6 and Sirach 24:10-22, where Wisdom is the presence of God in the Jerusalem Temple and similarly issues an invitation to her feast (24:19-21). Some later Rabbinic interpretation linked Proverbs 9:1 with Wisdom's role in the creation of the world (Pr. 8:22-31) and took the pillars to be those which support the earth (*cf.*

---

[103]R.D. Aus, 'Three Pillars and Three Patriarchs: A Proposal Concerning Gal 2 9', *ZNW* 70 (1979) 252-61, relates Gal. 2:9 to the Rabbinic tradition of identifying Abraham, Isaac and Jacob with the pillars or foundations on which the world rested (with reference to 1 Sa. 2:8; Pr. 10:25; Mi. 6:2). Whether this view was current in the 1st century is uncertain. Philo, *Migr. Abr.* 122-5; *Quest. Gen.* 3:44, do not necessarily show that it was; they may be instances of the general metaphorical use of 'pillar.' But in any case, it is not at all clear why the early church should have had three patriarchs. The Twelve were not the sons of Jacob, ancestors of the tribes, but phylarchs, playing a role in the constitution of the eschatological Israel; so it is hard to see why three persons equivalent to the three patriarchs (who were the ancestors of Israel, rather than playing a role in its constitution) should have had such a role. For the apostles as pillars of the world, see Pseudo-Ignatius, *Philad.* 9.

[104]The two pillars, called Jachin and Boaz, which stood in front of the Temple building in Solomon's Temple (1 Ki. 7:21; 2 Ch. 3:17; Je. 52:21) did not support anything. Although Johanan b. Zakkai was later compared with Jachin (*b. Ber.* 28b), the fact that there were only two such pillars means they cannot be the model for the usage in Gal. 2:9. In 1 Enoch 90:28-29, describing the removal of the old 'house' and the erection of the new (eschatological) 'house', pillars are prominent. Strictly, the house may symbolize the new Jerusalem, not the new Temple (*cf.* 89:36, where the house is the tabernacle; 89:50-56, where the house seems to be Jerusalem and the tower the Temple), but whatever the original meaning, it could readily be understood as referring to the eschatological Temple. Note also 4Q403 1/1:41 (C. Newsom, *Songs of the Sabbath Sacrifice: A Critical Edition* [HSS 27; Atlanta: Scholars Press, 1985] 209, 212), where with reference to the heavenly Temple, both the foundations of the holy of holies and the pillars supporting it are mentioned. It is especially interesting that these architectural features are regarded as animate and exhorted to praise God.

1 Sa. 2:8).[105] But an interpretation of Wisdom's house as the Temple and the banquet she prepares as the sacrificial banquet of Ezekiel 39:17-20 is also attested (*Lev. Rab.* 11:2). This evidence is late, but shows that to a Jewish exegetical mind such an interpretation was plausible. More chronologically relevant is the evidence of *Joseph and Aseneth.* Here Joseph's bride Aseneth is described in terms which make her an allegory of the eschatological Zion, in which all the nations will take refuge with God (15:7; 19:6, with allusion to Zc. 2:10 [LXX]; Is. 54:15 [LXX]). Though the term used is 'the City of Refuge,' it is preeminently the place of God's eschatological presence, and so the eschatological city and the eschatological Temple are not sharply distinguished (*cf.* Rev. 21). A further element in the allegory is that Aseneth's seven virgins are promised: 'you shall be the seven pillars (κίονες) of the City of Refuge and all the (female) fellow inhabitants of the elect of that city will rest upon you for ever' (17:6). Evidently in the same interpretative tradition is the third *Vision* of Hermas, in which he sees a tower (the church) being constructed of various kinds of stones (various categories of Christians). The tower is supported by seven women, who represent seven qualities such as Faith, Self-Control, Simplicity and so on (3.8.2-5).

As we have noted, there is no reason at all to assume that there were only ever three pillars (Gal. 2:9) in the early church.[106] The 'pillars' could have been once a larger group, now depleted, or a larger group of whom Paul and Barnabas consulted only with the three most important. We may presume that, on the basis of Proverbs 9:1, the pillars were a group of seven. That the group would overlap with the Twelve is not a problem. The Temple imagery was not used with rigid literalness. Peter could be both one of the twelve foundations (Rev. 21:14) and the unique rock on which the Temple was built (Mt. 16:18). Perhaps the seven pillars were originally, before the death of James the son of Zebedee, composed of the three most prominent of the Twelve (Peter, James, John) and the four brothers of the Lord (James, Joses,

---

[105]*B. Ḥag.* 12b; *Lev. Rab.* 11.1. Probably also indebted to this line of interpretation is *Clem. Hom.* 18.14, where the seven righteous patriarchs from Adam to Jacob are 'the seven pillars of the world.'

[106]But *cf.* the argument of D. Wenham and A.D.A. Moses, '"There Are Some Standing Here...": Did They Become the "Reputed Pillars" of the Jerusalem Church? Some Reflections on Mark 9:1, Galatians 2:9 and the Transfiguration', *NovT* 36 (1994) 146-63. They think the three pillars were originally Peter, John and James the son of Zebedee (the last replaced by the Lord's brother after his death), and connect the term 'pillars' with Mark 9:1 (which, however, says: 'there are some of those standing here...').

Jude, Simon). If so, the concept of the seven pillars would testify to the prominence of the brothers of Jesus alongside the Twelve already before the dispersal of the Twelve. Alternatively, perhaps the seven pillars were constituted after the persecution of Herod Agrippa when the Twelve no longer existed as a body. It would fit what we know of Peter from the time of the persecution onwards, both from Acts (12:17) and Paul (Gal. 2:11), if we thought of the seven pillars, not as a body permanently resident in Jerusalem and in charge of the church there, but as the group which led the Jerusalem church's mission to the Jewish people, most members of which, apart from James, would be travelling missionaries. James, as the head of the mother church, would be pre-eminent in this group. On this hypothesis, the elders, as the ruling group in the Jerusalem church itself, would be a different body of people. We cannot be sure. But James' place among the pillars (Gal. 2:9) is certainly the first evidence of the remarkable preeminence he was to attain in Jerusalem.

Further testimony to this, within the same sphere of imagery identifying Christian leaders with architectural features of the messianic Temple, comes from Hegesippus, who reports 2nd-century Palestinian Jewish Christian tradition about James. Most is legendary, but the following sentence deserves attention: 'because of his excessive righteousness [James] was called "the Righteous (ὁ δίκαιος)" and Oblias (Ὠβλιας), which is, in Greek, "Rampart of the people (περιοχή τοῦ λαοῦ)", and "Righteousness (δικαιοσύνη)", as the prophets show concerning him' (*ap.* Eusebius, *Hist. Eccl.* 2.23.7). Among the many attempts[107] to solve the riddle of the unintelligible Ὠβλιας, which most scholars have rightly supposed must be a corrupt form of a Semitic word or words, none has yet provided a wholly satisfactory explanation which does justice to what Hegesippus says the term means in Greek. I suggest that a better explanation is to be found in Isaiah 54:11-12, which, as we have seen, describes the architectural features of the eschatological Zion. In v. 12, the word גבול, which elsewhere usually means boundary or territory, refers to the surrounding wall of the city or Temple: it is rendered in the LXX as περίβολος, while inTobit 13:16 and Revelation 21 τεῖχος is used.[108] περιοχή would be a very suitable

---

[107]See H.J. Schoeps, 'Jacobus ὁ δίκαιος καὶ ὠβλιας', in Schoeps, *Aus frühchristliche Zeit* (Tübingen, 1950) 120-5; C.C. Torrey, 'James the Just, and his Name "Oblias"', *JBL* 63 (1944) 93-8; H. Sahlin, 'Noch einmal Jacobus "Oblias"', *Bib* 28 (1947) 152-153; Barrett, 'Paul', 15 n. 2; K. Baltzer and H. Köster, 'Die Bezeichnung des Jakobus als Ὠβλιας', *ZNW* 46 (1955) 141-2; S. Gero, 'Ὠβλιας Reconsidered', *Mus* 88 (1975) 435-440; Pratscher, *Der Herrenbruder*, 116-8.

translation. Transferred from its context in Isaiah 54:12 to be used as a title for James, גבולך (your wall) would become גְּבַל־עָם (wall of the people). It is not difficult to see how this could become Ὠβλιας in Greek (the final ς being an assimilation to Greek name endings). This explanation takes seriously Hegesippus' reference to the prophets, which should probably be taken to refer to all three designations of James. A reference to James as 'the righteous one' was found in Isaiah 3:10 (*cf.* Hegesippus, *ap.* Eusebius, *Hist. Eccl.* 2.23.15; 2 Apoc. Jas. 61:14-19) and probably other texts. A reference to James as 'righteousness' was probably found in Isaiah 54:14, which would make James the means by which God builds the eschatological Zion, and/or Isaiah 28:17 (which continues the favourite early Christian text about Christ as the cornerstone of the messianic Temple), which would make James the plumbline which God uses to build the new Temple.[109]

The protective surrounding wall of the eschatological Zion was of considerable importance (*cf.* Jos. Asen. 15:7, 16; 19:6; Rev. 21:12, 17-18). It is unfortunate that we do not know how 4QpIsa^{d} interpreted this feature of Isaiah 54:12, but it is worth noticing that in 1QH 8:8 the Teacher of Righteousness apparently compares himself to a strong tower and a high wall in relation to the building which is his community. But the most important aspect of the use of this term for James may be that, of the various architectural features mentioned in Isaiah 54:11-12, it is the only one which occurs in the singular. It was therefore appropriate to describe the unique position James came to hold at the head of the mother-church in Jerusalem. As a singular feature of the new Temple, James as the rampart compares only with Peter as the rock. This claim for James does not compete with Peter's; it attributes to him a different but equally unique and distinctive role in the church. It seems probable that the use of this term for James does go back to his lifetime, and corresponds to the position which Acts 21:18 also implies that James had acquired. Later, in the light of the legendary developments which treated the fall of Jerusalem as consequent upon James' martyrdom (Eusebius, *Hist. Eccl.* 2.23.18-20) the term 'Rampart of the People' was held to mean that, by praying for the forgiveness of the Jewish people (*Hist. Eccl.* 2.23.6), he protected the city, while he still lived, from impending disaster. But originally it will have referred to

---

[108]In the parallel to Eusebius, *Hist. Eccl.* 2.23.7 in Epiphanius, *Haer.* 78.7.7, Oblias is said to mean τεῖχος.

[109]*Cf.* the use of this text in 1QH 6:26-27, which takes it as an image of God's building the community.

his role in relation to the eschatological people of God, the Christian community.

We have seen that—in relation to the pillars and the elders—some uncertainty must remain as to the relation between leadership within the Jerusalem church and the Jerusalem church's oversight, as mother church, of the Christian mission. But, as far as James goes, there is no uncertainty. As the permanent head of the mother church, he continued to symbolise the centre while other apostles now represented the movement of the gospel out from the centre. James in the period of his supremacy in Jerusalem was no merely local leader, but the personal embodiment of the Jerusalem church's constitutional and eschatological centrality in relation to the whole developing Christian movement, Jewish and Gentile. This makes the question of the attitude of the Jerusalem leadership and of James in particular to the Gentile mission a highly significant one.

IV. The Jerusalem Church and the Gentiles

1. Oversight of the Christian mission

Luke portrays the Jerusalem church as exercising oversight over the developing Christian mission, including, in particular, the Gentile mission. Barnabas acts as a key link between Jerusalem and developments in Antioch (Acts 11:22-24, 29; 12:25), as well as between the Twelve and Paul (9:27; 11:25, 29). The Jerusalem council presupposes the authority of Jerusalem to decide the issue of Gentile Christians' obedience to the Law (Acts 15). Its decision binds not only Antioch and its daughter churches (15:22-31) but also the churches founded by Paul and Barnabas (16:4). When James recalls the decision in 21:25, the effect is to imply that Paul's Gentile mission is still subject to it.

Two important pieces of evidence outside Acts show that some kind of authority of Jerusalem over the Christian mission elsewhere was widely recognised. Precisely what kind of authority Paul himself attributes to the Jerusalem leaders in Galatians 2:2 (perhaps more at the time of the meeting than when he wrote Galatians) is debatable, but probably he and Barnabas at this stage were acting on the view of the Antiochene church, which looked to the mother church as authoritative on such a key question.[110] Even if Paul's meaning is that he was concerned, not for the validity of his gospel, but for the practicability of his mission, which would be seriously impaired without recognition from Jerusalem,[111] this would at least imply that Jerusalem's authority in such matters was of great importance to others. The extent to which Paul acknowledges the authority of the pillars here is all the more striking in the context of an argument for the independence of his own apostolate.

The second piece of evidence, from a very different source, is logion 12 of the Gospel of Thomas:

> The disciples said to Jesus: 'We know that you will depart from us. Who is it who will be great over us?' Jesus said to them: 'Wherever you have come, you will go to James the Righteous, for whose sake heaven and earth came into being.'

In its present context, this saying may serve to authenticate Gnostic works bearing James' name (the Apocryphon of James, the First and Second Apocalypses of James), just as the following logion authenticates the Gospel of Thomas itself (and perhaps other Thomas literature). But it cannot have originated for this purpose. It is clearly a saying which presupposes the mission of the apostles (and probably therefore presupposes the sending out of the apostles by the risen Christ) and gives to James the authority at the centre to which, wherever their missionary travels take them, they are to look. The saying very probably dates from James' lifetime, in which it makes excellent sense as an expression of the Jerusalem leader's authority over the mission to the Diaspora. (An authentication of James' successors for post-70 Jewish Christians who retained this view is less likely, but in this case it would still be evidence of a view of Jerusalem's authority which would go back to James' time.) The saying probably reflects the outlook of the early Jewish Christian mission to east Syria, some of whose traditions were later taken over by the Gospel of Thomas which originates in that area.[112]

In Acts much the most important expression of Jerusalem's oversight of the developing Christian mission is the decision of the Jerusalem council (Acts 15), to which we now turn.

---

[110]*Cf.* N. Taylor, *Paul, Antioch and Jerusalem* (JSNTSS 66; Sheffield: JSOT Press, 1992) 97-103.

[111]So F.F. Bruce, *Galatians* (NIGTC; Exeter: Paternoster, 1982) 111.

[112]The reference to Addai in 1 Apoc. Jas. 36:15-24 is also evidence associating James with the founding mission to Edessa.

2. *The Speech of James (Acts 15:13-21)*

In Luke's account of the Jerusalem council, the issue is whether Gentile converts must be circumcised and thereby obliged to keep the Law of Moses (15:1, 5), *i.e.* whether, in order to belong to the eschatological people of God, they have to become Jews. The speakers present two kinds of argument. Peter argues that the miraculous charismatic phenomena which accompanied the conversion of the first Gentile converts constituted a declaration by God that Gentiles are acceptable to him as Gentiles (15:8-9; *cf.* 11:12),[113] and Paul and Barnabas support this argument by referring to the miraculous signs which attended their own Gentile mission (15:12). However, this line of argument cannot, for an assembly of Jewish Christians, be the finally decisive one: the issue is a matter of *halakhah*, which can only be decided from Scripture (*cf. b. B. Meṣ.* 59b). The clinching argument, provided by James,[114] is therefore a scriptural one. He argues that the prophets, when they predicted that Gentiles would join the eschatological people of God, also made it clear that they will do so as Gentiles (15:15-19). Gentile Christians are therefore not obligated to the Law of Moses as a whole, but four specific commandments are binding on them (15:19-20). These are the terms of the so-called apostolic decree (15:28-29; *cf.* 21:25). As we shall see, James' argument really means that the Torah itself requires Gentile members of the eschatological people of God to keep these, but only these four commandments. Summarised in James' brief speech is a very precise exegetical argument as to the relationship of Gentile Christians to the Law of Moses.

The most important question is not whether the speech of James in Acts 15 reports what James actually said at the council, which is not likely, but whether it accurately reflects both the considered view of the Jerusalem church leadership, in which James was pre-eminent, as to the relation of Gentile Christians to the Torah, and also the exegetical arguments on which this view was based and with which it was recommended. Although it is widely, though not universally, admitted that the apostolic decree does emanate from the Jerusalem

[113]*Cf.* P.F. Esler, 'Glossolalia and the Admission of Gentiles into the Early Christian Community', *BTB* 22 (1992) 136-42.
[114]J. Jervell, *Acts and the People of God: A New Look at Luke-Acts* (Minneapolis, Minnesota: Augsburg, 1972) 188-93, gives a good account of the way Luke's narrative makes James' speech, rather than Peter's, decisive, but his explanation for Luke's portrayal of the role of James (that James had more authority than Paul for Luke's readers) is unconvincing.

church led by James, most scholars have denied that James' argument in 15:14-21 can do so. The observation that, not only is the scriptural quotation in 15:16-18 dependent on the LXX of Amos 9:11-12, but also that its value for James' argument seems to depend on precisely the LXX text where it differs from the MT, has usually been thought sufficient evidence for this view, and the scriptural argument in James' speech is consequently attributed either to hellenistic Christian exegetical tradition, followed by Luke,[115] or to Luke himself.[116] I have argued at length elsewhere[117] that this view rests on a failure to appreciate both the way in which the scriptural quotation in 15:16-18 is composed and interpreted by the skilled use of contemporary Jewish exegetical methods and also the way the quotation is exegetically linked with the terms of the apostolic decree. In what follows I summarise the essentials of my fuller discussion.

Careful attention to the text of the quotation in Acts 15:16-18 shows that it is far from simply a quotation of the LXX text of Amos 9:11-12 'with small variations.'[118] It is a conflated quotation, combining Amos 9:11-12 with allusions to other, related texts (hence 'the prophets' in the introductory formula: 15:15), which assist its interpretation, and exhibiting a text-form which has been selected and adapted to suit the interpretation. These features are now familiar to us not only from the New Testament but also from the Qumran *pesharim*, and they must be understood as the product of skilled exegetical work. What appears to be merely a quotation of a scriptural text turns out to be in fact also an interpretation of the text.

The interpretation takes 'the dwelling of David' (τὴν σκηνὴν Δαυειδ) to be the eschatological Temple which God will build, as the place of his eschatological presence, in the messianic age when Davidic

---

[115]*E.g.* G. Lüdemann, *Early Christianity according to the Traditions in Acts*, tr. J. Bowden (London: SCM Press, 1989) 169-70; J. Dupont, *The Salvation of the Gentiles: Studies in the Acts of the Apostles*, tr. J.R. Keating (New York: Paulist Press, 1979) 139-40; *cf.* F. Bovon, *Luke the Theologian: Thirty-three Years of Research (1950-1983)*, tr. K. McKinney (Allison Park, Pennsylvania: Pickwick Press, 1987) 98, 101, 107.

[116]*E.g.* E. Richard, 'The Divine Purpose: The Jews and the Gentile Mission (Acts 15)', in P.J. Achtemeier (ed.), *Society of Biblical Literature 1980 Seminar Papers* (Chico, California: Scholars Press, 1980) 267-82.

[117]R. Bauckham, 'James and the Gentiles (Acts 15:13-21)', forthcoming in B. Witherington (ed.), *The Acts of the Historians* (Cambridge: Cambridge University Press, 1995).

[118]K. Lake and H.J. Cadbury, in F.J. Foakes Jackson and K. Lake (eds.), *The Beginnings of Christianity: Part I: The Acts of the Apostles*, vol. IV (London: Macmillan, 1933) 176.

rule is restored to Israel. He will build this new Temple so that all the Gentile nations may seek his presence there. Three major features of the text-form support this interpretation. In the first place, the opening words (μετὰ ταῦτα ἀναστρέψω) and the closing words (γνωστὰ ἀπ' αἰῶνος) of the quotation, which do not come from Amos 9:11-12, frame the main text with allusions to other prophetic texts (Ho. 3:5; Je. 12:15; Is. 45:21) which are closely related to Amos 9:11-12, both in subject-matter and by means of the kind of verbal resemblances which Jewish exegetes took to indicate a mutually interpretative relationship between scriptural texts (*gezērâ shāwâ*).

Thus the opening words 'after these things' (μετὰ ταῦτα)—at first sight a surprising form of addition to the text—allude to Hosea 3:5, which in the LXX reads:

> And *after these things* the children of Israel shall *return* and *shall seek the Lord* their God (μετὰ ταῦτα ἐπιστρέψουσιν οἱ υἱοὶ Ισραηλ καὶ ἐπιζητήσουσιν κύριον τὸν θεὸν αὐτῶν) and *David* their king.

The italicised words indicate the verbal links with Acts 15:16-17. Both passages associate the restoration of the Temple and seeking the Lord in it with the restoration of Davidic rule.

The third word of the Acts quotation (ἀναστρέψω) probably alludes to Jeremiah 12:15-16:

> And it shall be that, *after* I have cast them [the Gentile nations] out, *I will return* (ἐπιστρέψω)[119] and have mercy on them, and will cause them to dwell, each in his inheritance and each in his land. And it shall be that, if they will indeed learn the way of my people, to swear by my name, "The Lord lives," as they taught my people to swear by Baal, then also they *shall be built* (οἰκοδομηθήσονται)[120] in the midst of my people.

Here the obvious thematic link is the idea of the eschatological conversion of the Gentile nations, but significantly there is also the theme of building, used in Jeremiah 12:16 metaphorically with reference to people. Since, as we shall see, the new Temple which God will build, according to Amos 9:11, is understood in the use of this text in Acts 15

---

[119]The difference between ἐπιστρέψω (Je. 12:15 [LXX]) and ἀναστρέψω (Acts 15:16; but the D-text has ἐπιστρέψω) may be due to a desire to relate this verb to the following verbs (ἀνοικοδομήσω, ἀνορθώσω), but it might indicate that at this point our exegete was not dependent on the LXX.

[120]*V.l.* 'it shall be built': οἰκοδομηθήσεται.

to be the eschatological people of God, there is a close link again with the Temple theme in the Amos text. That the Gentile nations will be 'built in the midst of my people' (Je. 12:16) suggests that they will form, together with Jews, the eschatological Temple of which Amos 9:11 speaks.

The final words of the Acts quotation (ποιῶν ταῦτα γνωστὰ ἀπ' αἰῶνος) give a different sense to the closing words of Amos 9:12 [LXX] (ποιῶν ταῦτα) by conflating them with words from Isaiah 45:21 (not, in this case, from the LXX version). The effect is to show that God's purpose of incorporating the Gentiles into his eschatological people is one which predates even these prophecies (as we shall see, the Law of Moses already reflects it). But the reason Isaiah 45:21 is relevant is that its context is another prophecy that the Gentile nations will turn to God and be saved (Is. 45:20, 22). Thus the allusions to three other prophetic passages which frame the main quotation from Amos put the latter in a context of prophecies which associate the eschatological conversion of the Gentile nations with the restoration of the Temple in the messianic age.

The second feature of the text-form is the adaptation of the text of Amos 9:11, which diverges from the LXX in omitting two whole clauses[121] and in varying the translation of the main verbs. The general effect of these modifications is to facilitate the interpretation with reference to the eschatological Temple, by making quite clear that the text refers to the restoration of a *building* (so ἀνοικοδομήσω and ἀνορθώσω are used in preference to ἀναστήσω), and by eliminating words (καθὼς αἱ ἡμέραις τοὺ αἰῶνος) which would conflict with the eschatological Temple's superiority over previous Temples.

The final feature of the text-form is the selection of the text of Amos 9:12a. Here the LXX differs significantly from the MT. The words ἐκζητήτωσιν οἱ κατάλοιποι τῶν ἀνθρώπων (LXX, followed by Acts 15:17) must presuppose a Hebrew text which had ידרשו ('they will seek')[122] for MT's יירשו ('they will possess') and אדם ('humanity') for MT's אדום ('Edom'). When Lake and Cadbury remark that the LXX here is 'apparently based on a misreading of the original Hebrew,' and conclude that, 'It is incredible that a Jewish Christian could thus have used the LXX in defiance of the Hebrew,'[123] they entirely misunderstand the way in which Jewish exegesis of this period treated the

[121]For omissions from the text as an exegetical device in the Qumran *pesharim*, see G.J. Brooke, *Exegesis at Qumran: 4QFlorilegium in its Jewish Context* (JSOTSS 29; Sheffield: JSOT Press, 1985) 91-92.

[122]In LXX ἐκζητεῖν most often translates דרש.

biblical text, as the Dead Sea Scrolls in particular have now made clear to us. A Jewish Christian familiar both with the Hebrew and the LXX of this verse would not regard the latter as a misreading of the Hebrew. He may have known a Hebrew text like that translated by the LXX, but, even if not, would have recognised that the LXX represents, not a misreading, but either a variant text or a deliberate alternative reading of the text. Jewish exegetes were accustomed to choosing among variants the reading which suited their interpretation, or to exploiting more than one. But in a case such as ours, it is scarcely possible to distinguish a variant text which has arisen accidentally in the transmission of the text from one which results from the exegetical practice of deliberately reading the text differently by means of small changes (known as *'al tiqrê* in later Rabbinic terminology).[124] The 'misreading' of the Hebrew text presupposed by the LXX of Amos 9:12 is quite comparable with many examples of deliberate 'alternative readings' (*'al tiqrê*) in the Qumran *pesharim*.[125] Thus there is not the slightest difficulty in supposing that a Jewish Christian exegete, familiar with the Hebrew text of the Bible but writing in Greek, should have welcomed the exegetical potential of the LXX text of Amos 9:12 as a legitimate way of reading the Hebrew text of that verse.[126]

Having established the way in which the text-form of the quotation has been created for its specific purpose, we must now consider the two crucial points of interpretation which enable this text to prove James' case: that the Gentiles are included in the eschatological people

[123]In Foakes Jackson and Lake (eds.), *Beginnings*, vol. IV, 176; *cf.* C.K. Barrett in D.A. Carson and H.G.M. Williamson (eds.), *It Is Written: Scripture Citing Scripture* (B. Lindars FS; Cambridge: Cambridge University Press, 1988) 244: 'James appears to quote the LXX where it differs from the Hebrew. Is it conceivable that he would do this?'

[124]For a striking example of *'al tiqrê* in LXX, see D.I. Brewer, *Techniques and Assumptions in Jewish Exegesis before 70 CE* (TSAJ 30; Tübingen: Mohr [Siebeck], 1992) 178. For *'al tiqrê* in the Targumim, see Brooke, *Exegesis*, 29-36; for *'al tiqrê* in the Qumran literature, see Brooke, *Exegesis*, 281, 284, 288-9, 306, 327; A. Chester in Carson and Williamson (eds.), *It Is Written*, 143-4; G.J. Brooke, 'The Biblical Texts in the Qumran Commentaries: Scribal Errors or Exegetical Variants?', in C.A. Evans and W.F. Stinespring (eds.), *Early Jewish and Christian Exegesis: Studies in Memory of William Hugh Brownlee* (Atlanta, Georgia: Scholars Press, 1987) 95-7; Brewer, *Techniques*, 197-8. Brooke, 'The Biblical Texts', 85-100 argues in detail that, whereas some variant readings in the Qumran *pesharim* represent already existing textual variants, many were deliberately created for exegetical reasons.

[125]See especially those for 1QpHab listed in A. Finkel, 'The Pesher of Dreams and Scriptures', *RQ* 4 (1963-64) 367-8; Brooke, *Exegesis*, 288-9; Brooke, 'The Biblical Texts', 95-7.

of God as Gentiles, without having to become Jews. The first is that the messianic Temple (τὴν σκηνὴν Δαυειδ) will have been understood to be the Christian community. We have already seen that this interpretation of the eschatological Temple, widespread in early Christianity, goes back to the early Jerusalem church under James' leadership, as the term 'pillars' (Gal. 2:9) shows.

The second point of interpretation concerns the phrase: 'all the nations over whom my name has been invoked.' The expression ἐφ' οὓς ἐπικέκληται τὸ ὄνομά μου ἐπ' αὐτούς ('over whom my name has been invoked') is a literal rendering of the Hebrew idiom אשר־נקרא שמי עליהם (Am. 9:12). In its relatively frequent use in the Old Testament the idiom expresses ownership, and is used especially of YHWH's ownership of the ark, the Temple, the city of Jerusalem, and the people of Israel. Israel is the people 'over whom the name of YHWH has been invoked' (Dt. 28:10; 2 Ch. 7:14; Je. 14:9; Dn. 9:19; *cf.* Is. 43:7), whereas the Gentiles are 'those over whom your name has not been invoked' (Is. 63:19).[127] As an expression of God's election of Israel as his own people, the phrase is equivalent to the covenant term סגלה, which denotes Israel as God's 'special possession' (Ex. 19:5; Dt. 7:6; 14:2; 26:18; Ps. 135:4; Mal. 3:17). In post-biblical Jewish literature it seems to have become more common than the latter as an expression of Israel's covenant status (Sir. 36:17; 2 Mac. 8:15; Bar. 2:15; Pss. Sol. 9:9; LAB 28:4; 49:7; 4 Ezra 4:15; 10:22; *cf.* 2 Bar. 21:21).[128] Its use in Amos 9:12 with reference to 'all the nations' is very striking, even in the MT, where its original meaning no doubt referred to the subjection of Israel's neighbours to Davidic rule. Even the MT could easily have been understood by a Jewish Christian as predicting the extension of Israel's covenant status and privileges to the Gentile nations. The LXX merely makes this implication clearer.

It is in the light of this phrase that the very precise relevance of Amos 9:11-12 to the issue in debate at the council of Jerusalem becomes clear. Many other prophecies portrayed the Temple of the messianic age as a place where the Gentiles would come into God's presence (Ps.

---

[126]In addition to following the LXX text of the first clause of Am. 9:12, Acts 15:17 adds an interpretative gloss: τὸν κύριον. The verb ἐκζητήσωσιν clearly requires an object, lacking in the LXX, but the fact that Acts 15:17 adds τὸν κύριον, rather than με, may suggest that there is here another expansion of the text of Amos by allusion to another text with which it shares common words and themes. In this case the allusion would be to Zc. 8:22.

[127]In all these texts the LXX renders the Hebrew idiom literally, as in Am. 9:12.

[128]Note also Jas. 2:7, where the phrase is used of Christians as God's eschatological people and probably with specific reference to the invocation of the name of Jesus in baptism, as is also the case in Hermas, *Sim.* 8.6.4.

96:7-8; Is. 2:2-3; 25:6; 56:6-7; 66:23; Je. 3:17; Mi. 4:1-2; Zc. 14:16).[129] There were also prophecies predicting that Gentile nations would become, like Israel, God's own people (Zc. 2:11 [MT 2:15]; *cf.* Is. 19:25). But in most cases such texts *could* be taken to mean that these Gentiles would be proselytes, undergoing circumcision as the corollary of their conversion to the God of Israel.[130] These texts could not decisively settle the issue. But Amos 9:11-12 could, for it states that the nations *qua* Gentile nations belong to YHWH. Precisely as 'all the nations' they are included in the covenant relationship (God's name has been invoked over them). Thus whereas Gentiles could not enter God's presence in the old Temple without becoming Jews, in the new Temple of the messianic age, the Christian community, they could do so as Gentiles. Probably no other scriptural text could have been used to make this point so clearly.

While Amos 9:11-12 provides the exegetical basis for maintaining that Gentile Christians are not obligated to keep the Law of Moses, it is not obvious why this conclusion is then qualified in James' speech by the proviso that there are four prohibitions they must observe (15:20). Luke's summary has obscured the exegetical argument on which the terms of the apostolic decree are based, but it can be uncovered. It depends on the common Jewish exegetical practice of *gezērâ shāwâ,* which associates scriptural texts which share common terminology. In one of the prophecies cited above as having contributed to the conflated quotation in Acts, the Gentiles who join the eschatological people of God are said to be 'in the midst of my people' (Je. 12:16: LXX ἐν μέσῳ τοῦ λαοῦ μου, rendering בתוך אמי). Another prophecy closely related to this and to Amos 9:11-12[131] uses similar phraseology: 'Many nations shall flee for refuge to the Lord in that day, and shall be his people, and they shall dwell in your midst' (Zc. 2:11a LXX: κατασκηνώσουσιν ἐν μέσῳ σου, which must presuppose a Hebrew text ושבנו בתוכך rather than the MT's ושבנתי בתוכך [2:15a]).

---

[129]On this theme in OT prophetic literature, see D.L. Christensen, 'Nations', in D.N. Freedman (ed.), *The Anchor Bible Dictionary*, vol. IV (New York: Doubleday, 1992) 1044-7.

[130]T.L. Donaldson, 'Proselytes or "Righteous Gentiles"? The Status of Gentiles in Eschatological Pilgrimage Patterns of Thought', *JSP* 7 (1990) 3-27, argues that the predominant Jewish eschatological expectation was that in the end times the Gentiles would be converted to the God of Israel *as Gentiles*, rather than by having to become proselytes. But it is not at all clear that the evidence he examines really supports this conclusion.

[131]Note that the preceding verse (Zc. 2:10) refers to God's presence in the eschatological Temple.

These two texts establish that the Gentiles who join the eschatological people of God are technically described as those who are 'in the midst' (בתוך) of Israel. This catchphrase reveals that these Gentiles are also mentioned in the Torah. In Leviticus 17-18 (MT) there are five occurrences of the phrase 'the alien who sojourns in your/their midst' (Lv. 17:8, 10, 12, 13; 18:26, all using בתוככם or בתוכם). Since two of these occurrences (17:10, 12) refer to the same prohibition repeated, there are in fact four commandments in Leviticus 17-18 which not only the Israelite but also 'the alien who sojourns in your/their midst' is obliged to keep. These correspond to the four prohibitions of the apostolic decree,[132] in the order in which they occur in the apostolic letter (Acts 15:29; *cf.* 21:25):[133] (1) 'Things sacrificed to idols' (εἰδωλοθύτων) are prohibited in Leviticus 17:8-9, since these verses concern not only burnt offerings but also sacrifices whose meat could be eaten by the worshippers, and since it is assumed (*cf.* v. 7) that sacrifices not brought to the tabernacle are not offered to YHWH but to idols.[134] (2) 'Blood' is prohibited in Leviticus 17:10, 12. (3) 'Things strangled' (πνικτῶν) are prohibited in Leviticus 17:13. The difficulty with this term in the apostolic decree has arisen simply because Leviticus 17:13 is a positive prescription: that animals killed for eating must be slaughtered in such a way that their blood drains out. Abstention from πνικτά is the negative corollary, for an animal killed in such a way that the blood remains in it is 'choked.'[135] It is significant that πνικτῶν in the apostolic decree refers to Leviticus 17:13, not, as sometimes alleged, to Leviticus 17:15, which refers to the 'alien' (גר) but does not use the full phrase with בתוך ('the alien who sojourns in your midst'). (4) 'Sexual immorality' (πορνείας) refers to Leviticus 18:26, where all the forms of

---

[132]I agree with the majority of scholars who prefer the reading which has four prohibitions without the Golden Rule as the original text of the decree in Acts 15:20, 29; 21:25. Other major readings are evidence of later interpretation of the decree. Recent discussions of the complex textual problem are W.A. Strange, *The Problem of the Text of Acts* (SNTSMS 71; Cambridge: Cambridge University Press, 1992) 87-105; P. Head, 'Acts and the Problem of its Texts', in B.W. Winter and A.D. Clarke (eds.), *The Book of Acts in Its Ancient Literary Setting* (Grand Rapids: Eerdmans/Carlisle: Paternoster, 1993) 438-42.

[133]The order is different in Acts 15:20.

[134]The objection of S.G. Wilson, *Luke and the Law* (SNTSMS 50; Cambridge: Cambridge University Press, 1983) 87, that 'the specific issue of eating εἰδωλόθυτα, while not unrelated to Leviticus 17, scarcely catches the flavour of the passage' misses the point that the apostolic decree, like all Jewish interpretation of the Torah, is concerned not to read the Law like a modern historical critic but to apply it to contemporary circumstances.

sexual relations specified in Leviticus 18:6-23 (relations within the prohibited degrees, intercourse with a menstruating woman, adultery, homosexual intercourse, bestiality) are prohibited to 'the alien who sojourns in your midst.' The general term πορνεία covers all these.[136]

That the terms of the apostolic decree are based on Leviticus 18-19 has been widely recognised,[137] but it has never been explained why precisely these four laws should be regarded as binding on Gentile Christians, because the exegetical link between these laws and the prophecies of Gentiles joining the eschatological people of God has not been recognised. There is no known Jewish parallel to the selection of just these four laws as the Mosaic laws which Gentiles should keep, and no evidence that Gentile Godfearers were expected to keep precisely these four laws. The pragmatic desire to facilitate table fellowship between Jewish and Gentile Christians[138] cannot account for the choice of these laws, no more and no fewer· Not even the supposition that Gentile Christians are considered to be in the situation of the resident aliens to whom the Torah refers adequately explains the apostolic decree, for there are other laws, most notably the Sabbath

---

[135]Philo, *Spec. Leg.* 4:122: meat from which the blood has not been drained is meat killed by 'strangling and choking' (ἄγχοντες καὶ ἀποπνίγοντες); and *cf.* Jos. Asen. 8:5; 21:14; *m. Ḥull.* 1:2. Wilson, *Luke*, 88-92, finds quite unnecessary difficulty with πικτῶν in relation to Lv. 17, because he entirely misses the relevance of Lv. 17:13. In fact, having cited Haenchen, who correctly derives the two prohibitions against blood and things strangled from Lv. 17:10-4, Wilson then quotes, as the terms used in Lv. 17:13-4, the terms which are actually used in Lv. 17:15 (*Luke*, 88). See also J.T. Sanders, *The Jews in Luke Acts* (London: SCM Press, 1987) 115, for criticism of Wilson; and E.P. Sanders, *Judaism: Practice and Belief 63 BCE–66 CE* (London: SCM Press and Philadelphia: Trinity Press International, 1992) 216, 520 n. 11.

[136]It is often supposed that the connection with Lv. 18:26 requires πορνεία in the apostolic decree to mean marriage within the prohibited degrees (*e.g.* R.P. Martin, *New Testament Foundations*, vol. II [Exeter: Paternoster Press/Grand Rapids: Eerdmans, 1987] 113; J.A. Fitzmyer, *To Advance the Gospel* [New York: Crossroad, 1981] 88), but this is not the case. Lv. 18:26 refers to all the 'abominations' of 18:6-23, which (with the exception of v. 21) are all sexual, but by no means all forms of incest. Thus πορνεία in the apostolic decree can be allowed its ordinary general meaning, rather than the implausible specialized meaning of relations within the prohibited degrees (*cf.* G. Zuntz, *Opuscula Selecta* [Manchester: Manchester University Press, 1972] 228; the evidence discussed by Fitzmyer, *To Advance*, 95-7, does not really show that πορνεία without further explanation could be understood to mean marriage within the prohibited degrees).

[137]*E.g.* Haenchen, *Acts*, 469; J.T. Townsend, 'The Date of Luke-Acts', in C.H. Talbert (ed.), *Luke-Acts: New Perspectives from the Society of Biblical Literature Seminar* (New York: Crossroad, 1984) 50; Esler, *Community and Gospel*, 99; Sanders, *The Jews*, 115.

[138]*Cf., e.g.* Esler, *Community and Gospel*, 98-9; Taylor, *Paul*, 140-2; and for the problems with this view, Sanders, *Jews*, 120.

commandment (Ex. 20:10; Dt. 5:14),[139] which are specifically said to apply to resident aliens. But the use of the catchphrase בתוך explains the selection. Besides the laws in Leviticus 17-18, the only laws in the Torah which the alien resident 'in the midst' (בתוך) of Israel is obliged to obey are Leviticus 16:29; Numbers 15:14-16, 29; 19:10, but all these refer specifically to the Temple cult. We can well imagine that Jewish Christian exegetes who understood the eschatological Temple to which Gentile Christians are admitted to be the Christian community would not apply these laws literally to Gentile converts. The use of בתוך as the principle of selection may seem to modern minds an arbitrary method of determining which Mosaic laws apply to Gentile Christians, but to 1st-century Jewish hermeneutics it is not in the least arbitrary: it is a precise and disciplined use of a well-recognised exegetical method.

Once we recognise the exegetical basis of the apostolic decree, we can see that the two stages of James' argument hang together as based on two closely related exegetical arguments. In the first place, the conflated quotation in Acts 15:16-18 establishes that Gentiles who join the eschatological people of God are not obliged to be circumcised and obey the Law of Moses. But secondly, an exegetical argument which creates a link between closely related prophecies and Leviticus 17-18 establishes that the Law of Moses itself contains just four commandments which do explicitly apply to precisely those Gentiles.[140] The difference between the two exegetical arguments is that the first is clear in the text of Acts, whereas the second is not. But this also corresponds to another difference. The conflated quotation in Acts 15:16-18 has clearly been composed in Greek, using the LXX. This does not mean it is the work of a Greek-speaking Christian ignorant of the Hebrew text. The quotation could have been composed in Hebrew with the same effect, and the exegete who composed it probably referred to the Hebrew text as well as the LXX. But he composed the quotation as we have it in Greek. However, the exegetical argument behind the terms of the apostolic decree necessarily depends on the Hebrew text of Leviticus 17-18.[141] It could, of course, have been explained in Greek, but not by the use of the LXX. The probability is that Luke has based the speech of James on a document which explained the exegetical basis of the apostolic decree for the Gentile Christians to whom it applied and which was therefore composed in

[139]Note also Lv. 24:16-22.

[140]This understanding of the argument also explains the otherwise puzzling verse 15:21. These four laws which apply to Gentile Christians are not novel inventions, but have been read out in synagogues in every city from ancient times.

Greek. This may have been a fuller text of the apostolic letter which Luke has, in that case, abbreviated in Acts 15:23-29.[142] Perhaps this document itself did not fully explain the exegetical basis for the four prohibitions; perhaps Luke has omitted this. But in either case we can see that in the thinking of those who formulated the decree both the interpretation of Amos 9:11-12 and the argument linking related prophecies to Leviticus 17-18 must have featured.

The close coherence of these two stages of the exegetical argument supports the impression Luke gives that the terms of the apostolic decree were integral to a decision of the Jerusalem church leaders that Gentile Christians need not be circumcised. The four prohibitions of the decree are not simply a pragmatic compromise, dealing with the problem of table fellowship in a context where it is not debatable that Gentile Christians do not have to keep the Law. In the thinking of those who formulated them, the same exegetical case which demonstrates conclusively that Gentile Christians do not have to keep the Law also shows that they do have to observe these four prohibitions. Thus the material Luke has preserved as the speech of James does represent, in summary form, the arguments of those who formulated the apostolic decree. We need to ask whether he has correctly attributed this material to James, at least in the sense that it derives from the Jerusalem leadership group of which James was the foremost member.

3. *The Origin of the Apostolic Decree*

The argument which James' speech presents and presupposes is precisely the kind of argument about the relation of Gentile Christians to the Law of Moses that we should expect from the Jerusalem church leaders. It employs very precise exegetical argument which skilfully

---

[141]There is no verbal correspondence in the LXX between Je. 12:16; Zc. 2:11 and Lv. 17:8, 10, 12, 13; 18:26; nor does the LXX distinguish verbally between the resident alien of those verses and the resident alien in the Sabbath commandment (Ex. 20:10; Dt. 5:14). Moreover, the LXX calls the resident alien in those chapters, as elsewhere in the Torah, 'the proselyte (προσήλυτος) who sojourns among you.' But the point of the apostolic decree is precisely that Gentile Christians are not required to become proselytes, who would be obliged to keep the whole Law.

[142]Note that 15:29 lists the four prohibitions in the order in which they occur in Lv. 17-18, and is therefore closer to the decree's exegetical basis than is 15:20, where the second and fourth prohibitions are reversed. The latter is explicable as a change which puts the two prohibitions perceived as most important first (*cf.* Rev. 2:14, 20).

deploys the exegetical methods of contemporary Jewish exegesis.[143] It employs the notion of the Christian community as the messianic Temple, which we know to have been important to the Jerusalem church under James' leadership. It deals with the question of Gentile Christians in a way which by no means sets aside the authority of the Law of Moses but fully upholds it, by requiring of Gentile Christians obedience to the four commandments which the Law itself imposes on them.

These considerations make the Jerusalem church leadership, with James at its head, very plausibly the source of the apostolic decree. However, they do not entirely rule out the possibility of some other origin within Jewish Christian circles, even in the Diaspora. It is almost universally agreed, for good reasons, that the decree itself is not a Lukan invention,[144] and it is quite widely thought to have come from the Jerusalem church leadership,[145] though many scholars doubt that Luke can have correctly described the circumstances of its formulation. But Haenchen, for example, argues that the decree 'must have come into force in a strongly mixed community of the Diaspora.'[146] Such a view is based on two presuppositions: that the decree was essentially a compromise solution to the problem of table fellowship in mixed (Jewish and Gentile) Christian communities, and that Galatians 2:12 shows that James was not inclined to compromise on this issue. The question of precisely which Jewish food laws Peter and other Jewish Christians in Antioch had been disregarding when eating with Gentiles,[147] before the 'people from James' persuaded them not to do so, is very difficult and cannot be discussed here. But it is therefore debatable to what extent the requirements of the apostolic decree would in fact represent a compromise in this situation. It is possible

---

[143]For this kind of skilled exegesis as characteristic of the circle of the Lord's brothers, see Bauckham, *Jude and the Relatives*, ch. 4.

[144]*E.g.* Haenchen, *Acts*, 470; Townsend, 'The Date', 49-50, 55-6; Esler, *Community and Gospel*, 98; G. Lüdemann, *Paul: Apostle to the Gentiles: Studies in Chronology*, tr. F. Stanley Jones (London: SCM Press, 1984) 72-4.

[145]*E.g.* D.R. Catchpole, 'Paul, James and the Apostolic Decree', *NTS* 23 (1977) 428-44; R.E. Brown and J.P. Meier, *Antioch and Rome* (London: Chapman, 1983) 42-3 n. 102; Lüdemann, *Paul*, 73-4; *cf.* Taylor, *Paul*, 141.

[146]Haenchen, *Acts*, 471. Hill, *Hellenists*, 143-6, argues against Haenchen, though his argument is spoiled by his view that the apostolic decree was a compromise. *Cf.* W. Schmithals, *Paul and James*, tr. D.M. Barton (SBT 46; London: SCM Press, 1965) 81-85, who doubts whether the regulations of the apostolic decree were ever in force within Christian churches at all. Luke may have taken them over from Diaspora Judaism.

that if Gentiles observed the first three provisions of the apostolic decree, there would no longer be a problem. However, the decree certainly does not deal with all possible problems for Jews eating with Gentiles (for example, it does not require Gentiles to abstain from pork or shellfish; it does not require them to ensure that their wine and oil were produced in accordance with the purity rules of Lv. 11:37-38). Nor is the enabling of table fellowship between Jews and Gentiles its primary purpose. Galatians 2:11-14 may describe, at least in part, the situation that required a decision by the Jerusalem leaders, and the apostolic decree may in fact have resolved the problem there described. But the decision taken addressed in principle the issue of Gentile Christians' obligation to the Law of Moses. The four prohibitions would have been regarded as in principle binding on Gentile Christians quite irrespective of whether they had any contact with Jewish Christians.

Only if the decree had the supreme authority of the mother church in Jerusalem and were regarded, not as a pragmatic compromise, but as formulating in principle the extent of the authority of the Mosaic Law for Gentile Christians can the subsequent history of its observance be explained. The evidence shows that observance of the prohibitions was widespread for a long period. It is true that the common view that Christians should not eat εἰδωλόθυτα (Justin, *Dial.* 34.8-35.2; Aristides, *Apol.* 15; Irenaeus, *Adv. Haer.* 1.6.3; Clement of Alexandria, *Paed.* 2.1.8.3-2.1.10.6; *cf.* Pliny, *Ep.* 10.96.10; Celsus, *ap.* Origen, *C.Cels.* 8.28; Lucian, *De morte Peregrini* 16)[148] need not presuppose the apostolic decree.[149] But the conjunction of φαγεῖν εἰδωλόθυτα and πορνεῦσαι in Revelation 2:14, 10, strongly suggests that the decree is in mind,[150] as it is also in a command not to eat blood and to abstain from εἰδωλόθυτα (Sib. Or. 2:96 = Pseudo-Phocylides 31).[151] When the

[147]See especially J.D.G. Dunn, *Jesus, Paul and the Law* (London: SPCK, 1990) 137-158; E.P. Sanders, *Jewish Law from Jesus to the Mishnah* (London: SCM Press, 1990) 258-308; Esler, *Community and Gospel*, 73-89; Hill, *Hellenists*, 126-42; P.J. Tomson, *Paul and the Jewish Law* (CRINT 3/1; Assen/Maastricht: Van Gorcum and Minneapolis: Fortress, 1990) 228-236.

[148]For additional evidence from the acts of the martyrs, see A. Ehrhardt, *The Framework of the New Testament Stories* (Manchester: Manchester University Press, 1964) 286-87.

[149]The discussion in Clement of Alexandria, *Paed.* 2.1.8.3-2.1.10.6, makes considerable use of 1 Corinthians as its authority.

[150]So C.K. Barrett, 'Things Sacrificed to Idols', *NTS* 11 (1964-65) 139. However, against Barrett, 'Things', 139-40, I do not think it can be demonstrated that the decree lies behind texts in Jude and 2 Peter.

Didache advises 'concerning food, bear what you are able, but in any case keep strictly away from meat sacrificed to idols, for it is the worship of dead gods' (6:3), it seems likely that it refers, not to Jewish food laws in general, but to the terms of the apostolic decree. While it shows that avoidance of blood was not found practical by all Christians, it also maintains that ideally this is desirable. That Christians abstain from eating blood is taken for granted by the Letter of the Churches of Vienne and Lyons (*ap.* Eusebius, *Hist. Eccl.* 5.1.26), Minucius Felix (*Oct.* 30.6-7), Tertullian (*Apol.* 9.13; *De Pud.* 12.4-5; *De Mon.* 5) and Clement of Alexandria (*Strom.* 4.15). Origen (*C. Cels.* 8.29-30) refers explicitly to the decree and clearly sees no problem in regarding all three of the first three prohibitions as binding on and actually observed by Christians in his time. None of these writers relate the decree to table-fellowship between Jewish and Gentile Christians, which would, in any case, hardly have been a matter of concern in their contexts. Few of them (Origen is an exception) show any sign of knowing the decree from Acts, which is extremely unlikely in several cases. Such wide acknowledgement of the prohibitions in the decree could not have started when Acts became widely known, but must go back to widespread circulation of the terms of the decree from an early period, independently of Acts.

Abstention from blood could be justified by reference to the Noahic prohibition (Gn. 9:4; *cf.* Justin, *Dial.* 20; Tertullian, *De Mon.* 5), but it is interesting to observe that the exegetical basis of the decree in Leviticus 17-18 was not forgotten. When Tertullian writes that Christians not only abstain from blood but also from things strangled and from carrion (*suffocatis quoque et morticinis: Apol.* 9.13), he has extended the decree's references to Leviticus 17:12-13 to include also 17:15. This is a logical step, since, of course, carrion meat is another form of meat with blood in it, but the explicit reference to carrion is exegetically based in Leviticus. The references to the apostolic decree in the Pseudo-Clementine literature (*Clem. Hom.* 7.4, 8; *Clem. Rec.* 4.36; *cf. Clem. Hom.* 8.19, 23; 9.23)[152] make very careful use of Leviticus 17-18 in order to elaborate the terms of the decree, not only adding to things strangled both carrion and things torn by animals, from Leviticus 17:15 (*Clem. Hom.* 7.8; *cf.* also 8.19), but also stressing that, according to

[151]This line occurs in a section of the (Christian) second Sibylline Oracle, which is borrowed from Pseudo-Phocylides, but in Pseudo-Phocylides itself it is found in only one inferior manuscript, and so must be regarded as a Christian interpolation: see P.W. van der Horst, *The Sentences of Pseudo-Phocylides* (SVTP 4; Leiden: Brill, 1978) 135.

Leviticus 18:19, πορνεία includes intercourse during a woman's menstrual impurity (*Clem. Hom.* 7.8; *cf.* 11.28, 30; *Clem. Rec.* 6.10), and deriving from this element in the laws for Gentile Christians the implication that some requirements of ritual purification from sexual defilements were also binding on them (*Clem. Hom.* 7.4, 8). It seems very probable that such interpretation of the apostolic decree must derive from Jewish Christian circles,[153] where its basis in the text of Leviticus was studied and interpreted with halakhic precision. Such acceptance of the apostolic decree as authoritative in post-70 Jewish Christian circles is very significant for the question of the origin of the decree.

Finally, it should be noticed that the various variant readings[154] in the text of the decree of Acts do not necessarily show evidence, as is usually assumed, of a desire to interpret the decree in an 'ethical' rather than a 'ritual' way. Omission of πνικτόν could mean that it was not properly understood, rather than being an indication that the prohibition of αἷμα was being interpreted as referring to murder rather than food.[155] Addition of the Golden Rule, found in texts which retain πνικτόν as well as texts which omit it, is not an 'ethicizing' of the decree but an attempt to make the decree fully comprehensive. If what the decree commands is really all that is required of Gentile Christians, then the four prohibitions are not sufficient, and the Golden Rule conveniently supplies a well-recognised, concise way of summarizing all other obligations. It is probable also that the addition of the Golden Rule made the decree a summary of what would be required of Christian converts which could be used in catechetical instruction.[156] The conjunction of the Golden Rule with the terms of the decree in *Clem.*

---

[152]On these passages, see E. Molland, 'La circoncision, le baptême et l'autorité du décret apostolique (Actes XV, 28 sq.) dans les milieux judéo-chrétiens des Pseudo-Clémentines', *ST* 9 (1956) 1-39. In my view the argument of A.F.J. Klijn, 'The Pseudo-Clementines and the Apostolic Decree', *NovT* 10 (1968) 305-12, that dependence on the apostolic decree belongs only to the latest redactional level of the Pseudo-Clementines is unconvincing. The so-called *Grundschrift*, on which both the major Pseudo-Clementine works depended, must have known not only the apostolic decree itself but also a Jewish-Christian tradition of interpretation of the apostolic decree.

[153]Unfortunately, there is still no consensus as to the Jewish Christian character of the Pseudo-Clementines and their putative sources. See the very useful review of the history of scholarship: F. Stanley Jones, 'The Pseudo-Clementines: A History of Research', *SecCent* 2 (1982) 1-33, 63-96.

[154]There is a useful table of the readings in Strange, *The Problem*, 88.

[155]Note the quotations from Ambrosiaster and Gaudentius in Strange, *The Problem*, 100-101.

[156]*Cf.* Strange, *The Problem*, 103; and the literature he cites: 221 nn. 152, 153, 157.

Hom. 7:4, and with the prohibition of εἰδωλόθυτα in Aristides, *Apol.* 15, may suggest that this occurred in use of the decree quite independent of the text of Acts, and from such actual catechetical use of the decree entered the textual tradition of Acts. This is further evidence of the deep roots which the decree took in the life of the church in many areas. It is very difficult to suppose that a ruling which originated, say, in Antioch, with no more authority than that of the church in that city and with the purely pragmatic purpose of facilitating table fellowship between Jewish and Gentile Christians, could have acquired this status. But it is fully intelligible if the decree really was promulgated by 'the apostles and the elders' in Jerusalem, as a kind of halakhic ruling on the obligation of Gentile Christians to the Mosaic Law, at a time when unique authority was generally attributed to the Jerusalem church.

We have so far discussed the evidence that the four prohibitions in the apostolic decree were widely acknowledged and observed. But there is another side of the matter. Logically prior to the four prohibitions was the accompanying decision of the Jerusalem council that Gentile Christians did not have to be circumcised (and thereby be obligated to keep the whole Law). This decision was, if anything, more influential than the four prohibitions. It is remarkable how little evidence there is, after this decision must have been promulgated by the Jerusalem church, of Christians proposing that Gentile Christians should be circumcised. (The evidence will be discussed in the next section.) To attribute this to the influence of Paul is greatly to exaggerate the influence of Paul. It was not Paul so much as the Jerusalem leaders who ensured that this particular option was no longer taken by any but a very small minority even of Jewish Christians. James in particular should probably be given much of the credit for the policy which had such an extraordinarily determinative influence on the history of early Christianity.[157]

4. Before and after the Jerusalem Council

So far we have concluded that Luke's account of the origin of the apostolic decree is historically plausible insofar as it attributes it to the Jeru-

[157]Contrast Schmithals, *Paul and James*, 85: 'the "decree" has no great significance for the problem of the relationship between the Jewish and the Gentile Christians; for after all that has been said, it is not only open to doubt whether it originated in primitive Christianity but also whether it was ever recognized there at all'!!

salem church leaders, who promulgated it as a decision in principle on the relation of Gentile Christians to the Law of Moses intended for the guidance of all Christian communities.[158] Two further, very difficult historical problems arising from Acts 15 must be briefly discussed, though space precludes a full discussion here.

The first is the relation between the Jerusalem council described in Acts 15 and Paul's accounts in Galatians 2:1-14.[159] It seems that Galatians 2:1-10 must describe an agreement between Barnabas and Paul and the three 'pillars' which took place before the promulgation of the apostolic decree. It has frequently been argued that Galatians 2:10 excludes the possibility that the apostolic decree was formulated at the time of the meeting described in 2:1-10. This argument may not be entirely conclusive, but the further consideration that the events of Galatians 2:11-14 are very difficult to envisage as occurring after the promulgation of the decree surely is. In that case, Galatians 2:1-10 records an initial decision by the three 'pillars,' in a private consultation with Barnabas and Paul, to the effect that the latter need not require circumcision of their Gentile converts. But the continuing debate on this highly contentious issue soon necessitated that the

---

[158]The view sometimes taken (*e.g.* A.S. Geyser, 'Paul, the Apostolic Decree and the Liberals in Corinth', in J.N. Sevenster and W.C. van Unnik [eds.], *Studia Paulina* [J. de Zwaan FS; Haarlem: Bohn, 1953] 136-7; R.H. Stein, 'Jerusalem', in G.F. Hawthorne and R.P. Martin [eds.], *Dictionary of Paul and His Letters* [Downers Grove, Illinois/Leicester: InterVarsity Press, 1993] 470) that Acts 15:23 shows the decree was intended only for the churches of Antioch, Syria and Cilicia, is quite mistaken. It is quite clear that this was not Luke's view (16:4). The letter in 15:23-29 is addressed to Antioch and its daughter churches because it refers specifically to the problems there had been in Antioch prior to the council (15:24) and recommends those who took the decree to Antioch (15:25-7). But no doubt other letters were written and delivered, communicating the decree to other churches. Luke's narrative focuses on Antioch because it was the starting-point for Paul's Gentile mission, and so he narrates the result of the council solely in terms of Antioch (15:22) and the churches already founded by Paul in Asia Minor (16:4). But the Jerusalem church was also the mother church for many other churches where the Gentile mission may have already been beginning: Rome, Damascus, East Syria, Egypt. Since the decree was a decision in principle on Gentile Christians' relation to the Law it would certainly have been communicated widely.

[159]For recent discussions of this complex issue, see D. Wenham, 'Acts and the Pauline Corpus II. The Evidence of Parallels', in Winter and Clarke (eds.), *The Book of Acts in Its Ancient Literary Setting*, 226-43; Stein, 'Jerusalem', 465-71; L.A. Alexander, 'Chronology of Paul', in Hawthorne and Martin (eds.), *Dictionary*, 115-23; G.W. Hansen, 'Galatians, Letter to the', in Hawthorne and Martin (eds.), *Dictionary*, 327-9; Hill, *Hellenists*, 107-22; R.N. Longenecker, *Galatians* (WBC 41; Dallas: Word Books, 1990) lxiii-lxxxviii.

whole matter be the subject of a full discussion and authoritative decision by the Jerusalem church leadership as a whole, perhaps in the context of a full assembly of the Jerusalem church (*cf.* Acts 15:22).[160] This decision, as described in Acts 15, did not contradict the earlier decision but added precision to it, as well as the full and formal authority of a ruling to be officially communicated throughout the churches. Probably, then, the Antioch incident (Gal. 2:11-14) belongs to the events which led immediately to the Jerusalem council, which Luke describes in Acts 15:1-2a.[161] Galatians would have been written in the heat of this debate at Antioch, shortly before the Jerusalem council.[162] This explains Paul's failure to refer to the events of Acts

---

[160]Scholars who, objecting to the view that Gal. 2:1-10 and Acts 15 describe two distinct events, express surprise that the same issue should be discussed and decided by the same people on two occasions, clearly have little experience of university politics!

[161]There is a problem here. Whereas in Acts 15:1-2a the issue is that of Gentile Christians and the Law, it seems clear that for Peter, Barnabas and the Jewish Christians of Antioch, who withdrew from table-fellowship with Gentiles (Gal. 2:12-13), the issue was that of Jewish Christians' obligation to obey the Law. They were persuaded (for whatever reason) that they should not continue to compromise their own obedience to food laws by eating with Gentiles. Though this could imply that Gentile Christians must observe certain food laws when eating with Jewish Christians, it did not mean that Peter and Barnabas had changed their conviction that Gentile Christians did not need to be circumcized and to keep the whole Law. However, it is easy to see how some Jewish Christians from Jerusalem could have taken advantage of this issue of table-fellowship to press their own case that Gentile Christians must be circumcized. Paul accuses Peter of giving plausibility to this case, not by his words but by his actions. This explanation has the considerable advantage of making the issue at Antioch, from Paul's perspective, the same as the issue in Galatia, and explaining why he thought the Antioch incident relevant to the latter and could connect the two so closely, as he does in Gal. 2:14-3:5. Since the issue of table-fellowship had been used as the occasion for reopening the wider issue of Gentile Christians and the Law, the Jerusalem council took up the latter issue and dealt with the former only by implication.

[162]In support of this correlation between the events in Acts and Galatians and of the early date for Galatians, see F.F. Bruce, 'Galatian Problems 1. Autobiographical Data', *BJRL* 51 (1968-69) 292-309; *idem*, 'Galatian Problems 4. The date of the epistle', *BJRL* 54 (1971-72) 250-67; *idem*, *The Epistle of Paul to the Galatians* (NIGTC; Exeter: Paternoster, 1982) 43-56; Longenecker, *Galatians*, lxiii-lxxxviii; C.J. Hemer, *The Book of Acts in the Setting of Hellenistic History* (Tübingen: Mohr [Siebeck], 1989) chapters 6-7. For earlier literature defending this position, see R. Bauckham, 'Barnabas in Galatians', *JSNT* 2 (1979) 68 nn. 3, 4. Those who have advocated it include my St Andrews predecessor: G.S. Duncan, *The Epistle of Paul to the Galatians* (London: Hodder & Stoughton, 1934) xxi-xxxi. His comment is still true: 'The hypothesis of an early date for Galatians, though it has many friends in Britain and America, has not so far commended itself to Continental scholars' (vii).

15:2b-33 in Galatians. That Luke makes no reference to the consultation and decision described in Galatians 2:1-10 (which on this hypothesis took place at the time of the visit of Barnabas and Paul to Jerusalem described in Acts 11:30) is not at all surprising. That decision proved (shortly after the writing of Galatians) to have been a short-lived arrangement, very soon superseded by a fuller and more authoritative decision, which then remained permanently in force. None would have had cause to remember the earlier agreement once the Jerusalem council had promulgated the apostolic decree. For the continuing history of the Gentile mission, which Luke narrates, the agreement of Galatians 2:1-10 was of little significance, while the Jerusalem council of Acts 15 was epoch-making.

The second problem is Paul's attitude to the apostolic decree. It is not as difficult as is often supposed[163] to envisage Paul accepting the decree, at least initially. It gave the full weight of the Jerusalem church leaders to Paul's main concern: that Gentile Christians should not be required to be circumcised.[164] Even if Paul was not entirely happy with the four prohibitions, he may have been prepared to accept them as the price for securing the main point at issue. Even Paul's discussion of εἰδωλόθυτα in 1 Corinthians can be read, not as a rejection of the decree's first prohibition, but as Paul's interpretation of it. In 1 Corinthians 10:25, 27 he defines situations in which it does not apply, while in 10:6-22 he strongly endorses it in the situation where he holds that it does apply (linking it also to the fourth prohibition in 10:8).[165] The real problem is that Paul seems to ignore the prohibition on eating meat with blood in it. This prohibition would qualify his advice in 10:25, 27 to such an extent that it is difficult to suppose he simply takes it for granted. So it seems that if Paul initially accepted the decree, he came to regard the prohibition of blood as impracticable.[166] It is not

[163]*E.g.* Catchpole, 'Paul, James', 429-31.

[164]As we have seen, Catchpole's claim that 'the theology underlying the Decree is one which sees the Christian gospel as doing nothing about the Jew/Gentile distinction' ('Paul, James', 430) is mistaken. The theology underlying the decree holds (as Paul does) that uncircumcised Gentile Christians belong fully to the eschatological people of God. The requirements of the decree are not understood as those which Jews in general held to apply to Gentiles, but as those which the Law of Moses prescribed for Gentile members of the eschatological people of God.

[165]*Cf.* Tomson, *Paul*, chapter 5; B. Witherington, 'Not So Idle Thoughts about *Eidolothuton*', *TynBul* 44 (1993) 237-54, who thinks Paul is faithful to the original intention of the decree.

[166]*Cf.* Did. 6:3, discussed above.

impossible that his partnership with Silas foundered on a disagreement on this point.[167]

If Paul took a view of the relation of Gentile Christians to the Law which was a little more liberal than that of the Jerusalem leaders expressed in the decree, were there other Jewish Christians, especially in the Jerusalem church, who continued to take a more conservative view, in the sense of continuing to press the case that Gentile believers should be circumcised and keep the whole Law? It is frequently assumed that a significant body of Jewish Christian opinion took this view throughout the period up to AD 70, as well as beyond. It is even sometimes thought to have become the dominant view of the Jerusalem leadership in the period of James' preeminence. However, the evidence for such a view is very weak.

Both Acts (15:1, 5) and Paul (Gal. 2:4)[168] provide evidence that before the promulgation of the apostolic decree there was a significant group in the Jerusalem church which advocated the circumcision of Gentile believers, though neither provides any evidence that James or other leaders sympathised with this group.[169] The question is whether this group survived or had any influence after the Jerusalem council. It is clearly Luke's view that, whether or not any Jerusalem Christians continued to hold this position, they had no influence. This is quite clear from Acts 21:20-21, where the antagonism towards Paul on the

---

[167]For Silas' role in relation to the decree and in partnership with Paul, see Acts 15:22, 27, 32, 40; 16:4. He is last mentioned in connection with Paul at the time of Paul's initial missionary preaching in Corinth: Acts 18:5; 2 Cor. 1:19; 1 Thes. 1:1; 2 Thes. 1:1.

[168]The 'false brothers' were not, as is often supposed, present at the private (2:2) consultation between Barnabas and Paul and the Jerusalem leaders. They had been to Antioch to 'spy' on what was happening there, but presumably had come from the Jerusalem church. See W.O. Walker, 'Why Paul Went to Jerusalem: The Interpretation of Galatians 2:1-5', *CBQ* 54 (1992) 503-10.

[169]Here Gal. 2:12 is the only evidence ever cited for the view that James held this position. Several points can be made against such an implication: (1) τινας ἀπὸ Ἰακώβου need mean no more than that they came from the Jerusalem church (*cf.* Acts 15:24: τινες ἐξ ἡμῶν): Paul probably had no way of knowing whether the authority they presumably claimed really authorized their actions in Antioch, but it is significant he does not criticize James. (2) If it was on advice from James that Peter and the other Jewish Christians withdrew from table-fellowship with Gentiles, this by no means implies that James advocated the circumcision of Gentile Christians; his concern would have been that Jewish Christians obey the Law, not Gentiles. (3) τοὺς ἐκ περιτομῆς may be either the Jewish Christians of Jerusalem or non-Christian Jews (for the latter view, see especially Schmithals, *Paul and James*, 66-67), but in either case the expression simply means that they were Jews; it should not be translated 'the circumcision faction' (NRSV).

part of Jewish Christians zealous for the Law has nothing to do with Paul's preaching to Gentiles.[170] The objection to Paul is that (as they have heard) he teaches *Jewish* Christians in the Diaspora to give up observing the Law. The Gentile issue has been decided by the apostolic decree (as 21:25 reminds the reader) and is no longer an issue. This distinction between Jewish Christian obedience to the Law and Gentile Christian obedience to the Law is crucial for a proper understanding of the evidence. It is important to remember that Jewish Christians could be as insistent as any Jew on Jewish obedience to the Law without objecting at all to Paul's *Gentile* mission. It was also possible to be strongly opposed to Paul, not at all because he did not require Gentiles to keep the Law, but because he allegedly encouraged Jews to abandon the Law.

However, we may ask whether the Pauline letters show that Luke has suppressed the fact that a significant body of opinion in the Jerusalem church continued to advocate the circumcision of Gentile converts after the Jerusalem council. If, as we have argued, Galatians should be dated before the council it does not provide such evidence. Otherwise, only Philippians 3:2-4 provides evidence of a group who advocated circumcision. However, they may be non-Christian Jews.[171] If they are Jewish Christians, nothing indicates any connection with the Jerusalem church. As for 2 Corinthians, in view of the importance of the issue of circumcision to Paul and the vehemence with which he treats it in Galatians and Philippians, it is inconceivable that he should have passed over this (as well as the issue of the Law in general) in silence, if his opponents were advocating it. Whether or not these opponents had some connection with the Jerusalem church,[172] they cannot be convincingly portrayed as continuing the programme of the 'judaisers' in Galatians.

---

[170]Even Hengel, *Acts*, 116-7, fails to see this, as does Bruce, *Men*, 106-7. Both impose on the evidence the notion of 'a progressive narrowing in composition and temper' (Bruce, *Men*, 98) in the Jerusalem church, for which there is simply no evidence.

[171]So G.F. Hawthorne, *Philippians* (WBC 43; Waco: Word Books, 1983) xliv-xlvii.

[172]We cannot here enter the debate as to whether the ὑπερλίαν ἀποστόλοι (2 Cor. 11:5; 12:11) are the 'Jerusalem apostles.' For recent arguments that they are not, see J.L. Sumney, *Identifying Paul's Opponents: The Question of Method in 2 Corinthians* (JSNTSS 40; Sheffield: JSOT Press, 1990) 158-1; Hill, *Hellenists*, 165-70. It is remarkable that scholars who argue that they are do not seem to ask themselves the question who, apart from James, these 'apostles' supposedly in Jerusalem would be at the time of writing of 2 Corinthians. Often the observation that Paul's ironic reference to them compares with Gal. 2:6, 9 seems to assume that the leadership situation in Jerusalem must still be as it was in Gal. 2:1-10.

There is no other evidence relevant to the pre-70 period, but we shall turn briefly to the evidence about Jewish Christians after 70. (Jewish Christians here means those Christian Jews who continued to observe the Law of Moses, whereas from the 2nd century onwards most Christians of Jewish descent abandoned Torah-observance, as most Gentile Christians believed they should.) Here again the evidence that Jewish Christians who themselves were circumcised and observed the Law expected Gentile Christians to do the same is remarkably sparse. It is noteworthy that the judaising tendencies Ignatius opposed did not include circumcision (as *Philad.* 6.1 makes clear). The most interesting evidence is Justin's account of Jewish Christians (*Dial.* 47). Justin is alone among patristic writers in tolerating (but no more than tolerating) the continued observance of the Law by Jewish Christians who did not require Gentiles to be circumcised and to observe the Law and who associated freely with Gentile Christians, though he explains that not all Gentile Christians are as tolerant as he is. He is also alone in distinguishing between such Jewish Christians and others who require Gentile Christians to observe the Law, breaking off fellowship with those who do not. However, it is not entirely clear whether he actually knew examples of the latter type[173] or whether the discussion is purely hypothetical. Probably he knew of some, but they need not have been many, since his main concern is to distinguish categories, numerous or not. Later patristic writers, beginning with Irenaeus (*Adv. Haer.* 1.26.2), who report that Ebionites or other Jewish Christians practise circumcision and observe the rest of the Law, never tell us whether these Jewish Christians thought Gentiles should do the same.[174] Their own conviction that Jews who became Christians should abandon the Law probably prevented them from entertaining the possibility of such a distinction.

Epiphanius reports that the Ebionite work which he calls the *Ascents* ['Αναβάθμοι] *of James* polemicised against Paul, who (it claimed) was not a born Jew but a proselyte and, because he was angry at not being allowed to marry the daughter of the High Priest, 'wrote against circumcision, the Sabbath and the legislation' (*Pan.* 30.16.9). Although this sounds like objection to Paul's Law-free Gentile

---

[173]G. Lüdemann, *Opposition to Paul in Jewish Christianity*, tr. M.E. Boring (Minneapolis: Fortress, 1989) 150-154, assumes without argument that he did.

[174]Epiphanius, *Pan.* 30.26.1 reports the Ebionites as saying, 'Christ was circumcised; you also must be circumcised (καὶ συ περιτμήθητι).' Whether this is addressed to a Jew or a Gentile is unclear, but it is no doubt only Epiphanius' paraphrase of an Ebionite argument.

mission, we cannot be sure that it is. The objection to Paul might have been that he encouraged *Jews* to abandon observance of the Law. If such a view of Paul could set Jewish Christians against him in Paul's lifetime (as Acts 21:20-21 suggests), it is even more likely to have been the source of anti-Paulinism among later Jewish Christian groups. They would read Paul as he was read by the Catholic Christians of their time, who understood Paul to mean precisely that keeping the Law was incompatible with Christian faith and who regarded them as heretics for continuing to observe the Law.[175] It is widely supposed that the *Ascents of James* to which Epiphanius refers bears some close relationship to *Clem. Rec.* 1.33-71,[176] but if so, it does not help to resolve our question. This passage does contain a favourable reference to circumcision (1.33.5), almost unique in the Pseudo-Clementine literature, and refers to the Gentile mission (1.42.1; 1.64.2), but with no indication that Gentile Christians must be circumcised.[177] Paul appears as the opponent of James, but before Paul's conversion, within a wholly Jewish context. As it stands, this section is entirely consistent with the rest of the Pseudo-Clementine literature, which elsewhere expounds what is required of Gentile converts to Christianity by interpreting the apostolic decree (*Clem. Hom.* 7:4, 8; *Clem. Rec.* 4.36; *cf. Clem. Hom.* 8.19, 23; 9.23). The strongest opposition to Paul occurs in the *Epistle of Peter to James,* prefaced to the *Clementine Homilies:* 'some from among the Gentiles have rejected my Law-observant (νόμιμον) preaching, preferring a certain lawless (ἄνομον) and absurd teaching by the man who is my enemy' (2:3). The meaning is that, unlike Paul, Peter teaches the permanent validity of the Law of Moses which was confirmed by Jesus (2:4-6). But again there is no indication that this implies the circumcision of Gentiles.[178]

---

[175]It is therefore all the more impressive that some later Jewish Christians held an entirely favourable view of Paul: see R.A. Pritz, *Nazarene Jewish Christianity* (Jerusalem: Magnes Press, 1988) 64-65, on the Nazarene interpretation of Is. 9:1-4, preserved by Jerome, *In Is.*

[176]See R.E. Van Voorst, *The Ascents of James: History and Theology of a Jewish-Christian Community* (SBLDSS 112; Atlanta: Scholars Press, 1989), who argues for this view and includes a full history of research on this passage in source-criticism of the Pseudo-Clementines.

[177]J.L. Martyn, 'A Law-Observant Mission to the Gentiles: The Background to Galatians', *SJT* 38 (1985) 311, uses a quite illegitimate argument from silence to claim that the author's community required of Gentile converts no less than it did of itself.

[178]Elsewhere the Pseudo-Clementines treat all that relates to the Temple and sacrifices as not genuinely part of the Law of Moses.

There is only one Jewish Christian group, the Elchasaites, who we can be certain advocated and practised the circumcision of Gentile converts. They were in many respects a very distinctive group.[179]

Since it is widely assumed that from the time of Paul's ministry onwards there was a common Jewish Christian view that Gentile believers should be circumcised and keep the whole Law,[180] it has been necessary to show how very little evidence there is for such a position. The fact that it is so hard to document this view for post-70 Jewish Christianity strengthens the case for rejecting it for pre-70 Jewish Christianity also. There may well always have been some Jewish Christians who maintained this view of the matter, but it is unlikely that they were more than an unimportant minority in the Jerusalem church after the Jerusalem council.[181] All the evidence suggests that the apostolic decree was generally accepted by Jewish Christians as authoritatively defining the relation of Gentile believers to the Law of Moses. They did not think this meant abolishing the Law, as some supposed was Paul's position. They understood it to be upholding the validity of the Law, which itself distinguished between Jews, who were to keep the whole Law, and Gentile members of the eschatological people of God, on whom it laid only the four obligations specified in the decree.

5. *The Jerusalem Church and Paul's Last Visit to Jerusalem*

Finally, we need to ask about the attitude of James and the Jerusalem leaders to Paul himself. Clearly, they acknowledged his apostleship (*cf.* Gal. 2:7-9), though they probably considered Paul, like all Christian missionaries, subordinate to their own authority as leaders of the mother church. They approved his mission to the Gentiles, and would certainly have praised God for its success, as Luke depicts them doing (Acts 21:20). But there are two possible reasons why there could have been some tension between the Jerusalem leaders and Paul. One is that

---

[179]*Cf.* Lüdemann, *Opposition*, 129-39.

[180]The prevalence of this assumption may be partly due to the impression gained from traditional interpretation of Paul that 1st-century Jews held observation of the Law to be the necessary way to salvation. It is then easy to assume that non-Pauline Jewish Christians must have shared this approach.

[181]Hill, *Hellenists*, 115, also rightly rejects 'the popular notion that these hardliners came in subsequent years to *control* the church in Jerusalem.... [T]here is no evidence of a dominant conservatism in the Jerusalem church.'

Paul apparently did not insist on full observance of the apostolic decree among his converts. This point should not be exaggerated. Paul clearly forbade unequivocal breaches of the first prohibition (1 Cor. 10:20-22), as well as the kinds of sexual immorality intended in the fourth prohibition (*cf.* 1 Cor. 5:1). Moreover, his principles, though different from those of the decree, meant that Gentile Christians should not breach the first three prohibitions of the decree when eating with Jewish Christians (*cf.* 1 Cor. 8:13; 10:23-33; Rom. 14:13-15). Finally, we should remember that meat was a rare luxury for most people, and would not have been part of the regular fellowship meals of the churches. Perhaps more problematic for the Jerusalem leaders than the practice of Paul's converts would have been Paul's assumption of his independent apostolic authority which enabled him to ignore parts of the decree. But it must be said that we have no evidence that Paul's attitude to the decree created difficulties between him and the Jerusalem leaders.

Probably more important was the suspicion that Paul encouraged Jewish Christians in the Diaspora to neglect the Law. In this respect, it is often overlooked that one of the most important, historically plausible elements in Luke's account of what happened on Paul's last visit to Jerusalem is the information that he had this reputation among non-Christian Jewish pilgrims from Asia, who mistakenly thought he had taken the uncircumcised Ephesian Trophimus into the inner court of the Temple (Acts 21:28-29) because, in their view, this was logically what the antinomian Paul would have done.[182] The attempt by the crowd at summary execution of Paul (21:30-31) reflects both the well-evidenced contemporary Jewish sensitivity about protecting the sanctity of the Temple from Gentile contamination,[183] and the equally well-evidenced notion of the legitimacy of 'zealot' action against Jews caught in such outrageous violations of covenant holiness (following the example of the archetypal zealot, Phinehas:

---

[182]*Cf.* Bauckham, 'The Parting of the Ways', 146.

[183]M. Hengel, *The Zealots*, tr. D. Smith (Edinburgh: T. & T. Clark, 1989) 206-17.

Nu. 25; 31:6).[184] There is every reason to believe this account of the circumstances of Paul's arrest.

This means that what the *Christian* Jews of Judaea[185] have heard about Paul (Acts 21:20-21) must be put in the context of Paul's reputation among Jews more generally. His reputation in Jerusalem doubtless derived from what Diaspora Jews, like those of Acts 21:27, visiting Jerusalem for the festivals, reported about him. The reputation was not entirely without foundation. While it is very unlikely that Paul really encouraged Jewish Christians to stop observing the Law, he was capable of speaking of their freedom from the Law in terms that could easily be taken to remove any obligation to keep the Law (*e.g.* Gal. 4:21–5:1). It is notoriously difficult to know what Paul's principle of becoming all things to all people (1 Cor. 9:20-22: '...to those under the law I became as one under the law... to those outside the law I became as one outside the law...'; *cf.* also Gal. 4:12) actually meant with regard to his own observance of the Law in practice. But for our present purposes the facts of his behaviour are less important than his reputation as someone who so devalued the Law of Moses as to encourage Jews to forsake it. Arguably, this made him a *madiah,* someone who leads Israelites into apostasy, and therefore subject to the death penalty according to the Torah (Dt. 13:13; *m. Sanh.* 7:4). This further explains the 'zealot' activity against him in Jerusalem (Acts 21:30-31; 23:12-15): the allegation that Paul had defiled the Temple was merely the occasion for executing the penalty which 'zealous' Jews were already fully convinced he had merited. That Paul himself was fully aware of his reputation in Jerusalem is clear from Romans 15:31a.

Jewish Christians in Jerusalem would naturally be influenced by this common Jewish perception of Paul. Even if they did not share it, it could make Paul an embarrassment to them. It could raise suspicions about their own loyalty to the Law and the Temple and compromise their mission to their own compatriots. The advice of the elders to Paul is a well-considered attempt to enable Paul to counteract his reputa-

---

[184]This was a well-established sense of the term 'zealot' before it became the name of a specific party during the Revolt. *Cf.* M. Hengel, *The Zealots*, tr. D. Smith (Edinburgh: T. & T. Clark, 1989) 149-83; D. Rhoads, 'Zealots', in Freedman (ed.), *Anchor Bible Dictionary*, vol. VI, 1044-5. For the plausibility of Acts 21:28-31 in terms of the notion of summary execution by the priestly authorities of someone who defiled the Temple, see P. Segal, 'The Penalty of the Warning Inscription from the Temple of Jerusalem', *IEJ* 39 (1989) 79-84. Acts 23:12-15 is also a typical example of 'zealot' action.

[185]There is no reason why Acts 21:20 should refer only to Jerusalem.

tion in Jerusalem—primarily with members of their own Christian community, but no doubt also with others. By not only undergoing his own purification (from corpse-impurity inevitably contracted during such a long absence from the Temple) but also paying for the sacrifices required for the purification of four Jewish Christian Nazirites and accompanying them,[186] Paul would make very public not only his own careful observance of the Law, but also his positive encouragement of such observance by others, even at personal cost. In Luke's account this advice certainly does not mean that the elders themselves are other than fully supportive of Paul. So far from dissociating themselves from Paul, they propose an action in which he appears in public solidarity with members of their own community. The advice shows confidence that Paul could in fact defy his unjustified reputation and prove himself Law-observant. The suggestion sometimes made that they deliberately lured Paul into a trap[187] is absurd. What actually happened (which depended on Jews from Ephesus both recognizing Trophimus[188] and making a mistake) could not have been foreseen by anyone. No doubt the elders recognised that Paul was in some danger in Jerusalem, but their advice was calculated to dispel the danger, not to increase it.

This is how Luke represents the matter. Suggested reasons for supposing that according to Luke's source Paul's reception by the Jerusalem church leaders was much less cordial are two. One is that Luke can record no attempt by the Jerusalem church leaders to come to Paul's defence after his arrest: 'It looks very much as though they washed their hands of Paul, left him to stew in his own juice.'[189] This concludes far too much from Luke's silence. James and his colleagues had no influence with either the chief priests or the Romans.[190] Any attempt they made on Paul's behalf would surely have been unsuccessful.[191] Luke's narrative, which naturally does not record every-

[186]Most problems about the procedures in Acts 21:24-27 disappear when it is recognized that the Nazirites were not discharging their vows, but being purified after contracting corpse impurity. This meant that they went through the same seven-day purification procedure as Paul did (Nu. 19:13-20), but in their case sacrifices had also to be offered on the eighth day (Nu. 6:9-12).

[187]A.J. Mattill, 'The Purpose of Acts: Schneckenburger reconsidered', in W.W. Gasque and R.P. Martin (ed.), *Apostolic History and the Gospel* (F.F. Bruce FS; Exeter: Paternoster, 1970) 115-6.

[188]The point of Acts 21:29 is that these Jews knew Trophimus from Ephesus. Otherwise no one would have known that he was not a proselyte.

[189]J.D.G. Dunn, *Unity and Diversity in the New Testament* (London: SCM Press, 1977) 256; *cf.* Lüdemann, *Early Christianity*, 217.

thing that happened, had more important concerns than with actions of the Jerusalem elders which made no difference to the course of events.

A much more significant omission by Luke is the fact that he makes no reference to the collection, which we know from Paul's letters it was the main purpose of his visit to Jerusalem to deliver. It has therefore been suggested that the Jerusalem leaders refused to accept it, for fear of being compromised by the association with Paul and his churches.[192] Luke suppressed this evidence of disharmony between the Jerusalem leaders and Paul.[193] But in that case the advice to Paul in Acts 21:23-24, which implies a public association between Paul and the Jerusalem Christian community, cannot be historical. In effect this explanation must therefore reject the whole account of the reasons for Paul's arrest (Acts 21:20-36), which, as we have seen, is inherently extremely plausible. More probable is the suggestion that the collection was accepted only on condition that Paul follow the elders' advice, thus dispelling the reputation which would otherwise tarnish their acceptance of the collection.[194] This is reasonable, except for the implication that Paul would not have been willing to follow the advice unless it were imposed in this way as a condition. We need only suppose that the acceptance of the collection and the advice went hand-in-hand. But this provides no explanation for Luke's failure to refer to the collection. The reason may be quite different. If Luke knew about the collection (as 24:18 suggests), he knew that its significance was bound up, in Paul's thinking, with the continuing, indeed escha-

---

[190]Dunn, *Unity*, 256 refers to 'James' apparent high standing among orthodox Jews.' But this is misleading. Josephus, *Ant.* 20.197-203, may indicate that James was respected by Pharisees (this is debatable), but it shows that he would certainly have had no influence with the chief priests.

[191]Of course, some members of the Jerusalem church may have believed the accusation that Paul had defiled the Temple, but we have no way of knowing this.

[192]Romans 15:31b has often been thought to suggest that Paul had reason to fear that the Jerusalem leaders would not accept the collection: *e.g.* J.D.G. Dunn, *Romans 9-16* (WBC 38B; Dallas: Word Books, 1988) 883; Taylor, *Paul*, 214-5. It is possible that Paul means this, fearing that the hostility of non-Christian Jews to him (Rom. 15:31a) might have this spin-off effect on the Jerusalem church. However, Hill, *Hellenists*, 177-8, points out that the use of εὐπρόδεκτος in Rom. 15:31 is parallel to its use in 15:16, where it is cultic language (*cf.* also Phil. 4:18; 1 Pet. 2:5) referring to the acceptability of a sacrifice to God. In this case the language may be a formulaic expression of piety, which simply for reasons of humility does not presume on the acceptability of the offering.

[193]*E.g.* Dunn, *Unity*, 257; Lüdemann, *Early Christianity*, 216-7.

[194]Haenchen, *Acts*, 613-4; Georgi, *Remembering the Poor*, 125-6.

tological centrality of Jerusalem in God's purpose. Writing after AD 70, this made little sense to Luke. Despite his so-called 'Jerusalem bias,' for Luke Jerusalem was central as the centre from which the centrifugal movement of the gospel went out to the ends of the earth, but not as the centre to which, in a corresponding centripetal movement, the eschatological people of God must constantly look back. Paul's concern to cement his churches' fellowship with the mother church, still less the Jerusalem leaders' conviction of Jerusalem's authority over other churches, were no longer relevant in Luke's time. By allowing the Jerusalem council of Acts 15 its epoch-making place in the history of the Gentile mission, but omitting the collection from Paul's last journey to Jerusalem, Luke conveys the sense that Jerusalem had been but by his time was no longer of key significance for the developing worldwide church.

INDEX OF MODERN AUTHORS

INDEX OF ANCIENT SOURCES

PAPYRI

INSCRIPTIONS

EARLY CHRISTIAN LITERATURE

DEAD SEA SCROLLS

APOCRYPHA AND JEWISH PSEUDEPIGRAPHA

RABBINIC TEXTS

INDEX OF BIBLICAL REFERENCES

OLD TESTAMENT

NEW TESTAMENT

INDEX OF PLACE AND PERSONAL NAMES AND SELECTED SUBJECTS

(see also the table of contents for subjects in chapter sub-headings)